by
gar Publishing Limited
ts
vn Road
n
2JA

gar Publishing, Inc.
att House
ourt
on
etts 01060

e record for this book
from the British Library

Congress Control Number: 2011926843

85793 336 2 (cased)

bound by MPG Books Group, UK

An Evolutionary Appr
Entrepreneurship

Selected Essays by Howard E. Aldric

Howard E. Aldrich

Kenan Professor of Sociology, University o Hill, USA

© How

All rigl
system
recordi

Publish
Edward
The Lyp
15 Lans
Chelten
Glos Gl
UK

Edward
William
9 Dewey
Northan
Massach
USA

A catalo
is availa

Library (

ISBN 978

Printed an

Edward Elgar
Cheltenham, UK • Northampton, MA, USA

Contents

Acknowledgements

The author wishes to thank the following who have kindly given permission for the use of copyright material.

American Sociological Association (ASA), for permission to reproduce: M. Ruef, H.E. Aldrich, and N.M. Carter, 'The Structure of Founding Teams: Homophily, Strong Ties, and Isolation Among U.S. Entrepreneurs', *American Sociological Review*, **68** (2), 2003, 195–222.

Annual Reviews Inc, for permission to reproduce: H.E. Aldrich and R. Waldinger, 'Ethnicity and Entrepreneurship', *Annual Review of Sociology*, **16**, 1990, 111–35.

Ballinger Publishing Company (HarperCollins Publishers) for permission to reproduce: H.E. Aldrich and C. Zimmer, 'Entrepreneurship Through Social Networks', in Donald Sexton and Raymond Smilor (eds), *The Art and Science of Entrepreneurship*, 1986, 3–23.

The Academy of Management for permission to reproduce: H.E. Aldrich and C.M. Fiol, 'Fools Rush In? The Institutional Context of Industry Creation', *Academy of Management Review*, **19** (4), 1994, 645–70.

Emerald Group Publishing Ltd, for permission to reproduce: H.E. Aldrich, 'Lost in Space, Out of Time: Why and How We Should Study Organizations Comparatively', in Brayden King, Teppo Felin and David Whetten (eds), *Studying Differences Between Organizations: Comparative Approaches to Organizational Research, Research in the Sociology of Organizations*, **26**, 2009, 21–44; H.E. Aldrich, 'Beam Me Up, Scott(ie): Institutional Theorists' Struggles with the Emergent Nature of Entrepreneurship', in Wesley D. Sine and Robert J. David (eds), *Institutions and Entrepreneurship, Research in the Sociology of Work*, **21**, 2010, 329–64.

Elsevier Ltd, for permission to reproduce: P. Dubini and H.E. Aldrich, 'Personal and Extended Networks Are Central to the Entrepreneurial Process', *Journal of Business Venturing*, **6** (5), 1991, 305–13; H.E. Aldrich and E.R. Auster, 'Even Dwarfs Started Small: Liabilities of Age and Size and Their Strategic Implications', in Barry Staw and L.L. Cummings (eds), *Research in Organizational Behavior*, **21**, 1986, 165–98; C.S. Hunt and H.E. Aldrich, 'The Second Ecology: Creation and Evolution of Organizational Communities as Exemplified by the Commercialization of the World Wide Web', in Barry Staw and L.L. Cummings (eds), *Research in Organizational Behavior*, **20**, 1998, 267–301; H.E. Aldrich and J.E. Cliff, 'The Pervasive Effects of Family on Entrepreneurship: Toward a Family Embeddedness

Perspective', *Journal of Business Venturing*, **18** (5), 2003, 573–96; H.E. Aldrich, L.A. Renzulli and N. Langton, 'Passing on Privilege: Resources Provided by Self-employed Parents to Their Self-employed Children', in Kevin Leicht (ed.), *Research in Social Stratification and Mobility*, **16**, 1998, 291–317; H.E. Aldrich and P.H. Kim, 'A Life Course Perspective on Occupational Inheritance: Self-employed Parents and Their Children', in Martin Ruef and Michael Lounsbury (eds), *The Sociology of Entrepreneurship, Research in the Sociology of Organizations*, **25**, 2007, 33–82; S. Lippmann, A. Davis and H.E. Aldrich, 'Entrepreneurship and Inequality', in Lisa A. Keister (ed.), *Entrepreneurship: Research in the Sociology of Work*, **15**, 2005, 3–31.

John Wiley and Sons Ltd, for permission to reproduce: H.E. Aldrich and P.H. Kim, 'Small Worlds, Infinite Possibilities? How Social Networks Affect Entrepreneurial Team Formation and Search', *Strategic Entrepreneurship Journal*, **1** (1), 2007, 147–65; S.W. Bradley, H.E. Aldrich, D.A. Shepherd and J. Wiklund, 'Resources, Environmental Changes, and Survival: Asymmetric Paths of Young Independent and Subsidiary Organizations', *Strategic Management Journal*, **32** (5), 2011, 486–509.

Kluwer Academic Publishers, for permission to reproduce: A. Fortune and H.E. Aldrich, 'Acquiring Competence at a Distance: Application Service Providers as a Hybrid Organizational Form', *The Journal of International Entrepreneurship*, **1** (1), 2003, 105–21.

Sage Publications Inc, for permission to reproduce: H.E. Aldrich, 'Who Wants to Be an Evolutionary Theorist?', *Journal of Management Inquiry*, **10** (2), 2001, 115–27; H.E. Aldrich and A.L. Kenworthy, 'The Accidental Entrepreneur: Campbellian Antinomies and Organizational Foundings', in Joel A.C. Baum and Bill McKelvey (eds), *Variations in Organization Science: Essays in Honor of Donald T. Campbell*, 1999, 19–33; A.E. Davis, L.A. Renzulli, and H.E. Aldrich, 'Mixing or Matching? The Influence of Voluntary Associations on the Occupational Diversity and Density of Small Business Owners' Networks', *Work & Occupations*, **33** (1), 2006, 42–72.

Routledge, Taylor and Francis Group, for permission to reproduce: H.E. Aldrich, A.B. Elam and P.R. Reese, 'Strong Ties, Weak Ties, and Strangers: Do Women Owners Differ from Men in Their Use of Networking to Obtain Assistance?', in Sue Birley and Ian MacMillan (eds), *Entrepreneurship in a Global Context*, 1997, 1–25.

Springer Science and Business Media, for permission to reproduce: P.H. Kim, H.E. Aldrich and L.A. Keister, 'Access (Not) Denied: The Impact of Financial, Human, and Cultural Capital on Entrepreneurial Entry in the United States', *Small Business Economics*, **27** (1), 2006, 5–22.

Taylor and Francis, for permission to reproduce: T. Baker, H.E. Aldrich and N. Liou, 'Invisible Entrepreneurs: The Neglect of Women Business Owners by Mass Media and Scholarly Journals in the United States', *Entrepreneurship & Regional Development*, **9** (3), 1997, 221–38.

University of North Carolina Press, for permission to reproduce: L.A. Renzulli, H.E. Aldrich and J. Moody, 'Family Matters: Gender, Networks, and Entrepreneurial Outcomes', *Social Forces*, **79** (2), 2000, 523–46.

Introduction

When Francine O'Sullivan asked me about doing a book on entrepreneurship, I initially resisted. I had written many papers on the topic but was not sure how they would cumulate into a book. Nevertheless, when I looked over my essays from the past several decades, I realized that I had already produced a book's worth of words. My ideas were scattered across many articles, however, and so I looked to see whether I could identify some common themes. Reviewing what I had written since the mid-1980s, I found five themes that unified my articles and book chapters.

First, I had written about the need to develop better theories, particularly with regard to new venture creation and the composition of founding teams. Second, I had conducted a number of studies on the role of social networks in entrepreneurial startups and change. Third, I had written several conceptual and empirical papers on the prospects for developing and pursuing successful entrepreneurial strategies. Fourth, from a comparative and international perspective, I had written on gender differences in entrepreneurial startups and change, as well as the involvement of families in small firms. Finally, going back to my early days studying small firms in American cities, I had completed a number of projects that investigated the relevance of entrepreneurship to the causes and consequences of stratification and inequality. I had also written quite a few papers on improving entrepreneurship research methods, but I am saving that line of writing for another project.

How an evolutionary theorist came to study entrepreneurship

For this collection, I have selected 23 of my published papers covering the five themes. Thirteen of them are from the year 2000 and later, eight are from the 1990s, and just two are from the 1980s. To put these papers into historical context, I should note that I actually began doing research on small and young firms back in the 1960s, when I was a graduate student in sociology at the University of Michigan. My PhD dissertation began as a two-wave panel study of small businesses in the high crime rate areas of three US cities: Boston, Chicago, and Washington DC. Doing a lot of the interviewing myself, I spent the summers of 1966 and 1968 walking through inner-city areas, interviewing business owners about their operations and asking how they coped with difficult conditions. After I took my first job at Cornell University, I added two more waves of interviews to the project, resulting in a four-wave panel study of business dynamics in complex and turbulent environments.

While I was working on empirical papers from this large panel study, using an ecological framework, I was also developing ideas about applying evolutionary theory to organizations. Emphasizing how little control small business owners had over their environments, my writings tended to privilege context as a driving force in organizational change. The late 1960s and early 1970s were a fertile period for the development of what scholars at that time called an organization/environment perspective and which later branched into one field called 'population ecology' and another called variously 'a natural selection perspective' or 'an evolutionary perspective'. Donald Campbell (1969), Bill McKelvey (McKelvey and Aldrich 1983), Joel Baum (Baum and Amburgey 2002), and others were instrumental in helping me develop my own ideas along evolutionary lines.

In the fall of 1975, I began a year-long sabbatical in England that enabled me to test some of the ideas I had developed in the American context. Working with three social geographers on a sample of small firms in three English cities, our research team designed a four-wave panel study that followed hundreds of small firms – mainly retail and service establishments – from 1978 to 1984 (Aldrich, Cater et al. 1983). The dynamics of ecological succession that I observed in the United States fit very well the pattern we found in England. As in the American context, business turnover rates were quite high, as one set of business owners, mainly white, were replaced by another set of business owners, mainly South Asian. The contacts I made in Europe while that study was under way spurred me to join with Roger Waldinger and Robin Ward in writing a book on ethnic entrepreneurs (Waldinger, Aldrich et al. 1990). Roger and I also wrote an essay on ethnic entrepreneurship in which we offered a model of how small firms interacted with their environments (Aldrich and Waldinger 1990).

Even when Roger and I were working on this project in the mid-1980s, I still thought of myself simply as an organizational sociologist studying organizations from an evolutionary point of view. Like Monsieur Jourdain in Molière's *The Bourgeois Gentleman*, who discovered that he had 'been speaking prose all my life, and didn't even know it', it was not until a fortuitous conjuncture of circumstances that I realized I was actually studying 'entrepreneurship'. Two events converged to change my self-identity: (1) an invitation to write a paper for a conference on social indicators; and (2) an invitation to attend a state-of-the-art conference on entrepreneurship. Let me explain.

First, in the early 1980s, I began working with several graduate students at Cornell University, studying the origins of organizational forms. As a result, I was invited to Washington DC to give a paper at a conference on using organizational data in social indicator research. In preparation for the conference, I read David Birch's book, *The Job Generation Process*, and went to visit him at the Massachusetts Institute of Technology in Boston to learn more about the data set he had put together, using the proprietary Dun & Bradstreet Market Indicators Database. After spending a day with him, I began to see the potential of integrating ideas from organizational ecology with those from evolutionary theory to understand business dynamics. One of my Cornell students, Ellen Auster, was then teaching at Columbia Business School and she joined with me in writing a paper about the problems facing new and small firms (Aldrich and Auster 1986).

Second, in 1985, as Ellen and I were finishing our paper, I got an invitation from Don Sexton to attend his state-of-the-art conference on entrepreneurship in Austin Texas. I was invited to comment on a paper presented by Al Shapero, but when Al became ill, Don called me on the Friday before the conference began (which was on a Monday!) and asked me if I would be willing to present a paper, rather than act as a discussant. I had already been thinking about social networks because of my research on ethnic businesses and decided to accept his invitation. Cathy Zimmer agreed to help me and we quickly put something together over the weekend. That paper on entrepreneurship through social networks led to other invitations to present my work and I began to meet others in the entrepreneurship research community (Aldrich and Zimmer 1986).

The Austin conference was an eye-opening experience for me. The scholars I met were passionate about their work, energized about what they were finding, and cared deeply about the phenomena. Unlike the careerist and petty gossip that I heard at most professional meetings, the people studying entrepreneurship seemed to be genuinely interested in the research itself and eager to initiate new members into their group. Because of contacts I made in Austin, I began attending the Babson College Entrepreneurship Conference and gave my first paper at the 1987 meeting at Pepperdine University. (The paper was on a study of social networks among entrepreneurs in the Research Triangle Area of North Carolina, carried out with Ben Rosen and the late Bill Woodward.) I have missed very few meetings since then.

In the 1990s, my involvement in evolutionary theory grew hand-in-hand with my entrepreneurship projects. Now that I realized that I was actually studying 'entrepreneurship' rather than 'small businesses', I reframed my research questions and began teaching seminars on the topic. I became associated in people's minds with small firms and entrepreneurship and received many invitations to teach courses and seminars internationally. Bocconi University in Milan hosted me for several month-long courses and I visited the University of Economics in Vienna every spring for seven years in the 1990s to offer a course on entrepreneurship in their Institute for Small and Medium-Size Businesses. Spurred in part by my youngest son's interest in Japanese studies, I twice taught short entrepreneurship courses at Keio University in Japan.

As will be apparent from the essays in this volume, I became involved in a series of large-scale entrepreneurship projects that began in the late 1980s. With Pat Ray Reese, I conducted a panel study of several hundred potential and actual entrepreneurs in the Research Triangle area of North Carolina. My students Linda Renzulli and Amy Davis subsequently used that data set for their masters' projects. Nancy Langton and I carried out a multi-wave panel study of small firms in the Vancouver, British Columbia region, and in collaboration with Jennifer Cliff Jennings wrote a number of papers from that project. In North Carolina, Arne Kalleberg, Peter Marsden, and I obtained an NSF grant to study different methods of sampling organizations, one part of which included an attempt to find newly founded firms in Durham County and the Research Triangle area.

In the mid-1990s, Paul Reynolds began soliciting my participation in perhaps the most important research project carried out in the United States in the past several decades: the Entrepreneurship Research Consortium (ERC) project, which eventually became the Panel Study of Entrepreneurial Dynamics (PSED I). I was initially reluctant to get involved, knowing how difficult it is to manage such diverse multi-member collective action projects. However, to his credit, Paul never gave up and although I did not join the executive committee of the first PSED, Paul always referred to me as his 'over-enthusiastic volunteer'. That experience taught me that it was better to be on the inside of such projects, rather than criticizing from the outside, and so when he proposed PSED II, I signed up for the executive committee.

Even though I came to the field of entrepreneurship studies almost by accident, I have never regretted my choice. Many of the phenomena that interest organization scholars are actually much easier to study in entrepreneurial context, where things are fresh, new, and small. In larger settings, researchers are often overwhelmed by complexity and find it very hard to pin down what is happening. By contrast, startups constitute an instant organizational laboratory with thousands of replications every day. Moreover, the selection logic forming the theoretical core of evolutionary theory shows itself every day as new ventures form and disband. I turn now to a brief explanation of the core principles of evolutionary thinking as applied to entrepreneurship.

What is an evolutionary approach to entrepreneurship?
The evolutionary approach to entrepreneurship is an overarching framework permitting comparison and integration of other social scientific theories. As a metatheory, it encompasses theories as diverse as population ecology (Hannan and Freeman 1989), new institutionalism (Scott 2008), resource dependence (Pfeffer and Salancik 1978), and transaction cost economics (Williamson 1994). At the heart of evolutionary thinking is the assumption that a struggle by entrepreneurs and organizations to obtain scarce resources, both social and physical, drives evolutionary processes (Aldrich and Ruef 2006). Competition among social actors shapes the struggle to obtain resources ahead of competitors or to avoid competition altogether. In fact, the primary motivation of many activities, from marketing to inter-organizational alliances, arises from organizations' attempts to shield themselves from competitive pressures.

The fundamental axiom of evolutionary analysis is that outcomes result from the interaction between organizations and environments, rather than being attributable to either organizations or environments, taken separately. Every explanation is thus contingent, with the effect of organizations' actions dependent upon environmental contexts and the effect of contexts unknowable until analysts specify organizational properties. The 'fit' between organizations and their environments is the key to understanding trends in organizational foundings, transformation, and disbandings. Scholars usually evaluate 'fit' in terms of outcomes like survival, profitability and growth. A fit need not be perfect but rather just the best under the circumstances. As circumstances change, what is fit under one context may not be fit under the next.

Evolutionary accounts rest on identifying the selecting forces that interact with particular variations to produce organizational and population change. Compared to person-centric accounts, selection arguments can seem maddeningly indirect and impersonal. Perhaps the most difficult premise to convey is that selection derives from the *consequences* of actions, not the *intentions* of actors. Individual differences across actors are clearly still important, as some people are more highly skilled than others at judging, envisioning, and reshaping selection environments. Nonetheless, the consequences of action are what count. Because entrepreneurship researchers often overlook this feature of evolutionary models, it bears repeating.

Competitive struggles drive entrepreneurs and organizations to create new strategies, routines and structural elements, to select those elements that prove effective, and to copy or extend those selected elements to other areas. Some of these new elements may require cooperation with other organizations. Therefore, the dynamics of interactions between organizations and their environments include the processes of variation, selection, and retention. Variation, selection, retention, and struggle occur simultaneously rather than sequentially. Analytically, the processes may be separated into discrete phases, but in practice, they are linked in continuous feedback loops and cycles. Variation generates the raw materials for selection, by environmental or internal criteria, and retention processes preserve selected variations. However, retention processes also restrict the kinds of variations that may occur, and competitive struggles as well as cooperative alliances can change the character of selection criteria.

When driven by competitive struggles and cooperative actions, the processes of variation, selection and retention jointly shape the course of evolution. These processes drive change at multiple levels: within and between organizations, within organizational populations, and across communities of populations. These multiple levels of social structure are nested within each other, as sources of variation and selection. From the viewpoint of 'upward causation' – emergence – changes in individual organizations may affect populations, and changes in populations may affect communities. From the viewpoint of 'downward causation' – constraint – populations and communities are pivotal in shaping environmental forces for organizations, while communities constitute an important component of the environment for populations.

Variations in strategies and structures that give units at these levels advantages in extracting resources from their environments will be objects of positive selection. New types of organizations and organizational forms may emerge when entrepreneurs respond to specific threats and opportunities in their environments; organizations that are efficient at taking advantage of those opportunities and countering those threats tend to survive and be imitated by existing organizations or new entrants. In organizational communities, populations with different characteristics enter into relationships of competition and cooperation; those populations better able to deal with the environment are more likely to survive, and characteristics of the successful population may then be diffused to other populations in the same community.

The essays in this book
This book brings together almost two dozen essays I have written alone or with various co-authors over the past several decades. In Part I, an introductory essay lays out the evolutionary approach, examining the assumptions and principles of 'selection logic' that drive evolutionary explanations. It is based upon a talk I gave when the Academy of Management's Organization and Management Theory division gave me a 'Distinguished Scholar' award in 2000. I used that opportunity to offer prescriptive advice to my colleagues regarding three aspects of their work. First, I was concerned because too many people claiming expertise in organization studies did not seem to know some of the basic economic and demographic facts about organizational populations in modern societies. Second, I felt that investigators jumped too quickly to agent and intention-based explanations of organizational phenomena, rather than looking to context-based explanations. Third, following arguments I had previously

made in state-of-the-art review essays, I argued against the field's heavy reliance upon cross-sectional and retrospective research designs.

Part II offers essays on evolutionary theory as applied to entrepreneurship, emphasizing the role of historical and comparative analysis. The first essay is an elaboration and extension of the argument that Roger Waldinger and I made in our book, with Robin Ward, on the historical conditions under which ethnic groups succeed in business (Waldinger, Aldrich et al. 1990). We argued that investigators must put the fate of ethnic groups into historical and comparative context to understand why particular ethnic strategies succeed or fail. In the second essay, written for a book honoring Donald Campbell's contributions to evolutionary thinking in organization science (Baum and McKelvey 1999), Amy Kenworthy and I developed an argument that runs through much of my work: entrepreneurship researchers are too quick to turn to personal characteristics, intentions and heroic actions as explanations for entrepreneurial behavior. Instead, we noted that innovative entrepreneurship is an infrequent outcome and that most entrepreneurial efforts are unremarkable. Cultural and social conditions typically conspire against humans' truly engaging in innovative action.

David Whetten, my first doctoral student at Cornell University, has long been interested in comparative approaches to organizational research. His suggestion that I contribute a paper to a conference that he and his colleagues organized in Sundance, Utah, was the stimulus for the third essay in this part. Writing 'Lost in Space, Out of Time' gave me an opportunity to return to my graduate school interests in historical and comparative analysis. I tried out some of the arguments in this paper during presentations in China, Japan, and several European venues, and was reminded again of the substantial national differences that underlie approaches to organizational analysis. I developed the final essay in this part as a contribution to several conferences organized by Wes Sine and Robert David to investigate the utility of new institutional theory in organizational analyses. (Overlap between the McGill conference in the summer of 2008 and the Montréal Jazz Festival was purely a coincidence!) The title, 'Beam me up Scott(ie)', was meant as an appreciative tipping of the hat to my friend and fellow sociologist Dick Scott, my host for a 1973 summer stay at Stanford University that rekindled my interest in a genuinely sociological approach to organization studies.

Part III focuses on the importance of social networks, particularly as they affect the genesis of entrepreneurial teams. The part begins with an essay I wrote with Cathy Zimmer for a conference organized by Don Sexton and Ray Smilor, mentioned previously in this essay. Our intent was not to develop new theory but rather to show that some simple ideas from social network analysis generated insights into some commonly observed features of entrepreneurial activity. I have been pleasantly surprised at how much attention that essay has garnered over the years – I think it was a case of being in the right place at the right time. The second essay, written with Paola Dubini as a summary of some papers we had written for several Babson College Entrepreneurship Research conferences, uses some elementary ideas from social network theory to explain why particular networking strategies might work for new ventures. The third essay, with Amanda Elam and Pat Reese, takes on a shibboleth of the entrepreneurship and gender literature: the claim that women entrepreneurs are somehow different from men in their strategic approaches. Using data from the Research Triangle study I mentioned earlier, we showed that with regard to how entrepreneurial women sought help and evaluated it, they were indistinguishable from the men in our sample. In a subsequent paper using our data from the British Columbia study, Jennifer Cliff Jennings, Nancy Langton and I pursued this line of inquiry further and showed that while men and women entrepreneurs might differ in how they talk about what they do, their actual behavior is very similar (Cliff, Langton et al. 2005).

The fourth paper in this part uses data from PSED I to investigate the composition of organizational founding teams. For this paper, Martin Ruef developed an innovative statistical technique for comparing the composition of the teams we actually observed with teams that might have emerged, if sex, race, and occupation were not factors influencing team composition. We were able to show that homophily – people joining with similar others – seems to be a dominant principle of team formation. The fifth paper, written together with Amy Davis and Linda Renzulli, continues this theme of homophily in patterns of human association. We showed that the context in which business owners met other people heavily influenced the composition of their business discussion networks. Scattering memberships across multiple associations and choosing discussion network members from different associations produced highly diverse networks. The final paper in this part was prepared for the Strategic Management Society conference that launched the *Strategic Entrepreneurship Journal*. Using four mathematical models of network structures, Phil Kim and I showed that a model depicting social networks as mostly isolated clusters of tightly linked individuals offer the best explanation for the homophilous composition of entrepreneurial teams.

Part IV takes a strategic approach to the creation of new organizational populations and communities, using examples from the commercialization of the Internet and the collapse of the Internet bubble. My paper with Ellen Auster, 'Even Dwarfs Started Small', begins this part with a review of the liabilities facing small and new organizations versus the advantages of being older and larger. We note, however, that new and small organizations also have advantages, in certain contexts. The question then is under what conditions is being small and new beneficial and how might older and larger organizations take advantage of those benefits. The next paper in this part draws on one of the ideas from my paper with Ellen Auster to examine the relative advantages of being new and autonomous in stable versus turbulent environments. Steve Bradley, Dean Shepherd, Johan Wiklund and I used a unique Swedish data set to show that autonomous organizations had higher risks of mortality than subsidiary organizations in normal times. However, autonomous firms came through an exogenous economic shock more easily than subsidiary firms because they apparently had been free to develop their own capabilities whereas the subsidiaries had not.

The third paper, 'Fools Rush In?' written with Marlena Fiol, examines the institutional context of industry construction, focusing largely on legitimacy. We argue that organizations in new industries do best when they engage in collective action with other organizations to enhance the legitimacy of their entire industry. Subsequently, in our book, Martin Ruef and I balanced the emphasis on legitimacy with the recognition that organizational learning is also important to the success of new industries. Courtney Shelton Hunt worked with me on the fourth paper in this part, 'The Second Ecology', in applying the ideas from 'Fools Rush In?' to several examples of how the World Wide Web had been commercialized in the mid-1990s. Similarly, the last paper, written with Annetta Fortune, explored the growth of a new industry that took advantage of technological opportunities afforded by the Internet: application service providers. Today, this application goes by the name of 'cloud computing', and is well understood, whereas in the late 1990s, it was a novel and potentially risky way to sell software applications. Just as the paper with Courtney was apparently the first paper presented on this topic at the Academy of Management meetings, so too was the paper with Annetta the first in the organization's literature to explore the 'cloud computing' phenomenon.

Part V presents essays concerning gender and family, offering a 'family embeddedness' perspective. The three papers in this part investigate gender and entrepreneurship, but in very different ways. My paper with Ted Baker and Nina Liou began with the observation that women business owners had been relatively neglected by both the mass media and scholarly journals in the United States. We explored some of the causes and consequences of that neglect. The second paper, with Linda Renzulli and Jim Moody, began with the observation that startup rates for women are lower than for men and investigated the possible effects of kinship relations on startups. We found that potential entrepreneurs who had higher proportions of kin in their business discussion networks were much less likely to start a business then those with lower proportions. Because women tend to have higher proportions of kin relations in their social networks than men, we identified that as a possible cause of the gender gap. The final paper, with Jennifer Cliff Jennings, reviewed the state-of-the-art on families and entrepreneurship as of the beginning of the 21st century. We noted ways in which social and economic trends have opened opportunities for family-oriented and family-based businesses, as well as the challenges faced by entrepreneurial efforts strongly embedded within family contexts.

Part VI focuses on the implications of entrepreneurship for stratification and inequality in modern societies, combining an evolutionary with a life-course perspective. The first paper, with Linda Renzulli and Nancy Langton, used the British Columbia data set to look more closely at the way in which self-employed parents might affect the human, financial, and social accumulations of their children. We were interested in this question because many studies show that the children of self-employed parents are about twice as likely as other children to become self-employed. We noted some of the life-course constraints on what self-employed parents can do for their children, given the short spell of self-employment for many people and the diverse interests and time demands of their children. The second paper, written with Phil Kim, continues this theme, putting it in a larger context through a review of the life-course perspective – developed in part by one of my colleagues at UNC, Glen Elder – and the literature on genetic endowments. The third paper in this part, written with Phil Kim and Lisa Keister, demonstrates that financial resources do not seem to be much of a barrier to nascent entrepreneurship. Families provide very little in the way of subsidies to their children, and varying lifetime levels of accumulated wealth are not a constraint on people attempting to create businesses. The final paper in this part, with Steve Lippmann and Amy Davis, uses the Global Entrepreneurship Monitor (GEM) database to explore the link between a nation's level of economic inequality and its level of entrepreneurial activity.

Part VII concludes the book with some brief reflections on future directions.

Acknowledging the contributions of others

The selected essays in this book reflect the influences noted above, but I am especially grateful to the many family members, graduate students, colleagues, and co-authors who worked with me to generate the data and the papers reprinted here. My oldest son, Steven, majored in physics as an undergraduate and when he graduated in the early 1990s, went into investment banking. After working several years as an analyst on a nearly 24/7 schedule, he entered the MBA program at Stanford University where he took courses from many of my friends and colleagues. I will never forget the day I visited him at Stanford in the spring of 1995. He took me to the computer lab and showed me how a new program called Netscape enabled someone to quickly access information over the Internet. In his final year at Stanford, 1994–95, he created a business plan for an Internet site that would allow users to comparison shop for insurance policies and went on to found one of the first dotcom companies, supported by several million dollars from investors. After selling his firm to Intuit, he spent a decade learning the corporate ropes and then became the CEO of a technology-based startup that produced brain fitness software. I have learned a great deal about entrepreneurship and management from him during our many discussions over the years.

My youngest son, Daniel, majored in Asian studies, became fluent in Japanese, and spent several years in Japan doing fieldwork on his way to earning his PhD in government from Harvard University. His field of research, environmental politics, involves the application of concepts such as social capital, collective action, and the dynamics of social movements. Just as Steven and I share interests in the founding of new ventures, Daniel and I share interests in the conditions under which people come together around collective action projects (Aldrich 2008). His comparative and international interests, as well as his acquaintance with the sociological literature on social movements, mean that we share an overlapping set of friends and colleagues.

Several dozen graduate students and many other co-authors contributed to the 23 papers included in this collection. At Cornell University, I worked with several outstanding students, including David Whetten and Udo Staber, but only one of them was interested in entrepreneurship at the time because of her interest in ethnicity and small firms: Ellen Auster. I moved to the University of North Carolina at Chapel Hill in 1982 and discovered that many students were intrigued with the puzzles posed by the persistence of small entrepreneurial firms in modern capitalist economies. Cathy Zimmer and I wrote a series of papers on trade associations (with Udo Staber and Jack Beggs), small businesses, and entrepreneurship and I learned a great deal from her about the statistical analysis of longitudinal data. Bill Woodward did much of the work for a pilot study of small firms in the Research Triangle Park (RTP) area, and then Pat Ray Reese organized and executed an incredibly ambitious plan for a longitudinal study of RTP potential and actual entrepreneurs. Amanda Ellen, Amy Davis, Jim Moody, and Linda Renzulli help us maximize the value of that data set in a series of articles about entrepreneurship and social networks. Linda's interest in startups carried over into her research on the founding of charter schools in the United States. Amanda parlayed her interests in entrepreneurship into helping start a biotech company in the RTP.

Ted Baker came to the Department of Sociology at Carolina after an early career as an entrepreneur and manager and kept me on my toes with his insider knowledge, keen insights, and passionate commitment to the concept of bricolage (Baker and Nelson 2005). Amy Kenworthy found Donald Campbell's work just as fascinating as I did, and I was delighted when she agreed to join with me on our homage to his work. Courtney Sheldon Hunt was another student who had returned to graduate school after a successful career in business. The original title of our paper was 'Why Even Rodney Dangerfield Has a Homepage', but the editors nixed that idea. Annetta Fortune, completing her PhD at the Fuqua School at Duke University with Will Mitchell, was also interested in Internet commerce. Just as Courtney and I had done, we turned a paper for my organization seminar course into a published article. Phil Kim and Steve Lippmann entered graduate school at Carolina around the same time, but took very different research paths. Phil joined with me in a series of papers using the PSED I and wrote his dissertation on an emergent model of new ventures, whereas Steve built his own data set around the origins of the commercial broadcasting industry in the early 20th century.

Several former colleagues are represented in this volume. At UNC, Lisa Keister began as an assistant professor with research interests in Chinese corporate networks and simulation models of economic inequality in America (Keister 2005). She sparked my curiosity about the connection between entrepreneurship and inequality, and we used the PSED I to investigate that connection. Martin Ruef also began at Carolina as an assistant professor, bringing his incredible philosophical and social scientific understanding to our everyday conversations about organizations and entrepreneurship. We not only wrote papers together but also a book, *Organizations Evolving*. He is my 'go to expert' on just about any problem I face, statistical or theoretical.

Colleagues from other universities have also played an important role in furthering my understanding of entrepreneurship and evolution. When I taught at Bocconi University, Paola Dubini and I began collaborating on a social network research project that resulted in several Babson College Entrepreneurship Research Conference papers and published articles. Her cheerful approach to even the most difficult problems is infectious, as I recently learned when talking with her about a new project on the commercialization of 'mommy blogs' on the Internet. Nancy Langton is a long time friend of my wife and I who has not only hosted us at the University of British Columbia in Vancouver but also brought me into a collaborative project on the growth of small firms. Through that collaboration, I met Jennifer Cliff Jennings. Nancy Carter and I became friends through our joint work on the Entrepreneurship Research Consortium and she opened my eyes to the embeddedness of most new firms in a strong family context.

Steve Bradley, while still a student working with Dean Shepherd at Indiana University, invited me to join a project on how young firms coped with environmental jolts. I was delighted to learn that Johan Wiklund was also part of the research team, as I had known him for many years through our joint ties to Per Davidsson and Jönköping University. Martha Martinez, although not represented in this volume by any papers, has been working with me on review essays on entrepreneurship for more than a decade, ever since her days as a graduate student at Duke. Finally, I owe an enormous debt of gratitude to Marlena Fiol who not only co-authored 'Fools Rush In?' but also more importantly, continuously reminds me of the importance of other things in life besides work!

Those things, of course, involve family. My wife, Penny, not only teaches her own courses, does volunteer work, and plans our travel, but also makes certain that we keep in touch with our grandchildren through weekly Skype visits when we cannot see them in person. Our two sons, both Carolina graduates, also married Carolina graduates and so we have a total Carolina family! Our grandchildren are a never ending source of delight: Jackson, who's never seen a sport that he can't excel in; Gavriel Tzvi, a voracious reader and Kendo enthusiast; Yaakov, whose first fishing expedition with me showed that he was born to fish; Yehudis, through whose eyes the *Nutcracker* ballet has never seemed more magical; and finally, Dov-Ber, who is fast on his way to becoming an escape artist to rival Houdini.

References

Aldrich, D. (2008), *Site Fights: Divisive Facilities and Civil Society in Japan and the West* (Ithaca, NY, Cornell University).

Aldrich, H.E. and E.R. Auster (1986), 'Even Dwarfs Started Small', in B.M. Staw and L.L. Cummings, *Research in Organizational Behavior* (Greenwich, CT, JAI Press), **8**, 165–98.

Aldrich, H.E. and J. Cater, et al. (1983), 'From Periphery to Peripheral: The South Asian Petite Bourgeoisie in England', in I.H. Simpson and R. Simpson, *Research in the Sociology of Work* (Greenwich, CT, JAI Press), **2**, 1–32.

Aldrich, H.E. and M. Ruef (2006), *Organizations Evolving* (London, Sage Publications).

Aldrich, H.E. and R. Waldinger (1990), *Ethnicity and Entrepreneurship, Annual Review of Sociology* (Palo Alto, CA, Annual Reviews, Inc.), **16**, 111–35.

Aldrich, H.E. and C. Zimmer (1986),'Entrepreneurship Through Social Networks', in D. Sexton and R. Smilor, *The Art and Science of Entrepreneurship* (New York, Ballinger), 3–23.

Baker, T. and R.E. Nelson (2005), 'Creating Something from Nothing: Resource Construction through Entrepreneurial Bricolage', *Administrative Science Quarterly*, **50**(3), 329–66.

Baum, J.A.C. and T.L. Amburgey (2002), 'Organizational Ecology', in J.A. Baum, *Companion to Organizations* (Oxford, Blackwell Publishers Ltd), 305–26.

Baum, J.A.C. and B. McKelvey (1999), *Variations in Organization Science: In Honor of Donald T. Campbell* (Newbury Park, CA, Sage).

Campbell, D.T. (1969), 'Variation and Selective Retention in Socio-Cultural Evolution', *General Systems*, **14**, 69–85.

Cliff, J.E., N. Langton, et al. (2005), 'Walking the Talk? Gendered Rhetoric versus Action in Small Firms', *Organization Studies*, **26**(1), 63–91.

Hannan, M.T. and J.H. Freeman (1989), *Organizational Ecology* (Cambridge, MA, Harvard University Press).

Keister, L.A. (2005), *Getting Rich: A Study of Wealth Mobility in America* (Cambridge, Cambridge University Press).

McKelvey, B. and H.E. Aldrich (1983), 'Populations, Natural Selection, and Applied Organizational Science', *Administrative Science Quarterly*, **28**(1), 101–28.

Pfeffer, J. and G.R. Salancik (1978), *The External Control of Organizations: A Resource Dependence Perspective* (New York, Harper & Row).

Scott, W.R. (2008), 'Approaching Adulthood: The Maturing of Institutional Theory', *Theory and Society*, **37**, 427–42.

Waldinger, R., H.E. Aldrich, et al. (1990), *Ethnic Entrepreneurs: Immigrant Businesses in Industrial Societies* (Beverly Hills, CA, Sage).

Williamson, O.E. (1994), 'Transaction Costs Economics and Organization Theory', in N. Smelser and R. Swedberg, *The Handbook of Economic Sociology* (Princeton, NJ, Princeton University Press), 77–107.

PART I

INTRODUCTION

[1]

♦ ♦ ♦

Who Wants to Be an Evolutionary Theorist?

Remarks on the Occasion of the Year 2000 OMT Distinguished Scholarly Career Award Presentation

HOWARD E. ALDRICH

University of North Carolina–Chapel Hill

Heedless of Madonna's warning, Paul Hirsch urged me to use this occasion as an opportunity to preach a bit. The Organization and Management Theory (OMT) division gave me a great platform from which to put forward my sense of where we are, what we've accomplished, and where we have fallen short. Three decades ago, I was the first associate editor of the *Administrative Science Quarterly,* and Paul thought that I might have some ideas on where we might go over the next decade or so. In short, Paul asked me to give a "Leadership Sermon." I'm assuming that he also released me from the scholastic requirement that I must thoroughly document the intellectual history and empirical rigor of all my claims! I plead for a temporary suspension of disbelief while I make my arguments.

Having just published my book, *Organizations Evolving* (1999), I have given some thought to what's missing in OMT, as well as to what it would mean if we took the evolutionary approach seriously. What difference would evolutionary thinking make in the way we think about theoretical issues and design our research? As it happened, I came up with a mixture of complaints and challenges. I want to celebrate what we've accomplished, but also to note where more needs to be done. In particular, I want to encourage people to pay more attention to process-oriented theorizing and research. As space does not permit me to review the fundamental features of evolutionary theory itself, readers desiring more information will need to consult my book.[1]

Four questions constitute the organizing themes of my talk. First, how can we build a more realistic OMT? Currently, our theorizing and research seriously misrepresent the actual shape of the organizational landscape. Second, what's wrong with outcome-driven research, and why should we focus more on event-driven research? Many of us fall too easily into the trap of explaining outcomes by working backward in time. Third, does OMT have rhythm? The theme of

AUTHOR'S NOTE: For their invaluable contributions toward making this a better article, I thank Ted Baker, Joel Baum, Kim Boal, C. Marlene Fiol, Paul Hirsch, Candace Jones, Alessandro Lomi, Bill McKelvey, Kelly Shaver, Paul Reynolds, Linda Renzulli, and all those who ignored the fire alarm and sat through the entire presentation in Toronto. (Was that Bill Starbuck I saw by the fire alarm switch?) Richard Dawson designed the figures for this article.

JOURNAL OF MANAGEMENT INQUIRY, Vol. 10 No. 2, June 2001 115-127
© 2001 Sage Publications, Inc.

the 2000 Academy of Management meeting was time, and I agree that timing is everything. Our theories and research designs often leave the timing and pacing of change imprecise or ambiguous. Fourth, in our research and theorizing, we need to ask ourselves more often, "What happens next?" We need to face the fact that all empirical generalizations are about the past, and begin thinking about building models from our theorizing and research that help us understand what is likely to happen in the future.

TOWARD A MORE REALISTIC OMT: THE TRUE SHAPE OF THE ORGANIZATIONAL LANDSCAPE

Because you're reading this, you probably also read the major OMT journals and maybe even write for them. Accordingly, we might expect that you'd be fairly knowledgeable about the basic facts regarding the organizational landscape. To confirm my assumption, let's play a little game: "Who wants to be an evolutionary theorist?" Take out a piece of paper and number it from 1 to 9 or, if you're reading your own copy of *JMI*, just write the answers in the boxes in Table 1 (no fair looking ahead—if this is going to work, you must play the game honestly!). Now, answer the nine questions in Table 1. All questions are about businesses in the United States. Sorry, Jean-Claude!

I'll make it easy for you. Here are the answers, all of which are in my book: 20,000, 5,478,000, 0, 14,000, 7,300,000, 21,000,000, 510, 20,000, and 4,300,000. Of course, this list is out of order! I considered putting the questions in order by the magnitude of their answers, but that would make the quiz much too easy. The answers are in the appendix.

When I ask these questions in seminars around the world, I routinely find that most people get most of these answers wrong by at least one order of magnitude, and sometimes more. Because the audience for my OMT talk consisted of the more enthusiastic and committed members of the profession, they got many more correct than most of my previous audiences.[2]

If your answers were typical, you overestimated the number of large firms, initial public offerings (IPOs), mergers and acquisitions, and publicly held firms. By contrast, you underestimated the number of new firms and total business entities. You may have even thought that personality differences matter for entrepreneurs. I'm no longer surprised by such esti-

mates, as they simply reflect what the business press emphasizes, as well as the topics and research designs found in academic journals. Should we be concerned? Consider the following parable.

At a cocktail party, academics from across the campus of Beserkely University meet and commiserate about their declining standard of living, unworthy students, and the results of the recent presidential election. Their host has invited colleagues from many different colleges and departments, and so you're meeting scientists, humanists, and even a few coaches. The president is out of town on a fund-raising trip.

A balding, middle-aged man in a tweed jacket, blue jeans, and wearing a black belt with brown shoes introduces himself: "Hello, I'm a botanist. You know, the study of plants?" You suddenly revise your estimate of the evening's potential payoff, as you see a chance to get expert advice on a problem that's been bugging you. "Oh, I'll bet you can help me. I've been battling some type of really nasty weed in my lawn for the past 3 years. It's really tough. I keep planting new rye grass, using fertilizer, and pouring enough weed killers on the lawn to wipe out the songbird population of my neighborhood, and still the stuff persists. I can't stamp it out. What is it? How can those things survive these brutal winters? What can I do?"

The botanist looks surprised at your question. "Oh, I'm sorry. I really have no clue. You see, I only study redwoods." Disappointed, you move on.

A young woman dressed in what looks like a safari suit introduces herself: "I'm new here, in the zoology department. Just got back from some fieldwork and am looking forward to my first faculty meeting." You realize she *must* be new. She had yet to sit through a department meeting where colleagues spent an hour arguing over whether the minutes for the last meeting must show the names of *all* those who seconded a motion, or just that it *was* seconded.

"Oh good, so you study animals? I have a question for you. My lawn is infested with these little rodent-like creatures. Every spring, I notice raised mounds of earth all over the place, and after the dog digs them up, I catch the mower's wheels in the holes. When Teddy actually catches one of the creatures, they look like blind hairy rats. Between them and the weeds, they're ruining my lawn. What are those things, anyway? What makes them so hardy? What can I do?"

Another startled look, accompanied by what looks, for a moment, like a condescending smile. "Oh, I'm

Table 1
Who Wants to Be an Evolutionary Theorist?

1. Approximately how many business entities have filed tax returns with the Internal Revenue Service in recent years?
2. Approximately how many businesses had paid employees in the most recent reporting year?
3. About how many incorporated businesses are there?
4. How many business startups were attempted the past year? (Feeling lucky? How many were left after 1 year?)
5. About how many firms, per year, were acquired in mergers and acquisitions in the first half of the 1990s?
6. Approximately how many publicly traded firms are there? (On all the stock exchanges and over the counter.)
7. About how many firms employ 500 people or more?
8. How many Initial Public Offerings (IPOs, for those of you in Finance) were there in 1999?
9. On how many personality traits do successful entrepreneurs differ from unsuccessful ones?

terribly sorry. I have no idea. I only study elephants." You glumly head back to the kitchen for another glass of Chianti, wondering how all these damned narrow specialists ever got jobs at Beserkely, supposedly a truly diverse university.

Redwoods and Elephants: OMT's Dilemma

Our field's claimed domain is organizations, but, like the scientists at the Beserkely University cocktail party, in reality we fall far short of universal coverage. Our journals are filled with studies of mostly large organizations or the surviving members of much larger cohorts of all kinds of organizations.[3] Most members of our potential study populations exited prior to when the study was carried out, and our data sets consist of the remnants of selection processes we've overlooked. Many variables we'd like to use in our research are only available for large, publicly held firms. Consequently, we miss the true extent of variety, diversity, and heterogeneity in the organizational landscape.

Of course, we've known about this problem for years. For example, researchers interested in financial performance measures must limit themselves to publicly traded firms. Privately held firms don't have to make public reports of their financial performance, and they're also notoriously idiosyncratic in their accounting practices. Thus, strategy and finance researchers, and others looking for standardized financial accounting measures, have found themselves limited to just 20,000 publicly listed firms, constituting a tiny fraction of the organizational population.

Left truncation is another example of the problems that limit the representativeness of our data sets. Our understanding of the association between organizational "age" and various kinds of transformation has been seriously distorted by selection bias. If we examine only surviving firms, we don't observe organizations over the full range of ages during which they're at risk of transformation.

Summary

Limiting our studies to only a small fraction of the organizational world means that we ignore much of the historical process that generated such organizations. Most, after all, began small (Aldrich & Auster, 1986). We miss their aging and their evolution through periods when competitors were eliminated. We don't see the distinctive differences that made surviving organizations hardier than their peers. In research that showed the importance of taking account of historical periods, for example, Jones (in press) traced the evolutionary differences within and between technology and content firms as they battled for dominance in the film industry between 1911 and 1920. Such historical details are lost if only the oldest and largest firms constitute our samples. Moreover, by ignoring the smallest and most fragile organizations, we overlook the source of diversity in the organizational landscape and the pace of its reproduction. Indeed, our field's multidisciplinary nature is threatened if we ignore the incredible diversity of its subject matter.

The skewed nature of the research that appears in our journals constitutes the longer-term issue facing us, as does the skewed nature of the populations that scholars choose to study. Skewed samples, in turn, bias the kinds of theory that we do. The people who are writing theory are inevitably basing it, in part, on what they choose as empirical generalizations from the research literature. If those empirical generalizations are based on a very small subset of the universe, then theorizing is also inevitably skewed toward those larger organizations.

For me, one of the most exciting areas of strategic leadership is figuring out how millions of small firm

118   JOURNAL OF MANAGEMENT INQUIRY / June 2001

owners manage to keep their organizations intact from 1 day to the next through a variety of vexing circumstances. By contrast, the leadership literature mostly focuses on people who either manage very big firms or, worse still, people who are the CEOs of very big firms, not middle managers. Because they focus on huge established firms, researchers ignore the much larger pool of people who are also leaders by most definitions but who don't get any attention. Is there still life in the strategic leadership literature after Jack Welch retires?

WHAT'S WRONG WITH OUTCOME-DRIVEN RESEARCH?

Dynamic designs might compensate for some of the problems I mentioned, but a high proportion of OMT research is still cross-sectional and static. At times, we seem almost wedded to single-administration questionnaires and surveys. Evolutionary explanations focus on processes and are event driven, with events followed prospectively to outcomes. By contrast, nonevolutionary explanations are outcome driven, with outcomes followed backward to their preceding events. Outcome-oriented researchers ransack organizational histories for formative events that might have led to the observed outcomes.

Outcome-Driven Explanations

Outcome-driven explanations are built backward, from an awareness of observed outcomes to prior causally significant events. Two related problems are introduced with this strategy. First, it often leads to investigators selecting on the dependent variable, a well-known research bias. Second, even though we might include all organizations—those that have experienced the event and those that have not—we still observe them at only one point in time. Figure 1 gives a graphic example of an outcome observed at Time 1 that is then linked backward to events occurring earlier.

For example, in a survey study, we might ask respondents about their level of commitment to an organization, and then ask about previous events hypothesized to have affected their commitment. We might ask about promotions, experiences with coworkers, or lateral transfers within the organization. In another example, while doing an organiza-

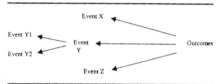

Figure 1:   Outcome-driven explanations
Source: Adapted from Elder, Caspi, and Burton (1988).

tional ethnography, we might conduct semistructured interviews and examine organizational archives to reconstruct relevant previous events.

Dutton's (1997) review of research on building strategic agendas mentioned several studies of major decision making that were outcome driven. For example, Hickson, Butler, Cray, Mallory, and Wilson (1986) studied 150 top decisions, Mintzberg (1978) studied 25 strategic decisions, and Eisenhardt (1989) examined eight firms in high-velocity environments by beginning with "endings" and then reconstructing the processes leading up to them. In each study, researchers conducted interviews with participants and also examined documents from company archives.

What difficulties might befall us in constructing outcome-driven explanations? First, of course, not everyone who was at risk of experiencing the event in the past is still around, thus introducing sample selection bias into our design. Organizations may have failed, disbanded, or otherwise gone out of existence. Even when studying large organizations, researchers will find that some have exited the field if the time span covered is lengthy. Individuals who took part in making key decisions are often no longer around for interviews. Second, relevant records from the past may have been lost or destroyed, leaving us unable to build a trail back from the outcome to relevant events. For example, bureaucracies keep records for administrative purposes, not research, and they often discard them after a set period of time (Reiss, 1992).

Third, humans are remarkably good at retrospective reconstruction, as recent incidents of "recovered memory" have shown. People like to put themselves at the center of the action—inflating their importance, excusing their mistakes, and settling scores with those no longer around to defend themselves.[4] Knowledge of the outcomes inevitably frames the explanations people offer when asked about the past (Kahneman, Slovic, & Tversky, 1982). Fourth, humans are also incredibly myopic creatures. Events whose importance was unrecognized at the time simply remain unacknowledged and left out of explanatory accounts subsequently offered.

I am not arguing against choosing research problems on the basis of observing significant outcomes.[5] Most of science is about studying what leads up to or causes outcomes. Much of the philosophy of science and epistemology is really about how to avoid making causal attribution errors, given outcome-based research. Problems arise when researchers forget that their underlying goal is to build event-driven explanations for outcomes, rather than to celebrate the outcomes.

Event-Driven Explanations

In contrast to outcome-driven explanations, event-driven explanations are built forward, from observed or recorded events to outcomes. Researchers pick certain kinds of events a priori and then record their occurrences over time. No simple rules exist for such designs, and some events can figure in more than one narrative. Moreover, most events we observe probably have no obvious consequences, thus requiring that researchers have strong a priori theoretically grounded notions of the expected causal process. Figure 2 gives a graphic example of events observed over time, which are then linked forward to outcomes occurring later. Note that later outcomes are themselves events with subsequent consequences.

For example, several event-driven survey research projects have been funded over the past three decades with notable success. Back in the 1940s, sociologists and political scientists studying voting behavior pioneered the study of political behavior over time. In 1940, three researchers studied 3,000 people in Erie County, Ohio, and followed about 600 of them with monthly interviews between May and November: "Interviews were spaced about a month apart to fit best the natural course of campaign events" (Lazarsfeld, Berelson, & Gaudet, 1944, p. 5).

Based on that groundbreaking study, many other panel studies followed. The Panel Study of Income Dynamics (PSID), initiated by John Lansing and Jim Morgan at the University of Michigan in the 1960s, followed people over many years, with interviews repeated at various intervals. Reports from the PSID, especially by authors such as Duncan and Coe (1984), allowed researchers to gain important new insights into the dynamics of economic status, especially poverty and welfare. Similarly, the National Longitudinal

Figure 2: Event-driven explanations
Source: Adapted from Elder, Caspi, and Burton (1988).

Study of Youth followed children from their early years in school up through adolescence, again with repeated interviews. By asking questions about the same events in successive surveys, researchers can link prior events to subsequent outcomes, such as getting a job or losing it, paying back a loan or welshing on it, and getting ahead or being held back in school.

In the field of entrepreneurship studies, Reynolds and his colleagues (Reynolds & White, 1997) have used multiwave panel studies to study the behavior of nascent entrepreneurs. A nascent entrepreneur is defined as someone who initiates serious activities that are intended to culminate in a viable business startup. Beginning with studies in several states, Reynolds (2000) and a large team of collaborators developed a method for conducting panel studies of the business startup process covering the entire United States. The model has been extended to Norway, Sweden, Canada, the Netherlands, Greece, and Argentina, and has been modified for cross-national comparisons of entrepreneurial activity and national economic growth in the Global Entrepreneurship Monitor Project (Reynolds, Hay, & Camp, 1999).

Event-based explanations can be built on archival records as well. We can seek evidence on events that have occurred by searching the files of organizations, using commercial directories, and tapping other publicly available sources of information. For example, many people are familiar with ecologists who use event history analyses based on archival data. Because of their dependence on archival data, they've been stuck with just a few events that can be studied that way. One of them is disbanding, whether through failure, bankruptcy, or another form of exiting a population. Another event recorded in company files and announced publicly by large firms is CEO succession.

Often, archival information will yield much of what we need. But there are other kinds of things that we are not going to find in the archives because the archives were collected for administrative purposes. Record-keeping bureaucrats in organizations keep records for themselves, not for researchers. Administrators keep records because they need to make decisions of some

120   JOURNAL OF MANAGEMENT INQUIRY / June 2001

kind, such as whether to tow your car to the city pound because you're a blatant traffic ticket scofflaw or to just put a notice on your windshield because you're an amateur offender. They don't care about your socioeconomic status or whether your parking problems stem from your attempt to hold down two jobs at opposite ends of the city. Thus, it's not so easy to take what they have in their archives and mold it to our purposes.

Research on interorganizational relations has been especially hampered by a lack of available information on events. Relations between organizations are often informal and undocumented, as Barley, Freeman, and Hybels (1992) discovered when they were trying to collect information on strategic alliances in biotechnology. When proprietary information is involved, organizational participants see researchers as one more source of technology leakage (Teece, 1980). In short, they may not trust us to keep our mouths shut. Indeed, in keeping with my first theme, privately held firms are loath to give up any sensitive information, leaving researchers to fall back on what they can find in public reports and government documents (e.g., Securities and Exchange Commission filings).

Summary

Cross-sectional designs and outcome-oriented data collection hamper our ability to construct evolutionary explanations. Dynamic designs enable us to separate the random noise in our data from the true underlying structural time trends (Dooley & Van de Ven, 1999). We need dynamic and event-oriented designs that leave room for unexpected historical conjunctures, blind alleys, and dead ends. Moving backward from organizational characteristics to "reasons" why it must have developed that way encourages the construction of arbitrary explanations.

For example, Fischhoff (1982) showed that people couldn't disregard what they already know about something when it comes to constructing an explanation about why something happened in the past. Once they know the outcome, people build stories that lead, inevitably, to that outcome. Fischhoff and his colleagues designed experiments in which they altered historical outcomes, using cases most people don't know much about. They took real historical data and simply changed the outcome of some series of events. When they asked people to estimate the probability with which they could have successfully predicted the outcome of the events, given knowledge only of the past, they consistently overestimated their abilities. Moreover, in writing up stories that justified their predictions, they were able to put together very coherent and compelling stories. Of course, they were wrong.

Moving forward with our explanations, using reliable information consistently collected on similar kinds of events allows us to avoid outcome-driven explanatory biases. However, we face another danger. Investigators may discover that their event-accounting schemes from early periods lose their explanatory power when circumstances change. When powerful period effects exist, our explanations will be historically contingent in the extreme (Aldrich, 1999, chap. 8). We need more dynamic research designs and fewer cross-sectional ones.

Growing interest in issues of organizational identity and continuity fits nicely into a concern for event-driven explanations (Whetten & Godfrey, 1998). Whether individuals develop a strong identification with an organization might depend on when they join and that organization's position in its life course. For example, we might expect that people who have experienced the ambiguity and struggle of a firm's formative days would identify closely with it. Indeed, they might even consider it a mirror of their own personal identities. Later arrivals might not feel the same.

Thus, depending on when they joined, employees may have very different images of the firm. Throughout its life course, an organization's identity and the emergent culture that shapes the selection and socialization of new employees remain contested. Looking forward, it may be very hard to predict which of many possible versions of firm identity will prevail. Unknown future events and contingencies create a selection environment through which some identities are likely to dominate others (Aldrich, 1999, chap. 6).

The extent to which an organization's identity affects its strategy depends, in part, on the trail of events established by its history. For example, research on top management teams has shown that a firm that experiences poor performance is more likely to replace a retiring—or ousted—CEO with an outsider, someone whose outlook has not been imbued with the firm's identity.[6] These outsiders are, in turn, more likely to make substantial strategic changes than are insiders. Poor performance events may thereby lead to broken connections between firm identity and strategy. In contrast, long periods of acceptable performance may lead to succession by long-time insiders and an unbroken marriage of firm identity and strategy. A tight bond between identity and strategy, however, does not guarantee a firm's survival. Strong identities can either blind organizations to changing environments, rendering them unable to adapt, or give them the cohesion they need to survive challenges brought on by change (Fiol, in press).

WHO'S GOT RHYTHM?

Time was the theme of the 2000 Academy of Management meeting, and in evolutionary theory, timing is critical. Theories of organizational change often leave the timing and pacing of change imprecise or ambiguous. We don't know whether the posited changes are accomplished in days, weeks, months, years, or decades. Research designs often further confound the issue, leaving a mismatch between a theory's implicit time frame and actual empirical indicators. For example, few theories of organizational change specify that change only occurs once a year, and yet researchers who rely on archival data often only have data available in 1-year chunks. As I've noted, researchers using archival data are at the mercy of administrators, whose demands for data are driven by organizational needs, not a theory of why things are happening.

Model Time Explicitly

Investigators should develop explicit models that specify the intervals of time during which transforming changes or events occur (McKelvey, 1997). What is the posited time trajectory? For example, how long should it take for new regulations to disrupt the established order of competition in an industry—weeks, months, or years (Haveman, 1992)? Why does it take that long? Are the regulators underfunded, incompetent, or in collusion with those they are supposed to regulate?

When investigators spell out a theory of the timing of events and outcomes, they can then decide on the frequency of observations needed and the time interval between them. For example, Lazarsfeld et al. (1944) decided that voters probably didn't change their minds about candidates more often than monthly, and then designed their data collection around that assumption. In an organizational example, Sastry (1997) showed how incorporating the notion of pacing into models of organizational change enriches our understanding of how organizations

adapt to environmental change. To do so, however, requires that we have an explicit theory of pace and duration.

Waiting, Pacing, and Duration

Time can be measure in clock time, but it is also embedded in people's interpretations of their situations. We can distinguish between two dimensions of time: pace and duration. Pace is the number of events in a given amount of time, whereas duration is the amount of time elapsed for a given event. Variations in pacing reflect the operation of cultural norms in evolutionary processes.

Merton (1949) coined the term *socially expected duration* to explain human's tendencies to base their decisions on how long they think a particular relationship or event will last. For example, officers in voluntary associations are usually elected to 1-year terms, and they plan their activities accordingly. In another example, normative expectations regarding career progress milestones are built into universities. Some universities have a reappointment clock in which faculty members have an initial 3-year appointment, and if they are renewed they come up for tenure in the 5th or 6th year. Those are socially expected categories in the sense that your career is now set up in 3- and 6-year chunks (for other examples, see Lawrence, 1997).

Gersick's (1991) research implies that if you give people a 3-year or 6-year duration in which they are meant to be working, they would typically take that expected duration and halve it. They would then time what they do with respect to the midpoint of that interval. So, for example, if a department gives a junior faculty member a 3-year appointment, we would expect that after 1.5 years, some kind of panic would set in. Assistant professors will begin to recognize that they have lost half of the time they've been allotted to prove themselves. Their behavior will change substantially in the second half of that period, compared with the first half.[7]

We can use the idea of expected duration to interpret business startup processes. For example, we can explain what happened in April 2000 as a change in investors' socially constructed duration expectations about dot-com firms. Many of the entrepreneurs who started dot-coms were thinking about their enterprises within a very long time frame. In fact, it's not clear that a closed-ended time interval was even salient to many of them. They might have been dreaming of an IPO, which would have meant that they were thinking, "Well, I probably have 5 or 6 years or so from startup time, to when venture capitalists get involved, to when we go public." They thus fantasized that they had 5 or 6 years to prove themselves. For them, 1 month, 6 months, or 1 year was really not a conspicuous time unit. Thus, they felt no pressure to do anything in a hurry, and they wouldn't have felt any pressure until they were halfway through that lengthy period.

In addition to duration effects, we must also be attentive to period effects—changes produced by historical events and forces that have a similar effect on all organizations, regardless of age (Aldrich, 1999, 201-216).[8] In April 2000, a classic period effect occurred. Suddenly, the perceptions of investors changed from "we are waiting for an IPO in 6 years" to saying that "we want to see results more quickly." The entrepreneurs who had been thinking about time in half-decade chunks were forced to think of time in terms of months: "I'm a new venture, and all of the sudden my investors say they want to see some positive cash flow inside of 18 months."

Nothing changed insofar as the fundamental issues about building a business were concerned. What changed was the expected duration during which people expect the building process to occur. The definition of a successful startup was no longer, "Take 6 years, build the company, and have a public exit event." Now, the normative expectation for the duration of a successful startup was, "Within 18 months we want to see positive cash flow, or at least we want to see a movement toward positive cash flow, maybe even profitability."

Thus, to understand the evolution of firms, we need to understand the social expectations they face regarding pacing and duration and how expectations change over time: What are the community or population expectations? Viewed historically, the definition of time is very context specific (Bartunek & Necochea, 2000). In particular, how time is defined in a particular era affects the urgency with which people carry out what they are doing. People slow down or speed up, depending on how close they are to expected timelines and guideposts. In describing the ecommerce world of the late 1990s, Kanter (2001) noted that "in the everything-faster e-world, where innovation is improvisational theater, opportunities become themes before the need is fully documented, the actors start the play while the producer is still finding backers, and the team celebrates milestones while the ending is still undetermined" (p. 280).

One interesting area of inquiry is the extent to which firms, when they experience a shift occur like the one in April 2000, have the ability to adapt and adjust to changes in social expectations. In the fall 2000, many observers predicted that something like 80% of the dot-coms would no longer be around by 2003. Observers were not talking like that before April.[9] Indeed, we heard few mentions of impending firm mortality. We knew that mortality was a likely ending event for many of these firms, but there was no sense of urgency. Now, in 2001, predictions of doom are being echoed over and over again, increasing the pressure on entrepreneurs to shorten their time horizons and not think about time in terms of half decades or even years.

Timing thus represents a critical part of the selection logic in evolutionary models. Survival often depends on small differences in the co-occurrence of several events (Carroll & Harrison, 1994). Rapid changes in selection environments can change the terms on which resources are available, thus altering the fate of organizations and populations. For example, in some technology fields, a new system or device introduced in September may garner few sales, although the same technology introduced the previous January might have come to dominate its market for some time. At the population level, in their study of San Francisco area hospitals' survival from 1945 to 1990, Ruef and Scott (1998) showed that powerful period effects can lead to historically contingent explanations. Outcome-based explanations and cross-sectional data thus put our empirical generalizations at risk by ignoring the importance of timing.

Summary

How can we study pacing and duration? We need information on when changes were initiated and completed, and on key events within the changes. Such information must be collected at the appropriate level and in a timely fashion. However, collecting timely information from archival and publicly available data is difficult. Often, such data can tell us when an event was completed, but not when people or organizations began working on it. So, we know the outcome but not the sequence and pacing of events leading up to it. For example, most corporate merger and acquisition negotiations begin in secret, and many never come to fruition. If we study only successful mergers and acquisitions, we might gain a false sense of the pacing and duration of the process. If we rely on public announcements, we also obtain only a partial picture of the process. Obtaining timely information will require that we develop alternative strategies for collecting it.

Fieldwork and real ethnography—the kind that goes beyond "data collection by walking around the office floor"—is costly, but it is critical to discovering the proper intervals for subsequent large-scale observation and data collection (Stewart, 1998). Fortunately, we have a number of exemplars of how to conduct rigorous process-oriented field studies and ethnographies, from Barley's (1990) intensive field immersion studies to Van de Ven, Polley, Garud, and Venkataraman's (1999) dynamic quantitative research. Barley spent months observing technicians in two Massachusetts' hospitals, and Van de Ven and his colleagues tracked the development of innovations in real time and in their natural field settings.

I recognize that investigators face resource constraints on the kind of information that they can collect. If we had unlimited resources, we would obviously choose representative samples and follow them over long periods of time. We would have an army of people documenting everything that happens in the organization. We don't have that available to us, so the question is, What kinds of compromises do we have to make? Van de Ven et al. (1999) and Barley's (1990) research shows us that questionnaire- or survey-based research is not the only way to think about the problem.

In planning survey-based research, researchers usually think about large N studies and of the need to compile sampling lists based on some known universe. But in event-driven research, we need a lot more information about micro-events whose consequences aren't yet known. That probably means spending more time in a smaller set of organizations, using other methods than survey research. Undoubtedly, our sample size will be smaller and more time will be required for that project than a survey. I recognize the inevitability of such constraints.

That's why, in my preconference seminars at Academy of Management meetings about the obligations of senior scholars, I've said that we don't just want to say to junior scholars, "Okay, we haven't done very well at this, and we haven't succeeded. Write us off and you do it better." Junior people could justifiably look at us and say, "Why didn't you do this stuff when you had the chance? If you didn't do it, why do you expect us to do it?" I recognize this contradiction, and

thus I'm also speaking to the more senior scholars who still have the energy to gear up for one last dash to the research frontier.

WHAT HAPPENS NEXT?

Picture a typical empirical article packed with regression coefficients or other measures of one variable's effects on another. If the authors were graphically inspired, their argument is probably illustrated by something like Figure 3, showing an arrow between several circles or boxes.[10] The figure and accompanying words in the text make an explicitly causal argument, although the time period represented by the arrow's flight is not usually spelled out. Looked at from an evolutionary point of view, the results merely describe a moment in time, captured as the people and organizations in the study were on their way to new destinations. I'm often puzzled by how the results are discussed and why several questions, in particular, are left unanswered.

First, if the form, direction, and magnitude of the relations discovered in the analysis continue to hold, what will the organizations look like a few time periods into the future? We often remind our students that the results of a single study don't constitute a sound empirical generalization. Only replications can tell us whether our theoretically based models have improved our understanding of the phenomenon. Overlooked in this formulation is the hidden truth that the coefficients in our research results are historical artifacts! Until we've tested the model on which the research is based in other periods, we don't know the extent to which our results are dependent on the unique historical circumstances in which the tests were run.

All our results are, in a sense, about the past. Critics often chide me that "evolutionary theory is backward looking—it only helps us understand what has already happened." They claim the higher ground and argue that they are engaged in a science of prediction. So I ask them, "When, exactly, did you collect your data? And when did you analyze it?" None of them ever claim to have written their results section before the data were collected. After all, building an explanatory model is easy once you know the outcome. But the strength of any claims about research results rests on our ability to project, using our understanding of the underlying process, what will happen

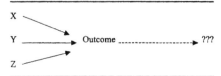

Figure 3:   What happens next?

next in the organizations we have studied. To do that, we have to understand relationship dynamics, not just the presence of relationships.

Second, if a positive or negative association is found between two variables, can it be sustained into the future indefinitely? Are there inherent limits on how strongly the two variables can become linked? For reasons I don't understand, thinking about organizations as complex adaptive systems has just not caught on in OMT, despite its obvious utility in diagnosing flaws in causal models (Anderson, 1999). I've never forgotten Buckley's (1967) admonition to look for deviation amplifying and deviation dampening feedback loops in organizations evolving. Decades later, Senge (1990) used well-understood principles of feedback loops in dynamic systems to create simple but powerful models of learning organizations. Simply put, most organizations evolve not only through positive but also negative, moderating, and balancing feedback processes. Knowing where you have been doesn't necessarily tell you anything about where you might be going (Boal, Hunt, & Jaros, in press).

I'm puzzled by discussions of research results that implicitly assume equilibrium has been reached in populations of people and organizations. For example, if diverse weak ties give entrepreneurs an advantage in competing for resources, does that mean that surviving entrepreneurs will eventually have only weak ties with others? If strong ties give entrepreneurs the emotional support they need to persist in the face of discouraging results, does that mean that surviving entrepreneurs will eventually have only strong ties with others? Clearly, balancing and moderating forces affect the mix of ties that entrepreneurs can sustain, and a complete picture of entrepreneurial networking must make room for such subtleties (Aldrich, 1999, 81-88).[11]

People tend to forget things they haven't used recently. Organizations aren't immune to memory loss either, as Argote (1999) and her colleagues have shown in a series of creative projects. Knowledge that goes unused decays quickly, although the process

might be arrested if means are found to institutionalize it. For example, Argote estimated that up to 80% of what an organization learned could be lost in a year or so, without continuous reinforcement. In models of organizational evolution, organizational learning needs to be complemented with organizational forgetting and other balancing processes. We might throw in a little laughter as well (Kundera, 1980).

I'm very hopeful that simulation and computational or agent-based modeling (ABM) can give us the additional tools we need to test the dynamic implications of our research results (Carley, 1991; Lomi & Larsen, 2001). In criticizing current practice in OMT, McKelvey (in press) noted that model building is the missing element in the theory-model-data trilogy of the scientific realism approach. In the best of all worlds, data would never touch theory directly. Instead, theory informs the modeling process, which in turn implies and is informed by research design and results. Simulation and ABM give researchers the opportunity to see what happens next without being constrained by meager research budgets and incomplete data sets (Keister, 2000). For example, an extremely clever simulation, showing the consequences of exploration and exploitation strategies, was a major reason for the appeal of March's (1991) scheme. Sterman and Wittenberg (1999) used dynamic modeling to explore the evolution of scientific paradigms, formalizing the propositions in Kuhn (1970).

In many respects, criteria for evaluating computational models are no different from those used for any other type of social science model, as Alessandro Lomi (personal communication, March 2001) reminded me. A model has to be expressive and accurate. The term *expressive* means that we must capture the crucially relevant aspects of the process in our model, and not just metaphorically. Models based on selection logic must spell out how the selection process actually works. The term *accurate* means that what is true in (or can be proven about) the model has to be true for the process as well. Expressiveness requires theoretical abstraction, whereas accuracy requires empirical grounding. Achieving both in the same model can be difficult.[12]

CONCLUSION

I've developed some of these themes at greater length in chapter 12 of my book, and so let me briefly summarize them here. First, we need to improve our mental maps of the organizational landscape. Currently, academic and popular writing on organizations is skewed toward the largest and most prominent organizations, distorting our vision. A more realistic view should include the full range of diversity found in organizational communities, especially the organizations struggling to emerge from what Kaufman (1985) called the "primordial soup" of creation.

Second, we should be wary of outcome-driven explanations. Think forward, not backward, and build event-driven explanations and research designs. Use outcome-driven interests to spark inquiries, but don't depend on them to build empirical generalizations. Third, we need to build time explicitly into our theories and models. Pacing and duration, when left unexamined, imply an equilibrium-based view and a static world. In this unrealistic scenario, organizations could not evolve, for nothing ever changes.

Fourth, we must recognize that all empirical generalizations are about the past. What differentiates an evolutionary view from others is an explicit recognition that the goal of organization studies is to build models of what happens next. The value of our research results depends on our ability to construct models of the underlying change process, use them to improve our theories, and then apply them to building better models. Accomplishing that goal requires that we understand the dynamics of relationships within an evolutionary framework.

APPENDIX
Answers to the "Who Wants to
Be an Evolutionary Theorist?" Quiz

1. In 1996, approximately 23 million taxable entities—nonfarm sole proprietorships, partnerships, and corporations—filed business returns with the Internal Revenue Service (U.S. Internal Revenue Service, *Statistics of Income*).
2. About 5.5 million businesses (not establishments!) employed at least one person for enough hours in at least one quarter of 1996 to pay Unemployment Insurance and Social Security taxes (U.S. Census, *County Business Patterns*).
3. In 1996, 4.6 million firms were incorporated as legal entities (U.S. Internal Revenue Service, *Statistics of Income*). Most were quite small, of course.
4. In 1999, according to the *Global Entrepreneurship Monitor* (Reynolds, Hay, & Camp, 1999), about 7.3 million startup attempts were made in the United States (P. Reynolds, personal communication, March 2001). Reynolds estimated that about 2.3 million would

become "baby firms" in 12 months, based on previous results.
5. According to the Business Information Tracking Series (BITS) database—formerly called Longitudinal Establishment and Enterprise Microdata (LEEM) of the Small Business Administration—about 0.5% per year of the establishments with employees in 1990 were acquired by another firm during 1990 to 1994 (Aldrich, 1999, 261-264; Small Business Administration, 1998). In round numbers, that's slightly fewer than 30,000 per year.
6. Aggregating across the NYSE, the AMEX, NASDAQ, and the various regional exchanges, shares of approximately 20,000 firms trade relatively freely in the public market.
7. In 1990, 14,023 firms in the United States employed 500 workers or more, employing more than 43 million people (Small Business Administration, 1994). At the top, 484 enterprises employed 10,000 or more.
8. In 1999, 510 firms had their Initial Public Offering, down from a high in 1996 of 758.
9. None. There are *no* thoroughly documented findings, based on rigorous research designs, showing that any personality traits consistently differentiate successful from unsuccessful entrepreneurs (Shaver, 1995). Gartner, Shaver, and Gatewood (2000) noted, "In short, the stereotype of the highly independent, financially-driven, risk-seeking entrepreneur may be nothing more than a distillation of the retrospective stories that entrepreneurs have told researchers in the past" (p. 10).

NOTES

1. Additional revenues earned from readers actually purchasing my book to learn more about evolutionary theory will be donated to my youngest son, Daniel. He's working on his Ph.D. in political science at Harvard and has become enamored of rational choice approaches, but is also finding that Theda Skocpol's (1984) arguments for the comparative-historical path are quite appealing.
2. As I recall, Gerry Davis and Mark Mizruchi came close to getting them all right. But I think most people got between half and three quarters correct. Of course, I used the honor system in scoring the answers.
3. As Bill McKelvey reminded me, we focus on large firms—especially those of us in business schools—because that's where the money is (e.g., in 1994, 9% of all corporations controlled about 97% of all corporate assets).
4. If you heard Joel Baum's introduction of me at the Organization and Management Theory (OMT) session that led to this article, you'll know what I'm talking about.
5. Bill McKelvey insisted I put this disclaimer into the body of the article.
6. I am indebted to Ted Baker for spelling this point out for me. I don't think any of his firms ever did poorly, however.

7. Think "sleepless nights" and "take-out dinners" and you get the picture.

8. In complexity theory terms, the basin of attraction might change in the middle of the historical era being studied. We could no longer assume that a single equilibrium point attractor was controlling a stable set of phenomena. McKelvey (1999, in press) makes this all abundantly clear.

9. There's a rumor that Jack Welch knew, however.

10. Journal editors seem to like graphical models, for some reason, even though most do little more than show, with boxes and arrows, what the text says in words—as I've done in Figure 3.

11. For a more general discussion of the emergence and persistence of order in complex systems, see McKelvey (in press).

12. Alessandro Lomi (personal communication, March 2001) noted that he is "dissatisfied by the metaphorical use of models borrowed from other fields and designed to address specific problems. I think that any model can be useful but has to be embedded in a detailed understanding of the phenomenon at hand."

REFERENCES

Aldrich, H. E. (1999). *Organizations evolving*. London: Sage.

Aldrich, H. E., & Auster, E. R. (1986). Even dwarfs started small. In B. M. Staw & L. L. Cummings (Eds.), *Research in organizational behavior* (Vol. 8, pp. 165-198). Greenwich, CT: JAI.

Anderson, P. (1999). Complexity theory and organization science. *Organization Science, 10*(3), 216-232.

Argote, L. (1999). *Organizational learning: Creating, retaining, and transferring knowledge*. Boston: Kluwer.

Barley, S. R. (1990). The alignment of technology and structure through roles and networks. *Administrative Science Quarterly, 35*(1), 61-103.

Barley, S. R., Freeman, J. H., & Hybels, R. C. (1992). Strategic alliances in commercial biotechnology. In N. Nohria & R. G. Eccles (Eds.), *Networks and organizations: Structure, form, and action* (pp. 311-347). Boston, MA: Harvard University Business School.

Bartunek, J. M., & R. Necochea. (2000). Old insights and new times: Kairos, Inca Cosmology and their contributions to contemporary management inquiry. *Journal of Management Inquiry, 9*(2), 103-113.

Boal, K. B., Hunt, J. G., & Jaros, S. J. (in press). Order is free: On the ontological status of organizations. In R. Westwood & S. Clegg (Eds.), *Point/counterpoint: Central debates in organization theory*. Oxford, UK: Blackwell.

Buckley, W. F. (1967). *Sociology and modern systems theory*. Englewood Cliffs, NJ: Prentice Hall.

Carley, K. (1991). A theory of group stability. *American Sociological Review, 56*(3), 331-354.

Carroll, G. R., & Harrison, J. R. (1994). On the historical efficiency of competition between organizational populations. *American Journal of Sociology, 100*(3), 720-749.

Dooley, K. J., & Van de Ven, A. H. (1999). Explaining complex organizational dynamics. *Organization Science, 10*(3), 358-372.

Duncan, G. J., & Coe, R. D. (1984). *Years of poverty, years of plenty: The changing economic fortunes of American workers and families*. Ann Arbor: Survey Research Center, Institute for Social Research, The University of Michigan.

Dutton, J. (1997). Strategic agenda building in organizations. In Z. Shapira (Ed.), *Organizational decision making* (pp. 81-107). Cambridge, UK: Cambridge University Press.

Eisenhardt, K. M. (1989). Making fast strategic decisions in high-velocity environments. *Academy of Management Journal, 32*(3), 543-576.

Elder, G. H., Jr., Caspi, A., & Burton, L. M. (1988). Adolescent transitions in developmental perspective: Sociological and historical insights. In M. R. Gunnar & A. Collins (Eds.), *Minnesota symposium on child psychology, 21* (pp. 151-179). Hillsdale, NJ: Erlbaum.

Fiol, C. M. (in press). Revisiting an identity-based view of sustainable competitive advantage. *Journal of Management*.

Fischhoff, B. (1982). For those condemned to study the past: Heuristics and biases in hindsight. In D. Kahneman, P. Slovic, & A. Tversky (Eds.), *Judgment under uncertainty: Heuristics and biases* (pp. 335-351). Cambridge, UK: Cambridge University Press.

Gartner, W. B., Shaver, K. G., & Gatewood, E. J. (2000). *Doing it for yourself: Career attributions of nascent entrepreneurs*. Paper presented at the Babson-Kauffman Entrepreneurship Research Conference, Babson Park, MA.

Gersick, C.J.G. (1991). Revolutionary change theories: A multilevel exploration of the punctuated equilibrium paradigm. *Academy of Management Review, 16*(1), 10-36.

Haveman, H. A. (1992). Between a rock and a hard place: Organizational change and performance under conditions of fundamental environmental transformation. *Administrative Science Quarterly, 37*(1), 48-75.

Hickson, D. J., Butler, R., Cray, D., Mallory, G., & Wilson, D. (1986). *Top decisions: Strategic decision making in organizations*. San Francisco: Jossey-Bass.

Jones, C. (in press). The coevolution of entrepreneurial careers, institutional rules, and competitive dynamics in American film, 1895-1920. *Organization Studies*.

Kahneman, D., Slovic, P., & Tversky, A. (1982). *Judgment under uncertainty: Heuristics and biases*. New York: Cambridge University Press.

Kanter, R. M. (2001). *Evolve! Succeeding in the digital culture of tomorrow*. Boston: Harvard Business School Press.

Kaufman, H. (1985). *Time, chance, and organizations*. Chatham, NJ: Chatham House.

Keister, L. A. (2000). *Wealth in America: Trends in wealth inequality*. Cambridge, UK: Cambridge University Press.

Kuhn, T. S. (1970). *The structure of scientific revolutions* (2nd ed.). Chicago: University of Chicago Press.

Kundera, M. (1980). *The book of laughter and forgetting*. New York: Alfred A. Knopf.

Lawrence, B. S. (1997). The black box of organizational demography. *Organization Science, 8*(1), 1-22.

Lazarsfeld, P., Berelson, B., & Gaudet, H. (1944). *The people's choice: How the voter makes up his mind in a presidential campaign.* New York: Columbia University Press.

Lomi, A., & Larsen, E. (Eds.). (2001). *Dynamics of organizations: Computational modeling and organization theories.* Menlo Park, CA: AAAI Press.

March, J. G. (1991). Exploration and exploitation in organizational learning. *Organization Science, 2*(1), 71-87.

Merton, R. K. (1949). *Social theory and social structure.* Glencoe, IL: The Free Press.

McKelvey, B. (1997). Quasi-natural organization science. *Organization Science, 8*(4), 351-380.

McKelvey, B. (1999). Avoiding complexity catastrophe in coevolutionary pockets: Strategies for rugged landscapes. *Organization Science, 10*(3), 294-321.

McKelvey, B. (in press). Model-centered organizational epistemology. In J.A.C. Baum (Ed.), *Companion to organization.* Oxford, UK: Blackwell.

Mintzberg, H. (1978). Patterns in strategy formation. *Management Science, 24,* 934-948.

Reiss, A. J., Jr. (1992). The trained incapacities of sociologists. In T. Halliday & M. Janowitz (Eds.), *Sociology and its publics* (pp. 297-315). Chicago: University of Chicago Press.

Reynolds, P. D. (2000). National panel study of US business start-ups: Background and methodology. In J. A. Katz (Ed.), *Advances in entrepreneurship, firm emergence, and growth* (Vol. 4, pp. 153-228). Stamford, CT: JAI.

Reynolds, P. D., Hay, M., & Camp, S. M. (1999). *Global entrepreneurship monitor.* Kansas City, MO: Kauffman Center for Entrepreneurial Leadership.

Reynolds, P. D., & White, S. B. (1997). *The entrepreneurial process: Economic growth, men, women, and minorities.* Westport, CT: Quorum Books.

Ruef, M., & Scott, W. R. (1998). A multidimensional model of organizational legitimacy: Hospital survival in changing institutional environments. *Administrative Science Quarterly, 43*(4), 877-904.

Sastry, M. A. (1997). Problems and paradoxes in a model of punctuated organizational change. *Administrative Science Quarterly, 42*(2), 237-275.

Senge, P. M. (1990). *The fifth discipline: The art and practice of the learning organization.* New York: Doubleday/Currency.

Shaver, K. G. (1995). The entrepreneurial personality myth. *Business & Economic Review, 41*(3), 20-23.

Skocpol, T. (Ed.). (1984). *Vision and method in historical sociology.* Cambridge, UK: Cambridge University Press.

Small Business Administration. (1994). *Handbook of small business data.* Washington, DC: U.S. Government Printing Office, Office of Advocacy.

Small Business Administration. (1998). *Mergers and acquisitions in the United States, 1990-1994.* Washington, DC: U.S. Government Printing Office, Office of Advocacy.

Sterman, J. D., & Wittenberg, J. (1999). Path dependence, competition, and succession in the dynamics of scientific revolution. *Organization Science, 10*(3), 322-341.

Stewart, A. (1998). *The ethnographer's method, qualitative research methods* (Vol. 46). Thousand Oaks, CA: Sage.

Teece, D. J. (1980). Economics of scope and the scope of the enterprise. *Journal of Economic Behavior and Organization, 1,* 223-247.

Van de Ven, A. H., Polley, D. E., Garud, R., & Venkataraman, S. (1999). *The innovation journey.* New York: Oxford.

Whetten, D. A., & Godfrey, P. C. (Eds.). (1998). *Identity in organizations building theory through conversations.* Thousand Oaks, CA: Sage.

PART II

THEORY

[2]

Annu. Rev. Sociol. 1990. 16:111–35

ETHNICITY AND ENTREPRENEURSHIP

Howard E. Aldrich

Department of Sociology, University of North Carolina, Chapel Hill, North Carolina 27599

Roger Waldinger

Department of Sociology, The City College, City University of New York, New York 10031, and Graduate School, City University of New York, New York 10036

KEY WORDS: ethnic stratification, entrepreneur, opportunity structure, immigrant, small business

Abstract

We examine various approaches to explaining ethnic enterprise, using a framework based on three dimensions: an ethnic group's access to opportunities, the characteristics of a group, and emergent strategies. A common theme pervades research on ethnic business: Ethnic groups adapt to the resources made available by their environments, which vary substantially across societies and over time. Four issues emerge as requiring greater attention: the reciprocal relation between ethnicity and entrepreneurship, more careful use of ethnic labels and categories in research, a need for more multigroup, comparative research, and more process-oriented research designs.

INTRODUCTION

The growth of new ethnic populations in Europe since 1945 as well as new waves of immigrants to the United States after the 1965 reform of immigration laws has made ethnic enterprise a topic of international concern. The new ethnic populations are growing at a time of restructuring in western econo-

111

mies, and large numbers of immigrant and ethnic minorities find themselves caught in the conjuncture of changing conditions. Members of some groups have entered business ownership in numbers disproportionate to their group's size, whereas others have shunned entrepreneurial activities.

In this chapter, we present a general framework within which the contributions of various approaches to explaining ethnic enterprise can be understood. The framework we propose is based on ethnic groups' access to opportunities, group characteristics, and emergent strategies, all of which are embedded within changing historical conditions. Within this framework, we review the concepts and research findings of the past several decades.

Focus of Our Review

"Ethnic" is an adjective that refers to differences between categories of people (Petersen 1980). When "ethnic" is linked to "group," it implies that members have some awareness of group membership and a common origin and culture, or that others think of them as having these attributes (Yinger 1985). We assume that what is "ethnic" about ethnic enterprise may be no more than a set of connections and regular patterns of interaction among people sharing common national background or migratory experiences. We emphasize the subcultural dimension of ethnicity—the social structures through which members of an ethnic group are attached to one another and the ways in which those social structures are used.

Entrepreneurship, in the classic sense, is the combining of resources in novel ways so as to create something of value. Much of the recent management literature on entrepreneurship focuses on business foundings, but the term has been expanded in the past few decades and used to encompass nearly all stages in the life cycle of businesses (Bird 1989). The entrepreneurial dimensions of *innovation* and *risk* are particularly salient when we examine ethnic businesses. Rather than breaking new ground in products, process, or administrative form, most businesses simply replicate and reproduce old forms. Simple reproduction is especially likely in the retail and services sector, where most ethnic enterprises are founded. Risks, however, are high for most businesses, regardless of whether they are innovative (Aldrich & Auster 1986). Liabilities of newness and smallness affect all businesses, ethnic or not.

Many writers have suggested making a distinction between entrepreneurs and owner/managers on the basis of either innovativeness or risk, but few have done a convincing job. Neither economists (Baumol 1968:66) nor sociologists (Wilken 1979:60) have been able to operationalize this distinction so that "entrepreneurs" are clearly differentiated from "owners" or even the self-employed. Therefore, in our review we follow the lead set by anthropologists and define entrepreneurs operationally as owners and operators of business enterprises (Greenfield et al 1979). This definition includes self-employed persons who employ family labor as well as those who employ outsiders.

Our review is based on the observation that some ethnic groups, particularly among first and second generation immigrants, have higher rates of business formation and ownership than do others. The historical record shows considerable disparities in self-employment among the various European ethnic groups in the United States; business participation rates are no less varied among contemporary immigrants in the United States and Europe today. To the extent that higher levels of entrepreneurship cannot be explained solely by the personal characteristics of owners, then we must turn to social structural and cultural conditions for an explanation.

Limitations of Current Research

What empirical research is available on which to build sound, cross-national, historically valid generalizations? Ideally, we would like information on multiple groups, spanning long periods, and from many different societies. Such information should include individual, group, and social context characteristics, with explicit attention paid to replicating and building on previous research.

In practice, information on ethnic enterprise comes from three sources: government censuses, survey research, and field studies. Using government census data is complicated because of political sensitivities over "ethnic origin" questions in government-sponsored information acquisition. Major controversy has erupted, for example, in Great Britain and West Germany in the past decade over whether such questions should be included, and if so, in what form. In the United States, unlike other industrialized nations, the government has maintained a *Survey of Minority and Women-Owned Businesses*, conducted every five years for the past two decades. That source is limited because the sociological definition of "ethnic business"—a business whose proprietor has a distinctive group attachment by virtue of self-definition or ascription by others—is more encompassing than the official definition of "minorities," which includes only black, Hispanic, Asian, and Native American groups.

The decennial Census of Population has been a fertile source of data on this wider range of ethnic entrepreneurial groups (Light & Sanchez 1987), especially with the addition of the ancestry item to the 1980 Census (Fratoe 1986, Lieberson & Waters 1988). However, the US Census has a major drawback—by law, the Census Bureau is forbidden to ask questions about religion. Thus, there are no official statistics about religio-ethnic groups— Jews, Muslims, and so forth—that are significant for the understanding of ethnic business. The Canadian census, which asks questions about religion and ethnic status, is a richer source, although it is rarely exploited for this purpose.

With these limitations in mind, many researchers have turned to community surveys and intensive case studies for in-depth information on specific groups. Investigators studying lengthy historical periods are forced to rely on incomplete and inconsistent information, or to draw dynamic inferences from cross-sectional surveys which include multiple generations of a group (Bonacich & Modell 1980). Survey research has provided valuable information, but as in other areas of sociology, the individual becomes de facto the unit of analysis, and the social context for behavior is lost.

A FRAMEWORK FOR UNDERSTANDING ETHNIC ENTREPRENEURSHIP

Our framework for understanding ethnic business development is built on three interactive components: opportunity structures, group characteristics, and strategies (Waldinger et al 1990). *Opportunity structures* consist of market conditions which may favor products or services oriented to co-ethnics, and situations in which a wider, non-ethnic market is served. Opportunity structures also include the ease with which access to business opportunities is obtained, and access is highly dependent on the level of interethnic competition and state policies. *Group characteristics* include predisposing factors such as selective migration, culture, and aspiration levels. They also include the possibilities of resource mobilization, and ethnic social networks, general organizing capacity, and government policies that constrain or facilitate resource acquisition. Ethnic *strategies* emerge from the interaction of opportunities and group characteristics, as ethnic groups adapt to their environments.

Opportunity Structures

The structure and allocation of opportunities open to potential ethnic business owners have been shaped by historically contingent circumstances. Groups can only work with the resources made available to them by their environments, and the structure of opportunities is constantly changing in modern industrial societies. Market conditions may favor only businesses serving an ethnic community's needs, in which case entrepreneurial opportunities are limited. Or, market conditions may favor smaller enterprises serving non-ethnic populations, in which case opportunities are much greater. Even if market conditions are favorable, immigrant minorities must gain access to businesses, and non-ethnic group members often control such access. Political factors may impede, or less frequently, enhance, the workings of business markets.

MARKET CONDITIONS   As the world economic system has evolved, opportunity structures have changed and immigrant ethnic groups have found
themselves facing very different market conditions. Markets in some business
sectors have opened, whereas others have closed. In almost all markets, small
businesses—once thought headed for inexorable decline—have shown remarkable resiliency and continue to attract new owners. Many immigrants
and their children have turned to small business enterprise, some in new
ethnic enclaves and others in businesses serving a wider market.

Ethnic consumer products   For a business to arise, there must be some
demand for the services it offers. The "protected market hypothesis" (Light
1972) posits that the initial market for ethnic entrepreneurs typically arises
within the ethnic community itself. If ethnic communities have special sets of
needs and preferences that are best served by those who share those needs and
know them intimately, then ethnic entrepreneurs have an advantage. Servic-
ing these special ethnic consumer needs involves a direct connection with the
immigrants' homeland and knowledge of tastes and buying preferences—
qualities unlikely to be shared by larger, native-owned competitors (Aldrich et
al 1985).

Immigrants also have special problems caused by the strains of settlement
and assimilation and aggravated by their distance from governmental mechanisms of service delivery. Consequently, the business of specializing in the
problems of immigrant adjustment is another early avenue of economic
activity. Ethnic consumer tastes provide a protected market position, in part
because the members of the community may have a cultural preference for
dealing with co-ethnics, and in part because the costs of learning the specific
wants and tastes of the immigrant groups discourage native firms from doing
so, especially at an early stage when the community is small and not readily
visible to outsiders.

Ethnic residential concentration has provided a strong consumer core for
many ethnic entrepreneurs, especially for immigrant groups in the early
decades of their settlement in their host country. Patterns of chain migration
and majority group discrimination lead to the build-up of ethnic residential
areas, presenting ethnic entrepreneurs with a captive market, thus adding a
second meaning to the phrase "protected market" (Aldrich et al 1985). The
initial clustering of migrants in cities has often led to long-term concentrations, facilitating recruitment networks for ethnic suppliers and workers.

If ethnic businesses remain limited to the ethnic market, their potential for
growth is sharply circumscribed (Aldrich et al 1983, Mohl 1985). The
obstacle to growth is the ethnic market itself, which can support only a
restricted number of businesses because it is quantitatively small and because
the ethnic population is often too impoverished to generate buying power

116   ALDRICH & WALDINGER

sufficient to fuel growth. Moreover, the environment confronting the ethnic entrepreneur is severe: Because exclusion from job opportunities leads many immigrants to seek out business opportunities, business conditions in the ethnic market tend toward proliferation of small units, intense competition, and a high failure rate, with the surviving businesses generating scanty returns for their owners.

However, under some conditions, ethnic markets may serve as an export platform from which ethnic firms may expand. One case in point is the experience of Cuban refugees in Miami, Florida (Portes 1987). The early refugees converged on a depressed area in the central city, where housing costs were low and low-rent vacant space was available. As the refugee population grew, and the customer base expanded, retail businesses proliferated (Mohl 1985). The availability of a near-by, low-cost labor force, linked together through informal networks, enabled Cuban entrepreneurs to branch out into other industries, such as garments and construction, where they secured a non-ethnic clientele. Once in place, these "export industries" served as a base for additional expansion of the ethnic economy: the export industries generated a surplus that trickled down to merchants serving the local, specialized needs of the Cuban communities. The export industries also enabled ethnic entrepreneurs to diversify, by moving backward or forward into related industries. The vibrant Cuban ethnic economy has turned Miami into a center for investments from Latin America as well as an entrepot for trade with that area, and Cuban entrepreneurs have been able to move into more sophisticated and higher profit fields (Levine 1985).

This example notwithstanding, we note that the growth potential of immigrant business hinges on its access to customers beyond the ethnic community. The crucial question, then, concerns the types of economic environments that might support neophyte immigrant entrepreneurs.

Non-ethnic markets   The structure of industry—number of businesses, capital and technological requirements—is a powerful constraint on the creation of new businesses. New firms are unlikely to arise in industries characterized by extensive scale economies and high entry costs. However, most western economies contain niches where techniques of mass production or mass distribution do *not* prevail. Researchers have identified four circumstances under which small ethnic enterprises can grow in the open market: underserved or abandoned markets, markets characterized by low economies of scale, markets with unstable or uncertain demand, and markets for exotic goods.

One such niche consists of *markets that are underserved* by the large, mass-marketing organizations. In the United States and some Western European nations, immigrants are heavily concentrated in the core areas of urban centers that are both ill-suited to the technological and organizational conditions of large enterprise *and* favorable to small enterprises. In Paris, London, New York, and Los Angeles, the core urban market is increasingly abandoned by the large food retailers, leaving a substantial consumer base for small local immigrant vendors.

Markets where *economies of scale* are low are another fertile field for immigrant business. In the absence of capital-intensive, high-volume competitors, small immigrant shopkeepers in urban cores can successfully pursue a strategy of self-exploitation. As Ma Mung & Guillon (1986) observed, the immigrant-owned neighborhood shops of Paris offer the same products as their French counterparts, but provide different services: longer hours, year-round operation, easily available credit, and sales of very small quantities.

A niche for immigrant firms also arises in markets affected by *instability or uncertainty*. When demand falls into stable and unstable portions, and the two components can be separated from one another, industries may be segmented into noncompeting branches (Piore 1980): one branch is dominated by larger firms, handling staple products; a second, composed of small-scale firms, caters to the unpredictable and/or fluctuating portion of demand. Immigrant garment firms—a ubiquitous presence in many of the major immigrant-receiving cities in the west—thrive on the availability of short-run products that larger firms cannot handle effectively (Morokvasic et al 1990).

A final niche in the general market arises where the demand for *exotic goods* among the native population allows immigrants to convert both the contents and symbols of ethnicity into profit-making commodities. Selling exotic goods and services offers a fruitful path of business expansion because immigrants have a special product that only they can supply or present in conditions that are seemingly authentic (Palmer 1984). Not only do immigrants lack competitors in "exotic markets," but they can also offer their products at relatively low prices and thereby capture a clientele priced out of the businesses run by native entrepreneurs (Ma Mung & Guillon 1986).

Market conditions, then, may be supportive of ethnic businesses either because ethnic owners enjoy a protected market position or because the environment is supportive of any neophyte capitalist willing to take higher than normal risks (abandoned markets, low economies of scale, and unstable demand). In this latter sense, ethnic owners truly are entrepreneurs, as they assume high risks under uncertain conditions.

ACCESS TO OWNERSHIP   Given the existence of markets, potential ethnic entrepreneurs still need access to ownership positions. Two conditions affecting access have been identified: (*a*) the level of interethnic competition for jobs and businesses; and (*b*) state policies, which have varied considerably among traditional, colonial, nation-building, and modern nation states.

Interethnic competition for vacancies   The likelihood of entering a supportive business niche is greatly affected by the level and nature of interethnic
competition for jobs and business opportunities. Competition may be direct,
in which case immigrants or ethnic minorities are likely to lose access to
desirable markets, or it may be mediated through processes of residential and
occupational succession, in which case vacancies open up in a predictable and
patterned way.

Research has found two outcomes of direct interethnic competition over
business opportunities: (*a*) when the competition is high, ethnic groups
concentrate in a limited range of industries, and (*b*) at very high levels of
competition, a group may be forced out of more lucrative activities, and either
squeezed into interstitial lines or pushed out of business altogether.

Two natural experiments, one involving Japanese and the other Chinese,
document the power of interethnic competition and state policies. First,
severe competition with whites in Canada in the late nineteenth and early
twentieth centuries led to the almost complete exclusion of Japanese from
major social institutions (Makabe 1981). For example, when the Canadian
government took away their right to vote, they lost access to the professions.
In Brazil early in this century, the lack of notable interethnic competition
meant that discrimination and exclusion movements did not materialize, and
the Japanese successfully entered a number of industries. Aided by the
Japanese government's friendly relations with Brazil, the Japanese developed
important social and financial skills. Second, consider the contrasting experience of the Chinese, originating from the same province, who settled in Lima,
Peru, and New York City in the early twentieth century. According to Wong
(1978), the level of discrimination was much higher in the United States than
Peru. For example, the US Chinese Exclusion Act of 1882 was not repealed
until 1943, and US miscegenation laws were not overturned by the Supreme
Court until 1967. By contrast, Peru placed few barriers in the way of Chinese
immigration and had no miscegenation laws, facilitating a very high in-
termarriage rate. Unlike the New York Chinese, who were heavily concentrated in a few industries in Chinatown, the Chinese in Lima were involved in a wide range of businesses. The associational structure of the
Chinese community in Peru was weak because it was not forced to contend
with the same level of interethnic competition as its counterparts in New
York, where ethnic identity was a salient issue for immigrants.

These contrasts draw attention to the relationship between context and
group responses. In general, economic exclusion strengthens group cohesion,
thereby increasing the density of ethnic networks, and in turn, increasing
access to group resources. Similarly, labor market disadvantage affects predispositions toward business opportunities. These issues are further developed
when we discuss group characteristics.

Interethnic competition may not only determine the range of accessible economic activities, but may also lead to expulsion or displacement from more valued niches. In these instances, dominant group members may follow strategies of social closure to reduce minorities' access to business or labor markets (Parkin 1979). Because ethnic monopolies are costly to some component of the dominant group population—whether employers, workers, or customers—recourse to state intervention is often sought.

Chinese immigrants to California in the nineteenth century encountered fierce competition from whites. In California, after the decline of mining in the late 1860s, Chinese workers went back to the cities, where they tried to enter the construction, manufacturing, and other better paying sectors. "Prompted by the leaders of the nascent unions and by political demagogues, white workers undertook a virulent and eventually successful campaign to drive 'the coolies' out. . . ." leaving the Chinese the laundry business and precious little else (Ong 1981:100).

The impact of competition was more severe on blacks than on Chinese in the United States (Lieberson 1980). Black businesses grew slowly after the abolition of slavery, initially developing in such lines as catering, tailoring, and barbering, following the patterns established prior to 1863. These businesses were mainly the province of a small mulatto elite who depended on connections to a white clientele. By the late 1800s, increased desire among whites for both physical and social distance from blacks, combined with greater competition from immigrants, pushed blacks out of their traditional trades and back into serving mostly black customers (Aldrich 1973).

Theories of *residential segregation and succession* point to forces *reducing* interethnic competition for business vacancies, although we recognize that segregation itself reflects a dominant group's success in insulating itself from a minority group. At the neighborhood level, replacement opportunities for immigrant owners selling to their co-ethnic neighbors emerge as a result of ecological succession. As the native group in a residential area no longer replaces itself, native entrepreneurs seek business opportunities outside the local area. Given a naturally high rate of failure among all small businesses, the absence of members from the older established group willing to open new firms in "changed" neighborhoods creates vacancies for potential immigrant business owners (Aldrich & Reiss 1976, Aldrich et al 1989).

Finally, we note that the classic pattern of *occupational succession*, observed in other areas of the labor market, also affects access to opportunities for ethnic entrepreneurs. In the general economy, the petite bourgeoisie often does not reproduce itself, but rather survives through the recruitment of owners from lower social classes (Bechhofer & Elliot 1981). To some extent, it is the very marginality of the small business position that discourages heirs from taking up their parents' modest enterprises (Berteaux & Berteaux-Wiame 1981).

In the central cities of the United States, where small business has been concentrated among European immigrants and their descendants, the changing social structure of Italian, Jewish, and other European ancestry groups has further diminished the allure of petty enterprise. As these native groups have faltered in their recruitment to small business, their share of the small business sector has inevitably declined, in part because of the high death rate to which all small businesses are prone. The exodus of Jewish or Italian petty merchants has provided replacement opportunities for Korean, Chinese, or Arab businessowners, who depend almost entirely on a non-ethnic clientele (Kim 1981).

Currently, indirect competition appears to characterize the relationship between immigrant entrepreneurs and members of dominant ethnic groups in most industrial societies. While occupational succession leads immigrants to move into positions vacated by whites, those same businesses are often coveted by members of nondominant ethnic groups. Thus, in the United States, interethnic competition among nondominant ethnic groups is an increasingly common phenomenon, as in black-Korean conflict (Kim 1987, Light & Bonacich 1988).

State policies   Elite sponsorship of middleman minorities is a characteristic of traditional, state-building, and colonial situations. The roles of Greeks and Armenians in the Ottoman Empire, and German and Jewish capitalists in tsarist Russia (Armstrong 1976), exemplify the traditional and state-building contexts: in these instances, middleman minorities were valued for their skills, and for their network of family and personal relations, which facilitated long-distance communications and transactions and thereby increased access to capital. In Southeast Asia and Africa, similar conditions led to the growth of Indian and Chinese trading networks (Curtin 1984), whose role was later transformed and enlarged by the integration of these areas into the European world economy (Yambert 1981).

Sociological accounts often emphasize that sponsoring elites benefit from the vulnerability of middleman minorities (Stone 1985), but middleman minorities are not necessarily easily dispatched. Though made in a Third World context, the argument that "business rivals are a prerequisite for business rivalries" (Horowitz 1985:116) holds for Europe as well: middleman minorities have hung on where they retain sufficient value to the dominant elite, where indigenous challengers are relatively few in number, and where the extraterritorial dimension of the middleman diaspora does not pose a political threat.

When these conditions no longer hold, the mobilization of lower strata of the dominant ethnic group upsets the alliance between middleman and dominant groups, especially under conditions of late and uneven modernization (Armstrong 1976). Thus, state sponsorship of middleman minorities has often been succeeded by policies designed to replace middlemen by indigenous capitalists. The interwar years in Europe saw numerous such cases, as when Polish government policies in the 1930s worked to benefit Poles at the expense of all other minorities (Goldscheider & Zuckerman 1984). Similar actions have been taken by newly independent states in the Third World.

Analytically, the concept of middleman minorities does not fit modern, multiethnic nation states, as the greater separation—or perhaps the more subtle and indirect linkages—of political and economic power in the United States and other capitalist countries limits the possibility of direct elite sponsorship (Jain 1988, Kashima 1982). Nonetheless, there is a close *descriptive* parallel between the classic middleman minorities and those contemporary ethnic groups—Koreans in the United States, East Indians in Britain, Moroccans in France—whose businesses are principally dependent on commercial transactions with out-group members. As noted, these latter opportunities arise as the consequence of occupational succession, and recent research has not provided evidence that these new immigrant entrepreneurs have significantly benefitted from elite sponsorship. Consequently, we propose the term "pseudo-middleman minorities" to distinguish contemporary ethnic groups that specialize in trade from the classic middleman of earlier periods.

Presently, the main impact of government policies on ethnic entrepreneurship in North America, Australia, and western Europe is *indirect*, derivative of broader immigration and labor market policies. A basic distinction can be made between countries in which labor recruitment was the dominant factor in immigration policy and countries in which other objectives—population growth, family reunification—have had higher priority. In the first instance, immigrants are subject to a high level of labor market control, which hinders rather than encourages immigrant entrepreneurship (Blaschke et al 1990). In Germany, for example, immigrant workers cannot open a business until they have obtained a residence permit, which they may only receive after more than eight years of labor migrant status in the country. By comparison, immigration countries, like the United States, place virtually no formal barriers to immigrant geographical or economic mobility and thereby increase the potential immigrant business start-up rate.

All western societies also maintain policies that implicitly *impede* ethnic business development. Policies that regulate business and labor markets, through licensing and apprenticeship requirements, health standards, minimum wage laws and the like, raise the costs of entry and operation for small firms—ethnic or not. The impact of these policies is most severe in countries like Germany and the Netherlands, where the small business sector continues to bear the imprint of its traditional artisanal, or guild-like past. In other countries, such as the United States, restraints on commercial competition are weak and apprenticeship requirements lax, with the result that ethnic entrepreneurs can more easily move into supportive markets.

Less significant than these indirect policy effects are those programs designed to provide economic assistance to immigrants and ethnic minorities. In the United States, minority businesses were ignored by the federal government until the 1960s, when "black capitalism" emerged in response to the black protest movement. Minority set-aside programs were introduced into government contracting procedures, and special minority enterprise investment programs were created. The amount of money allocated was never very large, but the effort was a significant symbol of minority business's importance in American society. Programs assisting Cuban and Indo-Chinese refugees have also provided financial and other forms of help for prospective business owners. However, the long-term economic significance of these various programs was small, and little concrete evidence of their consequences could be found in the 1980s.

Group Characteristics

Opportunity structures provide the niches and routes of access for potential entrepreneurs, but that is only half the picture. Group characteristics are emphasized by researchers concerned with why particular ethnic groups are disproportionately concentrated in ethnic enterprises (Portes 1987). We have identified two dimensions of group characteristics: predisposing factors and resource mobilization.

PREDISPOSING FACTORS   By predisposing factors we mean the skills and goals that individuals and groups bring with them to an opportunity. Hirschman (1982) argued that an ethnic group's socioeconomic achievements are partly a function of the human capital of individuals and the sociocultural orientation—motives, ambitions—derived from group membership. Selective migration has been particularly important for US ethnic groups, and favorable sociocultural orientations are often a reaction to conditions encountered in a new situation.

Selective migration   The selective nature of migration directs our attention to the human capital immigrants bring to their host societies. For example, the initial Cuban migration to the United States was highly selective, as middle and upper-middle class Cubans—many with substantial education, business experience, and capital—fled Castro's policies (Perez 1986). Similarly, in the post-1965 migration stream, the majority of Koreans worked in white collar or professional jobs before migrating to the United States (Min 1988). Before we invoke group-level explanations, human capital theorists suggest we control for individual-level endowments.

Frazier (1949) emphasized the importance of prior buying and selling experience for immigrants entering business. His argument focused on the negative consequences that *lack* of such experience had on black Americans, whereas most subsequent writers have focused on groups which have benefitted from prior business experiences. Capital, connections, and specific business skills expedited the rapid emergence of a Chinese subeconomy in Paris, following the arrival of Chinese refugees from Vietnam in the mid 1970s (Guillon & Taboada-Leonetti 1986). Senegalese traders have penetrated European and American cities in spite of lacking co-ethnic clients, higher education, and occupational training, because they could draw on prior business experience (Salem 1981).

Whether experience in the art of trading and selling is a *necessary* condition for business success is difficult to determine. Writers have often emphasized the prior business experience of turn-of-the-century Jewish immigrants to Western Europe and the United States. However, Jewish emigration from the Pale of Settlement was highly selective, and artisans, not business owners or traders, were the most likely to leave Russia. Merchants and dealers accounted for one third of the gainfully employed Jews in Russia, but only 6% of the immigrants in 1899–1910 were merchants or dealers (Rubinow [1905] 1975). The case of Greek immigrants is even more striking, as they have been a presence in urban restaurants in the United States since the early twentieth century (Fairchild 1911) though they apparently originated predominantly in fishing villages and rural areas (Herman 1979).

Some immigrant group members have not been able to turn their previous education and experience into positions comparable to those they held prior to migrating, because they had language problems or lacked proper credentials. These persons, finding their way into well-paying white collar work blocked, have sometimes turned to entrepreneurship (Min 1988).

Settlement characteristics   Settlement characteristics, of which group size and residential concentration are perhaps the most important, influence business development trajectories in a complicated way. Two business patterns have already been noted: the local ethnic market, arising as a consequence of residential clustering, and mainly dominated by retail and service businesses catering to a coethnic clientele; and the pseudo-middleman minority situation, in which geographically dispersed, ethnic businesses service an out-group clientele. A third pattern is the "ethnic enclave" (following the terminology coined by Portes). Though the enclave bears a resemblance to the local ethnic market in its spatial concentration and in the patronage it receives from nearby co-ethnic shoppers, it differs in two respects. First, the enclave's industrial structure is diversified beyond the "local economy" industries characteristic of a local ethnic market. Second, the enclave's industries are also linked to the general, nonethnic market (Portes & Bach 1985). Thus, population size and concentrations are necessary and sufficient conditions of local markets, but not of ethnic enclaves.

The turn-of-the-century Jewish immigrant community on Manhattan's Lower East Side—with its incredible concentration of retail and manufacturing firms in many business lines—presents the ethnic enclave in its classic form (Rischin 1962). Modern-day versions include the Chinatowns of New York (Wong 1987) and San Francisco (Godfrey 1988), as well as the Cuban subeconomy in Miami, which contains the single largest agglomeration of ethnic firms enumerated in 1982 (US Dept. of Commerce 1982).

The typology outlined above is, of course, an abstraction; in practice, multiple and overlapping patterns are likely. In Los Angeles, for example, Koreatown seems to fulfill the conditions of an ethnic enclave. However, the majority of Korean business owners in Los Angeles are in a pseudo-middleman minority situation, as the customer base needed to support the 21% self-employment rate of Koreans cannot be found in a Korean clientele alone (Light & Bonacich 1988:164). San Francisco's Chinatown can be classified as an enclave, but the emerging satellite Chinatowns in Richmond and Sunset best fit the description of a local ethnic market, and the many Chinese restaurants and laundry businesses fall into the pseudo-middleman minority category (Godfrey 1988:103–104). These patterns might be conceptualized as comprising stages in a developmental sequence (Waldinger et al 1990, Chapter 4). The very first Korean merchants to set up stores in emerging Hispanic immigrant neighborhoods in New York, for example, were veterans of an earlier Korean migration to Latin America (Kim 1981). As the Korean population in New York grew over the course of the 1970s and 1980s, it gradually provided the customer base for a dynamic, diversified local ethnic market (Kim 1987). By contrast, the Jewish ethnic enclave of the Lower East Side lasted for barely a generation. By the 1920s, with the decline of the Jewish working class, petty Jewish entrepreneurs increasingly sold to non-Jewish clients or employed a gentile labor force, producing a pseudo-middleman minority situation.

The interaction between such predisposing factors as settlement characteristics and opportunity structures emerges with particular salience when we examine intragroup differences in business activity. Though the Jewish Lower East Side exemplifies the ethnic enclave, self-employment rates for Russian Jewish immigrants were actually much higher outside New York. At the turn of the century, high self-employment rates for Russian Jews were positively correlated with small Jewish populations and low garment industry employment (Perlman 1983). Indeed, in small cities and towns, Russian Jewish migrants were almost entirely dependent on commercial transactions with outsiders, thereby reproducing the traditional patterns of Eastern Europe

(Morawska 1988). Thus, in large ethnic concentrations, intense competition from co-ethnics for an inherently limited number of small business opportunities imposes a significant ceiling effect, notwithstanding other group traits that provide a strong inclination toward business ownership.

Culture and aspiration levels Many researchers believe that some ethnic traditions contain economically useful practices. Others, however, warn that culture is fluid and adapts to changing circumstances: "An analysis that views cultural attributes as unchanging . . . cannot explain the differential socio-economic achievement of Chinese and Japanese Americans prior to and after World War II nor account for the differences between Asian Americans and other ethnic and minority groups" (Nee & Wong 1985; 287). Strictly cultural arguments also omit structural conditions that give rise to, and reinforce, attitudes favorable to economic achievement.

Attention to context highlights the fluidity of economic orientations and their responsiveness to changing conditions. Immigrant workers often begin as temporary workers in small businesses, seeking jobs that provide opportunities to work long hours and accumulate savings. Once their plans for return are postponed or abandoned, immigrants may have acquired skills which represent "sunk capital," and therefore provide an incentive to start up as self-employed (Bailey 1987). Native workers, not having "sunk capital," are far less likely to acquire entrepreneurial skills in businesses like restaurants or garments where the relative returns to investment in human capital are low. Immigrants will also be more satisfied than native-born workers with low profits from small business because of wage differences between their origin and destination countries (Light 1984).

The classic model of *middleman minorities,* as refined by Bonacich (1973) and others, includes three traits characterizing a group's cultural patterns: first, a sojourner orientation to their host country; second, distinctive social and cultural characteristics that promote solidary communities; and third, distinctive economic traits, including concentration in entrepreneurial roles, a tendency to keep capital liquid, and a preference for kin and co-ethnic labor (O'Brien & Fugita 1982).

The middleman minority model is subject to criticism on several counts. First, the model is ahistorical, ascribing traits that are abstracted from the social and economic structures in which either the classic- or the pseudo-middleman minorities have been found. For example, Jain (1988) showed that British colonialism had much to do with the preference of Indian traders for liquidity, because British imperial policy did not allow South Asians to own land for agricultural purposes; by necessity they concentrated on trade and commercial activities. Second, the argument that immigrants who move as sojourners will opt for business over employment, as the better way of rapidly

126   ALDRICH & WALDINGER

accumulating portable investement capital, is vulnerable on both logical and empirical grounds. Setting up a business is a more risky endeavor than working for someone else. When faced with the alternative of safely banking a nest egg to be returned back home, or investing in a business whose chance for success is always open to doubt, a prudent sojourner is likely to keep on working for someone else. Indeed, Ward's (1987) study of south Asians in Britain showed that they only resort to business in those cities where the available jobs are relatively poorly paid, preferring employment over business in high wage areas. Other research found that a sojourning orientation made no difference in the business operations of Asians in Britain (Aldrich 1977, Aldrich et al 1983), and that Korean pseudo-middleman minority store owners in New York were far less likely to be sojourners than their Hispanic counterparts who sold to an entirely co-ethnic clientele (Waldinger 1989). Third, the model's emphasis on distinctive economic traits, such as a preference for hiring co-ethnic workers or maintaining small firms when market conditions would allow for expansion, is based on the assumption that middleman minorities are not "modern capitalists in orientation" (Bonacich & Modell 1980:32). However, the empirical evidence speaks strongly to the contrary; for example, German Jewish department stores employed non-Jewish women in the inter-war period (Gross 1975), and Korean garment factory owners currently recruit Hispanic workers in New York and Los Angeles (Min 1989).

These specific criticisms also direct our attention to a broader observation: for every study that emphasizes an ethnic group's culture as a key factor in its economic achievements in business, another exists that emphasizes the often radical cultural changes occurring over a few generations. Separating the effects of the cultural values with which a group arrives in a host society from effects of the values generated by its post-migration experiences is extremely difficult. Clearly, some ethnic groups have high rates of entrepreneurship which persist over several generations. But as Steinberg (1981) has argued, structural factors limit the capacity of ethnic communities to preserve and pass on "traditional" ethnic customs and values. We remain skeptical of an oversocialized conception of an ethnic group's cultural heritage, apart from the social structure and institutions it constructs within the context of the larger society. Thus, we emphasize resource mobilization over cultural factors in our review.

RESOURCE MOBILIZATION   Founding and running a business, no matter how small, is a demanding task, and only a fraction of those who start are ultimately successful. The basic resources needed—labor and capital—are no different for ethnic entrepreneurs than others. Personalistic and familistic ties are part of business operation in all capitalist societies (Zimmer &

Aldrich 1987). Bechhofer & Elliot (1981) also noted that the general features of the petty bourgeoisie are much the same everywhere, particularly dependence on family labor and the use of hired labor as an extension, rather than a replacement, of the owner's labor.

Class versus ethnic resources   Light (1984) distinguished between "class" and "ethnic" resources in an attempt to separate the purely ethnic from the generic process of resource mobilization. Increased attention to class resources separate from ethnic resources was provoked, in part, by the emergence of middle-class entrepreneurs among recent immigrants, such as Cubans and Koreans. Light defined class resources as private property in the means of production and distribution, human capital, money to invest, and bourgeois values, attitudes, knowledge, and skills transmitted intergenerationally. Ethnic resources, in Light's model, are any and all features of their ethnic group that potential owners can use, such as cultural endowments, reactive solidarity, and sojourning orientation. In practice, few researchers have held to this distinction, but in theory, the distinction is critical, as it emphasizes the strong continuity between studies of small business in general and ethnic enterprise in particular.

We would expect *viable* business enterprises to look very much alike, regardless of ownership. Theories of ethnic businesses posit that such enterprises differ from others because of the social structure within which resources are mobilized. Researchers have focused on ethnic resource mobilization as a collective, rather than purely individual, activity, as ethnic entrepreneurs draw on family, kin, and co-ethnic relations for labor and capital. Because so many researchers have not compared their findings to non-ethnic business operations, they have tended to overstate the uniquely "ethnic" component in resource mobilization.

Ethnic social structures: social networks and organizing capacity   Ethnic social structures consist of the networks of kinship and friendship around which ethnic communities are arranged, and the interlacing of these networks with positions in the economy (jobs), in space (housing), and in society (institutions). Breton's (1964) concept of *institutional completeness* captures the spirit of much research on ethnic business, as it refers to the relative number of formal organizations in an ethnic community and the resulting complexity of relations between co-ethnics. We focus on the role of ethnic institutions in raising capital, recruiting labor, and dealing with suppliers and customers.

Information about permits, laws, management practices, reliable suppliers, and promising business lines is typically obtained through owners' personal networks and via various indirect ties that are specifically linked to their ethnic communities. The structure of such networks differs, depending upon the characteristics of the group. Some groups have very hierarchically organized families and a clear sense of family loyalty and obligation, whereas others have more diffusely organized families. Ritualized occasions and large-scale ceremonies also provide opportunities for acquiring information, and some groups have specialized associations and media which disseminate information. When co-ethnics supply such information, the consequence is often a piling up or concentration by an ethnic group within a limited number of industries. Newcomers finding employment among co-ethnics in these immigrant small business industries automatically gain access to contacts, opportunities to learn on the job, and role models. They therefore enjoy a higher probability of subsequent advancement to ownership than do their counterparts who work in larger firms among members of the dominant ethnic group.

Rotating credit associations are commonly used in many ethnic groups to raise capital (Ardener 1964). Light (1972) argued that traditional rotating credit associations among the Japanese and Chinese enabled locality-based groups to capitalize small businesses, whereas US blacks lacked such institutions and were thus at a disadvantage. Ethnic credit associations are based on levels of ethical accountability and frugality (Woodrum 1981) and have been found in a variety of guises among immigrants to the United States. Such associations were particularly important for groups that were discriminated against by regular financial institutions (Gerber 1982).

Rotating credit associations are important, but three research findings suggest their significance may have been overstated. First, entrepreneurs are often highly innovative in their search for capital, and ethnic owners have created many vehicles for raising capital other than rotating credit associations (Russell 1984). Second, some groups have many active rotating credit associations but do not use them to fund businesses (Bonnett 1981). Third, recent research has found that the great majority of ethnic owners fund their businesses from their own personal savings, with some money from their families (Min 1988).

Families, in addition to providing capital, are often the core workforce for small businesses. Thus, immigrants who arrive in a country with their families intact, or who can quickly reconstitute the family through subsequent migration, have an advantage over those who cannot. Similarly, ethnic groups with larger families, with high participation rates by family members, and with norms stressing collective achievement have some advantage over others.

Some research indicates that a strong family structure is not sufficient, nor perhaps even necessary, for ethnic entrepreneurs' success. In her study of

Mexican-American and Anglo-American families in three Southern California cities, Keefe (1984) found evidence of a strong extended family structure among the Mexican-American families, but no indication such strength was channelled into business activities. Chan & Cheung (1985) found that most Chinese businesses in Toronto either had *no* employees or no family members as employees. Zimmer & Aldrich (1987), in their research on South Asian and white shopkeepers in three English cities, found little difference between the two groups in their use of family labor.

Recent theoretical writings on ethnicity have stressed the advantages of ethnic over other forms of social organization (Glazer & Moynihan 1975, Olzak 1983), and some research on ethnic business supports this idea. Considerable attention has been paid to vertical and horizontal interfirm linkages that appear to reduce transaction costs and lower intraethnic competition (Wilson & Martin 1982). In contrast to the historical record (Light 1972), research on contemporary immigrant groups provides little evidence of price or entry regulation, vertical integration, or other joint monopolistic activities. Research on Korean retailers in the United States (Min 1988) does show that backward linkages to co-ethnic suppliers can be advantageous: transactions are made in the native language; co-ethnic wholesalers are more flexible on credit; and they carry the type of merchandise that appeals to Korean merchants' customers. However, in spite of these advantages, most Korean merchants make equal use of Korean and non-Korean suppliers. The common inability of ethnic trade associations to control competition between co-ethnics is additional evidence of the weakness of cultural constraints in the face of economic opportunities (Bailey 1987:55).

Ethnic institutions, such as churches and voluntary associations, are often supported by ethnic entrepreneurs for business reasons as well as a sense of in-group loyalty. For example, among Poles and Slavs, fraternal, mutual benefit societies sponsored by the Catholic Church have often contributed indirectly to ethnic businesses (Cummings 1980). Bonacich & Modell (1980) noted that the Nisei who had social bonds to their ethnic group in a variety of informal and formal contexts were more likely to participate in the ethnic economy, and vice versa. Boswell (1986:364) argued that "Chinese merchants subsidized traditional Chinese cultural and clan activities in part to maintain their trade monopoly."

As Bonacich (1973) observed, in-group solidarity is often a reaction to hostility from the host society. For example, Chicano used car dealers in the American Southwest are limited in their ability to cultivate interpersonal relations with people who could give them access to better automobiles because of white dealers' hostilities and ethnic stereotyping. Consequently, Chicano dealers "cannot accumulate sufficient capital to increase their credit

130   ALDRICH & WALDINGER

floor plan and thus trade in the high volume that would make them competitive with white dealers" (Valdez 1984:236). Instead, they sell to co-ethnics in the barrio who need credit.

Available evidence certainly indicates that many ethnic groups have a level of institutional completeness and internal solidarity that gives some of their members an advantage in mobilizing resources. The resources themselves are generic to the business founding and survival process, but models of ethnic entrepreneurship have probably exaggerated the unique advantage of certain groups because few studies are truly comparative—examining in detail both ethnic and non-ethnic businesses. The conditions facilitating resource mobilization are historically contingent, heavily dependent upon individual initiative, and subject to manipulation by dominant groups.

Ethnic Strategies

Strategies emerge from the interaction of opportunity structures and group characteristics, as ethnic entrepreneurs adapt to the resources available to them, building on the characteristics of their groups (Boissevain et al 1990, Boissevain & Grotenbreg 1986). Our use of the term "strategies" to characterize ethnic entrepreneurs' actions is in the same spirit as Hamilton's (1985:408) use of the term to explain patterns of temporary migration: strategy is a "technical term meaning the positioning of oneself to others in order to accomplish one's goals. Whereas one's reasons for action may be subjective and strictly personal, one's strategy is shaped by social circumstances . . . the strategy becomes social insofar as individuals recognize the actual or possible influence of others, their values and actions, upon their own goals."

Ethnic business owners commonly confront a number of problems in founding and operating their businesses, in addition to those we have already reviewed: acquiring the *training and skills* needed to run a small business; recruiting and managing efficient, honest, and cheap *workers;* managing relations with *customers* and *suppliers;* surviving strenuous business *competition;* and protecting themselves from *political attacks.*

Training and skills are typically acquired on the job, often while the potential owner is an employee in a co-ethnic or family member's business. Ties within the ethnic economy widen workers' contacts, increasing the probability of their moving up through a variety of jobs and firms in which skills are acquired (Portes & Bach 1985, Waldinger 1986). Family and co-ethnic labor is critical to most small ethnic businesses. Such labor is largely unpaid, and kin and co-ethnics work long hours in the service of their employers. Ethnic entrepreneurs manipulate family and co-ethnic perseverance and loyalty to their own advantage, but they also incur obligations in doing so.

Customers and clients play a central role in owners' strategies, as building a loyal following is a way of off-setting the high level of uncertainty facing small ethnic businesses. Some owners provide special services, extend credit, and go out of their way to deliver individual services to customers. Often, however, providing special services to one's co-ethnics causes trouble for owners, who then are faced with special pleading to take lower profits for their efforts (Aldrich et al 1983).

The intense competition generated in the niches occupied by ethnic businesses is dealt with in at least four ways: (*a*) through self-exploitation; (*b*) expanding the business by moving forward or backward in the chain of production, or by opening other shops (Werbner 1984); (*c*) founding and supporting ethnic trading associations (Light & Bonacich 1988); and (*d*) cementing alliances to other families through marriage (Sway 1988). Finally, ethnic entrepreneurs often need protection from government officials, as well as from rival owners outside their ethnic community. Government is dealt with by ethnic owners in much the same way that non-ethnic owners always have: bribery, paying penalties, searching for loopholes, and organizing protests.

Ethnic strategies, then, reflect both the opportunity structure within which ethnic businesses operate *and* the particular characteristics of the owner's group. Accordingly, ethnic strategies may be thought of as at the *center* of our framework, emphasizing their emergent character. The strategies adopted by the various ethnic groups in capitalistic societies around the world are remarkably similar.

CONCLUSIONS

We have used a framework based on three interactive components—opportunity structures, group characteristics, and strategies—to review recent scholarship on ethnic business development. Of necessity, we cast a wide net in our search for relevant research, as contributions have been made by investigators in many disciplines and from a variety of approaches. A common theme pervades most of this work: ethnic groups adapt to the resources made available by their environments, which vary substantially across societies and over time.

Among the many issues deserving greater attention, we include the following: the reciprocal relation between ethnicity and entrepreneurship, more careful use of ethnic labels, the need for more multiple group, comparative research, and the need for more process-oriented research designs. First, ethnicity, defined as self-identification with a particular ethnic group, or a label applied by outsiders, is neither primordial nor imported prior to contact

132   ALDRICH & WALDINGER

with a host society. Instead, ethnicity is a possible outcome of the patterns by which intra- and inter- group interactions are structured. The emergence of ethnic communities and networks may generate an infrastructure and resources for ethnic businesses *before* a sense of group awareness develops. In turn, an ethnic business niche may give rise to, or strengthen, group consciousness. Ethnic boundaries, as social constructions, are inherently fluid.

Second, much of the research on ethnic businesses fits Yinger's (1985:158) description of other research in the field of ethnic studies, as it is based on the "single fact of an ethnic (or state-origin) label, with little attention to the salience of the label, to the strength of identification with the ethnic group compared with other identities, or to the distinction between country of origin and ethnicity." Reliance on census data collected for other purposes is the culprit in most cases, and one remedy would be more studies specifically designed to measure multiple indicators of a person's ethnic identification, as well as involvement in entrepreneurship.

Third, as Miyamoto (1986) pointed out, we need more rigorous, detailed comparative data on multiple groups, studied over the same period, with comparable information collected on each group. Currently, studies using census data often include multiple groups, but as the census collects little information on entrepreneurial activities, and practically nothing on ethnic processes, they have limited utility for examining most questions of interest. The modal study using survey or field work data includes only one group, with only implicit comparisons made to others.

Fourth, almost no studies of ethnic enterprise have examined *performance* over time, and so we have little understanding of the contribution ethnic group structures and strategies make to entrepreneurial success. More dynamic research designs, such as panel studies, are clearly needed.

ACKNOWLEDGMENTS

Order of authorship is alphabetical, as this has truly been a collaborative effort. Comments from Melanie Archer, Judith Blau, Pyong Gap Min, David Torres, W. Richard Scott, Catherine Zimmer, and two anonymous reviewers helped us revise the manuscript. We thank Greg Floyd and Jane Scott for their bibliographic help, and Sharon Byrd and Deborah Tilley for preparing the final manuscript. Howard Aldrich's work on this article was facilitated by a grant from the Institute for Research in Social Science, University of North Carolina, Chapel Hill. Roger Waldinger's work on this article was made possible, in part, by a fellowship from the Robert F. Wagner, Sr., Institute on Urban Public Policy, Graduate Center, City University of New York.

Literature Cited

Aldrich, H. E. 1973. Employment effects of white-owned businesses in the black ghetto. *Am. J. Sociol.* 78:1403–26

Aldrich, H. E. 1977. *Testing the middleman minority model of Asian entrepreneurial behavior: Preliminary results from Wandsworth, England.* Pap. pres. Ann. Meet. Am. Sociol. Assoc., Chicago

Aldrich, H. E., Cater, J., Jones, T., McEvoy, D. 1983. From periphery to peripheral: The South Asian petite bourgeoisie in England. In *Research in the Sociology of Work,* Vol. 2, ed. I. H. Simpson and R. Simpson, pp. 1–32. Greenwich, Conn: JAI

Aldrich, H. E., Reiss, A. J. Jr. 1976. Continuities in the study of ecological succession: Changes in the race composition of neighborhoods and their businesses. *Am. J. Sociol.* 81:846–66

Aldrich, H. E., Cater, J., Jones, T., McEvoy, D., Velleman, P. 1985. Ethnic residential concentration and the protected market hypothesis. *Soc. Forc.* 63:996–1009

Aldrich, H. E., Zimmer, C., McEvoy, D. 1989. Continuities in the study of ecological succession: Asian business in three English cities. *Soc. Forc.* 67:920–44

Aldrich, H. E., Auster, E. R. 1986. Even dwarfs started small: liabilities of age and size and their strategic implications. In *Research in Organizational Behavior,* vol. 8, ed. B. M. Staw and L. L. Cummings, pp. 165–98. Greenwich, Conn: JAI

Ardener, S. A. 1964. The comparative study of rotating credit associations. *J. R. Anthropol. Inst.* 94:201–9

Armstrong, J. A. 1976. Mobilized and proletarian diasporas. *Am. Polit. Sci. Rev.* 9:393–408

Bailey, T. 1987. *Immigrant and Native Workers: Contrasts and Competition.* Boulder, Colo: Westview

Baron, S., 1975. *The Economic History of the Jews.* New York: Schocken

Baumol, W. J. 1968. Entrepreneurship in economic theory. *Am. Econ. Rev.* 58:64–71

Bechhofer, F., Elliot, B. eds. 1981. *The Petite Bourgeoisie: Comparative Studies of the Uneasy Stratum.* London: Macmillan

Bertaux, D., Berteaux-Wiame, I. 1981. Artisanal bakery in France: How it lives and why it survives. In *The Petite Bourgeoisie. Comparative Studies of an Uneasy Stratum,* ed. F. Bechhofer and B. Elliot, pp. 155–81. London: MacMillan

Bird, B. J. 1989. *Entrepreneurial Behavior.* Glenview, Ill: Scott, Foresman

Blaschke, J., Boissevain, J., Grotenbreg, H.,

Joseph, I., Morokvasic, M., Ward, R. 1990. European trends in ethnic business. See Waldinger et al 1990

Boissevain, J., Blaschke, J., Grotenbreg, H., Joseph, I., Light, I., Sway, M., Waldinger, R., Ward, R., Werbner, P. 1990. Ethnic entrepreneurs and ethnic strategies. See Waldinger et al 1990

Boissevain, J., Grotenbreg. 1986. Culture, structure and ethnic enterprise: the Surinamese of Amsterdam. *Ethnic Racial Stud.* 9(1):1–23

Bonacich, E. 1973. A theory of middleman minorities. *Am. Sociol. Rev.* 38:583–94

Bonacich, E., Modell, J. 1980. *The Economic Basis of Ethnic Solidarity in the Japanese American Community.* Berkeley: Univ. Calif. Press

Bonnett, A. W. 1981. Structured adaptation of black migrants from the Caribbean: An examination of an indigeneous banking system in Brooklyn. *Phylon* 42:346–55

Boswell, T. E. 1986. A split labor market analysis of discrimination against Chinese immigrants, 1850–1882. *Am. Sociol. Rev.* 51:352–71

Breton, R. 1964. Institutional completeness of ethnic communities and the personal relations of immigrants. *Am. J. Sociol.* 70:193–205

Chan, J., Cheung, Y. W. 1985. Ethnic resources and business enterprise: A study of Chinese businesses in Toronto. *Hum. Organ.* 44:142–54

Cummings, S. 1980. *Self-Help in Urban America: Patterns of Minority Economic Development.* Port Washington, NY: Kennikat Press

Curtin, Philip. 1984. *Cross-Cultural Trade in World History.* Cambridge: Cambridge Univ. Press

Fairchild, H. S. 1911. *Greek Immigration to the United States.* New Haven: Yale

Fratoe, F. 1986. A sociological analysis of minority business. *Rev. Black Polit. Econ.* 15:5–30

Frazier, E. F. 1949. *The Negro in America.* New York: Macmillan

Gerber, D. 1982. Cutting out Shylock: Elite anti-semitism and the quest for moral order in the mid-nineteenth century American market place. *J. Am. Hist.* 9:615–37

Glazer, N., Moynihan, D. P. eds. 1975. *Ethnicity.* Cambridge, Mass: Harvard

Godfrey, B. J. 1988. *Neighborhoods in Transition: The Making of San Francisco's Ethnic and Nonconformist Communities.* Berkeley: Univ. Calif. Press

Goldscheider, C., Zuckerman, A. 1984. *The*

134   ALDRICH & WALDINGER

Transformation of the Jews. Chicago: Univ. Chicago Press

Greenfield, S. M., Strickon, A., Aubey, R. T. 1979. *Entrepreneurs in Cultural Context.* Albuquerque: Univ. N. Mex. Press

Gross, N. 1975. *The Economic History of the Jews.* New York: Schocken

Guillon, M., Taboada-Leonetti, I. 1986. *Le Triangle de Choisy: Un Quartier Chinois a Paris.* Paris: Ciemi L'Harmattan

Hamilton, G. 1985. Temporary migration and the institutionalization of strategy. *Int. J. Intercultural Relat.* 9:405–25

Herman, H. 1979. Dishwashers and proprietors: Macedonians in Toronto's restaurant trade. In *Ethnicity at Work,* ed. S. Wallman, pp. 71–92. London: Macmillan

Hirschman, C. 1982. Immigrants and minorities: Old questions for new directions in research. *Int. Migrat. Rev.* 16:474–90

Horowitz, D. 1985. *Ethnic Conflict.* Berkeley: Univ. Calif. Press

Jain, P. C. 1988. Towards class analysis of race-relations-overseas Indians in colonial Post-colonial societies. *Econ. Polit. Weekly* 23:95–103

Kashima, T. 1982. Book review of Bonacich and Modell. *Am. Hist. Rev.* 87:1476

Keefe, S. E. 1984. Real and ideal extended familism among Mexican-Americans and Anglo-Americans: On the meaning of 'close' family ties. *Hum. Organ.* 43:65–70

Kim, I. 1981. *The New Urban Immigrants: The Korean Community in New York.* Princeton: Princeton Univ. Press

Kim, I. 1987. The Koreans: small business in an urban frontier. In *New Immigrants in New York City,* ed. N. Foner, pp. 219–42. New York: Columbia Univ. Press

Levine, B. B. 1985. The capital of Latin America. *Wilson Q.* 9:47–69

Lieberson, S. 1980. *A Piece of the Pie.* Berkeley: Univ. Calif. Press

Lieberson, S., Waters, M. 1988. *From Many Strands: Ethnic and Racial Groups in Contemporary America.* New York: Russell Sage

Light, I. 1972. *Ethnic Enterprise in America.* Berkeley: Univ. Calif. Press

Light, I., Sanchez, A. 1987. Immigrant entrepreneurs in 272 SMSAs. *Sociol. Perspect.* 30:373–99

Light, I. 1984. Immigrant and ethnic enterprise in North America. *Ethnic Racial Stud.* 7:195–216

Light, I., Bonacich, E. 1988. *Immigrant Entrepreneurs.* Berkeley: Univ. Calif. Press

Makabe, T. 1981. The theory of the split market labor market: A comparison of the Japanese experience in Brazil and Canada. *Soc. Forc.* 59:786–809

Ma Mung, E., Guillon, M. 1986. Les com- mercants etrangers dans l'agglomeration Parisienne. *Rev. Europeene des Migrations Int.* 2:105–34

Min, P. G. 1988. *Ethnic Business Enterprise: Korean Small Business in Atlanta.* New York: CMS

Min, P. G. 1989. *Some positive functions of ethnic business for an immigrant community: Korean immigrants in Los Angeles.* Final report submitted to the National Science Foundation, Washington, DC

Miyamoto, S. F. 1986. Book review of Ward and Jenkins. *Contemp. Sociol.* 15:142–43

Mohl, R. 1985. An ethnic 'boiling pot': Cubans and Haitians in Miami. *J. Ethnic Stud.* 13:51–74

Morawska, E. 1988. A Replica of the 'old-country' relationship in the ethnic niche: Eastern European Jews and Gentiles in small-town western Pennsylvania. *Am. Jewish Hist.* 77:87–105

Morokvasic, M., Waldinger, R., Phizacklea, A. 1990. Business on the ragged edge: immigrant and minority business in the garment industries of Paris, London, and New York. See Waldinger et al 1990

Nee, V., Wong, H. Y. 1985. Asian American socioeconomic achievement. *Sociol. Perspect.* 28:281–306

O'Brien, D. J., Fugita, S. S. 1982. Middle-man minority concept: Its explanatory value in the case of the Japanese in California agriculture. *Pac. Sociol. Rev.* 25:185–204

Olzak, S. 1983. Contemporary ethnic mobilization. *Annu. Rev. Sociol.* 9:355–74

Ong, P. 1981. An ethnic trade: The Chinese laundries in early California. *J. Ethnic Stud.* 8:95–113

Palmer, R. 1984. The rise of the Britalian culture entrepreneur. In *Ethnic Communities in Business,* ed. Robin Ward and Richard Jenkins, pp. 89–104. Cambridge: Cambridge Univ. Press

Parkin, F. 1979. *Marxism: A Bourgeois Critique.* New York: Columbia

Perlman, J. 1983. Beyond New York: The occupations of Russian Jewish immigrants in Providence, R.I., and other small Jewish Communities, 1900–1915. *Am. Jewish Hist.,* 72:369–94

Perez, L. 1986. Immigrant economic adjustment and family organization: The Cuban success story reexamined. *Int. Migrat. Rev.* 20:4–20

Petersen, W. 1980. Concepts of ethnicity. In *Harvard Encyclopedia of American Ethnic Groups,* ed. S. Thernstrom, pp. 234–42. Cambridge, Mass: Harvard

Piore, M. J. 1980. The technological foundations of dualism and discontinuity. In *Dualism and Discontinuity in Industrial Society,* ed. S. Berger and M. J. Piore, pp. 55–81. Cambridge: Cambridge Univ. Press

Portes, A., Bach, R. 1985. *Latin Journey.* Berkeley: Univ. Calif. Press

Portes, A. 1987. The social origins of the Cuban enclave economy of Miami. *Sociol. Perspect.* 30:340–72

Rischin, M. 1962. *The Promised City.* Cambridge, Mass: Harvard

Rubinow, I. 1975 [1905] *The Condition of the Jews in Russia.* New York: Arno

Russell, R. 1984. The role of culture and ethnicity in the degeneration of Democratic firms. *Econ. Indust. Dem.* 5:73–96

Salem, G. 1981. De la brousse senegalaise au Boul' Mich: le systeme commercial mouride en France. *Les Cahiers d'etudes africaines* 81–83:267–88

Steinberg, S. 1981. *The Ethnic Myth: Race, Ethnicity, and Class in America.* New York: Atheneum

Stone, J. 1985. *Ethnic Conflict in Contemporary Society.* Cambridge: Harvard Univ. Press

Sway, M. 1988. *Familiar Strangers: Gypsy Life in America.* Urbana Ill.: Univ. Ill. Press

United States Department of Commerce. 1982. *Survey of Minority and Women-Owned Businesses.* Washington, DC: US Govt. Printing Off.

Valdez, A. 1984. Chicano used car dealers: A social world in microcosm. *Urban Life* 13:229–46

Waldinger, R. 1986. *Through the Eye of the Needle: Immigrants and Enterprise in New York's Garment Trades.* New York: New York Univ. Press

Waldinger, R. 1989. Structural opportunity or ethnic advantage: immigrant business development in New York. *Int. Mig. Rev.* 23:48–72

Waldinger, R., Aldrich, H. E., Ward, R.

1990. *Immigrant Entrepreneurs: Immigrant and Ethnic Business in Western Industrial Societies.* Beverly Hills, CA: Sage

Ward, R. 1987. Small retailers in inner urban areas. In *Business Strategy and Retailing,* ed. Gerry Johnson, pp. 275–87. New York: Wiley

Werbner, P. 1984. Business on trust. Pakistani entrepreneurship in the Manchester garment industry. In *Ethnic Communities in Business: Strategies for Economic Survival,* ed. Robin Ward and Richard Jenkins, pp. 166–88. Cambridge: Cambridge Univ. Press

Wilken, P. 1979. *Entrepreneurship: A Comparative Historical Study.* Norwood, NJ: Ablex

Wilson, K., Martin, W. A. 1982. Ethnic enclaves. A comparison of Cuban and Black economies in Miami. *Am. J. Sociol.* 88: 135–60

Wong, B. 1978. A comparative study of the assimilation of the Chinese in New York City and Lima, Peru. *Comp. Stud. Soc. Hist.* 20:335–58

Wong, B. 1987. The Chinese: New immigrants in New York's Chinatown. In *New Immigrants in New York,* ed. N. Foner, pp. 243–72. New York: Columbia Univ. Press

Woodrum, E. 1981. An assessment of Japanese American assimilation, pluralism, and subordination. *Am. J. Sociol.* 87:157–69

Yambert, K. 1981. Alien traders and ruling elites: the overseas Chinese in Southeast Asia and the Indians in East Africa. *Ethnic Groups* 3:173–98

Yinger, J. M. 1985. Ethnicity. *Annu. Rev. Sociol.* 11:151–80

Zimmer, C., Aldrich, H. 1987. Resource mobilization through ethnic networks: Kinship and friendship ties of shopkeepers in England. *Sociol. Perspect.* 30:422–55

3

The Accidental Entrepreneur

Campbellian Antinomies and Organizational Foundings

HOWARD E. ALDRICH
AMY L. KENWORTHY

> The great heterogeneity and the tremendous numbers of variations make almost inevitable the "accidental discovery" of any strongly adaptive form.
>
> —*Donald T. Campbell (1965, p. 37)*

In the fall of 1994, Steven was in his second and final year of the MBA program at the Stanford Graduate School of Business, and things were going well. Over the summer, he had worked as an intern at McKinsey, and the company had offered him a permanent job for the following year, after graduation. He also was engaged to be married, and he and his fiancée were making coast-to-coast trips nearly every week to see each other and plan the wedding. As a break from his regular class work in the fall, he had arranged with two friends to take an independent studies course with Associate Dean Parker to develop a business plan for a new venture. The venture involved an innovation in the marketing of insurance products, using a Web site that allowed consumers to comparison shop between identical features of the policies they were considering. In his previous job, as an analyst at an investment banking firm, Steven had been involved in mergers and acquisitions in the insurance industry, and he had learned something about its practices. He thought he saw a way of creating a better

AUTHORS' NOTE: The authors shared equally in the challenging task of adequately contextualizing organizational emergence using Donald Campbell's ideas in one short chapter. We wish to acknowledge the helpful comments of Ted Baker, Bill Barnett, Jennifer Cliff, Bill Garner, Lisa Keister, Alessandro Lomi, Tammy Madsen, Bill McKelvey, Anne Miner, Hugh O'Neill, and Elaine Romanelli.

product, but for the moment it was just something to do as an intellectual challenge.

When the team members turned in their project, they were surprised when the dean told them that they were not yet finished. He said the idea had some promise and that they ought to shop the idea around to get reactions from possible funding sources. The dean's positive feedback piqued Steven's curiosity, and he followed up on an introduction to some New York City funding sources that the dean arranged. The investors were impressed and were ready to commit some funding up front, although not enough to guarantee the start-up's survival for more than a year or two. In spite of this reasonably good news, when the spring semester began, Steven's two colleagues dropped out of the project, with one deciding to take a job with a consulting firm and the other deciding to pursue more graduate work. Undaunted, Steven persisted in developing the plan, but now he needed to assemble a new team. He turned to an old college roommate and longtime friend who was a computer wizard, bringing him on to serve as the management information systems expert. Through his fiancée, he found the second person for his team—a person in his late twenties who was a marketing whiz and bored at his current job.

As the new team worked on the project, Steven finally decided to tell McKinsey that he was going to continue planning the new venture, rather than going to work for them. They were quite generous in their response, saying that they would wait for him if he wanted to pursue the idea further, and to check back with them if he changed his mind. In June, 1995, he graduated from Stanford, in July he was married, and in August he received his first measure of money from the investors, out of the $2.1 million they had pledged. He found a site in Alexandria, Virginia, hired his first employees, and launched the firm.

We draw several lessons from this story. First, entrepreneurship often happens when people are on their way to something else. Activities coalesce, and people find they have become entrepreneurs. Second, truly innovative start-ups are often the result of creative experimentation with new ideas by outsiders to an industry. Experience guides the choice of a domain for exploration, but indiffer-

ence to industry routines and norms gives an outsider the freedom to break free of the cognitive constraints on incumbents. Third, nascent entrepreneurs often encounter discouraging events along the way, but many persist and find ways around the obstacles. In their persistence, they often have a little help from their friends, acquaintances, and work associates. Fourth, regardless of their ambitions and skills, the fate of nascent entrepreneurs ultimately is still subject to external selection forces, such as demand, trends in technological regimes, and the actions of outsiders with legitimacy and money.

Our Objectives and Plan

Our goals in this chapter are rather modest: We want to pay homage to Donald Campbell and his work, and we want to draw on his ideas to build a simple model of innovative entrepreneurship. We pay homage to Campbell because of his influence on the field of evolutionary organizational studies. We try to invoke the spirit of Campbell by approaching the problem in a way we think he would appreciate, making liberal use of quotations from his work and creating an eclectic mix of ideas from diverse sources. In developing our model of innovative entrepreneurship, we draw on Campbell's ideas from his writings on evolutionary epistemology, creativity and experimentation, playfulness, altruism and clique selfishness, and more generally from his blind-variation-and-selective-retention (BVSR) model. We use the term "nascent entrepreneur" to refer to persons thinking about starting a new firm and involved in activities that could result in a new organization, distinguishing them from "entrepreneurs" who actually have created an operating entity (Reynolds & White, 1997).[1] We focus on explaining the degree to which nascent entrepreneurs, in creating new ventures, remain faithful to, or depart from, the established order of things.

Our chapter is structured as follows. First, using a strategy often adopted by Campbell, we list six empirical facts and puzzles characterizing entrepreneurship, choosing those that have a reasonable degree of empirical support. Second, for the sake of readers who may not be familiar with Campbell's work, we review his BVSR model. Third, we link the six puzzles to Campbell's BVSR model through a discussion of a reproducer-innovator continuum of organizational foundings. Fourth, drawing on Campbell's writings, we create two Campbellian antinomies (apparent contradictions) to explain why people fall at various points along the reproducer-innovator continuum. Finally, using the Campbellian antinomies and the reproducer-innovator continuum, we return to the six puzzles and interpret them using the BVSR model.

Six Empirical Facts and Puzzles Regarding Entrepreneurship

Our six facts and puzzles are drawn from a review of the entrepreneurship literature, with some based on extrapolations from existing work and others more firmly grounded in replicated studies. We chose them because they resonate with themes in Campbell's writings and because they represent the kinds of data that energized him in his debates with critics and doubters. The facts and puzzles reveal significant gaps in our understanding of organizational foundings as well as answering a question organizational and entrepreneurship theorists might well pose: "If we're so smart, why can't we find the one right way?"

1. In science, the arts, and even many spheres of everyday life, we find strong evidence of creative human endeavor (National Endowment for the Arts, 1997). In contrast, among entrepreneurs and the new ventures they create, we mostly find mundane replications of existing organizational forms (Aldrich & Fiol, 1994; Gartner, 1985; Low & Abrahamson, 1997).

2. Entrepreneurship is often discussed as an isolated, solo event, but research on entrepreneurship suggests that many people are implicated in the founding of new ventures (Reynolds & White, 1997). Some are founding team members, some are investors and employees, and others play a variety of supporting roles.

3. Some people appear much better at creating new firms and ensuring their survival than others,

as they own multiple firms and have been involved in multiple start-ups (Starr & Bygrave, 1992; Starr, Bygrave, & Tercanli, 1993). The knowledge of these habitual entrepreneurs, however, has proven very difficult to codify.

4. The gestation period of start-ups is lengthy and fraught with delays, in spite of the good intentions of the founders and the cost of procrastination. The average time for building a start-up is about 1 year, but the range is substantial (Reynolds & White, 1997). In the computer software industry, Van de Ven, Angle, and Poole (1989) found the process took about 4 years.

5. The more activities people engage in, the greater the chances of their starting, *but* also the greater their chances of quitting the process altogether (Carter, Gartner, & Reynolds, 1996; Gatewood, Shaver, & Gartner, 1995). The highest likelihood of persisting in "thinking about" starting a business, but not actually starting it, occurs among people who are less active than other nascent entrepreneurs.

6. Venture capital firms make their living from their investments and devote great effort to screening new business ventures, yet only a small portion of the firms they fund are successful (Gifford, 1997; Gorman & Sahlman, 1989). A great many fail, and of those that survive, many of them achieve, at best, an average rate of return on the capital invested. Venture capital firms appear unable to find a predictive template.

Two intriguing themes run through these puzzles. First, most entrepreneurs create organizations that look pretty much like all the other organizations in their population. Only a few create organizations that depart, in significant ways, from the current order of things. Second, the behaviors involved in getting any new venture up and running appear surprisingly difficult to master and codify, even for experienced hands.

BLIND-VARIATION-AND-SELECTIVE-RETENTION (BVSR)

One of Campbell's seminal contributions, especially for organization theory, was his selection model based on the analogy between "natural selection in biological evolution and the selective propagation of cultural forms" (Campbell, 1965, p. 26). There are three major components to this model (Campbell, 1965, p. 27, emphasis ours):

1. The occurrence of *variations*: heterogeneous, haphazard, "blind," "chance," "random," but in any event variable (e.g., the mutation process in organic evolution and exploratory responses in learning).
2. Consistent *selection* criteria: selective elimination, selective propagation, and selective retention of certain types of variations (e.g., differential survival of certain mutants in organic evolution, differential reinforcement of certain responses in learning).
3. A mechanism for the *preservation*, duplication, or propagation of the positively selected variants (e.g., the rigid duplication process of the chromosomegene system in plants and animals, memory in learning).

Campbell believed that the three conditions listed above, taken together, resulted in "evolution in the direction of better fit to the selective system" (Campbell, 1965, p. 27). Campbell went so far as to state that *no* fit or order would occur if any of the three components were missing. This proposition was based on his belief that (a) the possibility of all three components occurring simultaneously was minimal and (b) changes in environmental fit or order were, correspondingly, rare (Campbell, 1974b). One explanation for his "rare occurrence" belief is the tension he posited between variation and retention processes. He explained, "variation and retention are at odds in most exemplifications of the model. Maximizing either one jeopardizes the other. Some compromise of each is required" (Campbell, 1974b, p. 143).

Campbell used aspects of his selection theory to explain vision (1956b), problem solving (1956a), creative thought (1960), and sociocultural evolution (1965, 1979). Much of this work was done using what Campbell called his BVSR dogma (Campbell, 1960, 1974a, 1982a, 1990b), summarized as follows:

1. A blind-variation-and-selective-retention process is fundamental to all inductive achievements, to all genuine increases in knowledge, and to all increases in fit of system to environment.
2. The many processes that shortcut a fuller blind-variation-and-selective-retention process are in themselves inductive achievements, containing wisdom about the environment achieved originally by blind-variation-and-selective-retention.
3. In addition, such shortcut processes contain in their own operation a blind-variation-and-selective-retention process at some level, substituting for overt locomotor exploration or the life-and-death winnowing of organic evolution.

Although Campbell's BVSR dogma may appear somewhat tautological in nature (fit selects the learning that leads to further fit), it is a useful tautology (Scriven, 1959). Among other things, it leads us to ask interesting questions.

Why use the term "blind," as opposed to "random," to describe the generation of variations? Campbell did not want to confuse the statistically precise process of randomization with less precise variation mechanisms. Additionally, he wanted to capture the "accidental" nature of variation. Thus, he wrote:

"Deliberate" or "intelligent" variations would do as well as "blind," "haphazard," "chance," "random," or "spontaneous" ones. They might be better insofar as they could be pre-selected. But they might be worse in that they could be restricted to the implications of already achieved wisdom and would not be likely to go beyond it. One of the services of terms like "blind" and "haphazard" in the model is that they emphasize that elaborate adaptive social systems . . . could have emerged, just as did termite societies, without any self-conscious planning or foresightful action. It provides a plausible model for social systems that are "wiser" than the individuals who constitute the society, or than the rational social science of the ruling elite. It provides an anticipation of powerful "inadvertent" social change processes in our own day which may be adaptive in unforeseen or unwanted ways (Campbell, 1965, p. 28)

In Campbell's BVSR model, the cycle of variation, selection, and retention is repeated endlessly, as systems move toward greater fit with their environments. Most of the observed changes are rather small, serving mainly to perpetuate the existing order rather than displace it. We turn now to a closer consideration of the degree to which entrepreneurial outcomes also reflect a bias toward reproduction rather than innovation.

Figure 2.1. Organizational Founding Continuum

Innovator/Reproducer Continuum

The six puzzles we listed focus on the *behaviors* exhibited by individuals engaged in entrepreneurial endeavors and the *type* of entrepreneurial endeavors created. We will return to the issue of behaviors in a subsequent section. For the moment, we focus on the nature of the foundings themselves. Although the popular press portrays the typical entrepreneur as someone like Bill Gates of Microsoft, in fact the overwhelming majority of entrepreneurs are people starting small "reproducer" organizations. Reproducer organizations are defined as those organizations started in an established industry that are only minimally, if at all, different from existing organizations in the population. Most start-ups are reproducers. In contrast, the number of entrepreneurs creating innovative new firms that could potentially open up new niches or even entirely *new* industries is very small. As we saw in the example of Steven and insurance sold over the Web, innovation can, and does, happen. We will use the term "innovator" organizations to refer to this type of organizational founding, regardless of whether the venture actually succeeds.

As shown in Figure 2.1, the continuum of organizational foundings has "reproducer" organizations at one end and "innovator" organizations at the other.[2] Using Campbell's BVSR model, we attempt to explain why new ventures are found along the length of the continuum but mostly cluster at the reproducer end. First, we define the terms *reproducer* and *innovator*, using organizational knowledge to differentiate between them. Second, we use two Campbellian antinomies to explore why people fall at various points on the continuum. Following that discussion, in the next section we

return to the puzzles and interpret them through the lens of Campbell's BVSR environment.

Organizational knowledge is defined as "the patterns of cognitive associations developed by the organization's members," or the behavioral outcomes that result from patterns of cognitive associations (Fiol & Lyles, 1985, p. 805). We define "innovators" as those entrepreneurs who, through the development of new knowledge and consequent new organizational form, either transform an existing industry or create a new one. In the language of Anderson and Tushman (1990), innovative entrepreneurs have created competence-enhancing or competence-destroying innovations by departing from current knowledge. Although Anderson and Tushman do not label it, the implicit baseline in their scheme of organizational innovation is the *absence* of innovation. We extend their scheme by explicitly including a category of "reproducers," defined as those entrepreneurs who bring little or no incremental knowledge to the industries they enter. Reproducers create organizations in established industries by copying the received form and thus do not challenge the status quo.

Using the distinction between reproducer and innovator as developing incremental or new organizational knowledge, respectively, we can expand the reproducer-innovator continuum into the form of a ledger. We have labeled the ledger "Campbellian Antinomies," as shown in Table 2.1. In the ledger, we present two antinomies we have gleaned from the relevant 40-plus papers (of more than 200) that Campbell authored. We have listed only a subset of them in the reference section, to save space.

We use the term "Campbellian antinomies" to honor Campbell's influence over the ledger, as all the concepts and terms are his, and to represent the inherent paradoxes between the reproducer and

TABLE 2.1 Campbellian Antinomies

Reproducer	Innovator
Constructing Incremental Organizational Knowledge	Creating New Organizational Knowledge
Obedience to cultural routines, norms, habits	Creativity/experimentation & play/make-believe
Altruism	Egoism

innovator sides of the ledger. The term *antinomy*, defined as "a contradiction between two apparently equally valid principles or between inferences correctly drawn from such principles" (*Webster's New World Dictionary*, 1966, p. 39), describes the tension facing nascent entrepreneurs who could be reproducers or innovators. The two antinomies are (a) obedience to cultural routines, norms, and habits versus creativity/experimentation and play/make-believe; and (b) altruism versus egoism.

We selected these antinomies for two reasons. First, we believe that the contradictions represented by both antinomies clearly relate to the process of organizational founding. Second, the antinomies inform many of the behavioral and biological evolutionary processes to which Campbell devoted many of his papers.

Obedience to Cultural Routines, Norms, and Habits

Campbell was very clear about the overwhelming effects of culture and cultural routines on evolutionary processes. In describing the relationship of individuals to groups, he repeatedly mentioned the pressures toward conformity and cultural rigidity inherent in social processes. He wrote, "the social glue that holds . . . groups together has structure-maintenance requirements that limit and bias the portrait of the world such social groups sustain" (Campbell, 1979, p. 184). Campbell sometimes used the scientific community as an example of a self-perpetuating community constrained by social processes that often stifle individual variations. "Social processes in science can be seen as increasing or ensuring objectivity through providing a curb to individual 'subjective' biases or delusions. The 'objective' or the 'real' becomes that which can

be seen also by others. The logical positivist requirements of 'intersubjectivity' or 'intersubjective verifiability' make explicit this social role" (Campbell, 1979, pp. 181-182).[3]

He described the role of the individual in the social system of science as follows:

Not only is science conducted in the context of the elaborate social system of science, but its products "scientific knowledge" or "scientific truths" (or even more relativistically, "the accepted theories of physics as of May 11, 1977") are *social products*, incompletely specifiable in the beliefs of any one scientist or the writings in any one book. This remains true even for specialized areas and restricted topics. No matter how small the area, scientific knowledge is achieved in spite of minor disagreements, ignorances, and misunderstandings on the part of every one of its leading participants. This is analogous to the situation in a language, where, for the vast bulk of the working vocabulary, all speakers have some idiosyncratic usages and no one speaker adequately represents the language; where each individual speaker is soon replaced, yet the language persists as a coherent whole in spite of this. So too, each individual scientist is as replaceable as is any one cell in the body. The major innovations in any one epoch are independently invented by several persons, as sociology-of-science studies show. (Campbell, 1979, pp. 182-183)[4]

Campbell stressed the pervasiveness of cultural routines, and individuals' obedience to such routines, in his discussion of habits. Habits are the bedrock upon which evolutionary processes have been built, and in his discussion of the "evolutionary puzzle of instinct," also called the "Baldwin effect," Campbell noted that

Baldwin . . . proposed that for such instincts, learned adaptive patterns . . . preceded the instincts. The adaptive pattern being thus piloted by learning, any mutations that accelerated the learning, made it more certain to occur, or predisposed the animal to certain component responses would be adaptive and selected[,] no matter which component responses or in what order affected. The habit thus provided a selective template around which the instinctive components could be assembled. . . . In the habit-to-instinct evolution, the once-learned goals and subgoals become innate at a more and more specific response-fragment level. (Campbell, 1974a, pp. 425-426; reprinted in 1982a, p. 93)

We see in this discussion the importance of contextualizing learning as a "habit-to-instinct" cycle, structured by the environment. Learned adaptive patterns do not occur in isolation but rather are a result of the sociocultural environment in which the individual (i.e., animal) is immersed. Campbell used this argument to drive home his point about the constraints placed on individuals by their environments. If learning is grounded in a set of environmentally conditioned "learned adaptive patterns," then individual initiatives are severely fettered.

In contrast to the cultural conformity induced by social processes, Campbell identified creativity, experimentation, play, and make-believe as behaviors through which individuals "disobey" ingrained cultural routines, norms, and habits. The tension between conformity and creativity can be seen in the following quotation: "There is, perhaps, always a potential conflict between the freedom to vary, which makes advance possible, and the value of retaining the cultural accumulation" (Campbell, 1965, p. 35). We turn now to a description of these "deviant" behaviors.

Creativity/Experimentation and Play/Make-Believe

Why should we experiment? What value does creativity or make-believe have for organizational foundings? Campbell argued that the more "movement" or "experimental activity" in which an individual engages, the greater is the likelihood that innovative knowledge will result. Campbell believed that all creative thought has a BVSR component (Campbell, 1990a, p. 9) and that creativity is "a prime example of such a short-cut process using fallible vicarious selectors. Not at all do I deny the importance of creative thought. But I insist upon an explicit model for how it operates and require that this model fit in with radical selection theory" (Campbell, 1994, p. 31).[5]

The following quotations, on the importance of creativity/experimentation and play/make-believe, are taken from Campbell (1982a):

Truth is brought about through the "fundamental process of experimentation." The highest functions of thought are thus to be looked upon as experimental. (p. 92)

Play is a generalized native impulse toward the exercise of specific and useful activities. It is itself a functional character which has arisen by the selection, among the individuals of a very great number of animal forms, of variations toward the early and artificial use of their growing powers. It is a natural and powerful tendency in vigorous and growing young; in fact, it is an impulse of extraordinary strength and persistence, and of corresponding utility. (p. 90)

On the psychological side, a corresponding advance has been made in the interpretation of the state of "make-believe," which accompanies and excites to the indulgence of play. Make believe . . . leads to a sort of sustained imagination of situations, treated as if real—a playful "dramatization"—in which the most important principles of individual and social life are tentatively and experimentally illustrated. Play thus becomes a most important sphere of practice, not only on the side of the physical powers, but also in intellectual, social, and moral lines. (pp. 90-91)

Playfulness and experimentation are thus natural impulses that have been wired into humans because of their utility. The full expression of these tendencies is opposed, however, by another set of impulses—humans' tendencies to defer to the beliefs of others. Indeed, obedience to cultural routines can be powerful enough to intimidate individuals with dissenting beliefs. Campbell (1993) called unwarranted deference to others' beliefs "conformity-induced pseudo-confirmation" and noted the consequent loss of innovation:

Tremendously important in the establishment of both common-sense and scientific knowledge is consensual validation, the confirmation of observations by other persons. . . . There are two aspects to this process: On one hand, each person must describe the world as uniquely seen from his own particular point of vantage. On the other hand, each must take seriously the reports of others as to what they see. . . . These two essentials run counter to each other. Insofar as systematic biases have been observed. . . [there is] a tendency to contaminate one's reports in the direction of agreement with what others are reporting and thus to fail to report what is uniquely available from one's own perspective. The agreement achieved represents *pseudo-confirmation.* (1993, p. 37)

Thus, we see the reproducer/innovator tension: Individuals are torn between following the path of acceptance (i.e., least resistance) or the path of deviance, experimentation, and innovative risk.

How powerful are conformity-inducing forces? Campbell often noted the tension between "doubt" and "trust" in social systems, arguing that trust in the existing order played a critical role in stabilizing the system (Campbell, 1978; 1991b). The greater the propensity to doubts about current practices, the more likely individuals are to deviate and thus potentially destabilize the order. Although he could cite no experimental evidence in his favor, Campbell estimated the ratio of "trust to doubt" at about 99 to 1 (Campbell, 1987, p. 157). He arrived at that estimate using his own playful shortcut through the thicket of inductive logic thrown up by more data-driven theorists.

An alternative path to the nonconformist, innovative creation of new organizational knowledge is found via ignorance of existing cultural norms. Circumstances may occur where individuals simply do not know what the prevailing conformity-inducing forces dictate. We mentioned at the beginning of this chapter that *entrepreneurship often happens when people are on their way to something else.* For individuals who are outsiders to an industry or community of practice, the serendipitous, accidental emergence of a new organization will occur without knowledge of existing norms and practices. If an individual were ignorant of the norms, rules, and practices that dictate organizational forms within an industry or population, then conformity would be purely accidental. For these individuals, and the organizations they found, ignorance or blindness to (seen as deviance from) the norms of the population would be the root cause for creative, innovative organizational emergence (Cliff, 1997).

Altruism

Campbell's second antinomy is the tension between altruism and egoism. He believed that all individuals experience a tension between innate

altruistic tendencies toward the social community or "in-group" and a set of opposing tendencies involving egoistic/nepotistic drives. Campbell's (1986a) article proposed that this tension or conflict, at its most fundamental level, exists between cultural and biological behavioral tendencies.

> Previously (1975) my acceptance of the individual selectionist point of view for us vertebrates (but not for social insect cooperators) led me to dramatize self-denying altruism as a purely cultural product. Now, due to Axelrod, I am ready to credit our biological-dispositional inheritance with containing what some biologists call a "facultative polymorphism" on the selfish/cooperative dimension. Just as all male macaques have innate repertoires for both dominance and submission available for use in male-male encounters, so too biology may give us both cooperative and opportunistic-cheating proclivities, which may be differentially developed depending upon conditions (e.g., rural vs. urban) or cultures, but which remain ambivalently available in all of us. This facultative polymorphism could be the product of individual-level selection. (Campbell, 1986a, p. 795)

These inherent ambiguities, given the cultural pressures for "altruistic conformity" and the overwhelming majority of individuals who do, in fact, behave altruistically, result in unevenly distributed benefits/outcomes. Those who cooperate get less, whereas those who compete get more:

> While group selection no doubt occurs, its effects are undermined by individual selection. For example, individuals may sometimes have genes that lead to effective, group-survival-enhancing, self-sacrificial altruism. The chances of survival of the group as a whole are improved because of their presence. But the net benefits of this group-selection are greatest for non-altruists. For the altruists, their group-selection gains are reduced by the risks they run. No such costs, but only the benefits, accrue to non-altruists. Thus the relative frequency of non-altruists increases in the group in future generations. . . . I summarize the problem by the phrase "genetic competition among the cooperators." (Campbell, 1994, p. 24)

The tension between "what's best for the group as a whole" (altruism) and "what's best for the individual" (egoism) is not unidimensional. Campbell argued that conformity to group norms is a form of self-preservation. He used the term *clique selfishness* to describe this in-group protective behavior: "If we turn the phrase from 'reciprocal altruism' to 'clique selfishness,' we note that the internally altruistic groups are exploiting unorganized persons, or organized out-groups. . . . Each in-group can plausibly accuse the other group of clique selfishness and use this accusation to mobilize their own in-group solidarity. (Campbell, 1991b, p. 107).

The positive value that clique selfishness has for group maintenance and survival results in a rather high level of psychological ambiguity, as tendencies supporting both cooperative and competitive behaviors persist within individuals:

> To abbreviate a much longer argument (cf. Campbell, 1982a, 1983) for human complex social coordination that is achieved in spite of (rather than through eliminating) genetic competition among the cooperators, moral norms curbing ruthless intelligent individual optimization are rational selfish individual preferences as to how others behave. If the social organization is intact and if the collective goods are substantial, it is also rational to conform to such norms oneself if that is necessary for maintaining group membership. We probably have innate ambivalence (facultative polymorphism) on this score: an available repertoire of cooperative group solidarity and another one of individual optimization at the expense of the group. (Campbell, 1986b, pp. 360-361)

Having argued for the presence of altruistic tendencies in humans and their social systems, we next review the other side of the ledger—the pressure producing facultative polymorphism for individuals engaged in innovative, self-seeking behaviors—the "maximize my own benefits first and foremost" mind-set.

Egoism

An ongoing conflict exists between a social system's best interests and the interests of its members (Campbell, 1985). This conflict will be particularly salient when the individual is a creative, entrepreneurial member interested in challenging the dominant paradigm.

Even though the primary message of my chapter requires a continual ongoing conflict between behaviors that optimize organized groups and behaviors that optimize an individual's personal and nepotistic interests (which I pose as a conflict between the products of biological and cultural evolution), I do not want to deny that our biological history. . . has been increasingly social. (Campbell, 1994, p. 29)

Based on this apparent dichotomy, with each of the poles having deleterious effects (pure egoism leads to destruction, and pure altruism, as mentioned in the section above, results in nonadaptation and eventual extinction), Campbell argued against promoting pure egoism:

> In all social communities, narcissistic people with competitive egocentric pride are a problem. Cooperative people who defer to the majority, who get along and go along with others, and who hold the team together, get preferential treatment even if they are less competent. (Campbell, 1979, p. 194)

For Campbell, egoism, or "competition among the cooperators," results in secrecy and self-serving behaviors.

Campbell illustrated his point with an example of competition among scientists to be the first to report an innovative discovery:

> Our predicament as social animals who must achieve our sociality without inhibition of genetic competition among the cooperators (Campbell, 1975), and as social animals with a fundamental disposition to individual and clique selfishness, puts us in a special predicament insofar as public belief assertion is concerned. Were science designed only to guide our own behavior, then the value neutrality of our scientific conclusions would be complete. The model of the world best-suited to implementing our own values would also have the validity optimal for guiding others with different values. However, the fact that we are in varying degrees in competition with those others provides a motive to keep our knowledge, of our beliefs, private. This motive to achieve secrecy is inevitably characteristic of applied science, social or physical, industrial or national. (Campbell, 1982b, p. 335)

Competition for primacy thus drives scientists underground in their laboratory practices, but recognition for their achievements requires disclosure to the world. Disclosures, in turn, allow other scientists to learn about the discovery, and the shared knowledge—if replicated and validated—creates a new baseline for subsequent work.

Selection Rules: Campbellian Antinomies and Entrepreneurship Puzzles

Thus far, the quotations we have used from Campbell represent four different levels of analysis: individual, group, community, and population. In the following discussion of relationships among Campbell's antinomies, the BVSR environment, and our six entrepreneurial puzzles, we employ the *firm* as the unit of selection. Entrepreneurial variations in behaviors and activities, if successful, create a bounded entity that stands or falls as a unit. Campbell noted that

If, after all of this internal, structural selection an adult, fertile phenotype is produced, this phenotype is then subject to an *external* natural selection. Of all these many selective systems, only this last can involve an improvement in the fit of the organism to the environment, an increase in the "knowledge" which the genome carries in the external world. (Campbell, 1979, p. 185)

Selection of an entity does not imply that all of its components, taken in isolation, are viable. This is particularly significant to our discussion, given the underlying tension between variation and selection pressures.

To understand differences across entrepreneurial foundings with respect to variation and selection, we must first appreciate the complexity of the BVSR environment. Campbell believed that the environment was fluid and dynamic, and within this environment, adaptive and maladaptive organizational forms coexist.

The "wisdom" produced by biological and social evolution is retrospective, referring to past environments. It is only adaptive to the extent that these environments remain stable. Yet the rigid preservation systems essential for the process of evolution, also

provide for a retention of these systems long beyond their usefulness. (Campbell, 1965, p. 35)

We see, therefore, that at any given moment, both adaptive and maladaptive firms inhabit local environments—the enigma is that we cannot tell which is adaptive until the environment selects out maladaptive firms. The simultaneous existence of adaptive and maladaptive organizations is one of the inherent complexities of the BVSR environment:

Evolutionary theory—biological or cultural—does not automatically produce a "Panglossian" picture of perfect rationality or adaptedness. Indeed its theoretical resources can be assembled to understand and predict systematic dysfunction, and it may well be this potentiality that might most modify economic theory were the merger to be carried further. (Campbell, 1986b, p. 358)

One aspect of BVSR environmental selection we have ignored to this point is the required level of persistence on the part of nascent entrepreneurs (Gartner, Bird, & Starr, 1992). Campbell noted that environmental complexity and uncertainty imply a minimal chance of success for most new entities. Even highly focused, intentional behavior by motivated nascent entrepreneurs must contend with environments that reveal their structures only grudgingly. Repeated trials, over the lives of many nascent entrepreneurs, may be the only way to learn what environments have to offer:

There is bound to be a lot of the purely fortuitous or non-transferably specific in the life or death of a single biological individual or social system or culture item. For a systematic selective criterion to make itself felt above this "noise level," there must be numerous instances involved, and a high mortality rate. (Campbell, 1965, p. 31)

Persistence does not guarantee selection, but it keeps variations alive long enough for them to experience many different selection environments.

We now turn to an examination of the six entrepreneurial puzzles listed at the beginning of this chapter. Our goal is to provide interpretations of the puzzles, using Campbell's BVSR dogma and his antinomies, linking Campbell's theories to the literature on entrepreneurship. Our interpretations are not meant to be exhaustive or conclusive in nature. Instead, we hope that they will serve as a catalyst for further theoretical and empirical explorations. We repeat the puzzles, in greatly simplified form, for ease of exposition.

Puzzle #1: Most new organizations merely reproduce existing forms, rather than creating new ones. Campbell's description of the cultural routines, norms, and habits that restrict creative human activity may, in fact, be more relevant during the period of organizational founding than during succeeding periods. The tension between retaining cultural accumulation and an individual's "freedom to vary" often is resolved by forceful adoption of existing processes. Not only is it easier for entrepreneurs to follow accepted "recipes for success," but resource providers also frequently require it (Aldrich & Fiol, 1994; Suchman, 1995). Such recipes provide templates for the mundane reproduction of existing organizational forms. As Romanelli points out (this volume), to the extent that entrepreneurs blindly assume that copying from existing organizations will work, they fail to explore alternatives that might be more effective.

Innovation requires the ability to challenge, and often disregard, dominant cultural routines. Challenging the dominant paradigm is an overwhelming obstacle for many entrepreneurs. For example, resource requirements for founding, via loans or venture capital funding, may result in coercive isomorphism (DiMaggio & Powell, 1983) in which a new firm is forced to adopt a taken-for-granted form.

In-group pressures are a related reason we might observe a disproportionate number of reproducer organizations over innovator organizations. Individuals following the safer, more supported, in-group routes establish organizations in existing accepted industries. By contrast, we would expect to see innovator firms being established by individuals engaged in the less accepted, egoistic/nepotistic practices. Because they do not know the norms of a population well enough to be conceptually constrained by them, perhaps only outsiders can make radical breaks with tradition.

Finally, as described in the chapter by Miner and Raghavan in this volume, heterogeneous organizational copying or imitation may differentiate between reproducer and innovator organizations. Miner and Raghavan argue that copying and then implementing an eclectic mix of routines from other organizations might result in either increased *or* decreased adaptation. Using their terms, we believe that most firms are founded via simplistic imitation practices, resulting in reproducer organizations, but that foundings created using an extraordinary mix of routines occasionally may blossom into innovative organizations (see Gartner, Mitchell, & Vesper, 1989).

Puzzle #2: Most new ventures, even small ones, involve more than just the nascent entrepreneur during the start-up process. The altruism/egoism antinomy sheds light on this puzzle. The practitioner literature typically portrays entrepreneurial ventures as one-person foundings, but recent research suggests otherwise (Reynolds & White, 1997). Even though entrepreneurs may start their journey working alone, most successful entrepreneurial ventures require cooperative input from a variety of individuals. Entrepreneurs who try to manage their organizational founding as a single-person venture, rather than trading on their in-group status, forgo an array of potentially valuable resources. Campbell's discussion of the security/protection resulting from in-group membership highlights the value of maintaining a cooperative network during organizational foundings.

Involving other people in a founding, however, carries some costs. The more people involved, the greater the pressures on nascent entrepreneurs to follow well-understood routines and practices. What might have become a radically innovative approach to producing or selling a product/service may be so diluted by multiple contributions that it devolves into a replication of the familiar. Nascent entrepreneurs thus face a dilemma: Cooperative behavior facilitates resource acquisition and boundary construction, but egoistic/nepotistic behavior may be necessary to preserve the radical nature of the proposed venture. Because most new ventures involve groups rather than solo individuals (Reynolds & White, 1997), they face pressures pushing them toward the "reproducer" end of our continuum.

Puzzle #3: Habitual entrepreneurs are highly visible icons in many industries, yet their valuable knowledge has been difficult to codify and diffuse. Why is success not contagious? First, success across multiple start-ups requires repeated acquisition of tacit knowledge about local environments. Such knowledge is needed for an understanding of the influential customs, routines, norms, and habits that guide local environmental selection criteria. Deep understanding of tacit knowledge has the potential to mask egoistic drives as altruistic tendencies. Certainly, one of Campbell's strongest propositions relates variation to environmental fit (if there is fit, selection will follow), and one aspect of fit is local adaptation. Campbell argued that the peculiarities of language often obscure tacit knowledge, impeding people's efforts to transmit their local knowledge (Campbell, 1991a). Thus, successful entrepreneurs may not possess the language to codify their approach. If every speaker has an idiosyncratic usage and no two speakers use the same language pattern, then every speaker is constrained by the fit between her or his communication and the interpretations of others.

Second, the altruism/egoism antinomy may also shed light on this puzzle. Highly competitive business environments display what Campbell described as "the problem of competition among the cooperators." Why would successful entrepreneurs share their templates for success when they know full well that others replicating the templates would instantly become direct competitors? Our biologically (and culturally) determined competitive drives may be strong enough to inhibit codification of knowledge by successful entrepreneurs.

Puzzle #4: In spite of the best-laid plans, the gestation period of start-ups is lengthy and fraught with delays. Constructing a new entity takes a long time because nascent entrepreneurs make a lot of mistakes, pursue many blind alleys, and repeatedly retrace their steps. Why are mistakes and blind alleys so common? The direction in which "adaptive" lies, on the reproducer/innovator continuum,

is not readily apparent to most nascent entrepreneurs, so they are vulnerable to the social conformity pressures spelled out by Campbell's antinomy. Lacking strong evidence to the contrary, the path well traveled looks pretty good to nascent entrepreneurs, and they do what others have done. Because of local differentiation, however, much of what once worked no longer does.

Luckily for many nascent entrepreneurs, pressures for obedience to traditions and habits have not completely driven out tendencies toward experimentation and playfulness. Some deviant behaviors actually work. The result, over time, is a mix of start-ups containing mostly conformists or near-conformists, who eventually got it right, plus a few innovative deviants whose activities were rewarded. In the BVSR model, emergence as a coherent entity ultimately depends, of course, on fitness, and fitness is the interactive product of what nascent entrepreneurs offer and what local environments accept.

In addition, the process is lengthy only if some nascent entrepreneurs doggedly persist in their intentions to start a new firm. Discouraged entrepreneurs who give up quickly are of interest primarily if continuing entrepreneurs learn something by observing the dropouts, but learning from others is difficult without insider information. Environmental complexity and uncertainty create situations that take time for founders to learn and unravel. Repeated trials are required, over weeks and months, and may be the only way to place oneself in a position to be selected (Gartner et al., 1992).

Puzzle #5: The more activities people engage in, the greater the chances of their starting, *but* also the greater their chances of quitting the process altogether. Experimentation and persistence pay off for nascent entrepreneurs, although the payoff may be an early exit rather than a start-up. Campbell praised the virtues of experimentation by claiming that the "highest functions of thought" are experimental. In uncertain environments, playfulness and experimentation within the dark corners of an industry may reveal secrets not available to culturally obedient founders." We can also see, in Campbell's writings, the value of persistence. Those entrepreneurs who actively pursue organizational founding, regardless of what they do, will have a better chance of creating a firm than those entrepreneurs who remain relatively inactive.

With respect to the type of activities engaged in, the dynamic nature of the environment allows entrepreneurs to design any number of alternative paths to success. What works at one time may not work at another. Moreover, the degree of constraint between start-up activities is remarkably low. In one study of correlations between indicators of 14 different start-up activities, 60 of the 91 possible correlations were below 0.2 (Carter et al., 1996; Gatewood et al., 1995). Apparently, nearly anything goes, and effective mixes of activities exist in many different combinations.

Puzzle #6: Venture capital firms appear unable to find a predictive template for picking firms in which to invest.

This puzzle captures Campbell's overall message for those interested in organizational foundings. There is no predictive template that will guarantee success. Given the composition of the environment, containing both adaptive and maladaptive organizations, coupled with its fluidity, any template that would guarantee success would (a) apply only to the local environment (local culture-specific) and (b) be applicable at only one point in time (what is adaptive today may be maladaptive tomorrow). Venture capitalists would *seem* to be well placed to design a predictive template because they are in the business of designing them for evaluating business plans. They have not been able to do this for their own investments because no such generic template exists. Campbell's BVSR model explains why. The environment is far too fluid and contains complex antinomies that obviate any potential for developing "*the* right answer" or "*the* template for success."

Summary and Conclusions

Based on his BVSR dogma, Campbell's message to organizational and entrepreneurship theorists is clear: There is no *one right way* to found an organization, nor is the path necessarily straight.

The fluidity and dynamism of the environment create a situation in which success (i.e., founding) results from the interaction between organizational configuration and local environmental selection mechanisms. Because selection mechanisms are neither instantaneous nor perfect, adaptive and maladaptive firms coexist in every local environment. Only through post hoc analysis of what worked can we begin to understand the environmental selection mechanisms in place during any given period. Our understanding of what worked, however, will be constrained by the language in which we communicate and the vision derived from our past experiences.

We have used the terms *reproducer* and *innovator* to label differences among entrepreneurs and the types of organizations they found. Stated simply, reproducer organizations are severely constrained by the boundaries and institutional norms imposed by existing organizations, and they are dangerous models because they are a mix of adaptive and maladaptive forms. Innovator organizations face not only legitimization issues but also rigorous selection forces that may be impossible to overcome. The activities in which nascent entrepreneurs engage, as outlined in the Campbellian antinomies ledger, provide one overarching message for potential success: *Do something.*

Implications

Evolutionary theorists have not paid enough attention to entrepreneurship and the reproducer/innovator continuum (Aldrich & Fiol, 1994). Instead, evolutionary research has focused primarily on monumental discontinuities that occur only once or twice during a population's life cycle (Anderson & Tushman, 1990). Researchers need to turn their attention to nascent entrepreneurship and the founding process at the organizational level of analysis, not only to understand more about the processes and activities leading to organizational emergence but also to complement existing population-level theories.

More dynamic analyses of firm emergence and the founding process would strengthen all aspects of organization theory. We need methods for tracking founding processes, and thus we must find nascent entrepreneurs when they are just beginning to construct their ventures. One way of tackling this empirically is through random-digit dialing surveys of the entire adult population. Currently, the multi-university Entrepreneurship Research Consortium (ERC) is conducting such a longitudinal survey in an attempt to capture what happens during the gestation period when nascent entrepreneurs are only *thinking* about organizational foundings.

Epilogue

As for Steven, the entrepreneur with whom we began our story, over the fall of 1995, he continued to develop his firm. He mostly hired software engineers, but he also employed a few marketing specialists and salespeople. As the company grew, and as he searched for insurance companies as clients for his site, the tens of thousands of dollars per month from his investors no longer seemed like enough to sustain the firm through its early years of planned losses. On one of his trips to California, to look for strategic partners, the Intuit Corporation learned about his firm and asked if he was interested in being acquired. Over a period of several months, Steven and his partners hashed out the advantages of remaining independent and hoping for an early IPO (initial public offering) versus being acquired. Eventually, the choice became clear—be acquired or risk losing everything. In June of 1996, Steven and his partners sold the firm to Intuit for $8 million. His investors were handsomely rewarded for their 9 months of support.

Notes

1. Our chapter applies Campbell's ideas to entrepreneurship as a method of organizational emergence. For a discussion of Campbell's ideas as they relate to variation among existing organizations, see Romanelli's chapter in this volume.

2. Our reproducer/innovator continuum parallels March's (1991) exploiter/explorer discussion of organizational learning.

3. As McKelvey notes in his chapters in this volume, Campbell, in his later years, moved beyond logical positivism and

supported the scientific realist school (critical realism) that replaced positivism.

4. For a complete listing of the supporting cites provided by Campbell, see his 1979 article.

5. For a complete description of Campbell's BVSR dogma, as applied to creative thought, see Campbell (1990a).

6. We thank Bill Barnett for suggesting the expression "dark corner" to refer to unexplored but potentially profitable niches in a market.

References

Aldrich, H. E., & Fiol, M. C. (1994). Fools rush in? The institutional context of industry creation. *Academy of Management Review, 19*(4), 645-670.

Anderson, P., & Tushman, M. (1990). Technological discontinuities and dominant designs: A cyclical model of technological change. *Administrative Science Quarterly, 35*, 604-633.

Campbell, D. T. (1956a). Adaptive behavior from random response. *Behavioral Science, 1*(2), 105-110.

Campbell, D. T. (1956b). Perception as substitute trial and error. *Psychological Review, 63*(5), 330-342.

Campbell, D. T. (1960). Blind variation and selective retention in creative thought as in other knowledge processes. *Psychological Review, 67*(6), 380-400.

Campbell, D. T. (1965). Variation and selective retention in socio-cultural evolution. In H. R. Barringer, G. I. Blanksten, & R. W. Mack (Eds.), *Social change in developing areas: A reinterpretation of evolutionary theory* (pp. 19-48). Cambridge, MA: Schenkman.

Campbell, D. T. (1974a). Evolutionary epistemology. In P. A. Schilpp (Ed.), *The philosophy of Karl R. Popper* (pp. 413-463). La Salle, IL: Open Court.

Campbell, D. T. (1974b). Unjustified variation and selective retention in scientific discovery. In F. J. Ayala & T. Dobzhansky (Eds.), *Studies in the philosophy of biology* (pp. 139-161). London: Macmillan.

Campbell, D. T. (1975). On the conflicts between biological and social evolution and between psychology and moral tradition. *American Psychologist, 30*, 1103-1126.

Campbell, D. T. (1978). Qualitative knowing in action research. In M. Brenner, P. Marsh, & M. Brenner (Eds.), *The social contexts of method* (pp. 184-209). London: Croom Helm.

Campbell, D. T. (1979). A tribal model of the social system vehicle carrying scientific knowledge. *Knowledge, 2*, 181-201.

Campbell, D. T. (1982a). The "blind-variation-and-selective-retention" theme. In J. M. Broughton & D. J. Freeman-Moir (Eds.), *The cognitive-developmental psychology of James Mark Baldwin: Current theory and research in genetic epistemology* (pp. 87-96). Norwood, NJ: Ablex.

Campbell, D. T. (1982b). Experiments as arguments. *Knowledge: Creation, Diffusion, Utilization, 3*(3), 327-337.

Campbell, D. T. (1983). The two distinct routes beyond kin selection to ultrasociality: Implications for the humanities and social sciences. In D. L. Bridgeman (Ed.), *The nature of prosocial development: Interdisciplinary theories and strategies* (pp. 11-41). New York: Academic Press.

Campbell, D. T. (1985). Altruism: Biology, culture, and religion. *Journal of Social and Clinical Psychology, 3*(1), 33-42.

Campbell, D. T. (1986a). The agenda beyond Axelrod's *The evolution of cooperation. Political Psychology, 7*(4), 793-796.

Campbell, D. T. (1986b). Rationality and utility from the standpoint of evolutionary biology. *Journal of Business, 59*(4), S335-S364.

Campbell, D. T. (1987). Selection theory and the sociology of scientific validity. In W. Callebaut & R. Pinxten (Eds.), *Evolutionary epistemology: A multiparadigm program* (pp. 139-158). Dordrecht, The Netherlands: D. Reidel.

Campbell, D. T. (1990a). Epistemological roles for selection theory. In N. Rescher (Ed.), *Evolution, cognition, and realism: Studies in evolutionary epistemology* (pp. 1-19). Lanham, MD: University Press of America.

Campbell, D. T. (1990b). Selection theory and the sociology of scientific validity. In W. Callebaut & R. Pinxten (Eds.), *Evolutionary epistemology: A multiparadigm program* (pp. 139-158). Dordrecht, The Netherlands: D. Reidel.

Campbell, D. T. (1991a). Coherentist empiricism, hermeneutics, and the commensurability of paradigms. *International Journal of Educational Research, 15*(6), 587-597.

Campbell, D. T. (1991b). A naturalistic theory of archaic moral orders. *Zygon, 26*(1), 91-114.

Campbell, D. T. (1993). Systematic errors to be expected of the social scientist on the basis of a general psychology of cognitive bias. In P. D. Blanck (Ed.), *Interpersonal expectations: Theory, research, and applications* (pp. 25-41). New York: Cambridge University Press.

Campbell, D. T. (1994). How individual and face-to-face-group selection undermine firm selection in organizational evolution. In J.A.C. Baum & J. V. Singh (Eds.), *Evolutionary dynamics of organizations* (pp. 23-38). New York: Oxford University Press.

Carter, N. M., Gartner, W. B., & Reynolds, P. D. (1996). Exploring start-up sequences. *Journal of Business Venturing, 11*(3), 151-166.

Cliff, J. (1997). *Building on experience: A cross-level, learning-based approach to the design of new firms.* Unpublished manuscript, College of Commerce and Administration, University of British Columbia, Vancouver.

DiMaggio, P. J., & Powell, W. W. (1983). The iron cage revisited: Institutional isomorphism and collective rationality in organizational fields. *American Sociological Review, 48,* 147-160.

Fiol, C. M., & Lyles M. A. (1985). Organizational learning. *Academy of Management Review, 10*(4), 803-813.

Gartner, W. B. (1985). A conceptual framework for describing the phenomenon of new venture creation. *Academy of Management Review, 10*(4), 696-706.

Gartner, W. B., Bird, B., & Starr, J. (1992). Act as if: Differentiating entrepreneurial from organizational behavior. *Entrepreneurship: Theory and Practice, 16*(3), 13-32.

Gartner, W. B., Mitchell, T. R., & Vesper, K. H. (1989). A taxonomy of new business ventures. *Journal of Business Venturing, 4*(3), 169-186.

Gatewood, E. J., Shaver, K. G., & Gartner, W. B. (1995). A longitudinal study of cognitive factors influencing start-up behaviors and success at venture creation. *Journal of Business Venturing, 10*(5), 371-392.

Gifford, S. (1997). Limited attention and the role of the venture capitalist. *Journal of Business Venturing, 12*(6), 459-482.

Gorman, M., & Sahlman, W. A. (1989). What do venture capitalists do? *Journal of Business Venturing, 4*(4), 231-248.

Low, M. B., & Abrahamson, E. (1997). Movements, bandwagons, and clones: Industry evolution and the entrepreneurial process. *Journal of Business Venturing, 12*(6), 435-457.

March, J. G. (1991). Exploration and exploitation in organizational learning. *Organization Science, 2,* 71-87.

National Endowment for the Arts. (1997). National Medal of Arts press release [Announcement posted on the World Wide Web]. Retrieved from the World Wide Web: http://arts.endow.gov/Community/News/Medals98.html

Reynolds, P., & White, S. (1997). *The entrepreneurial process: Economic growth, men, women, and minorities.* Westport, CT: Quorum.

Scriven, M. (1959, August 2). Explanation and prediction in evolutionary theory. *Science,* pp. 477-482.

Starr, J. A., & Bygrave, W. D. (1992). The second time around: The outcomes, assets and liabilities of prior start-up experience. In S. Birley & I. C. MacMillan (Eds.), *International perspectives on entrepreneurship research* (pp. 340-363). Amsterdam: Elsevier.

Starr, J., Bygrave, W., & Tercanli, D. (1993). Does experience pay? Methodological issues in the study of entrepreneurial experience. In S. Birley & I. C. MacMillan (Eds.), *Entrepreneurship research: Global perspectives* (pp. 125-155). Amsterdam: Elsevier.

Suchman, M. (1995). Managing legitimacy: Strategic and institutional approaches. *Academy of Management Review, 20*(3), 571-610.

Van de Ven, A. H., Angle, H. L., & Poole, M. S. (1989). *Research on the management of innovation.* New York: Harper & Row.

Webster's new world dictionary. (1966). Cleveland, OH: World.

4

LOST IN SPACE, OUT OF TIME: WHY AND HOW WE SHOULD STUDY ORGANIZATIONS COMPARATIVELY

Howard E. Aldrich

Over the past few decades, there have been many calls for more "comparative research" in organization studies, and those calls have been answered so frequently that they have made possible this edited volume (Dobbin, 1994; Scott, 2001). I like to think of comparative research in terms of paying more attention to context, following Tsui's (2006) definition of contextualization as meaning the incorporation of context "in describing, understanding, and theorizing about the phenomenon within it." Indeed, scholars have offered so many possible dimensions of "context" that Von Glinow, Shapiro, and Brett (2004) proposed the term "polycontextualization" to cover all possible bases. In this chapter, I argue that "organizations" constitute a very heterogeneous set and that understanding the contextual effects of time and place gives us some leverage in explaining such heterogeneity.

I focus on just two dimensions of context, albeit big ones: time and space. I chose these two because of the substantial progress that's already been made in incorporating them into organization studies and because there is still so much that can be accomplished. I begin with a critique that McKelvey and I offered 25 years ago of the field's inattention to context,

Studying Differences between Organizations: Comparative Approaches to
Organizational Research
Research in the Sociology of Organizations, Volume 26, 21–44
Copyright © 2009 by Emerald Group Publishing Limited
All rights of reproduction in any form reserved
ISSN: 0733-558X/doi:10.1108/S0733-558X(2009)0000026003

especially the scope conditions surrounding research findings. I note that our critique fell short because it devoted insufficient attention to time and space as critical aspects of organizational environments. Despite considerable progress in the ensuing 25 years, the problem we pointed out persists, with many investigators still indifferent to reporting important contextual information about their projects.

Echoing the arguments of others in this volume, I then offer a brief defense for paying more attention to time and space in studying organizations and suggest how we might study them. I offer an amendment to the argument that McKelvey and I made, with the benefit of hindsight. With regard to time, I suggest a life course perspective and an historical perspective. With regard to space, I suggest looking at regional and national differences. Let me be clear about my purposes.

First, I am not making an argument for yet another taxonomy of organizations and organizational forms. Regardless of the taxonomy used, it must take account of time and space. Second, I am not making an argument for any radical changes in research designs. Instead, my arguments turn on making more effective use of the designs already available to us by explicitly taking account of time (clock time and constructed time) and space (local, regional, and national). Clearly, we have many examples of projects within the field of organizational studies that have emphasized "context." For example, the core idea of institutional theory is that cultural–institutional environments affect organizational practices and policies. Nonetheless, I believe that we have not paid enough attention to the temporal and geographical conditions that may account for the observable differences in organizational practices and policies. Consequently, we may have put too much faith in generalizations from our research projects.

THE ORIGINAL CRITIQUE OF MCKELVEY AND ALDRICH

In our 1983 paper, McKelvey and I (McKelvey & Aldrich, 1983) took the field of "organization science" to task for not paying sufficient attention to the scope conditions under which research findings are valid. (Today I would argue that the field also had not paid sufficient attention to matching theoretical ambitions with research designs.) We argued that the field fell short on three critical criteria: classifiability, generalizability, and predictability. We noted that samples of organizations were so poorly described that classifying them was impossible, that generalizations were being carelessly drawn, and that the predictive power of most theories was extremely weak.

With regard to classifiability, we noted that researchers mostly collected data on organizations conceptualized as legal entities, most of which were large firms. With regard to generalizability, we noted the extreme heterogeneity of many samples. Samples contained organizations from diverse industries, sizes, locations, and so forth, and we wondered whether generalizations could safely be drawn to some larger population. With regard to predictability, we noted that researchers were often content with finding weak patterns in their analyses.

When we looked more closely at the literature, we discerned two broad approaches investigators seemed to be using in designing their research: (1) treating organizations as all alike, or (2) treating organizations as all unique. Most studies followed the "all alike" approach, reporting their results as if one organizational form characterized all organizations. This tendency was evident in the haphazard way samples were drawn and in the expansive way generalizations were offered. We noted that a conservative conclusion from a typical project would be that generalizations applied only to these kinds of organizations. In spite of this, we found an implicit assumption that the results applied to all organizations, with no obvious qualifying statements. Lack of concern for representative samples was also evident, as was an overall cavalier attitude toward organizational differences and representativeness.

Today, we might characterize this "organizations are all alike" approach as one of extreme decontextualization. If organizations are all the same and if researchers are studying their own special samples, no detailed attention to "description" is required. I believe this is analogous to what Heath and Sitkin (2001) described as the "behavior is behavior" approach to organizational behavior. That is, it simply does not matter if the particular behavior someone is studying happens to be inside an organization. If investigators can ignore context and assume that "variables" mean the same thing across all contexts, then they can bring very high-powered results to bear on the data. However, is that a safe assumption to make?

The "all unique" approach was found less often in our 1983 survey, but we did find some studies reporting their results as if every organization possessed a unique form. Explicit statements of this position were hard to pin down but were nonetheless implicit. In particular, case studies of single organizations often seemed to follow this logic, as researchers carefully avoided generalizing their results to other populations. Today, we might characterize this approach as "extreme contextualization." We see clues to this approach in studies that essentially report no unexplained variance, instead offering very tidy explanations in which everything is fully accounted for.

As a remedy for the ills we diagnosed, McKelvey and I prescribed a population perspective, grounded in evolutionary theory, that emphasized research methods that improved the description and classification of organizational forms, defined more homogeneous groupings for purposes of improving generalizations, and focused on improving the power of explanations. We noted that change would not come easily, as the old ways were embedded in a research paradigm widely shared by organizational researchers. Nonetheless, we were cautiously optimistic.

Looking back, what we failed to note – but should have – was another feature of the evolutionary approach: all explanations of organizational outcomes must pay attention to organizations *and* their environments. Instead, we focused almost entirely on organizations and neglected to take account of the extent to which organizational outcomes are shaped by two aspects of their environments: time and space. By "time," I mean both "clock time," measured in days, weeks, months, and years, and "socially constructed time," measured in units that are meaningful to actors within a particular organizational and social context. For example, in high reliability organizations, "time" may be thought of in terms of how long it has been since an accident, rather than by a daily or weekly rhythm of work (Weick & Sutcliffe, 2001). By "space," I mean differences due to location in particular geographic units, such as cities, regions, and nation states.

As a thoughtful reader pointed out, there are several complementary definitions of time and space effects. In this chapter, I often link space to a bounded political jurisdiction, such as a city or nation, and thus my focus is on laws, regimes, and other institutional structures and practices. However, another way of thinking about the importance of time and space is in terms of resource constraints (Freeman & Audia, 2006). Hawley's (1950) classic treatise on human ecology noted that time and space impose considerable limits on what organizations and populations can do, as overcoming the friction imposed by time and space constraints requires resources. For example, in Galaskiewicz's study of children's use of urban facilities, time and space are important not only because of simple cost factors, but also because getting to places that offer activities for children requires overcoming the friction of distance caused by time and space constraints (Galaskiewicz, Inouye, & Savage, 2008).

Time and space, as discussed above, are important for the modeling and data analysis portions of our research projects and should be incorporated into our data collection and research designs. However, as my examples will reveal, they are often proxies for other processes, structures, and patterns that we theorize and that themselves vary across time and space (norms, laws, culture, and specific historical conditions). We won't be well served if we simply incorporate time and space as "variables" into our models. Instead, I will argue that we need to use the context of our cases to theorize the processes, structures, and patterns that vary across time and space.

Methodological Problems Persist: Time and Space in ASQ

Back in 1983, McKelvey and I were harshly critical of the skimpy information offered in the methods section of articles published in top journals, in addition to calling into question the choices made by investigators in designing their research. For this chapter, I examined all 128 empirical papers published in the *Administrative Science Quarterly* (ASQ) between 2000 and 2007. For each article, in keeping with my "space" theme, I noted whether more than one nation was sampled, and if so, whether that nation was the United States or some other country. For my "time" theme, I examined whether the authors reported when they had collected their data. I also noted if they collected data from more than one point in time and if so, I noted the length of time covered by the study. My results are shown in Table 1.

Somewhat surprisingly, given the increasing internationalization of the field of organization studies, as reflected in the proliferation of international journals and an increasing international representation at Academy of Management meetings, over 90% of the papers covered only a single nation. Not so surprisingly, 88% of the single nation studies were conducted in the United States. One might well ask whether organizational life is the same in the United States as in the rest of the world, but there are larger issues involved.

One possible effect of this single nation focus would be a failure to put research into an historical context, as we know that many organizational forms have diffused across nations. Thus, at any particular historical conjuncture, forms within a nation may be at different stages of development and implementation. Another effect of this single nation focus could be a misattribution of causal effects. Investigators could be led to argue that some features of organizations within a nation are "cultural,"

Table 1.   Space and Time as Reflected in Eight Volumes of the
Administrative Science Quarterly, Volumes 45–52.

Author Report	Percent	N (By Row)
1. More than one nation in sample	9	128
2. If one nation only: USA	88	118
3. Dates of data collection reported in methods section	65	128
4. Data collected from more than one time point	65	128
5. If data collected over time, time period covers:		
0–4 years	27	
5–9 years	19	
10–19 years	30	
20–29 years	11	
30–49 years	4	
50 years or more	9	
Not ascertained	1	
Total for panel 5	100	81

when in fact they are very similar for organizations of the same form in other nations. Lacking a comparative context, investigators may well be tempted to make an inappropriate cultural argument about what they have discovered.

Only about two-thirds of the papers published in ASQ over this time actually reported the dates covered by the research design. In about one-third of the papers, it was simply impossible to discern the years covered by the study. (Note that this was not a problem for authors who explicitly bounded their study interval with specific years, regardless of when they actually collected the data.) Indeed, given that my investigation began in the year 2000, I could even argue that we could not tell what *century* is covered by one-third of the papers.

What is the implicit claim being made by authors who do not tell us the years to which their data pertain? Does "time" make no difference to the generalizations being offered? Is the structure or process being investigated one that truly "stands the test of time" in the sense that it is invariant over the years, decades, and centuries? Although this proposition sounds absurd on its face, perhaps there are some principles of organizational life that change so slowly that we can safely ignore time. For example, the proposition that complexity increases with organizational size may well be the same in the 19th, 20th, and 21st centuries. However, that is a proposition that should be explicitly stated and defended, perhaps through multiple attempts at replication.

When I have presented these results at conferences, more than a few critics have suggested that for laboratory experiments, small group studies, and other investigations inside an organization, it may not matter if we are explicitly told in what year the data were collected. Although this comment sounds plausible at first, it rests on two strong assumptions. First, we must assume that the article was published within a few years of the data being collected and thus knowing the year of publication gives us the "period" for the behavior or structure under investigation. Second, we must assume that the "half-life" of the article is very short and that it will outlive its usefulness shortly after being published.

Otherwise, consider the consequences: imagine that several decades into the future, a scholar wants to examine the possible effects of economic downturns on the likelihood of "associative homophily" at parties in New York City involving business executives (Ingram & Morris, 2007). The scholar finds an article with an innovative research design published 20 years before and wants to replicate it, but because it does not indicate in what year the study was conducted, cannot decide if it was done before or after a major economic crisis that erupted around the time the paper was published. Does the desire to seek out others of the same race at business gatherings increase in turbulent times or is it a constant preference?

Just to be crystal clear: we either must assume that the patterns of attitudes, behaviors, structures, or other phenomena analyzed in an article are time invariant or that papers are published for immediate consumption only and have no value for future generations of scholars. If, by contrast, editors accept papers on the assumption that scholars will still be looking them up in the decades to come, checking to see whether anything has changed, then readers must be explicitly told when the data were collected.

In contrast with my discovery concerning missing information with regard to when data were collected, I was heartened to find that almost two-thirds of the studies reported data for more than one observation point. Approximately 27% used a narrow window of four years or less and another 19% followed cases between five and nine years. One quarter of the studies conceptualized the passage of time in terms of decades, following their cases for 20 years or more. At the extreme, 9% covered at least half a century.

Choosing a time frame for data collection requires investigators to consider the rhythm and periodicity of significant changes in what is being studied. For some processes, such as organizational failures, a decade or less might be sufficient. In contrast, for large-scale institutional changes, decades might be needed. Implicitly, then, the data in Table 1 show that few investigators were thinking in terms of large-scale changes.

My analysis of empirical papers published in ASQ since 2000 suggests that many of the concerns McKelvey and I expressed in 1983 are still relevant today. Investigators are still making implicit assumptions about the time and space invariance of the processes and structures they are studying, with most papers exemplifying a single nation short-term time orientation. Almost a third of them evidently feel their results are time-invariant.

Why Study Organizations Comparatively?

Perhaps my position is already clear from my review of what McKelvey and I argued and from my critique of what I found in ASQ, but let me make two points concerning why we need to pay attention to context in terms of scope conditions and theory testing. First, investigators need to make clear the *scope conditions* they claim for their generalizations. Adding time and space to one's research is not simply a way to explain more variation in organizational outcomes. That is a fool's errand. Instead, I believe that incorporating time and space into our comparisons improves the reliability and validity of our generalizations. Omitting a comparative context from our research can be a substantial threat to validity. In addition, studies of diffusion and population dynamics often chose empirical settings that "are biased toward large or otherwise significant industries, organizational populations, or phenomena" (Denrell & Kovács, 2008). Such biases threaten internal and external validity.

Second, with regard to *theory and model testing*, unlike the state of the field in the early 1980s, our theories today heavily emphasize organizational environments. So, whereas it made some sense to neglect time and space in 1983, it makes no sense now, when almost all our macroorganization theories concern time and space. As McKelvey (2002) has argued, our goal should be to improve each leg of the three-legged stool on which our field rests: theory, model, and data. We should use our theories to build models that we then test with data. Feedback from those tests allows us to fix the model and try again. Research is conducted, then, to set plausible parameter values for our models, rather than to "test theory."

Indeed, in the social sciences, it would be an extraordinary project that actually was able to challenge the fundamentals of a good theory. Instead, the best we can hope for is that repeated failures of models to be verified with data eventually call into question the theories. One excellent tool in this regard is simulation, such as through agent-based modeling. March (1991) made good use of this technique in his widely cited paper on exploration and exploitation.

Consider the role of time and space in two very popular approaches to organizational analysis. Organizational ecology research rests on the bedrock assumption that population dynamics depend on where a population is in its growth trajectory and also on the scale at which competition and cooperation are occurring. It is impossible to fully test ecological models without taking into account the full history of a population. Institutional organizational research at the population and field levels rests on the assumption that the diffusion of practices and forms over time depends on opportunities and constraints at multiple levels of analysis. It is impossible to fully test institutional models without taking into account the speed and shape of the diffusion curve over time and over diverse locations. Thus, from the viewpoint of setting the scope conditions and testing the models implied by our theories, we need to take time and space into account.

How do we Build Time and Space into Comparative Organizational Research?

In an unjustly overlooked celebration of the contemporary relevance of the Chicago school of sociology, Abbott (1997) argued that "no social fact makes any sense abstracted from its context in social (and often geographic) space and social time ... Every social fact is situated, surrounded by other contextual facts and brought into being by a process relating it to a past context." He argued that we should keep social facts in their contexts, describing the temporal and spatial structures of social contexts or "locatedness," to use his term. Abbott felt that a failure to take time and space into account made our work boring and reflected an unwillingness to take intellectual risks. Certainly, rising to the challenge posed by Abbott will be a major undertaking for most scholars. Nonetheless, it is a challenge worth meeting.

Time in Comparative Research: Two Scales

We can include "time" in our comparative analysis at several scales, and I will focus on two: at the level of the life course of specific organizations, and at the level of organizational populations. I focus first on the life course of organizations as a response to the question that Dave Whetten asked at our conference in Sundance, "what happens if we only focus on big and old versus new and small organizations?" In examining this question, I will treat time on a micro scale.

Time 1: Organizational Life Course

In my studies of entrepreneurship and organizational startups over the past several decades, I have become acutely aware of the difference between the mundane and the improbable. In the most recent decade, about 7 million startups per year have been launched by potential entrepreneurs in the United States. Within about six years, a little more than 2 million are left. During that time, only about half of those have managed to employ at least one person. Of the ventures that become sufficiently organized to qualify as truly viable businesses, only about 1 in 10 actually grow. Of those that grow, about 1 in 10,000 is lucky enough to have an initial public offering (IPO), at which time the founders are able to cash in on their success. Recently, the number of IPOs has been dwindling, with the number of high-technology IPOs at less than 50 per year. These 50 constitute the "black swans" (Taleb, 2007) of the entrepreneurial world. That is, they are highly improbable, have a high impact, and are predictable only after the fact.

Were we to focus only on the black swans, rather than comparing them with the mundane initial population of startups, or with any of the other population subsets I mentioned earlier, we would miss the critical feature of entrepreneurship in the United States: entrepreneurial success is difficult to attain. From a comparative point of view, we must consider two possible explanations for the process revealed by these numbers (Haveman & Rao, 1997). From a *selection perspective*, the data paint a picture of initial heterogeneity winnowed by time. The initial organizations in the population are simply overwhelmed by forces beyond their control, leaving a small set of lucky survivors. Note that testing this explanation requires we capture as much of the startup group's initial heterogeneity as possible. If we are studying startups within an existing population, identifying population members will be fairly straightforward. However, if we are farsighted and fortunate enough to recognize the potential development of a new population, not yet recognized by data gathering agencies and bureaus, then bounding the population to study will be a daunting task.

From an *adaptation perspective*, the story is one of organizations learning at each stage of the process, with some learning well and others not learning at all. Those that learn survive to go on to the next point in the life course, whereas most of those learning slowly or not at all are eliminated. From this perspective, the initial group of startups might still be heterogeneous, but with respect to their capability for learning. Plus, as in testing implications from the selection perspective, investigators must still capture as much of the initial heterogeneity as possible. Heterogeneity arises from multiple sources, including founders' goals and strategic preferences. For example, businesses started by families may not follow the same path as spin-offs from large corporations. Many owners of family businesses profess a desire to remain small, although circumstances may conspire against this wish. Conceptualizing "heterogeneity" thus requires us to have a deep understanding of what we are studying.

Notice several ways in which time figures into this narrative. First, to understand survival, we need to take a multiyear view, following organizations long enough to ascertain their fate. Second, because the factors affecting entrepreneurial success vary over time with changes in the economy, government regulation, the technological opportunity structure, and so forth, what enables some organizations to adapt in one era may be irrelevant in the next. Third, without following organizations over time, we cannot adjudicate between the selection and the adaptation models.

In keeping with my argument concerning the need for modeling, I note that "time" needs to be modeled explicitly when we are following organizations over time. At what scale should time be measured: minutes, days, weeks, months, or years? An examination of the papers published in *ASQ* and used for the analysis in Table 1 showed that very few were explicit about the units of time in which the investigators thought a process unfolded.

In his concept of "socially expected duration," Merton (1949) gave us a clue for making such decision about units of time. He noted that humans tend to base important decisions on how long they think a particular relationship or event will last. For example, in her study of committee work, Gersick (1988) found that members dawdled and frittered away time until they perceived that they were about halfway through the time allocated to them to complete their work. At the halfway point, such as two weeks into a one-month assignment, they suddenly began taking the assignment seriously. Another example of the fragility of any particular expectation regarding expected duration can be taken from the example of the market for IPOs in the late 1990s.

Before April 2000, entrepreneurs starting new high-tech ventures and seeking venture capital thought about the time to grow toward an IPO in years, rather than months. Typically, they could expect venture capitalists not to pressure them to prepare for an IPO until five or six years had passed. After April 2000, with the crash of the stock market and, in particular, the drying up of the market for IPOs, high-technology entrepreneurs found that expectations regarding duration had changed drastically. Whereas they had become accustomed to thinking in chunks of six years, they suddenly found themselves forced to think in six month chunks or less. Venture capitalists were asking for rapid results and were quick to pull the plug when entrepreneurs faltered. Thus, viewed from a socio-historical perspective, the very definition of time is context specific.

My second example concerns micro-level processes in which social interactions follow a daily rhythm and data collection and analysis must occur at the same scale. Black, Carlile, and Repenning (2004) reanalyzed ethnographic data from Barley's (1986) study of the implementation of computerized tomography in two hospitals. Barley documented the impact of the new technology on role relations and changing patterns of social interaction between doctors and technologists. Barley supplied enough information to allow Black et al. to create a dynamic simulation of how the changes unfolded over the nine months of Barley's observations. Their reanalysis provides an excellent example of a model in which time is conceptualized and measured at the level of the working day.

In generating the equations underlying their simulation, Black et al. modeled activities and interactions on a relatively fine-grained time scale of days. The resulting models, with their recursive interactions, revealed additional insights about the process of occupational boundary maintenance that were deeper and more complex than Barley's original analysis implied. As in the example of IPOs after April 2000, modeling these processes required that investigators grasp the natural rhythm of the interactions, necessitating a profound understanding of the context.

Time 2: The Long Sweep of History

My example of the market for IPOs takes us into historical territory. Following the lead of population demographers, Aldrich and Ruef (2006) classified historical influences into three types of effects: cohort, period, and maturation or aging. Aging or maturation effects describe the secular process of aging, a process I referred to in the previous section. For example, organizations might become less adaptable as they age. A cohort effect occurs when historical events have a differential impact on younger versus older organizations (or vice versa). For example, high oil prices might seriously weaken younger organizations but have little effect on older ones. Stinchcombe's (1965) classic paper on social structure and organizations developed this principle under the concept of "imprinting," noting that organizations founded in the same era tend to resemble one another. Johnson (2007) drew on this notion in explaining why the Paris Opera today still shows traces of its roots from the 17th century. A period effect occurs when historical events have similar consequences for different age cohorts.

For example, high oil prices might actually force organizations of *all* ages to economize on their operations.

Back in the 1940s and 1950, scholars of national economic development created models that rested on static, cross-sectional comparisons of "under-developed" economies with those of the "developed" Western nations. They assumed that the national institutions supporting developed economies needed to be replicated in the underdeveloped nations and that it was just a matter of time before such nations "caught up." Nations were grouped into stages and it was assumed that developing nations were merely in an early, more primitive phase along a path to development. These linear, one size fits all models were subsequently discredited. Scholars realized that "development" reflects not merely the internal conditions of a nation but also where it fits into the global economy. Moreover, a nation's historically determined past sets limits on where it can go next. Thus, current models recognize path dependence and global interdependence. In short, comparing organizations at one point in time does not necessarily reveal everything we should know about what makes them similar or different. We need to know the path along which each organization developed and where it fits into the larger context.

I have chosen three examples to illustrate the advantages of contextualizing organizational change in terms of what transpires over years and decades. First, to illustrate the power of taking age, period, and cohort into account, I have chosen an example from the health care field and changes in the hospice industry. Second, to illustrate the potential of focusing on diffusion processes within a single extended period, I have chosen examples from the field of corporate governance. Third, to illustrate the advantages of a multipronged project that investigates the genesis, shakeout period, and subsequent development of a population, I have chosen the radio broadcasting industry.

In studying the health care field after World War II, Scott and his collaborators (Scott, Ruef, Mendel, & Caronna, 2000) distinguished between three different historical periods. First, in the early era of *professional dominance*, physicians enjoyed high levels of prestige and a great deal of autonomy from external interference. Second, in the era of the 1960s, the *federal government* became heavily involved in health care. The national government began to play a major role in regulating health care and in controlling the allocation of funds to different kinds of health care facilities and equipment. Third, in the 1980s, a new era of *market orientation and managerial control* emerged, in which competition and market forces were seen by regulators and major corporations as the driving force behind how decisions ought to be made regarding health care.

Applied to the *hospice industry* between 1974 and 2006, Scott's characterization helps us understand how and why that industry changed. A major *period effect* occurred in 1983 with the passage of the Medicare Hospice Benefit Act, as it affected *all* hospices. The act enabled hospices to receive reimbursement for patient care from the federal government. However, hospices that chose to become Medicare certified opened themselves up to government oversight, an unwelcome development for many of them. A major *cohort effect* occurred in the 1980s with the onset of the era of market orientation, as it affected hospices differentially by age. Traditional hospices were nonprofit, whereas new hospices were profit oriented. Between 1992 and 1999, the number of for-profit hospices increased by 300%, whereas the number of nonprofit hospices rose by only 43%. Going forward, then, there was a substantial change in the mix of organizational forms in the population in response to the changed conditions brought on by market forces.

In contrast with the hospice example, which drew upon age, period, and cohort principles, my next example focuses on organizational changes within a single period: the spread of two governance innovations within corporate elite networks in the decade of the 1980s. Davis and Greve (1997) examined the impact of corporate board interlocks on the diffusion of poison pills and golden parachutes between 1980 and the end of 1989. So-called "poison pills" were adopted by some corporations as a defense against hostile takeovers, whereas golden parachutes were contracts that compensated executives who lost their employment when their firm was taken over. History figured into their analysis in several ways.

First, Supreme Court and U.S. Justice Department decisions in the early 1980s changed the institutional regulations governing mergers, significantly lowering regulatory barriers to hostile takeovers. Second, the rate of diffusion of the two practices differed significantly, with golden parachutes increasing gradually from 1980 to 1989, whereas poison pills shot up dramatically in the middle of the 1980s. At the end of the decade, both of them had been adopted by about half the large corporations in the United States. Differences in the rate of diffusion between the two practices allowed Davis and Greve to assess the relative importance of network contagion versus direct contact in the spread of innovations across the corporate network.

A related example of historical contingency comes from Mizruchi, Stearns, and Marquis's (2006) study of changes over a 22-year period in patterns of corporate borrowing. In the early 1970s, few large corporations had chief financial officers (CFO's). Instead, they had financial officers who acted more like bookkeepers than financial strategists. Bankers on their boards were expected to give advice on key financial matters, and Mizruchi et al. showed that ties to other corporations, through interlocking (shared) directors, influenced whether corporations decided to use debt financing. In the transformed economic environment of the 1980s, however, corporations began to internalize such decisions. Financial officers' positions were elevated and given the title of CFO as that role became increasingly professionalized and the "corporation as a bundle of assets" view took hold. By the early 1990s, the earlier network effect of being influenced by other corporations' borrowing behavior was gone. Thus, a claim that "interlocking directorates influence corporate behavior" could not be supported as a time-invariant empirical generalization. Instead, the network effect was contingent on a particular institutional and environmental configuration.

My third example of the advantages of historical analysis illustrates the advantages of investigating the entire life history of an industry. The radio broadcasting industry, with the benefit of hindsight, seems like an inevitable development, given the invention of wireless telegraphy in the late 19th century and subsequent innovations in the early 20th century. However, Kim and Lippmann (2008) showed that the development of the industry was substantially shaped by struggles between contending parties with very different conceptions of who should benefit from the new technologies. In the early days, wireless equipment manufacturers, comprising a group of inventors and entrepreneurs, tried to use patents and other devices to extend the old "point to point" telegraphy system, whereas the U.S. Navy defined the new technology as a national security issue and asserted their dominance over its uses. In contrast, amateur wireless operators framed the issue quite differently, taking advantage of the "point to many" broadcasting possibilities of the technology and arguing for an experimental and entertainment conception of its application.

Before 1920, amateur wireless operators also benefited from a more dynamic set of strategies, as their framing activities evolved over time, in response to changing conditions. In contrast, the inventors and entrepreneurs looked back in time and drew on the wired telegraphy industry as a model. Similarly, the Navy harkened back to an earlier age and tried to lock in the vision they had developed during World War I. Amateurs were continually reframing their conception of what "radio" could be and forging new alliances as field and environmental conditions evolved.

Although World War I gave the Navy a temporary advantage, developments after the war thwarted them as well as the wireless equipment manufacturers' attempts to frame the situation to benefit their interests. For a short time, between the war and the mid-1920s, innovation and entrepreneurship flourished across the radio spectrum as many diverse uses of radio broadcasting sprang up. Small businesses and commercial interests began using radio broadcasting to call attention to their offerings, and many noncommercial broadcasters, particularly religious broadcasters, also took advantage of the "one to many" opportunities offered by radio to reach a wider audience. Chaos ensued, as attempts by the federal government to limit the licensing of new stations were repeatedly rebuffed by the courts. Eventually, through a series of hearings held in Washington, DC, the federal government asserted centralized control, through the 1927 Federal Radio Act and the 1934 Federal Communications Act, which created the FCC.

In his analysis of the conflict and negotiation surrounding the various federal hearings and legislative acts, Lippmann (2005) coined the term "ideological capture" to describe the success commercial broadcasters had in framing the terms of the debate. At issue in the struggle over which stations should be licensed was the question of who represented "the public interest." Commercial interests succeeded in their attempts to frame their own broadcasts as being in the public interest through their dominance of the testimony at hearings, their representation on the initial commission, and disorganization among the noncommercial interests.

Lippmann (2007) showed that the consolidation of commercial broadcasters' interests, as enshrined in the legislation, had a devastating impact on the fate of noncommercial broadcasting. Whereas educational and religious broadcasters had made up a substantial portion of all stations throughout the early to mid-1920s, after the 1927 act the number of full-time commercial stations grew rapidly. In contrast, part-time commercial stations, educational, and religious stations gradually declined, both absolutely and proportionately. Failure rates for noncommercial stations increased, whereas those for full-time commercial stations decreased. Lippmann concluded that changes in the institutional environment of radio broadcasting shaped the way that market forces were allowed to play out in the industry. The 1927 Radio Act changed the institutional logic of radio broadcasting by bestowing legitimacy on a form supported by advertising, which only a few years before had been treated with hostility by many important individuals and groups (Lippmann, 2007). Full-time commercial broadcasters succeeded not because they had any direct competitive advantage but rather because competing uses of the radio spectrum were severely limited by federal legislation, which they played a major part in shaping.

Space in Comparative Research: Two Scales
I have already noted Abbott's anguish at the neglect of location as a context in social science research. He argued that research that examines organizational phenomena in only a single community, region, or nation runs the risk of producing decontextualized empirical generalizations. Under such conditions, researchers may mistakenly construct an explanation "about the way things are" that merely reflects the local manifestation of a process that is actually highly sensitive to contextual differences. Or, investigators may claim originality for a structure or process that is, in fact, quite generic. In this section, I will give examples of using "space" at two scales: at the level of cross-national differences and at the level of differences across regions within nations.

I offer three cross-national examples from Canada, Japan, and Sweden to illustrate the gains from using "space" in organizational analysis across national contexts. First, Litrico (2007) analyzed the emergence and diffusion of a "new" organizational form in Quebec from 1984 to 2007: the "collective kitchen." A collective kitchen is a group of people who meet regularly to prepare meals together. The participants create a number of meals that they take home to store for future consumption. Eventually, 1,400 of these new organizational forms were active in Quebec. As a collective action organization dependent on the continuing voluntary participation of its members, collective kitchens faced a classic problem of governance: avoiding shirking and eliciting effective efforts from participants. In short, such organizations need governance mechanisms that work.

From Litrico's description, it is clear that the collective kitchens in Quebec "invented" all the mechanisms of governance that previous forms of collective action at the small group and small organization level had already discovered: leadership by charismatic figures and a strong ideological bond between participants, based on the norms and values of "self-help" and "empowerment." The Quebec women responsible for collective kitchens made common cause with a similar movement in Peru, which also sprang up in the 1980s. (In 1988, approximately 1,500 collective kitchens existed in the Lima region of Peru.) For my purposes, what is important is that the basic organizing principle of a "collective kitchen" is the same as that of a "rotating credit association" (Light, 1972), which has been discovered periodically in various regions of the world. Taking a comparative view helps us see that the "new" organizational form was not unique to Quebec. Instead, when we recognize that its organizing principles are similar to those of other similar forms, we are led to ask "under what conditions does this collectivist form emerge and become successful?"

Second, a comparison between the United States and Japan illustrates the principle that "law constructs wealth patterns." The concept that stakeholders "own" a corporation was created by corporate law in the United States in the 19th century, with the law privileging stockholders as *the* owners of a corporation. However, one could simply call them "investors" instead, recognizing that others also have valid claims on a corporation, such as employees, citizens living nearby, and so forth. In contrast, in Japan, corporations have been run for the benefit of employees, not stockholders. Indeed, stockholders have historically been forced to accept lower rates of return on their investment because corporate managers have pursued a lifetime employment policy that retained people who "should" have been purged.

A comparative organizations project needs to recognize that corporate law varies over time and across nations. More importantly, law varies over time within a nation and thus what is "legal" in one era might not be so in another era. From a cross-national comparative point of view, we need to take account of the different legal regimes that constitute organizations in different forms across nations. Some of the differences in organizational forms across nations are caused by differences in law, rather than technology, managerial competence, and so forth.

Third, research on startups in the United States has found that about half are started by teams, and about half of the teams are spousal pairs (Ruef, Aldrich, & Carter, 2003). In contrast, a study of high-technology services firms in Sweden found a much higher proportion of husbands and wives as co-owners (Hellerstedt, Wiklund, & Aldrich, 2007). As many as 60% of the established firms were owned by couples. On first glance, one might ask whether the explanation for the higher proportion of family-owned firms is that Swedes are more "family oriented." However, the most likely explanation is that it is a response by Swedes to Swedish tax law regarding small firms. If the income of a firm goes over a certain threshold, the firm is taxed at a higher level. One way to keep a firm's income down is to pay out the profits as salary to two people, rather than just one. With a husband and wife on the payroll, income can be brought below the threshold. Thus, the difference between the United States and Sweden is not differential familism, but rather different tax structures.

As a reader pointed out, identifying differences between nations is only the starting point for a comparative analysis of organizational structures and processes. Differences at the national level, in aggregate, may conceal substantial heterogeneity at the population and organizational level. For example, Schneiberg, King, and Smith (2008) examined social movement

processes and outcomes (the institutionalization of alternative, noncorpo-
rate forms) across three industries. Similarly, national differences could be
disaggregated to the regional or community level, a point to which I now
turn.

A second spatial dimension involves differences across communities or
regions in the physical location of organizations (Freeman & Audia, 2006).
One important issue in this regard for organizational ecology concerns the
geographic scale at which population density should be measured.
Evolutionary theory proposes that we focus on the level at which variation
and selection forces are strongest. Some organizations compete at local
levels, some at regional levels, and others at a national or international level.
For instance, Ranger-Moore, Banaszak-Holl, and Hannan (1991) found
that increases in density had a stronger inhibiting effect on foundings of
banks, which were studied at a city level, than on foundings of insurance
companies, which were studied at a national level. Similarly, in his study of
bank branches and headquarters in Tokyo between 1894 and 1936, Greve
(2002) found that founding rates depended on local neighborhood density.

Note that we can link cross-national differences with the issue of
geographical scale. For example, Hannan, Carroll, Dundon, and Torres
(1995) argued that the geographic scale at which competition operated was
often more local than that at which legitimation processes transpired. The
cultural templates defining an organizational form tend to flow more freely
across spatial boundaries than the material resources invoked in competitive
interaction. Using a data set of automobile manufacturers in five European
countries between 1886 and 1981, Hannan et al. (1995) found some support
for this multilevel density-dependent model, with competition typically
occurring within country boundaries and legitimation occurring across the
European context as a whole.

In choosing to focus on geographic scale, a question arises as to whether
we should view spatial segregation in terms of discrete and discontinuous
boundaries or continuous distances between different regions. A discrete
boundaries approach seems most useful when political or cultural boundaries
generate meaningful constraints or advantages for organizational populations. For instance, Saxenian (1994) argued that California's Silicon Valley
and Boston's Route 128 have distinctive identities that cannot be reduced to
the physical or human geography of these regions. In comparing these two
regions, she argued that the high startup rate in Silicon Valley was due to its
culture of cooperation, in contrast with the culture of competition in the
Boston area that suppressed startup efforts. In a similar study, Molotch,
Freudenberg, and Paulsen (2000) compared Santa Barbara and Ventura,

California. They found dramatically different populations of voluntary and business organizations, despite the fact that both cities have an almost identical climate, topography, and early history in cattle ranching and citrus agriculture.

In contrast with this discrete perspective on space, economic geographers often view spatial segregation in terms of continuous, physical distances (Sorenson & Audia, 2000). Following classic location theory, geographers argue that physical distances impose real limitations on the ability of organizations to secure inputs from their logistical networks and to reach users or supporters. For instance, the spatial markets of acute-care hospitals are often represented as catchment areas, based on the distances that patients can feasibly travel to get to a hospital (Ruef, 1997). In health care, discrete political or cultural jurisdictions mean little because patients will travel across such boundaries to receive health care. However, in primary and secondary education, such jurisdictions mean a great deal because students do not typically travel more than 5 miles to school.

Regardless of the scale at which space is considered, it is an important contextual feature affecting organizational structures and processes. My argument is not that every research project should be cross-national or cross-regional, but rather that investigators must make decisions, a priori, as to whether their project makes sense if conducted within only one spatial unit. For many projects, where investigators have deep knowledge of other contexts, it might be sufficient if authors simply point out what is being taken for granted in framing the problem at the level of a single unit.

CONCLUSION

Comparing organizations not only shows us how organizations are alike but also how they are different from one another. How much can we learn from such comparisons? As it happens, what we learn depends very much on which organizations we choose to compare and what context we put them in. If "context" has a powerful influence on an organization's structure and all the organizations we pick for comparison are from the same spatial and historical context, we will see mostly the impact of the context. Or rather, we will not see it, because we will simply think that "all organizations are pretty much alike." Conversely, if we sample from "contexts" that are quite different, then we increase the likelihood of finding organizations that differ, as well. Again, this is under the assumption that "context" plays a major role.

But of course, until we compare organizations from differing "contexts," we will have no basis for drawing conclusions about contextual differences. Thus, paradoxically, if context really does not matter, we will have to sample from a wide range of context to figure that out! Although I have taken a strong position that most organizational processes vary across time and geographically, there may be some time and geographically invariant processes (e.g., density dependence appears to be one such process). However, unless we conduct comparative analyses, we cannot know that these processes are, in fact, temporally and geographically invariant. At the very least, we should request more replication studies.

To find out what is missing from the organizations in our samples, we will need to ensure that we sample from as wide a range of as possible, across time and space. How do we know how broadly to cast our sampling net, if we have never done it before? I would suggest letting evolutionary theory be our guide. It shows us that ecological pressures are a powerful differentiating force, and that whereas populations may comprise fairly homogeneous entities, the community level shows great diversity across populations.

Some may object that the skills required to find contrasting cases are daunting and perhaps beyond the reach of many scholars. I would argue that scholars who are willing to invest time in learning about the context, the history, and the full story behind their units of observation will always come out ahead. There are many skills that take time to learn, such as recognizing that after framing one's problem, it is best to try "backing out" one level. This requires being explicit about units of analysis, the main line of generalization, and so forth. Of course, I think everyone would benefit from learning a little more evolutionary theory, and not only for the benefits it confers with regard to understanding time and space!

In a related objection, some readers of this paper have pointed out the daunting challenges facing scholars seeking the data needed for explicit consideration of time and space in their research. Junior scholars may object that the time invested to collect comparative and dynamic data does not yield an adequate return, given that it is much easier to ignore time and space. I have heard this objection for many years, and my response has been twofold. First, senior scholars need to lead the way in showing what can be done and in using the freedom afforded by their tenured status to take more chances in creating research designs. Second, junior scholars should not attempt such work on their own, but rather should follow the model increasingly used across the sciences of creating collaborative research teams. Spreading the work across collaborators with diverse skills can make such projects feasible.

Finally, in a world of proliferating journals, online discussion forums, and conferences, organization studies researchers can be forgiven if they sometimes feel overwhelmed by information overload. How can scholars make their work stand out in all of this clutter? If we apply the "is this interesting" test to what we read, much of this work comes up short. It simply does not challenge what we thought we already knew. In contrast, bringing time and space explicitly into our research designs and analytic modeling opens a world of possibilities. I have implied that much of what we think we know about organizations is, in fact, heavily constrained to particular places and within particular times. In the new world I envision, iconoclastic organization studies scholars would make it their job to offer counterfactuals to received wisdom, challenging researchers not to get lost in space, out of time.

ACKNOWLEDGMENTS

I thank Susan Cohen, Frank Dobbin, Teppo Felin, Joseph Galaskiewicz, Phillip Kim, Brayden King, Steve Lippmann, Russell Nichols, Steve Vaisey, Dave Whetten, and several anonymous reviewers for their help in sharpening the arguments in this chapter. Nekia Pridgen provided excellent research assistance in the preparation of this chapter.

REFERENCES

Abbott, A. (1997). Of time and space: The contemporary relevance of the Chicago School. *Social Forces, 74*, 1149–1182.

Aldrich, H. E., & Ruef, M. (2006). *Organizations evolving.* London: Sage.

Barley, S. R. (1986). Technology as an occasion for structuring: Evidence from observations of CT scanners and the social order of radiology departments. *Administrative Science Quarterly, 31*, 78–108.

Black, L. J., Carlile, P. R., & Repenning, N. P. (2004). A dynamic theory of expertise and occupational boundaries in new technology implementation: Building on Barley's study of CT scanning. *Administrative Science Quarterly, 49*, 572–607.

Davis, G. F., & Greve, H. R. (1997). Corporate elite networks and governance changes in the 1980s. *American Journal of Sociology, 103*, 1–37.

Denrell, J., & Kovács, B. (2008). Selective sampling of empirical settings in organizational studies. *Administrative Science Quarterly, 53*, 109–144.

Dobbin, F. (1994). *Forging industrial policy: The United States, Britain, and France in the railway age.* New York: Cambridge University Press.

Freeman, J. H., & Audia, P. G. (2006). Community ecology and the sociology of organizations. *Annual Review of Sociology, 32,* 145–169.

Galaskiewicz, J., Inouye, J., & Savage, S. (2008). The effects of organizational demographics on the choice of activities and providers in the urban context. Presented at the American Sociological Association, Boston.

Gersick, C. J. G. (1988). Time and transition in work teams: Toward a new model of group development. *Academy of Management Journal, 31,* 9–41.

Greve, H. R. (2002). An ecological theory of spatial evolution: Local density dependence in Tokyo banking, 1894–1936. *Social Forces, 80,* 847–879.

Hannan, M. T., Carroll, G. R., Dundon, E. A., & Torres, J. C. (1995). Organizational evolution in a multinational context: Entries of automobile manufacturers in Belgium, Britain, France, Germany, and Italy. *American Sociological Review, 60,* 509–528.

Haveman, H. A., & Rao, H. (1997). Structuring a theory of moral sentiments: Institutional and organizational coevolution in the early thrift industry. *American Journal of Sociology, 102,* 1606–1651.

Hawley, A. (1950). *Human ecology.* NY: New York,.

Heath, C., & Sitkin, S. B. (2001). Big-B versus B-O: What is organizational about organizational behavior? *Journal of Organizational Behavior, 22,* 43–58.

Hellerstedt, K., Wiklund, J., & Aldrich, H. E. (2007). The impact of past firm performance on the exit of team members in young firms: The role of team composition. Presented at the Babson College Conference on Entrepreneurship Research, Madrid, Spain.

Ingram, P., & Morris, M. W. (2007). Do people mix at mixers? Structure, homophily, and the "life of the party". *Administrative Science Quarterly, 52,* 558–585.

Johnson, V. (2007). What is organizational imprinting? Cultural entrepreneurship in the founding of the Paris opera. *American Journal of Sociology, 113,* 97–127.

Kim, P. H., & Lippmann, S. (2008). *Standing on shaky ground: Institutional contests, delays, and interference in the U.S. wireless telegraphy field.* Unpublished paper, Business School, University of Wisconsin, Madison, WI.

Light, I. (1972). *Ethnic enterprise in America.* Berkeley, CA: University of California.

Lippmann, S. (2005). Public airwaves, private interests: Competing visions and ideological capture in the regulation of U.S. broadcasting, 1920–1934. In: H. Prechel (Ed.), *Research in political sociology* (14, pp. 111–150). Bingley, UK: Emerald.

Lippmann, S. (2007). The institutional context of industry consolidation: Radio broadcasting in the United States, 1920–1934. *Social Forces, 86,* 467–495.

Litrico, J.-B. (2007). Meaning inflation and identity maintenance in the diffusion of new organizational forms: The case of collective kitchens in Quebec. Presented at the The Cornell-McGill Conference on Institutions and Entrepreneurship, Ithaca, New York.

March, J. G. (1991). Exploration and exploitation in organizational learning. *Organization Science, 2,* 71–87.

McKelvey, B. (2002). Model-centered organization science epistemology. In: J. A. C. Baum (Ed.), *The Blackwell companion to organizations,* (pp. 752–780). Oxford, UK: Blackwell.

McKelvey, B., & Aldrich, H. E. (1983). Populations, natural selection, and applied organizational science. *Administrative Science Quarterly. 28.* 101–128.

Merton, R. K. (1949). *Social theory and social structure.* Glencoe, IL: Free Press.

Mizruchi, M. S., Stearns, L. B., & Marquis, C. (2006). The conditional nature of embeddedness: A study of borrowing by large U.S. firms, 1973–1994. *American Sociological Review, 71,* 310–333.

Molotch, H., Freudenberg, W., & Paulsen, K. E. (2000). History repeats itself, but how? City character, urban tradition, and the accomplishment of place. *American Sociological Review, 65,* 791–823.

Ranger-Moore, J., Banaszak-Holl, J., & Hannan, M. T. (1991). Density-dependent dynamics in regulated industries: Founding rates of banks and life insurance companies. *Administrative Science Quarterly, 36,* 36–65.

Ruef, M. (1997). Assessing organizational fitness on a dynamic landscape: An empirical test of the relative inertia hypothesis. *Strategic Management Journal, 18,* 837–853.

Ruef, M., Aldrich, H. E., & Carter, N. M. (2003). The structure of founding teams: Homophily, strong ties, and isolation among U.S. entrepreneurs. *American Sociological Review, 68,* 195–222.

Saxenian, A. (1994). *Regional advantage: Culture and competition in Silicon Valley and Route 128.* Cambridge, MA: Harvard.

Schneiberg, M., King, M., & Smith, T. (2008). Social movements and organizational form: Cooperative alternatives to corporations in the American insurance, dairy, and grain industries. *American Sociological Review, 73,* 635–667.

Scott, W. R. (2001). *Institutions and organizations.* Thousand Oaks, CA: Sage.

Scott, W. R., Ruef, M., Mendel, P. J., & Caronna, C. A. (2000). *Institutional change and healthcare organizations.* Chicago: University of Chicago Press.

Sorenson, O., & Audia, P. G. (2000). The social structure of entrepreneurial activity: Geograhic concentration of footwear production in the United States, 1940–1989. *American Journal of Sociology, 106,* 424–462.

Stinchcombe, A. L. (1965). Social structure and organizations. In: J. G. March (Ed.), *Handbook of organizations* (pp. 142–193). Chicago, IL: Rand McNally.

Taleb, N. N. (2007). *The black swan: The impact of the highly improbable.* New York: Random House.

Tsui, A. S. (2006). Editorial: Contextualization in Chinese management research. *Management and Organization Research, 2,* 1–13.

Von Glinow, M. A., Shapiro, D. L., & Brett, J. M. (2004). Can we *talk,* and should we? Managing emotional conflict in multicultural teams. *Academy of Management Review, 29,* 578–592.

Weick, K. E., & Sutcliffe, K. M. (2001). *Managing the unexpected: Assuring high performance in an age of complexity.* San Francisco, CA: Jossey-Bass.

[5]

BEAM ME UP, SCOTT(IE)! INSTITUTIONAL THEORISTS' STRUGGLES WITH THE EMERGENT NATURE OF ENTREPRENEURSHIP

Howard E. Aldrich

INTRODUCTION

Institutional theories of organizations in sociology have focused on exteriority and constraint over the past three decades, in keeping with their roots in macrosocial theory (Parsons, 1956). These theories have mostly examined the macrocontext for organization- and field-level activities, rather than the microprocesses through which humans accomplish particular actions. However, with the widespread diffusion and adoption of neo-institutional theory (hereafter NIT) as the default framework within organizational sociology, some authors have been unable to resist extending it to encompass microlevel change processes. In particular, people studying *entrepreneurship*, broadly defined, have created a new category of actors, called *institutional entrepreneurs* (hereafter IEs), along with associated new concepts, such as *embedded autonomy*. Organization studies journals now routinely publish papers on the topic of *institutional entrepreneurship*

Institutions and Entrepreneurship
Research in the Sociology of Work, Volume 21, 329–364
Copyright © 2010 by Emerald Group Publishing Limited
All rights of reproduction in any form reserved
ISSN: 0277-2833/doi:10.1108/S0277-2833(2010)0000021015

329

(Leca & Naccache, 2006), and special sections of mainstream management journals also regularly feature such papers.

Some might celebrate these developments, arguing that theories of entrepreneurship are finally being put on a solid theoretical footing. After all, NIT is one of the most widely used schemes in contemporary sociology. Skeptics, however, might wonder whether authors have distorted institutional theory in the process. Can concepts and principles originally used to explain the constraining influence of institutional structures on human behavior also be used to explain how individual humans generate new institutions? Even as they claim to know better, authors writing about IEs eventually endow them with strategic intentions, foresight, and well-rehearsed social skills. Along with Dick Scott (this volume) and John Meyer (Meyer, 2008), I am skeptical. Or as Hallett and Ventresca (2009) put it more prosaically, regarding institutional theory's struggle with microlevel processes, "what are we to do about people?"

I am quite willing to accept that institutional theory contributes to our understanding of the context within which humans create new entities, such as commercial enterprises and nonprofit organizations. (In this chapter, I limit my interest to the creation of new organizations, mainly businesses.) My quarrel is with overenthusiastic applications of the concept of "institutional entrepreneurship," and not with the value of an institutional approach as such. Simply put, I believe NIT should not be stretched to cover microlevel entrepreneurial processes. As Palmer, Biggart, and Dick (2008, p. 760) noted, "it seems possible that attempts to build up the new institutionalism's currently underdeveloped understanding of individual level phenomenon [sic] by drawing more on psychology and social psychology might result not in the articulation of new ideas but rather the re-labeling (as new institutionalism) of old ideas." Rather than create new concepts to make it so, I would prefer that theorists turn to other social scientific theories, especially from social psychology, learning theory, cognitive neuroscience, and behavioral economics, to explain the emergent nature of entrepreneurial phenomena. Why try to develop NIT as a comprehensive explanation of entrepreneurial actions, when it already has an important role to play in setting the context for entrepreneurial activities?

I have three goals in this paper. First, I want to remind us of the incredibly volatile and dynamic phenomena we are trying to explain, which I illustrate through a review of some statistics on the US business population. I present details about a highly visible case in which an entrepreneur appears to have been a pioneer in a movement that resulted in the transformation of an organizational population. I explain why I question whether we should lionize such individuals. Second, I want to make a positive case for the important contributions NIT can make to our understanding of entrepreneurship, defined as the creation of new organizations and new organizational populations. NIT helps us understand variations in rates of entrepreneurship over time and space, as well as variations in types of entrepreneurship.

Third, I call into question the usefulness of the term "IE" as an analytic tool. I argue that this label distorts our understanding of the capabilities of individual humans and leads to a misallocation of analytic resources. In particular, I suggest that analysts stop using the term "IE" when talking about people who create organizations and just call them "entrepreneurs." I argue for using the concept of *institutional entrepreneurship* to refer to the collective action of individuals and other entities that transform institutions (Aldrich & Fiol, 1994). I would prefer that analysts treat entrepreneurs involved in institutional transformation the same way as they treat other humans, using the same concepts and principles: no heroes, no farsighted visionaries. Institutional entrepreneurship is accomplished by entrepreneurs, but through collective action, not omnipotence and clairvoyance. I argue that an understanding of entrepreneurial processes requires that we focus on the emergence of organizations, a level of analysis that institutional theory is not well equipped to handle. I conclude by offering a few proposals for a better way to think about the characteristics and actions of entrepreneurs, whatever their achievements. Table 1 summarizes the terms I use and my proposed definitions of "institutional entrepreneur" and "institutional entrepreneurship."

Table 1. My Definitions of Terms Used in this Chapter.

Nascent entrepreneur: person who, alone or with others, attempts to create a new organization, regardless of whether the effort ultimately succeeds.

Entrepreneur: person who, alone or with others, actually creates an organization, regardless of whether it ultimately survives.

Institution: patterned behavior infused with meaning by normative systems and perpetuated by social exchanges facilitated by shared cognitive understandings (Greenwood, Oliver, Sahlin, & Suddaby, 2008).

Institutional entrepreneur: person who, alone or with others, is credited with helping to transform an institution: introducing new social or cultural forms logics into the world (typically embodied in organizations).

Institutional entrepreneurship: collective action by many people who jointly – in cooperation and competition – create conditions transforming institutions.

ENTREPRENEURSHIP: FROM POPULATION DYNAMICS TO GREAT CASES

I begin by noting the incredible volatility of the US business population and argue that any theory of entrepreneurship must contend with the harsh reality of staggering rates of entrepreneurial failure. Then, to illustrate the allure of IE's siren song, I examine the case of John Sperling, an entrepreneur who founded the most successful US for-profit higher educational venture: the University of Phoenix. I argue that NIT does have a role to play in explaining John Sperling's success, but at the level of collective action, rather than single IE's.

From the Mundane to the Improbable

The entrepreneurship literature is filled with examples of new ventures begun by pioneering entrepreneurs with little or no resources and which eventually made their founders very wealthy. Some of these entrepreneurs helped create entirely new industries, destroyed old ones, or both. Under the definition of "IE" I've found in the literature, many of these founders certainly qualify. However, focusing on these "black swans" (Taleb, 2007) can blind as to how improbable they are, compared to the mundane reality of a typical startup. The apparent easy success enjoyed by some highly visible IEs conceals considerable volatility caused by new ventures entering and exiting business populations at very high rates.

In this section, I offer an overview of the entrepreneurial landscape that tries to put into perspective the relatively rare successes represented by the cases of institutional entrepreneurship described in the literature. I first present some evidence regarding powerful selection forces at work on entrepreneurial processes. Such forces winnow the mundane efforts of everyday entrepreneurs down into the infinitesimally small handful of firms achieving outstanding financial success by going public. Then, I present some data from newly available Bureau of Labor Statistics' reports that document the considerable volatility in the US business population.

All Organizations Were Once New

Table 2 presents some statistics on new ventures in the United States, based on a variety of sources (Aldrich & Ruef, 2006). As shown in the first two rows, in recent years there have been roughly 7,000,000 startup attempts in the United States, involving around 12 million people

Table 2. Entrepreneurship in the United States: From the Mundane to the Improbable. Time Frame for Top Five Rows is the First Decade of the 21st Century.

No. of people involved yearly in startups	12,000,000
No. of startup attempts	7,000,000
No. of startups actually organized within 2 years	2,300,000
No. of new firms per year that hire at least 1 employee	1,400,000
No. of new ventures that grow	240,000
No. of angel investors (2006)	234,000
No. of firms receiving angel funds (2006)	51,000
No. of publicly traded firms (2010)	10,000
No. of new venture capital deals (2006)	3,600
No. of initial public offerings (2006)	202
No. of high-tech IPOs (2005)	50

(Reynolds & Curtin, 2007). Most of these are home-based, involve little or no outside funding, and face daunting challenges getting started. Fewer than half will succeed in creating an established business within three years, and perhaps a third will become stable financially. Only a small fraction will grow over their lifetimes, and many will add employees in one year only to shed them in the next. In addition to using their own funds and those of friends and family, some nascent entrepreneurs will succeed in attracting money from angel investors, comprising wealthy individuals, groups, or networks of investors that use their personal funds to take equity positions in young businesses.

In 2006, according to the best publicly available information, about a quarter of a million angel investors were active in the United States, and they invested in around 51,000 new firms. Angel investors are notoriously publicity-shy, and so these numbers are surely an undercount. Such investors pour more funding into startups and young firms than venture capitalists, but both groups face the same constraint on their exit opportunities: the number of publicly held firms in the United States is vanishingly small as a proportion of all firms. No more than 10,000 firms are publicly traded on various exchanges in the United States, and recently the number of initial public offerings has been dwindling (less than 200), with the number of high-technology IPOs at less than 50 per year. These 50 constitute the "black swans" of the entrepreneurial world.

Table 3 provides another perspective on the turbulent environment confronting entrepreneurs, displaying business dynamics for the four quarters of 2008. The Bureau of Labor Statistics compiles a database of

Table 3.   Volatility in the US Employer Business Population, 2008.
Number of Firms (in 000s).

	Openings	Expansions	Contractions	Closings
1st quarter	357	1,517	1,596	380
2nd quarter	355	1,479	1,633	391
3rd quarter	349	1,439	1,608	379
4th quarter	368	1,376	1,686	405
Total	1,429	5,811	6,523	1,555

Source: US Department of Labor, Bureau of Labor Statistics. Business Employment Dynamics (http://www.bls.gov/bdm/home.html).

Business Employment Dynamics (the BED) based on all firms with at least one employee ("employer firms"). It captures "openings" of establishments that hired at least one employee, "expansions" (hiring employees) and "contractions" (shedding employees) of existing establishments, as well as "closings" (shedding all employees). In the first quarter of 2008, 357,000 employer establishments opened, 1,517,000 expanded, 1,596,000 contracted, and 380,000 lost all their employees. The impact of the economic recession is apparent, as fewer firms were adding or keeping employees by the end of the year, compared to the beginning. Results for previous years in the series show the same high level of volatility, with a 10-year trend toward fewer openings and a dramatic spike in contractions between 2007 and 2009. Note that these statistics are for employer firms. For nonemployer firms – firms without employees – a new study indicates that rates of entry and exit are as much as three times higher (Acs, Headd, & Agwara, 2009).

The continuity of business dynamics over time suggests the presence of strong institutional forces shaping entrepreneurial actions. Each opening involves several people, either as members of an entrepreneurial team or as "helpers" without an equity stake in the new venture. Each opening also involves several people who are hired: the average opening establishment starts with 4.8 jobs, and the average expanding establishment adds 4.7 jobs. Each closing means about 3.7 jobs lost, and each contraction involves about 3.9 lost jobs. The remarkably high level of volatility shows that a large fraction of the economically active population in the United States is involved in making entrepreneurial decisions with serious consequences for others, as the economic landscape rises and falls under their feet. I turn now to a specific example of a new entrepreneurial venture that defied the odds portrayed in these tables.

Great Cases Make Bad Theory

Eisenstadt (1980) was apparently the first to use the concept of "institutional entrepreneurship" to describe people who were catalysts of structural change. Lawrence and Suddaby (2006, p. 217) credited DiMaggio (1988) with popularizing the notion that IEs were proactive agents in generating change, noting that "the concept of institutional entrepreneurship focuses attention on the manner in which interested actors work to influence their institutional contexts through such strategies as technical and market leadership or lobbying for regulatory changes." In this "actors and agency" perspective, it is clear that IEs are the people who get things done.

I found an extreme example of this perspective in a case study of a social rating agency in France. Taking a "critical realist approach," Leca and Naccache (2006, p. 634) argued that "institutional entrepreneurs are organized actors who *skillfully* use institutional logics to create or change institutions, in order to *realize an interest* that they value highly ... institutional entrepreneurs will *select* the structures depending on the context, to *ensure* that the causal powers of the structures that they intend to use *will work* [italics added]." Taking a slightly less heroic view and borrowing the concept of "embedded agency" from Emirbayer and Mische (1998), Mutch (2007, p. 1124) noted the paradox of viewing entrepreneurship as possible within the strong constraints posited by classical institutional theory: "to be consistent with an institutional framework, any consideration of agency has to consider the ways in which actors can escape the strong conditioning that is assumed to be supplied by institutional frameworks." Nonetheless, Mutch went on to use the language of institutional entrepreneurship in analyzing the success of Sir Andrew Barclay Walker (the Englishman who invented the concept of hiring paid managers for tied public houses).[1] Mutch also invoked the concepts of "autonomous reflexive" (Archer, 2003) and "agential reflexivity" to explain why some people can think independently of their contexts and thus take actions that oppose them. I will return to these issues when I examine the kinds of humans posited by these kinds of analyses.

Finding "IEs" in the Historical Record: The Phoenix Case

The historical record serves up many individuals who seem to exemplify the characteristics Mutch described. John Sperling was a tenured professor of economic history at San Jose State University (SJSU) in 1974 when he developed an idea for a degree program aimed specifically at working adults (Bartlett, 2009). When SJSU administrators nixed the idea, he took $26,000 of his personal savings, turned his home into an office, and created the

Institute for Community Research and Development. Within two years, revenues were almost $3 million. After a conflict with regulators in California, he moved his operations to Arizona and created what was to become the University of Phoenix. In 2009, his company was valued at about $10 billion, had more than 200 campuses and about 26,000 faculty members, and had made Sperling and his founding team very wealthy.

In the beginning, as an outsider to the professional academic community, he was ridiculed for his preposterous idea. He was a teacher, not an administrator, but he learned rapidly. As with many other successful high-growth ventures, the University of Phoenix was founded by a team: Sperling recruited two former students to work with him, thus mimicking other startup teams in which the founding members were well acquainted with one another. No angel money or venture capital funding was involved, but that didn't stop Sperling from creating a corporate entity – the Apollo Group – that held ownership of the University Phoenix and which went public in 1994 (594 firms had IPOs that year). Sterling subsequently created several other new ventures, such as Southwest Solar Technologies.

Was he an *entrepreneur*? Certainly, by most definitions, Sperling qualifies. Of the many definitions of entrepreneurship available, most turn on some notion of adding value to the world by creating a sustainable entity. Perhaps the most generic definition of entrepreneurship comes from Stevenson and Gumpert (1985): the pursuit of opportunities without regard to resources currently controlled. More expansive notions of entrepreneurship emphasize creating something new (Rindova, Barry, & Ketchen, 2009, pp. 477–478): "we define entrepreneurship ... as efforts to bring about new economic, social, institutional, and cultural environments through the actions of an individual or group of individuals." This expansive definition seems to be the one favored by institutional entrepreneurship theorists.

Going further, should we use the IE label for John Sperling? I don't think so. Consider several ways in which NIT can be brought to bear on the growth of the for-profit higher education sector. First, in the 1970s, the for-profit sector consisted of hundreds of small privately owned businesses that competed for the students not served by traditional four-year colleges and universities (Wilson, 2010). Strongly institutionalized forces rewarded organizational inertia and a strong commitment to tradition, and established colleges and universities were unable to recognize the profit opportunities of commercializing higher education. In short, institutional forces made established players unimaginative and restricted the number of actions they were willing to undertake. In contrast, no such constraints inhibited players who were outside the system.

Second, when new and more aggressive for-profit entities emerged, such as the University of Phoenix, they couldn't raise funds from venture capitalists or even from commercial banks. Moreover, they didn't fit within the conceptual categories used by regulators, higher education consultants, and other players in the established system. Over the ensuing three decades, thousands of for-profit entities were created, with many failing, and even today, the roughly 3,000 for-profit companies educate only about 7% of degree-seeking students (Wilson, 2010). However, collectively they have revenues of about $26 billion and are growing more rapidly than the traditional sector.

I would argue that an NIT approach should focus on the institutional constraints that hampered the traditional entities and left gaps for new entities to fill. Through sustained collective effort, for-profit organizations succeeded in obtaining federal grants for their students and accreditation for their degrees. Sperling benefited from the sacrifices endured by the many failing operations and pressure put on government agencies and regulators to accommodate the "new" student population served by the nonprofits. Sperling is an entrepreneur, but labeling him an IE deflects attention from the real institutional story. Following the logic of Aldrich and Fiol (1994), the emergence and growth of the for-profit sector is a story about institutional entrepreneurship, a project based on collective action, rather than heroic IE's. To appreciate the need for such an historical institutional analysis (Pierson, 2004), we must understand the larger organizational landscape in the United States as portrayed in Tables 2 and 3. Such understanding comes, I believe from an evolutionary perspective that draws heavily on NIT.

Selection Forces are Merciless: Beyond Black Swans
In 1974, John Sperling's new venture was one of millions created by nascent entrepreneurs and as such, would have attracted little attention, given how closely it resembled other startup attempts: home-based, no outside funding, and formed by a team of people well known to one another. In contrast, in 1994, when the Apollo Group went public, it was one of about 500 firms making the successful leap to public ownership. Taleb (2007) called such events "black swans" because they have high impact, are only retrospectively predictable, and are incredibly rare.

Were we to focus only on the black swans, celebrating their good fortune in emerging out of the mundane initial population of startups, we would miss the critical feature of entrepreneurship in the United States illustrated in Tables 2 and 3: success is exceedingly difficult to attain. With their focus on larger and well-established organizations, theories of IE emphasize agency and strategic action, suggesting that humans do fairly well in coping with uncertainty and turbulence. However, from a macroinstitutional viewpoint, we must consider two more disheartening explanations for the process revealed by these numbers (Haveman & Rao, 1997), neither of which is favorable to theories of strategic action. From an *adaptation perspective*, the story concerns whether humans learn something at each stage of the process, with disappointingly few learning well and most learning little or nothing at all. Those that learn survive to go onto the next event in their organization's life course, whereas most of those learning slowly or not at all simply fail. From a *selection perspective*, the story is one of initial heterogeneity in resources and capability being winnowed over time. From this perspective, the human tragedy is that forces beyond their control simply overwhelm nascent entrepreneurs in the population, leaving a small set of lucky survivors. Comprehensive theories of entrepreneurship must be cognizant of all possibilities, rather than just the heroic ones.

HOW DOES INSTITUTIONAL THEORY HELP US UNDERSTAND ENTREPRENEURSHIP?

I envision explanations of entrepreneurship that recognize and appreciate the full spectrum of entrepreneurial activities, from the mundane to the improbable. We need to take a multilevel long-term view, covering all facets of startup and survival. I believe that NIT can contribute a great deal to this effort: the factors affecting entrepreneurial success vary over time with changes in the economy, government regulation, the technological opportunity structure, and so forth.

Which Brand of Institutional Theory?

Anyone writing about "institutional theory" or "neo-institutional theory" must be cognizant of the rather large tent within which institutional theorists dwell. Noting that institutional theory as applied to organizations has relatively relaxed requirements, Davis (2006, p. 117) – co-author with W. Richard Scott of one of the leading organization theory textbooks – argued that "institutional theory is a generic perspective, a set of ideas and problems that serves as a rough guide to questions worth asking that seems to fit with the kinds of problems researchers find interesting these days."

Similarly, after observing that institutional theory is a way of thinking about social life rather than a "theory" as such, Czarniawska (2008, pp. 770–771) offered a simple definition of institution – "normatively justified patterns of action" – and a more complex one, from the Scandinavian school as influenced by Jim March: "institutions could thus be defined as collections of stable rules and roles and corresponding sets of meanings and interpretations."[2] Most definitions contain some notion of patterned behavior infused with meaning by normative systems and perpetuated by social exchanges facilitated by shared cognitive understandings (Greenwood, Oliver, Sahlin, & Suddaby, 2008).

From the classical institutional theory perspective, as exemplified in the work of John Meyer (Meyer & Rowan, 1977) and Dick Scott (2001), these definitions represent a form of "hard" institutionalism that downplays strategic action undertaken by self-interested actors and plays up the role of culture and constrained cognition. Indeed, one could almost read these accounts as positing humans as puppets programmed with culturally determined scripts. Although not as explicit as sociological institutionalism, institutionalism in political science and economics also views institutions as severely constraining. In the multidisciplinary field labeled "organizational institutionalism," most explanations emphasize the one-way influence of institutions on organizational actions, as in studies of diffusion across organizations and the consequences of adaptation to institutional constraints for organizational survival (Schneiberg & Clemens, 2006, p. 201). Over the past few decades, Meyer and Scott have diverged somewhat in their approach to NIT, and I think it is instructive to examine their views on institutions and agency.

John Meyer's Approach
In a spirited essay that concluded an historic edited volume on organizational institutionalism, Meyer (2008) assessed the several dozen contributed papers and offered a ringing defense of the new institutionalism against what he saw as "creeping realism" (my term, not his) in many of the contributions. He argued that the purposeful, forward-looking, intelligent actors identified as "IEs" represent an unrecognized intrusion of modernist ideas about human autonomy and control into institutional theory. Modernism in the social sciences, after the mid-20th century, championed a "rational choice" perspective on what humans could do, once they were freed by the expansion of free markets, the rule of democracy, and modern technology. Meyer argued that the term "actor" implies the notion of people making choices. although it is clear that NIT implies "actors" who

mostly follow prewritten scripts. Meyer advocated a hardline phenomen-ological approach to institutional analyses in which "actors" don't really need to make "choices" because they are embedded in environments that essentially leave them no choices to make.

In Meyer's view, the critical theoretical contest is between "realism" and "phenomenological" approaches, with realism positing actors who mostly create their own worlds and thus can change them. In the most extreme form of realism, people effectively must give their consent to whatever external forces influence them, whereas in the less extreme form, people are somewhat constrained by history, as in models positing path dependence (Garud & Karnoe, 2001). "Modern social science, following on modern ideology, celebrates a social world made up of strong actors, in the realist sense. Theory and ideology give great emphasis to notions of society as a product of such actors and their purposes" (Meyer, 2008, p. 795).

In an implicit swipe at DiMaggio (1988), he was critical of realist accounts that emphasize "power and interests" as the real forces behind observed changes, and he lamented the normative ideologies underlying accounts of individuals as "highly interested and agentic actors" (Meyer, 2008, p. 796). One implication of his view is that humans engaging in entrepreneurial activities are simply carrying out scripted actions authorized by the fields in which they are embedded. I return to this theme later in this essay, when I review DiMaggio's contributions.

Dick Scott's Approach
In an essay reviewing what he termed the "maturation" of NIT, Scott (2008) identified seven trends, two of which are particularly relevant to my argument: from determinant to interactive arguments, and from institutional stability to institutional change. Scott argued that early on, theorists overstated the extent to which institutional environments exhibited coherence and unity, treating institutional environments as imposing uniform requirements on passive organizations. As NIT matured, theorists observed that institutional effects differed by sectors and "organizational fields," with some more constraining than others. Theorists moved further to acknowledge heterogeneity within fields, calling them complex, frag-mented, and shot through with ambiguity, leading observers to ponder what would happen next, given competing alternatives. Another development was the recognition that laws and regulations could be resisted and reinterpreted by those to whom they were applied. In consequence, theorists began to write about opportunities for choice and the use of agency among "actors" (individuals and organizations). Scott cited with approval work by

DiMaggio, Giddens, and Oliver, all of whom emphasized power and strategic maneuvering as viable responses to institutional pressures.

Scott also noted that as NIT matured, it recognized change as well as stability and order. He argued that contemporary NIT is not only about constraint, but also empowerment, through the creation of particular roles and practices, because virtually all contemporary actors operate in multiple institutional environments offering them resources for creativity and innovation. Exogenous changes could come from shocks and jolts and from invasions of "foreign" ideas from other fields. Endogenous changes could come from conflicts between levels within fields, mismatches between juxtaposed elements of different fields, and organizations' failures to achieve their claimed goals. He noted that NIT scholars have adopted more dynamic research designs that capture institutional changes.[3]

Why Institutions Matter for Entrepreneurship

I want to point out several ways in which NIT helps us understand the dynamics of entrepreneurship, as exemplified in Tables 2 and 3. Perhaps the most important consideration is the extent to which NIT helps us understand the mundane, not just the improbable. Aldrich and Ruef (2006) argued that a host of institutional factors affect the organizational carrying capacity of a society and the likelihood of entrepreneurship, and I review two of them: cultural norms and values, and political and governmental activities and policies.

The Phenomenology of Entrepreneurship: Cultural Norms and Values

Using a phenomenological approach to institutional analysis, theorists recognize "the dependence of modern expanded actors on institutional scripts operating in their environments" (Meyer, 2008, p. 801). Phenomenologically, institutions affect the prevalence, intensity, and impact of entrepreneurs in at least two major ways. First, they structure the context within which entrepreneurs learn about entrepreneurship, search for resources, build their new ventures, and benefit from their efforts. Second, they provide the cultural resources with which entrepreneurs, public policy makers, investors, and others interpret the meaning of entrepreneurship. Changing norms and values shape and alter the construction of entrepreneurial identities, entrepreneurial intentions, and the willingness of resource providers to support new ventures. Institutions confer interpretive schema on entrepreneurs and others with which to make sense of actions taken by people creating new commercial and social entities. Thus, in some contexts, people who generate innovative solutions to problems may be viewed as positive agents of change, whereas in other contexts, such people may be viewed as threats to social order. Similarly, events seen as "problems requiring solutions" in some contexts, and thus as opportunities for entrepreneurial actions, may simply be taken for granted and endured in others.

For example, in their analysis of the emergence of the wind power industry, Sine and Lee (2009) showed that at the state level, changing attitudes about the environment motivated some entrepreneurs to create new firms for ideological reasons, reflecting the new cultural schema. Their actions and resulting sociocultural changes, in turn, opened up opportunities to entrepreneurs who were not ideological motivated. As the industry emerged over the following decade, most wind firms were founded in states where cultural norms and values, as well as government regulations, were very supportive, rather than in states with a greater expanse of wind-swept land amenable to wind power but less favorable norms and values. Sociocultural factors often exert a stronger influence than regulations, as Hiatt, Sine, and Tolbert (2009) observed in the emergence of the American soft drink industry. They found that legal disincentives, such as state prohibitions, were not as powerful as cultural strategies in causing the failure of breweries. Brewery failures, in turn, increased foundings of soft drink bottlers.

NIT emphasizes that selection of activities by humans is based on their appropriateness, not necessarily on pragmatic or instrumental criteria, and thus institutional researchers investigate the emergence of conventions regarding appropriateness (Biggart & Beamish, 2003). Norms and values influence nascent entrepreneurs' understandings of current conditions and help shape the way in which entrepreneurial ambitions are expressed, toward traditional lines of action or toward actions that challenge the status quo. Sine, Haveman, and Tolbert (2005) noted that institutional environments in new economic sectors shape perceptions of risk for nascent entrepreneurs, and thus affect the range of new technologies attempted. When nascent entrepreneurs perceive higher risk, they are less likely to found firms with novel technologies. For example, in the 1950s and 1960s, conventional accounts of higher education stressed its public good nature and took for granted the assumption that it had little commercial potential. John Sperling's founding of the University of Phoenix broke with conventional understandings and caused him great difficulties in dealing with the market and potential resource providers. The concept of a commercially oriented provider of higher education simply did not fit with current cultural understandings.

Entrepreneurs interpret opportunities while embedded in a system of cultural understandings, drawing upon and conditioned by their (learned) habitual responses to the situations they encounter. Entrepreneurs use many "social mechanisms" as they create new ventures, encountering problem situations and drawing upon social practices and available resources to solve the problems. Gross (2009, p. 359) defined social practices as "ways of doing and thinking that are often tacit, acquire meaning from widely shared presuppositions and underlying semiotic codes, and are tied to particular locations in the social structure and to the collective history of groups." Thus, to explain historical and comparative variations in entrepreneurship, we need to understand the social practices extant at particular times and places. Humans are creatures of habit, and entrepreneurs are no exception.[4] Institutional frameworks structure the context within which social practices emerge.

Political Processes and Events
Political–institutional factors affect entrepreneurship on a broad scale because they help shape values, alter expectations, and change public policies. Aldrich and Ruef (2006) noted that the creation of new organizations is particularly sensitive to four kinds of political processes. First, political turbulence can disrupt ties between established organizations and resources, rearranging organizational boundaries and freeing resources for use by new organizations. For example, the economic unification of Europe over the past three decades has had major effects on organizations' life chances, removing many of the barriers to trans-European marketing of goods and services. In particular, new business interest groups have formed as a reaction to increases in cross-border trade possibilities. In addition to taking collective action with regard to regulations, business interest associations can shape the cognitive categories used by organizations in their institutional environments. They can codify and spread best practices with regard to matters such as technology and tax advice and champion some organizational forms over others (Sine et al., 2005).

Second, regulation and deregulation significantly change the institutional context for nascent entrepreneurs. For example, the emergence of federal legislation in the 1930s regulating commercial broadcasting substantially affected the opportunity structure facing broadcasters. Nonprofit broadcasters were essentially shut out of the growing radio broadcasting market

(Lippmann, 2007). Malesky and Taussig (2009) showed how changes in political regulation at the institutional level in Vietnam affected entrepreneurial actions. Their research highlighted the impact of two legislative changes on rates of business creation: a 1986 law that launched reforms in the economy for private businesses, and a 2000 law that substantially reduced barriers for setting up a private company. Some forms of political regulation actually drive entrepreneurship outside the institutional framework of the formal economy altogether (Webb, Tihanyi, Ireland, & Sirmon, 2009, p. 575).

Third, direct government support encourages the creation of new organizations through enhanced legitimacy via the symbolic consequences of governmental action, as well as through direct subsidy (Schneiberg, 2005). In the United States, legislative initiatives have raised the founding rate of many populations. Kim, Lee, and Reynolds (2009) argued that government institutions may encourage employers and employees to invest in training, which in turn may spur entrepreneurial activity in knowledge-intensive industries, especially in countries with strong social protection policies. Fourth, macroeconomic policies indirectly affect the creation of new ventures to the extent that they affect unemployment rates and economic growth. Research in America and Western Europe shows the effect to be quite small, at least in the short run (Aldrich & Ruef, 2006, p. 236). However, Steier (2009) argued that at a global level, capitalist countries throughout the world show considerable variation in institutional arrangements and economic outcomes, such as rates of business creation by families. He argued against any simple breakdown of the world into a simple taxonomy of "varieties of capitalism," and instead pointed to substantial entrepreneurial heterogeneity even within "forms." For example, Kim and Li (2009) challenged the long-held notion that entrepreneurial activity occurs only in strongly regulated institutional environments. They argued that in regions where such institutions are in flux, such as emerging economies, entrepreneurship might flourish.

In this volume, Scott notes that an important connection between NIT and entrepreneurship is NIT's attention to the importance of legitimating processes. Simply creating something new is not sufficient for its survival. The response of external audiences is critical to any new social form's success, and some audiences are more critical than others in this process, as Aldrich and Fiol (1994) noted in their essay on the emergence of new industries. They posited multiple processes by which collective action by entrepreneurs in emerging organizational populations might build legitimacy for their new activities.

Celebrating Institutional Theory's Contributions

In this section, I have expressed my appreciation for the "hard" institutionalism of the theory group that emerged out of Stanford in the 1970s, a brand of institutional theory that stresses phenomenological institutionalism in which humans are seriously impeded from taking "strategic" action, including "institutional entrepreneurship." Cultural norms and values create the framework within which humans recognize some actions as appropriate and others to be avoided, making available particular social mechanisms and social practices that affect the likelihood and form that entrepreneurial action takes. These effects are most evident when we study entrepreneurship historically and comparatively. Political events and processes are perhaps the most constraining institutional factors, but they are often missed because entrepreneurship research tends to be carried out within a single nation, rather than comparatively (Aldrich, 2009).

GAPS AND PUZZLES: THE PARTS INSTITUTIONAL THEORY CAN'T REACH

I have noted that "hard" institutional theory provides a powerful analytic framework for understanding the macro- and mesocontexts within which humans must live and work. Its very success at explaining a great deal about social life has tempted some institutional theorists into extending the adjective "institutional" to a form of behavior that somehow seems to escape the serious constraints that institutional contexts ordinarily impose upon humans. What can it mean to use the concept of "IE" in other than a descriptive sense, that is, other than to characterize the humans involved in outcomes in which new social entities have been created? In this section, I want to again celebrate the gains in explaining entrepreneurship that are made salient by taking institutional theory seriously, but also to note the blind spots that arise when humans are credited with "embedded autonomy" and "autonomous flexibility." I emphasize the complexity and ambiguity facing nascent entrepreneurs at the microlevel of entrepreneurial processes. I advocate an emergence perspective, asking what kinds of humans are posited by institutional theorists and how do we build time, pacing, and duration into our models of emergence.

Emergence

New venture creation, from an evolutionary point of view, is a time-dependent heterogeneous process driven by myopically purposeful humans.

Whereas a small fraction of new ventures spring nearly fully formed out of the plans made by their founders, most of the new commercial entities depicted in Tables 2 and 3 have more prosaic origins. Even the minority of founding teams that create business plans normally do so only to satisfy the demands of external stakeholders who are seeking reassurance concerning the risks of dealing with new entities (Honig & Karlsson, 2004). Entrepreneurs rarely consult business plans once the founding process is underway. Baker and his collaborators (Baker, Miner, & Easley, 2003; Baker & Nelson, 2005) have convincingly made the point that "bricolage" – making do with what resources are available – is a much more apt description of the founding process than the term "designed." This dynamic aspect of organizational life has been overlooked or downplayed by institutional organization theory, shaped in part by the frameworks in key foundational articles.

For example, DiMaggio and Powell (1983), in an iconic institutional theory article that has been cited over 10,000 times, offered an explanation for convergence in forms within organizational fields. Their explanation turned almost entirely upon reflections about changes in existing organizations. In their model, isomorphism results primarily from organizational transformations, rather than the emergence of new organizations that challenge or disrupt forms in existing populations. They used the term "emergence" only three times in the paper and never in reference to new organizations. The word "entrepreneur" does not appear in the paper itself, but only in the title of one of the papers in the references section. The word "create" was used only to refer to "professions" as a group taking action to benefit itself, and the term "build" referred to managers seeking models. The terms "initiate," "start," and "generate" also did not appear. The paper is not totally bereft of reference to new organizations, as such references appear three times: they mention "new entrants" to a field once, "new organizations" entering a field once, and "new organizations" modeled on old ones once. On balance, however, their analysis concerns changes in entities that *already exist*, rather than entities that might come into being.

Although it heavily influenced ensuing theoretical developments, the paper did not totally dissuade subsequent analysts from considering emergent outcomes. For example, in a paper contrasting selection and adaptation arguments regarding why thrift institutions changed substantially from the mid-19th to the early 20th century, Haveman and Rao (1997) focused on the debate – a hot issue at that time – between theorists emphasizing "technical" versus "institutional" pressures for explaining changes in organizational populations. By bringing evolutionary theory's concern for organizational creation and population dynamics into the picture, they called attention to emergent outcomes. They made nine references to "institutional entrepreneurs," four references to "founders," and six references to "new organizations." They also made use of the verbs "create," "found," and "build," in reference to activities undertaken by humans as they went about "building up and tearing down" organizations in the thrift industry.

Even though they analyzed population dynamics in terms of starts and exits, Haveman and Rao did not actually study the microlevel processes involving "IEs." The only specific individual participant identified in the entire paper was the head of a national building and loan association's lobbying group. Otherwise, their analysis focused on changes in population composition through migration, different forms of collective action that affected the resources available to thrift institutions, legal and regulatory changes, and long-term trends in norms and values in the United States. Given the long sweep of history encompassed by their analysis, they clearly felt they could ignore the specific process through which particular associations and organizations rose and fell. Because of the data limitations in the historical record, they had little choice.

Thus, even though (1) "hard" institutionalism emphasizes constraints and downplays strategic action and (2) the highly influential conceptual apparatus offered by DiMaggio and Powell more or less ignored entrepreneurship, some researchers working within the stream of institutional thinking have occasionally evinced concern for emergent outcomes. However, such work is rare. Moreover, invoking the concept of "IE" does not, in my opinion, constitute sufficient recognition of the significance of emergent outcomes. Why haven't analysts taken "emergence" more seriously? Out of the many possible options, let me mention just two: theorists have been blinded by the high visibility of events in large organizations, and they have been too quick to imagine "purpose" and "intentionality" behind what they've observed.

Blinded by Bigness

Most institutional theory papers on organizations have dealt with relatively large units, writing about events that have happened within them or about the things that these large organizations did to other organizations (people, organizations, governments, and so forth). Institutional constraints in the well-structured fields inhabited by most large organizations make many events rather predictable, and they also make strategic action much easier to observe and document. However, when we switch the context to actions by humans outside of established organizations, not acting in the name of such organizations, it becomes much harder to trace the sources of constraints and their consequences. "Free range" entrepreneurs – the mundane, ordinary ones – are operating in turbulent environments. In trying to create a new entity, they encounter a great deal more uncertainty than representatives of large organizations ever face. Unlike the strategic actors pictured in much institutional research on organizations, where the ratio of successful to unsuccessful actions seems quite high, a high fraction of entrepreneurial probes end in futility.

The Allure of Agency

Fully embracing an evolutionary view of emergent outcomes requires that analysts accept the fact that sometimes "things just happen." Unluckily, humans are hardwired to attribute purpose and intentionality to everything they see around them (Tversky & Kahneman, 1981). As research has repeatedly demonstrated, assuming that structures were built for a purpose is a fundamental attribution error that even trained observers have a hard time overcoming (Lichtenstein & Slovic, 2006; Ariely, 2009). When people believe that something was designed and built, they often fail to search for exogenous selection forces that might actually have produced whatever it is they are observing. This problem has bedeviled evolutionary theorists for years and emboldened their opponents, as many people simply refuse to believe that small unplanned and incremental changes can have enormous consequences (Dennett, 1995). Large complex structures look massive, incontestable, and are thus taken for granted. Their mundane origins lie in an unexamined distant past. Looking for emergent outcomes does not mean that human intentionality is left out; far from it. But the humans resemble King Lear more than they do Rocky Balboa.

What Kinds of Humans Are Posited?

Initially, I found the concept of "IE" very appealing, with its iconic portrayal of autonomous and reflexive agents wreaking havoc on established orders as they brought new social entities into being. However, as I looked more closely at the characteristics attributed to these agents and at the cases selected as illustrative, I was reminded that institutional theorists are also humans. In that respect, they are as prone to selecting cases based on their visibility and prominence as the rest of us. The turmoil, ferment, and turbulence characteristic of everyday entrepreneurial activities is simply missing from these accounts. Instead, the concept of "IE" offers us a world designed by farsighted and clever humans that is as implausible as it is attractive.

What kinds of humans did DiMaggio posit in his influential article that popularized the concept of an IE? DiMaggio actually intended to *correct* what he saw as an overemphasis in institutional theory on the nonrational and noninstrumental aspects of behavior. He acknowledged that institutional theory's distinct contribution is its emphasis on people's preconscious understandings of phenomena, which lead them to either not recognize their own interests or, if they are recognized, to be unable to act upon those interests. He then put that argument aside and concentrated on an attempt to bring power and interest back into institutional theorizing, giving it more of a process orientation.

Although he didn't intend to overturn institutional theory's emphasis on the taken-for-granted aspects of institutions, in practice he presented a very strong portrait of self-consciously self-interested humans acting strategically to further their own interests and those of their groups. DiMaggio (1988, p. 13) argued that institutionalization results from the "political efforts of actors to accomplish their own ends," and their success depends upon the balance of power between opposing groups. Note how humans are empowered in these sentences: "creating new institutions is expensive and requires high levels of both interest and resources. New institutions arise when organized actors with sufficient resources (*institutional entrepreneurs*) see in them an opportunity to realize interests that they value highly" (DiMaggio, 1988, p. 14). Although his initial conceptualization seemed to be at the field level, he offered many examples of single organizations being transformed, and other examples in the paper included agencies, bureaus, social systems, and other entities apparently conceptualized as "institutions." He thus clearly intended to generalize his discussion to many different types of organizational entities.

In their appreciative citation of DiMaggio's paper and its impact, Lawrence and Suddaby (2006, p. 217) noted that "the concept of institutional entrepreneurship focuses attention on the manner in which interested actors work to influence their institutional contexts through such strategies as technical and market leadership or lobbying for regulatory changes." In addition, they credited Oliver with raising our awareness of institutional theory's potential to explain change by cataloging the kinds of strategic responses organizations make to institutional processes affecting them (Oliver, 1991, 1992). After cautioning that their advocacy of the concept of institutional work was *not* intended to imply "an understanding of actors as independent, autonomous agents capable of fully realizing their interest through strategic action," they nevertheless went on to say that their "practice approach" pointed toward "understanding the knowledgeable, creative and practical work of individual and collective actors aimed at creating, maintaining and transforming institutions" (Lawrence & Suddaby, 2006, p. 219). Moreover, in their identification of four specific categories of institutional work (defining, constructing identities, mimicry, and theorizing), they didn't seem to be writing of humans merely *trying* to do these things, but rather actually *accomplishing* them. Lawrence and Suddaby clearly were struggling with the paradox of positing self-aware and creative humans successfully working to disrupt and transform the very institutional frameworks that give them life.

Even so, the IEs in the work discussed above pale by comparison to those posited by rational-expectations economists who use the concept of "IE." In their book reviewing the economic literature on institutional entrepreneurship, Boettke and Coyne (2009) posited profit-motivated IEs who are able to engage in rational calculations to the extent that they can obtain accurate market signals. When this condition obtains, "entrepreneurs will tend to adopt institutions that are efficient" (Boettke & Coyne, 2009, p. 190). Perhaps anticipating such claims, Crouch (2005, p. 67) argued that "it is not possible for the rational expectations model to accept entrepreneurial activity, as entrepreneurialism involves a constant searching, which in fact changes the definition of the pursued optimum itself. Error and mistakes are essential to the process of business (and, one might add, scientific and technological innovation) ..." Rather than the logic of consequentiality, posited by rational-choice theorists such as Boettke and Coyne, institutional theory posits a logic of appropriateness in which humans work within preconceived classifications of situations (Czarniawska, 2008).

Hallett (2010, p. 70) noted the irony of attempting to use NIT in explaining entrepreneurial actions. NIT is very good for outlining the constraints that entrepreneurs face, but when NIT theorists introduce the concept of IEs, they "create a problematic imagery of heroic individuals (Maguire, Hardy, & Lawrence, 2004) inconsistent with NIT's important critique of atomistic, utilitarian, rational-choice models where actors' preferences and interests are treated as exogenous to the larger cultural order (DiMaggio & Powell, 1991)". As Powell and Colyvas (2008, p. 277) noted, "not all change is led by entrepreneurs, and surely heroic actors and cultural dopes are a poor representation of the gamut of human behavior."[5]

Although my brief review is selective rather than definitive, I believe it is sufficient to highlight my point that analysts using the concept of "IE" posit

human beings with properties that should make them unrecognizable to
neo-institutional theorists such as Meyer and Scott. As Rao, Greve, and
Davis (2001, p. 502) pointed out, "neoinstitutional research ... presumes a
model of human behavior in which people persist in a course of action that
they have copied from others even when it is against their own interests.
Such a model implies that actors are cognitive dopes ..." Despite their
moves into the "cognitive" terrain, I still think that institutional theorists
studying entrepreneurship work with a model of humans that is unrealistic.
The humans who populate the institutions described by institutional
theories of entrepreneurship are too aware of their options, too shrewd
with regard to strategies, and too willing to abandon old habits. Where are
the cognitive dopes?

Evolutionary theorizing, drawing upon modern cognitive psychology,
cognitive neuroscience, behavioral economics, and other fields paying close
attention to the microlevel of analysis, posits humans that are error prone
and myopic. They are embedded in organizational contexts that limit their
cognitive abilities and their awareness (Small, 2009). As John Meyer would
argue, individual variation does not *ipso facto* mean the individuals are
autonomous actors. If we are to conceptualize the creation of new social
entities as an emergent process, the humans in our models must be more
accurately portrayed. For example, nuanced models of entrepreneurial
actions can draw on the concepts of habits and social mechanisms to
emphasize the power of the status quo (Gross, 2009) and also draw on
cognitive psychology and behavioral economics to emphasize the everyday
occurrence of mistakes, accidents, and random variation (Aldrich &
Kenworthy, 1999; Ariely, 2009).

Time, Pace, and Process

One reason for NIT's struggle as a comprehensive theory of entrepreneurship is that it doesn't deal very well with duration, pacing, required levels of
effort, and so forth (Pierson, 2004). Although it posits causes and effects and
has "history" in many of its empirical models, we don't typically get a sense
of how long it takes to change or transform something. It is most time-
specific when it deals with legislation and legislative acts. In those cases,
we know *when* something happened and can read the back story –
retrospectively reconstructed – of how it happened. Even so, researchers
often don't give us a sense of "time passing" – how difficult the transformation, reconstruction, or new construction was, in the sense of why it took

days, weeks, months, or years, and whether that particular duration was necessary or merely sufficient.

In contrast, consider what we know about time and pacing with regard to creating new businesses. We have good data on nascent entrepreneurship and the startup process (Reynolds & Curtin, 2007). For example, we know that it takes, on average, about one and a half years to go from "initiating the effort" to "an established business," but also that there is a long tail to the process. Some nascent entrepreneurs spend years just contemplating a startup, and others spend years on the activities required. Still, on average, we know that a team of nascent entrepreneurs will invest more than a year, and occasionally more than two years, in a startup effort. (If it takes this long to start a small business, consider how much more difficult it is to create a large organization.)

We have several excellent exemplars who have studied the importance of timing in historically significant institutional transformations. For example, Starr (2004) made a powerful case for historical contingencies and path dependencies as factors in the evolution of communication media in the United States (telegraph, phone, newspaper, radio, and so forth). Change sometimes occurred in short bursts of frenzied activities, whereas at other times, it took decades for changes to occur. Eventually, many changes that were highly contested when first proposed came to be seen as inevitable, even natural and "the way things should be." In building his explanations, Starr wrote about "triggering events" and "pivotal moments." Of course, having knowledge of the outcome is a tremendous advantage when looking through the historical record to identify preconditions to change. Nonetheless, I believe Starr's lesson for entrepreneurship scholars is to recognize the importance of historical contexts and to try scaling explanations in as small a unit of time as possible.

Schneiberg and Clemens (2006) grappled with this issue in a review article recommending the "typical tools for the job" in conducting institutional analyses. They offered a rousing defense of "hard" institutionalism, offering observations such as institutions are "constraints on action" and "institutions as culturally constitutive of actors" (Schneiberg & Clemens, 2006, p. 196). However, because they were arguing for multilevel analyses and ways of bringing individuals into the picture, without committing "methodological individualism," they wanted to avoid positing humans as merely cultural dopes. They briefly mentioned "organizational entrepreneurs," but mostly wrote about humans who belong to *categories* of actors, rather than as individual change agents. Interestingly enough, in their comprehensive and sophisticated analysis of research strategies for

institutional analysis, there is no consideration of timing, pacing, and
the duration of change. They wrote about multiple levels of analysis
and patterns of association across institutional fields, but the analysis is
entirely formal and substantive. Certainly, context matters, but how long
does it take?

How might we develop theoretically grounded expectations regarding the
timing, pace, and duration of institutional change, as driven by entrepreneurial activities? Schneiberg and Clemens called for multilevel modeling,
and we can build on their suggestions by drawing on a contribution from
a long-time friend of (rational choice) institutional analysis from the
economics profession, Oliver Williamson. Boettke and Coyne (2009)
modified a scheme offered by Williamson (2000, p. 597), who had built on
a diagram originally developed by Scott (1995), and proposed a speculative
four-level institutional hierarchy, with changes at the "top" of the hierarchy
taking centuries and those at the "bottom" of the hierarchy occurring on
a continuous basis. Arguably, there is little systematic evidence to support
the specific durations he identified, but the scheme is a useful heuristic and
thus I show it in Table 4. If we accept Williamson's hierarchy, we can see
immediately that the domain for effective "institutional entrepreneurship" is
probably limited to the bottom two rows.

My point in this section is to call attention to the relatively
unsophisticated concepts of timing, pace, and duration in organizational
institutionalism and to note that this underdevelopment poses problems for

Table 4.   Williamson's Four-level Hierarchy of Institutions and
Projected Time to Change Them.

Institutional Level of Analysis	Examples	Expected Duration of Transformation Processes
Informal environment	Informal institutions, customs, traditions	Extremely long term (decades, centuries)
Formal environment	Formal rules of the game, especially regarding property	Very long term (years, decades)
Governance	How the game is played, especially regarding contracts	Long term (months, years)
Resource allocation and employment	Prices and quantities	Short term (days, weeks, months)

Source: Created with extensive modifications, from ideas in Williamson (2000), as modified in
Boettke and Coyne (2009), as originally developed by Scott (1995).

theorists wishing to build multilevel models in which "entrepreneurship" plays a role. Judgments regarding the degree to which "institutions" are stable or changing (incrementally or radically) rest upon observers' assessments along a variety of dimensions. From my reading of the empirical literature in NIT, two aspects of these required assessments stand out. First, they are usually categorical and lumpy, without much nuance. Second, the rate of change is not spelled out in much detail. Typically, data are collected in yearly chunks, and therefore changes can only be assessed every 12 months or so. More typical is a categorization covering multiple years, with "period," "eras," and "epochs" identified on the basis of limited evidence (Aldrich & Ruef, 2006).

A first step in coming to grips with emergence in institutional theories of entrepreneurship might involve developing an accounting scheme along the lines of that shown in Table 4. Although at first this might be mostly intuitive, at least it would help us appreciate the gap between the timescale for change implied by "hard" institutionalism and that posited by analysts employing the notion of "IE." Such a scheme might lead to greater awareness of the apparent communication gap between the "hard" institutionalists and those claiming they are also working in the institutional tradition.

FINDING INSTITUTIONAL THEORY'S PLACE

Institutional theory can contribute in many ways toward an understanding of entrepreneurship in capitalist economies. In this short chapter, I've only been able to identify a few examples of the context-setting analyses that I've found helpful. My concern is with the negative consequences of trying to transform institutional theory to deal with questions that are a bad fit for the assumptions underlying "hard" institutionalism. Others have identified similar concerns, as in this warning: "We think that too often the new institutionalism has served as a shade tree under which organization studies scholars, some of whom are only peripherally connected to the new institutionalism project, have found company and support with little in the way of self-criticism and self-improvement" (Palmer et al., 2008, pp. 755–756).

I have already noted two classes of problems with regard to institutional theory's ability to deal with the emergent nature of business startups and the astonishingly high level of social and economic turbulence associated with them. First, the most widely recognized problem commented upon by institutional authors themselves concerns the inherent contradiction between "institutions" and "entrepreneurship." Institutions are patterns of behavior that are reproduced without thinking or reflection by most people, most of the time. The people who inhabit them take institutional arrangements as exterior and constraining. Most important of all, they are extremely durable. If they did not last a long time, it would be pointless to identify them. If the norms regarding social behavior were constantly changing, it would be impossible to characterize them as an "institution" because behavior would be highly uncertain.

Therefore, in this respect, the concept of "institution" is fundamentally in conflict with the concept of "entrepreneurship" as an endogenous feature of institutions. Some theorists writing about institutional entrepreneurship have taken pains to point out the internal heterogeneity of many institutions, arguing that this internal incoherence provides space for tensions and contradictions that entrepreneurs can exploit. A counter-argument to this claim is that explanations for how and why such exploitation occurs typically draw from very different theoretical premises than "hard" institutionalism. A related issue concerns NIT's need to import explanations from other theories for why institutional arrangements become open to change. For example, in their study of the US electric power industry, Sine and David (2003) invoked NIT in pointing out that that *exogenous jolts* disrupted institutional logics and raised firms' awareness of flaws in current arrangements, thus increasing the salience of alternatives. Thus, the catalyst for change was a shock from outside the existing institutional arrangements, rather than emerging from within them.

Second, the less widely recognized problem of trying to extend concepts from institutional theory to the microlevel of entrepreneurial processes involves both the assumptions inherent in institutional theory concerning humans and the currently limited toolkit available to institutional theorists for studying timing, pacing, and duration. I have noted that institutional theory works very well as a macrolevel account, because it assumes that humans are, to a great extent, cultural dopes. In contrast, for better or worse, the humans in most entrepreneurship analyses are strategic actors, and theorists using the concept of "IE" have been unable to extricate themselves from that tradition.

Dilemmas in dealing with timing, pacing, and duration aren't inherent in institutional theory, but rather seem to be mostly a matter of inattention to their importance. Empirical research on entrepreneurship typically deals with time as calculated in hours, days, and weeks (Aldrich, 2001). With most neo-institutional empirical research projects treating "years" as the relevant timescale, researchers invoking the concept of "IE" have not yet recognized the gap.

Some Promising Lines of Inquiry

I've already noted the risk of trying to characterize central tendencies in a group of scholars as diverse as those calling themselves institutional theorists, and so I want to acknowledge a few significant recent contributions that hold out the promise of overcoming some of the difficulties I've reviewed. First, drawing more on concepts from American pragmatism than NIT, Mutch (2007) offered several ideas worth emphasizing. He noted that crediting institutional change and innovation to IEs places too much emphasis on the intentions and skills of individual entrepreneurs, and not enough on the emergence of practices that no individual foresaw or intended. He argued for attention to "personal projects" that may aggregate across individual actors to create unforeseen and unintended institutional changes. "Project," a term generated by existential Marxists, assumes that people can invest their time and effort to pursue goals that are projected as being realized in the future. Clearly, this is well outside the range of "hard" institutionalism, but it is a concept that process-oriented entrepreneurship scholars can embrace, although some of them will do so at arm's length!

Second, in the single article devoted solely to "institutional entrepreneurship" in the encyclopedic *Sage Handbook of Organizational Institutionalism*, Hardy and Maguire (2008) argued that it was possible to incorporate "agency" in ways that preserved some of the key insights of institutional theory. They acknowledged the paradox of positing "change" and "innovation" as occurring in highly institutionalized fields, but they argued that both central and peripheral actors could push for new ways of doing things. At the core of their argument was a distinction between two strains in the institutional entrepreneurship literature: (1) an actor-centric focus on how and why particular entrepreneurs are able to transform fields; and (2) a process-centric focus and concern for the microlevel struggle to change institutions. Employing concepts I've already mentioned – embedded agency, autonomous reflexive, and so forth – they discussed approaches as to who becomes an IE and how such people carry out their activities.

Two of their arguments fit with points I've made and are worth repeating. First, they noted the importance of distinguishing between intentions and outcomes: the messiness of institutional entrepreneurial processes shows the "potential for outcomes which are not necessarily those originally intended by the actors involved. It thus stands in contrast to the bulk of work on institutional entrepreneurship which seeks to explain the effectiveness or success of IEs in bringing about intended institutional change, usually with reference to specific strategies for intervening in a field ..." (Hardy & Maguire, 2008, p. 206). Second, in their emphasis on interpretive struggles by actors who contest the meaning of myths, logics, and discourses, they departed substantially from "hard" institutionalism.

Nonetheless, Hardy and Maguire conspicuously struggled with how to distance themselves from "hard" institutionalism. First, the apparently inescapable influence of traditional NIT was apparent in their description of how an institutional field "produces" peoples' interests, skills, and stocks of knowledge. Note the deterministic view of humans' relationship to structures. Second, although the mainstream field of entrepreneurship is almost entirely about the creation of new organizations, almost all of their arguments and examples concerned *new practices*, rather than new organizations. Third, in keeping with the practices of other institutional scholars, they made little direct reference to the fields of social psychology, psychology, and other behavioral sciences and instead wrote about cognition in terms of language and discourse. Fourth, their call to implement a process-centric approach to research on institutional entrepreneurship runs up against major methodological challenges.

Methodologically, many of the researchers reviewed by Hardy and Maguire favor ethnographic and other fieldwork-based approaches that involve obtaining information directly from participants through observation, interviews, and so forth. Cognitive psychology tells us that from the "inside," entrepreneurs are likely to perceive that they are the masters of their own destiny, creating organizations from the resources they control and responsible for the outcomes that emerge from the startup process. It is unlikely they will attribute their success to the favorable local, state, and national infrastructures that support their efforts, although they would no doubt nod in recognition, were it described to them. I suspect that as we move down the hierarchy identified in Table 4, from top to bottom, entrepreneurs become increasingly resistant to the idea that events at the local level are critical factors in their successes.

At the microscale, it is easy for humans to imagine that they are directly responsible for what they see around them. This phenomenon means that entrepreneurs themselves are probably unreliable reporters on why they have succeeded or failed. This would be a major problem with research if it only selected and interviewed "successful" entrepreneurs. However, if research on entrepreneurs were "fully ethnographic," involving observations of actual practices in various situations and over time, as well as interviews with entrepreneurs and other people involved, ethnographers would be able to triangulate their data and findings such that the end product would not be a methodological artifact. Using fully ethnographic methods, entrepreneurs' reports on their views would become one among many data points needed to understand how macroinstitutional forces affect entrepreneurial processes.

In this regard, perhaps Meyer should be given the last word. He noted that globalizing forces entice humans into constructing themselves as *actors*: "in an expanding and globalizing world society, people and groups everywhere seem to be eager to be actors – this often takes precedence over other goals, and can produce assertions of actor identity far from any actual actor capability. People, in short, may put more effort into being actors than into acting" (Meyer, 2008, p. 803). From the perspective of "hard" institutionalism, asking people why they want to become entrepreneurs is ultimately futile: they don't really "decide" to become entrepreneurs. Instead, they are caught up in institutional scripts that have them playing the role of entrepreneurs in capitalist economies. However, from a microlevel entrepreneurial process viewpoint, taking on an entrepreneurial identity is only the beginning of the struggle! Building up from this level, in our models, probably means abandoning institutional theory in favor of theories in which human actions – singly and collectively – play a more central role (Sewell, 1992).

CONCLUSIONS

I have argued that institutional theory is useful in explaining entrepreneurship to the extent that it sets the context within which humans create new entities, rather than engaging in a totalizing attempt to provide a comprehensive account of entrepreneurship. In these concluding remarks, I offer three suggestions for realigning the relationship between NIT and research on entrepreneurship.

Curb Injudicious Use of the Term "Institutional Entrepreneur"

The adjective "institutional" as applied to "entrépreneur" typically refers to people who have accomplished some major change. Applied after the fact, the term *always* fits. In papers I have reviewed for this chapter, the label has been applied to people who create new practices, found new organizations, pioneer new institutional fields, and so forth. Indeed, there seems no limit to the domain for this concept. The term almost always implies *intentional* human action, as the entrepreneurs wanted to do something, assembled the necessary power and resources, and then did it. As the Apollo moon mission control officer Eugene Kranz said, apparently "failure is not an option." This usage not only reinforces the heroic image of entrepreneurs that has plagued entrepreneurship research for decades, but also takes for granted a connection that should be made problematic: the link between intentions and outcomes. As Blute (2010, p. 18) pointed out, "there is no evidence in any area of human endeavor that, as a statistical body, innovations are biased in the direction that would be required for them to spread successfully. In fact, most fail." Surely, some personal projects that ended in organizational creation began as something else, and some projects that began with the best of intentions came to naught.

Multilevel Models Should Mix Modes of Theorizing

The multilevel model portrayed in Table 4 reminds us that "hard" institutional theories proceed from the top level downwards, with higher order institutional structures setting the conditions within which lower order structures must operate. Purely emergent models, which are hard to find these days outside of just-so stories regarding how economic markets emerged, proceed in the other direction. More sophisticated models, such as those found in modern evolutionary theorizing, posit a two-way causal street: complex entities can emerge from simpler entities, but with the range of possible emergent developments constrained by higher order structures (Dennett, 1995).

Adding timing, pace, and duration into a model complicates theorizing enormously, as the timing of processes at one level need not align with those at a different level. Researchers might acknowledge the multilevel nature of processes they are studying by invoking institutional theory to set up the slowly changing macrocontext within which more rapidly changing lower order processes are unfolding. For example, an institutional view might help researchers explain how and why discretionary wealth and other resources are unequally distributed in a set of local communities. A "process-centric" study might then focus on how teams of nascent entrepreneurs are assembling resources within these communities by calling upon strong ties in their local networks.

360   HOWARD E. ALDRICH

Humans as Heroes, Villains, and Fools

Even as they claim to know better, authors writing about IEs sooner or later endow them with strategic intentions, foresight, and well-rehearsed social skills. In a field where one of the foundational texts, March and Simon (1958), posited myopic purposefulness as a condition from which humans saved themselves by constructing organizations, it is strange to read about entrepreneurs who hit their intended targets with such accuracy. I have suggested that a more accurate rendering of the humans in our models will require that we make room for the kind of blundering that March (1971) and Weick (1979) have so eloquently described in their work. Ordinary humans spending their life savings on ill-fated mundane ventures may not be the stuff of *Harvard Business Review* articles, but they are the people that drive the entrepreneurial dynamics I've described. We need more of them in our models.

NOTES

1. "Tied houses" are public houses – bars, in American English – that can only sell beer and spirits from one brewery.
2. Czarniawska (2008) felt that the "strength of institutional theory lies in the tolerance of its propagandists."
3. As a contributor to NIT's development, Scott cited Giddens (1986), who viewed structures as both contexts and products of social action. However, I think using Giddens' work within NIT as a way to "bring change back in" gives up too much. It would seem, from an NIT view, that structures cannot continually be "up for grabs," as Giddens implies. Whereas it might make sense to posit locally significant innovative changes on an ongoing basis, Giddens' claims make no sense when generalized up to the field level. It is not that "structures only exist if and to the extent that they are continually produced and reproduced (Scott, 2008, p. 438). Rather, in my view, to be consistent, NIT must emphasize that local actions *do* reproduce institutional structures because that's what institutions *require* of their subjects. Otherwise, we cannot truly speak of "institutionalization." Within NIT, the reproduction of structures is collective, not individual. (Imagine a "tea party" taxpayer telling the Internal Revenue Service (IRS) that she objects to paying her taxes because otherwise she is helping to reproduce a structure she does not believe in – what are the consequences for her versus the IRS?) Nonetheless, some NIT theorists have embraced Giddens' work, although it makes more sense to me if used as a kind of orienting notion for people analyzing individual behavior at the social–psychological level.
4. Note that I am purposefully using the term "humans" rather than "actors" in this context.
5. Interestingly enough, in their review of possible microfoundations for institutional theory, Powell and Colyvas did not actually invoke institutional theory.

Instead, they turned to ethnomethodology and its variants, promulgated by Goffman, Garfinkle, and others. Scholars in that tradition worked with a very "active" view of humans: humans as actors authoring their own scripts, although with lots of intrusions and interventions by other authors. These authors do make mistakes, but only of interpretation, not blindness or biased perceptions. Indeed, they are very savvy "actors."

ACKNOWLEDGMENTS

I wish to acknowledge the incredibly helpful comments of Ted Baker, Barbara Czarniawska, Robert David, Jerry Davis, Raghu Garud, Mary Ann Glynn, Royston Greenwood, Tim Hallett, Phil Kim, Steve Lippmann, John Meyer, Woody Powell, Huggy Rao, Martin Rueff, Dick Scott, Wes Sine, and Lloyd Steier. Sadly, a gap exists between the paper they envisioned I should write and the paper that I was capable of writing. Nonetheless, they tried their best.

REFERENCES

Acs, Z. J., Headd, B., & Agwara, H. (2009). *Nonemployer startup puzzle.* Working paper. Office of Advocacy, Small Business Administration, Washington, DC.

Aldrich, H. E. (2001). Who wants to be an evolutionary theorist? Remarks on the occasion of the year 2000 OMT distinguished scholarly career award presentation. *Journal of Management Inquiry, 10*(2), 115–128.

Aldrich, H. E. (2009). Lost in space, out of time: How and why we should study organizations comparatively. In: B. King, T. Felin & D. A. Whetten (Eds), *Studying differences between organizations: Comparative approaches to organizational research* (Vol. 26, pp. 21–44). Bingley, UK: Emerald Group.

Aldrich, H. E., & Fiol, C. M. (1994). Fools rush in? The institutional context of industry creation. *Academy of Management Review, 19*(4), 645.

Aldrich, H. E., & Kenworthy, A. (1999). The accidental entrepreneur: Campbellian antinomies and organizational foundings. In: J. A. C. Baum & B. McKelvey (Eds), *Variations in organization science: In honor of Donald T. Campbell.* Newbury Park, CA: Sage.

Aldrich, H. E., & Ruef, M. (2006). *Organizations evolving.* London: Sage Publications.

Archer, M. S. (2003). *Structure, agency, and the internal conversation.* Cambridge, UK: Cambridge University Press.

Ariely, D. (2009). *Predictably irrational: The hidden forces that shape our decisions.* New York: Harper.

Baker, T., Miner, A. S., & Easley, D. T. (2003). Improvising firms: Bricolage, account giving and improvisational competencies in the founding process. *Research Policy, 32*(2), 255–276.

Baker, T., & Nelson, R. E. (2005). Creating something from nothing: Resource construction through entrepreneurial bricolage. *Administrative Science Quarterly, 50*(3), 329–366.

Bartlett, T. (2009). *Phoenix risen: How a history professor became the pioneer of the for-profit revolution* (Vol. 55). Washington, DC: The Chronicle of Higher Education.

Biggart, N., & Beamish, T. (2003). The economic sociology of conventions: Habit, custom, practice, and routine in market order. *Annual Review of Sociology, 29*, 443–464.

Blute, M. (2010). *Darwinian sociocultural evolution: Solutions to dilemmas in cultural and social theory*. Cambridge, UK: Cambridge University Press.

Boettke, P. J., & Coyne, C. J. (2009). Context matters: Institutions and entrepreneurship. *Foundations and Trends in Entrepreneurship, 5*(3), 135–209.

Crouch, C. (2005). *Capitalist diversity and change: Recombinant governance and institutional entrepreneurs*. New York: Oxford University Press.

Czarniawska, B. (2008). How to misuse institutions and get away with it: Some reflections on institutional theory(ies). In: R. Greenwood, C. Oliver, R. Suddaby & K. Sahlin (Eds), *The Sage handbook of organizational institutionalism* (pp. 769–782). Los Angeles, CA: Sage.

Davis, G. F. (2006). Mechanisms and the theory of organizations. *Journal of Management Inquiry, 15*(2), 114–118.

Dennett, D. (1995). *Darwin's dangerous idea: Evolution and the meanings of life*. London: Penguin Books.

DiMaggio, P. (1988). Interest and agency in institutional theory. In: L. G. Zucker (Ed.), *Institutional patterns and organizations: Culture and environment* (pp. 3–21). Cambridge, MA: Ballinger Publishing Company.

DiMaggio, P. J., & Powell, W. W. (1983). The iron cage revisited: Institutional isomorphism and collective rationality in organizational fields. *American Sociological Review, 48*(2), 147–160.

DiMaggio, P. J., & Powell, W. W. (1991). Introduction. In: W. W. Powell & P. J. DiMaggio (Eds), *The new institutionalism in organizational analysis* (pp. 1–40). Chicago: University of Chicago Press.

Eisenstadt, S. N. (1980). Cultural orientations, institutional entrepreneurs, and social change: Comparative analysis of traditional civilizations. *American Journal of Sociology, 85*(4), 840–869.

Emirbayer, M., & Mische, A. (1998). What is agency? *American Journal of Sociology, 103*(4), 962–1023.

Garud, R., & Karnoe, P. (Eds). (2001). *Path dependence and creation*. Mahwah, NJ: Lawrence Erlbaum and Associates.

Giddens, A. (1986). *The constitution of society: Outline of the theory of structuration*. Berkeley, CA: University of California.

Greenwood, R., Oliver, C., Sahlin, K., & Suddaby, R. (2008). Introduction. In: R. Greenwood, C. Oliver, K. Sahlin & R. Suddaby (Eds), *The Sage handbook of organizational institutionalism* (pp. 1–46). Los Angeles, CA: Sage.

Gross, N. (2009). A pragmtist theory of social mechanisms. *American Sociological Review, 74*(3), 358–379.

Hallett, T. (2010). Recoupling processes, turmoil, and inhabited institutions. *American Sociological Review, 75*(1), 52–74.

Hallett, T., & Ventresca, M. J. (2009). Inhabited institutions: Social interactions and organizational forms in Gouldner's *Patterns of Industrial Bureaucracy*. *Theory and Society, 35*(2), 213–236.

Hardy, C., & Maguire, S. (2008). Institutional entrepreneurship. In: R. Greenwood, C. Oliver, R. Suddaby & K. Sahlin (Eds), *The Sage handbook of organizational institutionalism* (pp. 198–217). London: Sage.

Haveman, H. A., & Rao, H. (1997). Structuring a theory of moral sentiments: Institutional and organizational coevolution in the early thrift industry. *American Journal of Sociology*, *102*(6), 1606–1651.

Hiatt, S., Sine, W. D., & Tolbert, P. S. (2009). Pabst to Pepsi: Social movements, entrepreneurial opportunity, and the emergence of the American soft drink industry. *Administrative Science Quarterly*, *54*(4), 635–657.

Honig, B., & Karlsson, T. (2004). Institutional forces and the written business plan. *Journal of Management*, *30*(1), 29–48.

Kim, P. H., Lee, C.-S., & Reynolds, P. D. (2009). *Backed by the state: Social protection and entrepreneurial entry in knowledge-intensive industries*. Madison, WI: University of Wisconsin-Madison.

Kim, P. H., & Li, M. L. (2009). *Seeking riches amid uncertainty: Institutional incentives for starting businesses in emerging economies*. Madison, WI: University of Wisconsin-Madision.

Lawrence, T. B., & Suddaby, R. (2006). Institutions and institutional work. In: S. Clegg, C. Hardy, T. Lawrence & W. Nord (Eds), *The Sage handbook of organization studies* (pp. 215–254). London: Sage.

Leca, B., & Naccache, P. (2006). A critical realist approach to institutional entrepreneurship. *Organization*, *13*(5), 627–651.

Lichtenstein, S., & Slovic, P. (Eds). (2006). *The construction of preference*. Cambridge, UK: Cambridge University Press.

Lippmann, S. (2007). The institutional context of industry consolidation: Radio broadcasting in the United States, 1920–1934. *Social Forces*, *86*(2), 467–495.

Maguire, S., Hardy, C., & Lawrence, T. (2004). Institutional entrepreneurship in emerging fields. *Academy of Management Journal*, *47*, 657–679.

Malesky, E., & Taussig, M. (2009). Out of the gray: The impact of provincial institutions on business formalization in Vietnam. *Journal of East Asian Studies*, *9*(2), 249–290.

March, J. G. (1971). The technology of foolishness. *Civiløkonomen*, *18*(4), 4–12.

March, J. G., & Simon, H. A. (1958). *Organizations*. New York: Wiley.

Meyer, J. W. (2008). Reflections on institutional theories of organizations. In: R. Greenwood, C. Oliver, R. Suddaby & K. Sahlin (Eds), *The Sage handbook of organizational institutionalism* (pp. 790–811). Los Angeles, CA: Sage.

Meyer, J. W., & Rowan, B. (1977). Institutionalized organizations: Formal structure as myth and ceremony. *American Journal of Sociology*, *82*(3), 340–363.

Mutch, A. (2007). Reflexivity and the institutional entrepreneur: A historical exploration. *Organization Studies*, *28*(7), 1123–1140.

Oliver, C. (1991). Strategic responses to institutional processes. *The Academy of Management Review*, *16*(1), 145–179.

Oliver, C. (1992). The antecedents of deinstitutionalization. *Organization Studies*, *13*(4), 563–588.

Palmer, D., Biggart, N. W., & Dick, B. (2008). Is the new institutionalism a theory? In: R. Greenwood, C. Oliver, R. Suddaby & K. Sahlin (Eds), *The Sage handbook of organizational instutitionalism* (pp. 739–768). London: Sage.

Parsons, T. (1956). Suggestions for a sociological approach to the theory of organization, I and II. *Administrative Science Quarterly*, *1*(1/2), 63–85, 225–239.

Pierson, P. (2004). *Politics in time: History, institutions, and social analysis*. Princeton, NJ: Princeton University Press.

Powell, W. W., & Colyvas, J. A. (2008). Microfoundations of institutional theory. In: R. Greenwood, C. Oliver, K. Sahlin & R. Suddaby (Eds), *The Sage handbook of organizational institutionalism*. London: Sage.

Rao, H., Greve, H. R., & Davis, G. F. (2001). Fool's gold: Social proof in the initiation and abandonment of coverage by Wall Street analysts. *Administrative Science Quarterly, 46*(3), 502–526.

Reynolds, P. D., & Curtin, R. (2007). Panel study of entrepreneurial dynamics II: Data overview. *SSRN eLibrary.*

Rindova, V., Barry, D., & Ketchen, J. D. J. (2009). Entrepreneuring as emancipation. *Academy of Management Review, 34*(3), 477–491.

Schneiberg, M. (2005). Combining new institutionalisms: Explaining institutional change in American property insurance. *Sociological Forum, 21*(1), 93–137.

Schneiberg, M., & Clemens, E. S. (2006). The typical tools for the job: Research strategies in institutional analysis. *Sociological Theory, 24*(3), 195–227.

Scott, W. R. (1995). *Institutions and organizations.* Thousand Oaks, CA: Sage Publications.

Scott, W. R. (2001). *Institutions and organizations.* Thousand Oaks, CA: Sage Publications.

Scott, W. R. (2008). Approaching adulthood: The maturing of institutional theory. *Theory and Society, 37,* 427–442.

Sewell, W. H., Jr. (1992). A theory of structure: Duality, agency, and transformation. *American Journal of Sociology, 98*(1), 1–29.

Sine, W. D., & David, R. J. (2003). Environmental jolts, institutional change, and the creation of entrepreneurial opportunity in the U.S. electric power industry. *Research Policy, 32*(2), 185–207.

Sine, W. D., Haveman, H. A., & Tolbert, P. S. (2005). Risky business? Entrepreneurship in the new independent-power sector. *Administrative Science Quarterly, 50*(2), 200–232.

Sine, W. D., & Lee, B. (2009). Tilting at windmills? The environmental movement and the emergence of the U.S. wind energy sector. *Administrative Science Quarterly, 54*(1), 123–155.

Small, M. (2009). *Unanticipated gains: Origins of network inequality in everyday life.* New York: Oxford University Press.

Starr, P. (2004). *The creation of the media: Political origins of modern communication.* New York: Basic Books.

Steier, L. P. (2009). Familial capitalism in global institutional contexts: Implications for corporate governance and entrepreneurship in East Asia. *Asia Pacific Journal of Management, 26*(3), 513–535.

Stevenson, H. H., & Gumpert, D. E. (1985). The heart of entrepreneurship. *Harvard Business Review, 63*(March/April), 85–94.

Taleb, N. N. (2007). *The black swan: The impact of the highly improbable.* New York: Random House.

Tversky, A., & Kahneman, D. (1981). The framing of decisions and the psychology of choice. *Science, 211,* 453–458.

Webb, J. W., Tihanyi, L., Ireland, R. D., & Sirmon, D. G. (2009). You say illegal, I say legitimate: Entrepreneurship in the informal economy. *Academy of Management Review, 34*(3), 492–510.

Weick, K. E. (1979). *The social psychology of organizing.* Reading, MA: Addison-Wesley.

Williamson, O. E. (2000). The new institutional economics: Taking stock, looking ahead. *Journal of Economic Literature, 38*(3), 595–613.

Wilson, R. (2010). For-profit colleges change higher education's landscape. *The Chronicle of Higher Education, 56*(22), 1, 16–19.

PART III

SOCIAL NETWORKS

[6]

ENTREPRENEURSHIP THROUGH SOCIAL NETWORKS

Howard Aldrich
Catherine Zimmer [1]

The formation of new businesses can be conceptualized as a function of opportunity structures and motivated entrepreneurs with access to resources. On the demand side, opportunity structures contain the environmental resources that can be exploited by new businesses as they seek to carve out niches for themselves. On the supply side, motivated entrepreneurs need access to capital and other resources so that they can take advantage of perceived opportunities. A cursory examination of this formulation reveals two essential issues that research on entrepreneurship must address: (1) entrepreneurship is a process and must be viewed in dynamic terms rather than in cross-sectional snapshots; and (2) entrepreneurship requires *linkages or relations* between key components of the process.

Entrepreneurs must establish connections to resources and niches in an opportunity structure, and at some point they must have been affected by relations with socializing agents who motivated them. Stevenson[2] noted that entrepreneurs are driven by opportunity-seeking behavior, not by a simple desire to "invest" resources. By contrast, managers are driven by a concern to invest the resources they manage, treating resources as an end in themselves rather than as a means to an end the way entrepreneurs do. Thus, for entrepreneurs the critical connection is to opportunities, whereas for managers it is to resources.

3

4   ENTREPRENEURSHIP CHARACTERISTICS

Traditional approaches to research on entrepreneurship neglect the relational nature of the process. Instead, they treat entrepreneurs either as atomized decisionmakers, operating as autonomous entities, or as prisoners of their cultural environment, predisposed to entrepreneurship. The approach we take, by contrast, focuses on entrepreneurship as embedded in a social context, channelled and facilitated or constrained and inhibited by people's positions in social networks. Our critique of traditional approaches and our proposed alternative are based on Mark Granovetter's thoughtful and thorough critique of explanations for "economic action."[3]

TRADITIONAL CONCEPTIONS OF ENTREPRENEURS

Traditional views of entrepreneurship have emphasized psychological and economic models, and a special kind of social-cultural model. In this paper we cannot do full justice to each model and so our objective is to highlight the deficiencies of each in dealing with the embedded nature of social behavior. (The embedded nature of social behavior refers to the way in which action is constrained or facilitated because of its social context.)

Following Granovetter, we have identified two undersocialized approaches to entrepreneurship that treat entrepreneurs as though they were "free agents," operating atomistically in an environment where their cognitions and beliefs drive their behavior.

Personality Theories

Personality-based theories of entrepreneurship posit that people's special personal traits make them prone to behaving and succeeding as entrepreneurs.[4] The list of traits is nearly endless but includes internal locus of control, low aversion to risk taking, aggressiveness, ambition, marginality, and a high need for achievement.

Problems with the Personality Approach

Three problems plague personality-based approaches to explaining entrepreneurship: empirical research does not find strong evidence supporting such approaches, similar approaches in the leadership field have made little progress in finding a generic "leadership" trait, and personality-based models underpredict the true extent of entrepreneurship in the United States.

First, rigorous empirical research has had trouble identifying any traits strongly associated with entrepreneurship, as Brockhaus and Horwitz pointed out at our conference. Most research on entrepreneurs suffers from selection bias—picking successful people and not evaluating their attributes against a comparison group. Research using appropriate comparison groups and other controls has uncovered inconsistent and weak relationships between personality characteristics and entrepreneurial behavior.

Second, a companion tradition in psychology studying leadership has foundered on a similar problem: After three decades of study, using a personality-based approach, investigators still have difficulty identifying leaders outside of the group context in which leadership is displayed. A fair summary would be that no one style of leadership is successful all the time—leadership is very much a contingent phenomenon, with different people exhibiting leadership in different situations.[5]

Third, the personality approach substantially underpredicts the extent of entrepreneurship in the United States as it overstates the extent to which entrepreneurs are different from others. Over their lifetimes, many people attempt, or at least strongly consider, setting up their own business. Hundreds of thousands try every year, and tens of thousands succeed in carrying through by establishing businesses that survive and prosper. All these people cannot be deviant, different, or special, possessing personality traits that the rest of us lack. Considering both the proportion of adults expressing an interest in self-employment and the proportion that actually attempt it, well over half the population must possess "entrepreneurial traits"!

Economic, Rational Actor Theories

Neoclassical economic theories view entrepreneurs as rational, isolated decisionmakers. These models assume that, with clear vision of one's goals and all the required information, a person makes a *decision* to enter self-employment. The motivated person scans the market and chooses the niche that will maximize his or her returns

6   ENTREPRENEURSHIP CHARACTERISTICS

on assets invested in the business. Recent modifications of the neo-classical approach take account of cognitive limits to rationality and information processing, recognizing the level of uncertainty involved in most economic decisions. However, even models of bounded rationality and satisficing behavior retain an emphasis on individual decisionmakers and fail to recognize the embedded nature of economic behavior.

Problems with Economic Approaches

Two problems confront investigators choosing economic, rational actor models of entrepreneurship: Cognitive limits on human behavior are much more stringent than typically recognized, and a strong research tradition in social psychology demonstrates the powerful influence of social factors on cognitions and information processing.

First, empirical research on cognition, perception, and decision-making by social psychologists has found that people do not behave the way atomistic models predict they should. A collection of papers edited by Kahneman, Slovic, and Tversky[6] has brought together a vast body of studies showing that people trying to make decisions have problems with (1) judging the representativeness of the information they receive; (2) making proper causal attributions; (3) limiting themselves only to information easily available, rather than searching for the information necessary to make informed decisions; (4) mistaking covariation for causal connections; (5) being overconfident; and (6) wildly overestimating their ability to make multistage inferences. Treated as isolated individuals, people do not measure up to the standards set by atomistic models.

Second, a person who behaved the way atomistic models describe would be an example of social pathology, not a rational decision-maker, as the person would have to reject all social contact. Ever since the original Sherif[7] autokinetic experiments, social-psychologists have been aware of the effect of social influence on decision-making. Persons do not make decisions in a vacuum but rather consult and are subtly influenced by significant others in their environments: family, friends, co-workers, employers, casual acquaintances, and so on.

American farmers are often cited as a classic example of how decisionmakers behave in a true competitive market, atomized and confined to taking individual actions that are futile in the face of unintended collective outcomes. However, the current predicament of American farmers is *not* because they made decisions as atomized individuals over the past decade but rather because they were influenced by their relations with significant others: bankers and commercial credit lenders, agricultural extension agents, and the farm-oriented business press. Farmers borrowed money to expand when they were advised to do so by persons whom they trusted. Paradoxically, we suspect that those farmers who are best off today are precisely those few who *were* most uninformed and socially isolated over the past decade, thus avoiding the influence of expansionist-oriented influentials!

Deterministic, Oversocialized Models of Entrepreneurship

Some theories posit a "propensity to entrepreneurship" based on national origins, culture, or religion. Certain groups are believed to possess beliefs, values, and traditions that predispose them to succeed in business, regardless of where they find themselves. At one time or another, various groups have been labeled this way, including the Jews, Chinese, Japanese, and Lebanese. Such models are deterministic and oversocialized because they presume the existence of a stereotypical standard that all members of the group display, and presume that behaviors are evoked regardless of the group member's situation.

Problems with the Sociocultural Approach

The major problem with this approach is that the groups alleged to possess a propensity to entrepreneurship display their predisposition only under limited, country-specific and historically specific conditions. Prior to immigration, persons originating from alleged entrepreneurial cultures are mostly indistinguishable from others around them, but in their new surroundings they take on entrepreneurial characteristics. For example, (1) Koreans in their native land versus

8   ENTREPRENEURSHIP CHARACTERISTICS

those migrating to Los Angeles, Atlanta, or Chicago[8] (2) Dominicans in their native land versus those migrating to New York City[9] ; and (3) Indians on the Indian subcontinent versus those migrating to England, many of whom come from farming or peasant backgrounds.[10] Research findings strongly suggest that we should attribute the flowering of a group's predisposition to situational, rather than deterministic, conditions.

A strong case is often made for "American exceptionalism," alleging that America is "the land of opportunity" that socializes its citizens into becoming aggressive risk takers. Popular magazines and self-help manuals published today tout the entrepreneurial character of Americans and the rebirth of the entrepreneurial spirit. Were such arguments valid, we would expect the rate of business formation in the United States to be much higher than, say, in Western European nations, and the rate of failure to be lower. In fact, accumulating evidence shows that the rates of business formation and dissolution in Western European nations are much the same as in the United States. Pom Ganguly's research for the British government's Department of Trade and Industry has found that new businesses are being added to the British economy at a rate of about one for every ten existing businesses, and businesses are being dissolved at a rate of about one for every twelve existing businesses.[11] These rates are nearly the same as those found by the U.S. Small Business Administration, using the newly constructed Small Business Data Base.[12] Similar results are emerging for other Western nations.[13] "National character" arguments must give way to models based on an underlying similarity in the economies of all Western advanced industrial societies. Rather than posit overdeterministic models, we should turn our attention to the situational conditions under which entrepreneurs enter business.

THE EMBEDDEDNESS OF ENTREPRENEURIAL BEHAVIOR

As an alternative to under- and oversocialized models of entrepreneurship, we propose a perspective that views entrepreneurship as embedded in networks of continuing social relations. Within complex networks of relationships, entrepreneurship is facilitated or constrained by linkages between aspiring entrepreneurs, resources,

and opportunities. We take a population perspective[14] on organizational formation and persistence, recognizing the interaction of
chance, necessity, and purpose in all social action.

The Population Perspective

From the population perspective, net additions to populations of
businesses reflect the operation of four evolutionary processes:
variation, selection, retention, and diffusion, and the struggle for
existence.[15]

Any kind of change is a *variation*, and the evolutionary process
begins with variations that may be intentional or blind. Some entrepreneurs are driven by a single-mindedness of purpose as they attempt to adapt their plans to environmental exigencies. Other entrepreneurs stumble onto opportunities and resources by chance, perhaps never intending to create a new enterprise until an accidental
conjuncture of events presents itself. The process of organizational
creation depends only on the occurrence of attempted variations and
not on the level of ambitions, foresight, or intelligence people bring
to the process. (Of course, whether the attempts succeed is another
matter.) The higher the frequency of variations, whatever their
sources, the greater the chances of net additions to organizational
populations.

Some variations—attempts at forming new enterprises—prove
more beneficial than others in acquiring resources in a competitive
environment and are thus positively selected. *Selection* criteria are
set through the operation of market forces, competitive pressures,
the logic of internal organizational structuring, and other forces
usually beyond the control of individual entrepreneurs. Organizations founded through maladaptive variations in technology, managerial competence, or other attributes are likely to draw fewer resources from their environments and are therefore more likely to fail.
Over time, populations of enterprises are more apt to be characterized by the attributes of surviving organizations than by the attributes of those that failed.

What is preserved through *retention* is the technological and managerial competence that all enterprises in a population use, collectively, to exploit the resources of their environment. The survival of
a particular business is not terribly consequential to the survival of

10   ENTREPRENEURSHIP CHARACTERISTICS

the population as a whole, as the total population's survival depends on the total pool of technological and managerial competence. The variations possessed by a particular enterprise contribute to the total pool but do not determine its collective fate.

The competencies of a population are held by the entrepreneurs and their employees. Retained variations are passed on, with more or less variation, from surviving entrepreneurs to those who follow and from old to new employees, some of whom may leave to form their own businesses. Linkages between enterprises facilitate the *diffusion* of beneficial variations, whereas isolated organizations contribute little or nothing to future generations. Not all variations are diffused to new entrepreneurs (because of hostility, pique, mistakes, stupidity, unwillingness to learn, etc.), introducing a large element of uncertainty into the process.

A competitive *struggle over resources and opportunities* occurs, fueling the selection process. Sometimes opportunities are so diverse and resources so abundant that a high proportion of entrepreneurs are successful and the business population grows rapidly. In new industries, first movers have substantial advantages and enjoy rapid growth. As industries evolve, however, or resources become more scarce, shakeouts occur and competition increases the mortality rate, with populations stagnating or declining.

Using evolutionary principles, the population perspective explains how particular forms of organizations come to exist in specific kinds of environments. A specific environment constitutes an opportunity structure containing a resource pool uniquely suited to organizational forms that adapt to it or help shape it. A form well-adapted to a specific environment is probably not the fittest form imaginable and is vulnerable to entrepreneurial successes in founding new organizations with more adapted forms. Nonetheless, it is tolerably fit and probably more fit than previous failed forms.

The population perspective makes minimal assumptions about the cognitive capabilities of humans as information-processors and renders practically irrelevant any speculations about entrepreneurial personalities. People become entrepreneurs through the conjuncture of the four processes outlined above, and entrepreneurship takes on meaning only within the context of these processes. People are intentional or purposeful in their actions, but social conditions are such that we usually cannot attribute organizational formation to any particular, identifiable, intentional act or set of acts.

Environments, as opportunity structures, are diverse, uncertain, and imperfectly perceived, and it is seldom true that a particular individual will both have an accurate view and be aware of it. People are limited by bounded rationality, suffer from limited or biased information and poor communication, and are subject to processes of social influence and reconstructions of reality. Hence, comprehensive explanations of entrepreneurship must include the social context of behavior, especially the social relationships through which people obtain information, resources, and social support.

The Characteristics of Social Networks

The starting point for studying entrepreneurship through social networks is a relation or transaction between two people. Relations may be treated as containing: (1) communication content, or the passing of information from one person to another; (2) exchange content, or the goods and services two persons can exchange; and (3) normative content, or the expectations persons have of one another because of some special characteristic or attribute. The strength of ties depends on the level, frequency, and reciprocity of relationships between persons, and varies from weak to strong. Most research has focused on single content types of relations, and so there is a paucity of information about the effects of types of relations on one another and on the durability of relations composed of different combinations of relations.

Relations between pairs of individuals—entrepreneurs, customers, suppliers, creditors, inventors, and so forth—whatever their content and whatever a person's social role, could be extended and persons included in ways that would expand a unit of analysis indefinitely. A central interest of network theorists, therefore, has been to find ways to set meaningful limits to the scope of a social unit under investigation. The concept of role-set, action-set, and network provide us with some tools for setting such boundaries.

A *role-set* consists of all those persons with whom a focal person has direct relations. Usually the links are single-step ties, but indirect links can be considered by specifying how many steps removed an interacting person can be from the central focal person and still be treated as in the set. We have borrowed the concept of a role-set from Merton, who defined it as "that complement of role relation-

12   ENTREPRENEURSHIP CHARACTERISTICS

ships which persons have by virtue of occupying a particular social status."[16] Merton gave an example of the status of public school teacher and its role-set, relating the teacher to pupils, colleagues, school principal and superintendent, board of education, and professional organizations of teachers. For entrepreneurs, we could think of partners, suppliers, customers, venture capitalists, bankers, other creditors, distributors, trade associations, and family members.

 One of the interesting issues highlighted by the role-set concept concerns conflict produced by divergent expectations from members of an entrepreneur's role-set. Entrepreneurs stand at the center of potentially conflicting demands and expectations from their role-sets, such as between expectations from spouses that some time will be spent at home versus demands from partners that weekends be used to catch up on paperwork. Business survival may depend upon the strategies entrepreneurs adopt to resolve such conflicts.

An *action-set* is a group of people who have formed a temporary alliance for a limited purpose. The concept of action-set has been used by anthropoligists, who have found a specific action or behavior, rather than status, helpful as a frame of reference in studying social change. Rather than the ego-centered analysis of role-set studies, action-set research examines the purposeful behavior of an entire aggregate of persons. Action-sets may have their own internal division of labor, behavioral norms vis-à-vis other persons, or clearly defined principles for the recruitment of new members. An action-set may be centered around the behavior of one individual, as in consortia of high-tech firms led by the enterprise with the most market power, but that is an empirical question.

A *network* is defined as the totality of all persons connected by a certain type of relationship and is constructed by finding the ties between all persons in a population under study, regardless of how it is organized into role-sets and action-sets. Given a bounded system, investigators identify all the links between people within the boundaries. Network analysis assumes that a network constrains or facilitates the action of people and action sets and thus is more than the sum of the individual links that comprise it.

Critical Dimensions of Networks

Before demonstrating the application of network concepts to the explanation of entrepreneurship, let us briefly review three dimensions of networks that are useful in social analysis: density, reachability, and centrality.

The *density* of a network refers to the extensiveness of ties between persons and is measured by comparing the total number of ties present to the potential number that would occur if everyone in the network were connected to everyone else. The simplest measures of density just consider the presence or absence of a tie, but more sophisticated measures take account of the strength of ties.

Reachability refers to the presence of a path between two persons, of whatever distance. Persons can be ranked by how many intermediaries a path travels before one person is indirectly linked with another. An example of the use of indirect ties in connecting distant individuals was provided by Travers and Milgram in their experimental study of communication channels, referred to as the small-world phenomenon.[17] Arbitrarily chosen persons in Nebraska were given letters to send to a target person in Boston, with the stipulation that the letters had to be channeled only through persons known to the senders. Out of 296 starts, 64 letters reached the target person, with the mean number of intermediaries being 5.2. The importance of linking pins was shown in that 48 percent of the completed chains passed through three central individuals before reaching the target.

The *centrality* of a person in a network is determined by two factors: (1) the total distance from a focal person to all other persons, and (2) the total number of other persons a focal person can reach. (For a comprehensive review of the centrality concept, and alternative definitions, see an article by Linton Freeman.[18]) The more persons that can be reached and the shorter the aggregate distance to these persons, the higher the centrality of a focal person. Persons who have extensive ties to different parts of a network can play a key role in entrepreneurial processes. Persons playing central roles may have ties to more than one action-set or other subset of a network, and they can serve three important functions: (1) they serve as communication channels between distant persons; (2) they may provide brokerage services linking third parties to one another by transferring resources; and (3) if they are dominant or high-status individuals, they may serve as role models for others or may use their position to direct the behavior of action-sets or individuals.

14   ENTREPRENEURSHIP CHARACTERISTICS

NETWORKS AND ENTREPRENEURSHIP

We turn now to four applications of network concepts to the study of entrepreneurship. The first application focuses on the effect of social forces that increase the density of networks, and the second application focuses on the role of "brokers" and other persons or organizations that increase reachability in networks. The third application applies Granovetter's discussion of the importance of linkage diversity to the question of which positions in networks are most likely to produce entrepreneurs.[19] The fourth application focuses on the importance of the social resources embedded in entrepreneurs' networks.

Increasing Density through Raising the Salience of Group Boundaries and Identity

Conditions that raise the salience of group boundaries and identity, leading persons to form new social ties and action-sets, increase the likelihood of entrepreneurial attempts by persons within that group and raise the probability of success. Increasing density can operate at two levels. First, at a local level, increasing density may lead to coalition formation between persons, thus enhancing their collective action capability. Repeated action-set formation, in turn, enhances the institutional infrastructure facilitating entrepreneurship. Second, if density increases not just at a local level but also at the system level—such as for an entire ethnic group or as a result of infrastructural development—then everyone is in a position to collect the combinations of resources necessary for successful ventures. The advantages of local action-sets would thus be eliminated and the entire group would have an advantage over outsiders.

Opportunities are irrelevant unless taken advantage of, and people vary widely in their ability to seize opportunities. Auster and Aldrich, Bonacich, Light, and others have argued that the possibility of exploiting opportunities is linked to a group's internal organizing capacity.[20] Ethnic groups with a high level of self-organization—a densely connected network—provide co-ethnics with a collective capacity for organizing new ventures. Indeed, the most salient feature of early business efforts by immigrant groups is their dependence on an ethnic community for support. Support is provided at two levels: informal support from the friends and relatives of aspiring business owners, and support from the larger network of ethnic institutions, including religious associations, fraternal organizations, and other small businesses. Strong community support, based on ethnic ties, allows small firms some degree of independence from the host community.[21]

Immigration, especially chain migration, may establish densely connected communities of co-ethnics who cooperate when confronted with host hostility.[22] The early opposition towards Japanese immigrants on the west coast of the United States by labor unions, who feared that Asians would replace them at lower wages, obstructed Japanese entry into the mainstream economy. In response, the Japanese pooled their resources and ultimately captured a significant portion of California's agricultural sector until their internment during World War II. The strong ethnic solidarity formed by union and public hostility generated ethnic networks that supported subsequent generations.[23]

Mutual aid, in the form of capital, credit, information, training opportunities, and the regulation of competition, gave Chinese and Japanese immigrants to the United States a strong base on which to develop small business. In contrast, black migrants from the South to Northern cities after World War I and continuing into the 1950s had few collective organizational traditions to follow, except for religion.[24]

Strong ties carry with them a history of past dealings in or out of a business setting that can form a basis for trust. Whereas banks and other formal institutions outside an ethnic group may have little or no objective credit history for an aspiring entrepreneur, within the group strong ties keep alive the memory of past experiences from which to infer trustworthiness, and these relationships may carry strong expectations of trust.[25] Another strength of strong ties is that "strong ties have greater motivation to be of assistance and are typically more easily available."[26]

Mutual benefit associations, cooperative housing and buying arrangements, joint capital raising activities, and other collective actions provide support for potential entrepreneurs. Recent groups in the United States who have followed this model include Cubans in Miami; Dominicans in New York City's garment trade; Koreans in Los Angeles's liquor, wig, and other retail stores; and Indians in Cali-

16   ENTREPRENEURSHIP CHARACTERISTICS

fornia's motel business. Most small firms are capitalized from the owner's savings, but other sources of funds are often sought. The Chinese *hui*, the Japanese *ko* and *tanomoshi*, and the Korean *kye* — rotating credit associations clothed in their respective cultural traditions—have provided simple mechanisms for immigrants to raise business capital.[27] In these cases, social conditions have raised the salience of group boundaries and identity, leading persons to form stronger ties with one another and often to the creation of effective action-sets.

Increasing Reachability and Connectedness Facilitate the Spread of Information and Resources in Networks

Broker roles are central positions in networks, resulting from people's attempts to minimize their transactions costs. Such positions exist because of their function of linking persons having complementary interests, transferring information, and otherwise facilitating the interests of persons not directly connected to one another. Many entrepreneurs enjoy a broker's position, and indeed Schumpeter's classic definition of an entrepreneur as someone who combines old resources in novel ways seems to equate the entrepreneurial with the broker role. However, we are interested in brokers who are not themselves entrepreneurs but who facilitate the actions of entrepreneurs. (Also, we believe many entrepreneurs do not themselves enjoy the advantages of a broker role.) For example, venture capitalists are as important for their broker role as for the funds they provide to struggling entrepreneurs because they bring together technical experts, management consultants, and financial planners to supplement the entrepreneur's limited knowledge and experience.

To illustrate the importance of broker roles, let us consider an example of a population divided into two major types of social roles—such as entrepreneurs and venture capitalists—where some method of interrole communication is desired by persons in each role. Communication is possible if all entrepreneurs are directly linked to all venture capitalists, thus creating a very complex set of relations. The total number of relations established would equal the number of entrepreneurs times the number of venture capitalists, assuming a link is established in each direction. If there were five entrepreneurs and five venture capitalists, the total number of links would be twenty-five.

Each new person added to either side would increase the number of required links linearly (e.g., if another entrepreneur is added, five more links are created). If another person were added to both sides, the number of linkages would increase as the square of the number added (e.g., if one pair is added, the number of ties jumps from twenty-five to thirty-six). In a large population, the maintenance of such a large set of linkages would be extremely costly, especially if the number of entrepreneurs and venture capitalists were increasing rapidly.

The evolutionary model from the population perspective would predict that any innovation or random variation that created a less costly solution to the problem would be quickly selected. Any cost-saving variation would give the entrepreneur using it a relative advantage, and thus a selective survival advantage, over other entrepreneurs in a resource-scarce environment. Similarly, any new organizational form that enabled entrepreneurs and venture capitalists to communicate with one another more quickly would be in a niche with an initially overwhelming advantage, as there would be a strong demand for its services.

If an intermediary or broker organization were created, linking entrepreneurs and venture capitalists—such as venture capital "fairs" or the joint seminars described by David Brophy[28]—the number of connections in the network would be reduced to the number of entrepreneurs plus the number of venture capitalists. That is, five plus five, joined by a central organization, rather than the five times five situation previously. Each person or organization would have one link to the broker, and the process of sorting out the various messages and information channels between them would be internalized by the broker. This is a complex task, but the broker specializes in the role and only a fraction of the ties would have to be active at any one time. Once introduced into a population, we would expect this function to persist, and the concept of the broker should become part of our industrial culture, passed on via imitation and tradition.

Voluntary associations, trade associations, public agencies, and other social units increase the probability of people making connections with one another. Rates of entrepreneurship should be higher in highly organized populations (i.e., populations with a high orga-

18   ENTREPRENEURSHIP CHARACTERISTICS

nizing capacity). The complex pattern of social organization described by Everett Rogers and Judith Larson in their book *Silicon Valley Fever* illustrates the synergistic effects of brokers, central meeting points—such as well-known "watering holes" and restaurants—and family and friendship networks that supported the high start-up rate in the Silicon Valley.[29]

Social networks build slowly, and thus it could be years before an area reaches a density threshold where reachability and hence entrepreneurship is facilitated. Formal studies are lacking, but it is our impression that the time to maturity for the Silicon Valley and the Route 128 complex in Boston was several decades. Accordingly, we expect the Research Triangle of North Carolina to age another decade or so before any significant entrepreneurial activity occurs. At present, the spin-off and new start-up rate appears very low.

The Importance of Diversity in an Entrepreneur's Network: Too Much Solidarity Stifles the Entrepreneurial Soul

Mark Granovetter has developed an argument linking the diversity of ties in which a person is implicated to the scope of opportunities open to that person.[30]

> The argument asserts that our acquaintances ("weak ties") are less likely to be socially involved with one another than are our close friends ("strong ties"). Thus, the set of people made up of any individual and his or her acquaintances will constitute a low-density network (one in which many of the possible relational lines are absent), whereas the set consisting of the same individual and his or her *close* friends will be densely knit (many of the possible lines present).[31]

A potential entrepreneur may have a small group of friends he or she knows well, each of whom knows the others quite well. He or she may also have many casual acquaintances, each of whom also has a circle of close friends. These close friends of his casual acquaintances are unlikely to be known to the potential entrepreneur, and thus his or her only possible ties to them are through the casual acquaintance. The weak tie between the potential entrepreneur and his or her acquaintance is therefore "not merely a trivial acquaintance tie, but rather a crucial bridge between the two densely knit clumps of close friends. . . . It follows that individuals with few weak ties will be deprived of information from distance parts of the social system and will be confined to the provincial news and views of their close friends."[32]

Research in the Boston area by Granovetter has documented that lack of access to the information provided by weak ties puts people at a competitive disadvantage in the labor market, as such people will obtain only redundant information from close acquaintances, who travel in the same circles as the job seeker.[33] People with a more diverse role set, connected to distant others via brokers or other intermediaries, will have access to a wider range of information.

Following the logic of this argument, entrepreneurs are more likely to be found in positions whose centrality is high and which are connected to lots of diverse information sources. Entrepreneurs activate their weak ties for at least two purposes: to gain access to business information and to attract customers. First, information about new business locations, potential markets for goods and services, sources of capital or potential investors, innovations, and standard business practice is likely to be spread widely among individuals. Other things being equal, someone with a small role-set of overlapping ties is at a disadvantage when competing for information with someone who has a large role-set of divergent ties. There is also a disadvantage we might call the "weakness of strong ties," wherein those persons with whom we are tightly linked lead to the introduction of extraneous socio-emotional content into information exchanges, clouding their meaning.

Second, entrepreneurs ask both their strong and weak ties to become customers. Then, in turn, these new customers may tell their strong and weak ties about the new venture. It is the weak ties who can expand the pool of customers; strong ties deliver redundant information.

Perhaps these ideas are a way of rethinking the traditional relation posited between "marginality" and entrepreneurship. Marginality is important but as a characteristic of the social structure, not as a personal characteristic of entrepreneurs. Instead, marginality refers to the weak ties potential entrepreneurs have to diverse information sources and to potential customers, putting them in positions to capitalize on opportunities that remain unknown to the less marginal person.

20   ENTREPRENEURSHIP CHARACTERISTICS

Nine studies reviewed by Granovetter have tested the strength of the weak ties argument and have provided partial support for it.[34] None of these studies, however, focused on entrepreneurs or on persons classified as self-employed. The theoretical importance of weak ties would be broadened by specific research on how small businesses are founded and how they subsequently fare.

The Importance of Social Resources: It is not just What You Know but Who You Know

Lin and his colleagues have added a component to the strength of ties literature.[35] In his theory of instrumental action, Lin suggested that in a hierarchical social structure, a person in a "position nearer to the top of the structure has greater access to and control of valued resources not only because more valued resources are intrinsically attached to the position, but also because of the position's greater accessibility to positions at other (primarily lower) rankings."[36] He defined social resources as valued resources that are accessible through ties with others. Therefore, all weak ties are not equally useful for acquiring social resources. Weak ties to those contacts with the most social resources—that is, contacts as high in the social hierarchy as possible—will provide the greatest access to social resources. Lin's research on the status attainment of job seekers has weakly confirmed the social resources argument, but his research must be replicated before we can place high confidence in his results.

Extending the argument, successful entrepreneurs will be found in positions with weak ties to people who are in positions to provide timely and accurate information, to people with the resources to act as a customers, and/or to people with resources to invest.

Entrepreneurship is a social role, embedded in a social context. Investigators cannot treat entrepreneurs in isolation as autonomous decisionmakers or lump them together with others with similar social characteristics, without regard to context. It is the effects of social networks in facilitating or inhibiting the activities of potential entrepreneurs.

ENTREPRENEURSHIP THROUGH SOCIAL NETWORKS　　21

NOTES TO CHAPTER 1

1. We are deeply indebted to Valerie Haines and Peter Marsden, colleagues at the University of North Carolina, for their comments and suggestions.
2. Howard Stevenson, "A Perspective on Entrepreneurship," Harvard Business School, No. 9-384-131, November 1984.
3. Mark Granovetter, "Economic Action and Social Structure: A Theory of Embeddedness," *American Journal of Sociology* (forthcoming); see also Ronald S. Burt, "Tertius Gaudens, Structurally Autonomous Entrepreneur," Columbia University, 1983. (Unpublished.)
4. See Robert J. Brockhaus and Pamela S. Horwitz, "The Psychology of the Entrepreneur," in this volume.
5. Richard Hall, *Organizations: Structure and Process* (Englewood Cliffs, N.J.: Prentice-Hall, 1982).
6. Daniel Kahneman, Paul Slovic, and Amos Tversky, *Judgment under Uncertainty: Heuristics and Biases* (New York: Cambridge University Press, 1982).
7. M. Sherif, "A Study of Some Social Factors in Perception," *Archives on Psychology* 187 (1935). The autokinetic effect is a visual illusion—a fixed pinpoint of light shown to subjects in a totally darkened room appears to move, smoothly or erratically. Subjects' judgments of the extent to which the light moves are strongly influenced by the reports of others in the room—typically, persons who are confederates of the experimenter.
8. Pyong Gap Min and Charles Jaret, "Korean Immigrants' Success in Small Business: Some Cultural Explanations," Department of Sociology, Georgia State University, August 1984. (Unpublished.)
9. Roger Waldinger, "Immigrant Enterprise and Labor Market Structure," Working paper, Joint Center for Urban Studies, MIT and Harvard University, 1982.
10. Howard Aldrich, John Cater, Trevor Jones, and Dave McEvoy, "From Periphery to Peripheral: The South Asian Petite Bourgeoisie in England," in Ida Harper Simpson and Richard Simpson, eds., *Research in the Sociology of Work*, Vol. 2 (Greenwich, Conn.: JAI Press, 1983), pp. 1-32.
11. Pom Ganguly, "Births and Deaths of Firms in the UK in 1980," *British Business* 29 (January 29-February 5, 1982).
12. U.S. Small Business Administration, *The State of Small Business* (Washington, D.C.: USGPO, 1984).
13. Robert Brockhaus, personal communication,
14. See Howard Aldrich, *Organizations and Environments* (Englewood Cliffs, N.J.: Prentice-Hall, 1979); and Bill McKelvey and Howard Aldrich, "Populations, Natural Selection, and Applied Organizational Science," *Administrative Science Quarterly* 28: 1 (March 1983): 101-28.

22   ENTREPRENEURSHIP CHARACTERISTICS

15.   See McKelvey and Aldrich, "Populations"; and Howard Aldrich, Bill McKelvey, and Dave Ulrich, "Design Strategy from the Population Perspective," *Journal of Management* 10: 1 (Spring 1984): 68–86.

16.   Robert Merton, "The Role-Set: Problems in Sociological Theory," *British Journal of Sociology* 8 (1957): 106–20.

17.   Jeffrey Travers and Stanley Milgram, "An Experimental Study of the Small World Problem," *Sociometry* 32 (1969): 425–43.

18.   Linton C. Freeman, "Centrality in Social Networks: Conceptual Clarification," *Social Networks* 1 (1979): 215–39.

19.   Mark Granovetter, "The Strength of Weak Ties," *American Journal of Sociology* 78: 6 (May 1973): 1360–80.

20.   See Ellen Auster and Howard Aldrich, "Small Business Vulnerability, Ethnic Enclaves, and Ethnic Enterprise," in Robin Ward and R. Jenkins, eds., *Ethnic Communities in Business: Strategies for Economic Survival* (New York: Cambridge University Press), pp. 39–54; Edna Bonacich, "A Theory of Middleman Minorities," *American Sociological Review* 38 (October 1973): 583–94; and Ivan Light, *Ethnic Enterprise in America: Business and Welfare among Chinese, Japanese, and Blacks* (Berkeley, Calif.: University of California Press, 1972).

21.   Kenneth Wilson and Alexandro Portes, "Immigrant Enclaves: An Analysis of the Labor Market Experiences of Cubans in Miami," *American Journal of Sociology* 86: 2 (September 1980): 295–319.

22.   Bonacich, "A Theory of Middleman Minorities."

23.   Edna Bonacich and John Modell, *The Economic Basis of Ethnic Solidarity* (Berkeley, Calif.: University of California Press, 1980).

24.   See E. Franklin Frazier, *Black Bourgeoisie* (New York: The Free Press, 1957), and Nathan Glazer and Daniel Patrick Moynihan, *Beyond the Melting Pot* (Cambridge, Mass.: MIT Press, 1963).

25.   Light, *Ethnic Enterprise*.

26.   Granovetter, "Economic Action" (forthcoming), p. 14.

27.   Mark Granovetter, "The Strength of Weak Ties: A Network Theory Revisited," in Peter V. Marsden and Nan Lin, eds., *Social Structure and Network Analysis* (Beverly Hills, Calif.: Sage, 1982), p. 113.

28.   David Brophy, "Venture Capital Research," in this volume.

29.   Everett Rogers and Judith Larson, *Silicon Valley Fever* (New York: Basic Books, 1984).

30.   See Granovetter, "The Strength of Weak Ties," (1973); Mark Granovetter, *Getting a Job: A Study of Contacts and Careers* (Cambridge, Mass.: Harvard University Press, 1974); Granovetter, "The Strength of Weak Ties," 1982; and Granovetter, "Economic Action" (forthcoming).

31.   Granovetter, "The Strength of Weak Ties," 1982, p. 105.

32,   Ibid., p. 106.

33. Granovetter, *Getting A Job*. Scott Boorman has suggested that Grano-vetter's findings may apply only when jobs are scarce. Strong ties may well be more valuable in other labor market conditions, such as when one needs to have influence exercised on one's behalf. See Scott A. Boorman, "A Cominatorial Optimization Model for Transmission of Job Information through Contact Networks," *The Bell Journal of Economics* 6: 1 (Spring 1975): 216–49.

34. Granovetter, "The Strength of Weak Ties," 1982.

35. See, for example, Nan Lin, W.M. Ensel, and J.C. Vaughn, "Social Resources and Strength of Ties: Structural Factors in Occupational Status Attainment," *American Sociological Review* 46: 4 (August 1981): 393–405; and Nan Lin, J.C. Vaughn, and W.M. Ensel, "Social Resources and Occupational Status Attainment," *Social Forces* 60: 59 (June 1981): 1162–81.

36. Nan Lin, "Social Resources and Instrumental Action," in Marsden and Lin, *Social Structure and Network Analysis*, p. 131.

[7]

EXECUTIVE FORUM

PERSONAL AND
EXTENDED NETWORKS
ARE CENTRAL TO THE
ENTREPRENEURIAL PROCESS

PAOLA DUBINI
Università Commerciale "L. Bocconi," Milan, Italy

HOWARD ALDRICH
University of North Carolina, Chapel Hill

F ROM A PRACTITIONER'S VIEWPOINT, NETWORKING IS A USEFUL TOOL FOR ENTRE-
preneurs who wish to enlarge their span of action and save time. Admonitions to
"network," however, may not be enough. "Networking" may result in a time-consuming
and fruitless effort, and leave potential partners highly frustrated (Turati 1988). From a
theoretical point of view, it thus becomes necessary to specify the conditions under which
networking contributes to business effectiveness, and to link it to the contingencies facing
firms.

In this executive forum, we propose a way of generating networking strategies for
entrepreneurs. First, we introduce general network concepts by considering personal networks; thus, we take the role set of individual entrepreneurs as the unit of analysis. Second,
we discuss the aggregation of personal networks into extended networks, which in turn can
be analyzed within firms (intra-firm relations) or between firms (interfirm relations).

We define entrepreneurship as "the process by which individuals—either on their own
or inside organizations—pursue opportunities without regard to the resources they currently
control" (Stevenson and Jarillo 1989). Networks are patterned relationships between individuals, groups, and organizations.

Entrepreneurs, in contrast to managers, thrive on unsettling and turbulent conditions.
Their greatest gains are made when discontinuities and gaps appear in society's economic
fabric, making traditional modes of doing business or traditional products and services
obsolete. Even under normal conditions, hidden opportunities for linking new products or
services to untapped markets may be available, if only entrepreneurs could obtain information
about where they lie. Mobilizing resources to pursue opportunities requires entrepreneurial

Address correspondence to Professor Howard Aldrich, Department of Sociology, University of North
Carolina at Chapel Hill, CB 3210 Hamilton Hall, Chapel Hill, NC 27599-3210.

The authors wish to acknowledge William B. Gartner, José Carlos Jarillo, and Gianni Lorenzoni for their
comments and insights.

Journal of Business Venturing 6, 305–313
© 1991 Elsevier Science Publishing Co., Inc., 655 Avenue of the Americas, New York, NY 10010

0883-9026/91/$3.50

contacts, knowledge, and confidence. Mobilizing resources also involves asking others to raise money, labor, and effort for a venture with an uncertain future. Entrepreneurship is thus inherently a networking activity.

The organization and management theory literature usually makes a sharp distinction between individuals, organizations, and environments. These units are demarcated by assuming strong breaks between each, with people acting "within" organizations, and organizations acting "within" environments. By contrast, a network approach emphasizes the threads of continuity linking actions across a field of action that includes individuals, organizations, and environments as a totality. Organizations are *in* environments, and environments are *in* organizations, penetrating them through the personal networks of boundary spanners and other members (Aldrich and Herker 1977; Weick 1979). Even though "networking" is used as a verb, network concepts themselves depict only a static pattern of relations. Adding *entrepreneurship* to the equation compels theorists to include *process* in their framework, as entrepreneurs and firms pursue opportunities opened to them, or withheld, because of their network positions.

TWO TYPES OF NETWORKS

In theory, any model of entrepreneurial networking should weave a seamless web in which the distinctions between individuals, organizations, and networks are blurred or even ignored. In practice, we have found it necessary to create a language for keeping track of individuals and their context, in order to discipline our thinking when we shift between individuals, groups, organizations and environments. Thus, we distinguish between personal networks—centered on a focal individual—and extended networks, focusing on collectives.

To take a simple example, an entrepreneur's personal tie to a friend not involved in his business may, by chance, lead to contacts with persons with information or resources his firm needs. Searching for these resources via normal organizational channels might cost more time or funds than the organization could spare. So, if the right connections are successfully made across the firm's boundaries into the extended network, two major constraints are cut: time and money (Melin 1987). Other costs related to the assembling of required resources may also be cut if links to them are present within personal or extended networks. In turn, the company itself may become network-oriented by incorporating network concepts in its structure and operating mechanisms, perhaps by creating strategic alliances (Lorenzoni 1983).

NETWORK PROPERTIES

The starting point for studying entrepreneurship through networks is a relation or transaction between two people. Relations between pairs of individuals—entrepreneurs, customers, suppliers, creditors, investors—whatever their content and whatever a person's social role, could be extended indefinitely. A central interest of network analysts, therefore, has been finding ways of setting meaningful limits to the scope of a social unit under discussion. The concepts of *personal network* and *extended network* provide us with some tools for setting such boundaries.

Some aspects of personal and extended networks are embedded in social structures relatively impervious to human intervention in the short term, but many other aspects are readily influenced by personal action. We thus assume that social networks are, in a large measure, enacted by their participants. Accordingly, we can treat networking like any other social skill that can be learned, involving making contacts, building relationships, and activating linkages (Grieco and Hosking 1987; Johannisson 1987).

Personal Networks

A *personal network*, or role set, consists of all those persons with whom an entrepreneur has direct relations (or, for some purposes, indirect relations via direct relations). For entrepreneurs, we could think of partners, suppliers, customers, venture capitalists, bankers, other creditors, distributors, trade associations, and family members.

The simplest kind of personal network includes direct ties linking entrepreneurs with persons with whom they have direct dealings. Typically, these are persons whom entrepreneurs meet on a face-to-face basis, and from whom they obtain services, advice, and moral support.

When we use the term "networking" as a verb, describing entrepreneurial behavior, we are usually thinking of special kinds of relations within personal networks—a network built on *strong ties*, relations entrepreneurs can "count on." By contrast, *weak ties* are superficial or casual, and people typically have little emotional investment in them. Brief examination of this idea gets at the heart of why networks are important for entrepreneurs.

"Networking" is often mentioned because people feel the need to distinguish "networking" behavior from ordinary business behavior. Picture behavior at two extremes: first, one-of-a-kind, quick and dirty, market-mediated transactions between people who never expect to see each other again (e.g., buying a magazine at a corner newsstand in St. Louis); and second, contact between two persons who expect to see each other frequently and who are in a relation "for the long term" (e.g., taking a machine-tool shop owner to lunch in Philadelphia to discuss specifications for a new piece of equipment).

The first kind of behavior is just a straightforward pragmatic transaction between people whose personal characteristics count for very little. It does the job, in most circumstances, and can be an efficient way of doing business. However, there are three problems associated with market-mediated transactions: opportunism, uncertainty, and exit.

First, *opportunism* is always a possibility. The other party, expecting never to deal with you again, may engage in "self-disbelieved" statements of competence or performance (Williamson 1981). Second, the problem of opportunism is heightened under conditions of *uncertainty*. It may be impossible to predict all the conditions under which a contract will have to be carried out, or to know precisely all the specifications a piece of equipment will have to meet. Third, when problems crop up, the other party may simply *exit* the situation, leaving you with a loss (Hirschman 1972).

"Networking," by contrast, refers to the expectation that many times both parties are investing in a long-term relation. Consider three benefits that follow from creating a social context in which people expect to deal with each other frequently over an extended period: trust, predictability, and voice, rather than exit.

First, regardless of what popular fiction says about business, *trust* is an important component of business dealings. Business would grind to a halt if parties to transactions always treated each other the way they are portrayed in works of fiction. Trust is enhanced—purely through self-interest—under conditions in which people feel that there is a good chance of dealing with each other again.

Second, *predictability* is increased when long-term relations are established. The inherent uncertainty in a situation is not reduced, but what *is* reduced is the uncertainty about whether the other party will do something to assist you when things do not go according to plan. Uncertainty is also reduced when someone's network contacts tell them where to go for assistance.

Third, people are more likely to use *voice* rather than exit in response to problems when relations are implicitly long-term. *Voice* means making one's complaints known and negotiating over them, rather than sneaking silently away.

Thus, "networking" with one's direct ties to turn them into strong ones is first and foremost a way of overcoming some of the liabilities inherent in purely market-like transactions with other people. "*Networking" involves expanding one's circle of trust.* In network terms, relations of trust are *strong ties,* as opposed to casual acquaintances, who are *weak ties.*

Trust is the basic element determining the solidity of the link and the permanence of the tie, reducing the risks for the involved parties. Mutual behavior is highly predictable and both parties are initially driven by a strong opportunism, which evolves into shared trust. Relationships evolve in a slow process, starting with minor transactions in which little risk is involved and thus little trust is required, and continuing on through transactions in which both partners can prove their trustworthiness. The accumulation of such acts enables the parties to expand their relation and eventually engage in major transactions (Blau 1964).

The *diversity* of entrepreneurs' networks is crucial to the scope of opportunities open to them. People with whom we have weak ties, such as casual acquaintances, are less likely to know one another than are persons with whom we have strong ties, such as close friends. Therefore, a personal network made up of a person's direct and indirect *weak* ties will be a low-density network, with many persons unknown to each other, whereas a personal network made up of a person's *strong* ties will be a high-density network, with most persons known to each other (Granovetter 1973). Of course, most personal networks will include a mix of weak and strong ties, and it is the relative balance of weak to strong that is crucial.

An entrepreneur may have a small group of friends she knows well, each of whom knows the others quite well. Information known to one person in this group is rapidly diffused to the others, and the entrepreneur learns little from talking to one friend beyond what she already knows from talking to another. She may also have many casual acquaintances, each of whom also has a circle of close friends. These close friends of her casual acquaintances are unlikely to be known to her, and thus her only possible ties to them are through the casual acquaintance. Thus, if these strangers have information of value, her only possible access to the information will be through weak ties.

Individuals with few *weak* ties "will be deprived of information from distant parts of the social system and will be confined to the provincial news and views of their close friends" (Granovetter 1982, p. 106). *Alternatively,* having enough diversity in one's *strong* ties, such that one's immediate network includes strongly linked people who have ties to very different parts of the social system, could provide information channels otherwise unavailable.

Successful entrepreneurs are more likely, therefore, to be found in positions that are connected to lots of diverse information sources (Aldrich et al. 1987). Information about new business locations, potential markets for goods and services, sources of capital or potential investors, and innovations is likely to be spread widely among individuals. Other things being equal, someone with a small set of overlapping ties is at a disadvantage when competing for information with someone with a large set of divergent ties.

In summary, entrepreneurs can increase their span of action through their personal networks and gain access at a limited cost to resources otherwise unavailable.

Extended Networks

Personal networks are constructed from the viewpoint of a particular individual; extended networks are the collective result when interconnected personal networks are examined. Within firms, extended networks consist of all the relations between owners, managers, and employees, as they are structured by patterns of coordination and control. Between firms, extended networks consist of relations between all the members of each firm who fill boundary-spanning roles. Given a bounded system—within a single organization or a set of many organizations—we construct a network by identifying all the relations (of whatever type) between people within the boundaries.

The logical shift from personal networks to extended networks becomes crucial if we are considering very small firms. Small companies are often considered as part of the family, or as "personal property." For a big corporation, by contrast, the difference between a company's set of relations and its shareholders' is quite evident. The need for separating the two concepts is not just formal, as such things as a company's goals, values, culture—all of which have a large effect on the type of linkages a company establishes—might at a certain point conflict with its owner's (Masini 1978; Coda 1988).

If we look at network activity in process, at the beginning of the development of the business idea, the company does not exist, and the object of study is the entrepreneur as a person putting all necessary resources together. However, when the first exchange of goods and services takes place, the focus of the attention shifts to the company itself (Colombo and Dubini 1988). The use of network concepts applied to firms rather than to individuals enables us to study also organizations that, due to their size or to their extreme specialization in the manufacturing process, would not otherwise be taken into consideration. Companies become relevant *because* they are part of a network (Lorenzoni 1983, 1987). This is rather typical in some areas in Italy that are heavily dominated by a single traditional industry (leather, textile, and glass). Through the initiative of an entrepreneur, the network of firms is first created, and then its efficiency and effectiveness are maximized.

The shift from personal to extended networks can be examined through the path followed to reach a final destination. Direct ties, especially strong ones, are significant not only for the persons directly linked, but also for the *indirect* access they provide to persons and organizations beyond the direct contacts. Indirect links can be considered by specifying how many steps removed from the entrepreneur an analyst wishes to include. Including indirect ties takes us closer to the essence of networks, as we begin to see how entrepreneurs and firms can leverage their direct connections by judicious choice of contacts who have access to others. The use of networks allows a firm, not only to increase its span of action, but also to reduce the uncertainty related to other companies' behaviors, because the existence of a relation increases the predictability of the behavior of the firms involved.

Indirect ties enable entrepreneurs and firms to substantially increase their access to information and resources, multiplying by many times over what is available through their direct ties.

Density

The density of a network refers to the extensiveness of ties between persons or organizations, and is measured by comparing the total number of ties present to the potential number that would occur if every unit in the network were connected to every other unit. The simplest measure of density considers just the presence or absence of a tie, but more sophisticated measures take account of the strength of ties. For example, a joint venture is a stronger tie than a gentlemen's agreement.

Reachability

Reachability refers to the presence of a path between two persons or firms, of whatever distance. Persons and firms can be ranked by how many intermediaries a path travels before one person is indirectly linked with another. Some units are completely isolated from others, as no path can be constructed to link them. For most units, however, there probably is a path to many others, although it may be quite lengthy.

Brokers

Brokers are people or firms who link units having complementary interests, transferring information or resources, and otherwise facilitating the interests of those not directly connected to one another. For example, venture capitalists are probably as important for their broker role as for the funds they provide to struggling entrepreneurs, because they bring together technical experts, management consultants, and financial planners to supplement an entrepreneur's limited knowledge and experience.

Some social settings facilitate brokerage, and some associations and organizations are themselves brokers in the role they play. Many voluntary associations, trade associations, public agencies, and other organizations increase the probability of people making contact with one another. The complex pattern of social organization in Silicon Valley illustrates the synergistic effects of brokers, central meeting points (bars and restaurants), and family and friendship networks in supporting high start-up rates (Rogers and Larson 1984). Brokers allow people to forge contacts that help them leap over otherwise unbridgeable gaps in their marshalling of resources.

HYPOTHESES CONCERNING NETWORKS AND ENTREPRENEURIAL EFFECTIVENESS

Personal networks and extended networks are simple but powerful ideas, allowing us to conceptualize the opportunities and constraints facing entrepreneurs and firms in the pursuit of their goals. Applied to the issue of entrepreneurial strategies, they provide new insight into what adaptive strategies entrepreneurs might pursue as they enter business.

Based on our review of network principles, we have formulated two general principles linking network behavior and entrepreneurial success:

- Effective entrepreneurs are more likely than others to systematically plan and monitor network activities
- Effective entrepreneurs are more likely than others to undertake actions towards increasing their network density and diversity.

We elaborate these hypotheses more fully, spelling out sub-hypotheses.

Planning and Monitoring Network Activities

Many of the divisions and barriers limiting the effectiveness of networks are unplanned, institutionalized structures and processes that can be overcome with proper planning (Welch

1980) to use networks as a competitive weapon. With regard to networking, viewed as part of the entrepreneurial process, we have formulated the following hypotheses:

- Effective entrepreneurs are able to *chart their present network* and to discriminate between production and symbolic ties (Johannisson 1987). Viewed in process at the first stages of development of a business idea, they are able to identify key persons, especially brokers, necessary to the start-up. To use MacMillan's (1983) concept, this means that effective entrepreneurs are able to prepare a political plan in addition to a business plan.

- Effective entrepreneurs are able to *view effective networks as a crucial aspect for ensuring the success of their company*. Although saying that networks become part of corporate values is perhaps too strong a statement, what it implies is that networking is a concept general enough to include all dimensions at present considered relevant for success: attention to customers, understanding of the business, market orientation, stress on quality, and so forth. From the entrepreneur's viewpoint, this means that the problem is not simply "to work on personal networks," but rather to work on personal networks *internally* consistent with his or her business idea.

- As a direct consequence of the latter hypothesis, effective entrepreneurs are able to *stabilize and maintain networks*, in order to increase their effectiveness and their efficiency. Because they are so relevant for the success of the company, enabling it to increase its span of action, its efficiency, and its possibility of controlling an unstable environment, good networks become a precious asset for the company. Thus, a shared interest in a prolonged relationship motivates the parties in a relation to solve conflicts that may arise by "voice," not by "exit" (Johannisson 1987, p. 17; Johanson and Mattsson 1987).

Because they are action-sets, inter-firm networks have a division of labor and a role structure, thus resembling small groups. Over time, firms play a variety of roles (Johnson and Mattsson 1987). For firm-based networks, one company initially may take the lead in brokering relations. Then, other firms may begin playing a more active role, creating a more mutually based network. Finally, responsibility for the network is diffused throughout the entire constellation of firms (Lorenzoni and Ornati 1988). As firms accumulate a history of positions within networks, their future activities are increasingly constrained. Thus, the process of network development "is not only a learning process but also an adaptation process" (Johanson and Mattsson 1987, p. 38).

Increasing Network Diversity

The great danger facing all business persons is that the daily struggle to cope with pressing problems and keep up with expected routines gradually eliminates time and energy spent in innovative activity (Mintzberg 1974).

- Effective entrepreneurs set aside time for purely "random" activities—things done with no specific problem in mind. Often joint projects are started between companies quite unexpectedly, just because opportunities arise. We offer this hypothesis to emphasize that personal and extended networks are mixtures of pragmatic, instrumental ties *and* emotional, spontaneously formed bonds.

- Effective entrepreneurs are able to *check network density*, so as to avoid too many overlaps (because they affect network efficiency) while still attaining solidarity and cohesiveness.

- Entrepreneurs in the process of starting companies are more effective to the extent that they economize on time and energy devoted to networking activity by planning a structure and operative mechanisms, enhancing communication with the external environment. They thus multiply, through extending the reachability of their networks, the stimuli for better and faster adaptation to change.

CONCLUSIONS

Unlike earlier approaches to entrepreneurship, the picture we have drawn focuses on entrepreneurs as embedded in a social context, channelled and facilitated, or constrained and inhibited, by their positions in social networks (Aldrich and Zimmer 1986; Granovetter 1985). We see entrepreneurship as intimately linked to other aspects of life, especially pre-entrepreneurial careers and non-workplace relationships. Not only is networking an individual—i.e., an entrepreneur's—activity, but it can also become part of a company's—as a separate entity—activity and structure. In this way, an entrepreneur is not the sole person responsible for seizing opportunities, as the whole company develops an awareness about its environment that allows it to better monitor its territory (Normann 1977).

So, two networking processes coexist: the extended networks associated with organizations, and the informal, personal networks associated with individuals. Taken together, these two processes affect the fate of entrepreneurs and their companies. Johannisson (1987, p. 7) noted that "formal organizations influence their members much less than, for example, the communities in which the organization members live. This also implies that much of importance to each separate organization takes place *among* organizations, realized through different inter-organizational networks."

We identified two strategic principles from our review of the network literature that apply to personal networks: systematically plan and monitor networking activities, and attempt to increase network density and diversity. As for company networks, organizational structures and operating systems can enhance a company's capabilities to interact with its environment and facilitate change and growth within its competitive arena.

We hypothesized that the most effective firms are those in which the two principles we have previously stated are pursued by the entrepreneurs in their personal networks, in the firm's internal structuring, and in the firm's relations with other firms. These strategies work best if there is an internal consistency between personal and extended network strategies. Thus, it becomes crucial to investigate *how* an extended network is created, developed, and strengthened over time, and how an entrepreneur manages to embed the concept of personal network in the company's "culture," so that the company itself becomes "network oriented."

REFERENCES

Aldrich, H., and Herker, D. 1977. Boundary spanning roles and organizational structure. *Academy of Management Review* 2:217–230.

Aldrich, H. and Zimmer, C. 1986. Entrepreneurship through social networks. In D.L. Sexton and R.W. Smilor, eds., *The Art and Science of Entrepreneurship*. Cambridge, MA: Ballinger, pp. 3–23.

Aldrich, H. Rosen, B., and Woodward, W. 1987. The impact of social networks on business foundings and profit. In N. Churchill, J. Hornaday, O.J. Krasner, and K. Vesper, eds., *Frontiers of Entrepreneurship Research 1987*. Wellesley, MA: Babson College Center for Entrepreneurial Studies, pp. 154–168.

Blau, P. 1964. *Exchange and Power in Social Life*. New York: Wiley.

Coda, V. 1988. *L'Orientamento Strategico di Fondo Delle Imprese*. Torino: UTET.

Colombo, G., and Dubini, P. 1988. *I Servizi per la Nascita e lo Sviluppo di Nuove Imprese: Condizioni di Efficacia e di Convenienza Economica*. Milano: Giuffré.

Granovetter, M. 1973. The strength of weak ties. *American Journal of Sociology* 78:1360–80.

Granovetter, M. 1982. The strength of weak ties: A network theory revisited. In P.V. Marsden and N. Lin, eds., *Social Structure and Network Analysis*. Beverly Hills, CA: Sage, pp. 105–130.

Granovetter, M. 1985. Economic action and social structure: The problem of embeddedness. *American Journal of Sociology* 91:481–510.

Grieco, M.S., and Hosking, D.M. 1987. Networking, exchange and skills. *International Studies of Management and Organization XVII* 1:75–87.

Hirschman, A.O. 1972. *Exit, Voice, and Loyalty*. Cambridge, MA: Harvard University Press.

Johannisson, B. 1987. Beyond processes and structure: Social exchange networks. *International Studies of Management and Organization XVII* 1:3–23.

Johanson, J., and Mattsson, L.-G. 1987. Inter-organizational relations in industrial systems: A network approach compared with the transaction-cost approach. *International Studies of Management and Organization XVII* 1:34–48.

Lorenzoni, G. 1983. La costellazione di imprese: Una base di indagine sui processi di sviluppo. *Economia e Politica Industriale* 38:283–309.

Lorenzoni, G. 1987. Costellazione di imprese e processi di sviluppo. *Sviluppo e Organizzazione* 102:59–72.

Lorenzoni, G., and Ornati, O. 1988. Constellations of firms and new ventures. *Journal of Business Venturing* 3(1):41–58.

MacMillan, I. 1983. The politics of new venture management. *Harvard Business Review*.

Masini, C. 1978. *Lavoro e Risparmio*, 2nd Ed. Torino:UTET.

Melin, L. 1987. The field of force metaphor: A study in industrial change. *International Studies of Management and Organization XVII* 1:24–33.

Mintzberg, H. 1974. *The Nature of Managerial Work*. New York: Harper & Row.

Normann, R. 1977. *Management for Growth*. New York: John Wiley and Sons Ltd.

Rogers, E.M., and Larson, J.K. 1984. *Silicon Valley Fever: Growth of High-Technology Culture*. New York: Basic Books.

Stevenson, H. and Jarillo, J.C. 1989. A paradigm of entrepreneurship: Entrepreneurial management. Working paper #89-040, Harvard Business School.

Turati, C. 1988. Joint ventures: Una corsa ad ostacoli. *Economia & Management*, 3:40–57.

Weick, K. 1979. *The Social Psychology of Organizing*, 2nd Ed. Reading, MA: Addison-Wesley.

Welch, M. 1980. *Networking: The Great New Way for Women to Get Ahead*. New York: Harcourt Brace Jovanovich.

Williamson, O. 1981. The economics of organization: The transaction cost approach. *American Journal of Sociology* 87:548–77.

STRONG TIES, WEAK TIES, AND STRANGERS

Do women owners differ from men in their use of networking to obtain assistance?

Howard E. Aldrich, Amanda Brickman Elam and Pat Ray Reese

INTRODUCTION

The growing number of woman-owned businesses has sparked debate on how men and women business owners differ and, more specifically, on the strength of the gender-based disadvantages women business owners face (Brush 1992). Such questions are critical to policy-makers, educators and potential entrepreneurs. Answers to these questions may provide guidelines for training and support programs designed to meet the needs of new business owners. Do women business owners have special needs? How different are their experiences?

Despite past evidence suggesting that male and female entrepreneurs share similar personality traits and demographic profiles, a growing body of research suggests that women entrepreneurs differ from men on some key dimensions. Brush (1992: 16) noted that: 'significant differences have been found in reasons for business start-up/acquisition, timing and circumstances of start-up, educational background, work experience and business skills. More differences are apparent in business goals, management styles, business characteristics and growth rates. These variations suggest that women perceive and approach business ownership differently than men.' Many studies have not been comparative, however, as they examined only men or women but not both, and many have not examined details of the resource mobilization process that lies at the heart of business operations.

In this chapter we examine the impact that gender-based differences in networking behavior have on the ability of men and women entrepreneurs to mobilize the support and resources they need for the survival and growth of new businesses. We believe that business networking is critical to the

1

STRONG TIES, WEAK TIES AND STRANGERS

success of new ventures, and thus we present a framework for understanding network relations between owners and key resource providers. Within the context of this framework, we review some current research and its implications for the success of women-owned businesses. We ask why some of the findings from past research do not correspond to current data describing the actual survival chances of women-owned businesses. After presenting our findings, we consider their implications for policies and programs designed to meet the needs of new business owners.

IMPORTANCE OF NETWORKS

New businesses are founded as a result of motivated entrepreneurs gaining access to resources and finding niches in opportunity structures. From the beginning, social networks are crucial assets for business owners struggling to make a place for themselves in competitive markets. Networking allows them to enlarge their span of action, save time and gain access to resources and opportunities otherwise unavailable. From start-up to stability, the structure of owners' networks affects the life chances of their businesses (Aldrich and Zimmer 1986; Zimmer and Aldrich 1987).

Even though many studies have found very similar psychological profiles and 'traits' for men and women entrepreneurs, this does not necessarily translate into similar patterns of social networking (Chaganti 1986; Goffee and Scase 1985; Hertz 1986; Sexton and Bowman-Upton 1990). Men have more opportunities for meeting higher status individuals (other males) than do women (Aldrich 1989). Because women are subject to occupational and voluntary organizational sex segregation, we might expect limits on women's access to business resources. Work experience and education may partially reduce organizational sex segregation, but marital status and childcare responsibilities may isolate women and increase their separation from business opportunities (McPherson and Smith-Lovin 1986). The social and institutional forces that shape networking opportunities may thus make matters very difficult for individual women entrepreneurs.

Do women differ systematically from men in how they use networks to obtain resources and assistance for their businesses? In particular, are men business owners more systematic and instrumental in network building than women? Answering these questions calls for a comprehensive framework.

NETWORK FRAMEWORK

Entrepreneurs are embedded in networks of social relationships, some of which are personal, such as ties to family, friends and neighbors, and others which are business related, such as ties to customers, vendors and creditors. Social relations are, to varying extents, purposive: some arise because of accidental or unplanned encounters with individuals, some are created via

2

STRONG TIES, WEAK TIES AND STRANGERS

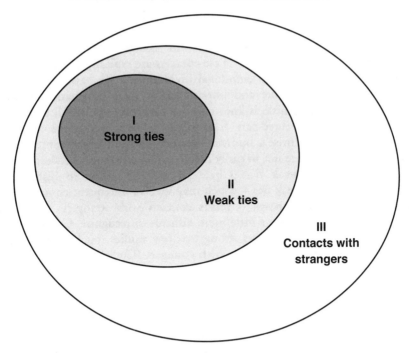

Figure 1.1 Framework of network relationships

organizational memberships, and others emerge as planned interactions to obtain access to specific information. In this sense, then, all entrepreneurs must construct networks of social relations in the process of obtaining resources for their firms.

We find it helpful to organize the types of relationships that make up a person's total set of relations into three circles, according to the strength of a tie, as shown in Figure 1.1 (see Granovetter 1985).

The inner circle (I) represents a business owner's advisor circle and includes a fairly small set of strong tie relationships. Strong tie relationships are usually of long duration and are based on a principle of implicit reciprocity. Individuals tend to make heavy investments in this type of relationship, requiring fairly frequent contact with the other person. Strong ties are typically more reliable than other ties and involve trust and emotional closeness.

The next circle (II), working outwards, involves weak tie relationships. These relationships are of much shorter duration and involve a lower frequency of contact. Weak ties are less reliable and more ambiguous and uncertain than strong ties. They often fade into dormancy, only to be revived when assistance is required.

3

STRONG TIES, WEAK TIES AND STRANGERS

The third outer circle (III) represents those relationships entered into for pragmatic purposes and may be best described as 'contacts' rather than as ties. Pragmatic contacts usually occur with strangers, or individuals with whom no prior ties have existed. These contacts are typically fleeting in duration and require little or no emotional involvement. We have only limited understanding of the value and importance of these pragmatic ties with strangers. In fact, very little is known about how they are established.

We proposed this three-part framework to help clarify the types of relationships that comprise a business network. In reality, however, the lines between these circles are not so easily defined. The differences between strong ties (Circle I) and weak ties (Circle II) are the easiest to distinguish. Differences between weak ties – which may involve infrequent contacts with other who are barely known – versus contacts with strangers – who are completely unknown – are a little more difficult to recognize. Consequently, most current research addresses strong ties, few studies touch on weak ties, and none really focus on contacts with strangers (Circle III).

CURRENT RESEARCH – HOW DOES IT FIT?

Even though men and women owners may be similar in many respects, some studies suggest that key differences still remain. For example, Sexton and Bowman-Upton (1990), searching for possible disadvantages of women entrepreneurs, found that men and women business owners differed on only two of nine psychological traits relevant to entrepreneurship. According to their results, women business owners scored lower on risk taking and endurance (energy level). Their findings may indicate that women business owners, when faced with limited abilities to develop strong tie networks through the usual channels (Circle I), may be less inclined to seek out the resources and information they require from strangers (Circle III).

Studies examining strong tie relations have found that women business owners are indeed embedded in different social relations than men. Aldrich *et al.* (1989) found significant differences in the sex composition of networks for men and women entrepreneurs in the USA and Italy. They suggested that structural constraints found in the workplace, in marriage and family roles, and in organized social life restricted the social networks of women business owners. Women-owned businesses are typically much smaller and limited to particular sectors of the economy, namely retail and services, as well as the lower status portions of the job market. Essentially, women appear to be left out of the informal, strong tie networks that provide men entrepreneurs with access to the resources and support needed for success and survival. Women entrepreneurs are thus left with the challenge of meeting their own needs through formal, weak tie channels.

Men simply do not include women in their business advisor circles. In a study of Circle I ties in five industrial nations in the late 1980s, Aldrich

STRONG TIES, WEAK TIES AND STRANGERS

and Sakano (1995) found that only 10 percent of the people mentioned by men as being relied upon for advice and assistance were women. By contrast, approximately 40 percent of the advisor networks of women business owners were women. Thus, men were involved in mainly same-sex networks, dealing almost entirely with other men, whereas women were involved in mainly cross-sex networks, dealing mostly with men but also with a high proportion of women.

Signs of a higher proportion of cross-sex ties in women's than in men's networks was interpreted by Aldrich and Sakano (1995: 25) as indicating that 'women are seldom found in the personal strong-tie networks of all owners, probably because of women's place in the existing distribution of economic resources and power in these nations.' Furthermore, they found that cross-sex ties were of a shorter duration than same-sex ties and that women entrepreneurs were twice as likely as men to have used a broker or third party to meet more powerful (men) network members. Based on these results, we could conclude that women business owners must rely on other strategies of network building, involving weaker ties, to gain the resources and support they need.

According to Brush (1992), women's domestic responsibilities and limited mobility chances at work, together with other institutional factors such as sexism and patterns of childhood socialization (Gilligan 1982), combine to produce a different way of approaching business ownership. Building on work by Aldrich (1989) and others, Brush (1992: 16) suggested a new perspective on women entrepreneurs – the integrated perspective – which posits that 'women perceive their businesses as "cooperative networks of relationships" rather than separate economic units. In this conception, business relationships are integrated rather than separated from family, societal and personal relationships.' If women experience their personal reality as a seamless web of interconnected social relationships spanning work, family and other domains, whereas men view reality in separate and autonomous domains, then it seems likely that women would be less comfortable if they had to rely on weak ties and contacts with strangers.

In summary, past research indicates that the effects of structural constraints and gendered socialization may force women to rely more on relationships with weak ties and contact with strangers. Such relations could have two consequences:

- reluctance to seek out assistance from these relationships;
- fewer resources and less support from their networks than men.

However, these implications have not been put to an empirical test.

Implications

Strong tie networks are critical to the success of small business. Small business owners are in a difficult position in modern economies and strong

5

STRONG TIES, WEAK TIES AND STRANGERS

ties of intimate friendship can provide social support than enables owners to weather crises and hardship. Strong tie relations of long duration are cemented by loyalty and trust and stand as a bulwark against an owner's being exploited by people out only for short-term gain. Past research suggests that women business owners are 'out of the loop.' Women are constrained by structural factors as well as by socialization. Not only do they apparently fall outside of the famed 'old boy's network,' but the business reality they face, or the more integrated approach they take to business, may further constrain their ability to succeed.

Given the importance of strong tie networks to the success of new ventures and women's exclusion from men's advisor networks, we might infer that women business owners have special needs. Based on prevailing evidence, policy-makers might conclude that programs should be designed to educate and support women business owners differently from men. Before jumping to any conclusions, however, we should examine these implications in the context of the actual success of women-owned businesses, relative to those of men. In particular, we need to look more closely at weak ties and contacts with strangers, to determine whether the pattern of gender disadvantage in strong ties carries over into other areas of women owners' social relations.

WHAT'S MISSING?

In their panel study of small businesses in Indiana, Kalleberg and Leicht (1991) actually found that, all things being equal, businesses run by women were just as likely to succeed as those run by men. They acknowledged that some gender differences do exist, that some factors seem to operate more favorably for one gender than the other, and that women do appear to face barriers originating from socialization practices, education experiences, family roles and weaker networks. Nonetheless, it appeared that women-owned businesses were generally able to survive and succeed, in spite of these gender barriers. Reese and Aldrich (1995), in their panel study of business survival in the Research Triangle Park Area of North Carolina, came to a similar conclusion.

These findings seem to contradict the dire implications of the research and theorizing we reviewed earlier. What produces such contradictions? Much of the research in the past has primarily considered the value and importance of strong tie circles, rather than weak ties or stranger contacts. Despite the indicated gender barriers and disadvantages, women entrepreneurs appear to be succeeding. Are women business owners, in fact, capable of mobilizing the necessary resources and support through their social relationships in Circle II and Circle III? Our results suggest that, indeed, this is the case.

STRONG TIES, WEAK TIES AND STRANGERS
STUDY OVERVIEW

Using data from a two-wave panel study on the networks of potential and active entrepreneurs in the Research Triangle Park Area of North Carolina, USA, we considered how women entrepreneurs compare to men in three areas: the process of acquiring information and assistance, relations with the people who supplied the assistance, and the cost and quality of assistance obtained. In this chapter we restrict our data analysis to the 217 entrepreneurs (157 men and 60 women) who were business owners at our initial contact in 1990 and whom we were able to interview again in 1992. We sampled most of them from the membership lists of organizations we found in the Research Triangle Area.

We wanted to study individuals in the early stages of organizational formation, as well as established organizations with a transaction history, and so in an exploratory phase of our project we located voluntary and non-profit organizations of interest to entrepreneurs in the Research Triangle Area of North Carolina. This area includes Raleigh, Durham, Cary, and Chapel Hill, and is well known because of the more than forty large firms and research institutes located in the Research Triangle Park, including IBM, Northern Telecom, Glaxo-Wellcome, BASF, the Environmental Protection Agency, Research Triangle Institute, and the SAS Institute.

Organizations differed in sex composition, purpose and membership interests, but they all focused on entrepreneurial or business activity:

1 the Council for Entrepreneurial Development (CED), based in Durham, included both entrepreneurs and service providers as members;
2 six networking organizations, all of which included both entrepreneurs and employees;
3 participants at Wake Tech Small Business Center classes, including entrepreneurs in very early stages of business start-up;
4 the National Association of Women Business owners (NAWBO), which is restricted to women entrepreneurs.

Our initial sampling list was constructed from members of those organizations. We added another subsample, randomly selected from business start-ups, to use as a reference. This sample was selected from new businesses that filed registration forms in Wake County, which includes Raleigh.

We collected the initial (Time 1) data in two phases. Phase I was a short questionnaire, which could be completed in about five minutes: Phase II involved in-depth, 30- to 40-minute telephone interviews that included structured and open-ended questions. We collected the Time 1 questionnaires and conducted interviews during a nine-month period in 1990 and 1991.

Combining all subsamples, we distributed 659 questionnaires and received 444 in a usable format, for an average response rate of 67 percent, as shown in Table 1.1. Response rates across the subsamples ranged from 41 percent

7

STRONG TIES, WEAK TIES AND STRANGERS

to 78 percent. We conducted a total of 353 telephone interviews, yielding completed interviews for 54 percent of those who received questionnaires and 80 percent of those who returned a questionnaire.

Our response rates compare favorably with other efforts to study entrepreneurs. Birley *et al.* (1990), using records similar to those we used in the business sample, achieved a 24 percent response rate; Cooper and Dunkelberg (1987) reported a 29 percent return; Aldrich *et al.* (1987) achieved less than a 41 percent return in a study of CED members; and Kalleberg (1986), using phone interviews which traditionally have a higher response rate than questionnaires, reported response rates between 55 percent and 68 percent, although he excluded non-working phone numbers in his calculation, whereas our rates include such cases as non-responses. Our response rates and tests of non-response bias (Reese 1992) increase our confidence in our findings.

Table 1.1 Sample size and response rates

| Sample source | Time 1 | | | Time 2 | | | |
| | Question-naire | | Follow-up phone interviews | Question-naire | Questionnaire and phone interview | | |
	Number distributed	% returned	Percent of return completing interview	Number mailed	Fully completed %	Partially completed %	Combined completion %
CED members	339	76	82	250	53	37	90
Networking organization members	67	78	83	49	43	43	86
Wake Tech students	78	68	79	52	25	58	83
Business sample	150	41	64	61	39	45	84
NAWBO sample	25	76	84	19	63	32	95
Total percent	—	67	80	—	64	24	88
Total number	659	444*	353	431*	203	177	380

Note: *The difference between the 444 questionnaires returned at Time 1 and the 431 respondents followed up at Time 2 is due to people who refused to participate further at the end of Time 1 or who were lost to the sample during interviewing for Time 1 for other reasons.

8

STRONG TIES, WEAK TIES AND STRANGERS

In June and July of 1992 we contacted respondents who had returned questionnaires two years earlier. Of the 444 returned questionnaires, we removed 13 cases from the Time 2 sample for a variety of reasons: six respondents had moved between the first and second phase of the Time 1 data collection and could not be tracked two years earlier, four questionnaires contained large amounts of missing data, and two people had explicitly notified us that they did not want to participate in any future studies. We mailed questionnaires to the remaining sample of 431.

We used a two-phase approach much like our Time 1 contact: we began with a short questionnaire and conducted short follow-up telephone interviews. We repeated several of our networking measures: we asked about the entrepreneur's business, whether they had made specific changes in their business, their use of resources, information about their business strategy and environment, their reasons for starting the business, and their business performance, as well as information on new businesses that entrepreneurs had begun in the two years since our initial contact.

We had a very good response from our second round of contacts, as shown in the four right-hand columns of Table 1.1. Of the 431 mailed questionnaires, we received questionnaires from 246 entrepreneurs and completed a short follow-up interview with 175 of them. We collected full information on an additional 28 respondents by asking the questionnaire and interview questions during a long telephone interview. Thus, we have extensive data on 64 percent of the sample and complete or partial information on 88 percent of the Time 1 participants.

Because few researchers have attempted this kind of panel study of entrepreneurs, we have little to compare with our response rates. Kalleberg and Leicht (1991), in the second wave of their panel study of small businesses in Indiana, completed interviews with 70 percent of their original businesses. They obtained information that 34 companies were out of business, giving them information about 78 percent of their original sample. For our study, collecting information on 88 percent of the sample respondents after a two-year period of time gives us increased confidence in our results. In this chapter we restrict our data analysis to the 217 entrepreneurs who were business owners at our initial contact in 1990 and whom we were able to interview again in 1992.

Sample characteristics

We first checked that the 27 percent of our sample that are women did not differ in fundamental ways from the men. Otherwise, the simple tables we present might show sex differences because subsample compositions differ drastically, rather than because women are using networks in different ways from men. The age, business age and industry distributions for men and women owners in our sample do not differ significantly, as shown in Table

9

1.2. About two-thirds of both groups are between the ages of 35 and 54, as we would expect from previous research on entrepreneurship, and almost none are under 25. Only about one in nine are over 55.

Age of the owner's current business was measured in 1990, and so the surviving businesses in our second wave of interviewing are about two years older, on average, than the business ages shown in Table 1.2. In 1990, almost one-third of the women and men had been in their current business less than two years, reflecting our success in finding businesses in their formative period. About 59 percent of the men and 51 percent of the women had been in business less than four years. In a previous paper (Reese and Aldrich 1995), we showed that the youngest businesses were the least likely to survive as active firms over the two-year study period: only 65 percent of those under one year old were still active in 1992, compared to 84 percent of those between three and four years old.

Most businesses were in the services sector, especially business and professional services. In our previous paper (Reese and Aldrich 1995), we found that survival rates varied slightly across industries, with retail firms the least likely to survive and finance, insurance, and real estate firms the most fortunate. For our purposes, the most important point to note is that the industry distribution does not differ significantly by sex. As we described in the section on research design, our main goal in sampling was to increase the number of women owners and to obtain a representative sample, not to produce a quota by industry. Nothing was done in our sampling plan to equalize numbers of firms by industries. Thus, our finding that there is no sex difference in the industry distributions suggests that men and women appear to have equal access to initial business opportunities in the Research Triangle.

The women owners in our sample have completed significantly fewer advanced degrees than the men, but both groups are fairly well-educated. Only about 10 percent of either group stopped their education with a high school degree, and 40 percent of the men and 29 percent of the women earned a post-graduate degree of some kind. One in eight of the men have a PhD or MD, compared to one in fourteen of the women. The high level of technical qualification of our sample reflects the industrial base of the Research Triangle, with many knowledge-intensive firms (such as Glaxo and IBM) as well as three major research universities, plus smaller colleges and universities. As we will show in our subsequent analyses, the more advanced educational qualifications of the men do not seem to have given them any substantial advantages over the women.

FINDINGS

In our analyses, we present information in graphic form. Full information on all analyses and more details on the study are available from the senior author.

STRONG TIES, WEAK TIES AND STRANGERS

Table 1.2 Personal and business characteristics of sample at Time 1 (1990)

Owner's age (yrs)	Sex of owner		Business age (yrs)	Sex of owner	
	Men	Women		Men	Women
Under 24	1	2	0–1.9	32	33
25–34	20	24	2–2.9	13	10
35–44	41	42	3–3.9	14	8
45–54	28	21	4–9.9	30	32
55+	11	11	10+	11	17
Total percent	101	100	Total percent	100	100
(N)	(229)	(84)	(N)	(230)	(84)
	$X^2 = 2.62$, N.S.			$X^2 = 4.20$, N.S.	

Industry	Sex		Business education	Sex	
	Men	Women		Men	Women
Construction	4	6	High school	9	11
Manufacturing	12	12	College (2 yr)	7	23
Transportation	2	4	College (4 yr)	44	37
Wholesale	4	4	MA, MS,		
Retail	8	12	MBA, JD	28	22
Finance, ins, RE	9	8	PhD, MD	12	7
Services	60	54			
Other	1	1			
Total percent	100	101	Total percent	100	100
(N)	(227)	(84)	(N)	(229)	(83)
	$X^2 = 3.35$, N.S.			$X^2 = 18.18$, p=.001	

The process of acquiring assistance

One implication of the critical literature on sex differences is that women might be less pro-active in pursuing opportunities than men, as their autonomy is constrained because they view business activity as integrated into the rest of their lives. A sociological perspective would argue that, regardless of their personal views, women's embeddedness in a network of obligations and responsibilities could limit their freedom of action. Men, by contrast, are said to see their businesses as independent from the rest of their lives and thus are free to follow opportunities wherever they may lead. Moreover, institutional arrangements permit such action. Our findings do not support these expectations, as shown in Figure 1.2.

We asked owners if, during the past year, they had asked for four different kinds of assistance: legal, financial or accounting, business loans or business financing, and advice from someone with experience in the same line of work. Legal and financial or accounting advice are consulting services usually provided by professionals, and business loans are almost always provided by banks, insurance companies, or other institutions. By contrast, advice from

11

STRONG TIES, WEAK TIES AND STRANGERS

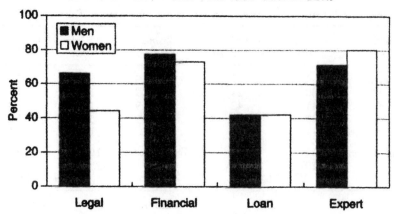

Figure 1.2 Percentage of owners who asked for assistance in obtaining four resources, by sex. Question: 'During the past year, have you asked for . . .?'

an 'expert' is more informal in nature. Thus, we have a range of types of assistance sought as well as possible types of providers. Nonetheless, entrepreneurs also need many other types of resources and our research is thus limited in its generalizability to the specific range that we were able to study.

In Figure 1.2, we show in bar graphs the percentage of men and women owners who reported they sought each type of assistance. In three of these four areas, we found no significant difference between men and women in the proportion asking for advice: about three-quarters of all owners asked for financial or expert advice, and about two-fifths asked for assistance with business loans. The only significant difference was in legal assistance. About 66 percent of the men, but only 44 percent of the women, had asked for legal assistance.

We explored this difference further by asking owners why they had asked for legal help and found no significant differences between men and women. As one might imagine, owners sought legal assistance for a variety of reasons and so we created a six-category scheme to code their responses. We found no significant gender differences in the reasons offered for seeking legal assistance. Men were no more likely to be involved in being sued, or suing someone, than were women owners. Similarly, very small proportions of both groups had sought legal assistance for creating incorporation papers or partnership agreements.

We also asked how many different people owners had sought out for assistance, testing the hypothesis that perhaps women had been more restrictive in their search than men. Again, however, in all of the four areas, we found no significant differences in the number of people contacted. Most owners had gone to only one or two people for legal, financial, and loan assistance, with men more active than women only in seeking loan assistance. Both groups were more active in seeking advice from someone in the

12

STRONG TIES, WEAK TIES AND STRANGERS

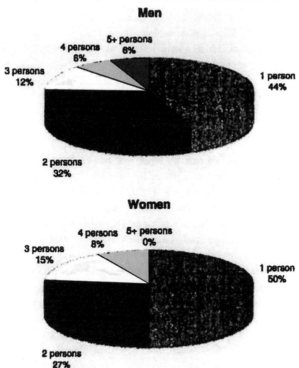

Figure 1.3 Number of lawyers who were contacted, by sex

same line of business, as about two-fifths sought assistance from five persons or more.

Because fewer women had sought legal advice than men, as shown in Figure 1.2, we looked more closely at those women who had searched for lawyers, comparing them with men who had sought legal advice. As shown in Figure 1.3, a detailed picture of the scope of the search engaged in by each group revealed very similar behaviors – women were essentially just as active as men in trying to find a lawyer to handle their business affairs. Thus, neither in the reasons they sought assistance nor in the intensity of their search – once they had decided on seeking legal assistance – did women owners differ from men.

We also looked more closely for possible difference as to why men and women owners were seeking assistance in obtaining business loans or business financing. We found no significant difference between men and women in the reasons they offered: about 20 percent of each group were concerned about their cash flow, another 20 percent were applying for a loan, and about one-quarter needed expansion capital. Indeed, the similarity in specific reasons mentioned was remarkable across the two groups.

13

STRONG TIES, WEAK TIES AND STRANGERS

Our results show that women were as active as men in networking activities in three of four critical areas: seeking financial, business loan, and expert assistance for their businesses. Only in the realm of seeking legal assistance were men more active and, even then, women owners who decided to seek such advice pursued as many leads as did men. The reasons they reported for seeking assistance were also indistinguishable.

The nature of relationships: who do owners seek out for assistance?

Instead of positing a difference in levels of networking activity, theories of sex differences sometimes assume that women seek assistance through different channels than men. Brush's (1992) 'integrative model,' for example, implied that women would be more likely to turn to family and friends than to work associates. If women are less opportunistic and prone to risk-taking, as some theories have suggested, then they may be less likely to seek assistance from strangers – people with whom they have no pre-existing tie (Sexton and Bowman-Upton 1990). To investigate this proposition, we asked owners about the last person they had contacted regarding a particular resource: 'Do you have a relationship with him/her, other than a consultant one – is he/she a family member, friend, a work associate or a member of the same organization?' Our results are displayed in Figure 1.4.

Three results stand out in Figure 1.4, which classifies the 'other' person by the primary relation identified: stranger, family member, friend, or business associate. First, women do not differ significantly from men in the proportion who sought assistance from strangers, ranging from a low of 25 percent of the men and 29 percent of the women seeking 'experts' to a high of 87 percent of the women and 88 percent of the men seeking business loan advice. Second, neither women nor men relied on family members for assistance for the four resources we asked about – in spite of Brush's (1992) arguments about business women living a more integrated life, women entrepreneurs show no greater inclination than men to ask family members for help. Instead, men and women apparently turned to people with the necessary qualifications, rather than relying on blood ties. Third, the overall pattern of relations is essentially the same for women and men – none of the differences in Figure 1.4 are statistically significant.

For legal and financial assistance, slightly less than half the owners turned to persons with whom they had a prior relationship. Almost no one turned to family members. Instead, they sought assistance from friends, work associates and people with whom they shared an organizational affiliation. Almost nine in ten owners of both sexes went to an accountant for financial assistance and all owners went to lawyers for legal advice, suggesting that most had no family members or friends in these professions.

About 42 percent of both groups sought assistance with business loans and almost all of them asked advice from people they did not know

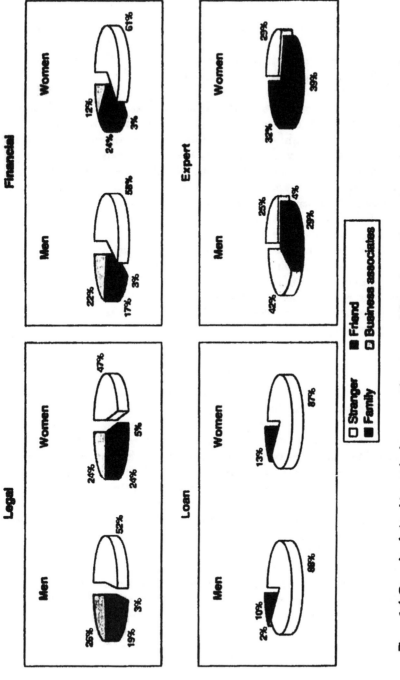

Figure 1.4 Owner's relationship to the last person they contacted for assistance, by sex. 'Percent who had specific type of relation to person contacted'.

STRONG TIES, WEAK TIES AND STRANGERS

previously. Only about one in ten made use of an existing non-consultative relationship to obtain assistance with business financing. Slightly more women than men, proportionately, used a bank loan officer for assistance, but the difference is not statistically significant.

Network ties played the biggest role in providing a channel for owners to seek advice from someone with experience in their own line of business. Only 25 percent of men and 29 percent of women owners turned to experienced persons with whom they had no prior ties. A slightly higher proportion of men than women sought advice from persons they had business relationships with, including competitors. Friends played a more important role in providing expert assistance than in any other domain, as 29 percent of men and 39 percent of women sought advice from them. About one-quarter of the friends were also identified as having some type of business relationship with the owner.

Clearly, when seeking assistance in obtaining crucial business assistance, men and women use similar channels: friends and business associates. Neither group relies on family members and neither shows a reluctance to seek out new persons with whom no pre-existing non-consultative tie has been established (i.e. the strangers we have placed in Circle III of our framework).

Cross-sex contacts

Might there still be a sex bias in the relationships relied upon by women owners? We investigated this possibility by asking owners the sex of the last person they had asked for assistance. In Figure 1.5 we show the percentage of men and women to whom the owners talked within each of the four domains. Men turned overwhelmingly to other men for assistance – for three of the four resources, three-quarters or more of the persons men asked for advice were men. Women also turned mostly to men for assistance, although not to the same extent as did male owners. In all four cases, the proportion of women asked for advice by women is higher than the percentage of women asked for advice by men, but in only two cases – loans and expert advice – is the difference statistically significant.

We noticed that the resource for which women owners turned most frequently to other women was business loan assistance and we also noticed that both men and women turned mostly to strangers for such advice. We speculated about whether women sought advice from other women more frequently when they had a pre-existing relation with the other party. Therefore, to test this idea, for each resource we examined whether having a prior relation affected the likelihood that a woman would be asked for assistance.

For men owners, the proportion of persons asked for advice who were women did not depend on whether a prior relation existed. For women

16

STRONG TIES, WEAK TIES AND STRANGERS

owners, however, when they had no prior ties to the person from whom they sought legal assistance, all ten advisors were men. By contrast, 45 percent of the 14 persons they turned to because they already had a prior relation were women. Prior relations made no difference for financial assistance and too few cases were available of prior relations concerning loan assistance to allow an analysis. For expert advice, there is a hint of an association, but it is not statistically significant: 46 percent of the 24 persons to whom women owners turned and with whom they had a prior relation were other women, whereas of the strangers from who they sought advice, only 20 percent (two out of ten) were women.

Thus, although men and women draw on the same types of social relations when seeking assistance and turn to the same organizational representatives when required (accountants, bank loan officers), women appear to seek out other women when it is possible. Note, however, that this same-sex bias is highly resource specific; when women owners rely on prior ties they are much more likely to ask a woman for advice than otherwise. For advice about business loans, women may perceive that other women have experienced more turn-downs in loan applications than men, and thus they want information from the most relevant population. For legal assistance, women seeking advice who did not know any lawyers with the required expertise ended up with only men as advisors. When they knew someone already in that domain, it was much more likely that they chose a woman advisor (although most were still men).

Figure 1.5 Percentage of owners who contacted a man to obtain specific assistance, by sex

STRONG TIES, WEAK TIES AND STRANGERS

Paying for the assistance obtained

We study networks in part because we believe that they take some business relations 'out of the marketplace,' allowing entrepreneurs to obtain resources without depleting their hard-earned capital. The 'old boy network' is said to favor men and disadvantage women. If true, then men using their network ties ought to secure favors not available to women. Thus, we investigated the extent to which women owners were as successful in obtaining assistance at below market rates as men.

We asked owners, 'Did you pay the market rate for the assistance you obtained?' Our results are shown in Figure 1.6.

Owners' abilities to avoid paying the market rate for advice differed dramatically by which resource they sought. Most paid market rates for legal and financial/accounting advice and many paid it for loan assistance, but almost no one paid the going rate for advice from others in their line of business. In two cases – financial and expert advice – women fared no better than men, having to pay the same rates as men. However, in the other two cases – legal and loan advice – women did better than men.

In every case, as we would expect, owners who had some type of prior relation with the provider were much less likely to pay market rates than other owners (analysis not shown). As we showed in Figure 1.4, women owners were as likely to have prior relations with advice providers as men, and so they benefited in equal measure from such relations. The most extreme case is expert advice: only 7 percent of owners with a prior relation to their advisor provider paid market rates, compared to 23 percent of those who went to strangers.

Quality of the assistance obtained and its consequences

Do women obtain the same quality advice as men? We asked owners to rate the quality of the advice they obtained on a scale from 0 to 100, a procedure that our respondents found easy to carry out. In essence, we were asking for a 'report card' on their service providers. Most were quite favorable, as shown in the average ratings they reported: 81.2 for legal assistance, 82.4 for financial assistance, 70.4 for loan assistance, and 79.4 for experts' advice.

In Figure 1.7, we show the ratings separately for men and women. In three of the four cases, women rated quality nearly identically to men. Only in the case of financial/accounting advice did women rate the advice they obtained significantly less favorably than men, although the difference is not large (8 points on a 100-point scale).

Another indicator of assistance quality is whether the assistance or advice received changed business practices. We asked owners to tell us whether they had changed the way they do business as a result of the assistance they obtained, and the results are displayed in Figure 1.8. in most cases, owners

STRONG TIES, WEAK TIES AND STRANGERS

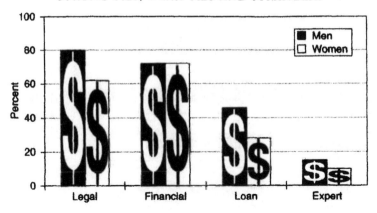

Figure 1.6 Percentage of owners who paid market rate for the assistance they obtained, by sex

did not change the way they did business, based on the assistance they received. Women were as unlikely to change as men in three of the four cases, but they differed from men in the way they used financial advice. Only one-fifth said they had changed the way they did business because of the financial advice they received, compared to about one-third of the men in our sample.

Curiously enough, the advice with the most powerful influence on business operations is that obtained from others in the same industry at below market rates. For women, advice from experts was the assistance most often sought, as shown in Figure 1.2; for men, it was the second most frequent type of assistance sought. Women owners conducted their most extensive search for assistance while looking for experts. Most owners – men and women – were able to find someone they knew, whether as a friend or work associate, who could provide expert advice, thus increasing the likelihood that they would not have to pay market rates for the assistance. Programs that bring established owners together with prospective owners should thus be a high priority for any economic development policies aiming to raise business founding and survival rates.

We have found that women do not seem to be disadvantaged by not being part of an 'old boys' network' when it comes to assistance that can be obtained from strangers or from experts known to them. Women seemed to benefit slightly more from their networks, as measured by being able to pay less than market rates for legal and loan assistance. They apparently received the same quality advice as men, regardless of what they paid, and they were no more likely to use the advice they received than men. We thus found no evidence that the material results of women's networking differ in any substantial ways from those for men. Both groups were able to find ways to obtain high-quality assistance at market rates for legal, business loan, and

19

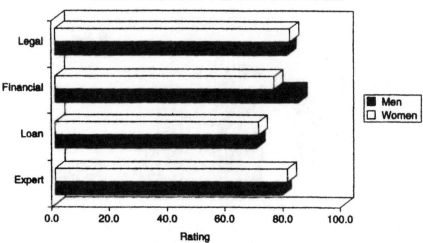

Figure 1.7 Owners' ratings of the quality of the assistance they obtained, on a scale of 0 to 100, by sex

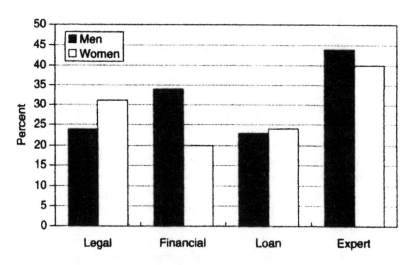

Figure 1.8 Percentage of owners who say that they changed their business practices as a result of the assistance they obtained, by sex

20

STRONG TIES, WEAK TIES AND STRANGERS

financial/accounting information, and high-quality assistance from other people in the same line of work at below market rates.

CONCLUSION AND RECOMMENDATIONS

From start-up to stability, the structure of owners' networks affects the life chances of their businesses, and thus studies of entrepreneurial networking have mushroomed in the past decade. Previous studies have told us a great deal about the personality and demographic characteristics of women owners, but few have focused on the comparative question we addressed: Do women differ systematically from men in how they use networks to obtain resources and assistance for their businesses? We reviewed some arguments for why women's networking might differ from men's, and used the previous literature to generate some guiding principles for our analysis.

Based on a two-wave panel study of 217 business owners in the Research Triangle Area of North Carolina, we conclude that women entrepreneurs are as active as men in networking to obtain assistance and as successful as men in obtaining high-quality assistance, some of which they obtain at below market rates.

Summary of findings

We examined entrepreneurs' networking activities in pursuit of four resources: seeking legal, financial, business loan, and expert assistance for their businesses. Our results show that women were as active as men in networking activities in three of these four critical domains. Only in the realm of seeking legal assistance were men more active and, even then, women owners who decided to seek such advice pursued as many leads as did men.

When entrepreneurs set off in pursuit of people who could help them, we found that men and women used similar channels: friends and business associates. Neither relied on family members and neither showed a reluctance to seek out assistance from strangers. Indeed, for some resources, especially business loan assistance, most entrepreneurs did not use pre-existing channels. Nonetheless, for the advice that ultimately paid the most dividends for owners – assistance from people already experienced in the entrepreneur's line of work – pre-existing ties were the main channel of resource acquisition. From other research we have conducted, we suspect such ties would fall into Circle II of our framework – weak ties, rather than strong ties.

Although men and women drew on the same types of social relations when seeking assistance and turned to the same organizational representatives when required (accountants, bank loan officers), women appeared to seek out other women when it was possible. Same-sex bias was highly resource specific and when women owners relied on prior ties, they were much more likely to ask a woman for advice than otherwise. For legal assistance, women

21

STRONG TIES, WEAK TIES AND STRANGERS

seeking advice who did not know any lawyers with the expertise they needed ended up with only men as advisors. When they knew someone already in that domain, it was more likely that they chose a woman lawyer (although most lawyers were still men).

In our assessment of the quality of assistance obtained via networking, we found that rather than being disadvantaged by not being part of an 'old boys' network,' women seemed to benefit slightly more from their networks, as measured by being able to pay less than market rates for legal and loan assistance. However, they apparently received the same quality advice as men, regardless of what they paid, and they were no more likely to use the advice they received than men. Both groups were able to find ways to obtain high-quality assistance.

We must be cautious in generalizing from our findings to the more general problem of resource mobilization facing all entrepreneurs. Entrepreneurs use networking to obtain customers, technology, suppliers, physical resources, financial resources, managerial and psychological support, and personnel. Entrepreneurs are almost always cash constrained when founding their firms and during any growth phases they experience. Thus, they make extensive use of networks instead of cash and seek cooperative arrangements whenever possible to get around their cash constraints. We have not investigated these other extremely important uses of networking and future research should certainly do so. We are especially interested in resources that are highly specialized or not commercially available, and therefore harder to obtain. Based on our results so far, we believe that the burden of proof has now shifted to those persons who assert that women entrepreneurs do seek assistance via different channels than men.

Implications

We thus find scant evidence that the results of women's networking – in patterns or in outcomes – differ in any substantial ways from those for men. Some structuralist theories posit that, regardless of their personal views, women's embeddedness in a network of obligations and responsibilities limits their freedom of action. Some personality and gender role theories posit that women might be less pro-active in pursuing opportunities than men, because they view business activity as wholistically integrated into the rest of their life. Some theories of sex differences in networking posit not a difference in activity, but rather a difference in the channels through which women, as opposed to men, seek assistance. Because of their pre-existing network ties, women are seen as more likely to turn to family and friends than to work associates.

Our results do not support the predictions of these theories. Instead, they support a view of women's networking as only marginally different from men's, with the main difference being that women are more likely than men

STRONG TIES, WEAK TIES AND STRANGERS

to turn to other women for some of the assistance they need. As in earlier studies, we found evidence for a sex bias in the composition of women's networks, but not in how they use them.

The entrepreneurship field's interest in networks has arisen in part because business strategists have asserted that personal networking can take some business activities 'out of the marketplace,' allowing entrepreneurs to obtain resources without depleting their hard-earned capital. These 'old boy networks' were formerly said to favor men and disadvantage women, but our results do not support this view. Instead, women now appear to be as good at playing them as the old boys themselves.

What are the implications for new/small business education programs? We believe that these programs should focus on skills sets, along with general education on issues of diversity, rather than on specialized agendas for special needs groups. There are two reasons why we feel this is important.

First, part of the battle against gender barriers in the world of new ventures involves changing stereotyped assumptions and low expectations about the capabilities of women entrepreneurs. Obviously, women business owners are just as capable as men at finding the assistance and support that they require for success. Until women are recognized as equally capable, they will continue to encounter resistance and obstacles in today's marketplace. Women-owned businesses continue to be smaller in size and lower in measures of profitability (Kalleberg and Leicht 1991), perhaps because of barriers in what we have labeled Circle I networks – strong tie advisor networks. Our results show that women are competing effectively in Circles II and III, but sex differences will persist as long as key positions are blocked to women.

Second, in a culture where gender roles are changing rapidly and work-places are becoming more heterogeneous, education about the potential barriers to success will benefit men as well as women. Building on Kalleberg and Leicht (1991), Fischer *et al.* (1993) found that innate gender differences were irrelevant to business success and that access to education was not a problem for women business owners. The area in which women entrepreneurs suffer most is access to start-up and industry experience, and subsequent exclusion from men's strong tie advisor networks. Because both men and women entrepreneurs will benefit from education on how to build their careers to gain necessary work experience, programs should be structured around agendas that focus on the development of business management skills.

Furthermore, educating men as well as women on the disadvantages faced by particular groups is also more likely, we believe, to lead to greater opportunities and access for these groups. For example, women know that, despite full-time employment, they carry more of the domestic burden than do their male counterparts. But what good is only raising the consciousness of the lower status group when much of the power for change lies higher up (Calas and Smircich 1992)? Improved chances for women business owners will

23

STRONG TIES, WEAK TIES AND STRANGERS

come when both men and women are taught the skills and information necessary to achieve success in new businesses and to promote equal opportunity in the marketplace.

ACKNOWLEDGEMENTS

We wish to thank Candida Brush, Neil C. Churchill, Umberto Lago and Nancy Langton for their excellent comments on earlier drafts of this chapter.

REFERENCES

Aldrich, H.E. (1989) 'Networking among women entrepreneurs', in O. Hagen, C. Rivchun and D. Sexton (eds) *Women Owned Businesses*, New York: Praeger: 103–32.

Aldrich, H.E., Reese, P.R. and Dubini, P. (1989) Women on the verge of a breakthrough? Networking among entrepreneurs in the United States and Italy, *Entrepreneurship and Regional Development* 1: 339–56.

Aldrich, H.E., Rosen, B. And Woodward, W. (1987) 'The impact of social networks on business foundings and profit', in N. Churchill, J. Hornaday, O.J. Krasner and K. Vesper (eds), *Frontiers of Entrepreneurship Research 1987*, Wellesley, MA: Babson College Center for Entrepreneurial Studies: 154–68.

Aldrich, H.E. and Sakano, T. (1995) 'Unbroken ties: how the personal networks of Japanese business owners compare to those in other nations', in Mark Fruin (ed.) *Networks and Markets: Pacific Rim Investigations*, New York: Oxford Press.

Aldrich, H.E. and Zimmer, C. (1986) 'Entrepreneurship through social networks', in D.L. Sexton and R.W. Smilor (eds) *The Art and Science of Entrepreneurship*, Cambridge, MA: Ballinger: 3–23.

Birley, S., Cromie, S. and Myers, A. (1990) *Entrepreneurial Networks: Their Creation and Development in Different Countries*, SWP 24/90, Bedford, UK: Cranfield School of Management.

Brush, C.G. (1992) 'Research on women business owners: past trends, a new perspective and future directions', *Entrepreneurship: Theory and Practice* 16: 5–30.

Calas, M. and Smircich, L. (1992) 'Using the "f" word: feminist theories and the social consequences of organizational research', in A.J. Mills and P. Tancred (eds) *Gendering Organizational Analysis*, Newbury Park, CA: Sage: 222–34.

Chaganti, R. (1986) 'Management in women-owned enterprises', *Journal of Small Business Management* 24: 18–29.

Cooper, A. and Dunkelberg, W. (1987) 'Old questions, new answers and methodological issues', *American Journal of Small Business* 11: 11–23.

Fischer, E.M., Reuber, A.R. and Dyke, L.S. (1993). 'A theoretical overview and extension of research on sex, gender, and entrepreneurship', *Journal of Business Venturing* 8: 151–68.

Gilligan, C. (1982) *In a Different Voice*, Cambridge, MA: Harvard.

Goffee, R. and Scase, R. (1985) *Women in Charge: The Experiences of Women Entrepreneurs*, London: Allen & Unwin.

Granovetter, M. (1985) 'The strength of weak ties', *American Journal of Sociology* 78: 1360–80.

Hertz, L. (1986) *The Business Amazons*, London: Deutsch.

STRONG TIES, WEAK TIES AND STRANGERS

Kalleberg, A. (1986) 'Entrepreneurship in the 1980s: a study of small business in Indiana', in G.D. Likecap (ed.), *Entrepreneurship and Innovation, Vol. I*, Greenwich, CT: JAI Press.

Kalleberg, A.L. and Leicht, K. (1991) 'Gender and organizational performance: determinants of small business survival and success', *Academy of Management Journal* 34: 136–61.

McPherson, J.M. and Smith-Lovin, L. (1986) 'Sex segregation in voluntary associations', *American Sociological Review* 51: 61–79.

Reese, P.R. (1992) *Entrepreneurial Networks and Resource Acquisition: Does Gender Make a Difference?*, PhD dissertation, University of North Carolina, Chapel Hill, NC.

Reese, P.R. and Aldrich, H.E. (1995) 'Entrepreneurial networks and business performance: a panel study of small and medium-sized firms in the Research Triangle', in S. Birley and I. McMillan (eds) *International Entrepreneurship*, London: Routledge.

Sexton, D.L. and Bowman-Upton, N. (1990) 'Female and male entrepreneurs: psychological characteristics and their role in gender-related discrimination', *Journal of Business Venturing* 5, January: 29–36.

Zimmer, C. and Aldrich, H.E. (1987) 'Resource mobilization through ethnic networks: kinship and friendship ties of shopkeepers in England', *Sociological Perspectives* 30(4), October: 422–55.

[9]

THE STRUCTURE OF FOUNDING TEAMS: HOMOPHILY, STRONG TIES, AND ISOLATION AMONG U.S. ENTREPRENEURS

MARTIN RUEF
Stanford University

HOWARD E. ALDRICH
University of North Carolina

NANCY M. CARTER
University of St. Thomas

The mechanisms governing the composition of formal social groups (e.g., task groups, organizational founding teams) remain poorly understood, owing to (1) a lack of representative sampling from groups found in the general population, (2) a "success" bias among researchers that leads them to consider only those groups that actually emerge and survive, and (3) a restrictive focus on some theorized mechanisms of group composition (e.g., homophily) to the exclusion of others. These shortcomings are addressed by analyzing a unique, representative data set of organizational founding teams sampled from the U.S. population. Rather than simply considering the properties of those founding teams that are empirically observed, a novel quantitative methodology generates the distribution of all possible teams, based on combinations of individual and relational characteristics. This methodology permits the exploration of five mechanisms of group composition—those based on homophily, functionality, status expectations, network constraint, and ecological constraint. Findings suggest that homophily and network constraints based on strong ties have the most pronounced effect on group composition. Social isolation (i.e., exclusion from a group) is more likely to occur as a result of ecological constraints on the availability of similar alters in a locality than as a result of status-varying membership choices.

SOCIOLOGISTS have made major strides toward understanding the conditions under which new organizations and new organizational forms are created, as well as the kinds of social locations that are most likely to spawn their creators. Beginning with Max Weber's ([1904–1905] 1992) analysis of ascetic Protestantism's contributions to the entrepreneurial spirit, sociologists have offered both macro- and microlevel interpretations of entrepreneurial phenomena (Carroll and Mosakowski 1987; Ruef 2000; Stinchcombe 1965). Today, sociologists conduct multilevel investigations, ranging from the personal networks of individual entrepreneurs to the transition of entire societies from socialism to capitalism (Aldrich forthcoming). Yet the mechanisms that may connect individual founders to one another remain poorly explicated.

The emergence of a new formal organization invariably entails a decision regarding who will participate and what they will contribute. Many entrepreneurs begin entirely on their own, although they may turn to oth-

Direct correspondence to Martin Ruef, Graduate School of Business, Stanford University, Stanford, CA 94305–5015 (ruef_martin@gsb.stanford.edu). We gratefully acknowledge the National Science Foundation for research support to Nancy Carter and Howard Aldrich under grant SBR-9809841, and the Center for Entrepreneurial Leadership at the Kauffman Foundation for their assistance in making this data available. We benefited from responses to presentations at Princeton, Harvard, Boston College, and the

2002 annual meeting of the American Sociological Association in Chicago. In particular, we thank Holly Arrow, Paul DiMaggio, Nancy DiTomaso, Elizabeth Mannix, Mark Mizruchi, Richard Moreland, Howard Stevenson, and anonymous *ASR* reviewers for their suggestions. All opinions and findings expressed are those of the author(s).

ers for help with various aspects of the founding process. Others begin with a team, making the enterprise a collective effort. Framed in this way, new organizations are clearly social entities from the beginning, as even solo founders implicitly make choices—or face constraints—that lead them *not* to cooperate with others in the founding process. How an organization begins and whether others are recruited to join the effort can have lasting consequences for its survival and performance. Why do some entrepreneurs go it alone, rather than join with others? On what basis do entrepreneurs in multimember teams choose other founders?

Our interest in entrepreneurial founding teams is linked with two broad themes in recent sociological theory and research. First, new organizations ensure the reproduction of existing populations of organizations and lay the foundation for the creation of new populations. Organizational ecologists have generally focused on dynamics within existing populations, noting that most founding attempts reproduce existing forms of organizations and are incremental rather than novel additions to the organizational landscape (Carroll and Hannan 2000). By contrast, evolutionary theorists have focused on the generation of new organizational populations, analyzing the conditions under which new forms of organizations carve out niches for themselves (Aldrich and Fiol 1994). Whether a new business simply copies an existing form or strikes off into novel territory can depend on the extent to which its founding team exhibits diverse capabilities and perspectives (Ruef 2002b). Investigating the forces that generate variation within founding teams thus carries the potential for explaining organizational innovation more generally.

Second, new organizations affect stratification and inequality in a society by shaping the life chances of entrepreneurs and their employees. Organizational foundings and disbandings generate a great deal of employment volatility through job creation and destruction. Between 1992 and 1996, about 28 million jobs were created in the United States by newly founded organizations (Birch 1997). For employees, organizational foundings create opportunities for advancement and facilitate the acquisition of addi-

tional human capital (Carroll and Mosakowski 1987; Haveman and Cohen 1994). For entrepreneurs, new business formation represents a potential for upward social mobility (Bates 1997; Nee and Sanders 1985). Many business owners employ family members in their business ventures, and some pass on their businesses—or the wealth gained from them—to their families (Keister and Moller 2000). To the extent that mobility and status considerations are taken into account by nascent entrepreneurs, these processes will tend to be reflected in mechanisms of inclusion and exclusion among organizational founding teams.

In this article, we consider how achieved and ascribed characteristics of entrepreneurs affect the composition of founding teams and how these characteristics are mediated by the social context of the entrepreneurial effort. From the sociological literature on group formation, we identify five general mechanisms that could influence team membership, including considerations of homophily, functionality, status expectations, network constraint, and ecological constraint. Homophily refers to the selection of other team members on the basis of similar ascriptive characteristics, such as gender, ethnicity, nationality, appearance, and the like (for a review, see McPherson, Smith-Lovin, and Cook 2001).[1] Functional theories consider the extent to which team members possess valuable and complementary achieved competencies that help ensure the success of a collectivity (e.g., Bales 1953; Slater 1955). Drawing on lines of research in expectation states (Fisek, Berger, and Norman 1991) and structuralism (Skvoretz and Fararo 1996), theories of status variation address the greater capacity of high-status individuals (with respect to ascribed *or* achieved characteristics) to attract other team members, compared with low-status individuals. Network perspectives posit that team formation occurs within a preexisting network of strong and weak ties that constrains the

---

[1] Most classical treatments of homophily (e.g., Lazarsfeld and Merton 1954) have not restricted it to ascriptive characteristics. For a purely homophilous mechanism to apply to achieved characteristics, however, the functional contributions of those characteristics must be ruled out.

founding team's choice of members. Finally, ecological perspectives emphasize the importance of the spatial proximity and environmental distribution of potential group members.

We examine these mechanisms of team composition using the Entrepreneurial Research Consortium's panel study of entrepreneurial dynamics (Reynolds 2000), a unique, nationally representative sample of nascent entrepreneurs. Previous studies of group formation have tended to analyze informal groups that happen to be observed in particular public spaces (James 1953; Mayhew et al. 1995), student project teams that are created in particular classrooms (Mannix, Goins, and Carroll 2002), or more formal teams that are observed in particular industries (for reviews and critique, see Cooper and Daily 1997; Lechler 2001). It is unclear to what extent these samples yield generalizable findings.[2] Another shortcoming of previous research on founding teams is that it has usually included only teams that have already achieved some level of success in organizational development. Such a "success bias" causes investigators to miss numerous founding teams that form but subsequently abandon their entrepreneurial effort and leads researchers to ignore the impact of changes in composition following initial team formation. We avoid such success bias by tracking entrepreneurs from the point when they first begin to take serious steps toward creating a new formal organization.

In addition to this empirical contribution, we also offer a methodological innovation that allows us to avoid success bias in analyzing the composition of entrepreneurial teams. As Goodman (1964) first noted in a path-breaking paper on systems of groups, proper estimation of size distributions and other mechanisms concerning group formation requires that an analyst consider all possible combinations of group members, not

just those observed in a given sample. We employ *structural event analysis* (Ruef 2002a) to generate the distribution of possible entrepreneurial teams and compare chance expectations within that distribution to empirical counts of the 816 teams in the national panel study. Poisson regression models are applied to account for deviations from expectations of chance group membership, based on mechanisms of homophily, functionality, status expectations, network constraint, and ecological constraint. We conclude by drawing out the empirical implications of these mechanisms for the ostensible sociability of some entrepreneurs and the relative isolation of others.

MECHANISMS OF GROUP COMPOSITION

In analyzing the formation of entrepreneurial teams, we consider five general mechanisms of group composition (see Table 1), which yield a set of hypotheses (H), corollaries (C), and assumptions (A). The hypotheses follow from the claims associated with each mechanism and some basic empirical generalizations regarding American society; corollaries hold true as a consequence of empirical proof for particular hypotheses. Although our hypotheses are examined in the specific context of organizational foundings, we believe that they may apply more broadly to the formation of task groups within a variety of settings, including established formal organizations.

HOMOPHILY

The mechanism of homophily explains group composition in terms of the similarity of members' characteristics. In principle, these characteristics may refer to social identities that are attached externally to individuals (e.g., ascribed characteristics such as gender, race, or age) or to internal states concerning values, beliefs, or norms (Lazarsfeld and Merton 1954).[3] In either

---

[2] Arrow, McGrath, and Berdahl (2000, chap. 2) note that most small group research since the 1950s has emphasized experimental designs—with compositional properties manipulated in laboratory settings—rather than the study of naturally occurring groups. This trend has led scholars away from such issues as group formation and composition.

---

[3] Clearly, identity and cognitive orientation tend to be linked in this explanation. The mechanism of homophily implies that individuals sharing a common identity also tend to share values, beliefs, or norms.

Table 1. Five General Explanations of Task-Group Composition

Theory	General Claims	Empirical Hypotheses, Corollaries, and Assumptions [a]
Homophily	Task groups tend to be composed of members with similar ascriptive characteristics (e.g., gender, ethnicity).	H_1: All-male and all-female teams will be more common than will mixed-gender teams.
		H_2: Ethnically homogeneous teams will be more common than will mixed-ethnicity teams.
Functional	Task groups tend to be composed of members with diverse achieved characteristics (e.g., leadership, occupational competency).	H_3: Teams with occupational diversity will be more common than teams lacking diversity.
		H_4: Occupational diversity will increase as a function of team size.
Status expectations	Individuals with high-status characteristics are more likely to attract other task-group members than are individuals with low-status characteristics.	H_5: Teams composed only of high-status members will be more common than those composed entirely from lower statuses.
		C_1: Given H_5, low-status persons will be more likely to be isolated than those from other backgrounds.
Network	The presence of prior network ties in a task group affects the extent to which the group exhibits diversity in ascribed and achieved characteristics.	A_1: Teams including family ties will have less ethnic diversity than teams lacking such ties.
		A_2: Teams including partner pairs will have greater gender diversity than teams lacking such ties.
		H_6: Teams composed of prior business acquaintances will have less occupational diversity than teams lacking such ties.
Ecological	Task groups tend to be composed of members in the same geographic locale and/or industry.	H_7: Homogeneous teams become more likely under conditions of residential/industrial segregation.
		C_2: Given H_1 and H_2, individuals that represent the numerical minority in a region/industry will be more likely to be isolated than others.

[a] All hypotheses assume that the size distribution and marginal probability for each team are controlled for, under a model of statistical independence.

case, the similarity of individuals disposes them toward a greater level of interpersonal attraction, trust, and understanding—and, consequently, greater levels of social affiliation—than would be expected among dissimilar individuals. This tendency toward homophily should be especially noticeable in groups such as organizational founding teams, which require sizable investments of time and resources (Bird 1989).

Although homophily may be analyzed in terms of ascribed characteristics, achieved characteristics, or internal psychological states, we restrict our operational definition of homophily to ascribed characteristics for several reasons. First, by excluding achieved characteristics (education, occupation, income) we prevent arguments regarding homophily from slipping into functional arguments regarding the efficacy of a social group. This is especially pertinent for groups that are task-oriented, such as business founding teams. Second, the similarity of group members in terms of psychological states is often endogenous to the group-formation process itself. Moreover, homophily in this regard may result as much from the *misattribution* of shared understandings among affiliated individuals as from actual shared understandings, because individuals tend to assume that others with whom they have structural bonds think as they do (Jussim and Osgood 1989; McPherson et al. 2001).

One of the most widely studied ascriptive characteristics driving homophily is gender. Gender homophily has been identified in a variety of task-oriented settings, including work establishments (Kalleberg et al. 1996), voluntary organizations (McPherson and Smith-Lovin 1982, 1987), and managerial networks (Ibarra 1997). Although representative data for founding teams is sparse, researchers have found that men's business discussion networks contain few women and thus contribute to gender homogeneity (Aldrich 1999:85–86; Carter 1994). Women's business support groups, often formed as a reaction to male dominance in entrepreneurial activities (Aldrich 1989), may further enhance homophily. Insofar as gender is a highly visible ascribed characteristic driving attributions of similarity and difference in emergent organizations, we propose that:

Hypothesis 1: All-male and all-female organizational founding teams will be more common than will mixed gender teams.[4]

A second ascriptive dimension that generates strong network homophily is ethnicity (Marsden 1987; McPherson et al. 2001). Studies of many task-group settings—such as workplaces (Kalleberg et al. 1996; Reskin 1999) and classrooms (Schofeld 1995)—reveal substantial homogeneity in ethnic composition, especially among white ethnic majorities. For entrepreneurial founding teams, the literature has also tended to emphasize solidarity within ethnicities, but primarily

among minority and immigrant groups (e.g., Aldrich and Waldinger 1990; Wilson and Martin 1982). Variations of in-group preferences across ethnicities may result from a number of factors, including ecological constraints on the availability of other entrepreneurs sharing a common ethnicity, discriminatory status expectations, and unmeasured network effects. With respect to baseline expectations, however, the existing literature supports the proposition that:

Hypothesis 2: Ethnically homogeneous organizational founding teams will be more common than will mixed-ethnicity teams.

FUNCTIONALITY

In opposition to the principle of homophily, many functionalist theories of task-group composition argue for the importance of *diversity* among members, especially with respect to achieved characteristics, such as leadership skills and task expertise. Pioneering research by Bales (1953) and Slater (1955) on small-group settings emphasized the dual necessity of socio-emotional leadership and task leadership. Subsequent research and theorizing on organizational founding teams has explored the extent to which entrepreneurs draw on diverse, complementary skills that may lie beyond the abilities of any individual founder, especially in high technology industries (Gartner 1985:703; Vesper 1990). Eisenhardt and Schoonhoven (1990) linked team diversity to functional performance, noting that organizational growth among semiconductor firms was higher for organizations with heterogeneous founding teams. At a more microlevel, Ancona and Caldwell (1992) reported benefits of functional diversity for communication and innovation in their study of product teams.[5]

We anticipate that new formal organizations in general, rather than just those in high–tech environments, may benefit from having founders with a diverse set of work experiences and occupational backgrounds. Having a chef, a restaurant manager, and a

---

[4] All hypotheses are subject to the usual *ceteris paribus* conditions. In particular, this means that the marginal distribution of different groups (e.g. men and women) is controlled for, that the propability of joint occurrences from these groups is addressed, and that predictions are advanced net of group size.

---

[5] Ancona and Caldwell (1992) also identified a potential drawback in that functional diversity might impede successful collaboration.

marketing agent on the founding team, for instance, can enhance the success of a new restaurant. By the same token, a precision manufacturing facility may profit from the entrepreneurial skills of an industrial engineer, an experienced machine operator, and a shop-floor supervisor. Following a functionalist logic, if potential founders anticipate such benefits of skill diversity in advance, then we expect that:

Hypothesis 3: Teams with founders from diverse occupational backgrounds will be more common than will teams lacking functional diversity.

This hypothesis regarding diversity is subject to two important caveats. First, occupational attachments can be a source of homophily, as well as diversity, insofar as occupations provide a common basis of socialization and, possibly, interpersonal relationships. What predominates in a given situation may depend on contact opportunities among individuals from different occupations as well as on the functional salience of occupational diversity per se—as opposed, for example, to diversity in education, previous work roles, and nonoccupational skills. We address this issue in Hypothesis 6.

Second, the desire for a functional division of labor may be contingent on the size of an entrepreneurial team. As Durkheim ([1893] 1949) emphasized, functional specialization tends to increase with group size, largely as a mechanism for the reduction of interpersonal competition. In groups that are characterized by large numbers of members and intensive interaction, a lack of differentiation in functional competencies can lead members to engage in turf battles over resources or work responsibilities. Insofar as teams are subject to similar dilemmas resulting from overlapping competencies, a functionalist logic suggests that:

Hypothesis 4: The occupational diversity of founding team members will increase with team size.

STATUS EXPECTATIONS

Arguments about the mechanisms of homophily and functionality treat distinctions within task groups—based on ascribed or achieved characteristics—as simple nominal ones. However, an extensive literature in social psychology notes that such nominal distinctions tend to be translated into rank-ordered status relationships insofar as they become tied to performance expectations (Berger et al. 1977; Skvoretz and Fararo 1996).[6] Even those ascriptive characteristics that are logically irrelevant to task performance (e.g., gender and race in most task situations) become subject to a "burden of proof process" in which group members must demonstrate that those characteristics are, in fact, substantively irrelevant (Fisek et al. 1991). Consequently, widely held cultural biases regarding status (e.g., of men over women, of ethnic majorities over minorities, etc.) are likely to affect processes of task-group formation and composition.[7]

The principle impact of status expectations on group composition tends to involve differential homophily among status groups. Assuming that only two status groups (A and B) are salient, with A being high-status and B being low-status, we expect that A individuals will have a strong associative preference for other A individuals, while B individuals will also have an associative preference for A individuals (which may not always be fulfilled). One consequence of this pattern is that the observed level of homophily among the elite As will be high, while the observed level of homophily among the lower status Bs will be lower (or perhaps negligible, in the absence of a general homophily mechanism). Bs would rather associate with the higher status As than with one another. Operationally, such status-varying homophily may involve ascribed characteristics (e.g., gender) or achieved characteristics (e.g., occupation), leading to the following predictions for our sample of founding teams:

---

[6] Blau's (1977) theory of macrostructure likewise distinguishes between *nominal* and *graduated* parameters that may affect social interaction. Unlike the more micro-oriented theories in social psychology, however, he does not account for ways in which nominal parameters may be translated into graduated parameters (or vice versa).

[7] However, the gender effects found in early research on status expectations are probably weaker now in the general population than they were several decades ago.

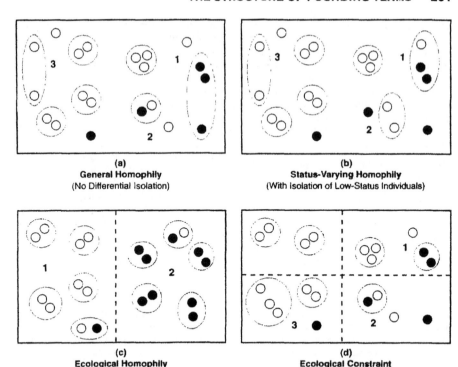

Figure 1. Patterns of Homophily and Isolation

Hypothesis 5: Organizational founding teams composed only of high-status persons (e.g., males, members of the ethnic majority, professionals) will be more common than those created entirely from other statuses.

For some sociodemographic dimensions, this tendency toward high-status homophily appears to be widely institutionalized in contemporary society. For example, the term "old boys network" connotes homophily among male managers and entrepreneurs. Similarly, the legal recognition of a professional partnership or corporation (Burke and Zaloom 1970) increases the likelihood of homophily within professional occupations—though it is more typically described in the guise of professional autonomy and self-determination (Freidson 1986). For other sociodemographic dimensions, the direction of status-varying homophily is less clear. Thus, the literature on ethnic entrepre-

neurship implies a tendency *away* from high-status homophily, as minorities and immigrants, regardless of occupation, form stronger in-group bonds than do whites in the face of discrimination and lack of alternative career opportunities (Aldrich and Waldinger 1990).

Status-varying homophily has a second general consequence that bears analysis. If members of an elite status group, A, tend to attract other members of A as well as some upstarts from a lower status group, B, it follows that individuals in B will be at higher risk of social isolation than those in A. Bs who are unable to affiliate with As may even prefer going solo, rather than working with other Bs. Notably, this consequence cannot be derived from general homophily alone (see Figure 1a). Given a population of 15 individuals in group A (white circles), five individuals in group B (black circles), and no status differentiation between the two, a general homophily effect predicts proportionate isolation of A and B individuals, with a relatively high proportion of other individuals in homogeneous groups (1 and 3) and only a few in heterogeneous groups (2). But with the activation of status differences (see Figure 1b), homogeneous low-status groups will seek to incorporate proximate high-status individuals in lieu of low-status ones (1) and formerly heterogeneous groups will tend to drop low-status members to conform to a homogeneous, high-status ideal (2). As a result, low-status individuals become disproportionately isolated.[8]

For entrepreneurs, isolation can pose both functional and social psychological problems. Multimember teams enjoy several benefits over solo entrepreneurs (Kamm and Nurik 1993; Lechler 2001), including a more diverse skill set (Vesper 1990), improved capacity for innovation (Ruef 2002b), and higher levels of social and emotional support (Bird 1989). Consistent with a theory of status expectations, empirical evidence suggests that entrepreneurs with a lower ascribed or achieved status are less likely to be members of teams and enjoy these benefits. For instance, while longitudinal trends in the United States point to the increasing proportion of female entrepreneurs, they also suggest that women are disproportionately involved in founding solo proprietorships, rather than partnerships or corporations (U.S. Department of Commerce 1996). More generally, if status-varying homophily applies to sociodemographic dimensions such as gender, ethnicity, and occupation (Hypothesis 5), it follows that:

Corollary 1: Low-status entrepreneurs (women, minorities, blue-collar workers) will be more likely to be isolated than will those from other sociodemographic backgrounds.

NETWORK CONSTRAINT

During the process of group formation, the choice of members based on shared identities, functional considerations, or status expectations is inevitably constrained by struc-

tural opportunities for social contact. One conduit of structural opportunity involves prior network ties among group members. These ties can be characterized broadly in terms of three concentric circles of social relationships: family members (strong ties), acquaintances and friends (weak ties), and strangers (Aldrich, Elam, and Reese 1996; also see Granovetter 1973). The extent to which the relational composition of a group relies on one concentric circle rather than another has crucial implications for the operation of other mechanisms of group composition.

Family members, particularly spouses and domestic partners, fulfill many requisites of shared identity that are otherwise generated through homophily. They interact frequently and tend to share rewarding experiences. With respect to entrepreneurial activity, family members have many opportunities to discuss the possibility of starting a new organization together. Ideas that might be superficially discussed and dismissed in other contexts often lead, among kin, to more cumulative plans for action. These considerations suggest that a failure to control for the presence of kinship ties in founding teams may lead to inflated estimates of homophily along certain ascriptive dimensions, particularly ethnicity.

For one ascriptive characteristic, however, the reverse is true. The substantial number of heterosexual spouse pairs that attempt to start business or nonprofit organizations together will deflate estimates of gender homophily (Aldrich, Carter, and Ruef forthcoming). To separate choice homophily from the gender heterogeneity induced by spouse pairs, we recognize that teams including spouse pairs will have greater gender diversity than teams lacking such ties. As with kinship ties, we treat this effect not as a hypothesis, but instead as an assumption about the gender composition of spousal pairs.

Among individuals who are not related but who know each other fairly well—such as work associates working for the same employer or in the same industry—some of the same interpersonal dynamics apply as with family members, but with less intensity. Work associates also have opportunities to develop trust and observe one another's strengths and weaknesses. Nevertheless,

---

[8] Note that a dynamic consequence of Bs' preferences for affiliations with As and their difficulty of doing so is to further raise the already high status of As.

such functional benefits may be offset to some extent when work associates share overlapping competencies. If many work associates have similar work experiences or occupational backgrounds, the principle of functional diversity (Hypothesis 3) is compromised. Functional complementarity depends, in part, on team members having diverse occupations because they come from different organizations with distinctive divisions of labor. On the other hand, when entrepreneurial teams are developed on the basis of collegial ties, we expect that:

Hypothesis 6: Teams including prior business acquaintances will have less occupational diversity than teams lacking such ties.

ECOLOGICAL CONSTRAINT

Aside from network constraint, the sheer numbers and spatial distribution of individuals having distinctive characteristics will influence what associations are likely to form. The importance of geographic proximity in group formation has long been recognized in both the microsociological (Goffman 1963) and macrosociological (Hawley 1950) literatures. Blau's (1977, 1980) program of macrostructural research develops theorems explicitly on the basis of which nominal or rank-ordered characteristics tend to be more common among the population of a region, leading to ecological constraints on patterns of association. Similar ecological constraints operate at a microlevel, but many are so fundamental to processes of group formation that they constitute baseline expectations about which individuals are expected to be found together in a group, rather than predictions of theoretical interest.

Several implications of ecological constraints on association merit further analysis. Organizational ecologists have emphasized the impact of industrial, as well as spatial, context on founding processes (Carroll and Hannan 2000). With respect to individual entrepreneurs, both industry and spatial constraints can generate aggregate tendencies toward homophily or isolation, independently of the group membership choices being made by the entrepreneurs. For purposes of explication in our hypothetical system of 20 individuals in Figure 1, we now assume

that group formation is feasible only within two local "quadrants," which may be geographic or industry-based (Figure 1c). Because of residential or industrial segregation, one quadrant (1) is heavily dominated by individuals in group A (white circles), while the other (2) is dominated by individuals in group B (black circles). If we think of the two quadrants as representing car repair shops and beauty salons, for example, then this pattern might be observed for industry sex segregation, with entrepreneurs in the car repair industry having a 90/10 male-female ratio and entrepreneurs in the beauty salon industry having a 10/90 male-female ratio.[9]

Such extreme cases of industrial segregation can lead to pronounced levels of homophily at an aggregate level, even when teams are constituted by random mixing within industries. Eighty percent of the two-person dyads shown in the figure are homophilous, although we would only expect 50 percent to be homophilous given the marginal gender distribution across industries.[10] When the industries are analyzed separately, however, the number of homophilous dyads in each quadrant reproduce statistical expectations, calculated as $.9 \times .9 \times 1$ combination $= 81$ percent of dyads composed of dominant group members. This reasoning leads to the proposition that homophily—at an aggregate level—can be induced by ecological constraints, as well as network and social psychological mechanisms:

Hypothesis 7: Homogeneous founding teams become more likely under conditions of strong residential and/or industrial segregation among entrepreneurs.

Ecological constraint may have implications for isolation as well as team homo-

---

[9] We assume that entrepreneurs choose from a restricted range of options when considering which industries to enter. Thus, in the short run, they succumb to the constraints we have identified.

[10] The overall gender distribution is a 50/50 mix. Under a model of random mixing, we would expect 25 percent $(.5 \times .5 \times 1$ combination) of the dyads to involve two males, 25 percent $(.5 \times .5 \times 1)$ to involve two females, and 50 percent $(.5 \times .5 \times 2$ combinations) to involve a mixed gender dyad.

phily. In his macrostructural theory, Blau (1977) notes that a population representing the numerical minority along some socio-demographic characteristic would be forced into greater levels of association with a population representing the numerical majority, as the minority population becomes proportionately smaller. In an elaboration on this model, Blau (1980) considers the possibility that members of a numerical minority may be at disproportionate risk of isolation, given the effects of homophily and propinquity (see Figure 1d). The likelihood that members of different groups will associate with one another is affected not only by their relative proportions in the population, but also by their degree of geographical dispersion or segregation. Group formation may only be feasible within local geographic "quadrants." In contrast to a system lacking ecological constraints (see Figure 1a), some geographically dispersed groups that are members of a numerical minority may not be able to find one another, leaving their solo members isolated. Naturally, the problem of ecological constraint also affects groups composed of members from the numerical majority (quadrant 3 in Figure 1d), but in those cases it is easier for the resulting isolates to reorganize themselves with proximate and similar alters. These considerations suggest that:

Corollary 2: Individuals who represent the numerical minority along any socio-demographic dimension will be more likely to be isolated than will those in the numerical majority.[11]

For many ascribed and achieved characteristics, Corollary 2 produces consequences similar to those anticipated because of status-varying homophily (Corollary 1). Our nationally representative sample suggests that female nascent entrepreneurs in the United States are only half as common as

---

[11] In contrast to Hypothesis 7, Corollary 2 assumes a relatively low level of residential or industrial segregation. High levels of segregation can reduce isolation among members of a numerical minority, while the random dispersion of a minority group among the majority necessarily leads to the former's isolation under conditions of general homophily and ecological constraints on association.

male entrepreneurs. Corollary 2 predicts, therefore, that female nascent entrepreneurs will be less likely to find associates with whom to found a new organization, given conditions of general homophily and ecological constraint. The same result, however, could be derived from a status-varying pattern of group formation in which women are less willing to associate with other women, even when geographic proximity is not a significant issue. Distinguishing between the two causes of isolation thus requires careful attention to the salience of general homophily and status-induced differential homophily.

DATA, MEASURES, AND METHOD

DATA

We use data from the Panel Study of Entrepreneurial Dynamics (PSED) to analyze the compositional properties of organizational founding teams. Between July 1998 and January 2000 a total of 64,622 individuals in the United States were contacted by telephone using a random-digit dialing process to identify those in the process of starting a business ("nascent entrepreneurs"). The data employed here are organized into three subsamples, which correspond to different funding sources and different data collection periods. The Entrepreneurial Research Consortium (ERC), which consisted primarily of academic institutions, financed data collection for a mixed-gender sample of nascent entrepreneurs. Another subsample was limited to an oversample of women entrepreneurs and funded by the National Science Foundation (NSF). Subsequently, the National Science Foundation provided funding for a third subsample—an oversample of minorities engaged in business start-up activities.

The research design for the PSED specified two phases for data collection. In the first phase, a marketing research firm telephoned households as part of a national survey that involved contacting 1,000 adults (500 females and 500 males 18 years of age or older) each week. Multiple phone calls (at least three) were made to contact each person. When an adult 18 years of age or older was identified and agreed to respond to the survey, a phone interview was administered. Two items were randomly inserted at different points in the survey and were used to determine whether the respondent qualified as a nascent entrepreneur: (1) "Are you, alone or with others, now trying to start a business?" and (2) "Are you, alone or with others, now starting a new business or new venture for your employer?" If the respondent answered yes to either of the questions, two additional questions were used to qualify whether the respondent was actively involved with the start-up process, and whether he or she would share ownership in the business. Affirmative responses to both additional questions were necessary for individuals to be considered "nascent entrepreneurs." Individuals who qualified as nascent entrepreneurs were invited to participate in a national study conducted through the University of Wisconsin and promised a cash payment.[12]

In the second phase of the data collection, the names, telephone numbers, and basic sociodemographic information of individuals who met the screening criteria were forwarded to the University of Wisconsin Survey Research Laboratory (UWSRL), where a detailed phone interview was conducted followed by a mailed questionnaire. More complete details about the sampling procedures can be found in Shaver et al. (2001).

SAMPLE AND WEIGHTS

The final sample of PSED respondents totals 830 nascent entrepreneurs. Of these, 7 respondents indicated that "nonpersons" expected to own more than 50 percent of the venture. We removed these cases from analyses, reasoning that they were influenced unduly by corporate interests rather than by the initiative of individual entrepreneurs. Six respondents indicated that their new venture had positive cash flow for more than 90 days before the initial interview by

UWSRL. We considered these efforts to be infant businesses and removed them from the analyses. Finally, one respondent indicated that their start-up involved a team, but failed to provide sociodemographic information that could be used to classify the respondent's gender or race/ethnicity. The case was disqualified. The elimination of these 14 cases reduced the sample size to 816 nascent entrepreneurs.

Because several of the subsamples described above involved oversampling of certain subgroups of the population, we employed post-stratification weights for each respondent based on estimates from the U.S. Census Bureau's Current Population Survey. The post-stratification scheme was based on gender, age, education, and race/ethnicity. More complete details about the computation of the weighting scheme can be found in Reynolds (2000).

MEASURES

The data of interest here come from items on the phone interview that were designed to collect information about: (1) characteristics of people who were helping to start the venture, and (2) relationships among the founding members (if applicable). During the UWSRL phone interview, respondents were asked, "How many people will legally own this new business—only you, only you and your spouse, or you and other people or businesses?" If the respondent indicated others would share ownership in the venture, they were asked to identify up to five who would have the highest level of ownership, and the ownership percentage to be held by each team member.[13] The respondent was then asked to provide information about each cofounder, including gender, ethnicity (white, African American, nonwhite Hispanic, Asian, other), primary occupation (open-ended response later classified into four categories: professional/technical; administrative/managerial; sales/service; operative/production), and the nature of the

---

[12] Offering incentives to gain participants, or to convert nonrespondents, has become a common practice in survey organizations (Singer, Van Hoewyk, and Maher 2000). A traditional method used to increase response rates in mail surveys, the practice has been expanded to telephone projects using random-digit dialing.

[13] Although this data collection procedure may truncate the team size distribution, less than 1 percent of the teams in the ERC sample involved more than six members (Reynolds 2002, personal communication).

Table 2. Descriptive Statistics for Organizational Founding Teams: Panel Study of Entrepreneurial Dynamics, 1998 to 2000

Variable	Number of Cases	Response	Weighted Count/Proportion
Size of team	816	One member	395
		Two members	312
		Three members	55
		Four members	31
		Five+ members	23
Industry of team	800	Primary/manufacturing	.19
		Personal service	.17
		Retail/wholesale	.28
		Business/professional Service	.36
Gender of member	1,423	Male	.62
		Female	.38
Gender composition of multimember team	421	All male	.29
		All female	.07
		Mixed-gender	.64
Ethnicity of member	1,347 [a]	White	.72
		Black	.17
		Hispanic	.09
		Asian	.02
Ethnic composition of multimember team	399 [a]	Single ethnicity	.86
		Multiple ethnicities	.14
Occupation of member	1,089 [b]	Professional	.30
		Administrative	.28
		Sales/service	.21
		Operative/production	.21
Occupational composition of multimember team	303 [b]	Single occupation	.32
		Multiple occupations	.68
Relational composition of multimember team	421	With spouses/partners	.53
		With nonspouse family member	.18
		With business associates	.15

[a] Excludes multimember teams involving other ethnicities or with missing information.

[b] Excludes multimember teams with any missing information on occupational composition.

relationships among all team members (spouses/partners; relatives/family members; business associates/work colleagues; friends/acquaintances; strangers before joining the team; other).

The dependent variable in our analysis involves the number of founding teams conforming to a particular combination of sociodemographic and relational characteristics. In turn, those characteristics—and the design parameters that describe how they are combined—serve as the independent variables. Our methodological approach employs the 816 sampled founding teams as its units of analysis, while incorporating information on the 1,423 individual persons that make up the teams (see Table 2).[14]

The size distribution of the teams in our weighted sample follows the truncated Poisson distribution that has been noted more

---

[14] A few teams also involved institutional founding members; these members are ignored in the following analyses.

generally for free-forming groups (Coleman and James 1961; White 1962), with a substantial number of solo entrepreneurs (395) and relatively few large teams (e.g., 23 founding teams involving five or more entrepreneurs). The majority of the entrepreneurs in the sample are white (72 percent) males (62 percent) involved in professional (30 percent) or administrative (28 percent) occupations. We also report some aspects of team composition for the 421 multimember founding teams (i.e., excluding "solo" entrepreneurs). These statistics indicate that most multimember teams involve a mixture of men and women (64 percent), relatively few incorporate members from more than one ethnicity (14 percent), and over half include married couples or cohabitating partners (53 percent). The majority of multimember teams (68 percent) display some functional diversity, drawing on more than one occupational category.

STATISTICAL METHODOLOGY

We employ a structural event analysis (Ruef 2002a) to predict the number of entrepreneurial teams matching some set of compositional characteristics, considering all possible teams (not just those that actually form). The risk set of possible teams is enumerated using counting rules drawn from combinatorial analysis (see Appendix A). Each potential team is treated as a case for purposes of analysis, leading to a Poisson distribution of team counts (Goodman 1964). These counts can then be predicted via the following Poisson regression:

$$P[f(E_i) = y] = e^{-\lambda}(\lambda^y / y!), \qquad (1)$$

where λ is defined in terms of the conditional probability for structural event occurrence $\lambda = f (p[E|r], r)$, and r specifies the size of each team. A baseline probability for each group, under an assumption of random population mixing (see Appendix A), is included as a fixed parameter in every Poisson regression. All other design parameters reflect deviations from random mixing and are estimated using maximum-likelihood techniques.

Because the number of possible teams grows exponentially for analyses involving multiple sociodemographic dimensions,

bootstrap techniques are used to analyze large, sparse matrices. In these cases, we construct a sample by selecting all cells with a nonzero observed count of founding teams, all other cells involving solo entrepreneurs or dyads, and one percent of the cells with an expected team size of three or greater and no observed team counts.[15] Structural zeros—those cells where a marginal frequency is zero—are removed from the sample. Weighted maximum-likelihood techniques are used to derive the corresponding estimates.

RESULTS

We test the theoretical claims advanced in Table 1 via a series of analyses that address compositional properties among entrepreneurial founding teams, beginning with a simple descriptive analysis of gender homophily (see Table 3). Using rote enumeration, we see that there are 20 possible teams involving unrestricted combinations of the two gender roles ([M]ale and [F]emale). The same quantity can be derived from the respective counting rule (see Appendix A, equation A-1), which yields 2 + 3 + 4 + 5 + 6 = 20 structural events for a system of two roles ($|N| = 2$) and no more than five participants per group ($r(H) = 5$). Categorizing teams further by the presence of spouse/partner ties, there are 20 possible gender combinations with no spouses or partners, 18 possible combinations with one spouse/partner pair (i.e., excluding solos), and 11 possible combinations with two spouse/partner pairs. The corresponding 49 structural events are shown in Table 3.

Inspection of the observed counts indicates that over a third (18) of the possible structural events are not actually realized for this sample; one gender combination (MFFFF) is not observed for any of the subsamples based on the presence of spouse/partner pairs. The expected counts in the table are derived using the multinomial formula (Appendix A, equation A-2) and knowledge of the marginal distributions.

---

[15] The sampling rate for the bootstrap methodology is based on the low sampling error anticipated for this sample size. The results are virtually identical when the rate is doubled or tripled.

Table 3. Observed and Expected Cell Counts for Gender Composition of Founding Teams: Panel Study of Entrepreneurial Dynamics, 1998 to 2000

Structural Event	Observed Count	Expected Count	Structural Event	Observed Count	Expected Count
Teams without Spouses/Partners			*Teams with One Spouse/Partner Dyad (Continued)*		
M	228	245.9	(MFF)	4	2.9
F	166	148.1	(FMM)	7	4.8
MM	73	46.7	(MMMM)	0	1.5
FF	27	17.0	(FFFF)	0	.2
MF	20	56.3	(MMFF)	1	3.3
MMM	28	10.7	(MFFF)	2	1.3
FFF	2	2.3	(FMMM)	7	3.7
MFF	3	11.7	(MMMMM)	0	.3
FMM	11	19.3	(FFFFF)	0	.0
MMMM	9	2.4	(MMFFF)	1	.6
FFFF	1	.3	(FFMMM)	1	1.0
MMFF	2	5.3	(MFFFF)	0	.2
MFFF	2	2.1	(FMMMM)	1	.9
FMMM	2	5.8	*Teams with Two Spouse/Partner Dyads*		
MMMMM	10	1.6	(MMMM)	0	.8
FFFFF	1	.1	(FFF)	0	.2
MMFFF	0	3.5	(MMFF)	5	1.7
FFMMM	2	5.8	(MFFF)	0	.7
MFFFF	0	1.1	(FMMM)	0	1.8
FMMMM	4	4.8	(MMMMM)	0	.3
Teams with One Spouse/Partner Dyad			(FFFFF)	0	.0
(MM)	2	25.1	(MMFFF)	1	.4
(FF)	0	27.4	(FFMMM)	1	.7
(MF)	191	90.5	(MFFFF)	0	.1
(MMM)	0	2.7	(FMMMM)	0	.6
(FFF)	0	.6			

Note: The sum of observed counts may not equal marginal totals because of rounding errors. Parentheses indicate spouse/partner relationships; N = 816.

Shaded areas indicate homogeneous multimember teams.

Men make up 62 percent of the entrepreneurs in the weighted sample, while women make up the remaining 38 percent. The distribution for the five size categories is: 395, 312, 55, 31, and 23. Finally, we note that 52 percent of the four-person founding teams do not include any spouse or partner pairs. Thus, to use one illustrative example, the expected number of founding teams without a spouse/partner pair composed of two men and two women is calculated as $[4!/(2! \times 2!)]$ $(.62^2 \times .38^2)(31)(.52) \approx 5.3$, more than twice the observed cell count. In many cases, we find that observed counts of single-gender teams (see shaded areas in table) exceed expectations, while counts of mixed-gender teams are lower than expectations. Exceptions to the rule tend to occur when spouse/partner ties exist within the founding teams.

To further examine the interaction of gender homophily and network constraint, we conducted a structural event analysis using Poisson regression models (see Table 4, Models 1 through 3). Model 1 illustrates

Table 4. Coefficients from Poisson Regression Models Testing Gender Composition of Founding Teams: Panel Study of Entrepreneurial Dynamics, 1998 to 2000

Independent Variable	Baseline Models			Models Controlling for Network Ties	
	Model 1	Model 2	Model 3	Model 4	Model 5
Intercept	5.976***	6.894***	8.207***	6.714***	6.725***
	(.050)	(.069)	(.189)	(.244)	(.244)
Team size	—	−.782***	−1.188***	−1.052***	−1.056***
		(.034)	(.069)	(.068)	(.068)
Size Category					
1 member	—	—	−1.043***	.315	.232
			(.135)	(.201)	(.205)
2 members	−.230**	—	—	—	—
	(.076)				
3 members	−1.969***	—	—	—	—
	(.144)				
4 members	−2.542***	—	—	—	—
	(.187)				
5 members	−2.886***	—	—	—	—
	(.219)				
Homophily					
Gender homophily	—	—	−.355+++	1.611+++	1.457+++
			(.104)	(.171)	(.236)
Status-varying homophily	—	—	—	—	.195
					(.201)
Minority isolation [a]	—	—	—	—	.189+
					(.102)
Opportunity Structure					
Partners/spouses × Gender homophily	—	—	—	−6.258+++	−6.253+++
				(.730)	(.730)
Model fit (G^2)	438.94	517.43	458.90	78.72	74.34
Degrees of freedom (design/fixed)	5/7	2/7	4/7	5/8	7/8

Note: Numbers in parentheses are standard errors. Number of structural events = 49; number of teams = 816.

[a] Women represent the gender minority.

*$p < .05$ **$p < .01$ ***$p < .001$ (two-tailed tests)
+$p < .05$ ++$p < .01$ +++$p < .001$ (one-tailed tests)

how a structural event analysis can be used to recover the distribution of group sizes for a particular sample. The specification implicitly includes a fixed parameter log $p(E|r)$ with a coefficient constrained to 1.0, which accounts for the probability of observing a given gender composition under an assumption of random mixing (see Appendix A, equation A-2). The fixed parameter is calculated based on the marginal distributions of gender and of spouse/partnership ties across

different team sizes (d.f. = 7).[16] The specification also includes an intercept and four design parameters for different team sizes.

[16] One degree of freedom is employed for the marginal gender distribution, four degrees of freedom are employed for the distribution of groups with a single spouse/partner dyad across team sizes two through five, and two degrees of freedom are employed for the distribution of groups with two spouse/partner dyads among team sizes four and five.

Adding the intercept (which corresponds to the number of founding "teams" with only a single member) to the respective coefficient estimates and taking the antilog allows us to recover the marginal size distribution (e.g., the number of four-member founding teams is $e^{5.976-2.542} = e^{3.434} = 31$).

Following the distributional implications of Goodman's (1964) model for group formation, Model 2 replaces the four size dummy variables with a single parameter for group size. Consistent with previous observations of free-forming groups (e.g. Coleman and James 1961; Mayhew et al. 1995), the parameter estimate reflects the fact that the observed frequency of founding teams varies inversely with size. This parsimonious model specification is then used as a baseline for a test of the homophily mechanism in Model 3, which adds two new design parameters. The parameter for homophily identifies whether a team is all-male or all-female (= 1) or of mixed composition (= 0). Surprisingly, the results suggest a strong *negative* effect for gender homophily ($p < .001$), with homogeneous groups appearing at a rate that is .70 ($e^{-.355}$) times that of comparable heterogeneous groups. This apparent tendency away from gender homophily seems to reflect the large number of heterosexual spouse and partner dyads on these entrepreneurial teams: 217 teams in the weighted sample included one spouse/partner pair and 7 teams included two.[17]

To what extent is gender heterogeneity induced by structural opportunity (e.g., selection of spouses as team members), and to what extent does it occur because of choice of dissimilar alters? Models 4 and 5 explore this issue by including a design parameter for single-gender teams with partner or spouse dyads. The results provide a more accurate picture of tendencies toward homophily (Model 4). Consistent with Hypothesis 1, there is now significant *positive* gender

homophily ($p < .001$), with homogeneous teams being five times ($e^{1.611}$) more likely than heterogeneous teams, net of romantic relationships. The specification in Model 4 illustrates the importance of separating the effect of the network constraint mechanism from the homophily mechanism.

Model 5 extends the analysis, considering whether there is substantial status-varying homophily—with all-male teams being more common than all-female teams—and whether female entrepreneurs tend to become disproportionately isolated. Contrary to status expectations theory (Hypothesis 5), there is no evidence that male entrepreneurs are more likely to band together than are female entrepreneurs. Nevertheless, there is disproportionate isolation of women in this sample, with solo female entrepreneurs appearing 1.21 times as often as expected based on the marginal distribution of gender. Given that entrepreneurial team formation is subject to general homophily but not status-varying homophily, we suggest (following Corollary 2) that the principal reason for the isolation of women may be ecological constraint. Because female entrepreneurs are far less common than male entrepreneurs, they may experience greater difficulty in finding other women with whom to start a business in their industry.

This explanation of gender homophily and differential isolation assumes that there is not a strong tendency toward gender segregation, particularly across industrial sectors. If gender segregation is high, then homophily may result as an artifact of ecological constraints on contact opportunities (Hypothesis 7). To explore this possibility, we split our founding team sample into subsamples based on industry categories—primary/manufacturing, retail/wholesale, personal services, business/professional services—and examined the gender distribution and level of homophily within each category (see Table 5).[18] There is some evidence of industrial sex segregation, with one sector—including primary and manufacturing industries—exhibiting a skewed gender distribution and no significant

---

[17] The other new parameter in Model 3 controls for "teams" composed of a single entrepreneur, which are tautologically homophilous. The corresponding parameter estimate is not substantively interesting in and of itself, but permits consistent estimation of the model independently of the way that gender homophily is coded for solo entrepreneurs.

[18] To eliminate the confounding influence of network constraint, this analysis excludes teams with spouse or partner dyads.

Table 5. Gender Composition and Coefficients for Gender Homophily of Founding Teams by Industrial Sector: Panel Study of Entrepreneurial Dynamics, 1998 to 2000

Industrial Sector	Gender Composition (Percent Male)	Gender Homophily Coefficients		Number of Events
		Coef.	(S.E.)	
Primary/manufacturing	88	.618	(.422)	105
Personal services	64	1.790***	(.438)	97
Retail/wholesale	61	1.323***	(.321)	163
Business/professional services	65	1.849***	(.304)	216
All sectors		1.570***	(.179)	581 ᵃ

Note: Numbers in parentheses are standard errors.

ᵃ Limited to teams reporting start-up industry (N = 800) and excluding teams with spouses/partners.

$^{*}p < .05$ $^{**}p < .01$ $^{***}p < .001$ (two-tailed tests)

intraindustry homophily. On the whole, however, estimates of intraindustry homophily tend to be similar to the level of homophily for the sample as a whole. This suggests that gender homogeneity is not generally an artifact of ecological constraints on team formation.

Table 6 presents a structural event analysis for a second major dimension of ascriptive homophily—ethnic composition. The basic risk set of structural events is again determined by counting rule (equation A-1 in Appendix A), calculated as $4 + 10 + 20 + 35 + 56 = 125$ potential events for a system of four ethnic identities ($|N| = 4$) and maximum team size of 5. Differentiating between teams that contain kinship ties and those that do not, we obtain another 121 potential events (the basic risk set minus the four types of ethnicity for solo entrepreneurs), for a total of 246 structural events. Because of incomplete ethnic information among some founding teams, we restrict our sample to 778 teams for this analysis.

Models 1 and 2 again illustrate how the team size distribution can be modeled using nonparametric and parametric specifications, respectively. These models are substantively identical to the first two shown in Table 4, except they take account of data attrition owing to missing information on ethnicity. Model 3 addresses the prediction that ethnically homogeneous teams will be more common than heterogeneous teams (Hypothesis 2). We enter a parameter into the model based on the Shannon-Weaver entropy (H)

of ethnic composition in each team.[19] The estimated level of ethnic homophily is high, with homogeneous teams being 46 times as likely to occur as expected by chance. In particular, this finding reflects the fact that homogeneous minority teams are common, despite the relative rarity of minority entrepreneurs in the population as a whole. For instance, we observe four teams composed of four African American entrepreneurs, although only .02 team is expected under a model of random mixing.

To some extent, ethnic homogeneity may be generated through kinship ties in the entrepreneurial teams. Model 4 reveals that family networks do increase ethnic homophily, as we assumed, but are not the only source of it. Teams involving both familial networks and ethnic diversity are extremely rare—only one case in our weighted sample matches this pattern. However, even controlling for this opportunity structure, ethnically homogeneous teams occur at a rate that is 27 times expectations. Examining differential levels of homophily among ethnic groups (Model 5), we find that minorities have a significantly higher tendency toward homogeneity than do whites. White entrepreneurs

---

[19] The measure of diversity is computed as:

$$H = -\sum_{i=1}^{n} \left(\frac{\log y_i}{\log n} \right) y_i,$$

where n is the number of ethnic categories, and y_i is the proportion of team members within each category i (Shannon and Weaver [1949] 1963). Ethnic homophily is simply $1 - H$.

Table 6. Coefficients from Poisson Regression Models Testing the Ethnic Composition of Founding Teams: Panel Study of Entrepreneurial Dynamics, 1998 to 2000

Independent Variable	Baseline Models			Models Controlling for Network Ties	
	Model 1	Model 2	Model 3	Model 4	Model 5
Intercept	5.938*** (.051)	6.864*** (.071)	4.078*** (.352)	4.533*** (.351)	2.770*** (.390)
Team size	—	-.791*** (.036)	-.909*** (.070)	-.887*** (.072)	-.818*** (.072)
Size Category					
1 member	—	—	-1.064*** (.122)	-1.005*** (.122)	-2.448*** (.153)
2 members	-.248** (.078)	—	—	—	—
3 members	-1.946*** (.145)	—	—	—	—
4 members	-2.548*** (.191)	—	—	—	—
5 members	-2.997*** (.235)	—	—	—	—
Homophily					
Ethnic homophily	—	—	3.833+++ (.297)	3.297+++ (.304)	6.378+++ (.382)
Status-varying homophily	—	—	—	—	-1.693+++ (.133)
Minority isolation [a]	—	—	—	—	.184+ (.111)
Opportunity Structure					
Family ties × Ethnic homophily	—	—	—	4.990+++ (1.552)	5.498+++ (1.580)
Model fit (G^2)	557.70	627.45	335.95	315.07	194.56
Degrees of freedom (design/fixed)	5/7	2/7	4/7	5/8	7/8

Note: Numbers in parentheses are standard errors. Number of structural events = 246; number of teams = 778. Ethnic information is missing for 38 teams.

[a] Blacks, Hispanics, and Asians represent ethnic minorities.

*$p < .05$ **$p < .01$ ***$p < .001$ (two-tailed tests)

+$p < .05$ ++$p < .01$ +++$p < .001$ (one-tailed tests)

are only .18 times as likely to develop mono-ethnic teams as are African Americans, Asians, and nonwhite Hispanics. Nevertheless, despite the propensity of many minority entrepreneurs to work within ethnic enclaves, they are still 1.20 times more likely to be isolated than white entrepreneurs, given ecological constraints on contact opportunities with other minority entrepreneurs (Corollary 2).

We turn next to the question of functional diversity, examining occupational composition within these founding teams (Table 7). Model 3 addresses the prediction that functionally diverse teams will be more common than expected under a model of random mixing (Hypothesis 3), again using an entropy measure of team composition (see footnote 19). The resulting coefficient estimate suggests a statistically nonsignificant effect for occupational diversity. Moreover, contrary to Hypothesis 4, there is a pronounced ten-

Table 7. Coefficients From Poisson Regression Models Testing the Occupational Composition of Founding Teams: Panel Study of Entrepreneurial Dynamics, 1998 to 2000

Independent Variable	Baseline Models			Models Controlling for Business Ties	
	Model 1	Model 2	Model 3	Model 4	Model 5
Intercept	5.892***	6.872***	6.846***	6.865***	6.907***
	(.053)	(.078)	(.418)	(.418)	(.427)
Team size	—	−.889***	−.537**	−.564**	−.568**
		(.041)	(.181)	(.183)	(.184)
Size Category					
1 member	—	—	−.418	−.409	−.498
			(.251)	(.251)	(.265)
2 members	−.447***	—	—	—	—
	(.084)				
3 members	−2.323***	—	—	—	—
	(.176)				
4 members	−2.826***	—	—	—	—
	(.222)				
5 members	−3.223***	—	—	—	—
	(.269)				
Functionality					
Occupational diversity	—	—	.466	.415	.323
			(.838)	(.836)	(.858)
Diversity × team size	—	—	−.850*	−.766*	−.754*
			(.337)	(.340)	(.342)
Status-varying homophily	—	—	—	—	−.103
					(.214)
Minority isolation [a]	—	—	—	—	.224*
					(.122)
Opportunity Structure					
Business ties × Occupational diversity	—	—	—	−.928	−.932
				(.607)	(.609)
Model fit (G^2)	245.76	294.47	225.71	223.28	219.78
Degrees of freedom (design/fixed)	5/7	2/7	5/7	6/8	8/8

Note: Numbers in parentheses are standard errors. Number of structural events = 246; number of teams = 665. Occupational information is missing for 151 teams.

[a] Operations/production workers represent the occupational minority.

*$p < .05$ **$p < .01$ ***$p < .001$ (two-tailed tests)

+$p < .05$ ++$p < .01$ +++$p < .001$ (one-tailed tests)

dency *away* from occupational specialization with increases in team size. Rather than emphasizing complementarities among different functions, larger founding teams seem to be characterized by homophily, even for achieved attributes such as occupation, once baseline interaction probabilities are taken into account.

Models 4 and 5 examine the extent to which this low level of occupational diver-

sity is induced by prior network relationships—in particular, the presence of former business associates on founding teams.[20] We

---

[20] Simple bivariate statistics suggest that the network density of business relationships in multimember teams has a slight (nonsignificant) negative correlation with the number of occupations represented ($r = -.04$). The lack of association between the two variables suggests that we

Table 8. Occupational Composition and Coefficients for Occupational Diversity of Founding Teams by Industrial Sector: Panel Study of Entrepreneurial Dynamics, 1998 to 2000

Industrial Sector	Occupational Composition				Occupational Diversity Coefficients	Number of Events
	Percent Production/ Operative	Percent Sales/ Service	Percent Adminis- trative	Percent Professional		
Primary/manufacturing	41	20	21	17	−.980 (.583)	110
Personal services	24	23	25	29	−1.513** (.549)	117
Retail/wholesale	21	22	28	29	−.540 (.506)	167
Business/professional services	14	22	31	33	−1.530** (.468)	218
All sectors					−1.312*** (.260)	613 [a]

Note: Numbers in parentheses are standard errors.

[a] Limited to teams reporting occupational composition and start-up industry ($N = 654$); excludes teams with business associates.

*$p < .05$ **$p < .01$ ***$p < .001$ (two-tailed tests)

constructed our measure of business ties within founding teams by counting any prior business-related association between two members of the team as an indication that the team's founding was influenced by business ties. As shown in Model 4, business ties do not decrease occupational diversity significantly (cf. Hypothesis 6). Inclusion of this effect only slightly attenuates the level of homogeneity from other structural and psychological mechanisms. The entrepreneurs in larger teams continue to show a pronounced tendency to congregate based on occupational similarity, rather than attention to functional diversity.

Model 5 completes the model specification, estimating parameters for the extent of disproportionate homophily among high-status occupations (professionals and paraprofessionals), as well as disproportionate isolation among low-status occupations (production and operations workers). Consistent with our findings for gender and ethnicity, there is no evidence of differential homophily among high-status entrepreneurs (contrary to Hypothesis 5), whereas there is evidence of a tendency toward differential isolation for blue-collar operatives

are not dealing with occupational subcultures. Network density is computed using the conventional formula for undirected graphs (Wasserman and Faust 1994).

and production workers. More specifically, entrepreneurs from a blue-collar background are 1.25 times more likely to be isolated than would be expected under a model of random mixing. Again, following Corollary 2, we suggest that this is a likely consequence of ecological constraint combined with a general tendency toward occupational homophily. Because organizational founders from a blue-collar background represent only 21 percent of all nascent entrepreneurs, they are slightly less likely to find other blue-collar workers with whom they can go into business.

As for the case of gender composition, occupational homophily may result from the segregation of occupations across industrial sectors or from the homogeneous selection of team members within sectors. A cross-tabulation of team member backgrounds and start-up industries reveals some segregation in this respect, with those founders having production or operative experience being more common among primary/manufacturing start-ups and those founders having administrative or professional experience being more common among business service/professional firms (see Table 8). Still, the sector-specific marginal distributions suggest that there is considerable potential for occupational diversity, even considering the ecological constraints imposed by industry.

Table 9. Coefficients from Poisson Regression Models Testing the Gender, Ethnic, and Occupational Composition of Founding Teams: Panel Study of Entrepreneurial Dynamics, 1998 to 2000

Independent Variable	Model 1		Model 2		Model 3	
	Coef.	(S.E.)	Coef.	(S.E.)	Coef.	(S.E.)
Intercept	3.082***	(.554)	2.602***	(.571)	.777	(.607)
Team size	−.269	(.193)	−.370	(.199)	−.306	(.197)
Size Category						
1 member	−1.017***	(.259)	.021	(.329)	−1.550***	(.358)
Homophily						
Gender homophily	−.580+++	(.125)	1.362+++	(.222)	1.263+++	(.273)
Status homophily (males)	—		—		.275	(.222)
Ethnic homophily	4.056+++	(.341)	3.599+++	(.337)	6.734+++	(.421)
Status homophily (whites)	—		—		−1.732+++	(.147)
Functionality						
Occupational diversity	.550	(.847)	.528	(.882)	.533	(.882)
Diversity × Team size	−.869*	(.359)	−.848*	(.378)	−.867*	(.367)
Status homophily (professionals)	—		—		−.126	(.220)
Isolation						
Women	—		—		.214+	(.115)
Ethnic minorities	—		—		.150	(.116)
Blue-collar workers	—		—		.289+	(.131)
Opportunity Structure						
Partners × Gender homophily	—		[F] [a]		[F] [a]	
Family Ties × Ethnic homophily	—		[F] [a]		[F] [a]	
Business ties × Occupational diversity	—		−.731	(.578)	−.699	(.585)
Model fit (G²)	1514.65		1274.63		1162.44	
Degrees of freedom (design/fixed)	7/33		8/38		14/38	

Note: Numbers in parentheses are standard errors. Number of structural events = 23,110; number of teams = 639. Occupational or ethnic information is missing for 177 teams.

[a] Indicates parameters that are fixed due to empirical zeros.

*p < .05   **p < .01   ***p < .001 (two-tailed tests)

+p < .05   ++p < .01   +++p < .001 (one-tailed tests)

Further evidence concerning the impact of ecological constraint can be found in the sector-specific estimates of occupational diversity. To simplify these analyses, we ignore interaction effects with team size and only estimate a single design parameter for occupational diversity. Founding teams in some industrial sectors—such as personal, business, and professional services—display the same trend away from occupational diversity observed in aggregate-level analyses. For other industrial sectors—including extractive, manufacturing, and retail/wholesale businesses—the tendency away from occupational diversity is not statistically significant. Although there is still no support for Hypothesis 3, the variability in sector-specific levels of occupational composition suggests that a small amount of the homogeneity observed among larger teams in the aggregate analysis is generated through ecological constraints (consistent with Hypothesis 7).

Given that occupation tends to be correlated with gender and ethnicity, the question remains whether the apparent occupational homophily within these teams is not simply derivative of homophily along ascriptive dimensions. We examine this issue using a combined *structural event analysis of all three factors*. Considering gender, occupation, and ethnicity together yields 32 role combinations at the individual level—white male professionals, white female professionals, black male professionals, black female professionals, etc. The basic risk set is therefore $s(H) = 32 + 528 + 5,984 + 52,360 + 376,992 = 435,896$ possible structural events (equation A-1). Because prior network ties may influence diversity and homogeneity in these groups, we parse multimember teams further into those that contain romantic, familial, and/or business ties and those that do not, leading to $2 \times 2 \times 2 \times 435,896 - 224 = 3,486,944$ structural events. After bootstrap sampling, 23,110 cases are considered in the analysis (see Table 9).

Controlling for structural opportunity, the impact of homophily and functional considerations on team composition can be seen in Model 2.[21] The tendencies toward ascriptive homophily and away from occupational diversity (in larger teams) are highly significant and comparable in magnitude to estimates from models that exclude other factors (see Tables 4, 6, and 7). As shown in Model 3, there is no evidence of differential homophily among males or professionals, while in-group preferences among whites are substantially lower than those observed for ethnic minorities. The variation of in-group preferences explains why ethnic minorities do not exhibit disproportionate levels of isolation, but women and blue-collar workers are likely to become solo entrepreneurs. The relative magnitude of isolation among the latter two social identities also provides additional support for the existence of ecological constraints on team formation, as isolation is predicted to be a function of the numerical prevalence of each identity under conditions of general homophily (Corollary 2). Accordingly, women, who repre-

sent 38 percent of the entrepreneurial population, should be less isolated than entrepreneurs from blue-collar backgrounds, who *represent only 21 percent of the population*. While our findings are consistent with this pattern of prevalence, it should be emphasized that the difference in the magnitude of the two estimates is quite small (an incidence rate ratio of 1.24 as opposed to 1.34, respectively).

As in previous analyses, strong network ties have a substantial impact on team composition, with ties among spouses/partners decreasing the gender homophily of entrepreneurial teams and ties among family *members increasing ethnic homophily* (cf. Models 1 and 2 in Table 9). Weak ties, on the other hand, do not play a statistically significant role in this analysis. Specifically, the presence of business acquaintances on the teams does not reduce occupational diversity markedly, once other factors are taken into account.

DISCUSSION

Using a nationally representative sample of organizational founding teams, we have tested for the operation of five mechanisms affecting the composition of entrepreneurial groups. We found strong support for one mechanism that influences group composition: homophily with respect to both ascriptive *and* achieved characteristics (in particular, gender, ethnicity, and occupation). We found mixed support for two other mechanisms—network and ecological constraint. The network constraint imposed by "strong" ties, such as romantic relationships and family ties, was quite pronounced, but "weak" ties, measured in our study by business acquaintances, imposed no significant network constraint. Our findings also suggest that ecological constraint contributes to the disproportionate isolation of numerical minorities—such as women and blue-collar workers—in the population of entrepreneurs. On the other hand, ecological segregation of these groups by industry does not appear to be a dominant factor driving team homophily.

We found little empirical support for two other mechanisms of group composition: functional diversification of achieved char-

---

[21] After removing cases with missing information on occupation and ethnicity, there are no founding teams with same-sex partners or with multi-ethnic family members. Consequently, the corresponding interaction effects are included as fixed, rather than empirical, parameters.

acteristics and differential homophily based on status expectations. Although baseline estimates of functional diversity were consistently insignificant, we found an unexpected tendency *away* from occupational specialization in larger teams. Contrary to Durkheim's ([1893] 1949) familiar argument, pressures for solidarity in these groups do not seem to favor the weak bonds of functional interdependence but instead contribute to functional homophily. Additional longitudinal research is required to identify how growth (or decline) in each team may lead to evolutionary changes in the mechanisms of group composition.

Our results concerning minority isolation are also provocative, suggesting that isolation in a founding team formation process can proceed without recourse to the stereotyped performance expectations associated with status-varying homophily. In short, social isolation can be produced largely by ecological, rather than psychological, mechanisms. However, as observed for the nonwhite ethnicities in our sample, *reverse* status homophily—particularly that producing greater in-group preferences among numerical minorities—may help combat the effects of ecological isolation.

IMPLICATIONS FOR THEORY

We studied naturally occurring groups involved in activities of fundamental importance to market-based economies: the emergence of new business start-ups. Our investigation thus goes beyond previous work on groups, which has mainly focused on concocted or well-established social units, such as work teams within established firms (Arrow et al. 2000). Within organizations, individuals usually have little choice in which teams to join or whom they will associate with on such teams. By contrast, the composition of entrepreneurial teams is likely to reflect the influence of patterns of association in which people are embedded within families, friendship circles, workplaces, and residential areas. As such, they provide an excellent context in which to observe the operation of basic social processes, such as homophily.

Our results represent a significant contribution to the accumulated set of empirical generalizations regarding homophily in social relations (McPherson et al. 2001). Even in a situation where we might reasonably expect stringent economic rationality to prevail—and thus lead to choices based on the functional diversification of achieved characteristics—we find that team composition is driven by similarity, not differences. Founders of organizations appear more concerned with trust and familiarity, at this early stage, than with functional competence, leading to a "competency discount" in founder recruitment. Just as in other areas of economic life, commercial exchanges involved in organizational foundings are strongly influenced by socially embedded patterns of associations (DiMaggio and Louch 1998; Zelizer 1994).

Our findings underscore a paradox of group formation that parallels similar structural dynamics identified in dyadic relationships (Burt 1992; Granovetter 1973). Granovetter (1992) described two aspects of network embeddedness that highlight the processes involved in team formation. Relational embeddedness refers to the depth of single dyadic ties, such as their degree of multiplexity and positive emotional investment. Structural embeddedness refers to the extent to which the mutual contacts of a dyad are themselves connected to one another. Our results show that relational embeddedness—prior ties along several dimensions—apparently dampen the functional diversity that Granovetter argued is achieved by weak ties or that Burt (1992) argued is achieved by structural holes.

During team composition, entrepreneurs seek out trusted alters, as well as those with whom they already have strong interpersonal relationships, while avoiding strangers who could bring fresh perspectives and ideas to the organizational founding process. Only 10 percent of the dyadic relationships within the PSED sample involve strangers (Aldrich et al. forthcoming). Interestingly, the number of distinctive occupational categories in teams involving strangers (mean = 2.1) is significantly higher than the number found in teams without strangers (mean = 1.3; *t*-statistic = 6.5; $p < .001$). Thus, entrepreneurs' tendency to avoid the inclusion of strangers on founding teams tends to decrease functional diversity and may, in the long run, inhibit the success of new formal organizations.[22]

At the outset, we noted that new organizations can reproduce and challenge the existing social order and that the kinds of organizations people construct are culturally embedded. The composition of entrepreneurial founding teams reflects the tendency toward gender, ethnic, and occupational homophily in the contemporary United States. Our results point to the emergence of social units that, if they persist, will exacerbate the already strong tendencies toward homophily in social relationships. Organizations are a significant sorting point along many dimensions of membership, especially gender and occupation. Our results confirm this tendency. Although McPherson et al. (2001) argue that organizations often create heterogeneity on the dimension of race, our results strongly suggest that, at least for organizational founders, teams are highly homogeneous by race and ethnicity. If homogeneous founding teams also hire employees similar to themselves, then new organizations represent a potent force for solidifying homophily within commercial relationships.

CAVEATS AND FUTURE CONSIDERATIONS

Our knowledge of organizational founding teams is still at a preliminary stage. A more complete description of compositional properties would consider additional characteristics, particularly other achieved characteristics that may be linked to functional diversity. It could be argued that our current occupational measure fails to capture more subtle functional properties of team member contributions. Thus far, we have also had little to say concerning the consequences of team composition and the evolution of compositional properties over time. Team composi-

tion may have a substantial impact on the problem of "collective action" in emergent formal organizations—that is, the problem of balancing the contributions of individual team members against the rewards they expect to receive from the collective enterprise (Simon 1945). Is the balance of contributions influenced only by the ascribed, achieved, and network characteristics of individual members? Or is the balance influenced by the composition of the organizational founding team as a whole, or by ecological properties of other teams in a given industry or geographic region? In turn, the balance of contributions and inducements—along with the initial composition of the teams—may influence the evolution of group composition. What members tend to stay and what members tend to leave organizational founding teams? Who is added to these groups? What mechanisms (homophily, functionality, status expectations, network or ecological constraint) govern this evolutionary process? Answering these questions represents an essential step in developing a more comprehensive understanding of the emergence of formal groups and organizations.

Martin Ruef is Assistant Professor of Organizational Behavior and (by courtesy) of Sociology at Stanford University. His research considers processes affecting the origin of new organizations, organizational forms, and institutions. With W. Richard Scott, Peter Mendel, and Carol Caronna, he is the co-author of Institutional Change and Healthcare Organizations: From Professional Dominance to Managed Care *(University of Chicago Press, 2000), which won the ASA's Max Weber and Eliot Freidson Awards in 2001 and 2002, respectively. In addition to studying contemporary entrepreneurs, his current projects include historical analyses of U.S. medical schools and institutional transformation in the postbellum South.*

Howard E. Aldrich is Kenan Professor of Sociology at the University of North Carolina, Chapel Hill, where he won the Caryle Sitterson Award for Outstanding Teaching in 2002. In 2000, he received two honors: The Swedish Foundation of Small Business Research named him the Entrepreneurship Researcher of the Year, and the Organization and Management Division of the Academy of Management presented him with an award for a Distinguished Career of Scholarly Achievement. His latest book, Organizations Evolving *(Sage, 1999), won the Academy*

---

[22] Whether the benefits of recruiting trusted alters as team members outweigh the possible costs of excluding strangers can only be assessed via a longitudinal study. If emerging businesses benefit from strong, in-group–based ties among their members, then homophily should have a positive effect on survival. If, however, such ties reduce a team's ability to respond to unforeseen or radically changing circumstances, then homophily may be a handicap for teams.

of Management George Terry Award as the best management book published in 1998–1999, and was co-winner of the Max Weber Award from the American Sociological Association's Section on Organizations, Occupations, and Work.

Nancy M. Carter is the Richard M. Schulze Chair in Entrepreneurship at the University of St. Thomas, Minneapolis, Minnesota, where she directs the MBA entrepreneurship program. She also has worked professionally in advertising and marketing research. Her research interests include the emergence of organizations, with a special emphasis on women- and minority-owned initiatives, and the founding strategies of new businesses. She works closely with government and private-sector initiatives promoting women entrepreneurs.

APPENDIX A

Structural Event Analysis

COUNTING RULES

The risk set $s(H)$ of a structural event analysis enumerates all possible combinations over a set of roles (N), subject to group size (r) and restrictions on permissible role combinations (Ruef 2002a). When roles within a group can be repeated an indefinite number of times, the number of combinations for a multiset of N roles is calculated as:

$$s(H) = \sum_{r=1}^{r(H)} \binom{r+|N|-1}{r}$$

$$= \sum_{r=1}^{r(H)} \frac{(r+|N|-1)!}{r!(|N|-1)!}, \quad (A\text{-}1)$$

where r varies over all observed group sizes—including singletons—up to $r(H)$ members (Brualdi 1992:71–73). Thus, a system of two gender roles N = {male, female} allows for three discrete forms of gender composition in structural dyads (r = 2): male-male dyads, male-female dyads, and female-female dyads. Using the counting rule, these combinations are calculated as ($r + |N| - 1$) choose r = ($2 + 2 - 1$) choose $2 = 3!/2! = 3$. To obtain arrangements for the two gender roles not exceeding three persons in size $r(H) = 3$, one simply sums the respective number of combinations for each possible size category: $s(H) = 2 + 3 + 4 = 9$ structural events.

Given multiple role dimensions, the role set should identify all possible combinations that may be held by any given group member. For two gender roles {[M]ale, [F]emale} and four occupational roles {[P]rofessional, [A]dministrative, [S]ervice, [O]perations}, there are eight unrestricted role combinations for each individual: N = {MP, MA, MS, MO, FP, FA, FS, FO}. If there are a priori restric-

tions imposed on role combinations (for instance, if women in a given society are not allowed to hold certain occupations), then the role set must be reduced accordingly.[a]

EVENT PROBABILITY

Probability theory provides the rules for calculating the expected chance of occurrence for any structural event under an assumption of random mixing. We designate the roles (or role combinations) in a set N as elementary events for purposes of statistical analysis and apply the rule of multiplication to determine the probability of joint events. Provided that the roles included in a particular structural event are events in N occurring with probability $p(n_1)$, $p(n_2)$, ... $p(n_k)$, the sampling distribution of joint structural events is given by the multinomial formula:

$$P(E|r) = \frac{r!}{|n_1|!|n_2|! \cdots |n_k|!}$$

$$\times \left[p(n_1)^{|n_1|} \times p(n_2)^{|n_2|} \times \ldots p(n_k)^{|n_k|} \right], \quad (A\text{-}2)$$

where $r = |n_1| + |n_2| + \ldots |n_k|$. It should be noted that the calculation of all joint event probabilities is conditional on structural events being of a particular size, r. For example, consider a structural analysis of organizational founding teams formed among three occupations: manual workers (n_1), service workers (n_2), and professionals (n_3). If structural events are drawn from a population of entrepreneurs that is 40 percent manual, 30 percent service, and 30 percent professional, then the expected probability of obtaining a three-member founding team with one manual worker and two service sector workers under an assumption of statistical independence is $p(E|3) = (3!/(2! \times 1!)) (.40^1 \times .30^2) = .108$. The event probability reflects the fact that there are three different ways to draw the participants. By comparison, the probability of obtaining a three-member team that consists only of manual workers is $p(E|3) = (3!/3!) (.40^3) = .064$.

For some analyses of structural events, joint event probabilities are not only conditional on group size but on other parameters as well. In analyzing the gender composition of groups, for instance, it may be important to control for the presence of romantic relationships that serve to deflate the observed level of gender homophily. Structural events involving these relationships can be separated from other events, and fixed effects can be introduced into models to control for the relationships present within each group-size category.

---

[a] Relational and group-level characteristics—and the restrictions imposed on them—can also be considered in generating the risk set of structural events. For instance, analyzing a set of two gender roles {M, F} and the presence or absence of a spousal/partner relationship (indicated by parentheses) yields six unrestricted combinations for a dyad: MM, FF, MF, (MM), (FF), (MF).

REFERENCES

Aldrich, Howard E. 1989. "Networking among Women Entrepreneurs." Pp. 103–32 in *Women-Owned Businesses*, edited by O. Hagan, C. Rivchun, and D. Sexton. New York: Praeger.

———. 1999. *Organizations Evolving*. Thousand Oaks, CA: Sage.

———. Forthcoming. "Entrepreneurship." In *Handbook of Economic Sociology*, 2d ed., edited by R. Swedberg and N. Smelser. Princeton, NJ: Princeton University Press.

Aldrich, Howard E., Nancy Carter, and Martin Ruef. Forthcoming. "With Very Little Help from Their Friends: Gender and Relational Composition of Nascent Entrepreneurs' Startup Teams." In *Frontiers of Entrepreneurship Research 2002*, edited by P. Reynolds et al. Wellesley, MA: Center for Entrepreneurial Studies, Babson College.

Aldrich, Howard E., Amanda Elam, and Pat Ray Reese. 1996. "Strong Ties, Weak Ties, and Strangers: Do Women Business Owners Differ from Men in Their Use of Networking to Obtain Assistance?" Pp. 1–25 in *Entrepreneurship in a Global Context*, edited by S. Birley and I. MacMillan. London, England: Routledge.

Aldrich, Howard E. and Marlene C. Fiol. 1994. "Fools Rush In? The Institutional Context of Industry Creation." *Academy of Management Review* 19:645–70.

Aldrich, Howard E. and Roger Waldinger. 1990. "Ethnicity and Entrepreneurship." *Annual Review of Sociology* 16:111–35.

Ancona, Deborah and David Caldwell. 1992. "Demography and Design: Predictors of New Product Team Performance." *Organization Science* 3:321–41.

Arrow, Holly, Joseph McGrath, and Jennifer Berdahl. 2000. *Small Groups as Complex Systems: Formation, Coordination, Development, and Adaptation*. Thousand Oaks, CA: Sage.

Bales, Robert. 1953. "The Equilibrium Problem in Small Groups." Pp. 111–61 in *Working Papers in the Theory of Action*, edited by T. Parsons, R. Bales, and E. Shils. Glencoe, IL: Free Press.

Bates, Timothy. 1997. *Race, Self-Employment, and Upward Mobility: An Illusive American Dream*. Baltimore, MD: Johns Hopkins University Press.

Berger, Joseph, M. Hamit Fisek, Robert Z. Norman, and Morris Zelditch. 1977. *Status Characteristics and Social Interaction: An Expectation States Approach*. New York: Elsevier.

Birch, David. 1997. *Small Business Research Summary*. RS Number 183. Washington, DC: U.S. Small Business Administration.

Bird, Barbara. 1989. *Entrepreneurial Behavior*. Glenview, IL: Scott, Foresman.

Blau, Peter. 1977. *Inequality and Heterogeneity*. New York: Free Press.

———. 1980. "A Fable about Social Structure." *Social Forces* 58:777–88.

Brualdi, Richard. 1992. *Introductory Combinatorics*. 2d ed. Englewood Cliffs, NJ: Prentice Hall.

Burke, William and Basil Zaloom. 1970. *Blueprint for Professional Service Corporations*. New York: Dun and Bradstreet.

Burt, Ronald. 1992. *Structural Holes: The Social Structure of Competition*. Cambridge, MA: Harvard University Press.

Carroll, Glenn and Michael Hannan. 2000. *The Demography of Corporations and Industries*. Princeton, NJ: Princeton University Press.

Carroll, Glenn and Elaine Mosakowski. 1987. "The Career Dynamics of Self-Employment." *Administrative Science Quarterly* 32:570–89.

Carter, Nancy. 1994. "Reducing Barriers between Genders: Differences in New Firm Startups." Presented at the annual meeting of the Academy of Management, August, Dallas, TX.

Coleman, James and John James. 1961. "The Equilibrium Size Distribution of Freely-Forming Groups." *Sociometry* 24:36–45.

Cooper, Arnold C. and Catherine M. Daily. 1997. "Entrepreneurial Teams." Pp. 127–50 in *Entrepreneurship 2000*, edited by D. Sexton and R. Smilor. Chicago, IL: Upstart Publishing.

DiMaggio, Paul and Hugh Louch. 1998. "Socially Embedded Consumer Transactions: For What Kinds of Purchases Do People Most Often Use Networks?" *American Sociological Review* 63:619–37.

Durkheim, Emile. [1893] 1949. *Division of Labor in Society*. Reprint, Glencoe, IL: Free Press.

Eisenhardt, Kathleen and Claudia Bird Schoonhoven. 1990. "Organizational Growth: Linking Founding Team, Strategy, Environment, and Growth among U.S. Semiconductor Ventures, 1978–1988." *Administrative Science Quarterly* 35:504–29.

Fisek, M. Hamit, Joseph Berger, and Robert Z. Norman. 1991. "Participation in Heterogeneous Groups: A Theoretical Integration." *American Journal of Sociology* 97:114–42.

Freidson, Eliot. 1986. *Professional Powers: A Study of the Institutionalization of Professional Knowledge*. Chicago, IL: University of Chicago Press.

Gartner, William. 1985. "A Conceptual Framework for Describing the Phenomenon of New Venture Creation." *Academy of Management Review* 10:696–706.

Goffman, Erving. 1963. *Behavior in Public Places: Notes on the Social Organization of Gatherings.* Glencoe, IL: Free Press.

Goodman, Leo. 1964. "Mathematical Methods for the Study of Systems of Groups." *American Journal of Sociology* 70:170–92.

Granovetter, Mark. 1973. "The Strength of Weak Ties." *American Journal of Sociology* 78: 1360–80.

———. 1992. "Problems of Explanation in Economic Sociology." Pp. 25–56 in *Networks and Organizations: Structure, Form, and Action*, edited by N. Nohria and R. Eccles. Boston, MA: Harvard Business School Press.

Haveman, Heather A. and Lisa E. Cohen. 1994. "The Ecological Dynamics of Careers: The Impact of Organizational Founding, Dissolution, and Merger on Job Mobility." *American Journal of Sociology* 100:104–52.

Hawley, Amos. 1950. *Human Ecology.* New York: Ronald.

Ibarra, Herminia. 1997. "Paving an Alternative Route: Gender Differences in Managerial Networks." *Social Psychology Quarterly* 60:91–102.

James, John. 1953. "The Distribution of Free-Forming Small Group Size." *American Sociological Review* 18:569–70.

Jussim, Lee and D. Wayne Osgood. 1989. "Influence and Similarity among Friends: An Integrative Model Applied to Incarcerated Adolescents." *Social Psychology Quarterly* 52:98–112.

Kalleberg, Arne, David Knoke, Peter Marsden, and Joe Spaeth. 1996. *Organizations in America: Analyzing Their Structures and Human Resource Practices.* Thousand Oaks, CA: Sage.

Kamm, Judy B. and Aaron J. Nurik. 1993. "The Stages of Team Venture Formation: A Decision Making Model." *Entrepreneurship Theory and Practice* 17:17–27.

Keister, Lisa A. and Stephanie Moller. 2000. "Wealth Inequality in the United States." *Annual Review of Sociology* 26:63–81.

Lazarsfeld, Paul and Robert K. Merton. 1954. "Friendship as Social Process: A Substantive and Methodological Analysis." Pp. 18–66 in *Freedom and Control in Modern Society*, edited by M. Berger, T. Abel. and C. Page. New York: Octagon Books.

Lechler, Thomas. 2001. "Social Interaction: A Determinant of Entrepreneurial Team Venture Success." *Small Business Economics* 16:263–78.

Mannix, Elizabeth, Sheila Goins, and Susan Carroll. 2002. "Starting at the Beginning: Team Formation, Composition, and Performance," Working Paper. Graduate School of Management. Cornell University. Ithaca. NY.

Marsden, Peter. 1987. "Core Discussion Networks of Americans." *American Sociological Review* 52:122–31.

Mayhew, Bruce, J. Miller McPherson, Thomas Rotolo, and Lynn Smith-Lovin. 1995. "Sex and Race Homogeneity in Naturally Occurring Groups." *Social Forces* 74:15–52.

McPherson, J. Miller and Lynn Smith-Lovin. 1987. "Homophily in Voluntary Organizations: Status Distance and the Composition of Face to Face Groups." *American Sociological Review* 52:370–9.

McPherson, Miller, Lynn Smith-Lovin, and James Cook. 2001. "Birds of a Feather: Homophily in Social Networks." *Annual Review of Sociology* 27:415–44.

Nee, Victor and Jimy M. Sanders. 1985. "The Road to Parity: Determinants of the Socioeconomic Achievements of Asian Americans." *Ethnic and Racial Studies* 8:75–93.

Reskin, Barbara. 1999. "The Determinants and Consequences of Workplace Sex and Race Composition." *Annual Review of Sociology* 25:335–61.

Reynolds, Paul D. 2000. "National Panel Study of U.S. Business Start-Ups: Background and Methodology." Pp. 153–227 in *Advances in Entrepreneurship, Firm Emergence, and Growth*, vol. 4, edited by J. Katz. Stanford, CT: JAI Press.

Ruef, Martin. 2000. "The Emergence of Organizational Forms: A Community Ecology Approach." *American Journal of Sociology* 106: 658–714.

———. 2002a. "A Structural Event Approach to the Analysis of Group Composition." *Social Networks* 24:135–60.

———. 2002b. "Strong Ties, Weak Ties, and Islands: Structural and Cultural Predictors of Organizational Innovation." *Industrial and Corporate Change* 11:427–49.

Schofeld, J. W. 1995. "Review of Research on School Desegregation's Impact on Elementary and Secondary School Students." Pp. 597–616 in *Handbook of Research on Multicultural Education*, edited by J. Banks and C. McGee. New York: Macmillan.

Shannon, Claude and Warren Weaver. [1949] 1963. *The Mathematical Theory of Communication.* Urbana, IL: University of Illinois Press.

Shaver, Kelly G., Nancy M. Carter, William Gartner, and Paul Reynolds. 2001. "Who Is a Nascent Entrepreneur? Decision Rules for Identifying and Selecting Entrepreneurs in the Panel Study of Entrepreneurial Dynamics (PSED)." Technical Paper. Jönköping International School of Business. Jönköping, Sweden.

Simon, Herbert. 1945. *Administrative Behavior.* New York: Macmillan.

Singer, Eleanor, John Van Hoewyk, and Mary P.

222   AMERICAN SOCIOLOGICAL REVIEW

Maher. 2000. "Experiments With Incentives in Telephone Surveys." *Public Opinion Quarterly* 64:171–88.

Skvoretz, John and Thomas Fararo. 1996. "Status and Participation in Task Groups: A Dynamic Network Model." *American Journal of Sociology* 101:1366–1414.

Slater, Philip. 1955. "Role Differentiation in Small Groups." *American Sociological Review* 20:300–10.

Stinchcombe, Arthur L. 1965. "Social Structure and Organizations." Pp. 142–93 in *Handbook of Organizations*, edited by J. G. March. Chicago, IL: Rand McNally.

U.S. Department of Commerce. 1996. *Economic Census: Survey of Women-Owned Businesses*. Washington, DC: U.S. Government Printing Office.

Vesper, Karl. 1990. *New Venture Strategies*. Englewood Cliffs, NJ: Prentice Hall.

Wasserman, Stanley and Katherine Faust. 1994 *Social Network Analysis: Methods and Applications*. New York: Cambridge University Press.

Weber, Max. [1904–1905] 1992. *The Protestant Ethic and the Spirit of Capitalism*. Reprint, London: Routledge.

White, Harrison. 1962. "Chance Models of Systems of Casual Groups." *Sociometry* 25:153–72.

Wilson, Kenneth and W. Allen Martin. 1982. "Ethnic Enclaves: A Comparison of the Cuban and Black Economies in Miami." *American Journal of Sociology* 88:135–60.

Zelizer, Viviana A. 1994. *The Social Meaning of Money*. New York: Basic.

[10]

Mixing or Matching?

The Influence of Voluntary Associations on the Occupational Diversity and Density of Small Business Owners' Networks

Amy E. Davis
University of North Carolina, Chapel Hill
Linda A. Renzulli
University of Georgia
Howard E. Aldrich
University of North Carolina, Chapel Hill

Most employees work in large organizations, enjoying the potential benefits of forming career-enhancing intraorganizational networks. By contrast, small business owners must look to external contexts such as voluntary associations for their business-enhancing ties. This research discusses ways through which involvement in voluntary associations can enhance or diminish occupational diversity and density for owners' networks. Whether owners met their alters (members of respondents' business discussion network, individuals they nominated as persons with whom they would discuss business matters) in voluntary association memberships and whether comemberships are concentrated in one or dispersed among several organizations influence the occupational diversity and density of their networks. The article concludes that voluntary association memberships help owners overcome some of the career isolation produced by their social location.

Keywords: social networks; voluntary associations; business owners

While organizational work environments provide wage and salary workers with a context in which to create networks to help them obtain promotions and raises (Campbell, 1988; Ibarra, 1992), small business owners have to rely on other contexts to form and maintain occupationally important networks. In this regard, social ties formed through contacts external to a business can be a crucial resource for entrepreneurial activity.

42

Research on small business owners has found that network characteristics, particularly low density and high occupational diversity, are important for economic success (Renzulli & Aldrich, 2005; Renzulli, Aldrich, & Moody, 2000); however, because most network research on work has focused on wage and salary workers (e.g., Campbell, 1988; Ibarra, 1992; Podolny & Baron, 1997), we still know little about how small business owners form and maintain occupationally important networks.

Our research breaks new ground by examining the extent to which voluntary associations contribute to the occupational diversity and density of business discussion networks. Voluntary associations that bring people together, such as civic clubs, chambers of commerce, charities, and networking groups, can be important social spaces for the "formation and maintenance" of interpersonal ties (McPherson & Smith-Lovin, 1986, p. 62; Popielarz, 1999a), particularly for owners who may not have similar opportunities in their workplaces. Many researchers agree that voluntary associations influence their members' social networks; however, the question remains as to how voluntary associations affect the business networks of small business owners. Specifically we ask: Given the relatively high level of segregation found in voluntary associations, under what conditions can business owners enhance the diversity and reduce the density of their networks through voluntary association membership and participation?

Using a unique data set on small business owners and nascent owners,[1] we were able to examine the effects of belonging to multiple organizations along two specific network dimensions: occupational diversity and density of ties. We argue that simply joining several different organizations has little impact on owners' network characteristics. Instead, the composition of social networks depends on the sorts of people members encounter and with whom they form ties in their organizations. Therefore, we examined owners' comemberships with alters (members of respondents' business discussion network, individuals they nominated as persons with whom they would discuss business matters) in the set of associations to which they belong. We focus not just on one organization but instead on peoples' ties in multiple organizations. Using theories and hypotheses developed in the more general literature on networks, we offer three hypotheses regarding the conditions under which we expect voluntary associations to promote more occupationally diverse and less dense networks for small business owners.

Authors' Note: We would like to thank Jennifer Glanville, Jeremy Reynolds, Martin Ruef, Daniel Cornfield, and the anonymous reviewers for their helpful comments on earlier drafts of this article. Direct all correspondence to Amy Davis, 155 Hamilton Hall CB#3210, University of North Carolina at Chapel Hill, Chapel Hill, NC 27599; e-mail: amy_davis@unc.edu.

Voluntary Associations and Social Networks

Previous work on the effects of voluntary organizations, in populations other than owners, has produced contradictory findings regarding their sorting versus their integrating effects (Babchuk & Edwards, 1965; McPherson & Smith-Lovin, 1986; Popielarz & McPherson, 1995). Some studies have suggested that voluntary association membership enhances network diversity, supporting the integration view. Other studies have suggested that voluntary associations are socially segregated and provide few opportunities to interact with diverse others. They thus promote network homogeneity, supporting the sorting view (see McPherson & Smith-Lovin, 1986, for a review of the integration and sorting hypotheses).[2] Below we outline the two hypotheses.

Voluntary Associations as Enhancers of Network Homogeneity: The Sorting Hypothesis

Although voluntary associations would seem to provide opportunities for individuals to meet a variety of new people, many authors argued that voluntary associations can actually decrease network diversity (Brady, Schlozman, & Verba, 1999; McPherson & Smith-Lovin, 1986; Popielarz, 1999a). They asserted that memberships in homogeneous associations primarily provide opportunities to meet types of individuals already encountered in other social situations (Kaufman, 2002). For example, several researchers have found that voluntary associations tend to be segregated by sex, age, education, and occupation, and they have concluded that segregated voluntary associations limit members' opportunities to develop diverse networks (McPherson & Rotolo, 1996; McPherson & Smith-Lovin, 1986, 1987; Popielarz, 1999a, 1999b).

Why Are Voluntary Associations Homophilous?

Homophily refers to the tendency for people to associate with those like themselves with regard to social characteristics (McPherson, Smith-Lovin, & Cook, 2001). Theorists have used the principle of homophily to explain why the members of voluntary associations are so often similar to each other. Researchers taking this view argued that members do not necessarily intentionally create segregated voluntary associations. Instead, segregation largely results from the ways in which people are selectively recruited and become committed members of organizations (Kaufman, 2002). Although some individuals may join an organization in response to an advertisement or independent inquiry, research has shown that individuals are more likely to participate in an organization if a friend is also a participant (Brady et al., 1999; McPherson, Popielarz, & Drobnic, 1992; Popielarz & McPherson, 1995). If existing members conscript friends who resemble themselves, the recruitment process thus reproduces organizational homogeneity. In addition, organizations rarely recruit individuals who would boost their diversity.

Beyond recruitment, segregation in voluntary associations increases because homophilic tendencies influence the duration of individuals' affiliations. The strength and number of ties within and outside of organizations, and token status within them, influence people's commitments to organizations and, hence, the length of their memberships (McPherson et al., 1992; Popielarz & McPherson, 1995). Dissimilar members are not necessarily excluded from or pushed out of the organization. Instead, friends pull their colleagues toward them; if friends are located inside the organization, then persons are likely to join and stay in the organization. If friends are located outside the organization, then persons are likely to be pulled out. Accordingly, to the extent that individuals join and remain in organizations with members who are similar to them, organizational homogeneity increases (Liedka, 1991; McPherson & Rotolo, 1996).

Voluntary Associations as Enhancers of Network Diversity: The Integration Hypothesis

Although some have argued that voluntary associations do little to enhance network diversity, others have claimed that voluntary associations are diverse and, hence, promote diversity in members' personal networks (Babchuk & Edwards, 1965; Eastis, 1998; Olsen, 1982; Putnam, 2000; Wellman, 2000). In addition, some researchers have shown that voluntary association activity enhances the diversity of someone's personal network, whether individual organizations are diverse or not. For example, researchers have found that individuals who belong to one or more voluntary associations have larger and more diverse networks (Bekkers, Völker, Van der Gaag, & Flap, in press; McPherson et al., 1992; Popielarz, 1999a; Putnam, 2000; Rotolo, 2000; Wilson, 2000; Wilson & Musick, 1997). However, none of these studies effectively demonstrated that voluntary associations cause more diverse networks, and some have argued for reverse causation. For example, Bekkers et al. (in press) argued that diverse networks lead to more memberships because those with diverse networks are more likely to be recruited into organizations.[3] Therefore, empirical research providing strong, unequivocal support for the integration hypothesis is limited, with the balance of empirical research suggesting that voluntary associations produce segregated rather than integrated social networks.

Occupational Diversity and Density:
Sorting or Integrating?

The integrating and sorting hypotheses are not necessarily mutually exclusive. In fact, it may be the case that voluntary associations can be integrating on one dimension and sorting on another (McPherson & Smith-Lovin, 1986, pp. 61-62) with their net effect dependent on the strength of each force.

We focus on density and occupational diversity because past research has shown that these network characteristics have important consequences for the range of resources available to individuals engaged in business activities (Renzulli & Aldrich, 2005; Renzulli et al., 2000). First, occupational diversity in social relationships constitutes an important avenue through which people acquire new viewpoints and information. Occupations vary in the extent to which their holders have opportunities to interact with others, express creativity and solve problems, and acquire knowledge through on-the-job training or continuing education. As a result, people's occupations have an effect on how valuable they are to others in providing resources through social relationships (Lin & Dumin, 1986). Networks with high occupational diversity have been associated with positive outcomes in a number of studies. For example, occupational diversity has been shown to produce advantages for organizational boards (Sicilano, 1996), job seekers (Campbell, 1988), and business owners (Renzulli & Aldrich, 2005).

Occupationally diverse networks formed through voluntary association memberships may be evidence for the integration hypothesis, suggesting that voluntary association memberships enable business owners to build networks that contain people of different occupations. Support for the opposing sorting hypothesis may be found, however, if voluntary associations bring together occupationally similar individuals.

Second, density refers to the extent to which alters in an individual's network know one another. High-density networks can be useful because they provide social support and facilitate the transmission of complicated information (Nahapiet & Ghoshal, 1998; Pescosolido & Rubin, 2000). Some research has also claimed that high-density networks foster economic relations through the creation of trust (see Coleman, 1988, for his discussion of closure; and Granovetter, 1985, for his discussion of embeddedness). High-density networks, however, can also be detrimental to the extent that they induce conformity and constrain individuals' autonomy, creativity, and innovation (Burt, 1997; Gould, 1993; Hansen, 1999; Putnam, 2000). When networks are dense, the potential assistance available from different members is often redundant because information and potential contacts are likely to be widely shared (Glanville, 2004). Additional network members in a dense network fail to provide novel information and resources.

Low-density networks, on the other hand, contain structural holes, indicating that a person knows two or more people not directly connected to one another (Burt, 1992; Finlay & Coverdill, 2000). Low-density networks have been characterized as beneficial because they increase individual autonomy and the potential for novel information from network alters. For example, people with low-density networks are more likely to experience early promotion or advancement (Burt, 1997; Podolny & Baron, 1997) and McEvily and Zaheer (1999) found that organizations with low-density ties were more likely to know about and implement new technologies.

Whatever the outcome of density for business success, high-density business discussion networks formed through voluntary association memberships may be evidence for the sorting hypothesis. However, if owners add previously unconnected alters to their networks, voluntary associations may connect members to diverse sources of information. Thus, less dense business discussion networks formed through voluntary association memberships may be evidence for the integration hypothesis.

Addressing Limitations of Previous Research

The debate over voluntary associations' effects on personal networks has been hampered by a focus on studying individual memberships, in the case of the sorting studies, and by a focus on simple presence or absence of memberships (i.e., the number of different memberships one has), in the case of the integration hypothesis. Sorting-hypothesis research compares members to members, whereas integration-hypothesis research compares members to nonmembers. Both approaches could overestimate or underestimate the homogenizing effects of voluntary associations.

To better understand the effects of voluntary associations on business owners' networks, we must examine membership sets that include zero, one, or several memberships, following the lead of Popielarz (1999b). She recommended studying multiple memberships to better illuminate whether voluntary associations are sorting or integrating (see also Glanville, 2004; McPherson & Smith-Lovin, 1982). Although individual memberships tend to encapsulate people within homogeneous contexts, belonging to several homogeneous voluntary associations located in different niches could actually produce diverse and low-density networks. A single membership will only enhance a member's personal network diversity if the organization is diverse and the member pursues opportunities to interact with people from different backgrounds in that organization. Conversely, a single membership will not enhance a member's personal network diversity if the organization is homogeneous or if the member lacks or does not pursue opportunities to interact with diverse people in the organization.

Furthermore, multiple memberships will not enhance the diversity of someone's personal network if each organization is homogeneous and contains the same types of members. In contrast, if someone belongs to multiple associations with different membership characteristics, they may have more opportunities to meet different types of people. For example, a woman who belongs to a political group, a chamber of commerce, a religious organization, and a hobby group might meet different people in each of the organizations, even if each of the organizations is internally homogeneous.

Hypotheses

If the sorting hypothesis is correct, then involvement in voluntary organizations will not provide opportunities to meet diverse people and will provide even fewer occasions to meet diverse others, compared to other contexts. If, on the other hand, the integration hypothesis is correct, then individuals who owners meet through voluntary associations are different from individuals they may meet in other contexts, such as their neighborhoods. Moreover, individuals met through voluntary associations may share a common interest that has nothing to do with their gender, race, or occupation. Such interest-based connections are, therefore, more likely to join diverse individuals, compared to people met in settings dominated by homophily (Wellman, 2000).

We illustrate how the arguments differ in the three panels of Figure 1. In this figure, persons in Panels A, B, and C are each tied to five alters.[4] In the three panels, the social spaces of work, school, and neighborhood are represented as overlapping, in that alters located in such spheres may know each other, resulting in increased network density. In addition, neighborhoods, schools, and workplaces may provide limited opportunities to increase occupational diversity. Research has shown that neighborhoods and schools are often homogeneous places with regard to social class and race. For example, Glanville (2004) found that memberships in voluntary associations located within respondents' neighborhoods were associated with more dense and less diverse networks than voluntary associations located outside their neighborhoods. Workplace networks are likely to be homogeneous with regard to occupation. In the case of small business owners, workplaces may also limit the numbers of sparse ties one can form.

Given ego's involvement in three different social spaces, what differences are voluntary association memberships likely to generate? To determine if

Figure 1
Two Potential Effects of Memberships in
Voluntary Associations on Ego's Social Network

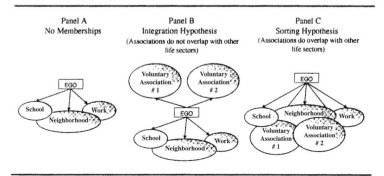

voluntary associations do, in fact, have an effect, we must consider where owners meet their alters. To highlight the difference between the sorting and integrating perspectives, we offer alternative Hypotheses 1a and 1b. Panels B and C demonstrate the logic behind our alternative hypotheses. Whereas ego in Panel A has no voluntary organization memberships, Panels B and C show egos who belong to two organizations and know alters in each organization. In Panel B, representing the integration hypothesis, voluntary associations do not overlap with neighborhood, work, or school, and thus provide opportunities to encounter people not otherwise accessible through these domains. Not only having but also actually forming ties through voluntary association memberships should increase occupational diversity and decrease density in business discussion networks. According to the integration hypothesis, ego in Panel B would have greater occupational diversity and less density than ego in Panel A.

Hypothesis 1a (Integration): Occupational diversity will increase and density will decrease as the number of alters owners meet through association memberships increases.

By contrast, in Panel C, voluntary organizations are represented as overlapping with the social spheres of work, school, and neighborhood, and persons encountered in such memberships would be likely to be encountered through other means. In this case, voluntary association membership does not provide a means of increasing occupational diversity and decreasing density in owners' networks. In addition, members of voluntary associations may be more homogeneous than members of other social spheres, given the relative ease with which individuals can leave voluntary associations, compared to neighborhood, work, or school. According to the sorting hypothesis, ego in Panel C would have less occupational diversity and more density than ego in Panel A with no memberships.

> *Hypothesis 1b (Sorting):* Occupational diversity will decrease and density will increase as the number of alters owners meet through association memberships increases.

Voluntary associations may also influence owners' business networks when persons share memberships with alters who were not met in the organizations. We argue that comemberships can produce sorting or integrating effects on owners' networks, depending on whether shared ties are concentrated within one organization or dispersed among several organizations. We illustrate two scenarios that would likely produce differing degrees of occupational density and diversity in the panels of Figure 2. Although ego in Panel A has three memberships, each of which could be a potential source of ties, three of ego's alters belong to the same voluntary association. The three alters with whom ego shares a membership are quite likely to know one another. Hence, any information one alter may have is likely shared with the other two, and thus several of the ties are redundant. In addition, the network may have low occupational diversity to the extent that the organization attracts individuals from particular occupations. By contrast, ego in Panel B shares a different membership with each of three alters, and thus we would expect a low-density and occupationally diverse network.

> *Hypothesis 2:* The more alters with whom owners share the same organizational membership, the lower the occupational diversity and the greater the density of their business discussion network.

To determine the sorting or integrating effects of voluntary organizations, we must know the pattern of affiliations and comemberships. Ego in Panel B has comemberships spread across different organizations, likely resulting in a more diverse and less dense network. With this pattern of affiliations and comemberships, a person draws on different organizations to connect with persons of varied interests and backgrounds. Ego in Panel B has the same network size, number of memberships, and number of comemberships as ego in Panel A. However, each alter with whom he or she shares a membership

Figure 2
The Effect of Concentrating Versus Dispersing Association
Memberships on Ego's Social Network

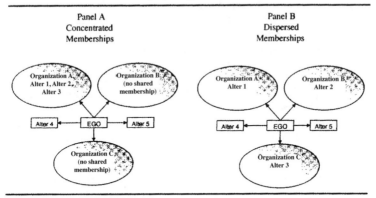

belongs to a different organization, unlike the three alters in Panel A. In Panel B, the three alters are less likely to know one another than people sharing memberships, and they may be very different from one another. Hence, ego in Panel B is more likely to receive novel information and resources from each alter than ego in Panel A.

Hypothesis 3: The more sources of comemberships with alters, the greater the occupational diversity and the lower the density of owners' business discussion networks.

Research Design

Data

We used data from the Research Triangle Entrepreneurial Development Study to explore the effects of voluntary associations on the networks of economically engaged individuals—nascent owners and business owners (see Reese, 1993; Reese & Aldrich, 1995; Renzulli et al., 2000, for a full description of the data). Participants were located in the Research Triangle area of North Carolina. The sample included information on current small business owners with active businesses and people who are in the process of trying to start businesses. The owners in this sample have, on average, 9.5 full-time employees ($SD = 29.3$). The modal number of employees is 0, and 90% of the owners had 20 or fewer employees. Our sample included not only people who were owners but also nascent entrepreneurs. "Nascent entrepreneurs" are people who are taking active steps to start a business but who have not yet succeeded in creating an operating entity (Reynolds & White, 1997). We included nascent owners and owners because the importance of voluntary associations in forming and maintaining relationships with others in voluntary associations is fundamentally different for businesses owners and those seeking business ownership compared to wage and salary workers.

The respondents were located through business organizations in the North Carolina counties of Durham and Wake, small business classes in a technical college in Wake County, and a random sample of new business owners in Wake County.[5] The randomly chosen subsample of new business owners in Wake County allowed Reese (1993) to show that sample source was significantly associated with network composition and networking activities. Thus, the multiple methods of recruiting participants increased heterogeneity in the variables of interest to us. When we added a dummy variable for the randomly chosen subsample of business owners to our regression equations, it was not significant, thus showing that our sampling process produced no significant selection bias (Renzulli et al., 2000).[6]

Two waves of information were collected; the first between 1990 and 1991, and the second in 1992. We used data from the first wave, which were collected in two phases. Phase 1 was a short mailed questionnaire in which 659 questionnaires were sent out and 444 returned. Phase 2 involved an in-depth telephone interview with 353 of the 444 respondents that returned the mailed questionnaire. The survey thus had a completion rate of 67% of those who received a mailed questionnaire and a response rate of 54% of the original sample that completed a mailed and telephone questionnaire. These response rates are comparable to those in other studies of entrepreneurs (Cooper & Dunkelberg, 1987; Kalleberg & Leicht, 1991). We used only those Wave 1 respondents who completed a phone interview, as only they were asked the questions we used to construct our independent and dependent variables. We also dropped cases that had missing values for our variables. Furthermore, we dropped from our regression analyses owners with a network size of less than two (22 respondents) because, by definition, these respondents have an undefined value for density. Respondents with zero or one alter cannot have any shared ties among alters and can only have a value of one for occupational diversity. We excluded those who reported having no plans of starting a business (31 respondents). The final sample used in this article includes 261 owners or nascent owners.

Measures

Our measures of network composition concerned respondents' business discussion networks. Business discussion networks comprised up to five persons whom respondents nominated as individuals with whom they would discuss business matters. Definitions and descriptive statistics of our variables are shown in Table 1.

We excluded kin from our measures characterizing the business discussion network. Kin ties are fundamentally different from other types of ties because they are either inherited or acquired via marriage. Organizations are unlikely to be the source of kin relationships, although respondents may share an organizational membership with kin. Therefore, to avoid mixing the impact of kinship and organizational memberships, we excluded from our analysis the 13% of alters who were related by kinship to the respondents.[7]

Dependent Variables

We define *occupational diversity* as the number of occupations represented in social networks. Our definition is the same as Campbell's (1988) definition of *occupational range* and Lin and Dumin's (1986) definition of *number of occupations accessed*. Occupational diversity is a count variable measuring the number of different occupations represented in respondents' business discussion networks.[8] Empirical work has shown that the occupations we chose in creating our diversity measure have an effect on the business owners' access to resources and nascent owners' abilities to start a business (Renzulli & Aldrich, 2005; Renzulli et al., 2000). We examined several ways of measuring occupational diversity, including the index of qualitative variation and entropy measures (Lieberson, 1969). The different measures produced similar findings, and we feel that the count measure provided the most straightforward interpretation. This measure nicely captured the extent to which respondents can reach varied occupations through their business discussion network. Respondents have an average of 2.8 different occupations represented in their networks. We control for network size, as we discuss later.

Density measures the extent to which respondents' alters know one another. After respondents were asked to nominate up to five people with whom they discuss business matters, they were then asked if "alter 1" knew alters 2 through 5, if alter 2 knew alters 3 through 5, and so on. These questions assume the relationship is nondirectional: if alter 1 knows alter 4, then alter 4 knows alter 1, for example.

Table 1
Definitions and Descriptives

Name	Description	M	SD
Voluntary organization variables			
Total number of memberships	Number of named organizations (0 to 5)	3.26	1.56
Potential connections	The natural log of the number of members in all of respondent's memberships (0 to 6.62)	5.63	1.36
Monthly activity in voluntary organizations	Summed number of meetings attended annually across the memberships. 1 = attended at least 12 organizational meetings (at least once a month) 0 = not active	.85	.35
Proportion women members	Proportion of members in respondent's memberships that are women (0 to 1)	.34	.15
Network and/or membership variables			
Network size	Number of named alters in business discussion network, excluding kin (2 to 5)	4.20	.95
Alters met in memberships	Number of alters met in memberships (0 to 5 potential; 0 to 4 actual)	1.88	1.54
Shared memberships	Number of comemberships in business discussion network (0 to 5)	.73	1.06
Sources of shared memberships	Number of organizations represented in business discussion network (0 to 5 potential; 0 to 4 actual)	1.16	.90
Controls			
Woman	Respondent's sex: 1 = woman, 0 = man	.27	.44
Married	Respondent's marital status: 1 = married, 0 = not married	.79	.41
Children	Respondent's number of children (0 to 8)	.88	1.14
Minority	Respondent's racial identity 1 = minority, 0 = White	.07	.25
Business owner	1 = owns a business 0 = nascent owner	.85	.36
Bachelor's degree	Respondent's education: 1 = at least a BA, 0 = less than a BA	.80	.40
Age	Respondent's age, in years (22 to 78)	41.45	8.78
Dependent variables			
Occupational diversity	Number of different occupations represented in business discussion network (1 to 5)	2.84	0.93
Density	The percentage of possible ties actually present in the business discussion network. Formula = $100 \times ([2 \times \text{number of shared ties}]/[\text{network size} \times \text{network size} - 1])$, (0 to 100)	50.01	32.26

Note: $n = 261$.

54

We used the Wasserman and Faust (Wasserman & Faust, 1994, p. 101) measure of density, which is

$$\Delta = 2L + g(g - 1),$$

where: Δ = density
L = Number of ties among alters
g = network size

For ease of interpretation, we calculated a percentage by multiplying density by 100. The highest possible value for our measure was 100, representing a network in which all alters know one another. The lowest value is 0, representing a sparse network in which no alter knows each other. Respondents have an average score of just over 50% for density within their business discussion network.

Independent Variables

Respondents were asked to list up to five voluntary associations in which they held memberships. Rather than examining the effects of each membership on respondents' networks in isolation, we considered how their overall voluntary association activity influenced their occupational diversity and density. Therefore, our measures regarding voluntary association membership and activity are summary measures of respondents' membership sets. We summed across the named organizations to obtain the total number of memberships. They were subsequently asked about various aspects of these organizations and their memberships, including their size, sex composition, type, and frequency of attendance. Respondents were asked if they met their alters through the membership (alters met in memberships), which of their alters belonged to the same organizations as they did (shared memberships), and the number of sources of shared memberships through different organizations (sources of shared memberships).

Alters met in memberships. Respondents indicated whether they initially met an alter through their membership (1) or not (0). We then summed across the (up to) five alters.

Shared memberships. Respondents indicated whether they shared a membership with their alter (1) or not (0). We then summed across the five alters to determine how many alters shared a membership with the respondent. In the examples shown in Figure 2 , each ego's score on this measure is 3.

Sources of shared memberships. Respondents were asked to indicate in which organization an alter shared a membership with them. Each organization is counted as either 0, meaning no shared membership with an alter, or 1, meaning one or several alters belong to the organization with ego.[9] We then summed the number of different organizations in which a respondent and an alter share a membership. For example, we refer the reader back to Figure 2. In panel A, ego's value for sources of shared memberships is 1, and in Panel B it is 3.

Controls

Demographic and human capital controls. Researchers have found that demographic and human capital characteristics influence network composition and voluntary association participation. Therefore, we controlled for these influences.

Studies have found that the characteristics of men's and women's networks differ; and, therefore, we control for gender. For example, Campbell (1988) found that women have less occupational diversity in their networks than do men. Married persons may engage in activities and social circles primarily of interest to their partners in which they are relatively separated from their other friends and colleagues, hence reducing network density and increasing occupational diversity. Having children may increase density and reduce occupational diversity because parents become involved in child-related activities through which they repeatedly meet other parents whom they know (Munch, McPherson, & Smith-Lovin, 1997; Rotolo, 2000).

Age, educational level, and race have a demonstrated effect on network composition and voluntary association activity. Marsden (1987) found that those with the most diverse networks are young to middle age, educated, and live in heavily populated areas. Campbell, Marsden, and Hurlbert (1986) found that low-density networks are associated with high socioeconomic status. Age was measured by respondents' ages in years, and education was a dummy variable coded 1 if respondents have at least a bachelor's degree and 0 otherwise. We also control for ethnicity and ownership status because of possible differences between Whites and minorities and between owners and nonowners. Minority is measured as an indicator of whether the respondent is a member of a minority group: Asian, African American, or Hispanic.[10]

To control for ownership, we used a variable that indicates whether a respondent owns and runs his or her own business (business owner). The reference group was those who were nascent owners. Actual business ownership may increase density because owners are embedded within a business community for their given industry and interact with suppliers, customers, vendors, distributors, creditors, and others who are likely to know one another. Controlling for business ownership allows us to understand if ownership in and of itself is key to creating these types of networks or if nascent owners are also able to use voluntary organizations to create particular network configurations.

Organizational and network controls. In addition to human capital, demographic, and family characteristics, we controlled for characteristics of respondents' business discussion networks and voluntary association memberships. We control network size, the number of alters a respondent nominated for his or her business discussion network. The average respondent has a network size of 4.24. We also included several characteristics of respondents' voluntary association memberships. The total number of memberships and size of respondents' voluntary association memberships may influence their opportunities to meet diverse people who themselves are not connected. Potential connections was computed as the natural log of the total number of members in all of respondents' memberships.[11] McPherson and Smith-Lovin (1982) created a similar measure they called "potential weak ties." Respondents were asked to estimate the number of members in each organization.[12] We summed their answers across the organizations they named (up to a maximum of five). The people in our sample have an average of 276 potential connections through their organizational memberships (mean of the logged value is equal to 5.6). Finally, we controlled for the frequency of attendance to separate the effects of belonging to voluntary associations from the effects of being "active." Respondents were asked how often they attended each of their memberships. We summed the number of meetings attended annually across the memberships. If respondents attended at least 12 organizational meetings (at least once a month), they were given a 1 for "active." Our definition is similar to that of McPherson and Rotolo (1996) who defined *active memberships* as those attended more than 1 hour per month.

Several researchers have focused on the effect that a voluntary association's sex composition has on opportunities to form diverse networks (McPherson & Smith-Lovin, 1986; Popielarz, 1999a, 1999b). Given the level of occupational sex typing in the United States, (see Reskin, 1993, for a review of the literature) we expected that organizational sex composition would particularly affect occupational diversity. Therefore, we control for the proportion women members in respondents' memberships.[13]

Analytic Strategy

To test the integration and sorting hypotheses for owners, we use nested models for our two dependent variables. In the first models, we consider the characteristics of respondents' affiliations (number, size, sex composition, and attendance) without the measures concerning shared memberships. As other research has shown, the more voluntary associations to which one belongs, the greater the likelihood that he or she will have diverse networks (Bekkers et al., in press; McPherson et al., 1992; Popielarz, 1999a; Popielarz & McPherson, 1995; Putnam, 2000; Rotolo, 2000; Wilson, 2000; Wilson & Musick, 1997). If such were the case, then the integration hypothesis would be supported. However, the sorting hypothesis predicts that recruitment into organizations is more important than the number of voluntary organizations to which one belongs. The second set of models includes the three independent variables pertaining to the way people know one another in their voluntary organizations. In this two-step analysis, we can examine the effects of voluntary association memberships; however, more important, we can show how meeting, sharing, and patterns of comembership affect network characteristics.

Our first dependent variable is a count of the number of different occupations that are represented in the respondent's network—occupational diversity. The range of the dependent variable was 1 to 5. The mean of 2.8 and the variance of .84 were not equal; therefore, our dependent variable was an overdispersed count, and we used a negative binomial model (Long, 1997). Diagnostics revealed heteroskedasticity, in which errors are correlated biasing the standard errors and thus making statistical inference problematic. We ran negative binomial regression with the Huber/White/Sandwich estimator of the variance to correct for heteroskedasticity and ensure the accuracy of interpretation of statistical significance. The expected percentage change for a unit change in the independent variable, holding other variables constant, can be computed as $100*[\exp(\beta_k * \delta)] - 1$ (Long, 1997).[14] The second dependent variable, density—measured as a percentage from 0 to 100—was continuous. Ordinary least squares (OLS) models are appropriate for such a dependent variable. After running OLS analysis in STATA, Cook–Weinberg diagnostic tests revealed that the density models also contained heteroskedasticity. We, therefore, used regression analysis with robust standard errors for density.

Our equation for density and occupational diversity is

$$\hat{y} = \beta_0 + \beta_1 \Pi + \beta_2 \Sigma + \beta_3 \Omega + \beta_4 \Theta + \beta_5 \Psi + \varepsilon,$$

where: $\hat{y}$ = the predicted value of the dependent variable

β_0 = a constant
Π = background characteristics
Σ = network and organizational controls
Ω = alters met in memberships
Θ = shared memberships
Ψ = sources of shared memberships
ε = error term

Our variables measure several related aspects of voluntary association membership: size, sex composition, alters met in memberships, shared memberships, and sources of shared memberships. Variance inflation factor levels are well below the conventional threshold for indicating problematic results, thus indicating that we do not have a problem with collinearity.[15] In addition, a correlation matrix for all of our variables is included in the appendix.

Results

Model 1 in Tables 2 and 3 indicates that simply joining several organizations has little effect on occupational diversity and density. The number of memberships is not significantly related to occupational diversity or density. These models, therefore, fail to provide clear support for either the sorting or integrating hypotheses. Model 2 in Tables 2 and 3, however, supports Hypotheses 1a and 2 (for density only) and Hypothesis 3 for density and occupational diversity.

Occupational Diversity

In our first set of hypotheses, we posited that meeting people in voluntary associations could have either an integrating (Hypothesis 1a) or sorting effect (Hypothesis 1b) on the number of different occupations people have in their network. However, because alters met was not significant, we found neither a positive (integrating) nor a negative (sorting) effect of meeting contacts in voluntary organizations. We are, thus, unable to confirm that simply meeting alters in organizations integrates dissimilar people or sorts people by homophily.

Hypothesis 2 posited that the more alters with whom people share organizational memberships, the lower the occupational diversity of their business discussion network. However, Model 2 indicates that shared memberships neither significantly increase nor decrease occupational diversity. In other words, knowing alters who are in the same voluntary organizations does not necessary increase or decrease the range of different occupations one can

Table 2
Negative Binomial Analysis With Robust Standard Errors Predicting Occupational Diversity by Comembership

	Model 1			Model 2		
	%Δ	Coefficient	SE	%Δ	Coefficient	SE
Network and/or membership variables						
Total number of memberships	.16	.00	.01	−.30	.00	.02
Potential connections	1.99	.02	.02	1.75	.02	.02
Monthly attendance in voluntary organizations	16.68	.15	.06**	15.53	.14	.06**
Proportion women members	−32.61	−.39	.16**	−33.05	−.40	.16**
Network size	15.29	.14	.02***	15.03	.14	.02***
Alters met in memberships	—	—	—	−.13	.00	.02
Shared memberships	—	—	—	−2.59	−.03	.03
Sources of shared memberships	—	—	—	7.86	.08	.04**
Controls						
Woman	4.97	.05	.05	4.78	.05	.05
Married	−.04	.00	.04	−.11	.00	.04
Children	.71	.01	.02	.88	.01	.02
Minority	−3.30	−.03	.07	−2.99	−.03	.07
Business owner	−3.22	−.03	.05	−4.37	−.04	.05
Bachelor's degree	1.62	.02	.05	.13	.00	.05
Age	.47	.00	.00**	.50	.00	.00**
Constant	13.20	.12	.17	15.41	.14	.16
N		261			261	
Log likelihood		−407.26			−406.60	

**p < .05. ***p < .01, two-tailed tests.

Table 3
Regression Analysis With Robust Standard Errors Predicting Density by Comembership

	Model 1			Model 2		
	Coefficient	SE	p	Coefficient	SE	p
Voluntary organization variables						
Total number of memberships	-.30	1.83	.87	.40	1.82	.83
Potential connections	-.41	2.76	.88	-1.43	2.80	.61
Monthly attendance in voluntary organizations	1.25	7.63	.87	1.25	7.73	.87
Proportion women members	14.11	20.58	.49	18.22	20.19	.37
Network and/or membership variables						
Network size	-2.28	2.82	.42	-4.00	2.94	.18
Alters met in memberships	—	—	—	-5.56***	2.01	.01***
Shared memberships	—	—	—	7.98***	2.17	.00***
Sources of shared memberships	—	—	—	-7.43**	3.26	.02**
Controls						
Woman	2.41	5.90	.68	1.92	5.64	.73
Married	-6.39	5.30	.23	-6.33	5.20	.22
Children	1.00	1.99	.62	1.43	1.95	.46
Minority	-13.94*	7.71	.07*	-13.74*	7.70	.08*
Business owner	13.48**	5.35	.01**	12.62**	5.20	.02**
Bachelor's degree	-11.92**	5.63	.04**	-11.85**	5.44	.03**
Age	.25	.25	.33	.24	.25	.33
Constant	49.36***	18.21	.01***	56.86***	18.76	.00***
N	261			261		
F	2.20			3.47		
df	12, 248			15, 245		
R^2	.08			.12		

$*p < .1. **p < .05. ***p < .01.$ two-tailed tests.

61

reach. Together, merely meeting and sharing memberships with alters do not play significant roles in the occupational diversity of owners' networks.

Hypothesis 3 was supported: sources of shared membership, or the number of different organizations in which a respondent shares a membership with an alter, does affect occupational diversity; that is, the more sources of shared memberships people have with their alters, the greater the occupational diversity of their business discussion networks (see Table 2, Model 2). For each unique organization in which a respondent shared a membership with an alter, the expected count of occupations represented in the business discussion network increased by 7.86%. Thus, having five different organizational affiliations in which an alter is also a member is associated with a 55% increase in the number of occupations in a respondent's business discussion network.[16]

Two organizational affiliation control variables have significant effects on occupational diversity: organizational attendance and sex composition. Attending organizational meetings once a month is associated with a 15.53% increase in occupational diversity. Having all women members is associated with a 33.05% decrease in occupational diversity, compared to having all men members. We did not offer specific hypotheses regarding these variables; however, the results suggest that further research should examine their effects on members' network characteristics.

Our results for occupational diversity thus provide some support for the integration hypothesis, but no support for the sorting hypothesis. Although simply meeting alters in voluntary associations does not improve business owners' occupational diversity, occupational diversity is enhanced when owners hold multiple memberships and share memberships with alters in different associations. Memberships in multiple organizations in which each is used to sustain relationships with different alters can thus be an important way to increase the occupational diversity of owners' networks.

Density

Our results for density show that voluntary associations can have either integrating or sorting effects, depending on the nature of owners' comemberships with alters in their business discussion networks, as we hypothesized. In Model 2 of Table 3, all three variables of interest have significant influences on density. As predicted by Hypothesis 1a, the integration hypothesis was supported when alters are met in memberships. Table 3 Model 2 shows that each alter that a respondent met in an organization was associated with a decrease in density of 5.56%. Through voluntary associations, owners go beyond their current ties and meet new people they would not encounter in other situations. Associations also may be places in which owners' existing alters are unlikely to share ties with most members.

In addition, sources of shared memberships decrease density, supporting Hypothesis 3. Recall that our measure of different organizational sources of shared memberships reflects how dispersed respondents' discussion alters are in their memberships. Each unique organizational source of shared memberships was associated with a 7.43% decrease in density.

However, we also found some support for the sorting hypothesis. Shared memberships with alters increased density within a respondent's business discussion network. Each additional shared membership was associated with an increase in density of 7.98%. Our results thus paint a complex picture of associations' effects. Meeting many alters in different voluntary associations decreases someone's social network density whereas having several alters in the same voluntary association increases network density, regardless of the relationships' origins.

Discussion

The purpose of the current study was to empirically examine the role voluntary associations play in shaping the occupational density and diversity of business owners' networks. In particular, we were interested in the sorting and integrating effects of voluntary associations. Previous research either examined single memberships in isolation and found sorting effects (McPherson & Smith-Lovin, 1986, 1987) or examined individuals' membership counts and found integrating effects (Putnam, 2000). Both types of research, however, were somewhat misleading. Uncovering the actual effects of association membership on networks required that we adopt a new analytic strategy (Popielarz, 1999b). Therefore, we examined business owners' sets of memberships and found that the ways in which alters are met and embedded in shared memberships tend to drive the integrating and sorting effects of voluntary associations on business discussion networks. Indeed, our analysis shows that voluntary associations can have sorting and integrating effects.

In studying business owners' sets of memberships, we hypothesized that voluntary associations' effects depended on whether they are sources of new relationships and whether comemberships with alters are concentrated in one or dispersed among several memberships. We first offered competing hypotheses. In Hypothesis 1a, we suggested that voluntary associations will have an integrating effect on networks if the number of alters owners met through associations increased, whereas in Hypothesis 1b we offered that voluntary associations will have a sorting effect on networks if the number of alters owners met through associations increased. In Hypothesis 2, we suggested that voluntary associations will have a sorting effect on networks if owners and their alters share memberships. Finally, in Hypothesis 3, we suggested an integrating effect if owners had many sources of comembership.

We found that simply adding persons through association contacts lowered discussion network density, supporting Hypothesis 1a. Offsetting this tendency, however, was a propensity for shared memberships to increase network density, supporting Hypothesis 2. Thus, if all of someone's business discussion alters were also comembers in the same organization, organizational involvement would raise network density, although it would not lower occupational diversity. These findings suggest that the sorting effects of voluntary associations are not an inevitable consequence of involvement in associations, particularly for business owners.

Therefore, despite compelling research that has demonstrated not only that many voluntary associations are segregated but also why they become segregated, we find voluntary association activity can, indeed, produce integrating effects on owners' business discussion networks. Memberships in multiple, dissimilar organizations enable owners to meet occupationally diverse others and those not part of the same circle of friends and acquaintances. Thus, associating with different people in different organizations could enable individuals who are economically engaged to increase the occupational diversity and reduce the density of their networks, potentially providing them with new information, resources, and assistance for their business ventures.

Our work does not show unequivocal support for the integration hypothesis, however. Owners are unlikely to enhance diversity and reduce density in their social networks simply by joining several organizations or even one large organization. Rather, support for the integration hypothesis is conditional on active involvement in several associations in which they do not already know many people. These findings suggest that, in strategic terms, owners can enhance the occupational diversity and decrease the density of their personal networks by joining several organizations and actively participating in those organizations; for example a religious organization, a service organization, a business or professional association, and a sociable organization, provided that they interact with different people in each.

Conclusion

Our analysis provides a partial explanation for why some researchers have argued that voluntary associations are segregating, whereas others have asserted that they are integrating. By collecting and analyzing detailed information about owners' multiple memberships and the interpersonal connections they make within those organizations, we were able to clarify the conditions leading to segregating or integrating effects of voluntary association participation. We found that voluntary associations could produce either effect on members' social networks. In addition, our research shows that focusing on shared memberships and sources of shared membership is helpful in explaining network configurations. We believe we are now closer to understanding the role voluntary association membership plays in owners' opportunities to cultivate linkages with disparate others. Because owners are, by definition, not situated in large establishments, they have few opportunities within their firms to create and maintain economically important networks. Similarly, the ties that nascent owners may be able to access in their current employment may not be useful for ownership. Accordingly, voluntary associations represent an alternative context in which owners can create business discussion networks.

Focusing on networking behaviors within owners' memberships also helps to clarify issues of causal ordering and spurious effects. Research demonstrating that membership in organizations, or particular types of organizations, shapes network composition is vulnerable to questions of causal ordering; that is, do voluntary association memberships increase network diversity or are those with diverse networks more likely to be association members? Bekkers et al. (in press) argued that enhanced networks could be a cause and an effect of voluntary association membership, with individuals having larger or more diverse networks more likely than other people to be recruited to voluntary associations. They argued that only organizations characterized by regular face-to-face meetings are likely to influence members' networks.

Our research strategy reduces the possibility that voluntary association participation and network characteristics are spuriously related because of unmeasured characteristics such as personality. First, by knowing if an alter was met in a voluntary association, we know the time order of the tie formation and membership in the organization. Second, we focused on comemberships, the extent to which owners share memberships with network alters. Examining comemberships' effects on occupational diversity and density of owners' networks provided an enhanced understanding of the types of people voluntary associations actually bring together.

Our work also has implications for understanding how organizations play a mediating and moderating role in the formation of networks and possibly even implications for how owners can be strategic in their networking efforts. Gaps between organizations represent perhaps the most important structural holes in social networks, rather than just those between individuals. Owners seeking strategic links to bridge holes in their networks would do well to search for organizations in which they have no friends or acquaintances. They might also, in concert with allies, found new organizations and associations to which they recruit dissimilar others. On the other hand, if density is important for the formation of trust and riskless transaction, then owners might do well by becoming important fixtures in their professional organizations.

Based on our findings, we see four possibilities for future research on the topic of network formation for owners. First, although we examined voluntary association memberships' effects on a particular set of ties for economically engaged individuals, further research should examine their effects on a random sample of the population's networks, examining a large set of ties. Using a position generator, in which respondents are given a list of occupations and asked to name people they know in the occupations, rather than a name generator that asks respondents to name people with whom they discuss important or business matters, may help researchers assess the degree to which respondents have access to people who are high status in voluntary organizations.

Second, a great deal of attention has been paid to the relative exclusion of women and minorities from informal networks and the relative level of gender and racial segregation observed in voluntary associations. Because of our relatively small sample size and the relatively small number of women and ethnic minorities in our sample, we were unable to examine possible interaction effects between our measures and gender and race nor were we able to explore race and gender diversity of networks. We did, however, find that organizational sex composition influences the occupational diversity of members' networks. Future research should examine interactions between race, gender, and voluntary association memberships and their effects on social network diversity and density to determine if involvement and comemberships in multiple organizations enhances network occupational diversity and reduces network density for all members, or only for some.

Third, our work brings us closer to understanding how voluntary organizations are important places for helping configure networks along two dimensions. The next research step is to examine the extent to which networks formed prior to business ownership overlap with voluntary association membership and help shape network configuration. In doing so, researchers can begin to examine network dynamics for owners and nascent owners. It would be useful to know, for example, if owners remain in voluntary associations even when they are not receiving short-term benefits. To what extent do owners recognize the long-term consequences of associating with diverse others?

Finally, though past research has shown that diversity, particularly occupational diversity, and low density are useful network configurations for positive outcomes at work and in business, our work did not explicitly test if the networks formed through voluntary associations were practically useful for owners to gain resources, find employees, and make contacts with clients and contractors. The next step in this line of research is to examine the extent to which the networks formed in voluntary associations are more or less beneficial for owners than other sources of ties.

Appendix
Correlation Matrix of Variables

	1	2	3	4	5	6	7	8	9	10	11	12	13	14	15	16	17
1. Total memberships	1.00																
2. Potential connections	.68	1.00															
3. Monthly attendance in volunteer organization	.52	.59	1.00														
4. Proportion women members	.22	.46	.33	1.00													
5. Network size	.28	.19	.19	-.15	1.00												
6. Alters met in memberships	.24	.18	.20	.09	.21	1.00											
7. Shared memberships	.36	.34	.31	.06	.42	.63	1.00										
8. Sources of shared memberships	.42	.37	.34	.09	.34	.48	.79	1.00									
9. Woman	-.18	-.18	-.07	.41	-.26	-.07	-.14	-.12	1.00								
10. Married	.04	.07	-.03	-.14	-.02	.05	.03	.03	-.20	1.00							
11. Children	.04	.00	-.03	-.04	.00	.03	-.06	-.06	-.14	.28	1.00						
12. Minority	-.09	-.12	.03	-.01	-.03	-.10	-.14	-.13	.07	-.16	.03	1.00					
13. Business owner	.13	.04	.13	-.06	.10	.05	.17	.19	-.03	.07	-.04	-.14	1.00				
14. Bachelor's degree	.24	.20	.06	-.14	.08	.08	.16	.21	-.27	.09	.05	-.13	.00	1.00			
15. Age	.18	.20	.11	.05	.13	.07	.11	.08	-.05	.13	-.13	-.03	.13	.03	1.00		
16. Occupational diversity	.22	.18	.22	-.11	.45	.12	.25	.29	-.15	.03	.00	-.03	.05	.09	.19	1.00	
17. Density	-.03	-.01	.02	.11	-.07	-.05	.06	-.03	.12	-.07	-.02	-.09	.16	-.17	.06	-.14	1.00

Notes

1. Throughout the article, we use the term *owner* to refer to current owners and potential owners, also called *nascent entrepreneurs* in the entrepreneurship literature. We do this to avoid repeated use of the cumbersome phrase *owners and potential owners*.

2. In our literature review and analysis, we use the terms *integrating* and *diversifying* as synonyms. As Putnam (2000) might suggest, one could use the term *integrated* to connote people becoming more tightly incorporated into a society through joining voluntary organizations. However, we use the term the same way it is used for characterizing the impact of busing on previously homogenous schools. When Black children were bused to previously all-White schools, their presence integrated the schools and created a more diverse student body than before.

3. Specifically, Bekkers et al. (in press) excluded network alters that respondents had met through memberships and thus only examined relationships formed prior to memberships.

4. Our panels resemble Pescosolido and Rubin's (2000, p. 62) spoke network structure characteristic of "the current form of social network formation" in which people are loosely connected to their organizations.

5. The organizations included Center for Entrepreneurial Development (CED), National Association for Women Business Owners (NAWBO), and varied networking organizations (NET).

6. In analyses not shown here, we replicated and extended Reese's (1993) test for possible selection bias in our sample. We found that sample source was a significant predictor of our independent and dependent variables before respondents' characteristics were introduced into the equations, but not afterward.

7. Originally, there were 1,255 alters. When kin are excluded, there were 1,096 alters. Because kin were excluded from our network measures, some of the excluded respondents had large networks but had fewer than two nonkin alters. Of these 22 excluded respondents, one half included individuals with networks of four or five alters, and one half included individuals with only one or two alters and, thus, would have been excluded anyway.

8. The 15 possible occupations represented in respondents' business discussion networks are business owner, president of a business, investor, lawyer, accountant, banker, scientist and/or professor, medical doctor, real estate professional, consultant, manager, miscellaneous employee, retired and/or unemployed, student, and homemaker.

9. Although it is possible for an alter and a respondent to share more than one membership, this was a rare occurrence in the data. Fourteen respondents reported that one of their alters belonged to more than one of their memberships. Four respondents reported that two of their alters belonged to more than one of their memberships. In the analysis, we counted these "multiple shared memberships" as a distinct membership. For example, if a respondent reported that one alter belonged to Organization 1, another alter belonged to Organization 3, and a third alter belonged to "multiple organizations", then the value for sources of shared memberships would be 3. We ran the analysis including and excluding these 18 cases, and the models were not changed.

10. We recognize that the vast majority of our sample was White. We ran our analysis three alternate ways: with race as a control, without race as a control, and deleting the 20 minorities from the sample and analyzing data for the Whites in the sample. The results are virtually identical in all three instances, and we chose to keep the minority respondents but control for race.

11. Values of 0 (when owners reported no memberships) were recoded as 1 to make computation of the natural logarithm possible.

12. The categories were less than 20, 20 to 50, 51 to 100, and more than 100 members. We recoded these variables to their midpoints: 10 members for the first category, 35 members for the second category, 75 members for the third category, and 150 members for the last category.

McPherson and Rotolo (1995) found that organizational members' estimates of organization size were similar to those of organization leaders and, thus, are a sensible way to measure organization size. Cross-tabulations indicate that respondents in this sample gave reliable answers with regard to organizational size, meaning that multiple members of the same organization give similar reports of organization size.

13. Respondents were asked to estimate the gender composition of their organizational memberships: all men (0), mostly men (.25), half and half (.50), mostly women (.75), and all women (1.00). We multiplied these proportions by organization size and summed for all memberships. We divided this number by potential connections (not logged).

14. We calculated the percentage change before we rounded the coefficient to the second decimal place.

15. We ran the occupational diversity model in ordinary least squares (OLS) to get variance inflation factors and tolerance because such diagnostics do not exist for negative binomial models. The variance inflation factor (VIF) and tolerance were well below the conventional threshold of 10.

16. To calculate this number, we used the percentage change formula $100 \times (\exp [b] - 1)$. We multiplied the coefficient .075 by 5, so the resulting formula was $100 \times (\exp [5 \times .075] - 1)$.

References

Babchuk, N., & Edwards, J. N. (1965). Voluntary associations and the integration hypothesis. *Sociological Inquiry, 35*(2), 149-162.

Bekkers, R., Völker, B., Van der Gaag, M. P. J., & Flap, H. D. (in press). Social networks of participants in voluntary associations. In N. Lin & B. Erickson (Eds.), *Social capital: Advances in research*. New York: Aldine de Gruyter.

Brady, H. E., Schlozman, K. L., & Verba, S. (1999). Prospecting for participants: Rational expectations and the recruitment of political activists. *American Political Science Review, 93*(1), 153-168.

Burt, R. S. (1992). *Structural holes: The social structure of competition*. Cambridge, MA: Harvard University Press.

Burt, R. S. (1997). A note on social capital and network content. *Social Networks, 19*(4), 355-373.

Campbell, K. E. (1988). Gender differences in job-related networks. *Work and Occupations, 15*(2), 179-200.

Campbell, K. E., Marsden, P. V., & Hurlbert, J. S. (1986). Social resources and socioeconomic status. *Social Networks, 8*(1), 97-117.

Coleman, J. S. (1988). Social capital in the creation of human capital. *American Journal of Sociology, 94*, S95-S120.

Cooper, A., & Dunkelberg, W. (1987). Old questions, new answers and methodological issues. *American Journal of Small Business, 11*(3), 11-23.

Eastis, C. M. (1998). Organizational diversity and the production of social capital. *American Behavioral Scientist, 42*(1), 66-77.

Finlay, W., & Coverdill, J. E. (2000). Risk, opportunism, and structural holes: How headhunters manage clients and earn fees. *Work and Occupations, 27*(3), 377-405.

Glanville, J. (2004). Voluntary associations and social network structure: Why organization location and type are important. *Sociological Forum, 19*(3), 465-491.

Gould, R. V. (1993). Collective action and network structure. *American Sociological Review, 58*(2), 182-196.

Granovetter, M. (1985). Economic action and social structure: The problem of embeddedness. *American Journal of Sociology, 91*(3), 481-510.

Hansen, M. T. (1999). The search-transfer problem: The role of weak ties in sharing knowledge across organization subunits. *Administrative Science Quarterly, 44*(1), 82-111.

Ibarra, H. (1992). Homophily and differential returns: Sex differences in network structure and access in an advertising firm. *Administrative Science Quarterly, 37*(3), 422-447.

Kalleberg, A., & Leicht, K. (1991). Gender and organizational performance: Determinants of small business survival and success. *Academy of Management Journal, 34*(1), 136-161.

Kaufman, J. (2002). *For the common good? American civic life and the golden age of fraternity.* New York: Oxford University Press.

Lieberson, S. (1969). Measuring population diversity. *American Sociological Review, 34*(6), 850-862.

Liedka, R. V. (1991). Who do you know in the group? Location of organizations in interpersonal networks. *Social Forces, 70*(2), 455-474.

Lin, N., & Dumin, M. (1986). Access to occupations through social ties. *Social Networks, 8*(4), 365-385.

Long, J. S. (1997). *Regression models for categorical and limited dependent variables.* Thousand Oaks, CA: Sage.

Marsden, P. V. (1987). Core discussion networks of Americans. *American Sociological Review, 52*(1), 122-131.

McEvily, B., & Zaheer, A. (1999). Bridging ties: A source of firm heterogeneity in competitive capabilities. *Strategic Management Journal, 20*(12), 1133-1156.

McPherson, J. M., Popielarz, P. A., & Drobnic, S. (1992). Social networks and organizational dynamics. *American Sociological Review, 57*(2), 153-170.

McPherson, J. M., & Rotolo, T. (1995). Measuring the composition of voluntary groups: A multitrait-multimethod analysis. *Social Forces, 73*(3), 1097-1115.

McPherson, J. M., & Rotolo, T. (1996). Testing a dynamic model of social composition: Diversity and change in voluntary groups. *American Sociological Review, 61*(2), 179-202.

McPherson, J. M., & Smith-Lovin, L. (1982). Women and weak ties: Differences by sex in the size of voluntary organizations. *American Journal of Sociology, 87*(4), 883-904.

McPherson, J. M., & Smith-Lovin, L. (1986). Sex segregation in voluntary associations. *American Sociological Review, 51*(1), 61-79.

McPherson, J. M., & Smith-Lovin, L. (1987). Homophily in voluntary organizations: Status distance and the composition of face-to-face groups. *American Sociological Review, 52*(3), 370-379.

McPherson, J. M., Smith-Lovin, L., & Cook, J. M. (2001). Birds of a feather: Homophily in social networks. *Annual Review of Sociology, 27,* 415-444.

Munch, A. J., McPherson, M. J.. & Smith-Lovin, L. (1997). Gender, children, and social contact: The effects of childrearing for men and women. *American Sociological Review, 62*(4), 509-520.

Nahapiet, J., & Ghoshal, S. (1998). Social capital, intellectual capital, and the organizational advantage. *Academy of Management Review, 23*(2), 242-266.

Olsen, M. E. (1982). *Participatory pluralism: Political participation and influence in the United States and Sweden.* Chicago: Nelson-Hall.

Pescosolido, B. A., & Rubin, B. A. (2000). The web of group affiliations revisited: Social life, postmodernism, and sociology. *American Sociological Review, 65*(1), 52-76.

Podolny, J. M., & Baron, J. N. (1997). Resources and relationships: Social networks and mobility in the workplace. *American Sociological Review, 62*(5), 673-693.

Popielarz, P. A. (1999a). (In)voluntary association: A multilevel analysis of gender segregation in voluntary associations. *Gender & Society, 13*(2), 234-250.

Popielarz, P. A. (1999b). Organizational constraints on personal network formation. *Research in the Sociology of Organizations, 16*, 263-281.

Popielarz, P. A., & McPherson, J. M. (1995). On the edge or in between: Niche position, niche overlap, and the duration of voluntary association memberships. *American Journal of Sociology, 101*(3), 698-720.

Putnam, R. (2000). *Bowling alone: The collapse and revival of American community.* New York: Simon & Schuster.

Reese, P. R. (1993). *Entrepreneurial networks and resource acquisition: Does gender make a difference?* Unpublished doctoral dissertation, University of North Carolina, Chapel Hill.

Reese, P. R., & Aldrich, H. E. (1995). Entrepreneurial networks and business performance. In S. Birley & I. C. MacMillan (Eds.), *International entrepreneurship* (pp. 124-144). London: Routledge.

Renzulli, L. A., & Aldrich, H. E. (2005). Who can you turn to: Tie activiation within core business discussion networks. *Social Forces, 84*(1), 323-341.

Renzulli, L. A., Aldrich, H. E., & Moody, J. (2000). Family matters: Gender, networks, and entrepreneurial outcomes. *Social Forces, 79*(2), 523-546.

Reskin, B. (1993). Sex segregation in the workplace. *Annual Review of Sociology, 19*, 241-270.

Reynolds, P. D., & White, S. B. (1997). *The entrepreneurial process: Economic growth, men, women, and minorities.* Westport, CT: Quorum Books.

Rotolo, T. (2000). A time to join, a time to quit: The influence of life cycle transitions on voluntary association membership. *Social Forces, 78*(3), 1133-1161.

Sicilano, J. I. (1996). The relationship of board member diversity to organizational performance. *Journal of Business Ethics, 15*(12), 1313-1320.

Wasserman, S., & Faust, K. (1994). *Social network analysis: Methods and applications.* New York: Cambridge University Press.

Wellman, B. (2000). Changing connectivity: A future history of y2.03k. *Sociological Research Online, 4.* Available from www.socresonline.org.uk/4/4/wellman.html

Wilson, J. (2000). Volunteering. *Annual Review of Sociology, 26*, 215-240.

Wilson, J., & Musick, M. A. (1997). Who cares? Toward an integrated theory of volunteer work. *American Sociological Review, 62*(5), 694-713.

Amy E. Davis is a Ph.D. candidate in the Department of Sociology at the University of North Carolina, Chapel Hill. Her research focuses on gender, family, and social networks in entrepreneurial and organizational contexts. Her dissertation examines the causes and consequences of participation in startup teams by low-status entrepreneurs.

Linda A. Renzulli is an assistant professor in the Department of Sociology at the University of Georgia. Her research focuses on organizational processes and stratification. She is currently studying organizational formation for charter schools and women-owned businesses.

Howard E. Aldrich is Kenan Professor of Sociology at the University of North Carolina, Chapel Hill, where he won the Carlyle Sitterson Award for Outstanding Teaching in 2002. He is chair of the Department of Sociology and adjunct professor of management in the Kenan Flagler Business School.

[11]

Strategic Entrepreneurship Journal
Strat. Entrepreneurship J., **1**: 147–165 (2007)
Published online 21 November 2007 in Wiley InterScience (www.interscience.wiley.com). DOI: 10.1002/sej.8

SMALL WORLDS, INFINITE POSSIBILITIES? HOW SOCIAL NETWORKS AFFECT ENTREPRENEURIAL TEAM FORMATION AND SEARCH

HOWARD E. ALDRICH[1]* and PHILLIP H. KIM[2]
[1]*Department of Sociology, University of North Carolina at Chapel Hill, Chapel Hill, North Carolina, U.S.A.*
[2]*School of Business, University of Wisconsin-Madison, Madison, Wisconsin, U.S.A.*

The social network perspective has become an important analytical lens for understanding strategic actions among entrepreneurs. Social theorists offer two competing visions of networks' configurations: one of infinite opportunities for individuals to develop heterogeneous circles of affiliations and the other of constrained opportunities privileging only certain individuals. We draw on this tension to describe three models of network formation – random, small world, and truncated scale free – and apply them to entrepreneurial team formation and resource mobilization strategies undertaken by entrepreneurs. We compare and contrast two models of team formation – a rational process model and an interpersonal relations model – and identify the network contexts under which each is most applicable. Mundane entrepreneurial teams arise within localized clusters and appear unlikely to take advantage of what network theorists have called small world networks, which depend upon bridging ties between clusters. Nonetheless, there are entrepreneurial strategies through which new ventures might achieve the advantages of small world networks. To the extent that new ventures emerge in truncated scale free networks, their founders must work within a highly centralized structure, with its institutionalized standards making team formation and entrepreneurial search more instrumental than within small worlds. Copyright © 2007 Strategic Management Society.

Early in the twentieth century, Georg Simmel (1955) published his classic essay on the intersection of social circles (translated into English as 'the web of group affiliations'). Contrasting social life in a metropolis with life in a village, he analyzed the impact of modernity on individuals' chances of meeting dissimilar others and moving to new social positions. Joseph Schumpeter (2003), writing in the same era, argued that the old economic order was being transformed by ambitious people behaving entrepreneurially and improving their economic positions. For many other social theorists of that era, the early twentieth century was a time of turmoil and change in which 'traditional' ways were giving way to the 'modern,' a transformation that met with their approval.

By midcentury, the sense of optimism conveyed by early modernist writings had given way to more

Keywords: social network; entrepreneurship; team; new venture; broker; startup
*Correspondence to: Howard E. Aldrich, Department of Sociology, University of North Carolina at Chapel Hill, Chapel Hill, NC 27599-3210, U.S.A.
E-mail: howard_aldrich@unc.edu

cautious sentiments. Two world wars and the onset of the cold war made theorists wary of promoting too optimistic a worldview. Publications on themes such as *The Organization Man* (Whyte, 1956) and *Small Town in Mass Society* (Vidich, 1958) suggested that individuals were heavily constrained by social structures, rather than agents of their own fate. Managers, rather than entrepreneurs, were the economic actors lionized by the news and entertainment media.

Over the past several decades, however, social theorists have once again returned to the issues raised by Simmel's analysis. One of the most highly cited papers ever published in sociology, Granovetter's (1973) 'The Strength of Weak Ties,' posed the question of the extent to which people's locations in social structures enabled them to escape the constraints of their social origins. Scholars who cite Granovetter's work often overlook one of his key themes, which was whether 'modernization' increased the likelihood that the job seeking and recruiting process operated on a universalistic, as opposed to a particularistic, basis. Like Simmel, Granovetter (1973) wondered whether modernization and structural differentiation emancipated people from ascriptive constraints. He studied employees, not entrepreneurs, but subsequent researchers saw value in extending his perspective to entrepreneurship.

In one of the first explicit calls for a social network perspective on entrepreneurship, Aldrich and Zimmer (1986) argued that putting entrepreneurial intentions into action requires that entrepreneurs establish connections with others who control resources. They argued that social structures played a major – if not dominating – role in who tries to become an entrepreneur and who succeeds. In this paper, we build on their argument, adding Simmel and Granovetter's concerns for social inequality and achievement to Aldrich and Zimmer's analysis. We argue that a theory of entrepreneurship and social networks must encompass the entire life cycle of new organizations, and that the best place to begin is with understanding the role that social networks play in business startups: the formation of entrepreneurial teams and the mobilization of resources via social relations. We present three simple models of network structure: random networks, small world networks, and truncated scale free or 'fat tail' networks. In describing each, we introduce concepts central to the literature on social network analysis, highlighting areas where we think network

analysis has something to say to entrepreneurship scholars.[1]

WHAT DO NETWORKS DO?

Social network scholars in the early 21st century have clearly been inspired by Simmel's work of more than a century ago. In his essay on the web of group affiliations, Simmel (1955: 151) wrote, 'opportunities for individualization proliferate into infinity also because the same person can occupy positions of different rank in the various groups to which he belongs.' This passage on *infinite opportunities* appeared toward the end of the book, in a section on 'Individualism and Multiple Group Affiliations' in which Simmel contrasted the 'modern pattern' of social webs with the earlier pattern of 'concentric affiliations.' Concentric affiliations cosseted people in successively larger rings of attachment, such as immediate family, extended kin, other village members, and the entire local community. The new web pattern gave people fresh choices and created opportunities for them to vary their positions across the various groups with which they affiliated. Individuals were no longer 'stuck' in fixed positions for their entire lives. The business strategy literature has echoed Simmel's positive characterization of the potential inherent in social ties over the past several decades (Hoang and Antoncic, 2003).

Social networks in the startup process

The term 'network' is now firmly embedded in the business strategy literature, generally seen in a positive light. Most strategic network research focuses on network structures and their consequences within and between established firms. There are very few papers on the genesis of ties and even fewer that consider the role of networks in the founding of new ventures, with the exception of a few works

---

[1] We present the three models in sufficient detail so that they serve as baselines against which to analyze observed networks. In entrepreneurship research, model building is often the missing element in the theory-model-data trilogy of the scientific realism approach (McKelvey, 2002). In this approach, theory is used to inform the modeling process, which in turn informs analysts' research designs and data collection. Comparisons of research findings with models implied by theory allows us to improve the models and ultimately to build better theory.

such as Beckman, Burton, and O'Reilly's (2007) paper on the gains to new ventures from founding team members' career histories. In this paper, we extend social network concepts and principles to the early stages of a firm's life, focusing on the team formation and resource mobilization strategies in new ventures.

First, new ventures derive many instrumental and social-psychological benefits from teams (Aldrich, Carter, and Ruef, 2004; Birley and Stockley, 2004). Studies uniformly find that teams do better than solo founders, regardless of the measured outcomes. Second, when founders do not have direct access to the resources they need via team members and their ties, they often turn to indirect ties for help. For example, one group studying new ventures, noted that founders 'relied on pre-existing networks as the primary means of access to the welter of resources needed during and after founding' (Baker, Miner, and Easley, 2003: 265). Specifically, we are interested in the way in which entrepreneurs can strategically search for resources using indirect ties.

Team formation

Two principles of team formation dominate the strategic management literature on teams, although most research concerns the upper echelons of *established* firms, rather than startups (Forbes *et al.*, 2006). First, a rational process model of team formation emphasizes selecting members based on pragmatic instrumental criteria, such as complementary skills or work experiences. From this viewpoint, competency should shape team formation so that new ventures possess the capabilities needed to manage complexity and growth. Second, a social psychological model emphasizes the interpersonal fit between team members and the need for smoothly functioning group processes. Many scholars have pointed to the important role that social and emotional support play in affecting human behavior (Thoits, 1984). For example, positive social relations within a team can create a supportive context within which people are encouraged to undertake innovative actions.

The two sets of principles are not mutually exclusive. Within the constraints of interpersonal attraction, teams can still search instrumentally for members. Similarly, within the constraints of resource-based needs, teams can still choose people who are 'attractive.' Nonetheless, as a normative principle, the business strategy literature seems to

privilege the rational process model over the social psychological model, claiming that new members *ought* to be chosen based on knowledge demands and resource connections, whereas accumulating evidence shows that 'new member addition, *as it actually occurs*, may be better explained by social-psychological theories' (Forbes *et al.*, 2006: 232). A social network view of team formation explains why such theories are a better fit to the realities of team formation.

We turn now to three models of network structure that are useful templates for understanding the social structural context within which teams form and entrepreneurs maneuver for opportunities and resources.

HOW DO SOCIAL NETWORKS ARISE?

Entrepreneurship scholars have embraced the optimistic message conveyed by much of the social network literature, viewing networking as the key to evading constraints on entrepreneurial action. Peter Blau (1977) gave scholars reasons for optimism, arguing that in modern society, people are able to participate in multiform heterogeneous circles and create many weak but integrative ties across diverse groups. Individuals thus gain numerous opportunities to experience diverse points of view. By implication, entrepreneurial opportunities are available to all.

In contrast, Pescosolido and Rubin (2000) argued that modern groups are so transitory and contingent that they do not really give people a basis for stable ties. Instead, people experience serial, ephemeral, short-term, contingent relations with others, mostly through indirect rather than face-to-face contacts. Pescosolido and Rubin cited growing temporary and part-time work as an example of increasing tenuousness and fragility in social relations. In describing the consequences of this postmodernist turn in the structure of contemporary social life, Pescosolido and Rubin (2000: 65) wrote, 'the expansion of roles that require flexibility, skill, and adaptability advantages some individuals while disadvantaging others. Those who profit from the new social forms are likely to be those in power (as in all social forms), those who are resource rich, and those on the cutting edge of societal developments (e.g., technology).' Note how they have taken Simmel's optimistic view of the transformation in the structure of social relations, as well as Blau's image of society as integrated through cross cutting ties, and turned it into an expectation that the benefits from the new structures will fall unequally across social locations.

We use these musings on the changing social order to introduce our three network models. For each model, we focus on two issues: (1) the extent to which the social world is organized into local clusters of densely connected individuals who interact primarily with one another, and (2) the average path length between individuals in the network, conceptualized as the average number of intermediaries it takes to connect any two randomly chosen individuals. The first issue speaks to the issue of recruitment into entrepreneurial teams across social locations and the second sheds light on the dilemmas involved in entrepreneurial searches for opportunities and resources.

The first model we present, one of random networks, presumes a highly individualized world in which everyone has nearly unlimited access to everyone else, constrained only by limits on the resources that can be devoted to the search for new social ties. Paths between distant people are short because there are no constraints on who can interact with whom and so everyone is available as an intermediary or broker. The second model, one of small world networks, presumes a highly clustered world in which people's searches for new ties are highly circumscribed by their environments, with people's ties connecting them mainly to others in their same social context. Despite the potential for many failed connections between clusters, small world theorists posit that bridging ties serve as short cuts connecting many of these local clusters to other clusters, potentially reducing average path lengths to those found in random worlds. In *some* small worlds, the distribution of ties follows a power law and they are therefore an instance of our third model, the 'truncated scale free' network.

A scale free network model presumes that social networks arise through a process that results in a robust and highly structured hierarchical system that is highly resistant to disruptive events. Path lengths are short because a small number of highly connected nodes dominate the distribution, with many nodes having a small number of ties. These networks may also have local clusters, making them also small worlds. Empirical observation of social networks has found that few resemble pure scale free networks. Instead, the distribution of ties follows a power law

distribution with a 'fat tail,' and thus some analysts call them 'truncated scale free' networks.[2]

Model 1: Random Networks

Beginning with a random network seems counterintuitive, as most people certainly do not think of themselves as behaving randomly as they go about their daily activities. How can we justify this choice? In fact, statistics based on random graphs are the baseline against which social network researchers judge observed graphs, as well as alternative models of social ties. By first considering a world without order or design, researchers are better able to appreciate the extent to which an observed network is truly special or unusual. Indeed, researchers follow the same principle whenever they conduct a statistical analysis of quantitative data. Analysts conduct tests of statistical significance against a baseline model of random association between variables, and when patterns of association depart significantly from randomness, search for reasons why. In the case of social networks, a random graph makes an interesting baseline because it exhibits a short average path length between nodes. Understanding why that is the case helps us appreciate the extent to which clustering, by itself, *reduces* global connectivity within nonrandom networks.

The structure of random networks

Two characteristics of random networks are central to our discussion. First, there is no clustering of nodes − nascent entrepreneurs in our case − and thus we have the most 'egalitarian' network in the sense that people's current locations do not limit their access to others. Neither prestige nor wealth affects someone's ability to connect to anyone else in the network. Second, average path length between nodes in random graphs is quite short because of indirect ties.

To convey a sense of the potentially unlimited connectivity in a world of randomly structured social networks, we offer a simple scenario. Consider a

---

[2] In truncated scale free networks, the degree distribution of ties is scale free over a significant portion of its range but it is not strictly scale free in the tails. In particular, at the 'high' end of the degree distribution, there are fewer extremely well-connected nodes that would be expected. Instead, the distribution bunches up short of the high values; hence the term, 'fat tail.'

situation in which an entrepreneur seeks resources from providers beyond his or her immediate set of direct ties – people known directly on a face-to-face basis. Assume that the entrepreneur ('ego') has 100 direct ties with other individuals ('alters') in his or her network. Then assume that each of the 100 alters has 100 direct ties in their networks. At this point, ego can access 10,000 additional individuals indirectly through the 100 alters with whom ego has a direct tie (i.e., $100 \times 100 = 10,000$ ties). If we assume each of the 100 first-order alters also has 100 direct ties with a second-order alter, ego can access an additional one million individuals indirectly (i.e., $100 \times 100 \times 100 = 1,000,000$ ties).[3]

Mathematically, we can formalize the logic underlying our example as follows. Define k as the number of ties from each person. Define N as the total number of people in the population under study. In a random network, the average number of steps needed to connect anyone to everyone else, defined as d, can be determined by the formula:

$$d = \ln N / \ln k$$

In the case of our example shown in Figure 1, $d = \ln 1,000,000 / \ln 100$, with d thus equal to 3. We can also solve for $N = k^d$. Simply put, in a random world, everyone is connected in a very small number of steps and so the average path length is very short. For example, in a world of 10 billion people, with $k = 100$, d is only five![4]

To the extent that nascent entrepreneurs inhabit a world structured through random connections, two interesting implications follow. First, the lead founders of new ventures would face few social constraints on the recruiting of new team members. A random world would give them access to everyone and the potential of building a 'dream team' of founders. Second, although nascent entrepreneurs would face few constraints on their search, they would also find navigating in such a world highly problematic. The potential benefits of enacting new direct ties would be obscured by an entrepreneur's inability to predict

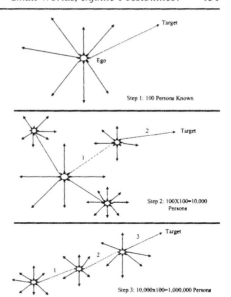

Figure 1. The potential of indirect ties

the payoff of indirect ties lying beyond them.[5] We turn now to the much more structured networks of small worlds.

Model 2: Small World Networks

The 'small world' concept had been around for some time when Stanley Milgram began his ingenious series of experiments (Milgram, 1967). Milgram argued that even individuals who appear to have a constricted set of relationships could actually be connected to socially and geographically distant individuals. He derived the famous proposition that a person appeared able to reach any other person in just six steps. Subsequently, Watts and Strogatz (1998) identified the mathematical conditions under

---

[3] As we note later, strictly speaking, these specific results obtain only if there is no overlap between direct ties, that is, at each step, ties are extended 'without replacement.'

[4] Higher values of k decrease d, but at a decreasing rate. In our example of $N = 1,000,000$, when $k = 500$, $d = 2.2$, and when k increases to 1000, d drops only to 2. By contrast, for $k = 10$, d rises sharply to 6.

[5] One reader of our paper wondered whether knowledgeable and skilled entrepreneurs would do better than others, even in a random world, because they would pick 'the best' direct ties. Unfortunately for these skilled entrepreneurs, knowing a direct tie's personal characteristics is of no help whatsoever in a random world, because they provide no information about *that* person's direct ties.

which it made sense to speak of a network as a 'small world.'

Despite the enthusiasm with which the public and some academic researchers embraced the concept, many remain skeptical about the empirical incidence of small worlds. Kleinfeld (2002) became interested in the empirical basis for the six degrees of separation principle and so looked into the archives of Milgram's studies. She found that the vast majority of the chains begun at originating sites did not reach their destination sites. She searched for other studies that had replicated the small world study and found only one that spanned at least two disconnected cities. Its completion rate was also very low. Moreover, that study underscored a substantial racial divide in the extent to which connections were completed. Kleinfeld's skepticism encourages further assessment of the assumptions underlying the 'small world' phenomena. Thus, in this section, we will examine those assumptions and what they might tell us about the conditions under which nascent entrepreneurs form startup teams and search for resources.

The structure of small world networks

Models of small world networks differ from models of random networks in two important ways (Watts, 1999). First, rather than connections being formed randomly across entire populations, relationships are clustered together in local networks, such as neighborhoods, friendship circles, or workplaces. Such clusters form because socio-cultural constraints substantially limit the extent to which any two persons might encounter one another. Most ties are based on homophily, rather than randomness (Ruef, Aldrich,

and Carter, 2003). These conditions increase the density of connection within clusters and reduce the chances that people in one cluster will have contacts with people in other clusters. By making it more difficult to enact ties with dissimilar others, such clusters potentially raise the average path length in social networks.

Second, to meet the condition of low average path lengths within small worlds, theorists posit that local clusters of nodes are linked to other local clusters through bridging ties. These bridging ties link clusters together to form a global network. Small world theorists have shown that a surprisingly *small* number of long-distance bridging ties have to be added to otherwise fragmented social networks to create a small world (Watts, 1999). The bridging ties jump over otherwise broad gaps in the network, thus lowering the average path between any two points. Note that small world theorists do not make claims about the *frequency* with which small world networks occur in the real world, but only that networks meeting these two conditions will be small world networks. Whether any particular network meets the conditions is an empirical question.

In Figure 2, we display two networks. For both networks, we calculate the clustering coefficient (based on the number of complete triads divided by the total number of potential triads where at least two out of the three nodes are directly linked) and the average path length (based on the number of links between all pairs of two nodes that could be reached from one another and the total number of linked nodes). The network in panel A does not have any nontrivial clusters and lacks bridging ties across distant nodes. In contrast, the network in Panel B

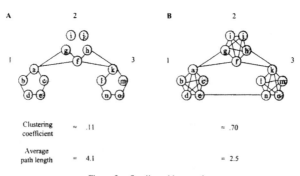

	A	2		B	2	
Clustering coefficient		≈ .11			≈ .70	
Average path length		= 4.1			= 2.5	

Figure 2.   Small world examples

contains several small world clusters and bridging ties joining these clusters. As a result, the clustering coefficient increases significantly between the two networks. Clustering coefficient values can range from a low of zero to high of one, and given the values in the figure, it is clear that a much higher percentage of nodes in panel B are connected to each other. Additionally, the average path length decreases substantially with the addition of a few bridging ties. In principle, people are much closer together in Panel B than in Panel A.

Homophily and clustering

Social science research strongly supports the proposition that social structural conditions generate densely linked local clusters. Researchers have extensively documented the generalization that 'birds of a feather flock together' since the early 20th century. Studies range from research on friendships (Lazarsfeld and Merton, 1954) and teams (Ruef *et al.*, 2003) to studies of cultural and voluntary associations (Emerson and Smith, 2000; McPherson and Smith-Lovin, 1986) and business organizations (Ibarra, 1995; Kanter, 1977). *Homophily* constitutes the central principle behind these consistent findings: 'Homophily is the principle that a contact between similar people occurs at a higher rate than among dissimilar people' (McPherson, Smith-Lovin, and Cook, 2001: 416). In the language of social networks, the 'friends of our friends' are already our friends, rather than strangers unknown to us.

Local clusters form in ways that sustain and amplify homophily. Strong boundaries deflect social relationships back upon themselves, thus fostering highly concentrated social networks. For example, instead of extending an open public invitation to join, existing clusters recruit new members either by specifically recruiting them (e.g., LinkedIn users send an invitation via email to other potential users) or through drawing on their current ties in other domains (e.g., through kinship ties). Because individuals who share similar characteristics are more likely to know each other, these individuals tend to form dense clusters in which everyone knows everyone else.

Dense local networks can lead to three self-reinforcing dynamics that reproduce and magnify their tendency toward narrow clustering. First, new people wishing to join an existing local network face potential barriers when they do not share common experiences and interests with current members. For example, kin-based network clusters may squeeze out

non-kin who would otherwise benefit from membership (Marsden, 1987). Second, similarities among individuals create stronger linkages and reduce the likelihood of turnover within a local network. Conversely, dissimilarities increase the likelihood of people leaving relationships. Third, if homophily serves as a basis for recruiting similar others, this common characteristic could be used as a screening mechanism. These three self-reinforcing dynamics, driven by homophily and propinquity, sustain the homophilous composition of local networks.

Bridges and short cuts

Because of clustering, people in discrete parts of a network will be unlikely to encounter people in other clusters without going to extraordinary lengths, such as working through many intermediaries. However, small world theorists have noted that it does not take many bridges between clusters to lower substantially the distance between people in different clusters. For our purposes in studying the creation of new ventures, we need to understand the process by which such bridges could be constructed. What strategies might entrepreneurs employ to shorten paths to potential opportunities and resource providers?

Constructing bridges across clusters poses a major challenge to most people. Although most of these boundaries are quasi-permeable, surmounting them requires work that people are often discouraged from undertaking. People's peer groups often actively discourage contact with dissimilar others, and settlement patterns create geographic separation that individuals must work to overcome.[6] Restrictions on associative activities create a recursive cycle – given knowledge constraints, individuals become habituated to seeking out similar others and uncomfortable with dissimilar others (McPherson and Smith-Lovin, 1987).

Overcoming these constraints requires that individuals proactively make strategic choices that push

---

[6] For example, Mouw and Entwisle (2006) used social network and spatial data from the National Longitudinal Study of Adolescent Health (Add Health) to examine the effect of racial residential segregation on school friendship segregation in the United States. They attributed about one third of the level of racial friendship segregation in schools to residential segregation, indicating that where students lived had a powerful effect on the likelihood that they were able to form cross-racial social ties. More of the effect resulted from residential segregation across schools than within them, implying that many students were not in a position to form inter-racial friendships because they had little chance of meeting people who were not like them. In short, they had few out-group choices to make.

them across social boundaries, or that individuals become involved in activities that expose them to dissimilar others. Individuals who pursue this strategy must be prepared to bear the additional costs generated by bridging differences (Arrow, McGrath, and Berdahl, 2000; Popielarz and McPherson, 1995). For example, Davis, Renzulli, and Aldrich (2006) found that nascent entrepreneurs who wished to increase the diversity of their social networks derived few benefits from simply joining a diverse set of voluntary associations. Instead, they gained network diversity by actively participating in the associations and aggressively seeking out new contacts at meetings. As another example, commercially oriented social network websites formalize the process of searching for bridging ties by showing members that a bridge exists between them and a desired contact whom they do not know personally. It is then up to them to convince the intermediary, whom they know, to make introductions for them.

Summary

The principle of small world networks reveals the tension hidden in calls for nascent entrepreneurs to 'use networking' to build entrepreneurial teams and seek opportunities. Being embedded in dense clusters of social relations that have emerged through homophily and propinquity creates a highly circumscribed world for entrepreneurs. However, to the extent that bridging ties allow entrepreneurs access to distant regions of a global network, the potential scope for entrepreneurial action expands enormously. Such ties can be an emergent consequence of forces beyond their control, but entrepreneurs can also reduce path lengths to valuable resources by taking strategic action. We will return to this point in a later section.

Model 3: Truncated Scale Free (or 'Fat Tail Distribution') Networks

Our third network model, of truncated scale free networks, differs in several ways from random and small world networks. Small world networks can also be scale free, whereas by definition, random networks are not. Thus, we begin by highlighting the differences between random and scale free networks and then discus their relation to small world networks. As we noted earlier, few networks studied by social scientists are purely scale free but rather

follow an exponential distribution with a 'fat tail.' For ease of exposition, we will keep the term 'scale free' as we describe the pure model.

Scale free compared to random networks

Scale free networks follow a power law in the distribution of their nodes and ties, unlike random networks, which follow a Poisson distribution. In scale free networks, some nodes have a very large number of ties (in and out) and most of the rest have very few. By contrast, random networks have a peaked distribution in the number of ties per node, and the distribution is very homogeneous, centered on the mean and mode. We illustrate the differences using the graphs displayed in Figure 3.

Panel A of Figure 3 shows a random graph with 36 nodes and 44 links, with an average in-degree of 2.42 ties per node and a very small standard deviation of 0.81 (Kurakin, 2007). Based on the figure in Panel A, Panel C shows the distribution of ties, $P(k)$, which is the probability that a randomly chosen node in a network has exactly k links. So, on the y axis, $P(k)$ is the fraction of nodes that have k links. Because Panel A is a random network, $P(k)$ in Panel C follows a Poisson distribution, which peaks at average k and exponentially decays as k increases, at rate $P(k) \sim e^{-k}$. The network in Panel A is not very highly interconnected, as only 44 out of 630 possible links are present. Using the formula we presented earlier in describing random graphs, the average path length between nodes would be about four.

Panel B shows a scale free network, also with 36 nodes and 44 links, with the same average in-degree of 2.42 as in the random network, but with a larger standard deviation of 2.63. However, in this case, the *average* is extremely misleading as an indicator of connectivity. As in all scale free networks, a small number of hubs dominates the distribution, with the top three having 9, 10, and 11 links to them, respectively. Panel D graphs the distribution of the figure shown in Panel B, and shows that $P(k)$ follows a power law distribution. There is no single peak, and the log/log plot in Panel D shows the $P(k)$ distribution follows the formula $P(k) \sim k^{-\gamma}$. Barabási (2002) noted that most of the power law distributions he studied had a γ of between 2 and 3. Thus, even though both networks have the same number of nodes and links, they are quite different in their organization. In the random network, the contribution of any particular node to the connectedness of the overall network is roughly equal, whereas in the

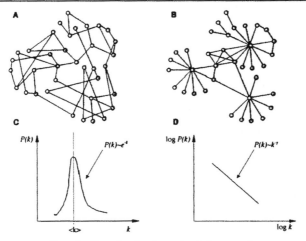

Figure 3. Examples of random and scale free networks

Note: Panel C graphs the degree distribution shown in Panel A. Similarly, Panel D
graphs the degree distribution shown in Panel B.
Source: Source: http://www.alexeikurakin.org/
Accessed June 26, 2007. Used with permission.

scale free network, a small number of nodes dominate the structure.[7]

Scale free compared to small world networks

Small world networks can also have a scale free distribution of ties. Unlike the small world networks we
described in the previous section, the connectivity of
a scale free network does not depend on shortcuts
closing long-distance gaps between clusters. As an
example, consider again the small world network
shown in Panel B of Figure 2. It has a much shorter
average path length than the network in Panel A,
but has a more uniform degree distribution than that
of Panel A. In Panel A, the average node has 2.13

ties and the standard deviation for the distribution
is 1.18, whereas the average node in Panel B has
4.73 ties and the standard deviation is only 0.88.
The reduction in path length between the two networks was not achieved through a small number of
highly connected nodes, as in Panel B of Figure 3,
but rather through a few links serving as short cuts
between clusters.

How might scale free networks emerge?

Barabási (2002) suggested that scale free networks
are best viewed dynamically, not statically. He and
his collaborators proposed two simple principles by
which to understand how scale free networks grow:
growth takes place one node at a time and new nodes
link to existing nodes following a principle of preferential attachment. As each new node is added to the
network, it links to a few others. These links are not
made randomly, but rather the node 'observes' which
nodes already have the most links and then link to
them. For example, investigators studying vicarious
learning have noted that firms can bypass the need
for trial and error learning by choosing a simple rule
of imitation, such as 'imitate the apparently most

---

[7] Not every highly centralized network has a scale free degree
distribution. In designed networks, such as those inside large
firms, there is an intra-organizational hierarchy, with a chief
executive officer at the top and then descending groups below,
in a ladder like structure. Thus, there is a uniform degree distribution by design, following guidelines about the number of
direct reports to any particular manager, and the distribution of
nodes does not conform to a power law. However, this is not a
generic result for centralized networks. It cannot be extended
to naturally emerging graphs in open networks.

successful individual or firm,' or 'imitate the fastest growing firm' (Miner and Haunschild, 1995). Thus, if entrepreneurs perceive that successful firms are funded by a top-tier Silicon Valley venture capital firm, such a rule would lead other entrepreneurs to seek investment with the same VC.

Following the principle of preferential attachment means, 'the rich get richer,' thus increasing inequality in a network. However, it is only probabilistic: not every new node links only to the most preferred. For growth to result in a scale free network, it is only necessary that a high proportion follow the preference principle. Some newcomers will *not* flock to the most highly connected nodes, because they have divergent preferences or because of capacity constraints on the ability of the most highly linked nodes to handle large numbers of ties arriving in a short interval. Nonetheless, if a large enough proportion of newcomers follow the principle of preferential attachment, the resulting network evolves into one with a few highly linked and many sparsely linked nodes.

What evidence do we have for the principle of preferential attachment driving network growth in the social world? We offer three examples. First, some ethnic business owners, in some communities, follow the principle of preferring to deal with other co-ethnics rather than outsiders (Aldrich and Waldinger, 1990). Second, studies of social movements and the 'bandwagon' effect, especially when driven by the mass media, show strong evidence for advantages accruing to pioneers (Low and Abrahamson, 1997). The race by dot.com firms to capture 'eyeballs' was premised on the existence of the preferential attachment principle, and studies have found that the structure of links to Web sites follows a power law distribution (Barabási, 2002).

Third, in fields where status and reputation effects strongly govern choices of which ties to form, we would expect scale free networks to form (Pollock, 2004; Pollock, Porac, and Wade, 2004; Stuart, Hoang, and Hybels, 1999). The venture capital industry represents a particularly promising place to look for scale free networks, based on status and reputation effects, given the high degree of uncertainty facing its participants. In their analysis of U.S. venture capital firms' investments, Sorenson and Stuart (2001) noted that frequent reliance on investment syndication, rather than solo investing, created a dense VC interfirm network that structured the flow of information in the industry.

Sorenson and Stuart's description of the network's evolution seemed to describe a preferential attachment pattern in which each syndication participation increased the likelihood of being invited again, as well as increasing trust in the syndication partners, thus raising the likelihood of future cooperation. New firms joining the network thus were at a disadvantage in linking with the most connected firms, in contrast to those already in the network. This pattern was confirmed in Kogut, Urso, and Walker's (2007) research on the development of the U.S. venture capital industry from 1960 to 2005, which revealed a more complex pattern of ties than a simple power law distribution. Rather than simply affiliating with the most connected firms, firms preferred to do new deals with incumbent firms that they had dealt with in the past. Thus, although the degree distribution itself deviated from a simple power law, the distribution of *repeated* ties followed a power law distribution. They suggested that the forces generating a nationally integrated venture capital network were more complex than simple preferential attachment and called for more research on the process (Kogut *et al.*, 2007).

Scale free networks and vulnerability to disruption

Scale free networks differ radically from random networks, and from small world networks that are *not* scale free, with regard to their vulnerability to failure. Random and non scale free small world networks are highly vulnerable to disruption, because dropping or cutting nodes randomly can disconnect the entire network, resulting in isolated fragments. In contrast, scale free networks are not vulnerable to failures at random. Many nodes can be removed randomly without disconnecting the overall network and breaking it into fragments. Most scale free networks studied by Barabási (2002: 115) and his students – who were explicitly looking at the issue of vulnerability – had a degree exponent smaller than 3 (the γ parameter in $P(k)\sim k^{-\gamma}$): 'Therefore, these networks break apart only after all nodes have been removed – or, for all practical purposes, never.' However, scale free networks are highly vulnerable to attacks directed at the most connected links – the top of the hierarchy, which has the nodes with the highest connectivity. As the most connected nodes are removed, the network eventually falls apart.

We can apply this idea to entrepreneurship in 'failed states' or in communities experiencing social upheaval. When a society or community experiences a major social upheaval, such as a civil war or a natural disaster, purely random failures will not threaten its overall stability. However, if civil war or terrorism results in the killing or emigration of top leaders, or natural disaster drives out the most well connected members of the community, the social fabric is threatened. Coordination between social entities will be much more difficult and path distances between nodes will increase substantially. In the United States, New Orleans seems to be experiencing this type of failure, as many business owners have left and entrepreneurs have created few new ventures. Thus, high growth oriented firms will be less likely to start up and less able to flourish in these troubled environments. However, very small-scale entrepreneurship will be much less affected and may even be more likely to thrive with so many dominant players removed or neutralized.

We can speculate that entrepreneurship will also be difficult, if, for some reason, a social network cannot grow scale free. In addition to the social upheaval already discussed, other forces may hamper scale free growth. If cultural or social constraints prevent ordinary nodes from becoming well-connected hubs, then the network will be more random than scale free. For example, if a society's or community's norms strongly encourage equality and the egalitarian distribution of resources, then 'leveling' will affect the nodes that began to accumulate resources and the network will remain fragmented or more small-world like than scale free.

Summary

Pure scale free networks display a degree distribution that follows a power law, as we showed in Figure 3. However, many degree distributions found among social networks are better characterized as exponential with heavy or 'fat' tails. That is, their degree distributions look very much like the line drawn in panel D of Figure 3, except that rather than continuing in a straight line down to the x-axis, the distribution is truncated and curves to the x-axis.[8] Commentators have offered various speculations on why this occurs, such as Kogut *et al.*'s (2007) observation about the tendency for repeated ties with the same players in the venture capital industry, rather than ties to the most linked players. For our purposes, we simply note that the truncated scale free

model is a good beginning point for understanding why average path length is so short in some kinds of networks.

APPLICATION TO ENTREPRENEURIAL TEAMS AND SEARCH

We turn now to two applications of the three network models we have reviewed. The first concerns the emergence of entrepreneurial teams and the consequences of network structures for team composition. The second concerns how network structures affect entrepreneurial search.

Entrepreneurship: Who's on YOUR team?

We noted earlier that the literature on entrepreneurial teams has proposed two principles by which teams might form. The rational process model of team formation emphasizes selecting members based on pragmatic instrumental criteria, whereas the social-psychological model emphasizes the interpersonal fit between team members. We argue that the instrumental model fits best those teams that emerge in well-institutionalized fields characterized by networks whose degree distributions resemble truncated scale free or exponential distributions with fat tails. By contrast, we believe the social-psychological model fits best for the vast majority of team foundings, in part because they are embedded in disconnected local clusters that only sporadically coalesce into small worlds that contain shortcuts to diverse other clusters.

Teams in well-institutionalized scale free networks

We can gain insight into the special social structural conditions under which most entrepreneurial teams form by examining teams emerging within networks characterized by power law distributions with fat tails: creative teams of coauthors in academic disciplines and creative teams in the Broadway music industry (BMI). In their work on team assembly mechanisms in four academic fields and the BMI, Guimerà *et al.* (2005) found that the set of people from whom teams were drawn was embedded in a larger network which acted as a storehouse of past knowledge created within the field. The large network of participants shared common professional standards, norms of collaboration, and was national in scope. Over time, the fields became increasingly

---

[8] They have fewer extremely well connected nodes than would be predicted by the exponent of the equation describing the log/log plot.

integrated, moving from semi-isolated small clusters to a single large connected cluster. A small number of very prestigious actors acted as brokers and created bridges between clusters, lowering the average path length for the entire network. Founders assembling teams thus had a very large community of practitioners from which to draw, with shared social identities.

Team sizes in all fields increased over time, reflecting the growing complexity of the fields and external performance pressures. Clearly, competence was a very important criterion in assembling teams and we would expect universalistic norms to govern recruitment. These teams exemplified many of the desired characteristics identified by the 'rational process' models of entrepreneurial team formation: adequate size, skill diversity, shared prior experiences, and high human capital. Even so, the investigators found a very strong tendency for people to repeat past collaborations, just as in the venture capital industry. At least for the BMI, the shape of the degree distribution could be characterized by a power law with an exponential tail, meaning it was highly skewed with a few people at the top with many ties and many people with only a few ties (Jarrett Spiro, personal communication). In this respect, it resembled the VC industry repeated tie distribution that we have already described (Kogut *et al.*, 2007), indicating that a process of preferential attachment seemed to be driving the national network for the BMI.

The social structural conditions underlying team emergence in these five fields provide a sharp contrast to the much more locally oriented networks out of which most entrepreneurial teams emerge. Nonetheless, they could well be descriptive of particular subfields of entrepreneurship, such as within regional clusters around Route 128 or Silicon Valley or within particular industries drawing on national talent pools where prestige and status affect the recruiting process.

Mundane entrepreneurial teams

In contrast to entrepreneurial teams formed in well-institutionalized fields, teams emerging under typical circumstances are deeply embedded in local clusters of social relations. We cannot assume that most nascent entrepreneurs are operating in a small world context in which ties to other clusters help them recruit diverse members for their founding teams. Whereas Guimerá *et al.* (2005) could take for granted an instrumental basis for team formation

as scientists searched for coauthors and Broadway producers sought choreographers and composers, we must acknowledge the priority of interpersonal relations in mundane foundings. Under such conditions, few teams will recruit out-of-cluster members. In this section, we review some evidence showing the extent to which homophily, familiarity, and propinquity dominate the dynamics of team formation, supporting the interpersonal relations model.

Interpersonal forces within local clusters powerfully mold team formation because they create conditions of high trust and positive social support. First, according to Coleman (1988), densely packed networks of social relations within a cluster constitute a primary source of 'social capital' because social norms are monitored and enforced more easily within closed networks. In dense networks, when people violate norms, they suffer the consequences of local sanctioning, such as loss of reputation. Within closed networks, violators will confront a 'united front' composed of members who call for a remedy. For example, nascent entrepreneurs in many developing nations use rotating credit associations to raise the capital they need. They rely on collective trust among their members and take advantage of the benefits of network closure (Biggart, 2001).

Second, local clusters in which a high proportion of alters know one another can be useful because they provide social support and facilitate the transmission of complicated information (Nahapiet and Ghoshal, 1998). Such networks, also called 'high density networks,' can foster economic relations through the creation of trust. For example, Portes and Sensenbrenner (1993) argued that social closure within immigrant communities gives individuals greater access to financial resources. Immigrant entrepreneurs are thus able to finance projects via ethnic-based cohesive ties.

Homophily and familiarity in team formation

Using data from the Panel Study of Entrepreneurial Dynamics, a representative national survey of 830 people who reported they were in the process of trying to start a new business in 1999–2000, Ruef *et al.* (2003) showed that two principles dominated team formation: homophily and familiarity. As we noted, in reviewing the forces generating clusters in small world networks, the homophily principle refers, in general, to a tendency for people with similar characteristics to associate with one another. In the PSED, teams were extremely homogeneous with respect to gender, race, and occupation. For example, racially homogeneous teams appeared in the data at a level 27 times that expected based on random mixing, and gender homogeneous teams – net of spousal pairs – were about 5 times more likely than expected. As we followed the founding efforts over time, we observed that they became more gender and racially homogenous as people left and new members joined the teams.

Familiarity is also a key social mechanism of in-group formation, and can be a result of pre-existing ties, such as through work or family. The principle of familiarity asserts that people who associate with one another, under certain conditions, become more likely to continue the association subsequently in other circumstances. How far outside their immediate circle are founders prepared to go in building a team? Research shows that people rarely establish 'relationships' with those they meet by chance (Grossetti, 2005). Instead, local clusters of family, friends, work, and neighborhoods will serve as the pool of people available for recruitment into entrepreneurial teams, if nascent entrepreneurs follow the principle of interpersonal relations in team building.

Following Simmel, we think it is useful to distinguish three concentric circles of inclusion for teams: family, others known personally to the lead founder or core founders, and strangers. Family members, particularly spouses and domestic partners, fulfill many of the requisites of shared identity that are otherwise generated by homophily. They are often in close proximity to one another and have had many opportunities to share rewarding experiences. Because they are likely to interact frequently, family members have many opportunities to discuss the possibility of starting a business together. They also have many occasions during which they can observe the reliability and trustworthiness of one another, perhaps predisposing them to a favorable response when asked to join in a new venture. If they see one another regularly, the chances for an escalation of commitment increase. Ideas that might be superficially discussed and dismissed in other contexts might lead, among kin, to the cumulative development of a plan for action.

Ruef *et al.* (2003) found that spousal and kinship ties were the most common basis of within-team relations: 65 percent of all teams had spouse/partner ties, other family ties, or both. Business ties seem to be an alternative to spouse/partner ties for team building, and about 39 percent of the non-spouse/partner teams had at least one such tie among its members. In

special analyses conducted for this paper, we found that only 4 percent of the teams organized around spouse/partner pairs also contained members linked by business or work relations. Larger teams were more likely to have such ties than two person teams.

To learn more about the way in which business ties influence team formation, we examined how the tie occurred. For the 173 ties reported in all 86 teams that had at least one business tie within the team, including eight spouse/partner based teams, we found that 51 percent were based on colleagues who worked at the same place and 49 percent were not. The process of workplace recruiting exemplifies the self-reinforcing pattern of homophily in social relations we mentioned earlier. In their work on hiring practices at a phone center, Fernandez, Castilla, and Moore (2000) reported that new hires referred by current employees were more likely to be similar to current employees than non-referred new hires.

We suspect that many of the ties not based on currently working together might reflect prior joint work experience in another workplace. Some of these ties might also reflect other kinds of business relations, such as clients, vendors, or consultants. Friendship and acquaintance ties were slightly more prevalent among the non spouse/partner teams than were business ties. About 44 percent of the non-spouse/partner teams had at least one pair of members who were friends or acquaintances prior to joining the team. By contrast, only 7 percent of the spouse/partner based teams also included at least one friends/acquaintance tie. Founders also call on others for help with specific problems, and our research shows that over 70 percent of founders have non-owner 'helpers' in their founding groups (Kim, Longest, and Aldrich, 2007).

Strangers need not apply

Strangers – people not related by kinship or known to one another prior to the initial interactions around the founding of a new venture – constitute the most interesting potential team members. Rational process theories of entrepreneurial team functioning strongly imply that interpersonal considerations are secondary to instrumental ones (Barney *et al.*, 1996; Mosakowski, 1998). If industry experience and technical or managerial competence are critical to the success of a team, then we would expect lead entrepreneurs to search widely for qualified people, using existing bridges to go beyond local clusters or creating new bridges if none exist. Well-qualified strangers might even be preferred over less-qualified family, friends, and business associates.

Accordingly, perhaps the most striking finding from the PSED concerns the nearly complete absence of any strangers whatsoever among two person teams, and their rarity among three person teams. They were also extremely rare among all spouse/partner based teams, with only 2 percent of such teams reporting any stranger ties. Only among the non spouse/partner based teams with 4 or 5 members, representing 18 percent of all the non spouse/partner teams, did we find a sizeable proportion of strangers. About half of the three and four person teams had at least one pair of strangers, and almost three-quarters of the five person teams did. Nonetheless, even in these large teams, most team members still knew each other prior to team formation. Clearly, these strangers carry the possibility of serving as bridging ties to other clusters. We suspect that these large teams, somewhat dependent upon people who were unknown to one another before forming the team, represent the kinds of more capital-intensive and growth-oriented teams that figure so prominently in the strategic literature on entrepreneurial teams.

Several studies of new venture performance suggest that pre-existing relationships might be an advantage within a team, rather than a source of concern (Francis and Sandberg, 2000). Forbes et als.' (2006) study of academic spinouts from two large public universities found new team members were selected for their similarity to existing team members, apparently driven by a desire for team consensus and harmony. Thus, local embeddedness in a cluster may not be a disadvantage, because the benefits of positive interpersonal dynamics offset the losses from a more homogenous team.

Summary

Clearly, the great majority of entrepreneurial teams emerge out of the local clusters described by small world networks but *without* the bridging ties necessary to reduce the social distance to strangers qualified for team membership. As such, we would expect them to be very stable, and follow-up studies over the subsequent three waves of the PSED bore out that expectation (Kim and Aldrich, 2004). Indeed, only 12 percent of the new ventures identified in the first wave experienced any changes in team composition over the four waves.

Unlike the creative teams assembled in increasingly institutionalized fields in the United States, as documented by Guimerá et al. (2005), most attempts at founding new ventures in the United States do not draw their members from a nationally-integrated pool of experts whose competence has been judged against agreed-upon standards. Strangers are rare, except for the largest teams, possibly hinting at a 'competency discount' that founders extend to potential members whom they know and trust. Instead, almost all startups assemble teams based on embedded ties from pre-existing relations within local clusters. We speculate – and we need more research on this issue – that founding team members use instrumental criteria mainly *within* networks of embedded ties. Apparently, bridging ties usually fail to bring in non-homophilous members. Most new ventures do not inhabit a 'small world.' To pursue this issue further, we turn now to the issue of bridging ties and entrepreneurial search more generally.

Search: Holed up in clusters?

At any given moment, the composition of entrepreneurial teams shows the impact of their embeddedness in local clusters and the constraints they face in breaking out of such clusters. However, networks are best viewed dynamically, not statically. If nascent entrepreneurs and founding team members find themselves closed off in clusters without indirect ties to the resources and opportunities they need, they can actively engage in resource mobilization through network-based search. Indeed, 'small worlds' depend upon bridges constructed through ties between clusters. In this section, we consider four questions: how does someone's location in a cluster affect their search behavior, how do people break out of clusters, what role does someone's social identity play in search, and how is search different in scale free networks?

Dense clusters inhibit search

High-density networks can be detrimental to the extent that they induce conformity and constrain individuals' autonomy, creativity, and innovation (Borgatti, 1997; Gargiulo and Benassi, 2000; Hansen, 1999; Putnam, 2000). When networks are dense, the potential assistance available from different members is often redundant because information and potential contacts are likely to be widely shared (Glanville, 2004). Additional network members in a dense network fail to provide novel information, although they might be able to supply other resources that entrepreneurs need.

Burt (2005) argued that people often provide others with information that they believe the person would like to hear, thus merely 'echoing' what the person already knows or believes. 'Echo' gives people a distorted view of what is really happening in their world, because it is redundant information, perhaps even deceptive. When coupled with people's failings with regard to self insight (Dunning, 2005), 'echo' falls well short of providing an accurate and reliable view of someone's environment. Social networks thus can affect the *meaning* that people find in their environments, by shaping and altering the information they receive and perhaps limiting their awareness of the need to search more widely for accurate information.

Breaking out of clusters

Consider a nascent entrepreneur contemplating recruiting a team of founders. Very few will methodically analyze their entire personal network, taking into account their weaker direct and potential indirect ties. Lacking clairvoyance, people will inevitably concentrate their investigations on their immediate circle of friends and any inferences about the value of new ties will depend heavily on personal intuition and experience. However, we note that networking software, such as LinkedIn, allows individuals to approach network searching in a much more systematic manner, and using such software seems on its way to becoming a 'best practice' in the high-technology sector.

Finding valuable information without the aid of sophisticated software may depend, in part, on a person's position in a social network. Indeed, Burt (2005) has forcefully argued that in explaining successful outcomes, investigators have given too much weight to human capital and not enough to location in social networks. His well-known argument about brokerage and closure stresses that advantages flow to people who recognize or at least take advantage of structural holes in networks. Throughout his analysis, he recognizes that people in 'good' locations might be different from others, and thus he always controls for the effects of human and social capital, e.g., age, experience, and job.

Implicit in his analysis is the assumption that people will recognize when they occupy bad locations and thus move to better locations. He seems to posit that, in the cross-section, we observe the consequences of people taking advantage of 'the kind of person he or she is, so motivation does not have to be measured once one has a measure of network structure' (Burt,

2005: 47). Nevertheless, he also goes to some lengths to point out that people often do not recognize their true situation. People seem not to be very good at seeing structural holes 'from the inside,' unless they already live in a hole-filled world. For example, in summarizing several studies (Freeman, 1992; Janicki and Larrick, 2005), he concluded, 'the summary conclusion from Freeman's and Janicik's experiments is that experience matters: people who live in a network that contains structural holes are more likely to recognize the holes in their next networks' (Burt, 2005: 77).

Burt's line of reasoning leads us to conclude that selection forces generated by structural ties, rather than strategic action, may account for much of an entrepreneur's structural advantage. Being able to recognize, acknowledge, or create opportunities may depend upon one's position within a social network. Having a non-homophilous entrepreneurial team, including strangers, could motivate and facilitate a search for structural holes. Random networks are full of structural holes, but most have no value and finding the few that do is a discouraging task. Truncated scale free social networks – if perceived for what they are – contain holes, but confront would-be opportunists with a daunting challenge, as we will point out shortly. Small world networks seem to be the most rewarding for those far-sighted entrepreneurs adept at building bridges between clusters.

Seeking short cuts

We can analyze effective entrepreneurial search behavior within social networks by drawing upon ideas from research on social identity. We noted the overwhelming task facing potential entrepreneurs who search for information and resources in truly random networks. A 'broadcast' search involves pursuing all possible social ties, a costly endeavor, given the lack of meaningful structure in the network. Even if we accept the implausible assertion underlying Figure 1 that we live in a world connected at random, knowing that *d* is only 3 is worthless to a person searching for unknown others. Because the paths to all others in the network are randomly generated, there is no *a priori* method for picking a path that will lead to any particular target. To ensure success, an entrepreneur would need to explore every single path at every single stage of *d*. Such a broadcast search would be incredibly costly and time consuming (Barabási, 2002).

By contrast, small worlds contain meaningful structures at the level of local clusters, and thus it would seem possible to engage in a 'directed' search that would economize on search costs. However, we have emphasized the high degree of redundancy in local clusters, implying that valuable information lies on a path that goes beyond the boundaries of the cluster and leads to other clusters. Therefore, people searching for resources and opportunities outside of their own cluster will need to find an indirect path to them.

In a small world, 'shortcuts' to unknown others *can* be found through directed search (Watts, 2003: 245). Initially, it might seem absurd to think that anybody in Nebraska would know to whom to send a letter, when the target is a stockbroker in the Boston area (Milgram, 1967). However, people use their knowledge of *social identities* to figure out where to start. They not only know who their friends are, but also to which social categories ('identities') they belong. Thus, in deciding on how to conduct their directed search, people pick categories such as 'works in finance' or 'travels a lot to the east coast.'

These social categories enabled people to bypass the need for a random search through all of their ties. Indeed, if they had to use a broadcast search—a way to take advantage of networks that might contain a high degree of randomness—they would overwhelm the system. Rather than a broadcast search, they choose people whose social identities might move the letter closer to the target. Milgram's subjects took advantage of their knowledge of local clusters plus their implicit recognition that there might be bridges across the gap between their local cluster and the target in Boston. Knowing someone in a particular identity class or cluster is a huge first step toward a search shortcut that jumps over the otherwise random steps required to complete a search for targets lying outside of local clusters.[9]

Searching in scale free/fat tail networks

In truncated scale free networks, centrally located actors occupy positions that give them many advan-

tages over less central actors. As Sorenson and Stuart (2001) observed, central actors can 'see' more of the network and spot potential opportunities before others. Their central position enables them to mobilize collective action quickly and efficiently, such as forming entrepreneurial teams, investment syndicates, and other collective commercial activities. They can treat some actors preferentially by granting them access to information and resources over other actors, such as competitors. Indeed, because of the role played by central actors, we speculate that the likelihood of developing successful 'high-growth' ventures increases if new ventures emerge in environments displaying scale free network characteristics.[10]

If entrepreneurs recognize that a network relevant to them has the property of being scale free, or nearly so, what strategies should they adopt? How does someone change standing in a truncated scale free distribution? One possibility is to form ties with relevant people who are further up in the distribution. For example, in academic scholarship, victors in the struggle for citations usually work in teams, rather than going solo. Junior scholars improve their chances by establishing coauthorship relationships with senior scholars, as shown by Guimerá *et al.* (2005). Another possibility is collective action, involving coalition formation with others to take collective action. For example, almost all high-tech new ventures involve teams, rather than solo entrepreneurs or partners.

Summary

Effective search behavior in small and truncated scale free worlds depends upon someone's network location, with densely connected clusters often leading to 'echo' rather than new information. Strategic responses to the constraints of clusters require people to break out, using technological assistance as well as deliberately seeking social locations in and around structural holes. Such locations increase the likelihood of someone recognizing opportunities and encountering non-redundant information. When entrepreneurs must search beyond their direct ties, they can use their knowledge of social identities as a starting point, rather than searching randomly. Search in scale free or fat tail networks is simpler

---

[9] We note that using 'social identities' in searching within networks resembles social network analysts' strategy of giving survey respondents 'position generator' lists. In such surveys, respondents are asked if they know people in certain categories. For example, in the Research Triangle Park area of North Carolina, Aldrich, Elam, and Reese (1996) asked about experts in law, accounting, and finance, along with an expert in the person's specific industry. Marsden (2005: 15) noted that 'studies suggest that respondents recall alters in social clusters when answering name generators. The basis for clustering likely varies across situations, but it is possible that foci of activities such as families, neighborhoods, workplaces, or associations offer a framework for remembering others.'

---

[10] For peripheral actors, over-reliance on a central actor creates potential vulnerabilities, unless they can create additional ties to others.

than in random or small worlds, insofar as uncovering the fundamental structural order is concerned. However, latecomers to well-institutionalized fields will have to wait their turn for a place at the table or else join with others in organizing an effective vehicle for collective action.

CONCLUSIONS

Our discussion of the differences between random, small world, and truncated scale free networks has highlighted key features of each. Identifying the concepts and principles for each provides analytic clarification, but we recognize that entrepreneurship researchers will not discover distinct cases of each. Instead, we recommend that investigators try to find the conditions under which each formulation is most useful in understanding a particular entrepreneurial issue.

Our review of the three network models raises the question of which model might be most useful in trying to describe the contexts in which most entrepreneurs live and work. Throughout our paper, we have emphasized the importance of covering the entire range of entrepreneurial activity, beginning with attempts to found ventures and continuing through their attempts to grow. To capture the dynamics and complexity of this process, we think it is important to keep an open mind regarding which network model is most appropriate and to specify under what conditions it might arise. Because of our training as sociologists, we have been drawn to the social conditions surrounding the founding of new ventures, particularly with regard to the kinds of teams that are assembled. Although these ventures are not the 'black swans' of the entrepreneurial finance literature (Taleb, 2007), they are the raw materials from which the economic system draws much of its vitality.

We suggest that investigators wishing to use network characteristics in their models should clarify what kind of network they are positing: random, small world, or scale free. We have argued that outcomes might well be different within each model and therefore network model type may act as a moderating condition. For example, we have hypothesized that the characteristics of entrepreneurial teams might differ across network context, with mundane entrepreneurial ventures more likely to arise in small world contexts and high growth oriented ventures

with larger and more nationally recruited founding teams arising in scale free networks.

To conclude, we offer some questions about the implications of the three models for entrepreneurial behavior. Are entrepreneurs in a random world, only a few steps from everyone else, but blind as to how they navigate in it? Are they in a very small world, sheltered and even trapped within narrow communities? Alternatively, are they in the small world that Milgram first described, clustered to a great extent but able to take advantage of a few 'long leaps' that connect their cluster to other clusters far removed, if only they knew how to search? Do they become better at searching as they learn to recognize structural holes and as they take on an entrepreneurial identity?

Are they in a truncated scale free world, where their fate depends upon where they stand in the pecking order of ties and affiliations? Are they in a complex scale free world, trapped somewhere between order and chaos? In such worlds, most of life is somewhat predictable, in the short run, but the significant big-impact events are rare and predictable only after the fact. In this world, entrepreneurs are plagued with various cognitive heuristics and biases, and rewards come in the form of very lumpy payoffs (the occasional 'black swan'). Which of these worlds did Simmel have in mind when he wrote of opportunities proliferating into infinity?

ACKNOWLEDGMENTS

We thank the Kauffman Foundation for their Sociology and Entrepreneurship disciplinary grant that supported this research. Comments and suggestions from Amanda Elam, Tom Elfring, Kyle Longest, Jim Moody, Lori Rosenkopf, Paul Reynolds, Martin Ruef, Olav Sorenson, Jarrett Spiro, Harry Sapienza, Toby Stuart, Steve Vaisey and Brian Uzzi greatly improved the paper.

REFERENCES

Aldrich HE, Carter NM, Ruef M. 2004. Teams. In *Handbook of Entrepreneurial Dynamics: The Process of Business Creation*, Gartner WB, Shaver KG, Carter NM, Reynolds PD (eds). Sage: Thousand Oaks, CA; 299–310.

Aldrich HE, Elam A, Reese PR. 1996. Strong ties, weak ties, and strangers: Do women business owners differ from men in their use of networking to obtain assistance? In *Entrepreneurship in a Global Context*, Birley S, MacMillan IC (eds). Routledge: London; 1–25.

Aldrich HE, Waldinger R. 1990. Ethnicity and entrepreneurship. In *Annual Review of Sociology*. Annual Reviews, Inc.: Palo Alto, CA; 16: 111–135.

Aldrich HE, Zimmer C. 1986. Entrepreneurship through social networks. In *The Art and Science of Entrepreneurship*, Sexton D, Smilor R (eds). Ballinger: New York; 3–23.

Arrow H, McGrath JE, Berdahl JL. 2000. *Small Groups as Complex Systems: Formation, Coordination, Development, and Adaptation* (1st edn). Sage: Thousand Oaks, CA.

Baker T, Miner AS, Easley DT. 2003. Improvising firms: bricolage, account giving and improvisational competencies in the founding process. *Research Policy* 32(2): 255–276.

Barabási A-L. 2002. *Linked: How Everything Is Connected to Everything Else and What It Means for Business, Science, and Everyday Life*. Plume: New York.

Barney JB, Busenitz LW, Fiet JO, Moesel DD. 1996. New venture teams' assessment of learning assistance from venture capital firms. *Journal of Business Venturing* 11(4): 257–272.

Beckman CM, Burton MD, O'Reilly C. 2007. Early teams: the impact of team demography on VC financing and going public. *Journal of Business Venturing* 22(2): 147–173.

Biggart NW. 2001. Banking on each other: the situational logic of rotating savings and credit associations. In *Advances in Qualitative Organization Research*, Vol. 3, Wagner JA, Bartunek JM, Elsbach KD (eds). JAI Press: Greenwich, CT; 129–153.

Birley S, Stockley S. 2004. Entrepreneurial teams and venture growth. In *Handbook of Entrepreneurship*, Sexton DL, Landstrom H (eds). Blackwell: Oxford, UK; 287–307.

Blau P. 1977. *Inequality and Heterogeneity*. Free Press: New York.

Borgatti SP. 1997. Structural holes: unpacking Burt's redundancy measures. *Connections* 20(1): 35–38.

Burt RS. 2005. *Brokerage and Closure: An Introduction to Social Capital*. Oxford University Press: Oxford, UK.

Coleman JS. 1988. Social capital in the creation of human capital. *American Journal of Sociology* 94(Supplement): 95–120.

Davis AE, Renzulli LA, Aldrich HE. 2006. Mixing or matching?: the influence of voluntary associations on the occupational diversity and density of small business owners' networks. *Work and Occupations* 33(1): 42–72.

Dunning D. 2005. *Self-insight: Roadblocks and Detours on the Path to Knowing Thyself*. Psychology Press, Taylor & Francis Group: New York.

Emerson MO, Smith C. 2000. *Divided by Faith: Evangelical Religion and the Problem of Race in America*. Oxford University Press: Oxford, New York.

Fernandez RM, Castilla EJ, Moore P. 2000. Social capital at work: networks and employment at a phone center. *American Journal of Sociology* 105(5): 1288–1356.

Forbes DP, Borchert PS, Zellmer-Bruhn ME, Sapienza HJ. 2006. Entrepreneurial team formation: an exploration of new member addition. *Entrepreneurship: Theory and Practice* 30(2): 225(224).

Francis DH, Sandberg WR. 2000. Friendship within entrepreneurial teams and its association with team and venture performance. *Entrepreneurship Theory & Practice* 25(2): 5–25.

Freeman LC. 1992. Filling in the blanks: a theory of cognitive categories and the structure of social affiliation. *Social Psychology Quarterly* 55(2): 118–127.

Gargiulo M, Benassi M. 2000. Trapped in your own net? Network cohesion, structural holes, and the adaptation of social capital. *Organization Science* 11(2): 183–196.

Glanville JL. 2004. Voluntary associations and social network structure. *Sociological Forum* 19(3): 465–491.

Granovetter MS. 1973. The strength of weak ties. *American Journal of Sociology* 78(6): 1360–1380.

Grossetti M. 2005. Where do social relations come from?: A study of personal networks in the Toulouse area of France. *Social Networks* 27(4): 289–300.

Guimerá R, Uzzi B, Spiro J, Amaral LAN. 2005. Team assembly mechanisms determine collaboration network structure and team performance. *Science* 308(29 April): 697–702.

Hansen MT. 1999. The search-transfer problem: the role of weak ties in sharing knowledge across organization subunits. *Administrative Science Quarterly* 44(1): 82–111.

Hoang H, Antoncic B. 2003. Network-based research in entrepreneurship: a critical review. *Journal of Business Venturing* 18(2): 165–187.

Ibarra H. 1995. Race, opportunity, and diversity of social circles in managerial networks. *Academy of Management Journal* 38(3): 673–703.

Janicki GA, Larrick RP. 2005. Social network schemas and the learning of incomplete networks. *Journal of Personality and Social Psychology* 88: 348–364.

Kanter RM. 1977. *Men and Women of the Corporation*. Basic Books, New York.

Kim PH, Aldrich HE. 2004. Teams that work together, stay together: resiliency of entrepreneurial teams. *Frontiers of Entrepreneurship Research* 24: 89–95.

Kim PH, Longest K, Aldrich HE. 2007. Can you lend me a hand? Social support, network structure, and entrepreneurial action. Working paper, University of Wisconsin: Madison, WI.

Kleinfeld JS. 2002. The small world problem. *Society* 39(2): 61–66.

Kogut B, Urso P, Walker G. 2007. Emergent properties of a new financial market: American venture capital syndication, 1960–2005. *Management Science* 53(7): 1181–1198.

Kurakin A. 2007. *The Image*. Kurakin Press: Novato, CA.

Lazarsfeld P, Merton RK. 1954. Friendship as a social process: a substantive and methodological analysis. In

Freedom and Control in Modern Society, Berger M, Abel T. Page C (eds). Octagon Books: New York; 18–66.

Low MB, Abrahamson E. 1997. Movements, bandwagons, and clones: industry evolution and the entrepreneurial process. *Journal of Business Venturing* 12(6): 435–457.

Marsden PV. 1987. Core discussion networks of Americans. *American Sociological Review* 52(1): 122–131.

Marsden PV. 2005. Recent developments in network measurement. In *Models and Methods in Social Network Analysis*, Carrington PJ, Scott J, Wasserman S (eds). Cambridge University Press: New York; 8–30.

McKelvey B. 2002. Model-centered organization science epistemology. In *The Blackwell Companion to Organizations*, JAC Baum (ed). Blackwell: Oxford, UK; 752–780.

McPherson JM, Smith-Lovin L. 1986. Sex segregation in voluntary associations. *American Sociological Review* 51(1): 61–79.

McPherson JM, Smith-Lovin L. 1987. Homophily in voluntary organizations: status distance and the composition of face-to-face groups. *American Sociological Review* 52(3): 370–379.

McPherson JM, Smith-Lovin L, Cook JM. 2001. Birds of a feather: homophily in social networks. In *Annual Review of Sociology*, Vol. 27, Cook K, Hagan J (eds). Annual Reviews, Inc.: Palo Alto, CA; 415–444.

Milgram S. 1967. The small world problem. *Psychology Today* 2: 60–67.

Miner AS, Haunschild PR. 1995. Population level learning. In *Research in Organizational Behavior*, Staw BM, Cummings LL (eds). JAI Press: Greenwich, CT; 115–166.

Mosakowski E. 1998. Entrepreneurial resources, organizational choices, and competitive outcomes. *Organization Science* 9(6): 625–643.

Mouw T, Entwisle B. 2006. Residential segregation and interracial friendship in schools. *American Journal of Sociology* 112(2): 391–441.

Nahapiet J, Ghoshal S. 1998. Social capital, intellectual capital, and the organizational advantage. *Academy of Management Review* 23(2): 242–266.

Pescosolido B, Rubin B. 2000. The web of group affiliations revisited: social life, postmodernism, and sociology. *American Sociological Review* 65(1): 52–76.

Pollock TG. 2004. The benefits and costs of underwriters' social capital in the U.S. IPO market. *Strategic Organization* 2(4): 357–388.

Pollock TG, Porac JF, Wade JB. 2004. Constructing deal networks: brokers as network 'architects' in the U.S. IPO

market and other examples. *Academy of Management Review* 29(1): 50–72.

Popielarz PA, McPherson JM. 1995. On the edge or in between: niche position, niche overlap, and the duration of voluntary association memberships. *American Journal of Sociology* 101(3): 698–720.

Portes A, Sensenbrenner J. 1993. Embeddedness and immigration: notes on the social determinants of economic action. *American Journal of Sociology* 98(6): 1320–1350.

Putnam R. 2000. *Bowling Alone: The Collapse and Revival of American Community*. Simon & Schuster: New York.

Ruef M, Aldrich HE, Carter NM. 2003. The structure of founding teams: homophily, strong ties, and isolation among U.S. entrepreneurs. *American Sociological Review* 68(2): 195–222.

Schumpeter J. 2003. Entrepreneur, translated by Becker MC, Knudsen T from Schumpeter JA, 1928, 'Unternehmer.' Handwörterbuch der Staatswissenschaften, 4th ed., Verlag von G. Fischer, Jena, VIII, 476 – 487. In *Advances in Austrian Economics*, Vol. 7, Koppl R, Birner J, Kirruld-Klitgaard P (eds). Elsevier: Amsterdam, The Netherlands.

Simmel G. 1955. *Conflict and the Web of Group Affiliations*. Translated by Wolff K, Bendix R. Free Press: Glencoe, IL.

Sorenson O, Stuart TE. 2001. Syndication networks and the spatial distribution of venture capital investments. *American Journal of Sociology* 106(6): 1546–1588.

Stuart TE, Hoang H, Hybels RC. 1999. Interorganizational endorsements and the performance of entrepreneurial ventures. *Administrative Science Quarterly* 44(2): 315–349.

Taleb NN. 2007. *The Black Swan: The Impact of the Highly Improbable*. Random House: New York.

Thoits PA. 1984. Explaining distributions of psychological vulnerability: lack of social support in the face of life stress. *Social Forces* 63(2): 453–481.

Vidich AJ. 1958. *Small Town in Mass Society*. Doubleday: New York.

Watts DJ. 1999. *Small Worlds: The Dynamics of Networks between Order and Randomness*. Princeton University Press: Princeton, NJ.

Watts DJ. 2003. *Six Degrees: The Science of a Connected Age* (1st edn). Norton: New York.

Watts DJ, Strogatz SH. 1998. Collective dynamics of small-world networks. *Nature* 393: 440–442.

Whyte WH. 1956. *The Organization Man*. Simon and Schuster: New York.

PART IV

STRATEGY

[12]

EVEN DWARFS STARTED SMALL:

LIABILITIES OF AGE AND SIZE AND THEIR

STRATEGIC IMPLICATIONS

Howard Aldrich and Ellen R. Auster

ABSTRACT

This paper links the organizational ecology and business strategy literatures by focusing on liabilities of age and size and their strategic implications. The first section discusses external and internal liabilities associated with age and size. We argue that the strengths of large, old organizations are often the weaknesses of small, new organizations and vice versa. The second section of the paper considers population-level and organizational-level strategic implications of liabilities of age and size. Loose coupling strategies such as subcontracting, and franchising and emulation strategies such as corporate entrepreneurship are examined. At the population level, these strategies create new forms which may improve the viability of whole populations of organizations. At the organizational level these strategies may help larger, older organizations and newer, smaller organizations compensate for their weaknesses.

Research in Organizational Behavior, Vol. 8, pages 165–198.
Copyright © 1986 by JAI Press Inc.
All rights of reproduction in any form reserved.
ISBN: 0-89232-551-8

165

INTRODUCTION

Unless organizations' environments are completely static, which is almost never the case, they must undergo transformations or they will be selected against. Transformation processes can be examined at two levels of analysis—the transformation of a specific organization or the transformation of whole populations of organizations. Research and writing in the business policy/strategy literature has tended to focus on the organizational level of analysis. It investigates how executive leadership can "initiate, shape, and direct" (Tushman & Romanelli, 1985) organizational transformation to enhance organizational efficiency. The business strategist's goal has been to understand the relative merits of different strategies that help organizations adapt to changes in their environment. Changes in strategy, in turn, dictate changes in structure and processes inside organizations. Business strategists assume, then, that organizations choose their strategies, reorient themselves based on those strategies, and then metamorphose their internal processes so they are consistent with the chosen strategies.

Population ecologists, on the other hand, have focused on how populations of organizations are transformed by environmental changes. Selection and retention, combined with the creation of new organizational forms, transform the composition of whole populations of organizations so that they are better suited to their environments. Some organizations fail and are selected out from the population, whereas other organizations survive and are retained in the population. In addition, new organizations are created, with some replacing old organizations and others embodying new forms. The volatility resulting from selective retention and creation at the organizational level of analysis creates metamorphosis at the population level, which then molds, alters, and constrains organizational-level metamorphosis.

Thus, we argue that both the business policy/strategy literature and the ecological literature focus on processes of metamorphosis, but at different levels of analysis. Moreover, metamorphosis at the organizational level of analysis is linked to population-level metamorphosis and vice versa. Based on these assumptions, we suggest that research and writing in both strategy and ecology would benefit from investigations which simultaneously consider both levels of analysis and how these levels are connected.

Our paper discusses the consequences and strategic implications of two variables which affect metamorphosis—age and size. The first section discusses the consequences of liabilities of age and size at the organizational level and the population level of analysis. At the organizational level of analysis, we argue that large, aging organizations face a number of constraints which severely limit their possibilities of metamorphosing and adapting to changing conditions. Liabilities stemming from developmental processes, internal inertia, and external dependencies all make transformation difficult for large, established organizations. New organizations, especially small ones, also face problems hampering their adaptation, but they are different problems than those of large, aging organizations. They must compete with already established organizations in their industries, and if they embody new forms, they must create a niche for themselves. At the population level, these external and internal liabilities of age and size produce a slowly changing aggregate number of organizations supported by a highly volatile underlying process involving millions of organizational births and deaths, and the creation of new forms.

The second section of the paper considers the strategic implications of liabilities of age and size. We consider both population-level and organizational-level implications. Two ways larger, established organizations attempt to cope with the consequences of liabilities of age and size are (1) through emulation of smaller, newer organizations and (2) through exploitation of smaller, newer organizations. Emulation strategies include internal venturing and internal entrepreneurship. Exploitation strategies include franchising, subsidized spin-offs, and subcontracting. Both strategies have implications at the population level. Emulation strategies create new forms—new "variations" within single organizational units that may aid survival for individual organizations and reduce overall population volatility. Exploitation strategies, when analyzed ecologically, can be viewed as means by which single organizations sustain themselves and metamorphose by feeding off smaller, newer organizations. The organizational survival prospects of larger, established organizations may be improved by being loosely coupled to population-level transformation processes. Although labeled *exploitation strategies*, it should be noted that these arrangements also offer advantages to some newer, smaller organizations because they become more sheltered from liabilities of newness and smallness.

LIABILITIES OF AGE AND SIZE

Liabilities of Aging and Bigness

Much of the research and writing on management and organizations is dedicated to the pursuit of organizational inertia. From the population perspective (McKelvey & Aldrich, 1983), a focus on retention mechanisms is sensible, as achieving organizational rationality is easiest when irrational potentials are closed off and uncertainty is minimized. Selection and placement, socialization and training, supervision and leadership, and other elements of business schools' curricula are oriented toward the persistence of routines. However, retention of routines makes aging organizations increasingly less fit for changing environments, compared to new organizations that are unencumbered by residues from the past. Aging organizations may survive, but with decreasing vitality, and their niche becomes increasingly vulnerable to invasion by newer forms of organizations.

Organizational limits to transformation and organizational inertia are the result of both internal and external factors. Some inertia stems from developmental processes internal to almost all large, aging organizations. As part of the "life cycle" or organizations, such transformations occur regardless of the nature of the environment. But, inertia is also partially a product of external selection processes, as large, aging organizations are differentially selected out of the population in ways that reward stable structures (Aldrich & Fish, 1981; Hannan and Freeman, 1984). These external and internal constraints are sometimes a consequence of aging alone, but often they result from a combination of the effects of age and size. Liabilities of aging and largeness are discussed in this section, although outcomes resulting primarily from the process of aging or from the effects of size will be distinguished when possible.

Internal conditions.

Four internal conditions associated primarily with aging that inhibit adaptation to change are (1) the retention of control in the hands of the original founders or members of their families, (2) pressures toward internal consistency as a basis of coordination and control, (3) the hardening of vested interests, and (4) homogeneity of members' perceptions. In selecting the preceding list of four internal conditions that limit adaptability, we chose forces that particularly constrain organizational variation. A central principle of the population perspective is that organizations cannot track changing external selection criteria when variation is limited (Aldrich, 1979), and therefore decreasing internal diversity ultimately renders an organization vulnerable to displacement, loss of efficiency, or failure.

First, the single most important factor constraining organizational transformation is the retention of control in the hands of the original founders or members of their families. The longer founders or their families hold onto control, the greater the probability that a crisis of succession will occur, especially if external conditions change (Boswell, 1973). As Chandler (1977) pointed out, there is a substantial difference between the behavior required of entrepreneurs and of professional managers, and owners who can make the transition between the two roles are rare. Allen (1981, 1983) found that chief executive officers (CEOs) who were principal stockholders in their firm had a much longer average tenure in their jobs than other CEOs, suggesting that controlling families may place retention of control above adaptability as a corporate priority. The precipitous decline of the Puritan clothing manufacturing firm, for example, after the firm had passed into the hands of the deceased founder's son, led to its acquisition by its major customer, Calvin Klein.

A nationally representative cross-sectional survey of 3000 firms in England found that 80% of the manufacturing and 87% of the nonmanufacturing firms were run by founders or their families (Bolton Committee, 1972). There was surprisingly little variation by size—for manufacturing firms, the figures were 1–24 employees—82%; 25–99 employees—75%; and 100–199 employees—70%. The very largest organizations in the United States and England have adopted professional management, but as firms with more than 200 employees constitute less than 2% of all businesses, organizations under family control are clearly the dominant form in the business population.

Second, as organizations age, pressures increase toward internal consistency as a basis for coordination and control. These pressures tend to be more pronounced as size increases. Specialization, a defining characteristic of bureaucratized organizations, restricts internal diversity. Patterns of behavior stabilize, individuals settle into characteristic roles, and standard operating procedures emerge and are institutionalized. Increasing emphases on producing reliable and accountable outputs magnify these tendencies (Hannan & Freeman, 1984). Formalization and specialization codify and thus preserve much of the successful past, but at the cost of mortgaging the future.

Starbuck (1965) used the metaphor of *organizational learning* in asserting that "older organizations have learned to ignore unimportant problems, and have accumulated mechanisms for tending to routine problems. They perceive stable problems and need stable structures" (p. 481). Increasing formalization of information-acquisition and -communication channels eventually constrains the information decision makers can take into account. Decreasing diversity and growing information gaps lead to ignorance of critical external information (Aldrich & Herker, 1977). Managers create programs to monitor problems but these programs become ritualized, add inertia, and inhibit reflection (Meyer & Rowan, 1977). Perceptions are categorized and simplified, further distorting and ridgifying what is observed. As organizations grow larger and become more complex, upper management becomes increasingly detached from persons more closely connected to the environment, and deviant perceptions may never be heard. Increasing age and size also may provide organizations with enough resources to buffer themselves from their environments, giving those in power more latitude in interpreting their views of the environment (Starbuck, 1983).

A review of research on small businesses' role in innovation, carried out by the Small Business Administration (1983), cited several studies supporting the argument that small businesses contribute a disproportionate share of product and process innovations. Gellman Research Associates (1982) studied 635 product innovations marketed during the 1970s in 121 industries, defined at the four-digit level. Of the 563 traced to firms whose size could be identified, 40% were generated by small businesses. The study also found that small firms produce 2.5 times as many innovations as large firms, relative to the number of people employed, and that they take less time to bring an innovation to market (Small Business Administration, 1983, p. 122). Similar results were found in a study of the food-processing and -manufacturing industries (Mueller, Culbertson, & Peckham, 1982). Unfortunately, the ages of firms studied were not reported, but the explanations offered are compatible with the arguments we have advanced regarding the higher flexibility and adaptability of younger organizations. We suspect that controlling for age would substantially reduce the "size" effect found in these studies.

Third, vested interests harden as organizations age and grow larger. Challenging perceptions, or suggestions for change, may be viewed as primarily mechanisms to gain power. It is likely that any alterations in organizational structure will be resisted because they will disturb existing distributions of resources and privileges (Hannan & Freeman, 1977). Members begin opposing changes in role structures and methods, unless they perceive direct personal benefits (Pfeffer, 1981). Adding tasks or functions to an organization may therefore require adding new subunits or divisions, a costly strategy compared to a straightforward reorganization of the existing structure.

Fourth, a variety of forces combine to induce a homogeneity of perceptions within organizations. Managers tend to recruit people who are compatible with the existing membership, and socialization and training continue the trend toward a uniformity in outlook. Closed social networks limit the inflow of new ideas and promote the development of a common frame of reference (Granovetter, 1973). Formalization and standardization of day-to-day activities and even internal career mobility creates organizational members whose experiences are similar. This internal homogeneity inhibits change by making organizations less sensitive to the unique characteristics of their local environments, inducing an often fatal myopia.

On occasions when the necessity for transformation can no longer be avoided—problems defined as "crises" by members—situational forces make it unlikely that strategic choices are made (March & Simon, 1958).

Under conditions of heightened uncertainty, social influence is a very important determinant of individuals' judgments. Under conditions where collective socialization has been most successful in inducing a uniformity of outlook, members are likely to acquiesce in judgements that continue past practices.

Carroll (1983) noted that "aging" may, in fact be a surrogate measure of organizations' exposures to turbulent environments, given that environments change rapidly and unpredictably: "When this occurs, organizational age will coincide roughly with the amount of environmental change experienced by an organization. In such instances, the probability of death should increase with accumulated uncertainty and, spuriously, age" (p. 313). His argument suggests that internal changes—developmental or otherwise—are not what render an organization vulnerable to negative selection, but rather the fact of having encountered a succession of environmental jolts until one finally does it in. This proposition can be tested, but only with data on both environmental changes and internal organizational structures and processes. A good example of such research is the event-history analysis of voluntary social service organizations by Tucker, Singh, and House (1984).

External Conditions.

Larger, older organizations also face external conditions which create resistance to change. As they age, organizations become more and more implicated in their surroundings, developing attachments and dependencies that constrain their freedom of action. We have singled our four liabilities beyond organizational boundaries for examination.

First, interorganizational arrangements and commitments may, in essence, constitute a guarantee on the part of management to continue past practices. Hannan and Freeman (1984) have argued that external selecting agents—banks, suppliers, customers, and other significant organizations—seek accountability and reliability in their dealings with other organizations. Consequently, those organizations achieving stability, by whatever route, will be favored over those that do not. Organizational inertia is thus partially a result of positive external selection, rather than only a cause of it.

Joint ventures, price-setting agreements, interlocking directorates, sponsorship, and other arrangements represent a partial loss of autonomy by an organization. Insofar as managers sacrifice control over their own affairs in exchange for the resources made available by such arrangements, their prospects for adaptive transformation are reduced. Some interorganizational arrangements carry the implication of a long-term sacrifice of an organization's interests in favor of a larger collectivity, as in certain kinds of business interest associations (Staber & Aldrich, 1983). Whether such sacrifices increase or decrease an organization's survival chances is always an empirical question.

Second, organizations in niches sheltered by government protection or support are under less pressure to adopt new forms, but they may also lose their ability to adapt when conditions change quickly. Among the more important forms of government support are tariff barriers and import quotas shielding firms against foreign competition; export subsidies; tax laws favoring certain types of investments that may lead to overcapitalization and waste; and military intervention. Sudden removal of government support often reveals the extent to which protected organizations had become inefficient in their use of resources, as new firms adopting a leaner organizational form cut into the market shares of the established firms; this recently was shown by developments in the airline, trucking, and telecommunications industries.

Third, support from social and political elites is often purchased at the price of compromises in objectives and practices. Many voluntary associations, public-sector organizations, and other nonprofit organizations with objectives not widely accepted or understood are highly vulnerable to external pressures. Such organizations may seek elite support as a way of stabilizing their position in a niche, making those changes necessary to ensure that support will be forthcoming when it is needed.

Fourth, barriers to entry into other niches may be too strong for most established organizations to surmount, thus eliminating the possibility of pursuing more attractive resource concentrations. Scale-economy, absolute-cost, and product differentiation barriers to entry are widely recognized as characteristic of many American industries, limiting entry for all but the largest and most powerful organizations. Of course, to the extent that these barriers prevent organizations from entering protected niches, organizations already in such niches will face fewer pressures for transformation.

Thus, aging organizations, even those that are growing, face a number of constraints that limit their prospects of transformation. Liabilities of aging include the retention of control by founders long after such control is effective, tendencies toward internal consistency and homogeneity, and the hardening of vested interests opposing changes. Beyond organizational boundaries, a variety of interorganizational arrangements create attachments and dependencies that make transformation difficult. New, unencumbered organizations, on the other hand, don't face these liabilities. They can respond more quickly to changing external conditions than can older and larger organizations. Aging organizations, as they accumulate commitments and experience, are less likely to undergo transformation than are younger organizations, which may or may not increase survival chances. (Indeed, Hannan & Freeman [1984] argued that successful transformations place organizations in a position of experiencing the liabilities of newness once again.) New and smaller organizations, although apparently better situated with regard to undergoing transformations, face many disadvantages that complicate the picture we have just drawn, as we argue in the next section.

Liabilities of Newness and Smallness

As a number of writers have pointed out, the literature on organizations and management fails to convey the extent to which organizational populations are highly volatile. Hannan and Freeman (1977), in their explication of the population ecology model of organizational change, noted that they were frustrated by "the lack of empirical information on rates of selection in populations of organizations—census data are presented in a manner that renders the calculation of failure rates impossible; and little longitudinal research on populations has been reported" (p. 959). Recently, theorists and researchers have begun to rectify this oversight, and we now have a much better picture of the obstacles damaging the survival chances of new and small organizations.

Most organizations are small, and are thus exposed to the liabilities of smallness. The Small Business Data Base (SBDB) of the Small Business Administration (SBA) for 1980 indicated that 86.0% of all establishments had fewer than 100 employees and were owned by firms with fewer than 100 employees, 11.3% of all establishments had fewer than 100 employees but were owned by firms with more than 100 employees, and the remaining 2.7% of all establishments had more than 100 employees and were owned by firms with more than 100 employees. (This latter category, although it constitutes less than 3% of all establishments, contains 52.1% of all employees, compared to 32.5% for firms with under 100 employees.) Most organizations begin as autonomous units, and are thus exposed to the liabilities of newness. The combination of smallness and newness means a very high early dissolution rate. Consequently, the age distribution of the U.S. organizational population is biased toward young organizations. According to Birch's (1979) figures, based on Dun & Bradstreet's DMI (Dun's Market Indicators) file, in 1969, 28% of all establishments were under 5 years old and 49% were under 10 years old.

The two most striking observations about new organizations are thus (1) their rate of dissolution and (2) their rate of formation. Although, aggregately, the organizational population is growing, this trend masks the underlying population volatility of organizations. Hundreds of thousands of organizations die each year and hundreds of thousands of organizations replace them. Currently, the rate of formation is higher than the rate of dissolution, thus resulting in overall growth. We will first examine formation rates and then turn to the dissolution rates of new organizations.

Creation of new organizations.   Until 1962, the U.S. Bureau of Economic Analysis made available data on the number of new businesses, based on information supplied by the Bureau of Old Age Survivors Insurance (OASI) and by the Internal Revenue Service (IRS). This series, beginning in 1940, showed that on average slightly more than 400,000 new businesses were created each year between 1955 and 1962. These figures cannot be taken at face value, as the OASI Bureau only reported information on businesses required to file social security tax forms for their employees, and it appears that the IRS data were only for incorporated businesses.

Since 1946, information on new business incorporations has been available from Dun & Bradstreet. Their figures show a steady increase in incorporations, beginning with 85,640 in 1949 and recently topping 600,000. This series is quite useful, but it confounds two very different events: the birth of a new organization, and a change in legal status from proprietorship or partnership to corporation. Only about one quarter to one third of the new certificates issued by the states represent actual new businesses. Businesses moving from one state to another inflate these totals, as they must seek a new certificate of incorporation from the Secretary of State in their new location. Some persons obtain certificates but never enter business, and others start new enterprises but fail so quickly that they never file a first year's tax return.

Dun & Bradstreet's DMI file, as modified by Birch (1979) and the Small Business Data Base, in its initial stages of formation by the Small Business Administration, provide fairly representative nationwide statistics on business formation. The DMI itself has some limitations, as Birch (1979) pointed out, but many of these are being overcome by the SBA's procedures.

Using the DMI data, Birch estimated birth rates for establishments as the proportion of new units added, relative to the existing population, for 2-year periods: 1972–1974 and 1974–1976. The figures for small establishments (20 employees or less) were 15.1% and 15.7%; for medium-size establishments (21 to 499 employees), 11.6% and 13.5%; and for large establishments (500 or more employees), 9.3% and 13.2%. Averaged across all sizes, the birth rate for the first period was 14.7% and for the second period, 13.4%. Information from other reports prepared by Birch indicates that birth rates vary slightly by geographic region. Using this same data source, Pennings (1982) found significant, explicable variations across the 70 cities he studied.

Using the SBDB for the period 1978–1980, the SBA estimated that the ratio of births to establishments ranged from a high of 13.5% in the Mountain states to a low of 9.3% in the East North Central region. Unfortunately, currently available SBDB information on business formation lacks information on two critical variables (although these problems eventually will be corrected): business size, and ownership—autonomous or subsidiary. The data also substantially undercount businesses without employees. When IRS data are used to count the self-employed, we find that self-employment increased about 2% to 3% annually between 1975 and 1980. About 35% of the 12.7 million proprietorship returns filed for 1980 indicated less than $10,000 in receipts, and thus quite a few of these ''businesses'' are not economically significant (Small Business Administration, 1983, p. 142).

The literature on organizational creation is extremely thin. Most research is of the case-study variety, and few attempts are made to obtain representative samples of new business start-ups or to relate business formation rates to the underlying business population distribution. In spite of these empirical shortcomings, information available demonstrates that the rate of business creation in the United States is substantial.

The dissolution of new organizations.   Carroll (1983) found 52 data sets on organizational mortality, and Shapero and Giglierano (1982) noted several others. In spite of substantial methodological differences between the studies, their findings are very consistent, as summarized by Carrol (1983): ''The most common finding is that organizational death rates decrease with age-dependence. That is, organizations are most likely to die in the first few years of operation'' (p. 304). However, the rate at which mortality declined with age varied substantially by industry; at one extreme, it took over 14 years for death rates to drop to half their initial rate, and at the other extreme, it took less than one year. The rate of decline was more rapid for manufacturing than for retail or service businesses. ''Several studies also point out that firms dying at young ages frequently have never experienced success. Typically, these firms did not experience a change in fortune from good times to bad times; they simply held out through bad times as long as possible'' (Carroll, 1983, p. 304).

One of the first widely cited studies was conducted by Crum (1953), based on an analysis of corporate statistics reported by the United States Treasury in 1945 and 1946, covering firms required to file income tax returns. In spite of severe data limitations, many industrial economists have used Crum's data, and recently Starbuck and Nystrom (1981) reconstructed the data in a way that permits a crude estimate of age dependence: 81% of the corporations did not survive their first 10 years; 53% of the first-decade survivors failed to survive their second decade, and in their third decade, 44% of the second decade's survivors did not survive. These figures show an increasing probability of survival given that a corporation has reached a certain age.

Mayer and Goldstein (1961) followed a small sample of business owners in Rhode Island over the first few years of their operations, and discovered that about half of them failed within the first 2 years. They concluded that less than 1 in 10 among small businesses could be considered "successful" after about 2 years of existence. McGarry (1930), in his study of retail stores in Buffalo between 1921 and 1928, found that 60% of the grocery stores were discontinued in the first year, 44% of the shoe stores, 34% of the hardware stores, and 27% of the druggists. Evans (1948), in a study of Maryland corporations between 1911 and 1938, found that 50% were discontinued within 2 years, and 70% within 10 years. Hoad and Rosko's (1964) research on manufacturing firms in Michigan found that 35% were discontinued within 3 years. Roberts and Wainer's (1968) research on 229 high technology firms in Boston found a lower discontinuance rate—20% after about 4½ years.

High reported death rates the first few years after organizations are created do not necessarily mean there is a liability of newness—the rate may be high and constant. Thus, subsequent cohorts of organizations must be followed over long periods of time to detect whether age-dependence is present. Additional methodological difficulties with many of these studies also make inferences difficult: many study only terminations, not the populations from which the terminated firms came (Star & Massel, p. 89), many study processes that are right-censored, (i.e., the population is not followed long enough to observe all the possible terminal events) (Tuma & Hannan, 1978), and some samples are very heterogeneous, with early deaths due to any number of factors apart from age (Carroll, 1983). Often the industries from which the businesses are drawn are not clear. Dun and Bradstreet, for example, publishes some of the most widely used statistics. Their data are the basic sources for the *Survey of Current Business,* the *Statistical Abstract of the United States,* and the Small Business Administration (Massel, 1978). Yet, "financial enterprises, insurance and real estate companies, amusement industries and many one-man services" are excluded from their samples (Auster, 1983).

Three studies that avoided some of these shortcomings and that provide nice illustrations of age-dependence are shown in Table 1. Churchill's (1955) study covered all U.S. businesses between 1947 and 1954, based on data prepared by the U.S. Department of Commerce, using a data base that eventually was discontinued because of the volume of errors discovered. Star and Massel's (1981) data is from the Illinois Retailers' Occupational Tax data base of 17,252 retail firms established in 1974 and followed until 1979. Shapero and Giglierano (1982) used telephone book yellow pages for Columbus, Ohio, between 1960 and 1974, counting all entries into and exits from the listings. Contingent nonsurvival rates are reported in Table 1, showing the percent of firms not surviving in a particular year, given that they had survived through the previous year.

Table 1. Age-Dependence of Business Survival Rates: Percent Nonsurvivors within Each Year from Date of Founding

Survival interval from founding	*Percent businesses not surviving over specified interval*				
	Churchill: all U.S. businesses	Massell: Retail firms in Illinois	Shapero and Giglierano: Columbia, Ohio		
			Business consultants	Machine shops	Restaurants
0 to 1 year	26%	19%	28%	17%	19%
1 to 2 years	34	26	23	16	16
2 to 3 years	26	20	15	10	14
3 to 4 years	19	17	11	5	14
4 to 5 years	14	13	2	11	15
5 to 6 years	12	5	0	8	9
6 to 7 years	NA	NA	6	5	11

All five columns in Table 1 show age-dependence of organizational mortality, as nonsurvival is highest in the 1st or 2nd year of a business's existence and then gradually drops off over the 6- or 7-year period. Two extreme patterns are apparent in Shapero and Giglierano's data: the non-survival rate is very high for business consulting firms in their first year of existence (28%) but then it drops off rapidly by the 5th year (2%); by contrast, the nonsurvival rate is almost constant across the years for restaurants, implying that there are few, if any, returns to experience in the restaurant business.

The preceding empirical evidence shows strong support for the presence of a liability of newness effect, but fails to explain why such an effect exists. We now turn to several external and internal processes that we believe cause the observed liability of newness.

Obstacles to survival. Emerging organizations face obstacles both externally and internally that make survival difficult. Stinchcombe (1965) labeled these problems "liabilities of newness." Externally, new organizations face a number of barriers to entry that may make movement into a new domain prohibitive, including (1) product differentiation, (2) technological barriers, (3) licensing and regulatory barriers, (4) barriers of entry due to vertical integration, (5) illegitimate acts by competitors, and (6) experiential barriers to entry.

New organizations may face product differentiation barriers to entry resulting from brand recognition and market acceptance of products of established firms. Overcoming these barriers requires enormous expenditures on advertising, whereas established organizations only need to spend to maintain their customer or client following. Existing organizations may be able to produce a product more cheaply than new entrants because they use a technology with significant returns to scale. Legitimacy is another problem for new organizations, especially when certification or licensing is a prerequisite to doing business. Product and worker safety, environmental protection requirements, and other laws and administrative regulations must be satisfied before new organizations begin earning a return on investment. New organizations also confront fierce competition from established organizations that make viability precarious. Established firms operating in more than one market can use profits from one area to subsidize cutthroat competitive practices in another. Vertically integrated firms can shut out new organizations by integrating backward to control sources of raw materials and forward to deny them retail outlets. Price-fixing agreements, cartels, and predatory price cutting also can be used by dominant firms to frighten off potential entrants or drive new organizations out of business. Finally, experiential barriers to entry also exist. Assuming that older organizations have survived mistakes in the process of aging, they acquire an advantage that new organizations lack. The significance of these returns on experience depends on the degree of instability in the environment. In environments that are more stable, experiential barriers to entry will be more powerful because learning from one's mistakes will have longer-run payoffs.

In addition to liabilities of newness arising from external constraints, new organizations also face internal liabilities of newness, which primarily revolve around the creation and clarification of roles and structures consistent with external constraints, and the ability to attract qualified employees. New organizations need to discover the most cost-effective and efficient ways of operating, for everything from plant layout to incentive systems for their employees. The quality of the employees attracted may be major factor in reducing the time and resources needed to get things running smoothly. To the extent that local organizations and institutions teach skills that are generalizeable, and the skills required of members are not unique to the organization, the availability of a disciplined and responsible work force will affect the liability of newness. For example, highly unionized work forces can be a help or hindrance in this process, depending on whether new structures of work fall within prevailing union definitions of work responsibilities. If new organizations adopt traditional forms, recognizing existing craft or industrial union job boundaries, their liability of newness is reduced. If, however, new structures require new job definitions challenging unions' jurisdictions, then the ensuing conflicts may raise liabilities of newness.

Thus, new organizations, especially if they use new forms, face many external and internal obstacles to survival. External liabilities of newness stemming primarily from various forms of barriers to entry make mobilization and acquisition of resources difficult. Workforce characteristics affect the types of communication and control structures new organizations adopt, and handicap their ability to create and clarify internal structures and roles consistent with external constraints. In addition to constraints that are a result of newness, many new organizations face liabilities of smallness. These processes often result in dissolution for new organizations, as indicated by the studies reviewed, although some of the processes which cause mortality for new organizations stem primarily from the effects of size.

Liabilities of smallness. Documenting the liability of newness, or decreasing age-dependence, is easier than presenting information on the liability of smallness, given the paucity of properly reported data. Many studies report the size of organizations failing to survive, but do not report the size distribution of the population at risk. Studies reporting size distributions, in turn, usually do not simultaneously control for size and age, thus confounding the two liabilities. Moreover, definitions of size vary across studies, making comparisons difficult. Some sources use total worth or relative size within an industry, whereas others use absolute numbers of employees with very different cut-off points. Finally, few studies include very small businesses that often operate without fixed sites, such as peddlers or venders or businesses run out of homes (Auster, 1983). As before, we report some illustrative studies to provide a flavor of the evidence, and also report results from some studies that are more comprehensive.

Using annual sales as a measure of business size, Star and Massel (1981) reported a direct relationship between size and survival: Between 1974 and 1979, survival rates by size were (1) under $240,000—31%; (2) $240,000–1,200,000—54%; (3) $1,200,000–2,400,000—64%; and (4) over $2,400,000—92%. The Small Business Administration (1983), using Dun & Bradstreet records for the entire business population of the United States, estimated that between 1978 and 1980, about 9.3% of almost 5 million establishments ceased operations or dissolved. Rates varied by industry, but in every case, the rate of dissolution was highest for smaller units and lowest for the largest units. By size classes, dissolution rates were as follows: (1) less than 5 employees—10.52%; (2) 5–19 employees—8.70%; (3) 20–99 employees—8.06%; (4) 100–499 employees—7.12%; and (5) 500 or more employees—5.13%.

Using the same source as the Small Business Administration, but for an earlier period, Birch (1979) reported dissolution rates for establishments by age and employment, as reported in Table 2. Unfortunately, the reported information suffers from several limitations, including highly aggregated size and age categories. Also, many of the larger establishments are actually branches of established organizations rather than independent organizations, and so the mortality rates may be underestimated. Finally, the data in Table 2 are for the period 1969 to 1976, following all estab-

Table 2.   Mortality Rates of U.S. Establishments, by Age and
Employment Size: Percent Establishments Active in 1969
that Were Out of Business by December 31, 1976

Establishment size (# employees)	Age (years)	Percent not surviving
0–20	0–4	63
	5–9	54
	10 +	50
21–50	0–4	46
	5–9	34
	10 +	26
51–100	0–4	44
	5–9	35
	10 +	25
101–500	0–4	44
	5–9	35
	10 +	23
501 +	0–4	33
	5–9	37
	10 +	16
Total, all sizes	0–4	62
	5–9	52
	10 +	48
All	All	52

Source: Dun and Bradstreet DMI file, as reported in Birch (1979, p. 37).

lishments alive in 1969, and there are some indications that this period
was a particularly favorable one for small business survival.

Nonsurvival rates are very high for small establishments, regardless of
age, as shown in Table 2. Dissolution rates are very high also for the first
5 years of operation, except for establishments with 500 employees or
more. The only categories in which more than three out of four establishments survive are those of establishments aged 10 years or more and
having 100 or more employees. With respect to the liability of smallness,
note that dissolution rates are highest for establishments with under 21
employees, *regardless* of age—the rate for establishments 10 years old or
more and with 20 employees or less is higher than that for *newly created*
organizations in any other size category.

One other study of organizational survival and size is of interest because
it used Makeham's model of the hazard function and examined age and
size effects simultaneously. Freeman, Carroll, and Hannan (1983) investigated death rates for national unions and local newspapers within the

United States, hypothesizing that initial organizational size would effect the initial dissolution rate—the "infant mortality" parameter, b_0, in the hazard function—but not the long-term death rate (the a_0 parameter). Newspaper size was measured by circulation and union size by number of members. They found that adding size to the equations explaining death rates significantly improved their fit, with size decreasing the initial death rate for unions but increasing it for newspapers; however, they advised readers to treat the latter finding cautiously, given missing data on size for almost 70% of the sample of newspapers, and inconsistency in estimates from other equations. The finding for unions, however, is robust and demonstrates a liability of both newness *and* smallness in their initial dissolution rates.

Thus, empirical evidence suggests that small size does make survival problematic. Often smallness is coupled with newness, but not all organizations are born small. Some have parent companies that provide for them financially, whereas others are fortunate and find substantial backing from investors and relatives. We will focus on factors that make survival problematic for small organizations whether they are new or old, although our major interest is in new organizations.

First, the most severe problem facing small organizations is raising capital. Most organizations begin with self-financing—money saved from previous jobs, inheritance, and selling or mortgaging possessions. Eventually, "seed capital," as it is called, is needed, whether for expansion or for use in meeting temporary cash-flow problems. Unfortunately, it is almost impossible for untried entrepreneurs to raise seed capital. Even the recent spurt of interest in new ventures, especially high-technology ones, has not changed the situation very much. "Venture capital" is available to owners *after* a track record has been established, when a small organization's founders decide they can no longer run the business or, more likely, when they cannot expand to meet from retained earnings and personal savings a perceived growth opportunity. Venture capital comes at a price, however, that many small organizations' founders are reluctant to meet. Interest rates are high (at least several points over the prime rate), investors' expectations are high, and the founder(s) may have to give up a great deal of equity in the company to outsiders. Moreover, venture capitalists often demand changes in the operation of the business, bringing it more into line with what they have come to expect from the successful businesses with which they have dealt.

Big organizations, then, have a substantial advantage in raising capital, as they pay lower interest rates and face fewer requests for changes that compromise the founder's concept of the organization. Ironically, many large firms borrow funds on the strength of their size, and then turn around and parcel it out to their many smaller operating units that are no larger than the small firms that are required by lenders to pay premium rates. Venture capital funds have improved small organizations' borrowing opportunities somewhat, but the total amount of venture capital available is still less than the borrowing requirements of the largest firms in the United States, such as (the reorganized) AT&T, General Motors, or Exxon.

Second, tax laws work against the survival of small organizations. When large firms borrow money that they use to acquire smaller ones, the interest charges are tax deductible (along with the cost of hiring investment advisors). On the other hand, the favorable tax treatment of capital gains, as opposed to ordinary income, gives small-firm owners a substantial incentive to sell out to larger firms. By selling out, they reduce the uncertainty of their own income and that of their heirs, and subject their gains to a lower tax rate (Bannock, 1981).

Third, government regulation weighs more heavily on small than on large organizations, as few concessions are made to "smallness." The administrative overhead expenses incurred by small organizations in dealing with at least four levels of government in the United States—city, county, state, and national—are substantial. Larger organizations have separate departments or specialists to deal with governmental rules and regulations involving occupational safety and health, environmental protection, zoning, product safety, consumer's rights, and so forth. Repeated surveys of small-business owners have found that "excessive governmental interference" is the single most mentioned complaint, rather than, for example, unfair competition from larger firms. Recent national administrations have made attempts to reduce the paperwork load on small businesses, but those efforts affect only one level of administration and they have been partially offset by the growth of the new "social" legislation (Vogel, 1983).

Fourth, small organizations face major disadvantages in competing for labor with larger organizations. Larger organizations, with their internal labor markets and perceived long-term stability, offer employees opportunities for career development and security of tenure that are lacking in smaller organizations. Internal labor markets offer employees incentives to remain with the employer that hired them. Increasing skill and experience are rewarded with the chance to move up to higher-rated and better-paying jobs. Small businesses are not absolutely disadvantaged, of course, as they offer employees a chance to learn a broader range of skills more quickly, but internal mobility opportunities are usually limited to relatives or co-ethnics of the owner(s).

Smallness compounds the liability of newness with regard to labor, as smaller organizations cannot afford the expenses of properly training new employees. Large organizations typically have separate personnel or human resource departments for selection and training of their work force, and new organizations established as subsidiaries or spin-offs of parent companies benefit from their sponsor's programs. Small organizations, by contrast, require that owners or managers combine the function of training and placement with all the other duties of managing the entire operation. Time that should be spent on research and planning is instead devoted to socialization and training.

Governmental requirements are often particularly troublesome for the relationship between small employers and their employees. Unemployment insurance, payroll taxes, and FICA contributions are collected quarterly by the IRS, and many small employers fall into arrears in their payments. Cash flow problems may leave owners short precisely at the time of the next required payment, forcing them to borrow money to meet the payment. The problem is compounded by most small organizations' inability to hire full-time accounting and legal assistance, and thus many financial problems go unnoticed until the time is past for simple solutions.

Thus, an examination of liabilities of age and size reveals that organizational populations are systematically decimated by liabilities of newness, smallness, and aging, and it also shows that this decimation is balanced by high replacement rates. We found that liabilities of newness produce a very high mortality rate for newly founded organizations, with the rate declining as organizations escape this very vulnerable state, and that liabilities of smallness produce a higher mortality rate for smaller than for larger organizations, regardless of an organization's age. Some of the liabilities that raise the risk of misfortune for small organizations revolve around a multitude of barriers to entry and hostile market forces combined with problems of recruiting and training a workforce. In addition, difficulties such as raising capital, meeting governmental requirements with regard to taxation and regulation, and competing with larger organizations for labor create liabilities that small organizations often cannot overcome. Accordingly, it would seem that older and larger organizations have a substantial advantage over younger and smaller organizations. However, we argued earlier that older and larger organizations also face a number of constraints that make metamorphosis difficult. Note the symmetry to our argument: The obstacles faced by new, small organizations often can be easily overcome by larger, more established organizations, whereas the constraints faced by larger, more established organizations can often be easily surmounted by new, small organizations.

STRATEGIC IMPLICATIONS

The strategic implications of our review of liabilities of age and size will be explored next. We take up the population implications first, pointing out that the liabilities of newness and smallness combined render ''life-

184   HOWARD ALDRICH and ELLEN R. AUSTER

cycle'' descriptions of organizational change problematic. Most organizations do not grow, and those that don't grow have high probability of dissolution. We then consider organizational-level strategic implications from two points of view—those of smaller and those of larger organizations. The implications are somewhat paradoxical, for they suggest that smaller organizations improve their chances of survival by becoming tightly coupled to bigger organizations, whereas bigger organizations avoid the liabilities of aging—which makes transformation problematic—by emulating or exploiting smaller organizations in loosely coupled arrangements.

Population-Level Strategic Implications

Some theorists have proposed ''life cycle'' models of organizational change, analogous to ''product cycle'' models from management science or even ''life course'' models from gerontology (Kimberly & Miles, 1980). Such models are useful in calling attention to the dynamics of organizational populations, and are thus a welcome corrective to the typical cross-sectional analysis reported in organizational studies journals. However, they can be misleading insofar as they imply that most organizations *experience* a complete life cycle. Our review of the literature on volatility in organizational populations showed that the ''life cycle'' of most organizations is truncated early. Moreover, even if liabilities of newness are overcome, growth does not always follow.

Survival should not be equated with growth. Organizations escaping the liabilities of newness still face an uncertain future. Between 1978 and 1980, for example, for all single-establishment enterprises in the Small Business Data Base, 14% were born during that period, 8% dissolved, 6% contracted in size, 63% showed no change in size, and only 10% expanded (Small Business Administration, 1983, p. 73). As Armington and Odle (1982) observed, net growth in employment within the U.S. business population is a result of ''violent growth (and shrinkage) in a minority of businesses, contrasted with stability in the majority of businesses'' (p. 1). Although major conceptual and methodological issues in the use of the SBDB are yet to be solved, it appears that new establishments created by multiestablishment and large firms are a significant factor in overall employment growth. Between 1978 and 1980, the ratio of births to deaths was much higher for the population of multiestablishment than for single-establishment businesses (2.48 vs. 1.66). Another issue still under discussion is the precise role of smaller versus larger organizations in overall employment growth, with researchers at the Brookings Institution at first skeptical of Birch's (1979) results—showing small independently owned businesses contributing disproportionately to employment growth—but recently moderating their views. Using a different way of classifying the

ownership status of units in the Dun & Bradstreet files, the Brookings
Institution investigators found that small autonomous businesses with less
than 100 employees in 1976 constituted 35.8% of the business population,
but accounted for 51.0% of total employment growth between 1976 and
1980 (Small Business Adminstration, 1983, p. 87).

From a population point of view, which is the vantage point of public
policy theorists and decision makers, we note several implications. First,
current economic policy, more or less by default, places a great deal of
emphasis on preserving existing organizations. Given the liabilites of aging
and the contrasting innovative potential of newer and smaller organizations,
perhaps more attention should be paid to the conditions under which new
organizational foundings occur. Could some of the liabilities of newness
and smallness be mitigated by public policies? The Small Business
Administration might be one place to start. A first step might be to increase
business owners' awareness of the sources of aid available to them. For
example, in a study of 658 black and white owners and managers in Chicago, Boston, and Washington, D.C., only 33% of the whites and 24% of
the blacks even knew what the initials SBA stand for (Auster, 1983). In
addition, an assessment of the effectiveness of the current resources and
how they're distributed might prove beneficial. Perhaps concentrating resources and extending aid for longer periods of time would be more effective. Perhaps more energy should be devoted to initial assistance in
locating a site and establishing a niche. Legislation can be an effective
tool also to enhance survival prospects. The impact of current taxation
and depreciation laws and recent antitrust legislation rulings on small and
new organizations are topics about which public policy makers should
know more.

Our argument for increased public policy intervention is that although
the consequences of the liabilities of newness and smallness are palpable
enough, as we have shown in our review, it is not clear that such liabilities
can be measured *ex ante*. Given current knowledge of organizational dynamics, identifying specific organizations that could be assisted at the
expense of others may be too daunting a task. Policy interventions are
better taken at the macro-level, rather than at the level of targeting particular organizations.

Organizational-Level Strategic Implications

Offering advice to owners and managers is a large and growing enterprise
in the United States, and we don't wish to add to the din, but we think
there are a few organizational-level strategic implications generated by
our review. The strategies themselves are not new, only their linkage to
the issue of organizational volatility. Two points should be kept in mind.

First, for simplicity's sake, we divide our remarks into those relevant for smaller and newer and those relevant for larger and older organizations, and thus are not concerned with establishing an exact boundary between the categories. Second, we treat actions as "strategies" when they have strategic consequences, rather than when they are generated by owners or managers with strategic motives. "Strategies" are thus treated as emergent as well a planned phenomena, and may well emerge as a result of external inducement rather than planned internal organizational initiative.

Smaller and newer organizations.   The central issue facing smaller and newer organizations, after their founding, is survival, with growth a close second (we ignore the constraints that kill most entrepreneurial ambitions before they lead to the assembling of resources). Survival will be enhanced to the extent that new and smaller organizations establish ties with older and larger organizations, shielding them from the liabilities they face. For brevity's sake, we discuss only three of the more common types of linkages: (1) franchising, (2) long-term contracts, and (3) mergers or acquisitions.

The number of retail franchise outlets grew by about 2% a year throughout the 1970s, accounting for about 28% of retail sales as early as 1973 (Johns, Dunlop, & Sheehan, 1978, p. 93). Although this aggregate figure indicates franchises' importance in the national economy, it obscures the variation in franchise growth and contracts by industry. In 1970, for example, franchised gasoline service stations represented 56% of all franchised organizations. By 1983, the number of franchised gasoline service stations had declined to 30% of all franchised organizations. On the other hand, between 1970 and 1983, the number of franchised business aids and services (accounting, tax preparation, employment services) more than quadrupled, and the number of franchised restaurants more than doubled (U.S. Department of Commerce, 1983). These differences by industry highlight the fact that the advantages and disadvantages of franchising as a strategy vary by population and niche.

In general, however, franchising provides certain benefits to the franchisee that help overcome liabilities of newness. Capital requirements may be partly met by the franchisor, and financial institutions apparently are more willing to lend to franchisees than to independent owners. Franchisees share in the economies of scale in marketing and administration gained through pooling expenses over dozens or hundreds of business units. Many of the liabilities of newness that involve learning new roles and creating control and communication structures are overcome by adopting standardized routines from the franchisor. This is not to say that operating in the manner prescribed by the franchisor is always most conducive to survival of the franchisee. Indeed, practices dictated by the parent company on everything from prices to territorial and employee restrictions often cause large numbers of franchisees to fail because those practices are not viable in their particular environments. Franchisees wishing to tailor their operating procedures to meet competition in their particular environments (change the hours they're open, prices, etc.) are often prohibited from doing so. Subtle coercion, reinforced with threat of termination of the franchising contract, allows parent companies to dictate the behavior of their franchisees (Hammond, 1979).

Long-term contracts are another method that smaller and newer organizations can use to overcome their liabilities. Long-term contracts give access to resources that are otherwise available only through continual competition with other organizations in the same niche. Contractors are especially prevalent in the services industries, providing legal, janitorial, computer, accounting, research, and other business services to larger organizations that wish to avoid the overhead involved in internalizing such services. Some businesses even assist the creation of new contracting organizations by guaranteeing a prospective contractor enough business to make entry into the field possible. As Peterson (1981) pointed out "many speciality firms in the auto, music, and chemical industries got their start in this way" (p. 74). Long-term contracts bring security to a business, but they also limit its autonomy and innovativeness. A survey of Australian small manufacturing firms found that about 25% sold half or more of their output to just two customers, and among these firms product innovation was much less likely than among less dependent firms (Johns, Dunlop, & Sheehan, 1978, pp. 48–49). Whether contracting is a feasible strategy largely depends on the volatility and competition in the environment. In those environments where price wars are frequent and technological changes are common, long-term contracts will be stifling unless the contracts are flexible and can be altered based on changes in the market.

Being acquired by or merging with an older or larger business is another self-protecting strategy adopted by smaller or newer organizations, but in cases where the acquired business is completely incorporated within the acquirer, it is also self-liquidating strategy. Comprehensive national data on mergers and acquisitions are not available, as the Federal Trade Commission publishes data only on the more economically significant actions in the mining and manufacturing industries. In spite of the widespread publicity accorded mergers and acquisitions, they have not totalled more than about 2000 a year recently. Acquisition fever in the Silicon Valley has sparked interest in "friendly take-overs" as a route to success for entrepreneurs who are luckly enough to start firms that attract the interest of larger businesses. We don't doubt that some small fraction of aspiring entrepreneurs begin their ventures with such a favorable dissolution in mind, but most entrepreneurs have more pressing matters on their minds.

A common thread runs through the survival strategies we've reviewed— owners and managers using them face a dilemma of losing control over their organizations in order to save them. The liabilities of newness and smallness are exchanged for the risk of control loss and increased dependence on external authority.

Larger and Older Organizations

Older and larger organizations face the problem of overcoming the liabilities of aging, although the data we reviewed showed that the rate of dissolution is much lower within this group than for newer or smaller organizations. (Older organizations that are *not* also large are apparently subject to substantial liabilities of smallness.) The liabilities of aging are overcome, we believe, by organizations that are able to emulate and/or exploit newer and smaller organizations. Strategies involving exploitation of more vulnerable organizations occur at the boundaries of older and larger organizations, whereas strategies involving emulation occur within organizations' internal structures.

Boundary-crossing strategies. Two boundary-crossing strategies involve creating ties with already established organizations: (1) acquisitions and mergers, and (2) contracting. We already have discussed these from the perspective of smaller and younger organizations, pointing out that they add security and continuity to the resource flow of otherwise highly vulnerable organizations. For older and larger organizations, acquisitions allow the by-passing of the high-risk start-up period during which new technologies or managerial practices are tried out. Rather than invest resources in internal experiments, managers can scan the business horizon and choose acquisition targets that have established a track record presaging future success. This strategy is deceptively simple—too simple, in fact, as the recent negative publicity given ill-conceived acquisitions attests. Three problems, in particular, increase the risk of the acquisition strategy. First, information distortions and opportunism by owners of acquisition targets may mislead acquirers into taking higher risks than they realize (Williamson, 1975). Second, taming an innovative autonomous firm by incorporating it into an established firm's corporate structure may kill the entrepreneurial dynamism that made it so attractive in the first place. Third, acquirers often forget that they obtain not only the sought-after product or process innovation but also a commitment to supporting many resource-consuming aspects of the target that are difficult to divest (Nees, 1981). Thus, although mergers and acquisitions are ways of externalizing the cost of product and process innovations, and of breaking into new markets, they also carry costs that may expose older and larger organizations to costs similar to the liabilities of newness.

Contracting with smaller and younger organizations avoids many of the problems associated with acquisitions and mergers, as long-term resource commitments are lessened. As Peterson (1981) noted, contractors can provide "a specialized technical service or offer a routine service in a novel way" (p. 74). From the perspective of larger and older organizations, business start-ups and failures in the surrounding organizational population represent cheap and highly visible experiments from which the best short-term opportunities can be plucked. Acquisitions create joint-fate commitments, whereas contracts decouple the highly doubtful long-term survival prospects of smaller and younger organizations from the contributions they make to the highly favorable survival prospects of larger and older organizations.

Two other boundary-crossing strategies require that larger and older organizations either create, or assist in the creation of, smaller organizations: (1) franchising, and (2) subsidized spin-offs. They are similar because both allow organizations to use entrepreneurs' desires for personal gain as an unobtrusive control mechanism, thus partially relieving the parent organization of investments in costly monitoring and control procedures. Franchising arrangements are most useful under conditions where "work sites are widely scattered and small, where customers must be sought out and actively solicited, where personalized service to customers is important, where spoilage or wastage is an important factor in costs, and where a low-paid and semiskilled work force requiring close supervision makes up a large part of operating costs" (Peterson, 1981, p. 74). Under these conditions, semiautonomous franchises will survive only if they are sensitive to local environmental conditions, and thus franchisors can allow markets to discipline their franchise network rather than relying upon internal control mechanisms (Eccles & White, 1983). Consumers spent an estimated $436 billion in franchise units in 1983, about 13% more than in 1982 (Farrell, 1984, p. 38). (A major key to success in franchising is to get the first units right, but that is a liability-of-newness problem, dealt with earlier.) The virtue of this strategy for the franchisor is that it provides a loosely coupled mechanism for coping with environmental fluctuations. The franchisor can adopt and metamorphose by feeding off the surviving franchisees.

Subsidizing spin-offs generally arise in two ways. First, established organizations sometimes develop new products or processes that, for a variety of reasons, they don't wish to produce or use internally—perhaps managers wish to limit the business's size, or full-scale development of the innovation would divert the organization from its major areas of competency. Under such conditions, an organization can still benefit from the innovation by creating a new business unit that is wholly or partially owned but which operates autonomously. Note that problems of opportunism and limited information, characterizing most acquisition decisions, are largely absent in the case of spin-offs. Second, many high-technology firms are finding that the entrepreneurial urges of their employees cannot be met internally, and a very high proportion leave every year to found their own businesses (Brittain & Freeman, 1981; Bruno & Cooper, 1979). In response, some firms have adopted policies of assisting employees to found spin-offs, in exchange for an equity position or a "most-favored supplier" arrangement with the new enterprise.

Internal emulation of smaller and younger organizations.　Boundary-crossing strategies allow older and larger organizations to exploit the flexibility and dynamism of younger and smaller organizations, while keeping them at arm's length. A second category of strategies involves older and larger organizations imitating smaller and younger organizations through internal restructuring, which creates conditions that generate or facilitate innovation and risk taking. A variety of labels have been assigned such conditions: loose-coupling (Aldrich, 1979; Weick, 1976), internal corporate venturing (Burgelman, 1983), entrepreneurial organization (Peterson, 1981), integrative organizations (Kanter, 1983), and so forth. Two common themes run through such descriptions: (1) organizations need a source of *aimless* variations—that is, variations that are produced without regard to their consequences, especially short-term ones; and (2) organizations must be structured so that at least some subunits have the autonomy to take substantial risks that do not jeopardize the existence of the whole organization.

First, consider the difference between what Burgelman (1983, p 1350) labeled *induced* versus *autonomous* strategic behavior, or what Ansoff and Brandenburg (1971), Van de Ven and Delbecq (1974) and Harrigan (1983) might label *strategic development* versus *strategic diversification*. Induced strategic behavior or strategic development fits into firms' existing approaches to strategic planning and is directed toward familiar environments and niches. Autonomous strategic behavior or strategic diversification falls outside firms' current conceptions of strategy, and does not fit into existing definitions or conceptions of markets or environments. Although autonomous strategic behavior may be purposeful to those engaging in it, its generation is decoupled from the currently understood purposes of a firm, thus providing a source of nearly pure variations— raw materials for "strategic renewal." "As such, autonomous strategic behavior is conceptually equivalent to entrepreneurial activity—generating *new* combinations of productive resources—in the firm" (Burgelman, 1983, p. 1350).

Although autonomous strategic behavior appears potentially dangerous to firms, Burgelman (1983) pointed out that it "provides the means for extending the frontiers of the corporate capabilities and for the discovery of additional synergies in the large, relatively unique resource combination constituted by such firms'' (p. 1354). Such behavior may lead to an exploration and elaboration of firms' distinctive competencies, as well as to clues indicating where further experimentation is not warranted.

Induced strategic behavior is implicit in the accumulated structures and processes of organizations, requiring little more from management than a continuation of what it is already doing. Indeed, whether such behavior should really be called *strategic* is open to question. In contrast, because of the liabilities of aging we described earlier, older and larger firms find that generating autonomous strategic behavior is extremely difficult. Burgelman (1983) argued that top management in large firms recognized strategic choices only after the fact, because corporate entrepreneurship is ''governed by a process of experimentation-and-selection spread over multiple, generic levels of management in the firm'' (p. 1360). He noted that managers need not encourage autonomous strategic behavior, but rather should take care not to suppress it. For those more strategically oriented, Burgelman (1984) offered nine design alternative for attempting to structure corporate entrepreneurship. These alternatives really represent nine points on a continuum where complete, direct integration of new changes falls at one end and complete spin-offs and detachment falls at the other end, with the development of new product departments, special business units, or new ventures divisions being typical examples of strategies in between the two extremes.

Although Burgelman implied that organizations can and will choose which form to adopt, it appears to us that the form entrepreneurship takes within an organization results from the combination of the external viability of new proposals combined with the degree of internal resistance. Moreover, many new ideas will be embodied in different forms at different times, and development is not always linear. For example, a tentative idea at t_1 may be the basis for a new division at t_2, and become a key component in the firm's domain of competence, or a loosely coupled satellite, or fizzle out at t_3. Finally, many organizations are multiform, hybrid organizations, and several divisions or subunits may be engaging in a number of these strategies simultaneously. One point is clear, however—organizations that discover such methods for processing new ideas will have a selective advantage over others, vis-à-vis the liabilities of aging.

Other theorists have identified organizational structures that facilitate innovative behavior, although not necessarily the pure variations discussed in the preceding sections. Differentiation is one structural dimension that may lead to increased innovation if communication exists between subunits. A greater diversity of expertise, techniques, and procedures may fuel experimentation (Wilson, 1966; Zaltman, Duncan, & Holbek, 1973). Unless upper management is committed to innovation, however, high levels of differentiation between subunits that are only slightly related may mean that proposals developed may tend to be radical and have a high probability of meeting resistance (Drazin & Kazanjien, 1984).

Others have proposed that Burns and Stalker's (1961) "organic firms" and Mintzberg's (1979) "adhocracies" are structures most conducive to innovation because of their flexibility. Miller and Friesen (1984) argue that these structures are particularly suited to demanding environments: "The more challenging the firms' environment, the greater their need to be entrepreneurial; the more organic their structures, the better they are able to recognize and fulfill this need" (p. 183). Similarly, Kanter (1983) proposed that the incentives for innovative behavior, are enhanced in situations where "*job charters are broad; assignments are ambiguous, non-routine, and change-directed; job territories are intersecting,* so that others are both affected by action and required for it; and *local autonomy is strong* enough that actors can go ahead with large chunks of action without waiting for higher-level approval" (p. 143). Note how closely this description resembles our description of the role structures that create a liability of newness in new organizations. Kanter's arguments and those advocating adhocracies and organic structures imply that established organizations can reinvigorate their structures by emulating newly created organizations, but perhaps at the risk of increasing their probability of dissolution.

Second, rather than creating an autonomous "entrepreneurial organization," in which transformation is a firm's *sine qua non,* managers can set up internal loosely coupled structures in which certain units carry the burden of innovative behavior (Aldrich, 1979). The degree of coupling between persons, roles, or subunits within organizations depends on the activity of their common variables. If two elements have few variables in common, or if variables common to both are relatively unimportant compared to other variables influencing the system, they are relatively independent of each other and thus loosely-coupled. As with external loosely-coupled arrangements such as franchising, internal loose-coupling makes it more difficult for changes in individual elements or units to affect the entire system than in tightly-coupled systems. External events therefore do not ramify throughout an entire system, and subcomponents can achieve their own adaptation with local subenvironments. Research and development laboratories are a common example of how organizations shield potentially disruptive activities from the rest of their activities. Experimenting with innovation through the use of temporary teams is another example (Kanter, 1983).

Some firms, especially in high-technology fields, attempt to retain the benefits of smallness, without its liabilities, by keeping their operating units small and loosely-coupled. "Hewlett-Packard and 3M are among the companies that find a wide variety of virtues in small-scale divisions, creating new ones when existing ones get too large'' (Kanter, 1983, p. 170). In 1982, the average 3M manufacturing plant had only 270 employees, and only five had more than 1,000 employees. Hewlett-Packard tries to keep its 60,000 employees in units below 2,000 people or $100 million in sales. The Mondragon confederation of employee-owned manufacturing and service firms follows a similar strategy, with its over 18,000 employees Units that grow larger than 1,000 or so are split in two.

Thus, the major problem facing smaller and younger organizations is survival, whereas larger and older organizations face the problem of strategic transformation. Franchising, long-term contracts, and being acquired increase the survival chances of smaller, newer organizations, buffering them from the liabilities others face. However, they lose a great deal of autonomy in the process. Long-established and larger organizations have escaped the liabilities of newness and smallness, but the liabilities of aging means decreasing efficiency, reduced profits, and barriers to transformation that ultimately lead to their dissolution (often by acquisition). We argued that the liabilities of aging are overcome when such organizations exploit or emulate smaller and newer organizations. In this process, ironically, they may expose themselves again to the liabilities of newness.

CONCLUSIONS

We first highlight some areas for future research and conclude with the theoretical and public policy implications of our arguments.

Areas for Future Research

First, additional research is needed on the effects of age and size on mortality (both the direct relationship of each on mortality, and their interaction effects), and how these effects differ by organizational type and the nature of the environment. For example, what is the impact of age and size on mortality, for generalists in highly turbulent environments? Do small, new generalists fare better than small, old generalists (interaction effects of age and size)? Does that pattern change for specialists (different types of organizations)? How do changes in the environment alter these relationships? Longitudinal data on multiple populations of organizations in different types of environment would be necessary to answer these questions.

Second, we need to understand more about what processes underlie the effects of age and size, the conditions under which they emerge, and their impact on organizational survival. For example, what are the most overwhelming liabilities of size for generalists? Do specialists face the same liabilities? How do the liabilities associated with largeness change over time? Do different liabilities emerge in different environments? How does their impact on survival differ by environment?

Third, organizations currently involved in emulation and imitation strategies require further investigation. In what types of organizations and environments are these different forms occurring? Are they effective in overcoming liabilities of age and size? For example, in what types of organizations and environments is franchising more likely to emerge as opposed to subcontracting? What are the implications of this strategy for the franchisor and for the franchisee? Do the effects on the franchisor and/or franchisees differ depending on the environment? Only when research accumulates on some of these issues can effective strategies be formulated by policy makers, organizational researchers, and individual organizations.

Summary and Implications

The apparent slow pace of aggregate change in the organizational population in the United States and the seemingly placid existence of familiar organizations often blind us to the volatility of the underlying processes. Tens of thousands of new organizations are founded each year, and tens of thousands are dissolved. Existing organizations, even large ones, experience problems that limit their potential for transformations to more adaptive states that would enhance survival prospects. We labeled those aspects of organizational inertia that are the result of developmental processes the *liabilities of aging*. They include retention of control by recalcitrant founders, increasing bureaucratization, the hardening of vested internal interests, and a growing uniformity of outlook among members. Other aspects of inertia result from developing interorganizational arrangements that commit organizations to established routines or protect them from the necessity of changing routines.

New and smaller organizations face different problems. The liabilities of newness result from workforce and market characteristics that give a selective advantage to experienced organizations. Recruiting and training workers for new organizations requires the overcoming of control and communication problems. Competing with established organizations affects new organizations' viability because it makes access to resources problematic. The liabilities of smallness include problems of raising capital, meeting a myriad of governmental requirements, and competing for labor with larger organizations.

Empirically, these processes produce a high level of volatility in the organizational population. Liabilities of newness produce a very high mortality rate for newly founded organizations, with the rate declining as organizations age. Liabilities of smallness produce a high mortality rate for small organizations, regardless of their age. The organizations removed from the population by these processes are replaced at a rate that is actually producing growth in the overall organizational population of the U.S.

Strategically, these processes pose some interesting paradoxes. At the population level, policy makers have been slow to recognize the dynamics linking organizational births and deaths to overall economic growth. Most strategies have been targeted on preserving existing organizations and on providing programs to meet their expressed needs. The important role played by organizational births and by small, autonomous organizations has been neglected. It is not clear, however, whether a greater awareness of these processes will lead to feasible policy recommendations. Births and deaths are, above all, a stochastic process in which picking winners and losers is extremely difficult. Even investment professionals, who are gradually expanding the range of their investments in expanding newer and smaller organizations, shy away from involvements in the initial formation of new businesses.

Smaller and newer organizations have several avenues of survival enhancement open to them, including franchising, contracting, and being acquired, but at the cost of increased dependence and possible loss of control. Owners and managers of larger and older organizations are probably more self-conscious in their consideration of strategies for survival, which include boundary-crossing strategies and strategies to emulate or exploit smaller and younger organizations.

So, smaller and younger organizations usually die young. If they grow, it is often at the expense of their autonomy. Bigger and older organizations, in contrast, survive more easily, and do so in part by preying on the smaller and younger organizations continually being created all around them.

ACKNOWLEDGMENTS

We want to thank the following people for their suggestions and criticisms on the manuscript and for helpful discussions of some of the ideas: Glenn Carroll, Robert Drazin, Donald Hambrick, Eric Leifer, and Everett Wilson. An earlier version of this paper was presented at the Annenberg School of Communications, University of Southern California. This project was funded in part by a Faculty Research Fellowship of the Graduate School of Business, Columbia University.

REFERENCES

Aldrich, H. (1979). *Organizations and environments.* Englewood Cliffs, NJ: Prentice-Hall.
Aldrich, H., & Fish, D. (1981, December). *Origins of new organizational forms: Births, deaths, and transformations.* Paper presented at the Social Science Research Council Conference on Organizational Indicators of Social Change, Washington, DC.

Aldrich, H., & Herker, D. (1977). Boundary spanning roles and organizational structure. *Academy of Management Review, 2,* 217–230.

Allen, M. (1981). Managerial power and tenure in the large corporation. *Social Forces, 60*(2), 482–494.

Allen, M., & Panian, S. (1982). Power, performance, and succession in the large corporation. *Administrative Science Quarterly, 27*(4), 538–547.

Ansoff, H. I., & Brandenburg, R. G. (1971). A language for organizational design (Pts. I & II). *Management Science, 17,* 705–731.

Armington, C., & Odle, M. (1982, Winter). Small business—How many jobs? *Brookings Review, 1,* 1.

Auster, E. R. (1983). *Social demographic, organization, and business location characteristics associated with small business survival: A comparison of blacks and whites.* Unpublished doctoral dissertation, Cornell University, Ithaca, NY.

Auster, E. R., & Aldrich, H. (1984). Small business vulnerability, ethnic enclaves and ethnic enterprise. In R. Ward & R. Jenkins (Eds.), *Ethnic communities in business: Strategies for economic survival* (pp. 39–54). London: Cambridge University Press.

Bannock, G. (1981). *The economics of small firms.* Oxford: Basil Blackwell.

Birch, D. (1979). *The job generation process.* Center for the Study of Neighborhood and Regional Change, Massachusetts Institute of Technology, Cambridge, MA.

Bolton Committee. (1972). *Small firms: Report of the committee of inquiry on small firms.* London: HMSO.

Boswell, J. (1973). *The rise and decline of small firms.* London: George Allen and Unwin.

Brittain, J., & Freeman, J. (1980). Organizational proliferation and density dependent selection. In J. Kimberly, R. Miles, & Associates (Eds.), *The organizational life cycle* (pp. 291–338). San Francisco: Jossey-Bass.

Bruno, A., & Cooper, A. (1979). *Patterns of development and acquisitions for Silicon Valley startups.* Unpublished paper, University of Santa Clara, CA.

Burgelman, R. (1983). Corporate entrepreneurship and strategic management: Insights from a process study. *Management Science, 29*(12), 1349–1364.

Burgelman, R. (1984). Designs for corporate entrepreneurship in established firms. *California Management Review, 26*(3), 154–166.

Burns, T., & Stalker, G. (1961). *The management of innovation.* London: Tavistock.

Carroll, G. (1983). A stochastic model of organizational mortality: Review and reanalysis. *Social Science Research, 12*(4), 303–329.

Carroll, G. (1984). The specialist strategy. *California Management Review, 26*(3), 126–137.

Chandler, A. (1977). *The visible hand.* Cambridge, MA: Belknap.

Churchill, B. (1955). Age and life expectancy of business firms. *Survey of Current Business, 35*(12), 15–19.

Crum, W. (1953). *The age structure of the corporate system.* Berkeley, CA: University of California Press.

Drazin, R., & Kanzanjian, R. (1984). *Organizing to support internal diversification.* Working Paper, Columbia University, New York.

Eccles, R., & White, H. (1983, November). *Control through markets and hierarchies.* Paper presented at the W. I. Thomas and Florian Szaniecki Conference on Social Theory, University of Chicago.

Evans, G. (1948). *Business incorporations in the United States: 1800–1943.* New York: National Bureau of Economic Research.

Farrell, K. (1984). Franchise prototypes. *Venture: The Magazine for Entrepreneurs, 6*(1), 38–43.

Freeman, J., Carroll, G., & Hannan, M. (1983). The liability of newness and age dependence in organizational death rates. *American Sociological Review, 48*(5), 692–710.

Gellman Research Associates. (1982). *The relationship between industrial concentration, firm size, and technological innovation.* Paper presented for the Office of Advocacy, U.S. Small Business Administration, Jenkintown, PA.

Granovetter, M. (1973, May). The strength of weak ties. *American Journal of Sociology, 78,* 1360–1380.

Hammond, A. (1979). *Franchise rights—A self-defense manual for dealers, distributors, wholesalers and other franchisees.* New York: Panel Publishers.

Hannan, M.. & Freeman, J. (1977, March). The population ecology of organizations. *American Journal of Sociology, 82,* 929–964.

Hannan, M., & Freeman, J. (1984, April). Structural inertia and organizational change. *American Sociological Review, 49,* 149–164.

Harrigan, K. R. (1983). Preparing the firm for transformational strategies. *Advances in Strategic Management, 1,* 133–142.

Hoad, W., & Rosko, P. (1964). *Management factors contributing to the success or failure of new small manufacturers.* Ann Arbor: University of Michigan Press.

Johns, B. L., Dunlop, W. C., & Sheehan, W. J. (1978). *Small business in Australia.* Hornstay: George Allen and Unwin.

Kanter, R. (1983). *The change masters.* New York: Simon & Schuster.

Kimberly, J., & Miles, R. (1980). *The organizational life cycle.* San Francisco: Jossey-Bass.

March, J., & Simon, H. (1958). *Organizations.* New York: Wiley.

Massel, M. (1978). It's easier to slay a dragon than kill a myth. *Journal of Small Business Management, 16,* 44–49.

Mayer, K., & Goldstein, S. (1961). *The first two years: Problems of small firm growth and survival.* Washington, DC: U.S. Government Printing Office.

McGarry, E. (1930). *Mortality in retail trade.* Buffalo, NY: University of Buffalo Press.

McKelvey, B., & Aldrich, H. (1983). Populations, natural selection, and applied organizational science. *Administrative Science Quarterly, 28,* 101–128.

Meyer, J. W., & Rowan, B. (1977). Institutionalized organizations: Formal structure as myth and ceremony. *American Journal of Sociology, 83,* 340–363.

Miller, D., & Friesen, P. H. (1984). *Organizations: A quantum view.* Englewood Cliffs, NJ: Prentice-Hall.

Mintzberg, H. (1979). *The structuring of organizations.* Englewood Cliffs, NJ: Prentice-Hall.

Mueller, W., Culbertson, J., & Peckham, B. (1982). *Market structure and technological performance in the food and manufacturing industries.* Madison, WI: College of Agricultural and Life Sciences, Research Division.

Nees, D. (1981). Increase your divestment effectiveness. *Strategic Management Journal, 2,* 119–130.

Pennings, J. (1982). Organizational birth frequencies: An empirical investigation. *Administrative Science Quarterly, 27*(1), 120–144.

Peterson, R. (1981). Entrepreneurship and organization. In P. Nystrom & W. Starbuck (Eds.), *Handbook of organizational design* (Vol. 1) (pp. 65–83). New York: Oxford University Press.

Peterson, R., & Berger, D. (1971). Entrepreneurship in organization: Evidence from the popular music industry. *Administrative Science Quarterly, 16*(1), 97–106.

Pfeffer, J. (1981). *Power in organizations.* Marshfield, MA: Pittman.

Roberts, E. B., & Wainer, H. A. (1968). New enterprises on Route 128. *Science Journal, 4*(12), 78–83.

Shapero, A., & Giglierano, J. (1982). *Exits and entries: A study in yellow pages journalism.* Unpublished paper, College of Administrative Science, The Ohio State University, Columbus, OH.

Small Business Administration. (1983). *The state of small business: A report of the president.* Washington, DC: U.S. Government Printing Office.

Staber, U., & Aldrich, H. (1983). Trade associations and public policy. In R. Quinn & R. Hall (Eds.), *Organizations and public policy* (pp. 163–178). Beverly Hills, CA: Sage.

Star, A., & Massel, M. (1981). Survival rates for retailers. *Journal of Retailing, 57*(2), 87–99.

Starbuck, W. (1965). Organizational growth and development. In J. G. March (Ed.), *Handbook of organizations* (pp. 451–533). Chicago: Rand McNally.

Starbuck, W. (1983). Organizations as action generators. *American Sociological Review, 48,* 91–102.

Starbuck, W., & Nystrom, P. (1981). Designing and understanding organizations. In P. Nystrom & W. Starbuck (Eds.), *Handbook of organization design* (pp. ix–xxii). New York: Oxford University Press.

Stinchcombe, A. (1965). Organizations and social structure. In J. G. March (Ed.), *Handbook of organizations* (pp. 142–193). Chicago: Rand McNally.

Tucker, D. J., Singh, J., & House, R. J. (1984). *The liability of newness in a population of voluntary social service organizations.* Paper presented at the American Sociological Association Annual Meetings, San Antonio, TX.

Tuma, N., & Hannan, M. (1978). Approaches to the censoring problem. In K. Schuessler (Ed.), *Sociological methodology* (pp. 209–240). San Francisco: Jossey-Bass.

Tushman, M., & Romanelli, E. (forthcoming). Organizational evolution: A metamorphosis model of convergence and reorientation. In L. Cummings & B. Staw (Eds.), *Research in organizational behavior* (Vol. 7). Greenwich, CT: JAI Press.

U.S. Department of Commerce, Bureau of Industrial Economics. (1983). *Franchising in the economy, 1981–1983.* Washington, DC: U.S. Government Printing Office.

Van de Ven, A., & Delbecq, A. L. (1974). A task contingent model of work-unit structure. *Administrative Science Quarterly, 19,* 183–197.

Vogel, D. (1973, January). The power of business in America: A reappraisal. *British Journal of Political Science, 13,* 19–43.

Weick, K. (1976). Educational organizations as loosely coupled systems. *Administrative Science Quarterly, 21,* 1–19.

Wholey, D. R., & Brittain, J. W. (1984). *Organizational ecology and strategy: A theoretical assessment.* Paper presented at the Western Academy of Management Meetings, British Columbia, Canada.

Williamson, O. (1975). *Markets and hierarchies: Analysis and antitrust implications.* New York: The Free Press.

Wilson, J. Q. (1966). Innovation in organization: Notes towards a theory. In J. D. Thompson (Ed.), *Approaches to organizational design* (pp. 193–218). Pittsburgh, PA: University of Pittsburgh Press.

Zaltman, G., Duncan, R., & Holbek, J. (1973). *Innovations and organizations.* New York: Wiley.

[13]

Strategic Management Journal

Strat. Mgmt. J., **32**: 486–509 (2011)

Published online EarlyView in Wiley Online Library (wileyonlinelibrary.com) DOI: 10.1002/smj.887

Received 11 September 2008; Final revision received 19 August 2010

RESOURCES, ENVIRONMENTAL CHANGE, AND SURVIVAL: ASYMMETRIC PATHS OF YOUNG INDEPENDENT AND SUBSIDIARY ORGANIZATIONS

STEVEN W. BRADLEY,[1]* HOWARD ALDRICH,[2] DEAN A. SHEPHERD,[3] and JOHAN WIKLUND[4]

[1] *Hankamer Business School, Baylor University, Waco, Texas, U.S.A.*
[2] *Sociology Department, University of North Carolina, Chapel Hill, North Carolina, U.S.A.*
[3] *Kelley School of Business, Indiana University, Bloomington, Indiana, U.S.A.*
[4] *Whitman School of Management, Syracuse University, Syracuse, New York, U.S.A., and Jönköping International Business School, Jönköping, Sweden*

Using an evolutionary model and a sample of 7,166 firms in the manufacturing and technology sectors of Sweden, we find that surviving organizations founded independent of a parent organization have lower long-term failure rates than their protected subsidiary counterparts. Specifically, we find that subsidiary organizations have low mortality rates when compared to independent organizations, but that their mortality rates increase more rapidly during a severe economic downturn. We also find evidence that surviving independent organizations are more capable than subsidiary organizations of using their resources to reduce mortality rates during an environmental jolt. Overall, our findings strengthen the notion that organizational adaptation is linked not only to ecological and strategic processes but also to organizational structure. Copyright © 2010 John Wiley & Sons, Ltd.

INTRODUCTION

Substantial changes in environments can undercut the appropriateness of developed routines and the attractiveness of protected positions, leaving organizations vulnerable (Dowell and Swaminathan, 2006; Ruef, 1997). However, whereas some organizations falter when their environments change, others thrive (Haveman, 1992; Haveman, Russo, and Meyer, 2001; Meyer, 1982; Sine and David, 2003). Understanding why organizations

Keywords: environmental jolt; parent; failure; resources; adaptation; structure
*Correspondence to: Steven W. Bradley, Hankamer School of Business, Baylor University, One Bear Place #98006, Waco, TX 76798-8006, U.S.A. E-mail: steve_bradley@baylor.edu

are affected so differently by environmental change is fundamental to theories of competitive advantage and survival (Aldrich and Ruef, 2006; Gimeno *et al.*, 1997; Henderson and Mitchell, 1997; Hrebiniak and Joyce, 1985; McDougall *et al.*, 1994; Romanelli, 1989; Shane and Stuart, 2002). One possible explanation for differential effects is that the impact of environmental change on performance and survival depends, to some extent, on an organization's relations with other organizations (Aldrich, 1979; Aldrich and Ruef, 2006).

Thus, a key strategic characteristic of organizations is their degree of independence, especially with regard to whether they are tied to a parent organization or not (Ito, 1995; Schrader and Simon, 1997; Scott, 2003; Zahra, 1996).

Organizational independence affects the autonomy an organization has in making 'its own decision about the use and allocation of its internal resources without reference or regard to the demands of potential linkage partners' (Oliver, 1991: 945–955), such as parent organizations. Organizations that stand in a subordinate relationship to other organizations via ownership ties have given up some degree of autonomy. Our interest lies in the extent to which surrendering autonomy affects an organization's development of its competitive strengths and in how such development affects its survival chances during founding, as well as following periods of sudden environmental change.

Organizational theories suggest several trade-offs with regard to giving up autonomy (Dill, 1958). Organizational dependence has been associated with potential *operating deficiencies*, including a diminished ability to reconfigure resources in the face of competing demands (Scott and Meyer, 1983), a loss of capacity to respond to unforeseen environmental changes (Zeitz, 1980), and an intensification of external control (Pfeffer and Salancik, 1978). For example, if a new corporate venture is too closely tied to its parent, it may lack the discretion needed to respond appropriately to its specific market conditions. Conversely, organizational dependence has also been associated with potential *operating benefits*, because dependent organizations gain from their strong ties to parent organizations, unlike independent organizations that may have only limited access to stable links with key stakeholders and fewer sources of knowledge for developing effective structures (Aldrich and Auster, 1986; Shepherd, Douglas, and Shanley, 2000; Stinchcombe, 1965). Independence means organizations must depend on their own limited resources for dealing with unforeseen environmental changes, with no parent organization to protect them from external threats.

To investigate this conundrum further, we test a model that examines differences between independent and subsidiary organizations at founding and during environmental change, while addressing the role of resources in this process. In doing so, we provide a tentative answer to our research question: *why do some organizations with seemingly strong initial positions fail when environments shift, whereas others with weaker initial positions survive?*

To anticipate our results, our findings support several key theoretical insights explaining 'deviations from what that [baseline] model [of selection and learning] would predict' (Barnett, Greve, and Park, 1994: 26). In Barnett's *et al.* (1994) model, 'selection' refers to competitive pressures that cause organizational mortality in the absence of managerial learning. Our results enable us to disentangle the effects of unobserved heterogeneity in selection and learning processes related to the presence or absence of ties to parent organizations. First, we show that new independent organizations are more likely to succumb to selection pressures than new subsidiaries, which benefit from being tied to a parent organization at founding. Second, we find that because they have weathered selection pressures early on, surviving independent organizations are more resourceful in coping with sudden environmental changes than subsidiary organizations, despite the subsidiary's greater resource endowments. Our study shows that selection and learning that lead to adaptation are both partially a function of organizational structure. Furthermore, we find that, over time, independent and subsidiary organizations differ in how effectively they use observable resources.

The paper proceeds as follows: we begin by noting that independent and subsidiary organizations are organizational structures with distinctive initial endowments. We apply theories of evolutionary competition to explain their differential survival chances at founding and during a negative environmental jolt. Next, we examine how differences in independence affect organizations' uses of resources to improve their survival chances, particularly with regard to how they cope with a negative environmental jolt. We then attempt to rule out possible alternative explanations to our model. We conclude with the implications of our results.

Organizational independence as a founding condition

Differences in their structures at founding likely lead to variation in the level of resources available to organizations. Resources at founding have survival value to the extent that they give new organizations time to establish effective operating processes (Chakravarthy, 1982; Galbraith, 1974), build slack resources (Cyert and March, 1963; Sharfman et al., 1988; Thompson, 1967), and strengthen ties to transaction partners

(Venkataraman and Van de Ven, 1998). With regard to initial endowments, *subsidiary organizations* have a number of advantages over *independent organizations*. First, ties to a parent organization confer valuable access to financial resources, such as providing assets accumulated through on-going operations (Hines, 1957; Miller, Spann, and Lerner, 1991). Organizational scholars have found that limited endowed resources and a lack of supporting institutions lead to a greater liability of newness (Stinchcombe, 1965) and higher failure rates (Baum, 1996; Carroll and Hannan, 2000). Second, subsidiary organizations may acquire debt capital at a lower cost than independent organizations through collateralization of loans by their parent organizations (Blanchflower and Oswald, 1988; Hines, 1957). Third, subsidiary organizations can draw strength from their parent companies' reputations, allowing them to hire employees and deploy established trademarks and copyrights that provide initial goodwill for the company (Caves and Porter, 1977; Zahra, 1996). Fourth, a parent firm's network of relationships can facilitate better pricing from suppliers and bestow an initial customer base from which to draw. In contrast, independent organizations are often self-funded, creating greater cash constraints at start-up and requiring them to develop their own key relationships over time (Aldrich, 1999; Blanchflower and Oswald, 1988).

Thus, survival rates may differ across organizations because they face different selection pressures within a population, depending on whether they have a relationship with a parent organization. Pursuing this theme, Barnett (1997) argued that organizational evolution depends in part on whether organizations are single units or parts of larger structures. In his model, independents as single units face competitive selection pressures on their own, resulting in the weakest units being eliminated and the strongest competitors surviving. In contrast, subsidiaries face a very different situation. As larger organizations undertake structural differentiation, they create a hierarchy of subsidiaries to carry out different functions. Unlike single independent units, subsidiaries that are parts of larger organizations will face altered selection processes because (1) they are shielded via structural differentiation within the larger organizations, and (2) they have ties to powerful institutions (Barnett, 1997).

If the subsidiaries were stand-alone organizations, their unit-specific performance would determine their survival chances. However, the aggregation of subsidiaries into 'groups' and 'divisions' means that selection often takes place at the corporate level, independent of the fitness levels of individual subsidiaries. In this manner, regardless of whether subsidiaries are performing well, they are selected *not* only by their local competitive environment but also by their *relationship* to a parent organization. Similarly, ties to powerful institutions available through the parent organization can provide protected positions or market opportunities that alter mortality rates (Baum and Oliver, 1991).

Given a sufficient initial stock of resources, the probability of mortality early on is relatively low for both subsidiary and independent organizations. As environmental selection pressures mount and organizations' structures become misaligned with their environments, their likelihood of failure increases. Selection pressures will weed out unfit organizations with fewer resource buffers to shield them. In principle, adaptation processes will eventually make surviving organizations less vulnerable to threats (Fichman and Levinthal, 1991). It is even likely that some new independent firms may have a number of attributes that make them more effective at adaptation than subsidiaries (Barnett and Carroll, 1995; Hannan and Freeman, 1984; Haveman, 1992; Henderson, 1993). However, we agree with previous investigators who have posited that differences in adaptation attributes 'become overwhelmed by resource differences in the startup period' (Carroll *et al.*, 1996: 120). Considering these differences in initial endowments between subsidiary and independent organizations, we expect the following:[1]

Hypothesis 1: Before a jolt, subsidiary entrants will have lower mortality rates than independent entrants.

Organizational independence and environmental jolts

Although we follow previous research in hypothesizing that dependent entrants will have lower

---

[1] We acknowledge that to the extent that independent organizations engage in extensive preproduction—such as market research, planning, and learning—their hazard rates will more closely resemble those of subsidiaries (Carroll *et al.*, 1996).

mortality rates than independents, we have reason to suspect that this initial advantage may not last. With time, advantages accrue to organizations that learn quickly (Carroll *et al.*, 1996), and, as we develop in our model below, this is more important under some environmental conditions than others. In particular, independent organizations may have an advantage over subsidiaries in the speed with which they learn in unstable environments. Specifically, we posit that differences in exposure to adversity from historical competition lead to asymmetric selection rates for independent and subsidiary organizations during an environmental jolt.

Environmental jolts are 'transient perturbations whose occurrences are difficult to foresee and whose impacts on organizations are disruptive and potentially inimical' (Meyer, 1982: 515). Natural disasters, unexpected tax hikes, and sudden economic downturns adversely affect the fortunes of almost all organizations within an economic niche (Venkataraman and Van de Ven, 1998). These disturbances in the environment can occur as a point in time event, such as a sudden employee strike (Meyer, 1982) or over identifiable periods, such as years of political upheaval (Carroll and Delacroix, 1982). Jolts may disrupt patterns of positional advantage, thus exposing formerly protected organizations to new environmental pressures. For example, in studies of Argentine newspapers, Swaminathan (1996) found that positional advantages at founding became liabilities during periods of environmental change. We propose that independent organizations have two advantages over subsidiary organizations during and after an environmental jolt: (1) they have great flexibility to learn by experimentation, and (2) they have fewer rules that inhibit absorbing new knowledge.

First, at founding, independent organizations typically have more flexibility than subsidiaries to experiment in the development of new processes. They are also more likely to maintain them as they evolve because they face no hierarchical pressures from parent organizations to adopt company-wide practices. Their flexibility allows independent organizations to swiftly adapt current processes or develop new ones by moving more decisively than subsidiary organizations and more quickly redeploying people, machines, and capital (Tushman and Anderson, 1986). In contrast, subsidiary organizations are likely shielded from selection pressures longer and have fewer

opportunities to learn vicariously from the failure of young independent organizations. As a result, they may find it difficult to adapt to events that require nonroutinized action (Henderson, 1993). Similar to Myer's (1982) 'prospector' hospital facing an employee strike, independent organizations become better able than dependent organizations to plan for contingencies because they are accustomed to solving problems through decentralized and cooperative decision making (Burt, 1992; O'Donnell *et al.*, 2001), which leads to greater awareness prior to a jolt and better exploitation of employee initiatives following a jolt's occurrence (Meyer, 1982).

Second, even when they are exposed to learning opportunities, before they can learn from events subsidiary organizations often must overcome greater bureaucratic constraints than independent organizations. They inherit modes of communication and structure imposed by their parent company, and these tend to focus on stability and reliability (Pfeffer and Leblibici, 1973). When negative environmental jolts occur, subsidiaries may revert to greater dependence on the parent corporation (Ito, 1995). Further, parent firms base resource allocations for subsidiaries on prior experience, long-range funding commitments reflected in strategic plans, and the rationale for creating the subsidiary in the first place (Burgelman and Sayles, 1986; Carroll *et al.*, 1996; Mintzberg, 1994). These resource commitments often increase the complexity of the organization (Haveman, 1992). Consequently, a subsidiary's flexibility to act may be constrained. In contrast, independent organizations have greater freedom to find or alter current resources to meet changing environments.

Thus, independent organizations have greater opportunities to learn and more flexibility to incorporate that learning into subsequent actions (Henderson, 1993; Rosenbloom and Christensen, 1994; Tushman and Anderson, 1986). We therefore expect that differences between independent and subsidiary organizations in their abilities to learn and rapidly incorporate learning into new practices will be particularly important when environments change. We hypothesize that:

Hypothesis 2: The mortality rate during an environmental jolt will be greater for subsidiary organizations than independent organizations.

Organizational independence and organizational resources

Our logic to this point suggests that organizational structure moderates the relationship between selection pressures and survival. Evidence for selection pressures can be derived by observing rates of organizational exit, but it is difficult to distinguish between selection based on organizational frailty (greater resources decreasing susceptibility to mortality) and selection based on learning (managers recognizing the need for action within their particular context and then using their resources to take appropriate actions) (Aldrich and Ruef, 2006; Swaminathan, 1996). While scholars have debated whether higher levels of resource availability help or have diminishing returns, it seems reasonable in the context of the new organizations (with more limited means) studied here to follow theory that has proposed a positive net effect for resource availability.[2] Thus, the approach we take infers that independent organizations have learned to more effectively use the resources available to them than subsidiary organizations and that this learning is particularly useful in surviving a jolt.

It is quite possible that the effect of resources is contingent upon the extent of an organization's dependence on other organizations. We thus reframe the issue as one of the conditions under which resources make the most difference to organizational survival. We consider four key observable organizational resources for subsidiary and independent organizations: levels of equity, financial slack, fixed assets, and employees. Subsidiaries receive *equity* primarily from parents with the

expectation that it will be applied toward the predefined strategic objectives of the larger organization (Burgelman and Sayles, 1986). Independent organizations, whether self-funded or supported by outside investors, must continually assess whether their current allocations are effective. Infusions of capital will be incremental and based on short feedback loops related to current knowledge and performance, rather than on long-term projections (Sorenson and Stuart, 2001). Incremental actions based on short feedback loops enable firms to more quickly obtain (and maintain) a 'fit' with the environment. This ability to quickly adapt enhances the likelihood of survival (March, 1995) and is probably more critical when firms face a jolt. In the event of an economic downturn, shorter evaluation cycles and fewer rules and regulations give independent organizations the freedom to redirect resources toward new opportunities and other adaptive actions.

In periods of relative stability, organizations amass slack resources (Cyert and March, 1963; Sharfman *et al.*, 1988). Here, slack refers specifically to financial resource availability in excess of resource demands. This *financial slack* can be used to smooth current processes or experiment with new opportunities (Cyert and March, 1963; Sharfman *et al.*, 1988). Subsidiaries will likely attempt to use financial slack to protect prior positions that have provided resource advantages, whereas independent organizations will likely take more experimental approaches to resource allocation (Meyer, 1982; Sine and David, 2003). Although both uses of slack can enhance the likelihood of survival, subsidiaries may protect prior positions for their parents' rather than their own (Barnett *et al.*, 1994).

Assets and *employees* have also been shown to increase chances for survival (Shane, 2003). For example, strategically acquired assets can improve a focal firm's position and capabilities, thus increasing its chance of survival (Greve, 2003), and a greater number of employees allows organizations to acquire information faster (Shane, 2003). Subsidiaries are likely to differ from independents in their acquisition and allocation of assets and employees because of past decisions they have made. Subsidiaries' decisions on the allocations of assets and employees are often shaped by organizational retention of parents' past policies and actions (Levinthal, 1997; Ocasio, 1997). Although subsidiaries can benefit to some

---

[2] Organizational theorists have argued that slack provides room for experimentation through changes in structure or management style, innovation in the development of new products or markets, strategic flexibility, and buffering from environmental jolts (Cyert and March, 1963; Meyer, 1982; Nohria and Gulati, 1996; Singh, 1986; Thompson, 1967). In contrast, agency theorists and resource constraints scholars indicate that slack introduces principal/agent conflicts, which induce managerial hubris, complacency, and inefficiency and the use of slack to pay for the mismatch between the organizational strategy and market demand (Brush, Bromiley, and Hendrickx, 2000; Jensen, 1986; Litschert and Bonham, 1978; Yasai-Ardekani, 1986)). Prior theoretical work has attempted to bridge these two research streams (Bourgeois, 1981; Sharfman *et al.*, 1988) by acknowledging that there may be an optimal level of slack after which performance will diminish. Empirical studies supporting this curvilinear relationship include the examination of slack effects on innovation (Nohria and Gulati, 1996), state-owned enterprise performance (Tan and Peng, 2003), and the performance of privately held firms (George, 2005).

degree from these retained routines and structures, they may not always be appropriate (Helfat and Lieberman. 2002). This potential mismatch diminishes the parent's potential for improving the survival chances of the focal subsidiary.

New independent organizations also have histories but they lie within the memory of founders (Nelson and Winter, 1982). Independent organizations develop routines and capabilities from this prior knowledge and are unfettered by modes of coordination and hierarchical control imposed by a parent. They can thus use their discretion to allocate assets and employees to match current environmental demands, rather than meet parent expectations. Even if fewer resources are available for independents, their effect on survival chances can be greater due to their flexibility in matching resources to the emerging environmental conditions. If the environment changes quickly, this flexibility allows organizations to more rapidly learn what works and what does not. For subsidiaries, by contrast, the impact of employee responsibilities and firm assets on survival will be diminished when there is an environmental jolt because they are tied to past policies and cannot be easily reconfigured from their original intent. Thus,

Hypothesis 3: Resources ([a] financial slack, [b] employees, [c] assets, [d] equity) will reduce mortality rates more for independent than subsidiary organizations.

Hypothesis 4: While resources ([a] financial slack, [b] employees, [c] assets, [d] equity) reduce mortality rates more for independent organizations than subsidiary organizations, this difference will be greater during than before an environmental jolt.

RESEARCH METHOD

Population/sample

We drew our sample from the complete population of all independent and subsidiary incorporated companies registered in Sweden from 1994 to 2005. inclusive. By law, incorporated companies must register with the Swedish patent office before commencing operations, and must file annual reports (which are certified by a chartered accountant). All data for this study were taken from these certified reports. We used multiple cohort panels of all new organizations within

selected industries from 1994 to 1998. By starting from an organization's founding, we minimize left censoring issues such as survivor bias. We strengthened our design by using all new organizations within a given industry, thus eliminating potential selection concerns. Organizations were selected from 117 three-digit International Standard Industrial Classification (ISIC) code industries, which included both high technology (aerospace, computers, electronics, pharmaceuticals, technical machinery) and low technology intensive industries (wood and paper products, materials manufacturing, manufacturing and recycling) to provide variability in the extent of industry competition, complexity, munificence, and dynamism (Statistics Sweden database [http://www.scb.se/default2154.aspx], accessed 15 September 2005). The panels contain 58,424 observations from 6,099 independent and 1,067 subsidiary organizations that were incorporated from 1994 to 1998. The proportion of independent to subsidiary organizations is similar to independent/subsidiary organization studies conducted in other countries (e.g., Schrader and Simon, 1997) as well as related work conducted on *de alio* and *de novo* firms (Carroll *et al.*, 1996). An additional sensitivity check using bootstrap resampling to generate estimates and robust standard errors did not alter the direction or significance of the results, with the exception that equity became nonsignificant in Model 2.1 below.

Variables

Hostile environmental jolt event

A global economic downturn began toward the end of 2000 and continued through early 2003, as evidenced by corrections in stock markets around the world that were a reaction to excessive optimism in technology sectors. The downturn in worldwide markets affected Sweden's growing telecommunications and information technology sectors as well as other manufacturing sectors that relied on exports (Hon, Strauss, and Yong, 2007). The events of September 11, 2001, exacerbated pessimism about the future and spread from the United States to other countries as described in business and trade journals (Polzehl, Spokoiny, and Starica, 2004). The drop in stock prices was mirrored by a decline in production. For example, according to the International Monetary Fund, the percent change in gross domestic product (GDP) for Sweden in 1999 and 2000 was 4.6 and 4.4 percent, respectively. By 2001, the GDP growth rate dropped to 1.1 percent and rose only to 1.9 percent in 2002. During the fiscal year 2000, only 10 percent of the three-digit ISIC Swedish industries studied received fewer new orders than the prior year. By 2001, over 82 percent of the industries received fewer new orders than the prior year. In fiscal year 2002, over 77 percent of the industries received fewer new orders than 2000. Signs of recovery appeared in 2003, with less than 50 percent of industries having fewer new orders than the 2000 fiscal year. Those experiencing recovery had substantial jumps in new orders compared to the prior year (Statistics Sweden database). We defined the jolt period as occurring from 2001 through 2002 and additional analysis based on defining the jolt period as 2001 through 2003 did not substantially alter our results.

To further justify the notion of a hostile jolt period and separate it from more common industry fluctuations, we conducted an empirical test. We generated a least squares estimate of new orders from data for all industries for the years 1995 to 2000 (indexed to year 2000). We then generated projected growth estimates for the years 2001 and 2002 and compared them to actual industry orders. In both 2001 and 2002, the observed indexed orders were below the 99 percent predicted confidence interval band, providing further evidence that the substantial drop in orders across industries was not due to random variance, but instead to a severe economic downturn.

Dependent variable

Our dependent variable is organizational failure. Organizations were coded 1 if they failed during the time period studied and 0 otherwise. Failures included completed bankruptcies, completed liquidations, closures based on company request, and merger or acquisition of organizations at risk of bankruptcy (Hannan and Freeman, 1989: 267). While we recognize that mergers and acquisitions are often not included in failure rate studies (e.g., Fischer and Pollock, 2004), we found that a large number of exits for subsidiary organizations fell into this category. We used the 'Z-score' multivariate financial model to investigate the likelihood of bankruptcy (Altman, 1968). If an organization that entered a merger had a Z-score that indicated

a high probability of bankruptcy (Z < 1.81), we coded that organization as a failure.[3] Mergers that did not have a high probability of bankruptcy were treated as right censored after the merger date. To test the sensitivity of our results to this cutoff, we also examined other cutoffs (Z < 2.99, which is considered a 'grey zone' for bankruptcy) as well as two other bankruptcy weighting factors used for private and manufacturing firms (Altman, 2002; Eidleman, 1995). Our results were essentially the same, with only one firm recoded in one case.

Industry variables

Environmental jolt was dummy coded 1 for the economic downturn years of 2001 and 2002 and 0 otherwise. *Cohort* included the population of organizations that incorporated in a given calendar year in Sweden for the industries studied. Dummy values of 1 were given for the specific entry years from 1994 to 1997 and 0 otherwise, with 1998 omitted in our models as the comparison year. These variables are intended to capture common characteristics of organizations founded in the same year beyond competition at founding, which is captured by founding density. The first sample cohort consisted of firms started six years before the jolt and the last sample cohort consisted of firms founded two years before the jolt. We ended with the 1998 cohort, rather than continue with 1999 and 2000 cohorts, to reduce confounding between founding hazards and hazards related to the jolt period. *Density* is the contemporaneous organizational population density for all organizations in a given three-digit ISIC industry. It indicates the total number of producer organizations in a given year. Greater density implies a higher likelihood of resource scarcity and a tighter market niche, leading to higher mortality rates at all ages (Carroll and Hannan, 1989).

Founding density or density delay is the organizational population density for all organizations in a three-digit ISIC industry in the year of entry.

---

[3] $Z = 1.2A + 1.4B + 3.3C + .6C + 1.0D$. Z = score; A = working capital divided by total assets; B = retained earnings divided by total assets; C = earnings before interest and taxes (EBIT) divided by total assets; and D = book value of preferred and common equity. A Z-score less than 1.81 means that for private companies there is a moderate to high probability of bankruptcy and a high probability for public companies. The Z-score has been used in multiple countries and provides a useful tool for predicting bankruptcy or financial difficulties (Eidelman, 1995).

Greater competition at founding is associated with higher mortality rates (Swaminathan, 1996). This covariate is fixed for each organization. Density x age was included with founding density to account for a potential 'trial-by-fire' effect in which organizations founded in adverse environments experience higher mortality rates but have lower mortality rates with age than organizations founded in less adverse environments (Swaminathan, 1996). Industry-level heterogeneity was considered for its effects on both the initial survival of firms and their ability to prepare for environmental jolts. We developed our measures from a slightly modified version of the conceptual framework of Dess and Beard (1984), based on Aldrich's (1979) scheme. We used three-digit ISIC codes for the population of Swedish organizations, calculated for each year of the period studied.

Dynamism, as a measure of instability in an industry, was operationalized by the standard error of the regression slope divided by the mean value of sales, using a moving five-year average prior to the panel year (Dess and Beard, 1984). *Munificence*, representing relative growth opportunity within an industry, was a moving five-year average of the slope divided by mean industry sales (Dess and Beard, 1984; Goll and Rasheed, 1997). *Industry concentration* was a measure of monopoly-like competition which may affect organization survival (Hannan and Freeman, 1984). This measure was operationalized using Herfindahl's index to measure the concentration of sales for each firm-year observation in a three-digit ISIC sector (George, 2005). *Industry indicator variables* were used to capture related industry level effects across the 117 three-digit ISIC manufacturing industries included in the study (001 to 379 ISIC range). The eight categories created were mining, wholesale, publishing and printing, materials manufacturing, machinery and equipment, technical equipment, transportation, and 'other,' with the latter used as the excluded category in the models.

Organizational variables

The organizational-level variables in this study were organizational structure, distinguished as independent or subsidiary, and resources specified as equity, employees, fixed assets, and financial slack. Organizations were dummy coded 0 if independent and 1 if a *subsidiary* organization. Consistent with Swedish law, subsidiaries indicated their

parent corporations' name and identifying number in audited statements submitted to the Swedish government. *Equity* was the owner's reported equity in the business (total assets minus total liabilities). With regard to *employees* as resources, we experimented with using both the absolute number of employees and the logarithm of employees. The resulting models did not differ in fit and so we report results based on number of employees for ease in interpreting the results. *Fixed assets* were nonliquid assets required for operations and include facilities, equipment, and real property.

Following prior work, *financial slack* is measured as the difference between current assets and current liabilities (Brealey and Meyers, 2003; Mishina, Pollock, and Porac, 2004). It describes short-term resource accessibility, indicating whether a firm is keeping excess resources that are not put into productive use (positive financial slack) or fueling growth that may include short-term deficits (negative financial slack) (Bhide, 1992; Mishina *et al.*, 2004). This measure is highly correlated (alpha = 0.99) with George's (2005) 'transient slack' measure of the difference between resource availability and resource demand. *Age* was current year minus founding year, with younger organizations assumed to have higher liabilities of newness (Hannan and Freeman, 1984; Stinchcombe, 1965).

Analyses

Organizational exit rates were assessed using continuous time event history analysis. The firm is treated as the unit at risk and the dependent variable is the probability of a firm's exit defined as:

$$r(t) = \lim_{\Delta t \to 0} \frac{P[t < T < t + \Delta t | T < t]}{\Delta t} \quad (1)$$

where T is a random variable for the time of the event of interest, t is the time period of interest, and P is the probability of the firm's exit from the market over the interval [t, t + Δt]. We used a piecewise constant exponential model to estimate the hazard rate of organizational exit, which allows the hazard rate of exit to vary across time periods, but the hazard rate is assumed to be constant within the time periods. This approach allows modeling time dependence without making strong parametric assumptions about its functional form and also allows model estimation without bias when the data are left truncated with known founding times (Barnett, Swanson, and Sorenson, 2003). In choosing a time scale, we had to decide between age and calendar time. Age dependent mortality has been shown to be an important factor in prior studies (Freeman, Carroll, and Hannan, 1983; Henderson, 1999; Swaminathan, 1996). In this study, the environmental jolt period of interest occurs at different ages for the five cohorts studied. Allison (1984) noted that if the hazard is thought to vary greatly with historical conditions that affect sample members in the same way, then calendar time might be the best clock. This logic suggests breaking the time period of observation into pieces consistent with our interest in examining period effects (prejolt, jolt and postjolt) on the hazard rate of failure while controlling for age effects. To estimate rate models with time-varying covariates, we interacted covariates with each time period following the approach proposed by Tuma (1980) and described in prior studies (Blossfeld, Golsch, and Rohwer, 2007; Singer and Willett, 2003). Typical interaction models include main effects and the interaction term with the assumption that the covariate changes linearly over the interaction term (in our case time). The approach we have taken uses the stpiece Stata module for piecewise constant hazard models (Sørensen, 1999) allowing covariate interaction with each period of interest. This approach fits better with our theoretical arguments and reveals trends over separate time periods that might not be captured by a standard interaction model. This approach also reduces multicolinearity problems and the number of models necessary to capture the effects of interest.

RESULTS

In Table 1 we provide descriptive statistics of the sample. There were a total of 1,664 independent and 143 subsidiary failures from the industries included during the time frame. Figure 1 shows average levels of four resources by year for independent and subsidiary firms. Differences between independents and subsidiaries appear to increase over time and a t-test comparison of differences, by year, confirmed that they are statistically significant (p < 0.01). Figure 2 shows average resources by cohort over time. Resource accumulation over time was similar by cohort, with the exception of the 1996 cohort year. The similarities across

cohorts give us confidence that all firms were influenced by overarching economic forces affecting every cohort.

In Table 2 we present the results of the piecewise constant exponential rate models of exits from Swedish manufacturing industries from 1994–2005 for organizations founded between 1994 and 1998. Model 2.1 represents a baseline for time period, age, and cohort effects along with key industry and organizational covariates affecting exit rates. The baseline model accounts for the influence of control variables on mortality rates. The amount and direction of variation in these and subsequent models indicates whether the mortality rate increases, decreases or remains steady for a spell of time. The mortality rate for a given coefficient in the exponential model can be interpreted as:

$$r(t) \equiv r = \exp{(\beta_t)} \qquad (2)$$

where β is the estimated coefficient for a given time t. Therefore, as the coefficient increases, the mortality rate increases. A more negative coefficient can be interpreted as a reduced mortality rate.

Organizational independence and jolts

In Model 2.2, we added the dummy variable indicating whether a firm was an independent or subsidiary. The coefficient is negative but not significant (p > 0.05). In Model 2.3 we add the interaction of the time period pieces with the subsidiary dummy. The subsidiary prejolt estimate is significant and negative (p < 0.001), indicating that the hazard rate is lower for subsidiaries during the prejolt period.[4] These results are consistent with our arguments that subsidiaries have lower mortality rates prior to the jolt and support Hypothesis 1.

The subsidiary jolt covariate in Model 2.3 captures the effect of organizational structure during the economic downturn. The interaction term is positive and significant (p < 0.001). The results confirm our expectation that while failures were greater for independent organizations prior to the environmental jolt, subsidiaries were hit hardest by the jolt, supporting Hypothesis 2. To interpret this interaction effect, we antilogged the coefficient

---

[4] We also generated cumulative survival functions and conducted log-rank tests for equality of survivor functions. Independents and subsidiaries were significantly different for the period prior to the jolt ($\chi2 = 229.63$; p < 0.001).

Table 1. Means, standard deviations and correlations of key variables

Variable	Independent firms Mean	Independent firms S.D.	Subsidiary firms Mean	Subsidiary firms S.D.	1	2	3	4	5	6	7
1 Failure	0.04	0.20	0.01	0.07							
2 Age	4.47	3.02	4.57	2.96	-0.155						
3 Founding density/100ᵃ	10.57	8.01	8.85	8.11	-0.009	0.013					
4 Density/100ᵃ	10.01	7.83	8.42	7.86	0.062	-0.461	0.000				
5 Concentration/1000	1.06	1.44	1.05	1.51	0.007	0.001	-0.366	0.035			
6 Dynamism	0.07	0.06	0.07	0.06	0.024	-0.124	-0.250	0.062	0.135		
7 Munificence	0.04	0.07	0.04	0.08	0.013	-0.087	0.066	0.079	0.075	0.112	
8 Mining	0.01	0.09	0.01	0.10	0.004	-0.038	-0.100	0.006	0.034	0.082	-0.016
9 Wholesale	0.10	0.30	0.09	0.29	0.042	-0.153	-0.249	0.052	0.089	-0.105	-0.132
10 Materials	0.21	0.41	0.23	0.42	0.048	-0.236	0.112	0.279	-0.160	0.014	0.076
11 Machine	0.06	0.24	0.09	0.29	-0.002	-0.118	-0.100	0.076	-0.070	0.275	0.023
12 High tech	0.05	0.23	0.08	0.27	0.024	-0.112	-0.215	0.026	0.206	0.172	0.149
13 Transport	0.02	0.15	0.04	0.20	0.016	-0.078	-0.158	0.027	0.035	0.144	0.049
14 Publishing	0.09	0.29	0.13	0.33	0.052	-0.153	0.328	0.176	-0.174	-0.287	-0.073
15 Financial slack/1000 (SEK)	0.92	22.24	7.52	153.16	-0.005	0.009	-0.021	0.000	0.017	0.012	-0.003
16 Employees (size)	4.11	14.41	24.22	115.66	-0.015	0.028	-0.058	-0.001	0.066	0.014	-0.007
17 Fixed assets/1000 (SEK)	2.62	56.17	19.16	132.40	-0.009	0.014	-0.029	-0.002	0.032	0.005	-0.009
18 Equity/1000 (SEK)	0.76	15.25	7.19	75.57	-0.006	0.044	-0.024	-0.015	0.032	0.008	-0.007
19 Subsidiary					-0.073	0.013	-0.080	0.012	-0.001	0.018	-0.024

Correlations above .009 are significant at p < 0.05.
ᵃ Orthogonalized variables (Means and SD shown non-orthogonalized).
N organizations = 7166; N independent org. = 6099; N subsidiary org. = 1067; N org.-years = 58, 424; 48,521; N subsidiary org.-years = 9, 903.
Independent org. exits = 1664; Subsidiary org. exits = 143.

Variable	8	9	10	11	12	13	14	15	16	17	18
8 Mining											
9 Wholesale	-0.030										
10 Materials	-0.047	-0.176									
11 Machine	-0.024	-0.089	-0.140								
12 High tech	-0.023	-0.084	-0.132	-0.067							
13 Transport	-0.015	-0.055	-0.086	-0.044	-0.041						
14 Publishing	-0.030	-0.111	-0.175	-0.088	-0.083	-0.054					
15 Financial slack/1000 (SEK)	-0.001	-0.006	-0.004	0.003	0.015	0.022	-0.008				
16 Employees (size)	-0.008	0.001	0.000	0.000	0.042	0.026	-0.026	0.193			
17 Fixed assets/1000 (SEK)	-0.002	-0.003	0.008	-0.006	0.011	0.008	-0.011	0.394	0.384		
18 Equity/1000 (SEK)	-0.004	-0.011	-0.018	-0.010	0.014	-0.003	-0.015	0.127	0.185	0.578	
19 Subsidiary	0.012	-0.012	0.014	0.044	0.041	0.050	0.039	0.037	0.151	0.083	0.071

to obtain an odds ratio finding that subsidiaries were 2.18 times (exp[0.779]) more likely than independents to fail during the jolt period (Singer and Willett, 2003). We also examined the fit of the model using the deviance statistic which is defined as $-2 \times$ log likelihood. The difference in the deviance statistic between Model 2.3 and 2.1 is 194 (p < 0.001, 3 d.f.) indicating an improved fit with the interaction terms included. Further evidence was provided by a Wald test for the subsidiary time period variables indicating that they are significant for Model 2.3 ($\chi 2$ [3 d.f.] = 82.18; p < 0.001).

Postjolt consequences

Although we offered no hypotheses about it, we were also interested in the longer-term consequences of the jolt on independent and subsidiary organizations. It seemed plausible that one of two scenarios might occur. The jolt effect might be temporary and then subsidiaries would recover with the help of their parent organizations. Alternatively, the jolt effect might persist because of subsidiaries' difficulties in realigning their strategies or resources because of patterns of operation imposed by their parent organizations. The estimated coefficient for the subsidiary postjolt period was positive and significant (p < 0.001), indicating that subsidiaries were 2.5 times more likely to exit than independents after the jolt period.[5]

Figure 3 depicts these differences between independent and subsidiaries in terms of a multiplier for the three time periods. The multiplier is obtained by exponentiating the coefficient and normalizing to a base comparison—in this case the independent jolt coefficient. We found that the mortality rate for independents prior to the jolt was 3.5 times the mortality rate during the jolt (exp(-0.447)/exp(-1.716)). The mortality rate of subsidiaries during the jolt was 2.18 times (exp(-1.716 + 0.779)/exp(-1.716)) that of independents during the jolt (matching the result we obtained earlier by antilogging the subsidiary jolt coefficient). The multipliers for the independents in the postjolt (0.19) and the subsidiaries postjolt (0.48) were lower in comparison to the independent jolt period. The figure illustrates that those surviving independent organizations become

---

[5] (exp(0.920) = 2.5.

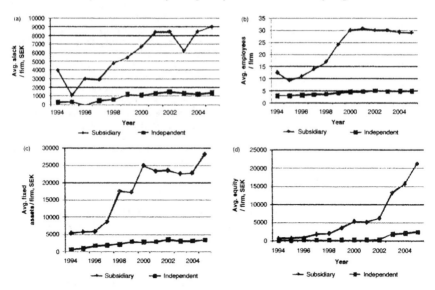

Figure 1.   Average (a) financial slack, (b) employees, (c) assets, and (d) equity for independent and subsidiary organizations by year

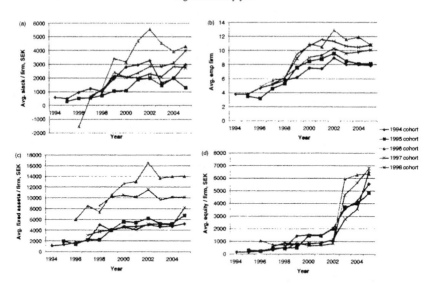

Figure 2.   Average (a) financial slack, (b) employees, (c) assets, and (d) equity by cohort

498   *S. W. Bradley et al.*

Table 2. Piecewise-exponential models of organizational failure in Swedish Manufacturing from 1994–2005[a] combined for independent and subsidiary organizations

Variable	Model					
	(2.1)		(2.2)		(2.3)	
Prejolt period (yrs 1994–2000)	−0.470	(0.168)**	−0.467	(0.168)**	−0.447	(0.168)**
Jolt period (yrs 2001–2002)	−1.490	(0.223)***	−1.485	(0.223)***	−1.716	(0.231)***
Postjolt period (yrs 2003–2005)	−3.099	(0.228)***	−3.091	(0.228)***	−3.377	(0.232)***
Age	−0.133	(0.027)***	−0.132	(0.027)***	−0.130	(0.027)***
Cohort						
Cohort entry yr. 1994	0.940	(0.139)***	0.936	(0.139)***	0.904	(0.139)***
Cohort entry yr. 1995	0.734	(0.136)***	0.730	(0.136)***	0.713	(0.136)***
Cohort entry yr. 1996	0.544	(0.153)***	0.543	(0.153)***	0.530	(0.152)***
Cohort entry yr. 1997	0.059	(0.154)	0.062	(0.155)	0.047	(0.154)
Industry						
Founding density/100	0.237	(0.044)***	0.237	(0.044)***	0.235	(0.044)***
Density/100	−0.272	(0.046)***	−0.272	(0.046)***	−0.268	(0.046)***
Density squared/10,000	0.001	(0.001)	0.001	(0.001)	0.001	(0.001)
Founding density × age/100	−0.004	(0.001)**	−0.004	(0.001)**	−0.003	(0.001)*
Concentration/1000	−0.086	(0.026)***	−0.087	(0.026)***	−0.074	(0.026)**
Dynamism	−0.143	(0.621)	−0.137	(0.621)	−0.116	(0.622)
Munificence	−0.959	(0.409)*	−0.963	(0.409)*	−0.926	(0.408)*
Mining	−3.623	(0.386)***	−3.615	(0.386)***	−3.491	(0.386)***
Wholesale	−3.676	(0.134)***	−3.669	(0.134)***	−3.577	(0.134)***
Materials	−3.462	(0.097)***	−3.453	(0.097)***	−3.328	(0.096)***
Machine	−3.905	(0.190)***	−3.895	(0.190)***	−3.747	(0.189)***
High tech	−3.606	(0.166)***	−3.595	(0.167)***	−3.446	(0.166)***
Transport	−3.902	(0.276)***	−3.888	(0.276)***	−3.682	(0.276)***
Publishing	−3.219	(0.130)***	−3.206	(0.132)***	−3.060	(0.130)***
Organization						
Financial slack/1000	−0.042	(0.012)***	−0.042	(0.012)***	−0.039	(0.012)***
Employees (size)	−0.007	(0.004)	−0.007	(0.004)	−0.008	(0.005)
Fixed assets/1000	−0.041	(0.012)***	−0.041	(0.012)***	−0.035	(0.012)**
Equity/1000	0.040	(0.012)***	0.040	(0.012)***	0.033	(0.013)*
Subsidiary			−0.074	(0.101)		
Subsidiary × prejolt					−4.387	(1.001)***
Subsidiary × jolt					0.779	(0.231)***
Subsidiary × postjolt					0.920	(0.127)***
Goodness-of-fit						
Log likelihood	−2789.38		−2789.11		−2692.39	
n parameters	26		27		29	

[a] Number of observations = 58,424; number of organizations = 7166.
Unstandardized estimates reported along with standard errors in parentheses.
* $p < 0.05$; ** $p < 0.01$; *** $p < 0.001$.

hardier and are less susceptible to environmental changes than subsidiaries.

Despite this result, it seems reasonable that there should be at least some mortality effect due to the jolt's effect on independent organizations. The prejolt time period for independents includes both early years for new firms where mortality is high as well as successive years where mortality drops, replicating patterns from prior studies (Freeman *et al.*, 1983). After founding, independents

in comparison to subsidiary firms generally have more financial funding available, less access to debt capital where collateralization is required, and fewer benefits from social networks. These initial hazards in the prejolt period could mask what might be an increase in exit due to the jolt period for independents. Therefore, we reconstructed our prejolt period as year 2000, leaving out years 1994 to 1999, to focus our comparison of the jolt period more directly with the time immediately preceding

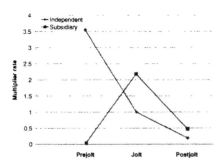

Figure 3. Multiplier rate plot from Model 2.5 comparing subsidiary and independent organizations across time periods

the jolt while reducing the effect of potential initial selection pressures in the prejolt period. Estimating Model 2.3 again, we found that the mortality rates were 1.62 times higher for independents during the jolt than prior to the jolt. Subsidiary mortality rates during the jolt were 2.6 times that of independents prior to the jolt. Mortality rates for subsidiaries were 1.60 times that of independents during the jolt period and were significantly different (p < 0.05). While our theoretical choice of time periods did not capture this finer difference, nonetheless, our hypotheses and results were robust to this additional analysis.

Resource effects

We also proposed that organizational structures (subsidiary or independent) affect the extent to which firms make effective use of their resources. We examined differences in the effect of observable resources for independent and subsidiary organizations across time (Table 3) and for three distinct time periods (Table 4). In Table 5 we report the independent and subsidiary Z-test significance difference comparisons for resources (Clogg, Petkova, and Haritou, 1995). Model 3.1 estimates the main effects of resources. Financial slack and fixed assets reduced hazard rates for independents (p < 0.01), but were not significant for subsidiaries (p > 0.05). Based on Z-test scores, the coefficient differences between independent and subsidiary firms for financial slack and fixed assets were significant (p < 0.05). The coefficients for employees and equity were not significant (p > 0.05) in Model 3.1 and the coefficient

differences between independents and subsidiaries were also not significant (p > 0.05) in Table 5. Hypothesis 3, that resources reduce mortality rates more for independents than subsidiaries, is thus supported for financial slack (Hypothesis 3a) and fixed assets (Hypothesis 3c) but not supported for employees (Hypothesis 3b) and equity (Hypothesis 3d).[6]

Models 4.1 to 4.4 estimate the respective effects of financial slack, employees, fixed assets, and equity on hazard rates across time periods. Model 4.1 estimates the effect of financial slack, which did not significantly reduce mortality in the prejolt period, but did so in the jolt (p < 0.001) and postjolt (p < 0.01) periods. Financial slack did not have a significant effect on mortality (p > 0.05) across the time periods for subsidiaries. Number of employees available in Model 4.2 did not reduce mortality rates until after the jolt period for independent firms (p < 0.001) and was not significant across time periods for subsidiaries (p > 0.10). Model 4.3 indicates a general trend of assets reducing hazard with time for independent firms (p < 0.05 prejolt and postjolt), although assets had no significant effect *during* the jolt period (p > 0.05). Assets had no significant effect on subsidiaries' mortality across the time periods. In Model 4.4, equity significantly increased mortality during the prejolt and the jolt period but was not significant in the postjolt period (p > 0.05). Equity did not significantly influence mortality rates with time for subsidiary firms (p > 0.05).

The results for equity with time period were contrary to Hypothesis 3d, as higher equity increased mortality rates during the jolt period for independent firms (p < 0.05). Financial slack had a negative, but nonsignificant effect on independents and subsidiaries prior to the jolt. Financial slack reduced mortality rates more for independent than subsidiary organizations during an environmental jolt (p < 0.001) providing evidence for Hypothesis 4a. The resources of employees, assets and equity were not significantly lower (p > 0.05) during the jolt period and thus did not provide support for Hypotheses 4b, 4c, and 4d, respectively.[7]

---

[6] We conducted analyses without controlling for cohort and the results were substantially the same as those reported.
[7] A final model including all the interactions was not reported because multicolinearity made the estimates unreliable.

500   *S. W. Bradley et al.*

Table 3.   Piecewise-exponential model of failure rates for independent and subsidiary organizations

	Model			
	(3.1)			
	Independent		Subsidiary	
Prejolt period (yrs 1994–2000)	−0.438	(0.186)*	−9.086	(1.412)***
Jolt period (yrs 2001–2002)	−1.572	(0.247)***	−6.356	(1.081)***
Postjolt period (yrs 2003–2005)	−3.206	(0.252)***	−6.455	(0.900)***
Age	−0.144	(0.028)***	0.415	(0.120)***
Cohort				
Cohort entry yr. 1994	1.063	(0.157)***	−1.346	(0.510)**
Cohort entry yr. 1995	0.876	(0.155)***	−1.173	(0.430)**
Cohort entry yr. 1996	0.660	(0.174)***	−0.556	(0.386)
Cohort entry yr. 1997	0.140	(0.182)	−0.578	(0.303)
Industry				
Founding density/100	0.197	(0.048)***	0.460	(0.122)***
Density/100	−0.002	(0.000)***	−0.003	(0.001)*
Density squared/10,000	0.001	(0.001)*	−0.004	(0.002)
Found. density × age/100	−0.003	(0.002)*	−0.011	(0.006)*
Concentration/1000	−0.077	(0.027)**	−0.036	(0.081)
Dynamism	−0.878	(0.709)	3.827	(1.353)**
Munificence	−0.683	(0.444)	−1.955	(1.123)
Mining	−3.608	(0.416)***	1.464	(1.266)
Wholesale	−3.614	(0.135)***	−0.953	(1.241)
Materials	−3.376	(0.098)***	−0.003	(0.806)
Machine	−3.781	(0.198)***	−0.175	(0.934)
High tech	−3.539	(0.173)***	0.337	(0.894)
Transport	−3.822	(0.297)***	0.461	(1.032)
Publishing	−3.109	(0.134)***	−0.354	(0.848)
Organization				
Financial slack/1000	−0.068	(0.023)**	−0.015	(0.016)
Employees (size)	−0.002	(0.007)	−0.014	(0.007)
Fixed assets/1000	−0.064	(0.021)**	−0.012	(0.014)
Equity/1000	0.038	(0.037)	0.011	(0.014)
Goodness-of-fit				
Log likelihood	−2380.51		−267.56	
n parameters	26		26	

Number of observations = 58, 424; number of organizations = 7166.
Standard errors shown in parentheses.
* $p < 0.05$; ** $p < 0.01$; *** $p < 0.001$.

Alternative explanations and robustness checks

We believe our theoretical arguments and empirical evidence for differences between independent and subsidiary organizations are compelling, but there are other possible explanations for our results. Alternative explanations might fall under two general categories. First, weaker independent organizations were selected out, leaving only the stronger ones, or second, the benefits accrued to subsidiaries through a parent organization were lost prior to the jolt, thus leaving them vulnerable. Our additional analysis (available as an Appendix from the first author) supports our results. We examined the first alternative by investigating relative changes in the resources of independent and subsidiary organizations over time. We did not find evidence, at least in terms of observable resources, that independents are 'more endowed' than subsidiary organizations leading into the jolt period. We examine the second explanation by investigating whether there is evidence of weakness in parent organizations prior to the jolt or evidence that there was buffering of poorly performing subsidiaries prior to the environmental jolt. The variance in mortality rates during an environmental jolt does not appear related

Table 4.   Piecewise-exponential model of failure rates including period specific effects for independent and subsidiary organizations

	Model							
	(4.1)		(4.2)		(4.3)		(4.4)	
	Independent	Subsidiary	Independent	Subsidiary	Independent	Subsidiary	Independent	Subsidiary
Prepit period (yrs 1994–2000)	−0.431 (0.186)**	−9.078 (1.411)***	−0.456 (0.186)*	−8.143 (1.510)***	−0.447 (0.186)*	−8.514 (1.530)***	−0.453 (0.186)*	−7.590 (3.563)*
Jolt period (yrs 2001–2002)	−1.525 (0.248)***	−6.361 (1.081)***	−1.616 (0.251)***	−6.315 (1.085)***	−1.576 (0.252)***	−6.303 (1.083)***	−1.581 (0.249)***	−6.362 (1.081)***
Posjolt period (yrs 2003–2005)	−3.163 (0.253)***	−6.453 (0.900)***	−2.973 (0.258)***	−6.478 (0.901)***	−3.193 (0.253)***	−6.451 (0.900)***	−3.165 (0.253)***	−6.465 (0.900)***
Age	−0.145 (0.028)***	0.415 (0.120)***	−0.145 (0.028)***	0.415 (0.120)***	−0.144 (0.028)***	0.414 (0.119)***	−0.144 (0.028)***	0.417 (0.119)***
Cohort								
Cohort entry yr. 1994	1.068 (0.157)***	−1.349 (0.510)**	1.058 (0.157)***	−1.345 (0.510)**	1.064 (0.157)***	−1.349 (0.510)**	1.071 (0.158)***	−1.354 (0.510)**
Cohort entry yr. 1995	0.879 (0.155)***	−1.176 (0.430)**	0.873 (0.155)***	−1.174 (0.430)**	0.876 (0.155)***	−1.174 (0.430)**	0.881 (0.155)***	−1.180 (0.429)**
Cohort entry yr. 1996	0.662 (0.174)***	−0.557 (0.386)	0.656 (0.174)***	−0.550 (0.386)	0.661 (0.174)***	−0.554 (0.385)	0.665 (0.174)***	−0.559 (0.385)
Cohort entry yr. 1997	0.140 (0.182)	−0.578 (0.303)	0.133 (0.182)	−0.577 (0.303)*	0.141 (0.182)	−0.580 (0.303)	0.145 (0.182)	−0.579 (0.303)
Industry								
Founding density/100	0.196 (0.048)***	0.460 (0.122)***	0.200 (0.048)***	0.460 (0.122)***	0.197 (0.048)***	0.459 (0.122)***	0.195 (0.048)***	0.461 (0.122)***
Density/100	−0.242 (0.049)***	−0.308 (0.146)*	−0.246 (0.049)***	−0.307 (0.146)*	−0.241 (0.049)***	−0.308 (0.146)*	−0.239 (0.049)***	−0.309 (0.146)*
Density squared/10,000	0.001 (0.001)***	−0.004 (0.002)	0.001 (0.001)*	−0.004 (0.002)	0.001 (0.001)*	−0.004 (0.002)	0.001 (0.001)*	−0.004 (0.002)
Found. density × age/100	−0.003 (0.002)*	−0.011 (0.006)	−0.003 (0.002)*	−0.011 (0.006)	−0.003 (0.002)*	−0.011 (0.006)	−0.003 (0.002)*	−0.011 (0.006)
Concentration/1000	−0.079 (0.027)**	−0.036 (0.081)	−0.076 (0.027)*	−0.034 (0.081)	−0.077 (0.027)**	−0.036 (0.081)	−0.077 (0.027)**	−0.036 (0.081)
Dynamism	−0.922 (0.711)	3.833 (1.353)**	−0.928 (0.708)	3.818 (1.352)**	−0.873 (0.709)	3.814 (1.352)**	−0.879 (0.709)	3.829 (1.353)**
Munificence	−0.671 (0.444)	−1.956 (1.124)	−0.688 (0.444)	−1.948 (1.123)	−0.678 (0.444)	−1.964 (1.122)	−0.679 (0.444)	−1.958 (1.123)
Mining	−3.610 (0.416)***	1.468 (1.266)	−3.591 (0.416)***	1.394 (1.269)	−3.608 (0.416)***	1.471 (1.266)	−3.606 (0.416)***	1.466 (1.266)
Wholesale	−3.621 (0.135)***	−0.957 (1.241)	−3.617 (0.135)***	−0.926 (1.242)	−3.613 (0.135)***	−0.977 (1.241)	−3.616 (0.135)***	−0.955 (1.242)
Machine	−3.384 (0.098)***	−0.004 (0.806)	−3.376 (0.098)***	0.033 (0.808)	−3.375 (0.098)***	−0.002 (0.805)	−3.379 (0.098)***	−0.002 (0.806)
High tech	−3.790 (0.198)***	−0.181 (0.933)	−3.773 (0.198)***	−0.124 (0.936)	−3.779 (0.198)***	−0.202 (0.934)	−3.785 (0.198)***	−0.173 (0.933)
Transport	−3.550 (0.173)***	0.333 (0.893)	−3.537 (0.173)***	0.340 (0.894)	−3.536 (0.173)***	0.309 (0.894)	−3.541 (0.173)***	0.338 (0.894)
Publishing	−3.828 (0.297)***	0.455 (1.031)	−3.821 (0.297)***	0.512 (1.034)	−3.821 (0.297)***	0.445 (1.031)	−3.822 (0.297)***	0.464 (1.031)
	−3.111 (0.134)***	−0.353 (0.848)	−3.097 (0.134)***	−0.351 (0.848)	−3.107 (0.134)***	−0.385 (0.849)	−3.110 (0.134)***	−0.357 (0.848)
Organization								
Financial slack/1000	−0.001 (0.007)	−0.014 (0.007)	−0.072 (0.025)*	−0.015 (0.016)	−0.073 (0.026)**	−0.013 (0.016)	−0.062 (0.024)*	−0.015 (0.016)
Employees (size)	−0.071 (0.022)***	−0.013 (0.014)	−0.065 (0.021)*	−0.011 (0.013)	−0.061 (0.007)***	−0.014 (0.007)	−0.001 (0.007)	−0.014 (0.007)
Fixed assets/1000	0.016 (0.041)	0.011 (0.015)	0.057 (0.031)	0.010 (0.014)	0.043 (0.035)	0.008 (0.015)	−0.068 (0.021)***	−0.012 (0.014)
Equity/1000								

Financial slack × prejolt/1000	−0.019 (0.032)	−0.021 (0.043)						
Financial slack × jolt/1000	−0.186 (0.051)***	−0.011 (0.028)						
Financial slack × postjolt/1000	−0.076 (0.027)*	−0.017 (0.018)						
Employees × prejolt			0.007 (0.007)	−0.308 (0.539)				
Employees × jolt			0.014 (0.014)	−0.024 (0.019)				
Employees × postjolt			−0.078 (0.023)***	−0.012 (0.008)				
Fixed assets × prejolt/1000					−0.058 (0.023)*	−0.899 (2.054)		
Fixed assets × jolt/1000					−0.065 (0.046)	−0.023 (0.034)		
Fixed assets × postjolt/1000					−0.081 (0.036)*	−0.009 (0.014)		
Equity × prejolt/1000							0.084 (0.032)*	−11.962 (32.718)
Equity × jolt/1000							0.060 (0.094)	0.010 (0.015)
Equity × postjolt/1000							−0.031 (0.056)	0.011 (0.014)
Goodness-of-fit								
Log likelihood	−2377.38	−264.13	−2371.19	−206.98	−2380.17	−267.14	−2378.32	−267.26
n parameters	28	28	28	28	28	28	28	28

Number of observations = 58, 424; number of organizations = 7166.
Standard errors shown in parentheses. * $p < .05$; ** $p < .01$; *** $p < .001$.

to firm resource differences, thresholds, or parent buffering, but instead reflect the consequences of differences in organizational independence.

DISCUSSION AND CONCLUSION

Why do some organizations that do well in stable environments become more vulnerable to selection pressures when environments shift? We proposed that organization independence at founding not only influences survival chances under 'normal' economic conditions but also affects organizations' abilities to weather a hostile environmental event. Using a large sample of firms in the manufacturing and technology sectors of Sweden, our expectations were confirmed. We found that the effect of organizational independence on survival rates was contingent on the nature of the environmental conditions, with subsidiaries doing better than independents prior to the jolt, but with independents outperforming subsidiaries during the jolt. We tested and rejected three alternative explanations for our results: independents 'catching up' with subsidiaries in resource availability, the past performance of the parent organization, or the buffering of poorly performing subsidiaries prior to the economic downturn.

Organizational independence and environments

Prior evolutionary models implied that advantages gained through strategic position or the development of competitive abilities are primarily a function of organizational size (Barnett, 1997; Barnett and McKendrick, 2004). Larger organizations often shield themselves from selection pressures through mutual forbearance and access to powerful institutional ties, whereas smaller organizations must learn to adapt and to survive. We extended previous arguments about the advantages of smaller organizations by examining additional possible returns to independence. We found that independent entrants have elevated liabilities of newness but that they benefit from their freedom to experiment and develop alternative routines. The value of such flexible structures may not become fully apparent until environments become unstable and established routines turn into potential liabilities.

Our findings reveal that the success of entry may be contingent on the independence of the entering

Table 5.   Significant difference tests of resource covariates as main effect and period specific effects

Model	Covariates	Independent		Subsidiary		Z-test[a]
		Coeff.	Std. Dev.	Coeff.	Std. Dev.	
3.1	Financial slack/1000	−0.068	(0.023)	−0.015	(0.016)	−1.92*
3.1	Employees	−0.002	(0.007)	−0.014	(0.007)	1.26
3.1	Fixed assets/1000	−0.064	(0.021)	−0.012	(0.014)	−2.09*
3.1	Equity/1000	0.038	(0.037)	0.011	(0.014)	0.68
4.1	Financial slack × prejolt/1000	−0.019	(0.032)	−0.021	(0.043)	0.02
4.1	Financial slack × jolt/1000	−0.186	(0.051)	−0.011	(0.028)	−3.02*
4.1	Financial slack × postjolt/1000	−0.076	(0.027)	−0.017	(0.018)	−1.82*
4.2	Fixed assets × prejolt/1000	0.007	(0.007)	−0.308	(0.539)	0.58
4.2	Fixed assets × jolt/1000	0.014	(0.014)	−0.024	(0.019)	1.65*
4.2	Fixed assets × postjolt/1000	−0.078	(0.023)	−0.012	(0.008)	−2.73**
4.3	Employees × prejolt	−0.058	(0.023)	−0.899	(2.054)	0.41
4.3	Employees × jolt	−0.065	(0.046)	0.023	(0.034)	−0.73
4.3	Employees × postjolt	−0.081	(0.036)	−0.009	(0.014)	−1.65*
4.4	Equity × prejolt/1000	0.084	(0.032)	−11.962	(32.718)	0.37
4.4	Equity × jolt/1000	0.060	(0.094)	0.010	(0.015)	0.52*
4.4	Equity × postjolt/1000	−0.031	(0.056)	0.011	(0.014)	−0.71

[a] Z-test: $= (\beta_1 - \beta_2)/\text{SQRT}(\text{SD}\beta_1{}^2 + \text{SD}\beta_2{}^2)$.
$Z = 1.65$ at $p < 0.05$, 2.33 at $p < 0.01$.

organizations. To pursue this issue in greater depth, we looked more closely at covariate effects on the mortality rates of independent and subsidiary organizations in Table 4.

Age and density showed distinct differences by organizational structure. Age reduced the hazard of mortality for independent organizations, but increased it for subsidiaries (diff. sig. $p < 0.05$). Arguably, the most influential view is that liability declines with age (Freeman *et al.*, 1983; Stinchcombe, 1965), with this pattern varying by such factors as prior levels of competition (Carroll and Hannan, 1989; Swaminathan, 1996), institutional ties (Baum and Oliver, 1991) or firm strategy (Henderson, 1999). The results of our study suggest that, at least in the short run, age effects can be quite different by structure—particularly when there are abrupt changes in the environment. Independents displayed a U-shaped relationship with density (a negative density term and a positive density squared term) while subsidiaries displayed declining mortality rates with density, though the difference in size of the main effect was not significant ($p > 0.05$).

Current ecological theory is still uncertain about the processes by which founding density affects age or time-dependent mortality (Lomi and Larsen, 1998). Swaminathan's (1996) empirical support for a 'trial by fire' hypothesis was unable to distinguish between selection and population-level learning as explanations of the lower long-run mortality for firms founded under greater adversity. Our study suggests that organizational structure plays a role in the effect of density delay. Founding density increased the odds of mortality for both structures across the Table 3 models, but was significantly ($p < 0.05$) greater for subsidiaries (1.58 times) than independent organizations (1.22 times). The greater effects for subsidiaries may be a result of parent ties that constrain them to a less than ideal market niche or less effective practices that become more evident when environments change. Our results also show the coefficient for founding density x age was significant and negative ($p < 0.05$) for independent organizations but not significant for subsidiaries ($p > 0.05$). Independent organizations follow a form of the 'trial-by fire–model' (Swaminathan,1996) with high early failure rates but with subsequently lower failure rates. Whether through selection or learning, the patterns are partially a function of structure. These differences between independent and subsidiary organizations deserve further inquiry.

It might seem surprising that industry concentration reduced mortality for independents but not subsidiaries, because some have argued that markets that are controlled by larger firms are likely to restrict newer firms' strategic choices in pricing, branding, distribution, and logistics (George, 2005). These constraints would appear to favor subsidiaries because of their ties to larger organizations. However, based on resource partitioning theory, Carroll (1985) argued that increasing concentration could actually favor smaller specialist firms because large generalist firms that try covering multiple market segments potentially leave many small specialized niches open. In less concentrated markets, generalists and specialists compete for the same resources, giving an edge to the generalists. However, as concentration increases, generalists fight for the center, whereas specialists exploit peripheral niches and avoid direct competition with generalists. Thus, specialists may actually do better in more concentrated markets. Using industry life cycle theory, Agarwal and Audretsch (2000) offered a similar argument: small firms enjoy survival advantages within mature technology-intensive industries because they occupy strategic niches in which they are somewhat protected from competition by larger firms. Extending these arguments, new independent firms, freed from the constraints of their parent companies, can move more quickly than subsidiaries to protected niches in concentrating markets in which they enjoy a survival advantage.

To investigate further, we examined a specific industry with a high concentration of market share: the furniture industry (ISIC 361) in Sweden, which is mature and dominated by a few key players. Technological innovations in manufacturing have allowed niche manufacturers into the market, similar to the rise of the minimills in the mature steel industry (Christensen, 1997). A separate analysis of this industry, though speculative due to the small sample size, suggested subsidiaries had a higher mortality rate with age than independents.[8] Survival advantages thus appear to accrue to firms able to rapidly find new opportunities in a market dominated by a few competitors, rather than to firms that are tied to past practices with diminishing returns.

The evidence that dynamic environments increase mortality rates more for subsidiaries than for independents supports the notion that more flexible organizational structures are beneficial in uncertain environments (Burns and Stalker, 1961; Carroll

et al., 1996). Both stochastic change and the sudden change examined in this study appear to favor flexible organizations. Greater uncertainty disrupts the benefits of established processes and designs, creating disadvantages for subsidiaries that lack the flexibility to alter codified knowledge received from their parent firms when environments change. These findings add to Barnett and colleagues' work (Barnett *et al.*, 1994), suggesting that organizational structure, in this case whether a firm is an independent or subsidiary, may play an important role in an organization's ability to cope with a competitive or a protected market position.

Effective use of resources

The adaptation literature indicates that organizational change can improve performance and survival chances if changes are built on established routines and competencies (Haveman, 1992). Our study extends this literature by showing that improvement depends upon the effective use of resources. Specifically, we found that independent organizations improved their survival chances through the deployment of discretionary financial resources and assets with time. Several interesting patterns emerge from the results in Tables 3 to 5. First, new organizations struggled to use resources effectively before the jolt. Employees and financial slack did not significantly reduce mortality prior to 2001 for independents or mortality for subsidiaries. This supports the notion that liabilities of newness occurs because of the costs introduced when employees have to learn new roles in an organization's early years (Stinchcombe, 1965). Second, we find evidence that more flexible forms of resources reduce mortality for organizations that have learned to use them with time (George, 2005). Financial slack reduced mortality during the jolt period for independents, while the effects of employees and assets were not statistically significant. Reassigning assets and employees for efficient use is difficult, particularly for young organizations still in the process of forming routines (Stinchcombe, 1965). Interestingly, employee contributions to survival only became significant for independents after the jolt period, possibly indicating that alternative routines and experimentation during turmoil revealed more effective uses for human capital moving forward. Third, we were surprised that equity capital increased hazard rates in the general models (2.3) as well as during the prejolt and jolt periods for independents (3.4). This result contradicts prior work that found that initial capital increases survival chances (Bates, 1998; Holtz-Eakin, Joulfaian, and Rosen, 1994). However, it does support both recent theorizing (Baker and Nelson, 2005; Mosakowski, 2002) and empirical work (Katila and Shane, 2005) suggesting that organizations may be more innovative when forced to *find a way* (Stevenson and Jarillo, 1990). Equity at founding is often allocated based on *a priori* strategies that may become outmoded when environments change, thereby constraining organizational adaptation. Future researchers might build on this study by investigating whether prior knowledge and experience (with processes and markets) change the role of initial equity in organizational survival.

The differences between independent and subsidiary organizations across observable resources suggest that routines and competencies developed under conditions of greater independence lead to enhanced flexibility and success in configuring resources to match changing environments. Our study is also, to our knowledge, the first to use changes in the effects of resource usage as indicators of organizational learning in models of competitive evolution and is worthy of future research.

Limitations and opportunities

Our panel study has several advantages over previous research designs studying organizational survival and environmental jolts, and its limitations lead to a number of interesting questions for future research. First, by choosing multiple cohorts of organizations for study, we substantially reduced problems associated with left censoring and selection bias. However, the data contained little variance in organization exits for subsidiaries up to the years just prior to the environmental jolt period and little variance in age with the sample containing young organizations. We speculate that the results generalize to these more heterogeneous conditions. However, future studies might further explore differences in organizational independence where more time has elapsed between founding and a jolt.

Second, we examined independence as a dichotomous state, rather than a continuous variable because we were constrained by the data available for the study. Being able to measure varying levels of autonomy within independent and subsidiary organizations would further enhance our understanding of whether freedom in decision making regarding the allocation of resources enhances or hinders survival chances in changing environments. Future studies may find other theoretically significant deviations from baseline evolutionary models by choosing other interesting organizational structures and forms than the 'independent' and 'subsidiary' classification used in this study. Third, our goal was to examine the role of independence in asymmetric selection rates at founding and during an environmental jolt. Our postjolt data revealed interesting patterns of lingering effects from the jolt on subsidiary selection rates. A separate and theoretically interesting future research study might examine the imprinting effects of a jolt on longer-term survival or performance (e.g., Freeman, 1984).

We note three scope conditions that may limit the generalizability of our findings. First, we assume that independent organizations have greater autonomy than subsidiaries. We acknowledge that parent-subsidiary relationships are heterogeneous with regard to formal and informal control (Birkinshaw, Hood, and Jonsson, 1998; Daniels, Pitts, and Tretter, 1984) and that independent organizations may have their autonomy diminished (for example by debt covenants [Gompers, 1995; Jensen, 1986]). Second, we assume that because of their ties to a parent, subsidiaries must deal with more bureaucratic rules and regulations than independent organizations, thus making change more difficult (Haveman, 1992; Lieberman and Montgomery, 1998). Nonetheless, it is possible that ties to a parent could enhance proactive behavior if the parent has a more entrepreneurial orientation (Covin and Slevin, 1991), is more risk seeking (Carpenter, Pollock, and Leary, 2003), or strategically benefits from a highly 'active' subsidiary (e.g., mutual forbearance [Greve, 2008]). Finally, we focus on a negative environmental jolt and assume that adaptation enhances survival. It could be that other types of jolts have positive effects (Shepherd *et al.*, 2000; Venkataraman and Van de Ven, 1998) and/or enhance the benefit of economies of scale and persistence rather than adaptation (although that was not the case with the jolt studied here). Therefore, our findings may not hold for situations when subsidiaries have greater autonomy and less organizational inertia than independent organizations and for jolts that are positive and/or jolts that do not reward adaptation.

506   *S. W. Bradley et al.*

CONCLUSION

Aldrich and Auster (1986) previously made the case that the strengths of large, old organizations are often the weaknesses of small, new organizations and vice versa. Our study suggests that independence may alter the nature of the contest between small, new organizations and large, old organizations. The liabilities and advantages of newness and smallness may be moderated by the extent to which new organizations are independent or dependent. Subsidiaries are likely to take on the characteristics, routines (including rules and regulations), and orientation of their parent organizations, thus undercutting the adaptive potential of the organization.

Our theory and results have important implications for evolutionary models of competition and adaptation to environmental change (Barnett *et al.*, 1994; Haveman, 1992). 'Although prior research has examined implications of environmental conditions for firm survival ..., little theorizing and empirical research at an organizational level has examined how firms can mitigate these threats' (Fischer and Pollock, 2004: 479). We find that independent organizations face higher initial selection pressures that apparently strengthen the resourceful capability development of survivors. In contrast, subsidiaries of larger parent organizations are shielded from competition but face higher risk of exit during a subsequent economic downturn. This finding lends empirical support to theories suggesting that exposure to adversity makes organizations stronger competitors (Barnett and Hansen, 1996; Swaminathan, 1996). It also provides an alternative example of asymmetric selection (Barnett *et al.*, 2003). Being a subsidiary leads to reduced flexibility and a reliance on positional advantages at founding that may leave organizations less competitive when environments change abruptly. Our findings suggest that scholars direct their attention not only to whether or how organizations adapt but also to the conditions under which organizational structures enable or inhibit adaptation when environments change.

ACKNOWLEDGEMENTS

We appreciate valuable comments from Jeff Covin, Will Mitchell, and two excellent, anonymous reviewers.

REFERENCES

Agarwal R, Audretsch DB. 2000. Does entry size matter? The impact of life cycle and technology on firm survival. *Journal of Industrial Economics* 49(1): 21–43.

Aldrich H. 1979. *Organizations and Environments*. Prentice-Hall: Englewood Cliffs, NJ.

Aldrich H. 1999. *Organizations Evolving*. Sage: London, UK.

Aldrich H, Auster ER. 1986. Even dwarfs started small: liabilities of age and size and their strategic implications. *Research in Organizational Behavior* 8(2): 165–198.

Aldrich H, Ruef M. 2006. *Organizations Evolving* (2nd edn). Sage: London, UK.

Allison PD. 1984. *Event History Analysis*. Sage: Newbury Park, CA.

Altman EI. 1968. Financial ratios, discriminant analysis and the prediction of corporate bankruptcy. *Journal of Finance* 23(4): 589–609.

Altman EI. 2002. *Revisiting Credit Scoring Models in a Basel II Environment* London Risk Books: London, UK.

Baker T, Nelson R. 2005. Creating something from nothing: resource construction through entrepreneurial bricolage. *Administrative Science Quarterly* 50(3): 329–366.

Barnett WP. 1997. The dynamics of competitive intensity. *Administrative Science Quarterly* 42(1): 128–160.

Barnett WP, Carroll GR. 1995. Modeling internal organizational change. *Annual Review of Sociology* 21: 217–236.

Barnett WP, Greve HR, Park DY. 1994. An evolutionary model of organizational performance. *Strategic Management Journal*, Winter Special Issue 15: 11–28.

Barnett WP, Hansen MT. 1996. The red queen in organizational evolution. *Strategic Management Journal*, Summer Special Issue 17: 139–157.

Barnett WP, McKendrick D. 2004. Why are some organizations more competitive than others? Evidence from a changing global market. *Administrative Science Quarterly* 49(4): 535–571.

Barnett WP, Swanson AN, Sorenson O. 2003. Asymmetric selection among organizations. *Industrial and Corporate Change* 12(4): 673–695.

Bates T. 1998. Survival patterns among newcomers to franchising. *Journal of Business Venturing* 13(2): 113–130.

Baum J. 1996. Organizational ecology. In *Handbook of Organization Studies*: Clegg S, Hardy C, Nord W (eds). Sage: London, UK; 77–114.

Baum J, Oliver C. 1991. Institutional linkages and organizational mortality. *Administrative Science Quarterly* 36: 187–218.

Bhide A. 1992. Bootstrap finance: The art of start-ups. *Harvard Business Review* 70(6): 109–117.

Birkinshaw J, Hood N, Jonsson S. 1998. Building firm-specific advantages in multinational corporations: the role of subsidiary initiative. *Strategic Management Journal* **19**(3): 221–241.

Blanchflower DG, Oswald AJ. 1988. What makes an entrepreneur? *Journal of Labor Economics* **16**(1): 26–60.

Blossfeld H-P, Golsch K, Rohwer G. 2007. *Event History Analysis with Stata*. Lawrence Erlbaum Associates: Mahwah, NJ.

Bourgeois LJI. 1981. On the measurement of organizational slack. *Academy of Management Review* **6**(1): 29–39.

Brealey RA, Meyers SC. 2003. *Principles of Corporate Finance* (7th edn). McGraw-Hill: New York.

Brush TH, Bromiley P, Hendrickx M. 2000. The free cash flow hypothesis for sales growth and firm performance. *Strategic Management Journal* **21**(4): 455–472.

Burgelman R, Sayles L. 1986. *Inside Corporate Innovation*. Free Press: New York.

Burns T, Stalker G. 1961. *The Management of Innovation*. Tavistock: London, UK.

Burt R. 1992. *Structural Holes: The Social Structure of Competition*. Harvard University Press: Cambridge, MA.

Carpenter MA, Pollock TG, Leary MM. 2003. Testing a model of reasoned risk-taking: governance, the experience of principals and agents, and global strategy in high-technology IPO firms. *Strategic Management Journal* **24**(9): 803–820.

Carroll GR. 1985. Concentration and specialization: dynamics of niche width in populations of organizations. *American Journal of Sociology* **90**(6): 1262–1283.

Carroll GR, Bigelow LS, Seidel MDL, Tsai LB. 1996. The fates of *de novo* and *de alio* producers in the American automobile industry 1885–1981. *Strategic Management Journal*, Summer Special Issue **17**: 117–137.

Carroll GR, Delacroix J. 1982. Organizational mortality in the newspaper industries of Argentina and Ireland: an ecological approach. *Administrative Science Quarterly* **27**(2): 169–198.

Carroll GR, Hannan M. 1989. Density dependence in the evolution of populations of newspaper organizations. *American Sociological Review* **54**(4): 524–541.

Carroll GR, Hannan MT. 2000. *The Demography of Corporations and Industries*. Princeton University Press: Princeton, NJ.

Caves RE, Porter ME. 1977. From entry barriers to mobility barriers: conjectural decisions and continued deterrence to new competition. *Quarterly Journal of Economics* **91**(2): 241–261.

Chakravarthy BS. 1982. Adaptation: a promising metaphor for strategic management. *Academy of Management Review* **7**(1): 35–44.

Christensen CM. 1997. *The Innovator's Dilemma: When New Technologies Cause Great Firms to Fail*. Harvard Business School Press: Boston, MA.

Clogg C, Petkova E, Haritou A. 1995. Statistical methods for comparing regression coefficients between models. *American Journal of Sociology* **100**: 1261–1293.

Covin JG, Slevin D. 1991. A conceptual model of entrepreneurship as firm behavior. *Entrepreneurship Theory & Practice* **16**: 7–25.

Cyert R, March J. 1963. *A Behavioral Theory of the Firm*. Prentice-Hall: Englewood Cliffs, NJ.

Daniels JD, Pitts RA, Tretter MJ. 1984. Strategy and structure of U.S. multinationals: an exploratory study. *Academy of Management Journal* **27**(2): 292–307.

Dess GG, Beard DW. 1984. Dimensions of organizational task environments. *Administrative Science Quarterly* **29**(1): 52–73.

Dill WR. 1958. Environment as an influence on managerial autonomy. *Administrative Science Quarterly* **2**(4): 409–443.

Dowell G, Swaminathan A. 2006. Entry timing, exploration, and firm survival in the early U.S. bicycle industry. *Strategic Management Journal* **27**(12): 1159–1182.

Eidleman GJ. 1995. Z scores–a guide to failure prediction. *CPA Journal* **65**(2): 52–54.

Fichman M, Levinthal DA. 1991. Honeymoons and the liability of adolescence: a new perspective on duration dependence in social and organizational relationships. *Academy of Management Review* **16**(2): 442–468.

Fischer H, Pollock T. 2004. Effects of social capital and power on surviving transformational change: the case of initial public offerings. *Academy of Management Journal* **47**(4): 463–481.

Freeman J. 1984. Dynamics of publisher succession. *Administrative Science Quarterly* **29**(1): 93–113.

Freeman J, Carroll GR, Hannan MT. 1983. The liability of newness: age dependence in organizational death rates. *American Sociological Review* **48**(5): 692–710.

Galbraith JR. 1974. Organization design: an information processing view. *Interfaces* **4**(3): 28–36.

George G. 2005. Slack resources and the performance of privately held firms. *Academy of Management Journal* **48**(4): 661–676.

Gimeno J, Folta TB, Cooper AC, Woo CY. 1997. Survival of the fittest? Entrepreneurial human capital and the persistence of underperforming firms. *Administrative Science Quarterly* **42**(4): 750–783.

Goll I, Rasheed AMA. 1997. Rational decision-making and firm performance: the moderating role of environment *Strategic Management Journal* **18**(7): 583–591.

Gompers PA. 1995. Optimal investment, monitoring, and the staging of venture capital. *Journal of Finance* **50**(5): 1461–1489.

Greve HR. 2003. *Organizational Learning from Performance Feedback: A Behavioral Perspective on Innovation and Change*. Cambridge University Press: Cambridge, UK.

Greve HR. 2008. Multimarket contact and sales growth: evidence from insurance. *Strategic Management Journal* **29**(3): 229–249.

Hannan M, Freeman J. 1984. Structural inertia and organizational change. *American Sociological Review* **49**: 149–164.

Hannan M, Freeman J. 1989. *Organizational Ecology*. Harvard University Press: Cambridge, MA.

508   *S. W. Bradley et al.*

Haveman HA. 1992. Between a rock and a hard place: organizational change and performance under conditions of fundamental environmental transformation. *Administrative Science Quarterly* 37(1): 48–75.

Haveman HA, Russo MV, Meyer AD. 2001. Organizational environments in flux: the impact of regulatory punctuations on organizational domains, ceo succession, and performance. *Organization Science* 12(3): 253–273.

Helfat CE, Lieberman MB. 2002. The birth of capabilities: market entry and the importance of pre-history. *Industrial and Corporate Change* 11(4): 725–760.

Henderson AD. 1999. Firm strategy and age dependence: a contingent view of the liabilities of newness, adolescence, and obsolescence. *Administrative Science Quarterly* 44(2): 281–284.

Henderson R. 1993. Underinvestment and incompetence as responses to radical innovation: evidence from the photolithographic alignment equipment industry. *RAND Journal of Economics* 24(2): 248–270.

Henderson R, Mitchell W. 1997. The interactions of organizational and competitive influences on strategy and performance. *Strategic Management Journal*, Summer Special Issue 18: 5–14.

Hines HH. 1957. Effectiveness of entry by already established firms. *Quarterly Journal of Economics* 75: 132–150.

Holtz-Eakin D, Joulfaian D, Rosen HS. 1994. Sticking it out: entrepreneurial survival and liquidity constraints. *Journal of Political Economy* 102(1): 53–75.

Hon MT, Strauss JK, Yong S-K. 2007. Deconstructing the NASDAQ bubble: a look at contagion across international stock markets. *Journal of International Financial Markets, Institutions and Money* 17(3): 213–230.

Hrebiniak LG, Joyce WF. 1985. Organizational adaptation: strategic choice and environmental determinism. *Administrative Science Quarterly* 30(3): 336–349.

Ito K. 1995. Japanese spinoffs: unexplored survival strategies. *Strategic Management Journal* 16(6): 431–446.

Jensen MC. 1986. Agency costs of free cash flow, corporate finance, and takeovers. *American Economic Review* 76(2): 323–329.

Katila R, Shane S. 2005. When does lack of resources make new firms innovative? *Academy of Management Journal* 48(5): 814–830.

Levinthal DA. 1997. Adaptation on rugged landscapes. *Management Science* 43(7): 934–950.

Lieberman MB, Montgomery DB. 1998. First-mover (dis)advantages: retrospective and link with the resource-based view. *Strategic Management Journal* 19(12): 1111–1125.

Litschert RJ, Bonham TW. 1978. A conceptual model of strategy formation. *Academy of Management Review* 3(2): 211–219.

Lomi A, Larsen ER. 1998. Density delay and organizational survival: computational models and empirical comparisons. *Computational & Mathematical Organization Theory* 3(4): 219–247.

March JG. 1995. The future, disposable organizations and the rigidities of imagination. *Organization* 2(3): 427–440.

McDougall PP, Covin JG, Robinson RB Jr, Herron L. 1994. The effects of industry growth and strategic breadth on new venture performance and strategy content. *Strategic Management Journal* 15(7): 537–554.

Meyer AD. 1982. Adapting to environmental jolts. *Administrative Science Quarterly* 27(4): 515–537.

Miller A, Spann MS, Lerner L. 1991. Competitive advantages in new corporate ventures: the impact of resource sharing and reporting level. *Journal of Business Venturing* 6: 335–350.

Mintzberg H. 1994. *The Rise and Fall of Strategic Planning*. Free Press: New York.

Mishina Y, Pollock TG, Porac J F. 2004. Are more resources always better for growth? Resource stickiness in market and product expansion. *Strategic Management Journal* 25(12): 1179–1197.

Mosakowski E. 2002. Overcoming resource disadvantages in entrepreneurial firms: when less is more. In *Strategic Entrepreneurship: Creating an Integrated Mindset*, Hitt M, Ireland D, Sexton D, Camp M (eds). Blackwell: Oxford, UK; 106–126.

Nelson RR, Winter S. 1982. *An Evolutionary Theory of Economic Change*. Belknap: Cambridge, MA.

Nohria N, Gulati R. 1996. Is slack good or bad for innovation? *Academy of Management Journal* 39(5): 1245–1264.

Ocasio W. 1997. Towards an attention-based view of the firm *Strategic Management Journal*, Summer Special Issue 18: 187–206.

O'Donnell A, Gilmore A, Cummins D, Carson D. 2001. The network construct in entrepreneurship research: a review and critique. *Management Decision* 39(9): 749–760.

Oliver C. 1991. Network relations and loss of organizational autonomy. *Human Relations* 44(9): 943–961.

Pfeffer J, Leblibici H. 1973. Executive recruitment and the development of interfirm organizations. *Administrative Science Quarterly* 18(4): 449–461.

Pfeffer J, Salancik GR. 1978. *The External Control of Organizations: A Resource Dependence Perspective*. Harper & Row: New York.

Polzehl J, Spokoiny V, Starica C. 2004. When did the 2001 recession really start? Econometric series at SSRN: http://129.3.20.41/eps/em/papers/0411/04110 17.pdf (14 July 2006).

Romanelli E. 1989. Environments and strategies of organization start-up: effects on early survival. *Administrative Science Quarterly* 34(3): 369–387.

Rosenbloom RS, Christensen CM. 1994. Technological discontinuities, organizational capabilities, and strategic commitments. *Industrial and Corporate Change* 3(3): 655–685.

Ruef M. 1997. Assessing organizational fitness on a dynamic landscape: an empirical test of the relative inertia thesis. *Strategic Management Journal* 18(10): 837–853.

Schrader RC, Simon M. 1997. Corporate versus independent new ventures: resource, strategy, and performance differences. *Journal of Business Venturing* **12**: 47–66.

Scott WR. 2003. *Organizations: Rational, Natural, and Open Systems*. Prentice Hall: Upper Saddle River, NJ.

Scott WR, Meyer JW (eds). 1983. *The Organization of Societal Sectors*. Sage: Beverly Hills, CA.

Shane S. 2003. *A General Theory of Entrepreneurship*. Edward Elgar: Northampton, MA.

Shane S, Stuart T. 2002. Organizational endowments and the performance of university start-ups. *Management Science* **48**(1): 154–170.

Sharfman MP, Wolf G, Chase RB, Tansik DA. 1988. Antecedents of organizational slack. *Academy of Management Review* **13**(4): 601–614.

Shepherd DA, Douglas EJ, Shanley M. 2000. New venture survival: ignorance, external shocks, and risk reduction strategies *Journal of Business Venturing* **15**(5/6): 393–410.

Sine WD, David RJ. 2003. Environmental jolts, institutional change, and the creation of entrepreneurial opportunity in the U.S. electric power industry. *Research Policy* **32**(2): 185–207.

Singer D, Willett JB. 2003. *Applied Longitudinal Data Analysis: Modeling Change and Event Occurrence*. Oxford University Press: New York.

Singh JV. 1986. Performance, slack, and risk taking in organizational decision making. *Academy of Management Journal* **29**(3): 562–585.

Sørensen JB. 1999. Stpiece: Stata module to estimate piecewise-constant rate hazard models. Unpublished ado-file. University of Chicago, Graduate School of Business: Chicago, IL.

Sorenson O, Stuart TE. 2001. Syndication networks and the spatial distribution of venture capital investments. *American Journal of Sociology* **106**(6): 1546–1588.

Stevenson HH, Jarillo JC. 1990. A paradigm of entrepreneurship: entrepreneurial management. *Strategic Management Journal*, Summer Special Issue **11**: 17–27.

Stinchcombe A. 1965. Social structure and organizations. In *Handbook of Organizations*, March JG (ed). Rand McNally: Chicago, IL; 153–193.

Swaminathan A. 1996. Environmental conditions at founding and organizational mortality: a trial-by-fire model. *Academy of Management Journal* **39**(5): 1350–1377.

Tan J, Peng MW. 2003. Organizational slack and firm performance during economic transitions: two studies from an emerging economy. *Strategic Management Journal* **24**(13): 1249–1263.

Thompson J. 1967. *Organizations in Action*. McGraw-Hill: New York.

Tuma NB. 1980. *Invoking RATE*. SRI International: Menlo Park, CA.

Tushman ML, Anderson P. 1986. Technological discontinuities and organizational environments. *Administrative Science Quarterly* **31**(3): 439–465.

Venkataraman S, Van de Ven AH. 1998. Hostile environmental jolts, transaction set, and new business. *Journal of Business Venturing* **13**(3): 231–255.

Yasai-Ardekani M. 1986. Structural adaptations to environments. *Academy of Management Review* **11**(1): 9–21.

Zahra SA. 1996. Technology strategy and new venture performance: a study of corporate-sponsored and independent biotechnology ventures. *Journal of Business Venturing* **11**(4): 289–321.

Zeitz G. 1980. Interorganizational dialectics. *Administrative Science Quarterly* **25**(1): 72–88.

[14]

© *Academy of Management Review*
1994, Vol. 19, No. 4, 645–670.

FOOLS RUSH IN?
THE INSTITUTIONAL CONTEXT OF
INDUSTRY CREATION

HOWARD E. ALDRICH
University of North Carolina
C. MARLENE FIOL
University of Colorado at Denver

New organizations are always vulnerable to the liabilities of newness, but such pressures are especially severe when an industry is in its formative years. We focus on one set of constraints facing entrepreneurs in emerging industries—their relative lack of cognitive and sociopolitical legitimacy. We examine the strategies that founders can pursue, suggesting how their successful pursuit of legitimacy may evolve from innovative ventures to broader contexts, collectively reshaping industry and institutional environments.

Founding a new venture is risky business under any conditions, but especially so when entrepreneurs have few precedents for the kinds of activities they want to found. Early ventures in the formative years of a new industry face a different set of challenges than those that simply carry on a tradition pioneered by thousands of predecessors in the same industry. Such foundings are risky, but are they also foolish? From an institutional and ecological perspective, founders of new ventures appear to be fools, for they are navigating, at best, in an institutional vacuum of indifferent munificence and, at worst, in a hostile environment impervious to individual action. In addition to the normal pressures facing any new organizations, they also must carve out a new market, raise capital from skeptical sources, recruit untrained employees, and cope with other difficulties stemming from their nascent status.

Among the many problems facing innovating entrepreneurs, their relative lack of legitimacy is especially critical, as both entrepreneurs and crucial stakeholders may not fully understand the nature of the new ventures, and their conformity to established institutional rules may still be in question. We capture these problems by using the term *legitimacy* in two related senses: (a) how taken for granted a new form is and (b) the

Critical comments and ideas came from all quarters, including Joel Baum, Jack Brittain, Neil Churchill, Moshe Farjoun, William Gartner, Heather Haveman, Christabel LaMotte, Ingrid Rasch, Elaine Romanelli, Jitendra Singh, Andrew H. Van de Ven, and David Whetten. Deborah Tilley shaped this manuscript into its final form.

extent to which a new form conforms to recognized principles or accepted rules and standards. The first form of legitimacy is labeled *cognitive*, and the second, *sociopolitical*.

In this article, we examine the social processes surrounding the emergence of new industries, from the early pioneering ventures through the early stages of growth, when the form proliferates as the industry becomes established. Legitimacy is not the only factor influencing whether an industry successfully moves beyond the stage of a few pioneers to fully realized growth. Clearly, many other factors are important to a new industry's success, such as the state of the economy, latent demand for the product or service, competitive pressures from related industries, and the skills of new venture owners and workers. Because only a few theorists have examined failed industries (e.g., Astley, 1985), and we have no systematic research in this area, our article is necessarily speculative. However, we believe that legitimacy is a more important issue than previously recognized, and so we focus our arguments and propositions on factors affecting an industry's legitimacy and on legitimating strategies pursued by innovating entrepreneurs.

Our aim is to identify factors hindering and supporting the progression from the founding of a completely new activity, in an institutional void, through its development as a legitimate industry. Our focus is on the development of independent new ventures that are not sheltered by sponsoring organizations. By definition, such ventures cannot rely on existing institutions to provide external legitimacy. Throughout the article, we refer to *new activities* as specific product/process innovations, one aspect of what ecologists refer to generally as new organizational forms; *new ventures* are independent organizations initiating the new activity; and *industries* are groups of organizations with similar products/processes.

Background

This paper extends current theories linking organizational legitimacy and industry creation. Ecological theorists have provided empirical evidence of lower founding and higher disbanding rates when industries are small (Hannan & Freeman, 1989). Borrowing from institutional theory (Meyer & Rowan, 1977; Scott & Meyer, 1983), they have argued that this pattern exists because firms initially lack external legitimacy due to their small numbers. Their strongest arguments have been based on findings from organizational populations with chronic problems of sociopolitical opposition and repression (e.g., labor unions and newspapers) (Delacroix & Rao, 1993). In the 1990s, they have begun to address legitimacy issues stemming from a lack of knowledge and understanding (Hannan & Carroll, 1992).

Theorists using economic models have challenged ecologists' legitimacy arguments, asserting that industry entry and exit patterns are the result of competition and industry consolidation (Delacroix, Swaminathan, & Solt, 1989). The focus of economic theories of industry creation has been on the risks and economic trade-offs that characterize new industry entry decisions (Klepper & Graddy, 1990; Winter, 1984), and they have given little weight to the social context within which those decisions are embedded. Klepper and Graddy's study, however, provided findings that strongly suggest the influence of other than purely economic-technical considerations in the growth of an industry. They found that some industries went from origin to stability (defined as the year when the number of firms reached a peak and remained more or less the same for a few years) in only two years, whereas others took more than 50 years. The average was 29 years, and the standard deviation was 15, indicating that there is an enormous range of variation in the time required for industries to become established. Some fraction of this time reflects the early founders' struggles in developing cognitive and sociopolitical legitimacy.

We begin by defining and describing the two forms of legitimacy. We note that there are many constraints facing innovating entrepreneurs. Framing the problem in this way portrays founders as confronting a seemingly insuperable obstacle course in their struggle for legitimation. We then reframe the problem, using an institutional framework to specify a set of conditions that calls for particular strategies on the part of founding entrepreneurs. Reframing the issue in this way highlights founders' opportunities for overcoming existing legitimacy barriers and establishing a new set of norms, paving the way for an emerging industry to grow. We emphasize the cumulative way in which entrepreneurial activity plays a role in reshaping the larger environmental context by beginning with the individual venture and working our way up the hierarchy.

Entrepreneurs and Legitimacy Constraints

New industries emerge when entrepreneurs succeed in mobilizing resources in response to perceived opportunities. Identifying opportunities, assembling resources, and recruiting and training employees are challenges facing all entrepreneurs, and all of these activities require the cooperation and strategic interaction of individuals and groups. However, founders of entirely new activities, by definition, lack the familiarity and credibility that constitute the fundamental basis of interaction. Many of the other constraints on a new industry's growth are thus magnified. Access to capital, markets, and governmental protection are all partially dependent on the level of legitimacy achieved by an emerging industry.

In the original formulation of the argument linking industries and legitimacy, Hannan (1986) identified increasing numbers of organizations as the primary force raising the legitimacy of a population. The empirical puzzle that Hannan grappled with is a pattern, in a population's growth, of low founding rates and high disbanding rates in its early years, followed by a gradual increase in founding rates and a decrease in disbanding rates. What contextual factors discourage potential founders and undermine the survival of many organizations that are founded?

Subsequent answers to this question have become more theoretically subtle and historically sophisticated (Hannan & Carroll, 1992; Ranger-Moore, Banaszak-Holl, & Hannan, 1991), but they still follow Hannan's early identification of industry size—net of other conditions—as a crucial condition.

When the number of organizations in a new industry is small, new organizations are thought to have a lower chance of survival because they must learn new roles without having role models, and they must establish ties with an environment that does not understand or acknowledge their existence (Hannan & Carroll, 1992; Stinchcombe, 1965). As an industry grows, increasing numbers of organizations raise its legitimacy along two dimensions: cognitive, or knowledge about the new activity and what is needed to succeed in an industry, and sociopolitical, or the value placed on an activity by cultural norms and political authorities (Ranger-Moore et al., 1991).

Cognitive legitimation refers to the spread of knowledge about a new venture. Hannan and Freeman (1986: 63) noted that when an activity becomes so familiar and well known that it is taken for granted, time and other organizing resources are conserved, "attempts at creating copies of legitimated forms are common, and the success rate of such attempts is high." One can assess cognitive legitimation by measuring the level of public knowledge about a new activity. The highest form of cognitive legitimation is achieved when a new product, process, or service is taken for granted. An example is the diffusion of knowledge about personal computers—how to use them and how to manufacture them—in the 1970s and 1980s that facilitated the spread of PC use in homes and schools and that helped spawn many start-ups. From a producer's point of view, cognitive legitimation means that new entrants to an industry are likely to copy an existing organizational form, rather than experiment with a new one. From a consumer's point of view, cognitive legitimation means that people are knowledgeable users of the product or service.

Sociopolitical legitimation refers to the process by which key stakeholders, the general public, key opinion leaders, or government officials accept a venture as appropriate and right, given existing norms and laws. One can measure sociopolitical legitimation by assessing public acceptance of an industry, government subsidies to the industry, or the public prestige of its leaders. An often-cited example is the passage of the Wagner Act in 1935, which gave special status under federal law to unions following the form specified in the Act (Hannan & Freeman, 1986). For U.S. unions, government approval was a symbol of a long struggle for legitimacy, waged first by craft and then industrial unions.

Studies of organizational legitimacy have focused primarily on the impact of controversial activities on a firm's ability to acquire and maintain sociopolitical approval (Elsbach & Sutton, 1993; Hannan & Carroll, 1992; Meyer & Rowan, 1977). However, this aspect of legitimacy may not be the most relevant to the legitimacy issues facing founders of entirely new activities. As Delacroix and colleagues (1989: 247) noted, there is a "diffuse belief that profit-seeking activities are valid, unless otherwise specified." Though it may be legally validated in the form of a legal charter, an entirely new activity begins, by definition, with low cognitive legitimacy. Without widespread knowledge and understanding of their activity, entrepreneurs may have difficulty maintaining the support of key constituencies.

SOCIAL CONTEXT AS OPPORTUNITY

Social contexts present entrepreneurs with many constraints, yet they also set the conditions that create windows of opportunity. Through processes of social construction, entrepreneurs can develop new meanings that may eventually alter institutional norms. Our arguments follow institutional constructionists, who emphasize how people in organizations act to produce and reproduce their environments (DiMaggio & Powell, 1983; Zucker, 1986). Social contexts, from this perspective, represent not only patterns of established meaning, but also sites within which renegotiations of meaning take place. Founding entrepreneurs of innovative ventures—the first stage in creating new industries—are initiators in this process of renegotiation. Table 1 proposes four levels of social context as progressively broadened sites within which founding entrepreneurs build trust, reliability, reputation, and, finally, institutional legitimacy.

We focus first on dynamics at the organizational level, and then we suggest how the progressive building of trust and reliability may work its way up the hierarchy, collectively reshaping industry and institutional

TABLE 1
Entrepreneurial Strategies to Promote New Industry Development

Level of Analysis	Type of Legitimacy	
	Cognitive	Sociopolitical
Organizational	Develop knowledge base via symbolic language and behaviors	Develop trust in the new activity by maintaining internally consistent stories
Intraindustry	Develop knowledge base by encouraging convergence around a dominant design	Develop perceptions of reliability by mobilizing to take collective action
Interindustry	Develop knowledge base by promoting activity through third-party actors	Develop reputation of a new activity as a reality by negotiating and compromising with other industries
Institutional	Develop knowledge base by creating linkages with established educational curricula	Develop legitimacy by organizing collective marketing and lobbying efforts

environments. A series of propositions summarizes our discussion of possible strategies for gaining legitimacy at each level of the hierarchy.

Entrepreneurs and Trust-Building Opportunities

What is trust? Early definitions refer to "assured reliance on the character, ability, strength, or truth of someone or something" (*Webster's New Collegiate Dictionary*, 1981: 1246). Later variants stress that trust is a belief, in the absence of any evidence, that things will "work out" (Gambetta, 1988; Gartner & Low, 1990). The role of trust is central to all social transactions (ranging from marriage to international affairs) where there is ignorance or uncertainty about actions and outcomes. Despite its pervasiveness, it is most often taken for granted as a background condition or "a sort of ever-ready lubricant that permits voluntary participation in production and exchange" (Dasgupta, 1988: 49).

Trust, reliability, and reputation are methods of attaining cooperation based on increasing familiarity and evidence (Bateson, 1988). Thus, the less information or evidence we have, the more we need to trust. As information accumulates and evidence mounts, we can increasingly rely on patterns of reliability and reputation. Trust is a critical first-level determinant of the success of founding entrepreneurs because, by definition, there is an absence of information and evidence regarding their new activity. Gartner and Low (1990: 18) argued that the concept of trust "provides a link between factors influencing organization formation at the individual level to factors influencing formation at the organizational and environmental levels." Specifically, they believed that the social process of gaining legitimacy is shaped by the interpersonal processes of achieving trust in the organizing process.

Entrepreneurs in a new industry face rather different conditions than those operating in the relative security of simply reproducing old activities. With their industry having achieved cognitive and sociopolitical legitimacy, most entrepreneurs in recognized industries do not have to build trust within a vacuum. In contrast, founders of ventures in new industries, without the advantages of a taken-for-granted activity and without widespread sociopolitical approval, must first call upon whatever personal and interpersonal resources they possess. They must interact with extremely skeptical customers, creditors, suppliers, and other resource holders, who are afraid of being taken for fools. With no external evidence, why should potential trusting parties "trust" an entrepreneur's claims that a relationship "will work out," given that an entrepreneur may be no more than an ill-fated fool?

Organizational Strategies

Entrepreneurs need strategies for encouraging a trusting party's beliefs in the shared expectations, reasonable efforts, and competence of the aspiring entrepreneur. Given the absence of information and prior behavior concerning a venture in a new industry, pioneering founders cannot base initial trust-building strategies on objective external evidence. Instead, they must concentrate on framing the unknown in such a way that it becomes believable. An "entrepreneur must engineer consent, using powers of persuasion and influence to overcome the skepticism and resistance of guardians of the status quo" (Dees & Starr, 1992: 96).

Cognitive legitimacy. Without clear guidelines for assessing performance in an emerging industry, a new venture's stakeholders find it difficult to consistently weigh risk/reward trade-offs. Founders cannot easily convince others to follow their directives, as they have no tangible evidence that such actions will pay off. In established industries, founders can simply cite tradition to their employees and other stakeholders as a justification for particular actions. No such appeal is available to founders in new industries.

Perceptions and evaluations of risk are highly subjective. The framing of an issue, rather than its actual content, often determines whether it is seen as a "foolish risk," especially in the absence of objective standards (Tversky & Kahneman, 1981). Brophy (1992: 396) noted that "new ventures by definition have no history and often provide an inadequate basis for making accurate predictions. 'Gut feel' and the netting of a lot of variables and complex relationships play vital roles in new venture financing decisions." When external tests of reliability are unavailable, cooperation is possible if issues are "simplified, stylized, symbolized, and given ritual expression: if, that is, they are coded in convention" (Hawthorn, 1988: 114). Founders who can behave "as if" the activity were a reality—producing and directing great theater, as it were—may convince others of the tangible reality of the new activity.

Research has documented the powerful psychological effects of issue framing (e.g., Link, 1987). Issue frames are important not only because of their psychological consequences, but also because of their value as legitimating and motivating symbols. In a study of the process by which charismatic leaders transform the beliefs of their followers, Fiol, Harris, and House (1992) stressed the importance of symbolic communication. Based on the results of their study, they concluded that charismatic leaders employ a number of specific rhetorical techniques to change social norms. First, charismatic leaders appeal to a common bond with followers, even when breaking established values, so as to appear trustworthy and credible to society. They do this through the frequent use of inclusive referents such as "we" and "us," as opposed to "I" and "you." Second, charismatic leaders frame issues using high levels of abstraction, thus fostering a degree of ambiguity around their innovative ideas. Howell and Higgins (1990: 336) similarly wrote of technology champions "appealing to larger principles or unassailable values about the potential of the innovation for fulfilling an organization's dream of what it can be." If entrepreneurs frame their innovation broadly enough to encompass existing knowledge, they will appear more credible.

Proposition 1: Founders who utilize encompassing symbolic language and behaviors will gain cognitive legitimacy more quickly than others.

Sociopolitical approval. Innovative founders also face the hurdle of winning the approval of organizational stakeholders for their activities. With institutional support precarious, with other industries mounting attacks on the new industry, and with other ventures within the industry battling over what direction the industry will take, stakeholders within an organization are understandably shy about giving their wholehearted commitment to an entrepreneur. On what basis should they trust the entrepreneur? To the extent that elementary claims of efficacy by innovative entrepreneurs are difficult to verify, because cognitive legitimacy is absent, stakeholders are likely to resist their escalating resource demands.

Founding entrepreneurs must build a knowledge base that outsiders will accept as valid, and yet they have no external source of validation from which to argue. Given the lack of externally validated arguments, they must draw on alternative forms of communication, such as narratives, to make a case that their ventures are compatible with more widely established sets of activities. Rational argument is based on inferential moves and deliberation; narration works by suggestion and identification. Both express reasons to believe.

Philosophers of science have often noted the unique ability of stories to explain events without explicit reference to external criteria (Nagel, 1961). Kaplan (1986) observed that stories provide a way to explain something without having to agree on explicit criteria; subsequently, stories can form the currency of communications to a wider public. "A political leader creates a story that helps persons structure their experience. He draws from their stories to make his more perfect, more encompassing, more capable of attracting a wider following and gaining greater allegiance" (Krieger, 1981: 75).

The validity of a story relies not on a set of external criteria, but on how well the story coheres and is free of contradictions (Fisher, 1985). A founding entrepreneur's "truth" may well contradict the "truth" people know. Stories can bridge the gap, by affirming the former without negating the latter. Based on their study of champions of technological innovations, Howell and Higgins (1990: 336) concluded that "the fundamental components of a champion's capacity to introduce innovations successfully are the articulation of a compelling vision of the innovation's potential for the organization, the expression of confidence in others to participate effectively in the initiative, and the display of innovative actions to achieve goals."

Entrepreneurs need to disguise the truly radical nature of their new activity and the challenge it may pose to established organizations, while simultaneously making a case that they are different enough to hold a comparative advantage. Later, as the emergent industry attains some stability, founders can look back and tell new stories about the "radical pioneers" in the early days of the industry's history.

> *Proposition 2: Founders who communicate internally consistent stories regarding their new activity will gain sociopolitical approval more quickly than others.*

Intraindustry Strategies

Intraindustry processes constrain the legitimacy of new industries by structuring the immediate environment within which new organizations operate. A lack of standard designs, for example, may block the diffusion of knowledge and understanding, thus constraining the new activities. Once founding entrepreneurs have developed a basis of understanding and trust at the level of their organizations, they must find strategies for establishing stable sequences of interaction with other organizations in their emerging industry.

Cognitive legitimacy. Intraindustry processes of competition and co-operation pose a challenge to new founders, not only because they must convince skeptics of their organization's staying power, but also because they must fend off organizations offering slightly different versions of their products/services, creating confusion in the minds of interested observers (Carroll, Preisendoerfer, Swaminathan, & Wiedenmayer, 1989). Founding entrepreneurs have no ready-made formula for persuading others that they have it right. As Delacroix and Rao (1993) pointed out, organizations founded later in an industry's life cycle benefit by vicariously learning from early successful foundings. The earliest founders have no such advantage.

Early on, founders of potential alternatives implicitly compete for the right to be taken for granted, appealing to potential customers, investors, and others to accept their version. Organizations attempting to copy a new activity, while starting up, are in a difficult position because poorly understood activities are only imperfectly imitable (Barney, 1986; Reed & DeFillippi, 1990). Much of the knowledge of a new industry is only implicit, held by the founders and their employees in uncodified form. Such knowledge is often complex, making it hard for others to identify causal relations (Nelson & Winter, 1982). Finally, knowledge is often bound up in assets that are very specific to a particular organization, creating relationships that are hard for others to duplicate. Thus, until cognitive legitimacy coalesces around a reduced set of accepted standards or designs, pioneering entrepreneurs assembling resources for their organizations will inevitably make frequent mistakes. Foundings will be inhibited and disbandings will be frequent.

The lack of convergence on a dominant design in new industries constrains the perceived reliability of founding firms by increasing confusion about what standards should be followed. Convergence toward an accepted design is facilitated if new ventures choose to imitate pioneers, rather than seek further innovation. Implicit agreement on a dominant design, common standards, and the interfirm movement of personnel made possible by conditions of imitability increase the level of shared competencies within an emerging industry. Imitation and borrowing from early foundings eventually spread knowledge of new activities beyond their point of origin and contribute to convergence on a dominant design (Anderson & Tushman, 1990). Imperfect imitability is thus reduced and disbanding rates drop as effective knowledge is more widely diffused. Of course, some organizations may gain more than others as an industry's legitimacy is strengthened, as Rao (1993) found in his study of the early years of the American automobile industry. As the auto industry struggled for acceptance, firms that won victories in reliability and speed competitions organized by third parties were more likely to survive than those that did not win.

A new venture's ability to imitate others depends on whether what is being copied is protected by legal instruments—patents, copyrights, and trade secrets—and on whether the innovation is codified (Teece, 1987). If an innovation cannot be legally protected, and it involves a product or process whose nature is transparently obvious to outsiders, others may freely copy the innovation. By contrast, if the innovation can be protected and its nature is difficult to understand, except through learning by doing, the innovation is unlikely to be imitated by others (Dosi, 1988). Discord over a dominant design is exacerbated under these conditions.

Industries with imitable innovations are more likely than others to generate collective action. As founders with imitable products or services realize their innovations are leaking to competitors and potential new entrants, they gain a strong incentive to cooperate on stabilizing conditions in the industry. By contrast, firm-centered actions are likely to increase under conditions of inimitability, as founders are able to protect their core competencies from being widely diffused. Fiercely competitive individual strategies hamper a united collective front by an industry.

Initial collaborations begin informally, in networks of interfirm relations, but some later develop into more formalized strategic alliances, consortia, and trade associations (Powell, 1990). Van de Ven and Garud (1991) noted that those who conducted studies of high-technology industries, such as the cochlear implant industry, have found that new-to-the-world innovations tend to be pursued by a handful of parallel, independent actors who come to know one another rapidly through personal interaction and through traveling in similar social/technical circles, such as attending the same industry conferences and technical committee meetings. This small handful of actors can generate networks that, in the aggregate, result in institutional-legitimating events. If founders can overcome the barriers to effective collective action, they can rise above the level of their individual ventures and run together "in packs" (Van de Ven, 1991).

Imitability's effects appear paradoxical unless we pay careful attention to different levels of analysis. For an industry, easier imitability means growth, because entry is facilitated, and an expanding market may mean that proportionately more entrants survive. For individual ventures, however, easier imitability makes survival more problematic, because their market becomes crowded with equally competent rivals, and survival becomes contingent on fairly small differences between ventures. One common pattern is that new entrants survive at the expense of early entrants who cannot learn fast enough to keep up. The net effect of imitability is contingent on where an industry is in its life cycle, as it will depend on the relative balance between underlying growth in a market, new entries, and exits from the industry.

> *Proposition 3: Industries in which founders encourage convergence around a dominant product/service design will gain cognitive legitimacy more quickly than others.*

Sociopolitical approval. Collective action is extremely difficult to organize early in the life of an industry due to free rider problems (Moe, 1980; Olson, 1965). To the extent that mistakes are frequent and a consistent body of knowledge emerges very slowly, and thus collective action is impeded, sociopolitical approval may be jeopardized.

Several conditions quite common to new industries impede the collective action needed to gain sociopolitical approval. First, intense competition over designs and standards may prevent any particular firm from growing much faster than the rest of the industry, thus reducing the chances that an industry champion will emerge to energize efforts toward collective action. Second, if competing designs emerge and subgroups form around them, conflict among the subgroups may cause confusion and uncertainty for potential stakeholders. Dissension and diversity within an industry may thus be mirrored by a similar pattern externally, hampering an industry champion's ability to form coalitions promoting the total industry (Bolton, 1993). For example, the nascent pay-per-call information-services industry (using 900-prefix phone numbers) was growing rapidly until it ran into political problems in the early 1990s because it lacked uniform standards and consistent government regulations. U.S. Sprint decided to stop carrying most pay-per-call services because of consumer complaints and difficulties in collecting from customers who disputed their bills. The industry was fortunate to have a trade association, the Information Industry Association, that was able to lobby for uniform federal regulations, although whether the industry will survive in its early form is still uncertain (Andrews, 1992).

The importance of finding avenues to collaborative action within an industry is well illustrated by the history of a new industry in Asia: American universities operating in Japan. In the 1980s, many American universities rushed to set up branch campuses in Japan, as Japanese educators welcomed them as models for educational reform of the Japanese system (Regur, 1992). By the early 1990s, the disbanding of some branches and well-publicized problems in others had eroded Japanese confidence in American university branches, and the industry's future was in doubt.

In response, in 1991, 20 of the strongest programs formed the Association of American Colleges and Universities in Japan, setting standards for quality and reliability for American programs in Japan. The new association markedly improved the image and reputation of such programs, and Japanese local governments have renewed their interest in helping sponsor these ventures.

Funeral home owners' successes in controlling state regulation of the industry kept the founding rates of technically superior alternatives very low (Torres, 1988), almost totally suppressing the emergence of competing industries. For almost a century, locally owned funeral homes in the United States blocked alternatives to traditional means of disposal of the dead, opposing crematoriums, burial societies, and chain-owned funeral homes. Locally owned homes, which controlled most state boards regulating the industry, imposed requirements that were intended to exclude alternative forms, such as prohibiting corporate ownership, requiring that all establishments be fully equipped, prohibiting establishments from sharing equipment, and requiring that all establishments employ a full-time embalmer.

In Europe, small retail shops resisted the growth of large shops located in suburban areas (called hypermarkets) by arguing that the long hours and weekend operations of such businesses threatened traditional values by disrupting family life. "Blue laws" in the United States have been used by small shops for the same ends.

> *Proposition 4: Industries in which founders mobilize to take collective action will gain sociopolitical approval more quickly than others.*

Interindustry Strategies

Interindustry processes—the nature of relations between industries, whether competing or cooperating—affect the distribution of resources in the environment and the terms on which they are available to entrepreneurs. Established industries that feel threatened are sometimes able to change the terms on which resources are available to emerging industries, either by questioning their efficacy or their conformity to the established order. Even after a new industry develops into a recognized entity, other industries may withhold recognition or acceptance of it. If a critical mass of founders unites and builds the reputation of their new industry as a visible and taken-for-granted entrant into the larger community, gaining sociopolitical approval is more likely.

Cognitive legitimacy. Established industries that feel threatened by a newcomer may undermine a new venture's cognitive legitimacy through rumors and information suppression or inaccurate dissemination. Though sometimes a low level of cognitive legitimacy may be an advantage for a new venture (when the activity is not taken as a serious threat), it is a detriment when older, competing firms spread rumors that a product or technology is unsafe, costly, or of inferior quality. For example, early mail- and phone-order computer supply stores in the United States were highly specialized, selling mainly to people very knowledgeable about electronics who were building or modifying their own equipment. When the industry began to grow rapidly in the 1980s, selling to "amateurs," traditional walk-in stores argued that such operators did not provide after-sales service and, thus, were an inferior form. Similarly, HMOs confronted bitter opposition from traditional physician practices, and they grew slowly until other organizations intervened on their behalf (e.g., large insurance companies) (Aldrich, 1989; Wholey, Christianson, & Sanchez, 1990). Traditional physicians argued that HMOs violated customary expectations about effective physician-patient relationships and, thus, delivered inferior services to patients. In the United States, high-technology firms, such as medical-equipment manufacturers, tried to use cognitive legitimacy arguments as a weapon against small, independent firms that wanted to service the machines the manufacturers sell to customers, such as clinics and hospitals (Naj, 1991). The manufacturers, such as Eastman Kodak, argued that third-party service technicians could not legitimately service their machines because they lacked the manufacturer's training and diagnostic service equipment. Had they been successful, they would have suppressed the growth of the independent repair industry, but the courts did not accept their claims.

Founders must build a reputation of the new industry as a reality, as something that naturally should be taken for granted by others. A new vocabulary must be coined, new labels manufactured, and beliefs engendered in an industry with no natural history. Although formulated in the context of examining behaviors and meanings within organizations, Fiol's (1991) proposition that identities link an organization's culture (consisting of unarticulated underlying beliefs and values) with the behaviors of its members, illuminates the task facing new founders. The actors who are the targets of entrepreneurs' legitimizing strategies (suppliers, distributors, bankers, and so forth) attempt to make sense of entrepreneurs' behaviors by drawing on current understanding of what they observe. This meaning-making process is mediated by what people perceive as the identities of the founders: gamblers, serious business leaders, cowboy entrepreneurs, high achievers, wild-eyed inventors, water-walkers, and so forth. Any of these labels is potentially applicable, but their meanings differ drastically.

Entrepreneurs can take advantage of the inherent ambiguity in interpreting new behaviors by skillfully framing and editing their behaviors and intentions vis-à-vis the trusting parties. They need to emphasize those aspects of their ventures and their own backgrounds that evoke identities that others will understand as risk oriented but responsible. Founders must do this work for their individual ventures as they negotiate with other firms, but a more powerful image can be invoked when founders work through interfirm associations.

Trade associations are "minimalist organizations"—they can be operated via low overhead and quickly adapted to changing conditions—and, thus, are easier to found than, for example, production organizations (Halliday, Powell, & Granfors, 1987). Many trade associations, following the example of state bar and other voluntary associations, operate out of the offices of member firms in their early years. Others are administered by law firms that represent some of the larger firms in the industry. Thus, the catalyst to an association's founding is often an industry champion who steps forward and volunteers to cover the costs of running the association as it recruits enough members to gain a stable dues base. Typically, the largest firms in an industry do this, and they are well represented on the association's board of directors.

Interfirm linkages such as trade associations play a critical role in helping entrepreneurs promote an industry's cognitive legitimacy (Aldrich & Staber, 1988). They help firms formulate product/process standards through trade committees, trade journals, marketing campaigns (to enhance the industry's standing), and trade fairs (where customers and suppliers can gain a sense of the industry's stability). Trade associations represent the industry to government agencies, and they play a critical role in times of crisis (when an industry's public image may be threatened).

> Proposition 5: *Industries in which founding firms promote their new activity through third-party actors will gain cognitive legitimacy more quickly than others.*

Sociopolitical approval. Insufficient cognitive legitimacy renders a new industry vulnerable to interindustry processes that may jeopardize its normative acceptance. Established organizations in related industries often strongly oppose the rise of new ventures seeking to exploit similar resources, and they may try to block these new ventures at every turn, including questioning their compatibility with existing norms and values. Established organizations usually do not challenge entrepreneurs' generic rights to create business organizations (such rights are assured in most Western political democracies), but rather they resist the creation of ventures that threaten the markets of established industries. In addition to questioning the knowledge base of a new industry, established industries may effectively oppose a newcomer by inducing legal and regulatory barriers.

The emergence and growth of new industries is thus partly dependent on the severity of attacks from established industries that may resist encroachment. They may raise doubts about the new activity's efficacy or its conformity with societal norms and values and, thus, change the terms on which resources are available to emerging industries. Beyond recognition, new industries need reliable relationships with other, established industries. Once cognitive legitimacy is achieved, tacit approval in the form of economic transactions is more likely. Some forms of interindustry cooperation emerge as the unintended consequences of competing industries pursuing their self-interests, whereas other forms are more deliberate. For example, in his study of three forms of cooperatives in Atlantic Canada, Staber (1989) found that increases in the density of several forms of cooperatives improved the overall climate for cooperatives to such an extent that founding rates for other types were increased. The cooperatives not only provided direct support to each other, but also created a positive image of cooperative activity that raised the salience of norms of cooperation in the region.

If a new industry faces overt conflict with an established industry, a trade association or an industry council is probably required to mobilize the newcomer's strength. However, many interindustry relations are more matters of education and negotiation than of zero-sum conflict. For example, new biomedical and health-care industries only survive if they can convince third parties (insurance companies and the government) to pay the costs that patients cannot bear, such as CAT scans or cochlear implants. Thus, firms in the industry must cooperate to educate and influence these third parties to include the product or service in their payment reimbursement systems (Van de Ven, 1991).

The paradox of individual versus collective benefits is again apparent: pioneering ventures that solicit or accept cooperative relations with established industries may succeed to such an extent that followers (so-called "second movers") enter the fledgling industry with lower costs and thus drive the pioneers out of business (Jovanovic, 1982). Osborne Computer, for example, was a pioneer in bundling other manufacturers' software with its products, but did not survive some costly marketing blunders that gave other firms a chance to surpass it. At the industry level, however, such cooperation often is essential for survival.

> Proposition 6: *Industries in which founding firms negotiate and compromise with other industries will gain sociopolitical approval more quickly than others.*

Institutional Strategies

Institutional conditions may constrain the rate at which an industry grows by affecting the diffusion of knowledge about a new activity and the extent to which it is publicly or officially tolerated. If founders have pursued effective trust-building and reliability-enhancing strategies within their emerging industry, and have established a reputation vis-à-vis other industries, the groundwork has been laid for attaining legitimacy at the institutional level. At this level, founders are no longer working as isolated individuals. Instead, industry councils, cooperative alliances, trade associations, and other vehicles for collective action are in place to achieve institutional legitimacy.

Cognitive legitimacy. Established industries enjoy an enormous benefit via the institutionalized diffusion of knowledge about their activities.

The "social space" (Delacroix & Rao, 1993) an industry has achieved in a society is sustained, in part, by a widespread understanding of how it fits into the community. At the beginning, organizations in the new industry are too rare to create the critical mass needed to begin raising the new industry's level of cognitive legitimacy. Reporters, newspaper and magazine editors, and other mass media gatekeepers are unfamiliar with the set of terms for describing the activity, and their depictions may be inaccurate. Thus, potential entrepreneurs (i.e., early followers) may be seriously misled if they rely on such reports, and mistakes in imitating the new activity will be common (Phillips, 1960).

The lack of general understanding of the new industry also makes it difficult to recruit and retain employees. People wonder what will happen to their careers if they join a persuasive entrepreneur in building a totally new organizational venture. Because new ventures tend to be specialized, the skills they require may not be easily transferable to other organizations that are searching for people with recognizable talents.

Educational institutions create and help spread information about the competencies these organizations need. Educational institutions, especially vocationally and professionally oriented ones, base their training on curricular materials prepared by mass market–oriented publishing houses. Without an accepted vocabulary or conceptual framework, writers and editors face serious difficulties in devising manuals and textbooks. Because such programs are backward-looking, training people in skills for which curricular material has already been prepared, founders cannot rely on existing programs to train their employees (Romanelli, 1989).

A new industry must either build on the competencies already supported or find ways to encourage the provision of new ones. In technology-based industries, the basic research on which firms draw often has been generated in university laboratories a decade or more before it was commercialized (Link & Bauer, 1989). For example, the basic ideas for cochlear implant devices were developed in the late 1950s and early 1960s, almost two decades before the ideas were fully commercialized. Thus, firms such as Nucleus and 3M had an already developed pool of scientific expertise from which they could draw consultants and employees (Van de Ven & Garud, 1991).

In the United States, new firms regularly establish partnerships with community and technical colleges, often at the request of local economic development agencies that are hopeful of the generation of new jobs. Because educational institutions are inherently conservative in their curriculum development, a new industry must achieve a fairly high degree of self-organization before curriculum materials will be written especially for them. Superconductor research was well underway in the United States before universities began putting science/industrial ceramics sequences into their applied sciences and engineering curricula. Shan, Singh, and Amburgey (1991: 82) noted that early in the history of the biotechnology industry in the United States, "there was only a limited supply of scientists with Ph.D.s and other specialized training so essential for an NBF [new biotechnology firm]." Eventually, as career prospects in the industry became known, more recruits were attracted, and the supply of scientists improved.

> *Proposition 7: Industries that create linkages with established educational curricula will gain cognitive legitimacy more quickly than others.*

Sociopolitical legitimacy. Lack of institutional support for the diffusion of knowledge about new industries also may undercut an industry's efforts to secure sociopolitical approval. Most forms of business enterprise have enjoyed at least institutional tolerance of their existence when they first emerged (Delacroix et al., 1989; Zucker, 1989), but this apparent easy success has blinded us to the occasions on which such support has not been forthcoming or has been lost. The first newspaper editor in the United States was jailed (Delacroix & Carroll, 1983), the life insurance industry was initially vilified as profaning the sacredness of life (Zelizer, 1978), and many forms of interbusiness alliances were ruled illegal in the 19th century (Staber & Aldrich, 1983).

Low sociopolitical legitimacy is still a critical barrier to many potential business activities today. For example, new schemes for burning or burying toxic waste often clash with U.S. communities' norms about local control over land-use decisions (Levine, 1982). A similar public controversy dogged attempts by chemical firms manufacturing fluoride to convince local community officials to purchase fluoridation systems for their public utilities (Coleman, 1957). In such cases, firms try to hire lobbyists with local connections and to form "citizens' groups" backing the proposed scheme.

New industries whose activities and long-term consequences are not well understood may have trouble in winning approval from cautious government agencies. In the 20th century, U.S. firms in the fledgling biotechnology industry, which based their technologies on manipulation of DNA, faced a major hurdle in winning FDA approval of their testing procedures. New industries whose production technologies may put workers at risk have to win approval from state and federal OSHA offices. Once an industry's activities are well understood, government regulatory agencies have shown considerable resistance to new industries whose activities challenge an older industry but which use unfamiliar or novel technologies. In the 1980s, the removal of federal regulations in many industries made us aware of how many new forms of organization were suppressed by implicit governmental strictures against their activities (e.g., cellular phones) (Haveman, 1990; Prentiss, 1984).

In the U.S. political system of divided executive and legislative branches, and with independent regulatory agencies, newly organized industries ultimately must co-opt, neutralize, form alliances with, and otherwise come to terms with, government agencies. The biotechnology industry developed in an environment of great uncertainty, because firms did not have a clear idea of what products would be regulated and what safety tests would be required by the Environmental Protection Agency, the Food and Drug Administration, and the Department of Agriculture. Accordingly, the Industrial Biotechnology Association lobbied the FDA, the EPA, and other agencies in an attempt to create a more certain regulatory environment. The first FDA ruling in 1981, approving the first diagnostic kit based on a monoclonal antibody, significantly raised the founding rate of biotech firms in the years that followed (Shan et al., 1991).

Biotechnology firms also appealed to the President's Council on Competitiveness to pressure federal agencies to weaken regulations perceived as hindering the growth of the biotech industry. In what we take as a sign that sociopolitical approval had finally been achieved at the highest levels of government, these efforts were rewarded in early 1992. President Bush issued a new government policy on biotechnology which said that genetically engineered products should not be assumed to be inherently dangerous and that regulations for biotechnology products should not receive greater scrutiny than products produced by conventional means (Fisher, 1992; Hilts, 1992).

The cochlear implant industry faced a similar problem as its products were brought forward for official scrutiny (Van de Ven & Garud, 1991). Contracts and grants from the National Institute of Health for basic cochlear implant research stimulated university-based research, and some discoveries were developed into potentially commercial products in the late 1970s and early 1980s. Five private firms initiated activities, but each had its own ideas about product standards, appropriate tests, and so forth. Conditions stabilized only when the FDA gained experience in testing the new technology and began systematically favoring certain kinds of evidence on product safety over others. Government agencies such as the FDA and EPA are important for any new industry whose products or services are costly, technically complex, and whose use may create an irreversible health or welfare condition for a user (Van de Ven, 1991).

Government agencies can play a role in structuring the interorganizational environment of new industries in ways that encourage trusting relations between firms. Rappa's (1987) study of the development of the gallium arsenide integrated circuit in the United States, Japan, and Western Europe found that more firms and scientists were involved in the United States, but in Japan there was greater coordination among the firms' and scientists' efforts. In Japan, MITI encouraged interfirm cooperation via industry and trade committees. The cooperating firms jointly formulated industrial governance policies, developed a competence pool of scientists and managers through training programs and informal information sharing, and also worked on commercial applications of the technology (see also Fransman, 1990). By contrast, U.S. firms stood on the sidelines and waited for an industry infrastructure to emerge on its own.

Proposition 8: Industries that organize collective market-
ing and lobbying efforts will gain sociopolitical ap-
proval more quickly than others.

The strategies for generating and sustaining trust, reliability, reputation, and finally, institutional legitimacy, are as interrelated as the
hierarchical contexts that spawn them. Gaining the trust of stakeholders
within and around the firm provides a basis from which to build a knowledge base via cooperative exchange rules with other similar organizations. Such interactions, in turn, make it easier for member firms to organize collectively and to build a broad reputation of their industry as an
enduring reality. An established reputation facilitates the co-optation of
institutional actors, ultimately leading to legitimacy.

Though we have emphasized the communicative aspects of trust
building at the organizational level, trust is the "lubricant" (Dasgupta,
1988: 49) that smoothes the way throughout the legitimacy-building process. As founders pursue legitimacy within successively broader social
sites, they must continually persuade without proof. Evidence of trustworthiness within one context does not automatically serve as evidence of
trustworthiness within a broader context. Fortunately for founders, trust
has the capacity to be self-fulfilling and self-reinforcing (Gambetta, 1988),
making it a powerful weapon against the vicious cycle of social barriers
to innovation.

DISCUSSION AND CONCLUSIONS

New organizations are always vulnerable to the liabilities of newness, but never more so than when entrepreneurs have few precedents for
their actions. The first organization of its kind faces a different set of
challenges than one which simply carries on a tradition pioneered by
many predecessors. Given the institutional, interindustry, intraindustry,
and organizational conditions facing pioneering founders, different strategies are called for than those used by imitators and borrowers. Such
foundings are risky, but they need not be foolish. We have highlighted the
conditions under which founders can pursue strategies that could culminate in an industry gaining legitimation at the institutional level. We
began with a discussion of the dynamics at the organizational level,
suggesting how the progressive building of trust may work its way up the
hierarchy, collectively reshaping the interindustry and institutional environments.

The period during which a new industry emerges deserves more theoretical attention, because the struggle to carve out a niche for a new
industry involves such strong forces that the events of that period may be
forever imprinted on the organizations that persist (Stinchcombe, 1965).
Indeed, the model of industry development implicit in Table 1 points
toward a new activity pattern that eventually is in harmony with its interorganizational and institutional environments. As a settled member of

the community, the new industry takes its place as a defender of the status quo.

Our examination of the early phases of an industry's life also implies that many promising new activities never realize their potential because founders fail to develop trusting relations with stakeholders, are unable to cope with opposing industries, and never win institutional support. Thus, understanding the strategies used by founders of new ventures helps us understand the forces contributing to industry variety in organizational communities.

Finally, the strategies that emerge from our reframing of ecological and institutional theories raise an important practical issue. Strategy theorists have long prescribed uniqueness and imperfect imitability as means of gaining a sustainable competitive advantage (Barney, 1986; Reed & DeFillippi, 1990). Our framework suggests that a single venture's uniqueness during initial stages of an industry's development must be counterbalanced with the collective efforts of all players in the emerging industry to portray the new activity as familiar and trustworthy, if they are to survive as a group.

Research Directions

Generating and sustaining trusting relationships are at the heart of overcoming low legitimacy. We have offered a number of propositions about effective strategies for achieving trust in the development of new industries. Researching these ideas will take us beyond the cross-sectional surveys that currently dominate methods of data collection in entrepreneurship research (Aldrich, 1992). The creation and institutionalization of new activities occurs through a dynamic process that cannot be captured in discrete snapshots. A number of additional research implications emerge from our study.

First, entrepreneurship researchers often attempt to distinguish between new businesses that copy well-known practices in their industry and businesses that are truly innovative, pioneering practices without precedent. However, such distinctions are almost always made within the context of an established industry, rather than calling attention to the possible origins of a new industry. Investigators thus conflate two very different events that pose very different problems for entrepreneurs: innovating within an institutionalized context versus striking out into uncharted waters, where industry boundaries are not yet secure. In the future, researchers of entrepreneurship need to separate these two forms of innovation.

Second, the debate in the ecological-institutional literature over "legitimacy" has focused, in part, on the issue of left-censoring of a population's history: Are data on the population available from its earliest days, when foundings were beginning to be observed? Left-censoring of data (i.e., not having the early years of an industry's history available) can lead to misspecification of models and biased conclusions regarding the pattern of population growth. However, such debates overlook a more serious form of selection bias: to the extent that researchers study only industries that survived long enough to make their mark upon the usual sources of archival information, they overlook the unsuccessful industries. Groups of firms that struggled and did not succeed in becoming institutionalized provide the best historical record for testing our ideas about the social context of industry formation. Indeed, only by comparing the strategies of terminated industries with those that completed their life cycles can we assess the relative importance of the forces we have identified in this article.

How can we avoid a bias against industries with truncated histories? Becoming aware of the issue is a good start. Just as evolutionary theorists have made us aware of the danger of focusing our research attention on cross-sectional studies of surviving organizations (Aldrich, 1979: 56–61), so too must we become aware of our tendency to focus on surviving industries. We must pay more attention to economic and business history, written not at the level of case studies of individual firms, but rather at the level of eras and epochs. Which activities have attracted entrepreneurs, speculators, investors, and others, only to lose out when support was not forthcoming from key stakeholders, other industries, and institutional forces? We have found that the business press is a good source of information on new activities that attract attention because they are challenging traditional industries, failing in spectacular fashion, or otherwise making short-run news.

Third, when a new industry's origin is identified, researchers must focus intensively on its early years. Ecologists have now collected information on fairly complete life histories for many populations, but only for such generic events as foundings and disbandings. In addition to these key events, researchers must also collect information on patterns of contact between the entrepreneurs who founded early ventures, and especially on any efforts they undertook to create vehicles for collective action. We also need information on how other groups of firms (possible competitors, regulatory agencies, local governments, etc.) responded to the first new ventures in a fledgling industry.

Fourth, a new industry's boundaries are ultimately determined by the balance it achieves between competition and cooperation vis-à-vis other groups of firms. Hannan and Freeman (1986) adopted the language of institutional theory in arguing that a population's boundaries are socially constructed. We have argued that whether a new population even finds a niche for itself in the community of populations is problematic. Research is needed on contacts at the boundary between industries: How are such contacts managed? Is there an implicit division of labor within new industries according to which founders negotiate boundaries? Have governments made this process easier or more difficult for new industries?

Fifth, within new industries, the key events affecting their emergence as stable entities involve the formation of other types of organizations

(Delacroix & Rao, 1993). These signs of an industry's success—industry councils, trade associations, joint university-industry research ventures—have been investigated, but they have not been linked to the life cycle of industries. By focusing on these independent markers of an industry's legitimacy, we can avoid the ambiguity inherent in trying to infer a social process from mere increases in the number of member organizations.

Finally, investigating these ideas will require expanding our disciplinary reach to take in anthropologists, political scientists, social psychologists, and others interested in understanding the genesis of contexts that give meaning to new behaviors. The social construction of organizational reality involved in building a new industry requires meaning making on a grand scale, and we suspect that those entrepreneurs who do it well are obsessed with the process. As such, they make fascinating subjects of study.

REFERENCES

Aldrich, H. E. 1979. *Organizations and environments.* Englewood Cliffs, NJ: Prentice Hall.

Aldrich, H. E. 1989. New paradigms for old: The population perspective's contribution to health services research. *Medical Care Review,* 44: 257–277.

Aldrich, H. E. 1992. Methods in our madness? Trends in entrepreneurship research. In D. L. Sexton & J. D. Kasarda (Eds.), *The state of the art of entrepreneurship:* 191–213. Boston: PWS-Kent.

Aldrich, H. E., & Staber, U. H. 1988. Organizing business interests: Patterns of trade association foundings, transformations, and deaths. In G. R. Carroll (Ed.), *Ecological models of organization:* 111–126. Cambridge, MA: Ballinger.

Anderson, P., & Tushman, M. 1990. Technological discontinuities and dominant designs: A cyclical model of technological change. *Administrative Science Quarterly,* 35: 604–633.

Andrews, E. L. 1992. House votes to put stricter rules on "900" pay-call phone services. *New York Times,* February 25: 1.

Astley, W. G. 1985. The two ecologies: Population and community perspectives on organizational evolution. *Administrative Science Quarterly,* 30: 245–273.

Barney, J. B. 1986. Types of competition and the theory of strategy: Toward an integrative framework. *Academy of Management Review,* 11: 791–800.

Bateson, P. 1988. The biological evolution of cooperation and trust. In D. Gambetta (Ed.), *Trust: Making and breaking cooperative relations:* 14–30. New York: Blackwell.

Bolton, M. K. 1993. Organizational innovation and substandard performance: When is necessity the mother of innovation? *Organization Science,* 4: 57–75.

Brophy, D. 1992. Financing the new venture: A report on recent research. In D. L. Sexton & J. D. Kasarda (Eds.), *The state of the art of entrepreneurship:* 387–401. Boston: PWS-Kent.

Carroll, G. R., Preisendoerfer, P., Swaminathan, A., & Wiedenmayer, G. 1989. *Brewery and Brauerei: The comparative organizational ecology of American and German brewing industries.* Working paper OBIR-34, Center for Research in Management, University of California, Berkeley.

Coleman, J. S. 1957. *Community conflict.* New York: Free Press.

Dasgupta, P. 1988. Trust as a commodity. In D. Gambetta (Ed.), *Trust: Making and breaking cooperative relations:* 49–72. New York: Blackwell.

Dees, J. G., & Starr, J. A. 1992. Entrepreneurship through an ethical lens: Dilemmas and issues for research and practice. In D. L. Sexton & J. D. Kasarda (Eds.), *The state of the art of entrepreneurship:* 89–116. Boston: PWS-Kent.

Delacroix, J., & Carroll, G. R. 1983. Organizational foundings: An ecological study of the newspaper industries of Argentina and Ireland. *Administrative Science Quarterly,* 28(2): 274–291.

Delacroix, J., & Rao, M. V. H. 1993. Externalities and ecological theory: Unbundling density dependence. In J. V. Singh & J. Baum (Eds.), *Evolutionary dynamics of organizations:* 255–268. Oxford, England: Oxford University Press.

Delacroix, J., Swaminathan, A., & Solt, M. 1989. Density dependence versus population dynamics: An ecological study of failings in the California wine industry. *American Sociological Review,* 54: 245–262.

DiMaggio, P. J., & Powell, W. W. 1983. The iron cage revisited: Institutional isomorphism and collective rationality in organizational fields. *American Sociological Review,* 48: 147–160.

Dosi, G. 1988. Sources, procedures, and microeconomic effects of innovation. *Journal of Economic Literature,* 26: 1120–1171.

Elsbach, K. D., & Sutton, R. I. 1992. Acquiring organizational legitimacy through illegitimate actions: A marriage of institutional and impression management theories. *Academy of Management Journal,* 35: 699–738.

Fiol, C. M. 1991. Managing culture as a competitive resource: An identity-based view of sustainable competitive advantage. *Journal of Management,* 17: 191–211.

Fiol, C. M., Harris, D., & House, R. 1992. *Charismatic leadership.* Working paper, College of Business, University of Colorado at Denver.

Fisher, L. M. 1992. Biotechnology industry rejoices with caution. *New York Times,* February 26: C2.

Fisher, W. R. 1985. The narrative paradigm: An elaboration. *Communication Monographs,* 52: 347–367.

Fransman, M. 1990. *The market and beyond: Cooperation and competition in information technology development in the Japanese system.* Cambridge, England: Cambridge University Press.

Gambetta, D. 1988. Can we trust? In D. Gambetta (Ed.), *Trust: Making and breaking cooperative relations:* 213–238. New York: Blackwell.

Gartner, W. B., & Low, L. 1990. *Trust as an organizing trope.* Paper presented at the annual meeting of the Academy of Management, San Francisco.

Halliday, T., Powell, M. J., & Granfors, M. W. 1987. Minimalist organizations: Vital events in state bar associations, 1870–1930. *American Sociological Review,* 52(4): 456–471.

Hannan, M. T. 1986. Competitive and institutional processes in organizational ecology. (Tech. Rep. 86–13). Ithaca, NY: Cornell University, Department of Sociology.

Hannan, M. T., & Carroll, G. R. 1992. *Dynamics of organizational populations: Density, legitimation, and competition.* New York: Oxford University Press.

Hannan, M. T., & Freeman, J. H. 1986. Where do organizational forms come from? *Sociological Forum,* 1: 50–72.

Hannan, M. T., & Freeman, J. H. 1989. *Organizational ecology.* Cambridge, MA: Harvard University Press.

Haveman, H. 1990. *Firm size, slack, and rates of change: The savings and loan industry after deregulation.* Unpublished paper, Durham, NC: Duke University, Fuqua School of Business.

Hawthorn, G. 1988. Three ironies in trust. In D. Gambetta (Ed.), *Trust: Making and breaking cooperative relations:* 111–126. New York: Blackwell.

Hilts, P. J. 1992. Bush to ease rules on products made by altering genes. *New York Times,* February 25: A1, B7.

Howell, J. M., & Higgins, C. A. 1990. Champions of technological innovation. *Administrative Science Quarterly,* 35: 317–341.

Kaplan, T. J. 1986. The narrative structure of policy analysis. *Journal of Policy Analysis and Management,* 5: 761–778.

Klepper, S., & Graddy, E. 1990. The evolution of new industries and the determinants of market structure. *RAND Journal of Economics,* 21: 27–44.

Krieger, M. H. 1981. *Advice and planning.* Philadelphia: Temple University Press.

Jovanovic, B. 1982. Selection and the evolution of industry. *Econometrica,* 50: 649–670.

Levine, A. G. 1982. *Love canal: Science, politics, and people.* Lexington, MA: Lexington Books.

Link, A. N., & Bauer, L. L. 1989. *Cooperative research in U.S. manufacturing: Assessing policy initiatives and corporate strategies.* Lexington, MA: Lexington Books.

Link, B. G. 1987. Understanding labeling effects in the area of mental disorders: An assessment of the effects of expectations of rejection. *American Sociological Review,* 52: 96–112.

Meyer, J., & Rowan, B. 1977. Institutionalized organizations: Formal structure as myth and ceremony. *American Journal of Sociology,* 83: 340–363.

Moe, T. N. 1980. *The organization of interests.* Chicago: University of Chicago Press.

Nagel, E. 1961. *The structure of science: Problems in the logic of scientific explanation.* London: Routledge & Kegan Paul.

Naj, A. K. 1991. Defending the turf: Medical-gear makers take harsh measures to keep service jobs. *Wall Street Journal,* October 8: 1, 6.

Nelson, R., & Winter, S. 1982. *An evolutionary theory of economic change.* Cambridge, MA: Belknap Press.

Olson, M., Jr. 1965. *The logic of collective action.* Cambridge, MA: Harvard University Press.

Phillips, A. 1960. A theory of interfirm organization. *Quarterly Journal of Economics,* 74: 602–613.

Powell, W. W. 1990. Neither market nor hierarchy: Network forms of organization. In L. L. Cummings & B. M. Staw (Eds.), *Research in organizational behavior,* vol. 12: 295–336. Greenwich, CT: JAI Press.

Prentiss, S. 1984. *Introducing cellular communications: The new mobile telephone system.* Blue Ridge Summit, PA: Tab Books.

Rao, H. 1993. *Certification mechanisms and trust: Reliability competitions in the American automobile industry, 1895–1912.* Unpublished paper, Emory University Business School, Atlanta, GA.

Ranger-Moore, J., Banaszak-Holl, J., & Hannan, M. T. 1991. Density-dependent dynamics in regulated industries: Founding rates of banks and life insurance companies. *Administrative Science Quarterly,* 36: 36–65.

Rappa, M. 1987. *The structure of technological revolution: An empirical study of the development of III-V compound semiconductor technology.* Unpublished dissertation, University of Minnesota, Carlson School of Management, Minneapolis.

Reed, R., & DeFillippi, R. J. 1990. Causal ambiguity, barriers to imitation, and sustainable competitive advantage. *Academy of Management Review,* 15: 88–102.

Regur, N. M. 1992. Japan loses faith in American branch campuses but its students still flock to universities in U.S. *Chronicle of Higher Education,* September 16: A43–44.

Romanelli, E. 1989. Organization birth and population variety: A community perspective on origins. In B. M. Staw & L. L. Cummings (Eds.), *Research in organizational behavior,* vol. 11: 211–246. Greenwich, CT: JAI Press.

Scott, W. R., & Meyer, J. 1983. The organization of societal sectors. In J. Meyer & W. R. Scott (Eds.), *Organizational environments: Ritual and rationality:* 129–154. Beverly Hills, CA: Sage.

Shan, W., Singh, J., & Amburgey, T. L. 1991. Modeling the creation of new biotechnology firms, 1973–1987. In J. L. Wall & L. R. Jauch (Eds.), *Academy of Management Best Papers Proceedings:* 78–82.

Staber, U. H. 1989. Organizational foundings in the cooperative sector in Atlantic Canada: An ecological perspective. *Organization Studies,* 10: 383–405.

Staber, U. H., & Aldrich, H. E. 1983. Trade association stability and public policy. In R. Hall & R. Quinn (Eds.), *Organization theory and public policy:* 163–178. Beverly Hills, CA: Sage.

Stinchcombe, A. 1965. Social structure and organizations. In J. G. March (Ed.), *Handbook of organizations:* 142–193. Chicago: Rand McNally.

Teece, D. 1987. Profiting from technological innovation: Implications for integration, collaboration, licensing, and public policy. In D. Teece (Ed.), *The competitive challenge:* 185–219. Cambridge, MA: Ballinger.

Torres, D. L. 1988. Professionalism, variation, and organizational survival. *American Sociological Review,* 53: 380–394.

Tversky, A., & Kahneman, D. 1981. The framing of decisions and the psychology of choice. *Science,* 211: 453–458.

Van de Ven, A. H. 1991. *A systems framework for studying the process of entrepreneurship.* Paper presented at a conference on Theories of Entrepreneurship, University of Illinois, Champaign-Urbana.

Van de Ven, A. H., & Garud, R. 1991. *Innovation and industry development: The case of cochlear implants.* Unpublished paper, University of Minnesota, Strategic Management Research Center, Minneapolis.

Webster's new collegiate dictionary. 1981. Springfield, MA: G. & C. Merriam Company.

Wholey, D. R., Christianson, J. B., & Sanchez, S. M. 1990. *The diffusion of health maintenance organizations: Density, competitive, and institutional determinants of entry.* Unpublished paper, University of Arizona, Department of Management and Policy, Tucson.

Winter, S. 1984. Schumpeterian competition in alternative technological regimes. *Journal of Economic Behavior and Organization,* 5: 287–320.

Zelizer, V. A. 1978. Human values and the market: The case of life insurance and death in 19th-century America. *American Journal of Sociology,* 84: 591–610.

Zucker, L. G. 1986. Production of trust: Institutional sources of economics structures, 1840–1920. In B. M. Staw and L. L. Cummings (Eds.), *Research in organizational behavior,* vol. 8: 53–122. Greenwich, CT: JAI Press.

Zucker, L. G. 1989. Combining institutional theory and population ecology: No legitimacy, no history. *American Sociological Review,* 54: 542–545.

C. Marlene Fiol received her Ph.D. in strategic management from the University of Illinois. She is an assistant professor of management at the University of Colorado at Denver. Her current research focuses on cognitive processes in organizations, especially as they relate to strategic change, organizational learning, and innovation.

Howard E. Aldrich received his Ph.D. in sociology from the University of Michigan. He is Kenan Professor of Sociology and Director of the Industrial Relations Curriculum in the College of Arts and Sciences, and Adjunct Professor of Management in the Kenan-Flagler School of Business, at the University of North Carolina, Chapel Hill. Currently, he is conducting research in three areas: a comparative study of the governance structures of research and development consortia in the United States and Japan (with Toshihiro Sasaki and Michele Bolton); a longitudinal study of human resource management practices in new ventures in two industries— environmental consulting and computer education and training, in the Research Triangle Area of North Carolina (with Ted Baker); and a panel study of small business survival and growth, also in the Research Triangle Area (with Pat Ray Reese).

THE SECOND ECOLOGY:
CREATION AND EVOLUTION OF ORGANIZATIONAL COMMUNITIES

Courtney Shelton Hunt and Howard E. Aldrich

ABSTRACT

Organizational ecology has mostly neglected the community level of analysis, and has focused instead on the organizational and population levels of analysis. Signs of change are evident, however, and in this chapter we join researchers who are promoting investigations at the level of organizational communities. We propose an updated model of community creation and evolution, using a model that builds on the theoretical tenets proposed by Astley and Fombrun in the mid-1980s, but updating them to reflect current economic realities as well as recent developments in organizational theory. Our model of community evolution is built around three themes: (1) the importance of technological innovation as a major catalyst for the creation of new organizational forms and new populations; (2) the central role of entrepreneurial activities in promoting and sustaining the growth of populations and communities; and (3) the dependence of community development on legitimization at multiple levels. In addition to these themes, our model also emphasizes the process of coevolution, as we argue that the dynamics inherent within each theme are mutually interdependent and exert reciprocal influence on one another. Throughout the discussion we illustrate our assertions with examples from the evolution of the World Wide Web as a commercial community.

Research in Organizational Behavior, Volume 20, pages 267-301.
Copyright © 1998 by JAI Press Inc.
ISBN: 0-7623-0366-2

267

INTRODUCTION

The study of organizational ecology has its roots in the pioneering work of Amos Hawley, whose 1950 book, *Human Ecology*, treated the development of human communities as a process in which people interacted with their environments through the use of technology. In the ecological tradition spawned by Hawley, researchers have focused on several levels of analysis, including individual organizations, populations of organizations, and organizational communities (Carroll, 1984; Hannan & Freeman, 1989). Most of this research has used a population ecology perspective and has focused on the population level of analysis, examining the contingencies affecting vital events in the lives of organizations, as documented in reviews of the literature by Carroll (1984), Wholey and Brittain (1986), Singh and Lumsden (1990), and Baum (1996).

In the past few years, however, the number of articles and book chapters taking a community ecology perspective has increased, focusing on the dynamics of organizational *communities*. Many of the current efforts were consolidated in a collection of writings on organizational ecology, Baum and Singh's *Evolutionary Dynamics of Organizations* (1994a). In contrast with previous collections, such as Carroll's *Ecological Models of Organizations* (1988) and Singh's *Organizational Evolution: New Directions* (1990), Baum and Singh devoted an entire section of their book (five chapters and two commentaries) to understanding the dynamics of community evolution. In Carroll (1988), by contrast, only two of the book's 12 chapters focused on the community level of analysis; and in Singh (1990) there was only one chapter on community dynamics, which was focused on voluntary organizations rather than commercial enterprises.

Given an increased interest in community ecology, our goal for this chapter was the creation of a revised model of how organizational communities emerge and evolve over time. This model is rooted in the early work of W. Graham Astley and Charles Fombrun; however, it has been updated to reflect developments in organizational theory during the past decade. In particular, our revised model is based on Information Age assumptions rather than Industrial Age assumptions, and emphasizes the importance of technological innovation as a major catalyst for the creation of a commercial community. The model also pays attention to the role of entrepreneurs in creating the new organizational forms that become the foundation for new populations and new communities, and describes how legitimization efforts by individual firms and organizational collectivities promote the development of foundling communities. Finally, recognizing that efforts to promote the development of organizational communities do not occur in isolation, we treat the ideas of interdependence and reciprocal influence under the rubric of coevolution.

We begin with a review and critique of Astley and Fombrun's early ideas regarding community creation and evolution. Next, we provide our working definition of organizational communities. In the third section we present our model of community evolution and discuss each of the four major themes included in the model. Throughout the paper our arguments are illustrated with examples from the evolution of the World Wide Web as a commercial community. We conclude with a summary of the revised model and a brief discussion of how our revised model can be incorporated into future research in organizational ecology.

ASTLEY AND FOMBRUN'S WORK ON COMMUNITY ECOLOGY

In 1985 W. Graham Astley published an essay that criticized the literature on population ecology for failing to adequately address the question, "Why are there so many kinds of organizations?" (Hannan & Freeman, 1977, p. 936). According to Astley, theories of population ecology did not adequately explain how new organizational forms are created and why a multitude of diverse organizations can proliferate in a given economic environment. Instead, ecological theories at that time focused on how selection processes create uniformity and stability in organizational forms, and how existing populations are sustained over time.

Astley contended that research on organizational ecology should also focus on the dynamics of community[1] ecology, particularly community evolution, to explain how new organizational forms arise. Advocating a punctuated equilibrium model of change, he asserted that basic innovations (Mensch, 1979), representing dramatic technological change, are a catalyst for the creation of new organizational forms, which in turn spawn new populations and, subsequently, new organizational communities. He further argued that the environments in which these new organizational forms emerge are munificent and forgiving, allowing diverse forms to proliferate and coexist before a dominant form emerges in later stages of population growth (Moore & Tushman, 1982). Given this environmental munificence, competition only becomes a factor of organizational life when the environment subsequently becomes saturated, resources are scarce, and selection forces begin to dominate, as posited by population ecology's density dependence model (Hannan & Freeman, 1989).

Capitalizing on the ideas put forward in Astley's essay, along with their earlier work on collective action among organizations (Astley, 1984; Astley & Fombrun, 1983a, 1983b), Astley and Fombrun continued to develop their ideas in several ensuing articles. Subsequently, they theorized about the development of communities via the evolution of interorganizational relationships (Astley & Fombrun, 1987), analyzed the importance of social structural embeddedness in influencing stability and change within communities over time (Fombrun, 1986), and advocated an expanded view of organizational ecology that more fully considered the social and institutional context of community evolution (Fombrun, 1988).

Astley and Fombrun's early writings made several unique contributions to the inchoate field of community ecology.[2] The main contribution of Astley's original essay was its focus on the creation of new organizational forms and the role these new organizational forms play in providing a foundation for the subsequent creation of organizational populations and communities. Astley concentrated on technological innovations, especially basic innovations, as the catalyst for the creation process. In addition to recognizing the importance of technological innovations, Astley and Fombrun also emphasized the importance of interorganizational relationships in community evolution. In contrast with an under-socialized view of human economic behavior (Granovetter, 1985), they postulated that actors within organizations often forge relationships with actors in other organizations in an effort to manage their environment and gain influence over their futures (Astley & Fombrun, 1987). They also stressed the role that institutional actors and institutional processes play in community evolution (Fombrun, 1988), as well as the social context within which communities emerge and evolve (Fombrun, 1986).

Although Astley and Fombrun offered many valuable ideas regarding community evolution, their ideas were limited in several respects, and we turn now to six criticisms of their approach. First, many of their conceptual assertions were rooted in an Industrial Age model of organizations. Consequently, many of their ideas were focused on processes of evolution within a manufacturing context, rather than on those communities that may be more oriented to delivering information or services. Discussing the role of technological innovation in community evolution, for example, Astley (1985, p. 231) wrote, "once made, technological choices entail large investments in equipment and know-how and so discourage subsequent changes in the course of industrial development." In a similar fashion, Astley and Fombrun (1987, p. 168) presented vertical integration as a series of relationships linking organizations from the "supply of raw materials [to] the delivery of end products."

Their Industrial Age perspective also led Astley (1985) to assume that innovation is spawned by technological stalemates, with the impetus for change rooted in crises such as economic depressions and stagnation. Although this picture of innovation may have been accurate in some historical periods, it does not fit an Information Age economy. As firms increasingly focus on gaining a strategic advantage through innovation and continuous improvement, and as computer technology provides them with the means to achieve these improvements within a short time frame, they are less resistant to change. Indeed, firms no longer need a crisis as a catalyst for pursuing new opportunities.

A third criticism of Astley and Fombrun's work is that it focused primarily on *competition* as a driving force behind organizational action. Although Astley (1985) asserted that open environmental space and environmental munificence were critical for the creation of a new organizational community, in the ensuing period Astley and Fombrun (1987) retreated from that assertion, assuming instead that resources are scarce and that organizations must find ways to minimize the risks they face in uncertain environments. Horizontal integration, for example, was proposed as a method of acquiring knowledge about competitors' actions and identifying ways to fend off environmental threats. However, when environments are open to new organizational forms, it is more likely that firms will pursue collective action as a way of achieving mutual benefit or joint gains. An emphasis on symbiotic and commensalistic relations, rather than competition, is more in keeping with the original principles of human ecology (Carroll, 1984).

Astley and Fombrun's theory of evolution also appears to be dependent on a structural-functional mode of analysis. They asserted that the development of interorganizational relations progresses in a hierarchical fashion from simple to complex, first as horizontal integration, then as vertical integration, and ultimately as "diagonal" integration (Astley & Fombrun, 1987). Much of their analysis consisted of attempts to classify actions and relationships into their hierarchical scheme, thus losing sight of the dynamic nature of organizational communities. They seemed to look at communities from the "top down," treating a community as a functionally integrated whole. Given the dynamics of business interactions in the Information Age, however, as well as the speed with which organizational change can now occur, it is unlikely that evolution will develop as slowly—and as neatly—as they suggested.

Fifth, Astley and Fombrun relied on a punctuated equilibrium model of change (Astley, 1985), and argued that innovations acting as catalysts for the creation of new communities were revolutionary and discontinuous. However, as Van de Ven and Garud (1994) noted, most technological innovations—even those that appear very dramatic—have well-established roots in a history of cumulative research and development. Models of technological paradigms, technological trajectories (Dosi, 1982), technological communities (Lynn, Reddy, & Aram, 1996), and other richly historical accounts of technological innovation paint a more evolutionary than revolutionary picture (Rosenberg, 1982).

A sixth and final criticism of Astley and Fombrun's work is that much of their writing focused on change within existing organizational communities, rather than the creation of new communities. Although Astley's initial essay emphasized creation, their subsequent work (e.g., Fombrun, 1986) tended to focus instead on a comparison of the conditions that promote stability versus the conditions that promote change within an established community. This perspective is similar to the perspective taken in much of the research on technological innovation—a presumption that a community exists to serve an established purpose and that it can either accommodate or resist a given innovation. Given current business conditions, however, such a presumption is increasingly implausible, as new technologies are introduced with accelerating frequency. Some of these technologies are related to existing products, services, and markets; however, a number of them are unique, creating opportunities for new products and services and opening new markets that are not necessarily in competition with existing products and services.

In summary, Astley and Fombrun's work provided a solid foundation for understanding how new commercial communities come into being and how they evolve over time. However, given recent changes in the economic landscape, as well as developments in organizational theory over the past decade, their ideas were limited in several key respects. Consequently, we felt it was time to create an updated theory of community creation and evolution, which we will attempt to do in the remainder of this chapter.

DEFINING "ORGANIZATIONAL COMMUNITY"

Before proceeding with our theoretical discussion, we need to provide a conceptual grounding for our assertions by offering a working definition of organizational community. Previous research on community ecology has been criticized for lacking a consistent definition of this construct. As DiMaggio (1994) noted in his critique of the community ecology chapters in the Baum and Singh volume, different authors often equate an organizational community with a population, a subcommunity, an interorganizational network, or an "industry." In some prior work (e.g., Astley, 1985; Baum & Korn, 1994) organizational communities have been considered as distinct units of analysis; however, in other work (e.g., Barnett, 1994; Wade, 1996) they have been examined in a more general sense, as sets of relationships or interdependencies among individual organizations or populations of organizations.

Given this lack of consensus, we felt compelled to devise our own definition as a focal point for our theoretical assertions. Our working definition is thus:

> An organizational community is a set of coevolving organizational populations joined by ties
> of commensalism and symbiosis through their orientation to a common technology.

We believe this definition retains the essence of Hawley's original conceptualization of community, which emphasized functional interdependence between units (i.e., commensalistic and symbiotic relations). Symbiosis can be defined as "the mutual benefit resulting when different types of producers transact in markets" (Barnett & Carroll, 1987, p. 401), and commensalism results when "similar organizations work together in concerted political action" (Barnett & Carroll, 1987, p. 401). This definition also preserves evolutionary theory's emphasis on a future that is constructed rather than designed; that is, communities *emerge* from relationships between units that involve competition and cooperation, rather than coming into being according to plan. To allow us to bound our unit of inquiry short of an entire regional or national economic system (Barnett, 1994), we limit ourselves to organizations and populations oriented toward a common technological core.[3] Finally, we recognize that the extent to which social actors are interdependent is ultimately an empirical question, and that investigators must make informed choices in setting boundaries around a set of "interdependent" activities.

Our definition of an organizational community can be illustrated through the example of the World Wide Web, a community that has evolved since 1993 as a result of the technological innovations that made possible widespread commercial

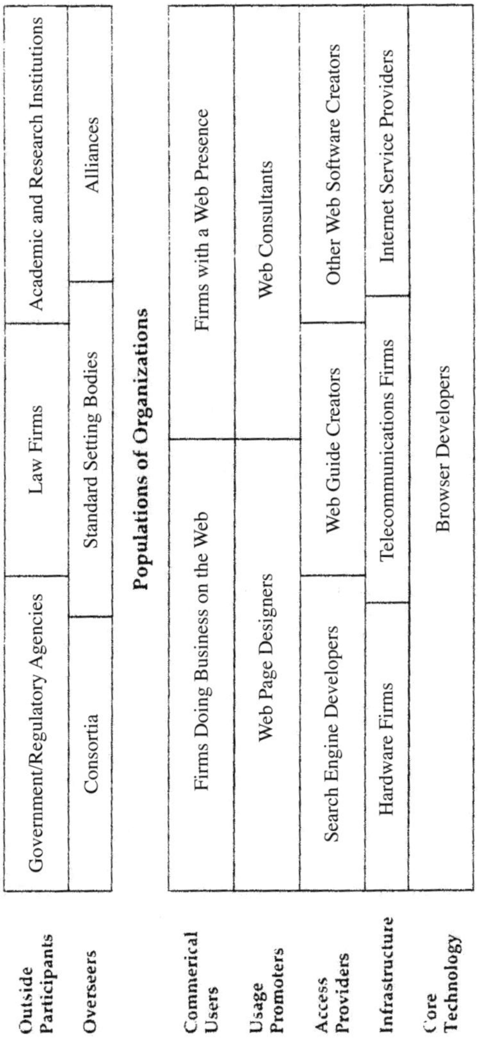

Populations of Organizations

	Government/Regulatory Agencies	Law Firms	Academic and Research Institutions

Outside Participants			
Overseers	Consortia	Standard Setting Bodies	Alliances

Commerical Users	Firms Doing Business on the Web		Firms with a Web Presence
Usage Promoters	Web Page Designers		Web Consultants
Access Providers	Search Engine Developers	Web Guide Creators	Other Web Software Creators
Infrastructure	Hardware Firms	Telecommunications Firms	Internet Service Providers
Core Technology		Browser Developers	

Figure 1. The Commercial Community of the World Wide Web

Table 1.   Populations and Other Participants in the
World Wide Web Commercial Community

Populations/Participants	Examples
Browser Developers	Netscape, Microsoft
Hardware Firms	SUN Microsystems, @Home
Telecommunications Firms	AT&T, MCI, NYNEX
Internet Service Providers	UUnet, Mindspring
Search Engine Developers	HOTBOT, DEC (Alta Vista)
Web Guide Creators	Yahoo, Excite
Other Web Software Creators	Digicash, Macromedia
Web Page Designers	Free Range Media Company WebZeit
Web Consultants	TopChoice Systems
Firms Doing Business on the Web	Interactive Insurance Services Amazon.com
Firms with a Web Presence	Coca-Cola, Toyota, Sears
Consortia	WWW Consortium, WWW Artist Consortium
Standard-Setting Bodies	Internet Engineering Task Force
Alliances	Silicon Graphics & Template Graphics
Government/Regulatory Agencies	FCC, FTC
Law Firms	Womble, Carlyle, Sandridge & Rice
Academic and Research Institutions	MIT, NCSA

use of the Internet. This community is depicted in Figure 1, which shows the various populations making up the Web, organized by their distance from the core technology. Figure 1 is supplemented by Table 1, which lists examples of organizations from the various populations, as well as other participants within the community.

To emphasize the importance of a core technology, at the base of Figure 1 we show the population of organizations that have developed browser software.[4] Extending beyond the population of browser developers, the community also includes populations of firms focused on creating and maintaining the technological infrastructure needed to support the community (e.g., hardware manufacturers like Sun Microsystems, telecommunications firms such as AT&T, and Internet Service Providers [ISPs] like UUNet). Additional populations provide enhanced access to Web technology, and consist of organizations that develop search engines (e.g., Digital Equipment Corporation), web guides (e.g., Yahoo), and other Web-related software (e.g., Digicash). Other populations of firms are focused on enhancing access to the Web, and include Web-page designers (e.g., Free Range Media Company), and Web consultants (e.g., TopChoice Systems).

Moving beyond those populations that are focused on Web-related products and services as one of their core competencies, other populations of firms are using the

Web as a medium for advertising or selling non-Web goods and services. One of these populations consists of firms that are doing business on the Web (e.g., Amazon Books, Interactive Insurance Services), whereas another population includes those firms that have a commercial presence on the Web but are not necessarily transacting business (e.g., Coca-Cola).

In addition to these populations there are also groups of organizations that concentrate on meeting the unique oversight needs of the Web community. These groups of organizations include consortia (e.g., the WWW consortium, the Internet Society), standard setting bodies (e.g., the Internet Engineering Task Force), and research and development alliances (e.g., between Silicon Graphics and Template Graphics Software). In addition to these groups there are also a number of outside organizations that have become involved in the Web community: government and regulatory agencies such as the U.S. Federal Communications Commission, the Federal Trade Commission, and the Securities and Exchange Commission (which became involved because of its interest in regulating the online trading of stocks), law firms (e.g., Womble Carlyle Sandridge & Rice, P.L.L.C., which has worked on issues such as trademark and copyright issues), and academic and research institutions (e.g., the Massachusetts Institute of Technology [MIT]) and the National Center for Supercomputing Applications [NCSA]).

As depicted in Figure 1, the Web community consists of organizational populations that are united by bonds of commensalism and symbiosis through their orientation to a common technology. Hardware firms, for example, must develop and market products that are compatible with browser technology, while concurrently providing the speed and power necessary to handle the high volume of transactions generated on the Internet. Internet Service Providers (ISPs) are dependent on hardware manufacturers, telecommunications firms, and software developers for the tools needed for customers' access to the Web. ISPs also rely on Web consultants to help create user-friendly interfaces between their services and end users. Commensalism is promoted by consortia, alliances, and standard-setting bodies, which are focused on creating a solid technological foundation for the Web, as well as representing the interests of the community to outsiders.

A REVISED MODEL OF COMMUNITY EVOLUTION

Our intent in writing this chapter was to propose a revised model of community evolution that capitalizes on the strengths of Astley and Fombrun's early ideas, modifying them where necessary to eliminate tenets based on outdated assumptions and expanding them to reflect conceptual and empirical developments from the last 10 years. Our ideas regarding community creation have their origins in our observations of the evolution of the Web as a commercial endeavor from 1993 through 1997. Early on, we recognized the Web as an organizational "community." However, we also realized very quickly that some of the community evolu-

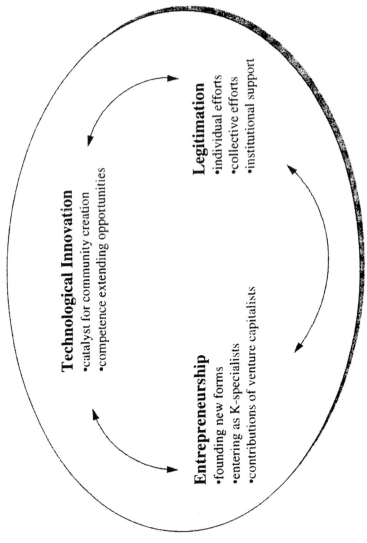

Note: Arrows represent coevolution.

Figure 2.   Themes of Community Creation and Evolution

276

tion dynamics proposed by earlier theorists fit poorly when applied to the Web. Upon further reflection, we recognized the potential for updating the theory of community evolution, based not just on the example of the Web but also on other communities that have emerged in recent years.

The dynamics inherent in the process of community evolution can be categorized into three main themes: (1) the importance of technological innovation, (2) the central role of entrepreneurial activities, and (3) the dependence of community development on the establishment of legitimacy. Each of these themes, which are depicted in Figure 2 and are the focus of the theoretical discussion to follow, can be used to describe and explain how commercial communities emerge and evolve over time. As Figure 2 reveals, however, the dynamics described by these themes do not occur in isolation. Instead, each of them influences the others through a process of coevolution involving not only the members of a given community, but also the technology around which the community is built and the social context within which the community is maintained. We discuss coevolution in more detail at the end of this section.

The Importance of Technological Innovation

Technological innovation is a major catalyst for the creation of a new organizational community to the extent that it prompts the creation of new organizational forms. New forms may become the basis for new populations that are linked together through the processes of commensalism and symbiosis by their shared orientation to a common technology (Astley, 1985). However, contrary to Astley's punctuated equilibrium view, we think it is unrealistic to assume that one could identify a single key event that generated a new organizational population, based on a technological breakthrough. Instead, Van de Ven and Garud (1994) proposed an evolutionary view that treats technological innovation as a cumulative series of interrelated acts of variation, selection, and retention, eventually culminating in a commercial application. Consequently, we take for granted that historical processes in the twentieth century, as described by many writers (e.g., Dosi, 1988; Rosenberg, 1982; Usher, 1954), continually generate technological innovations that have commercial potential. Some of the innovations are seized upon by entrepreneurs and pursued with such vigor that new populations are formed. Although many of these populations fail (Aldrich & Fiol, 1994), those that prosper may become the nucleus of new organizational communities.

For the Web, the introduction of Mosaic software in 1993 was the major technological innovation that facilitated its emergence as a commercial community, but there were many previous events that set the stage for Mosaic to become a catalytic event (Hafner & Lyon, 1996). Many firms (e.g., Digital Equipment Corporation, MCI Telecommunications) were working to find a way to exploit the technology of the Internet for commercial gain. In addition, Mosaic technology was itself an innovation that improved upon the earliest Web browser, which was created by CERN scientists to provide a more sophisticated means for getting information from the Internet. The dramatic effect of the innovation was not perceived at the time of Mosaic's introduction—it only became evident after the fact. Also, because there was an environment of open sharing and standard setting, many individuals contributed to the early enhancements of the Mosaic technology, thus enabling it to become the dominant standard very rapidly.

Technological innovations cannot be viewed in isolation, as pointed out by Tushman and Murmann (1998) in their chapter for this volume. Instead, innovations are generally related to some aspect of a technological system, which can be thought of as composed of core and peripheral subsystems. Innovations causing a discontinuity in a technological stream are often linked to changes in an existing core subsystem or the creation of a new one. Following a radical innovation, an era of ferment ensues in which struggles occur between contending designs. The era of ferment ends with the selection of a dominant design for the core subsystem, and it is then followed by an era of incremental change (Anderson & Tushman, 1990). Although the period of incremental change may be relatively stable with respect to the core subsystem, it may be quite dynamic with respect to innovations in peripheral subsystems because individuals and organizations compete to create subsystems that complement the core technology (Tushman & Murmann, 1998).

Although the Web is not a technological system in a traditional, manufacturing sense, the innovations that have occurred in the early days of the Web's evolution do fit Tushman and Murmann's ideas. In particular, the introduction of browser technology could be seen as the key innovation that created the core subsystem of the Web's commercial community. Because the community converged around this technology relatively swiftly and Netscape asserted its dominance within a year after the technology was introduced, the Netscape browser quickly became the standard within the community. Consequently, subsequent efforts at enhancing the technology of the Web focused on peripheral subsystems, such as browser add-ons and other user interfaces.

Astley (1985) also proposed that significant technological innovations emerge from crisis situations, such as an economic recession. This assertion is historically dubious, especially when applied to traditional manufacturing organizations, and it is even less convincing in the Information Age. As managers are continuously looking at ways to enhance their existing technology and/or create new technologies, many of which are information-based, crises are no longer major catalysts for innovation. In the case of the Web, for example, browser technology was unique in many respects, providing the opportunity for firms and individuals to do new things rather than promoting new ways to do old things. Browser technology was exploited because of the potential gains available by introducing new products and new services in an as-yet-undefined market.

For established populations, the consequences of innovations for particular organizations have typically been described either as incremental and therefore competence-enhancing, or radical and therefore competence-destroying (Methé,

Swaminathan, & Mitchell, 1996; Tushman & Anderson, 1986). Innovations that are based on new substantive knowledge presumably pose major problems for existing firms in mature populations, because their routines and competencies may not be flexible enough for them to adapt to the changes required. For example, Baum, Korn, and Kotha (1995) showed that the shift from analog to digital technology destroyed many incumbents in the facsimile transmission industry. By contrast, innovations that represent improvements, minor modifications, or extensions of existing knowledge presumably permit many existing organizations to survive by adapting to the minimal changes required (Abernathy & Clark, 1985; Utterback & Abernathy, 1975).

The distinction between competence-enhancing and competence-destroying innovations complements Astley's punctuated equilibrium model of change. When innovations are competence enhancing, they are readily adapted by existing firms, thereby eliminating the opportunity for new organizations to exploit the technology. By contrast, however, when innovations are competence destroying, existing firms are less likely to accommodate the new technology, which opens an access route for new players. This perspective presupposes that existing firms lack the flexibility to adapt their knowledge capabilities and resource capacities to significant changes.

Technological innovations need not be *either* competence enhancing *or* competence destroying, however. Instead, for new communities in the Information Age, technological breakthroughs not only mean the creation of a new population because of new substantive knowledge requirements, but also new opportunities for established populations to expand their competencies by participating in the new community. Thus, rather than a dichotomy between competence-destroying and competence-enhancing innovations, we propose a third category of innovations: *competence-extending*. From our perspective, competence extending innovations permit existing firms to pursue new opportunities that allow them to stretch their existing competencies into complementary ventures. Unlike competence enhancing opportunities, these new ventures are not a natural or logical extension of their current capabilities and cannot therefore be pursued with minimal effort. At the same time, however, these opportunities cannot be perceived as direct threats to their existing business pursuits and competencies. Instead, they are potential opportunities for expanding their domains by pursuing new markets through the exploitation of new competencies.

The evolution of the Web provides many examples of the ways in which existing firms jumped on the Internet bandwagon in an effort to establish new commercial niches for themselves. One of the most dramatic examples is Bill Gates's decision to officially change Microsoft's strategic direction from PC-based software to an almost-exclusive focus on Web-based technology, a decision he made after witnessing the phenomenal success of Netscape. AT&T also made a major strategic decision to become an ISP, a decision that was also made by almost all of the regional phone companies. Although these decisions involved the creation of new business units, they were logical extensions of their existing capabilities. In a similar fashion, many public relations and advertising firms decided to leverage their knowledge of the media into the Web environment by adding competencies for Web-site design and maintenance. These pursuits were not simply an enhancement of existing competencies, but rather were entirely new ways that these firms could capitalize on their existing skills/knowledge base, as well as their existing resources, to enter a new commercial niche.

The Central Role of Entrepreneurial Activities

Community evolution depends upon a steady stream of organizational foundings for the growth of new populations and the revitalization of established ones. In the early days of community creation, entrepreneurs produce many of the new organizational forms that initiate new populations (Romanelli, 1989; Thornton, 1998). Many of the Web populations identified in Table 1, for example, were opened up by pioneering entrepreneurial firms moving quickly and rather haphazardly, rather than established firms that were seeking to diversify. In the ISP population, for example, established firms were dwarfed in numbers by the thousands of local ISPs that were founded in the mid-1990s, as new firms took advantage of the slowness with which large firms, such as the telephone companies, responded to the new technology. Between 1996 and 1997, in fact, more than 1,000 new ISPs were founded (Yoshitake, 1997). Similarly, most of the Web consulting and design firms were created by young entrepreneurs fresh out of college; some were fleeing established advertising and marketing firms. Free Range Media Company, established in Seattle in 1994, grew to 65 employees by late 1996 and was building sites for firms such as Westin Hotels and Progressive Networks. Their recruiting strategy stressed their entrepreneurial nature: "We're a small, eclectic group of technologists, designers and business strategists located in Seattle's historic district, Pioneer Square. If you're interested in having an impact in the Internet world, then come be a part of a dynamic, entrepreneurial, growing group that will challenge you to push your own boundaries" (Free Range Media, 1997).

As the community evolves, the environment for potential entrepreneurs changes as new opportunities and constraints emerge (Aldrich & Wiedenmayer, 1993). Changes in the community context also affect the mix of favored organizational forms within established and emerging populations. As new populations achieve greater cognitive and sociopolitical legitimacy and founders learn the required competencies, founding rates increase because of enhanced entrepreneurial understanding of new forms and a more generous flow of resources to startups (Aldrich & Fiol, 1994). In some cases, technological progress toward greater reliability, breadth of application, efficiency of production, and ease of use may occur during this period, as well (Miner & Haunschild, 1995). Across the entire evolving interorganizational field, heightened legitimacy and organizational learning means that new populations generated at later stages in the community's growth will exper-ence more favorable founding conditions than earlier populations.

Even when a community has evolved to a mature stage, with commensalistic and symbiotic relations between its populations, foundings of new firms by entre-preneurs help maintain stability and growth within populations. Indeed, in estab-lished populations and communities, new firms play a much bigger role than is commonly realized. Entrepreneurs not only form the advance guard that opens to new populations, but they also replenish established populations, replacing exiting firms and sustaining competition (Dunne, Roberts, & Samuelson, 1988. Although most of the newly founded firms are small and do not survive as long as existing firms, they nonetheless are a major source of volatility and potential inno-vation in mature populations.

Favored Forms

Because communities contain multiple populations, which are at different stages of development, rates of entrepreneurship will differ across populations, as will the most favored organizational forms (Brittain & Freeman, 1980). When established populations become involved in relationships with other populations opportunities occur for specialized organizational forms. Thus, we cannot treat "foundings" as a homogeneous, unvarying group, but rather we need to take account of their complexity and diversity (Gartner, 1985). In addition, entrepre-neurs founding organizations in populations that are part of a larger organizational community are in a different context than entrepreneurs in more isolated popula-tions.

Within a community context we can use arguments about density dependence and resource partitioning to theorize about which forms will be favored during the early phase of community evolution, when ferment and lack of consensus over dominant designs still characterize core populations, and during a latter phase. when core populations have settled on dominant designs. Two kinds of population entrants are of interest: newly founded firms, and established firms that are diver-

Table 2. Organizational Form Most Likely to Be Successfully Adopted by Population Entrants, at Different Stages of Community Development

	Community Phase:	
Entrant is:	Ferment in Core Populations	Dominant Design in Core Populations
New firm	r-specialist	k-specialist
Old diversifying firm	unlikely to enter	k-strategist (specialist or generalist)

sifying into a new market or population. Using ecological theory's classification scheme for organizational forms, we can derive four kinds of forms and then link them to environmental conditions. The types of organizational forms most likely to be favored in different community stages are listed in Table 2 and discussed in the paragraphs that follow.

Ecologists have identified two dimensions of forms that vary with population density: *r* versus *K* strategists, and specialists versus generalists. The *r* versus *K* distinction is based on the kinds of organizations that do well in the early as opposed to the late stages of population density, with *r*-strategists favored early and *K*-strategists favored late. Organizations following an *r*-strategy reproduce rapidly and move quickly to obtain the resources available when carrying capacity is under-exploited, using their "first-mover" advantage. These organizations traditionally benefit during the era of technological ferment, when consensus is lacking on a dominant design (Rosenkopf & Tushman, 1994). *K*-strategists, in contrast to *r*-strategists, typically do well when a population is near its carrying capacity, and selection is based on efficient use of resources, rather than quickness (Brittain & Freeman, 1980, p. 312). In this more settled era, dominant designs are recognized, the pace of innovation has slowed to a more incremental rate, and firms can focus on production-process improvements. Under these conditions, where efficiency is presumably favored by market forces, *K*-strategists out-compete *r*-strategists and so *r*-strategists are typically replaced by *K*-strategists as a population matures.

The second dimension of organizational form—specialism versus generalism—is based on the breadth of the niche occupied by organizations, on the assumption that organizations sacrifice some degree of competitive edge when they spread their fitness over a wide as opposed to a narrow niche (Carroll, 1984; Hannan & Freeman, 1977). The two dimensions of *r* versus *K* and specialism versus generalism may be combined to produce four distinct form types: *r*-specialists, *r*-generalists, *K*-specialists, and *K*-generalists. Using these four combinations, a generic developmental pattern of forms within different population densities can be derived (Brittain & Freeman, 1980). Early in the life of a population, when a niche is first opened, the pioneers are likely to be *r*-specialists that multiply and move quickly. In the personal computer industry, pioneering firms such as Osborne and Franklin produced workable machines but were notoriously inefficient, and eventually failed when more efficient producers emerged. After an early period of development, so-called "early followers" can gain a large market share by being more efficient (and powerful) than *r*-specialists. Such early followers are likely to be *K*-generalists: divisions, subsidiaries, or other dependent units of established firms, as well as new firms. Later, *K*-specialists, with small market shares, can survive on the stable, narrow niches left to them by the *K*-generalists.

Mature populations contain *K*-specialists and *K*-generalists, with the mix depending upon how heterogeneous the market is, whether there are economies of scale in operations, and whether organizations can change strategies easily (Carroll, 1985). The more heterogeneous the market, the more difficult it is for a *K*-generalist to produce one product/service that appeals to all segments. Attempts to do so in one product/service will likely raise costs and could mean the loss of customers who are looking for more specialization. A *K*-generalist could try producing multiple products/services, but that becomes increasingly costly as differences grow between segments. *K*-generalists benefit from economies of scale, and producing multiple products/services rather than a single product/service robs them of their advantage. Thus, in heterogeneous, differentiated environments. *K*-specialists will typically be able to find niches that are not being exploited by *K*-generalists, an outcome Carroll (1988) called "resource partitioning."

Given these arguments, we would expect that in the early phase of a community's development, when new populations are emerging, only newly founded firms would enter in significant numbers, given the hazards facing firms when agreement is lacking over a dominant design. The newly founded firms that are successful will be *r*-specialists, rather than *r*-generalists, and these firms will be the pioneers with competence-destroying potential (Bryman, 1997). It would be extremely risky for entrepreneurs to found generalist firms under such conditions, as they would waste excess capacity in a situation where the future is almost totally unpredictable. Later, when some consensus has been achieved in core populations, established firms seeking to diversify will enter the various new populations. They have the luxury of adopting either a *K*-specialist or *K*-generalist strategy. By contrast, newly founded firms entering at a later stage will enter mainly as *K*-specialists. Thus, most of the firms specifically founded to transact business on the Web were *K*-specialists that focused on narrow and well-understood products, such as books, music CDs, and pornographic pictures, even though the channel through which products or services were sold was unprecedented.

New populations formed during the latter phase of the community's development may skip over, or move through rapidly, the period where *r*-specialists are favored. In this respect, selection dynamics within a community are not like selection dynamics within an isolated population. Rather than new populations being characterized by an early period of turmoil and uncertainty over standards, startup firms' entrepreneurs can recognize their place in the community and orient themselves to the dominant design in the core population, as represented in the *K*-generalists' products and processes. Computer software is perhaps the best Information Age example of this development, as the computing platform established by Microsoft Windows has stabilized the environment for startup software firms. *K*-specialists build on the dominant design, exploit slight variations and imperfections in it, and are competence-extending for the majority of firms in their populations.

Interrelations between populations in an evolving community may also promote the founding of *K*-specialists if firms in some populations are growing more slowly than others. As Brittain and Freeman (1980) pointed out, organizationally induced entrepreneurship may occur whenever a firm is not growing fast enough to satisfy the ambitions of employees in its middle ranks. If the firm is fairly young, with senior executives in their 30s and 40s, younger employees in the lower ranks may perceive their opportunities for upward mobility blocked. Some employees respond by leaving to found their own firms, because they can capitalize on their insider knowledge of their employing firm's product/service shortcomings. Working in a K-generalist is especially likely to put boundary-spanning employees in contact with organizations in other populations, giving them ideas about useful innovations that could be commercialized (von Hippel, 1988; see also Thornton, 1988). Similar opportunities are also likely in a K-specialist that is growing too slowly to bring all its new products/services to market.

The Role of Venture Capitalists

Formal sources of capital and funding are not essential for most entrepreneurs who start businesses, even technology-based ones (Hart & Denison, 1987; but for an exception, see Delacroix & Solt, 1988). However, venture capitalist firms have played several important symbiotic roles in the emergence of new, technology-based communities: (1) providing funding for firms to expand; (2) as early investors, legitimating a risky investment for other, more conservative investors; and (3) serving as facilitators or catalysts for the creation of alliances. Venture capital firms and stock underwriting firms are not the major suppliers of capital to growing firms in the United States, but nevertheless, their actions have had a disproportionate effect in certain population segments of American industry, such as the semiconductor, biotechnology, and Web communities (Brittain, 1994; Schoonhoven & Eisenhardt, 1993). As such, relations between the venture capitalists, underwriters, and Web populations are of special interest to us.

Venture capital firms disburse funds to firms that have established a track record, and stock underwriters assist firms with initial public offerings of stock—IPOs—only when they show solid potential for growth. Venture capitalists are generally interested in investing in firms in which they can achieve a solid return on their investment through IPOs, and their investment activity is tied to general economic prospects in the economy; however, even during periods of economic downturn, venture capital firms seek investment opportunities.[5] Venture capitalists provided funds for the expansion of entrepreneurial firms in a several emerging communities in the 1980s. The first biotechnology firm went public in 1980, and of the hundreds of new firms founded through 1996, slightly over 200 eventually went public. For the 100 firms on which Deeds, Mang, and Frandsen (1997) were able to obtain data, the average size of an IPO was $19.3 million. Deeds, Mang, and Frandsen (1997) found that the amount raised was influenced not only by a firm's characteristics but also by the industry's perceived legitimacy. Federal approval of new biotech-derived drugs substantially enhanced the chances for commercial success of the firms' products, and positive articles in the press about the biotech industry sharply raised the industry's legitimacy and investors' confidence in the offerings. The commercial viability of the products, as certified by the FDA, made the positive media coverage credible and thus increased the flow of funds to the industry.

Several of the core populations of the Web community—browser and search engine firms, Internet access providers—benefited from the very early positive evaluation of the Web's potential by venture capital firms. Beginning in 1995, Web-based firms launched IPOs at stock prices not economically justified by their current and projected earnings. The best-known example was Netscape, which had revenues of only $16.6 million in the first half of 1995 and had never made a profit. Nonetheless, the first day of public trading in August 1995 put a value of $2.2 billion on the company's stock. After its IPO in April 1995, UUnet, an access provider, was trading at 248 times its estimated 1996 earnings. Although many investment fund managers began expressing skepticism about these high multiples almost immediately, and the price of many firms tumbled in the months after their IPOs, investors continued to invest heavily through 1995 (Hylton, 1996).

In addition to helping emerging firms obtain needed funds, venture capital firms also contribute to community evolution through the mediating role they play in spreading knowledge of effective forms and linking firms in different populations by playing a gatekeeping and information diffusion role. "Venture capital firms invest their money largely on the basis of the potential value of an entrepreneur's idea, a collateral that conventional bankers consider worthless" (Larsen & Rogers, 1988, p. 108). With their commitments to very risky concepts, venture capitalists have a stake in making sure a young firm has excellent managerial, marketing, and financial talent, as well as innovative researchers. They often assemble such teams of skilled managers by selecting from diverse but related industries. Silicon Valley law firms have also been involved in facilitating new venture formation. For example, Suchman (1994) found that law firms worked with venture capital firms in playing an information-mediating role for startup companies, helping institutionalize routines in areas such as recruiting officers and structuring equity arrangements. Sequoia Capital and Kleiner Perkins Caulfield & Byers are two of the best-known venture capital firms playing a mediating role in the Web community. Sequoia Capital was involved in the IPO for Excite; Kleiner Perkins has made many investments in high technology companies, including Netscape, Excite, and @Home; and senior partner John Doerr has played a major role in bringing together many high technology firms.

The Dependence of Community Development on the Establishment of Legitimacy

As a community is becoming established, its continued viability depends on the extent to which its core populations gain cognitive and sociopolitical legitimacy (Aldrich & Fiol, 1994), given the embeddedness of organizational populations in their sociopolitical environments (Baum & Oliver, 1992; Dacin, 1997), as well as on the extent to which technological changes influence the actual or perceived value of the firms' products (Miner & Haunschild, 1995). The greater the dependence of the emerging community on new organizational forms and new populations, the more serious its legitimacy problems. Among the many problems facing innovating entrepreneurs, their relative lack of legitimacy is especially critical, as other entrepreneurs and crucial stakeholders may not fully understand the nature of the new ventures, and their conformity to established institutional rules may still be in question.

"Legitimacy" is at stake in two related senses: how taken for granted a new form is (i.e., *cognitive* legitimacy), and the extent to which a new form conforms to recognized principles or accepted rules and standards (i.e., sociopolitical legitimacy). *Sociopolitical* legitimacy includes two components: *normative* acceptance, referring to conformity with cultural norms and values, and *regulatory* acceptance, referring to conformity with governmental rules and regulations (Aldrich & Fiol, 1994). How does a developing organizational community achieve legitimacy? We assume there is no "guiding hand" at the community center, directing strategic moves toward legitimacy. Instead, the course of community legitimacy is determined by: (1) the extent to which new organizations and new populations achieve legitimacy in their own right, (2) the extent to which organizations and populations within the community are able to work together to establish standards and advance the interests of community members, and (3) the nature of the involvement of community-level institutional actors, such as government, educational organizations, and the media.

Legitimacy Efforts by Individual Organizations

Firms in newly created populations need to foster trust among the constituencies with which they interact, whether those constituencies consist of customers or other firms within the nascent community. Given the paucity of information concerning new ventures, however, pioneering firms cannot base their initial trust-building strategies solely on impersonal evidence such as technological efficiency. They must also concentrate on framing the unknown in such a way that it becomes credible (Aldrich & Fiol, 1994).

To enhance cognitive legitimacy, for example, firms need to connect their innovations to existing knowledge, often through the use of symbolic language and behaviors (Aldrich & Fiol, 1994). Evidence of such efforts was abundant in the early days of the Web community, especially through the use of *metaphors* and *jargon* that linked concepts with which individuals were familiar to the new Web-based concepts. For example, a common convention for indicating that a Web page had not been completely developed was a message that said "currently under construction," usually accompanied by hard-hat graphics that conveyed the idea that although Web pages are basically intangible, they do "get built." The Web was also sometimes referred to as "the Wild, Wild, Web," implying a comparison between the creation of the Web and the settlement of the U.S. western territories in the nineteenth century. In addition to using metaphors that linked images of the past and present with this commercial venue of the future, early promoters of the Web also created a whole new language that blended old words with new concepts. An "internaut/cybernaut," for example, is a person who travels in "cyberspace," a "cyberpreneur" is an entrepreneur on the Internet, and a "hotzine/ezine" is an electronic magazine.

To enhance their normative legitimacy, firms can develop and communicate internally consistent stories that advance a compelling vision that they are behaving in a reasoned and trustworthy manner, even though they are promoting an innovation that has potentially transformative power (Aldrich & Fiol, 1994). Early founders of new commercial enterprises on the Web were effectively invisible to their potential customers, who saw only the firm's home page, not the organization itself. Because they could not rely on a recognizable physical presence to help convey their promise, they had to find some other way of communicating the credibility of their enterprises to the potential market. For many of them, the solution to this problem meant devoting a portion of their home pages to providing an overview of the company's history, as well as statements about their current business strategy. The home pages of those firms that were more closely focused on the Web's infrastructure often included sales pitches, directed at other businesses, that described the commercial potential of the Web and described how they—as a company with both a well-articulated vision and a sound approach—could help any business create and maintain a viable and profitable Web presence.

Collective Efforts by Organizations

Although individual firms and populations may be able to achieve their own legitimacy, accomplishing community-level legitimacy is problematic if these firms engage in unbridled competition to advance their own interests and do not cooperate with each other to promote their mutual interests (Aldrich & Fiol, 1994; Garud, 1994). A lack of standard designs, for example, may block the diffusion of knowledge and understanding, thus constraining the new activities. Therefore, in addition to developing a basis of understanding and trust at the level of their organizations, founders of new firms must also find strategies for establishing stable sequences of interactions with other organizations in their emerging community.

To further enhance cognitive legitimacy beyond the level of the individual firm, emerging organizations can converge around a dominant product or service design and focus on developing community-wide standards through the establishment of industry councils, cooperative alliances, trade associations, and other vehicles for collective action that are required to achieve legitimacy (Aldrich & Fiol, 1994; Haunschild, 1993). Because of a growing interest in conflicts over standards within evolving technological communities, rich case histories are now available for a number of industries in the United States: the automobile industry (Rao, 1996), the radio systems industry (Rosenkopf & Tushman, 1994), the electrical supply system industry (David, 1992; David & Greenstein, 1998), the machine tool industry (Noble, 1984), the microprocessor industry (Wade, 1996), and the telephone industry in Pennsylvania (Barnett, 1994). These studies document the importance of interorganizational networks and alliances in socially constructing acceptable population-level standards.

In the case of the community surrounding the Web, a basic level of standardization was in place from the beginning because of the Web's foundation in the already-established Internet. In addition, many of the original Web browsers (e.g., Mosaic, Netscape), as well as the software for developing home pages (hypertext mark-up language or HTML) and other Web-related products, were available free of charge to any Internet user. Because of their availability as shareware, these products dominated the Web during its early years. Their domination was threatened by the emergence of proprietary packages (e.g., by Microsoft) that offered more features and greater ease of use. However, because there were so many already-established Web sites that relied on the "old" software, new competitors were under pressure from consortia and trade associations, as well as users, to ensure that their products maintained full compatibility with the old. In the fall of 1995, for example, Microsoft announced that it would design its products to work with Java, a new language for Web browsers developed by Sun Microsystems, rather than pursue a path outside the dominant standards. However, in a sign that the agreement might be in jeopardy, in October 1997, Sun Microsystems sued Microsoft, claiming that Microsoft had violated the terms of its licensing agreement and was trying to create a proprietary, Windows-based Java language.

To establish normative and regulatory legitimacy, firms pursue collective action to influence the standards and regulations controlling commercial activity. Van de Ven and Garud (1994, p. 436), for example, described how the American Association of Otolaryngology "initiated a committee of representatives from industry, clinics, audiology, psychoacoustics, and other disciplines to study and recommend technical standards for [the cochlear implant] industry." Within the Web community, groups that were formed to promote Internet standards included the Internet Engineering Task Force (IETF), the Internet Assigned Number Authority, the Federal Networking Council, and the Internet Society (Fox, 1995). Consortia and associations were also created, such as the European Microsoft Windows NT Academic Centre (EMWAC) at the University of Edinburgh, a consortium funded by Microsoft, DEC, Sequent, Datalink Computers, and Research Machines; and a consortium of Enterprise Integration Technologies, NCSA and RSA Data Security, which was dedicated to creating a secure protocol for communicating via the Web. Between 1993 and 1997 there were four International World Wide Web Conferences held in Europe and the United States, where Web service providers and businesses discussed ways to resolve some of the common issues they faced.

Almost all of the collective efforts by members of the Web community have been successful at promoting their interests, especially with respect to regulatory control over the community's activities. During the 1996-1997 session of Congress, for example, several efforts were made to enact legislation that would have forced independent service providers, such as America Online, to monitor messages sent through their servers to help control the dissemination of material (e.g., pornography) that was considered inappropriate. As a result of collective lobbying efforts by community members, however, none of these efforts were successful.

The Web is an interesting case precisely because collective action organizations—alliances, coalitions, consortia—formed so quickly and managed to recruit the largest firms in the affected industries to join. As a community of populations, many of the Web's interest groups have been multi-industry, rather than limited to membership from only one population. For example, the World Wide Web Consortium, which set standards for the Web, included more than 100 members. All major software firms joined, as did the major hardware firms, such as IBM, Sun Microsystems, and Silicon Graphics (Lohr, 1995, p. C1). Collective action organizations have made population-level learning much easier, as firms have shared hardware and software information and worked on solutions to common problems affecting many populations (Miner & Haunschild, 1995).

Institutional Support

In addition to individual and collective efforts at achieving legitimacy, organizational communities may benefit if a strong supporting infrastructure is already in place. Because of the roots of a community in technological innovation, the essential infrastructure often comes from research and development sponsored by the government. Several studies have documented the significant role of governmental support for the technological base of a new industry. These studies illustrate how governmental assistance can create a stable nucleus for an evolving organizational community and thus accelerate the speed with which new populations achieve legitimacy. In their study of the creation of the cochlear implant industry, for example, Van de Ven and Garud (1994) noted that there were 22 years of research and technological advancements before the first commercial activity took place. Research on electronically enhancing human hearing was conducted by academics, and sponsored by grants from public research foundations and philanthropists. Rosenkopf and Tushman (1994, pp. 413-414) noted that "the radio community grew not only from the entry of new firms and associations, but also from the emergence and active participation of military, legislative, and regulatory bodies...the U.S. Navy became a very large user of radio technology...[and] also lobbied for legislation that would prioritize their needs..." The U.S. Air Force played a major role in establishing numerically controlled machine tools as a standard, versus the record-playback standard that some firms wanted (Noble, 1984).

In the case of the Web, government agencies were involved early on in the development efforts. The Defense Department created DARPAnet, the forerunner of the Internet, and the National Science Foundation and other research agencies actively encouraged the Internet as a medium for communication between scientists (Hafner & Lyon, 1996). Eventually, scientists wanted to be able to exchange graphics as well as text, so two scientists at CERN in Switzerland created the first Web browser. Graphics technology was further developed by the NCSA, a research institution at the University of Illinois at Urbana/Champaign. As companies began to realize the commercial potential in the technology, NCSA began licensing the technology to commercial organizations for further exploitation and development.

The importance of obtaining governmental support for community activities cannot be underestimated. With it, a community is able to establish its legitimacy quickly and flourish. Without it, individual efforts to form organizations and create new populations can be severely hampered. The biotechnology community, for example, fought a long-running battle with government regulators, and only in late 1995 did the industry receive final FDA approval that eliminated special restrictions on drugs made by biotechnology companies and treated them the same as drugs made by traditional pharmaceutical firms (Shan, Singh, & Amburgey, 1991). Consequently, this community struggled for almost 20 years to achieve the kind of sociopolitical legitimacy that the Web community had apparently already won after only three years, even though investors poured billions of dollars into the biotech industry in the intervening years.

Educational institutions may also play a role in how rapidly some emerging communities achieve legitimacy. Budding populations can establish links with educational institutions by incorporating the skills and knowledge needed for success in the populations into their curricula. Rosenkopf and Tushman (1994) described a number of technological communities that benefited from government investment in university research, and Deeds, Mang, and Frandsen (1997) argued that biotechnology firms attempted to enhance their legitimacy by identifying themselves with elite research universities, such as Harvard, Stanford, and the University of California at San Francisco. Of course, in many cases faculty inventors of key technologies actually started new firms, and their perceived value arose from genuine technological advances, such as the use of restriction enzymes and recombinant DNA. In turn, the legitimacy of the firms and their technologies was heightened by links to elite research universities.

With respect to the Web, the community-university link exemplifies the type of mutualism that Hawley (1950) described in growing communities. In the beginning, the Internet and the Web were the sole province of academic and research institutions, and the establishment of commercial sites benefited from their early experimental efforts. After commercial enterprises discovered the Web, however, most of the developments and changes were initiated by private firms. Coming full circle, the Web itself now provides fodder for academic work of a different sort: scholars study it and seek to understand its impact on organizational life, and students use it to do research and entertain themselves in their off-hours. Many of the Web entrepreneurs founding organizations in the new Web-based populations shown in Table 1 have been young people in their 20s, many just out of college, who learned about computers in coursework and in part-time jobs. For example, one of the founders of Netscape was a student at the University of Illinois while he worked for the NCSA, and the founders of Yahoo were Stanford graduate students.

Populations in a symbiotic relationship with Web-based firms also contributed to the rapid legitimization of the Web. For example, established law firms initially assigned patent and copyright lawyers to Web cases, and many set up special divisions to handle Internet-related issues. Eventually, law firms devoted entirely to the Internet were founded. These efforts were key in paving the way for establishing some of the legal standards for commercial Web activities, in addition to helping the community obtain the normative and regulatory legitimacy needed to achieve success.

In a similar fashion, the media—especially print media—played a very key role in the early days of the Web to help it establish both cognitive and normative legitimacy. The rapidity with which information about the Web was disseminated by journalists is nothing short of astounding. In 1993, for example, there were only 34 magazine articles and 13 articles in major newspapers that mentioned the Web. During 1994, however, those figures had jumped to 686 and 743 respectively; and during 1995 they reached totals of 6,365 and 10,054.[6] In the early days many of the articles were published in technical journals and focused on describing what the Web was and how browser technology worked. Over time, the content evolved to discussions of how the Web could and would affect commercial activity, and the publication outlets became less technical and more mainstream. As the legitimacy of the Web became even more established, references to the Web (usually through provision of a home page address) became integrated into stories of all kinds, such as announcements of upcoming rock concerts and descriptions of new movie releases.

The Process of Coevolution

Coevolution is a key feature of community development. Using a Canadian metropolitan day-care community, Baum and Singh (1994b), described how organizations and populations of organizations can systematically influence their environments, in addition to being influenced by those environments. Rosenkopf and Tushman (1994) created a model of the reciprocal relationship between the evolution of a given technology and the community that has been built around that technology. They demonstrated how the actions of organizations and populations can promote and influence changes in the technology, in addition to having technological innovation prompt changes within an organizational community. Van de

Ven and Garud (1994) expanded on this notion of coevolution in their analysis of
the reciprocal influences among technology, organizations, and institutions in the
cochlear implant industry.

From our perspective, coevolution happens within and across all levels in an
organizational community, facilitating its development into a cohesive whole.
Coevolution is the dynamic force connecting the themes—technological innovation, entrepreneurship, and legitimacy—illustrated in Figure 2. Significant technological innovations, for example, are not likely to happen without institutional
support, especially research and development sponsored by the government.
Although institutional support is necessary for the creation of innovations, these
innovations are not usually exploited for commercial gain by the organizations
that created them. Instead, they are generally seized upon by entrepreneurs, who
are willing to take the risks necessary to commercialize the new technology.

Once exploitation of a technological innovation begins, new requirements for
institutional support emerge as the organizations sponsoring the innovation strive
to achieve legitimacy. Government and regulatory bodies, for example, are faced
with decisions regarding the extent to which they need to become involved in the
burgeoning community, as overseers and as supporters. Innovating organizations
must also consider how to modify the technology so that it is readily accessible to
end users, thereby enhancing its cognitive and normative legitimacy. In making
modifications, firms and regulatory agencies must engage in collective action to
establish standards, both within and across populations. Established standards, by
eliminating barriers to entry and partially leveling the playing field between established and start-up firms, provide enhanced opportunities for new groups of entrepreneurs to join the community. Often, because of their increased openness to
change and willingness to take risks, entrepreneurs can devise significant
improvements to the technology that further enhance its legitimacy.

The Web community was initiated by the introduction of Mosaic browser software, which was created by the NCSA as an enhancement to the graphics-based
interface technology developed by scientists at CERN. Although this software
was created by government-sponsored organizations, it was most successfully
exploited by Netscape, a start-up firm. The developers at Netscape, along with
other software developers in the early days of the community (few of whom were
from established firms), were able to make significant enhancements to the technology at an early stage, in addition to establishing a set of open standards to discourage competition and encourage knowledge sharing. These technological
improvements, as well as an early reliance on standards, enhanced the user friend-
liness of the technology, enabling the community to establish cognitive and normative legitimacy very quickly.

Improvements and shared standards promoted the additional entry into the community of entrepreneurs, who leveraged their time, rather than money, to establish
a presence on the Web. Entrepreneurial initiatives eventually led to changes by
established firms. Web consultants and Web-page design firms, for example,

drove established firms seeking a Web presence into creating sites that did much more than simply provide information to consumers (Schwartz, 1997). For example, some firms created sites allowing consumers to send feedback to the firm, sign up for e-mailed update bulletins, and click through to other firms offering complementary products or services. In addition, a new population of firms seeking to establish Web-based economic transaction standards (e.g. CyberCash, Clickshare, Digicash) pushed traditional credit card companies into alliances with Web-oriented software firms, such as Netscape and Microsoft. As these alliances grew, at the organizational and population levels, they further enhanced the technology and legitimacy of the Web. Strong alliances also prompted the increased involvement of organizations and groups outside of the Web community, such as government and regulatory agencies, and academic and research institutions.

The coevolution of an organizational community depends on the simultaneous processes of variation, selection, retention, and struggle at the population level. What emerges is a new phenomenon that has subsequent consequences for the populations within the community. Variation is a feature of each segment of the model portrayed in Figure 2, such as through technological innovations, proactive legitimization strategies adopted by entrepreneurs and firms, new firms founded by entrepreneurs, and collective action attempts by action-sets of firms and populations. Similarly, selection processes are represented in each segment of the circle, such as through the struggle over a dominant design, the fit between legitimization strategies and prevailing social and cultural norms, venture capitalists' responses to entrepreneurs' attempts to raise funds, and successful solutions to the free rider problem developed by organizations pursuing collective action. Retention processes are also a part of the circle, such as through the embedding of a dominant design in the architecture of new products and processes, the institutionalization of a population's human resource needs in a college's curriculum, the tacit and informal rules used by venture capitalists to evaluate applicants, and the bureaucratization of the associations created by collective action.

CONCLUSION

We believe our chapter has made several contributions to the organizational ecology literature in general, and community ecology in particular. First, we have provided a focused definition of what a community is, thereby delimiting the construct of interest. Our definition acknowledges that communities consist of interacting populations that are united by their common orientation to a particular technology, and recognizes the importance of commensalism and symbiosis in defining the nature of those interactions.

We have also provided an updated theory of community creation and evolution that builds on the early contributions made by Astley and Fombrun: (1) technological innovation is a major catalyst for the creation of a community; (2) open environmental space—discovered or constructed—in the early days of community creation provides the opportunity for entrepreneurs to create new organizational forms, and allows new organizations and populations to engage in collaborative rather than competitive activities; and (3) legitimacy and institutional support are critical processes for community development.

Revisions in the Model of Community Evolution

Our revised model also addresses a number of the deficiencies in Astley and Fombrun's conceptualizations. First, we no longer rely on a set of Industrial Age assumptions about how organizations are structured and related to one another, or how innovative or resistant they are to change. We do not assume that existing organizations are monolithic and inflexible, or that they resist significant technological innovations except in cases of severe economic crisis or technological stalemates. Second, although we believe that technological innovation is a major catalyst for the creation of a new community, we do *not* advocate a punctuated equilibrium model of change. Rather, we assume that innovations may be evolutionary as well as revolutionary in nature, and that they are often rooted in an established pattern of research and development efforts undertaken by government-sponsored organizations. Entrepreneurs who recognize the commercial potential inherent in a given technology often move an innovation from its discovery to its commercialization.

A third major difference between our model and Astley and Fombrun's is that we assume a different process of evolution than they did. Our emphasis is on community creation and early evolution, rather than on change within existing communities. In addition, we do not assume that the process of evolution is linear or follows a structural-functional pattern of change. Instead, we emphasize the dynamic and fluid nature of community evolution through the process of coevolution, in which changes in any given aspect of the community can influence changes in other aspects. Although we posited that technological innovation is a major catalyst for community creation, we also recognize that innovation cannot take place without institutional support, and generally will not be commercially exploited unless someone with an entrepreneurial spirit is willing to take a chance on realizing its commercial potential. Finally, we do not assume that competition is the only motivating force energizing the activities within a burgeoning community. Rather, we believe that the openness of the environmental space in the early days of the community opens a window of opportunity for firms and populations to engage in collective action.

We have stressed that opportunities for entrepreneurs to enter populations within an emerging community may be different in the Information Age than they were in the Industrial Age. For example, we have argued that new firms can enter as K-specialists in early stages of a community's evolution, rather than waiting for later stages, especially when a set of standards for the community has been well established early on. We have pointed to the role that venture capitalists play in supporting the growth of new firms directly, through the raising of funds, and indirectly, by enhancing their legitimacy.

Legitimacy is a crucial dynamic in ensuring that a community is fully established. Organizations act independently to promote their cognitive and normative legitimacy with individual stakeholders, within and outside of the community. Simultaneously, sets of organizations also engage in collective action (Aldrich & Whetten, 1981). Some of these collective efforts focus on establishing a set of standards for the community, whereas others are aimed at publicizing the community's needs to individuals and organizations, especially institutions, outside of the community. When information traveled slowly, was costly to obtain, and difficult to interpret, new populations and communities may well have waited years not only for technological competencies to diffuse across populations, but also to achieve full legitimacy. In the Information Age global communication networks and high-technology information delivery systems have dramatically increased the speed with which technological competencies and legitimating activities are spread.

Overlaid on the themes of technological innovation, entrepreneurship, and legitimation, the process of coevolution was introduced to comprehend how communities emerge and become established. Rather than assume that these dynamics occur in isolation or evolve in some hierarchical fashion, our model proposes that the dynamics change as the community evolves. Changes in technological innovation influence entrepreneurial opportunities as well as legitimization processes; entrepreneurs can create new innovations which may then also enhance the cognitive legitimacy of the community; and the process of promoting legitimacy through the establishment of standards provides opportunities for entrepreneurs to start new ventures.

The propositions implied by our updated model of community creation and evolution are exemplified in how the World Wide Web was formed as a commercial community. One could argue, however, that the Web is unique, and that the processes inherent in its evolution do not translate easily to other communities. In particular, the speed with which the Web developed and established its legitimacy is unprecedented in organizational history.[7] We concede that the community of the Web may be unique; however, we do not believe its uniqueness detracts from our theoretical assertions. In fact, we believe that the speed with which the Web evolved was due precisely to the synergistic effects of the dynamics portrayed in Figure 2.

Many processes and events facilitating the Web's legitimacy came together very early in its life cycle. Because the Web emerged from research on the Internet, which itself had been established for over 20 years, it began with a significant degree of institutional support. Its roots in the Internet also provided the Web with a certain degree of regulatory legitimacy from its earliest days. Because the technology was so accessible, both to developers and users, it not only quickly became available for use by many firms, but it also gained cognitive and normative legitimacy. The concerted effort early on to establish a set of technological standards not only enhanced technological compatibility but also increased the technology's normative legitimacy. And, because of the conjuncture of technological compatibility with enhanced legitimacy, entrepreneurs and established firms were encouraged to create new ventures that exploited the commercial possibilities inherent in the new technology.

The Future

We hope that the ideas developed in this paper are an impetus for further research on community ecology. In particular, we believe that the propositions implied by our revised model can be tested by exploring the evolution of other commercial communities, especially those that have arisen in recent years. The model could also be used to study the evolution of communities that are in the process of emerging, using a recent technological breakthrough as the focal point and potential catalyst. For example, in 1997 a number of start-up firms began to pursue the commercial possibilities of *combinatorial chemistry*, from both medical and manufacturing perspectives. As these firms continue their efforts, we may be able to monitor their successes and failures from a community ecology perspective to see whether they become the foundation for the emergence of new populations and a new community.

Our analysis of the commercialization of the Web has shown that technological evolution is intertwined with the dynamics of community legitimization. More generally, the development of technological standards for a particular industry may have widespread consequences for the entire community to which it belongs. In some cases, new technological change may represent a form of "collective learning" that can be distinguished from direct learning from experience by individual organizations (Miner & Haunschild, 1995). Through organizational units formed by collective action, populations of organizations may observe the impact of population-level routines on the fate of other populations, adopt new population-level practices, and thereby influence the fate of communities with which they are linked. For example, when U.S. semiconductor firms imitated Japanese research consortia in an effort to enhance population-level survival (Aldrich & Sasaki, 1995), their resulting activities influenced not only the semiconductor industry, but also the entire community of firms to which the industry belonged. Deliberate population-level learning thus influenced community evolution. We have emphasized the role of legitimacy in community development, and a next step for research may well be to examine the link between legitimacy and collective technological learning.

We end on a methodological note. In researching community evolution, researchers will need to guard against left-censoring of a community's history by collecting data on a community from its earliest days, when new populations were just beginning to coalesce. Left-censoring of data—not having the early years of an community's history available—can lead to misspecification of models and biased conclusions regarding patterns of community growth. Underlying this issue is a more serious form of selection bias: to the extent that we study only populations and communities that survived long enough to make their mark upon the usual sources of archival information, we overlook the unsuccessful ones. Groups of firms and populations whose actions seemed likely to result in the emergence of a new community, but that were subsequently thwarted, provide the best historical record for testing our ideas about the social context of community emergence. Indeed, only by comparing developments in terminated communities with those that completed their life cycles can we assess the relative importance of the forces we have identified.

ACKNOWLEDGMENTS

We are indebted to Barry Staw, Ted Baker, Bill Barnett, Tina Dacin, Marlene Fiol, Andrew Gold, Lisa Keister, Anne Miner, Leann Mischel, Annette Ranft, Anand Swaminathan, Patricia Thornton, and Mike Tushman for helpful comments and suggestions on earlier drafts of this chapter. We also wish to thank Heather Barton and Brad Spires for their research assistance. Leslie Whitley whipped the manuscript into its final form.

NOTES

1. Astley (1985) defined organizational communities as "sets of diverse, internally homogeneous populations (p. 224) that are linked together into functionally integrated systems by their orientation to a common technology."

2. Interestingly, however, this work has failed to generate significant interest among ecologists. In a search of the Social Sciences Citation Index, for example, we found only a handful of subsequent publications that cited Astley and Fombrun's 1987 article. In addition, although over 60 publications have cited Astley's 1985 essay, closer investigation indicated that most of the references to this work were honorific, focusing on specific aspects of the article rather than on the theory as a whole.

3. We recognize that Hawley's work implies many different kinds of communities, rooted in commensalistic and symbiotic relations, such as urban and regional communities, social and religious associations, and so forth. Legal developments and changes in values can also create a focal point around which a community might develop. However, for purposes of this paper we have chosen to focus on commercial communities, following the lead of most ecological writings on communities over the past decade.

4. Although this population is currently dominated by Netscape and Microsoft, many organizations have attempted to create and disseminate browser software over the past four years. In late 1996, in fact, over 50 different versions of browser software were identified on a Web site called Browser-Watch (1997), which is maintained by Mecklermedia Corporation.

5. For example, after a brief slowdown in the late 1980s, IPOs climbed again in the early 1990s, raising about $21 billion in 1992. In 1992, just before the boom in Web-based IPOs, venture capital

firms made new commitments of $2.5 billion to growing firms (United States Small Business Administration, 1994).

6.   These figures are based on a review of Nexis data files from 1993 through 1995.
7.   Some community insiders have even equated "Web years" to "dog years."

REFERENCES

Abernathy, W. J., & Clark, K. B. (1985). Innovation: Mapping the winds of creative destruction. *Research Policy, 14*, 3-22.

Aldrich, H. E., & Whetten, D. A. (1981). Organization sets, action sets, and networks: Making the most of simplicity. In W. Starbuck & P. Nystrom (Eds.), *Handbook of organization design* (pp. 385-408). New York: Oxford University Press.

Aldrich, H. E., & Wiedenmayer, G. (1993). From traits to rates: An ecological perspective on organizational foundings. In J. Katz & R. H. Brockhaus (Eds.), *Advances in entrepreneurship, firm emergence, and growth* (Vol. 1, pp. 145-195). Greenwich, CT: JAI Press.

Aldrich, H. E., & Fiol, M. C. (1994). Fools rush in? The institutional context of industry creation. *Academy of Management Review, 19* (4), 645-670.

Aldrich, H. E., & Sasaki, T. (1995). R&D consortia in the United States and Japan. *Research Policy, 24* (2), 301-316.

Anderson, P., & Tushman, M. L. (1990). Technological discontinuities and dominant designs: A cyclical model of technological change. *Administrative Science Quarterly, 35*, 604-633.

Astley, W. G. (1984). Toward an appreciation of collective strategy. *Academy of Management Review, 9*, 526-535.

Astley, W. G. (1985). The two ecologies: Population and community perspectives on organizational evolution. *Administrative Science Quarterly, 30*, 224-241.

Astley, W. G., & Fombrun, C. J. (1983a). Collective strategy: Social ecology of organizational environments. *Academy of Management Review, 8*, 576-587.

Astley, W. G., & Fombrun, C. J. (1983b). Technological innovation and industrial structure: The case of telecommunications. *Advances in Strategic Management, 1*, 205-229.

Astley, W. G., & Fombrun, C. J. (1987). Organizational communities: An ecological perspective. *Research in the Sociology of Organizations, 5*, 163-185.

Barnett, W. P. (1994). The liability of collective action: Growth and change among early American telephone companies. In J. A. C. Baum & J. V. Singh (Eds.), *Evolutionary dynamics of organizations* (pp. 337-354). New York: Oxford University Press.

Barnett, W. P., & Carroll, G. R. (1987). Competition and mutualism among early telephone companies. *Administrative Science Quarterly, 32*, 400-421.

Baum, J. A. C. (1996). Organizational ecology. In S. R. Clegg, C. Hardy, & W. Nord (Eds.), *Handbook of organization studies* (pp. 77-114). London: Sage.

Baum, J. A. C., & Korn H. J. (1994). The community ecology of large Canadian companies, 1984-1991. *Canadian Journal of Administrative Sciences, 11* (4), 277-294.

Baum, J. A. C., & Oliver, C. (1992). Institutional embeddedness and the dynamics of organizational populations. *American Sociological Review, 57*, 540-559.

Baum, J. A. C., & Singh, J. V. (1994a). *Evolutionary dynamics of organizations*. New York: Oxford University Press.

Baum, J. A. C., & Singh, J. V. (1994b). Organization-environment coevolution. In J. A. C. Baum & J. V. Singh (Eds.), *Evolutionary dynamics of organizations* (pp. 379-402). New York: Oxford University Press.

Baum, J. A. C., Korn, H. J., & Kotha, S. B. (1995). Dominant designs and population dynamics in telecommunications services: Founding and failure of facsimile transmission service organizations, 1965-1992. *Social Science Research, 24*, 97-135.

Brittain, J. W. (1994). Density-independent selection and community evolution. In J. A. C. Baum & J. V. Singh (Eds.), *Evolutionary dynamics of organizations* (pp. 355-378). New York: Oxford University Press.

Brittain, J., & Freeman, J. H. (1980). Organizational proliferation and density dependent selection. In J. R. Kimberly, R. H. Miles, and Associates, (Eds.), *The organizational life cycle* (pp. 291-338). San Francisco: Jossey-Bass.

Bryman, A. (1997). Animating the pioneer versus late entrant debate: An historical case study. *Journal of Management Studies, 34* (3), 415-438.

Browserwatch. (1997). Browser statistics. http://browserwatch.internet.com (10/14/97).

Carroll, G. R. (1984). Organizational ecology. *Annual Review of Sociology, 10,* 71-93.

Carroll, G. R. (1988). *Ecological models of organizations.* Cambridge, MA: Ballinger.

Carroll, G. R. (1985). Concentration and specialization: Dynamics of niche width in populations of organizations. *American Journal of Sociology, 90* (6), 1262-1283.

Dacin, T. M. (1997). Isomorphism in context: The power and prescription of institutional norms. *Academy of Management Journal, 40* (1), 46-81.

David, P. A. (1992). Heroes, herds, and hysteresis in technological history: Thomas Edison and the "battle of the systems" reconsidered. *Industrial and Corporate Change, 1,* 129-180.

David, P. A., & Greenstein, S. (1990). The economics of compatibility standards: An introduction to recent research. *Economics of Innovation and New Technology, 1,* 3-42.

Deeds, D. L., Mang, P.Y., & Frandsen, M. (1997). The quest for legitimacy: A study of biotechnology IPO's. Paper presented at the 1997 meeting of the Academy of Management, Boston, MA.

Delacroix, J., & Solt, M. (1988). Niche formation and foundings in the California wine industry, 1941-1984. In G. R. Carroll (Ed.), *Ecological models of organization* (pp. 53-68). Cambridge, MA: Ballinger.

DiMaggio, P. (1994). The challenge of community evolution. In J. A. C. Baum & J. V. Singh (Eds.), *Evolutionary dynamics of organizations* (pp. 444-450). New York: Oxford University Press.

Dosi, G. (1982). Technological paradigms and technological trajectories. *Research Policy, 11,* 147-162.

Dosi, G. (1988). Sources, procedures, and microeconomic effects of innovation. *Journal of Economic Literature, 26,* 1120-1171.

Dunne, T., Roberts, M. J., & Samuelson, L. (1988). Patterns of firm entry and exit in U.S. manufacturing industries. *Rand Journal of Economics, 19* (4), 495-515.

Fombrun, C. J. (1986). Structural dynamics within and between organizations. *Administrative Science Quarterly, 31,* 403-421.

Fombrun, C. J. (1988). Crafting an institutionally informed ecology of organizations. In G. R. Carroll (Ed.), *Ecological models of organizations* (pp. 223-239). Cambridge, MA: Ballinger.

Fox, B. (1995). Retailing on the Internet: Seeking truth beyond the hype. *Chain Store Age Executive with Shopping Center Age, 71* (9), 33.

Free Range Media. (1997). Free range media news. http://www.freerange.com (19 June 1997).

Gartner, W. B. (1985). A conceptual framework for describing the phenomenon of new venture creation. *Academy of Management Review, 10* (4), 696-706.

Garud, R. (1994). Cooperation and competitive behaviors during the process of creative destruction. *Research Policy, 23,* 385-394.

Granovetter, M. (1985). Economic action and social structure: The problem of embeddedness. *American Journal of Sociology, 91* (3), 481-510.

Hafner, K., & Lyon, M. (1996). *Where wizards stay up late: The origins of the Internet.* New York: Simon & Schuster.

Hannan, M. T., & Freeman, J. (1977). The population ecology of organizations. *American Journal of Sociology, 83,* 929-984.

Hannan, M. T., & Freeman, J. (1989). *Organizational ecology.* Cambridge, MA: Harvard University Press.

Hart, S., & Denison, D. R. (1987). Creating new technology-based organizations: A system dynamics model. *Policy Studies Review, 6*, 512-528.

Haunschild, P. R. (1993). Interorganizational imitation: The impact of interlocks on corporate acquisition activity. *Administrative Science Quarterly, 38*, 564-592.

Hawley, A. H. (1950). *Human ecology: A theory of community structure*. New York: Ronald.

Hylton, R. (1996). Making money in the tech market. *Fortune*, May 13.

Larsen, J. K., & Rogers, E. M. (1988). Silicon Valley: The rise and falling off of entrepreneurial fever. In R. W. Smilor, G. Kozmetsky, & D. V. Gibson (Eds.), *Creating the technopolis: Linking technology, commercialization, and economic development* (pp. 99-115). Cambridge, MA: Ballinger.

Lohr, S. (1995). Telecommunications giants joint Internet security quest. *New York Times*, December 18, C2.

Lynn, L. H., Reddy, N. M., & Aram, J. D. (1996). Linking technology and institutions: The innovation community framework. *Research Policy, 25*, 91-106.

Mensch, G. (1979). *Stalemate in technology*. Cambridge, MA: Ballinger.

Methé, D., Swaminathan, A., & Mitchell, W. (1996). The underemphasized role of established firms as the sources of major innovations. *Industrial and Corporate Change, 5* (4), 1181-1203.

Miner, A., & Haunschild, P. (1995). Population level learning. In L. L. Cummings and B. M Staw (Eds.), *Research in organizational behavior* (Vol. 17, pp. 115-166). Greenwich, CT: JAI Press.

Moore, W. L., & Tushman, M. L. (1982). Managing innovation over the product life cycle. In M. L. Tushman & W. L. Moore (Eds.), *Readings in the management of innovation* (pp. 131-150). Boston, MA: Pitman.

Noble, D. (1984). *Forces of production*. New York: Alfred A. Knopf.

Rao, H. (1996). The social construction of reputation: Certification contests, legitimation, and the survival of organizations in the American automobile industry, 1895-1912. *Strategic Management Journal, 15*, 29-44.

Romanelli, E. (1989). Organizational birth and population variety: A community perspective on origins. In L. L. Cummings & B. Staw (Eds.), *Research in organizational behavior* (Vol. 11, pp. 211-246). Greenwich, CT: JAI Press.

Rosenberg, N. (1982). *Inside the black box: Technology and economics*. Cambridge: Cambridge University Press.

Rosenkopf, L., & Tushman, M. L. (1994). The coevolution of technology and organization. In J. A. C. Baum & J. V. Singh (Eds.), *Evolutionary dynamics of organizations* (pp. 403-424). New York: Oxford University Press.

Schoonhoven, C. B., & Eisenhardt, K. M. (1993). Entrepreneurial environments: Incubator region effects on the birth of new technology-based firms. In M. Lawless & L. Gomez-Mejia (Eds.), *Advances in global high technology management* (Vol. 8, pp. 149-175). Greenwich, CT: JAI Press.

Schwartz, E. I. (1997). *Webonomics: Nine essential principles for growing your business on the World Wide Web*. New York: Broadway Books.

Shan, W., Singh, J. V., & Amburgey, T. L. (1991). Modeling the creation of new biotechnology firms, 1973-1987. In J. L. Wall & L. R. Jauch (Eds.), *Academy of management best papers proceedings 1991* (pp. 78-82). Miami Beach, FL.

Singh, J. V. (Ed.) (1990). *Organizational evolution: New directions*. Newbury Park, CA: Sage.

Singh, J. V., & Lumsden, C. J. (1990). Theory and research in organizational ecology. *Annual Review of Sociology, 16*, 161-195.

Suchman, M. C. (1994). On advice of counsel: Law firms and venture capital firms as information intermediaries in the structuration of Silicon Valley. Unpublished doctoral dissertation, Stanford University.

Thornton, P. H. (1998). The sociology of entrepreneurship. *Annual Review of Sociology, 24*, forthcoming.

Tushman, M. L., & Anderson, P. (1986). Technological discontinuities and organizational environments. *Administrative Science Quarterly, 31*, 439-465.

Tushman, M. L., & Murmann, J. P. (1998). Dominant designs, technology cycles, and organizational outcomes. In L. L. Cummings & B. M. Staw (Eds.), *Research in organizational behavior* (Vol. 20, pp. 231-266). Greenwich, CT: JAI Press.

United States Small Business Administration (1994). *Handbook of small business data.* Office of Advocacy, Small Business Administration, Washington, DC: U.S. Government Printing Office.

Usher, A. P. (1954). *A history of mechanical inventions.* Cambridge, MA: Harvard University Press.

Utterback, J. M., & Abernathy, W. J. (1975). A dynamic model of product and process innovation. *Omega, 3* (6), 639-656.

Van de Ven, A. H., & Garud, R. (1994). The coevolution of technical and institutional events in the development of an innovation. In J. A. C. Baum & J. V. Singh (Eds.), *Evolutionary dynamics of organizations* (pp. 425-443). New York: Oxford University Press.

von Hippel, E. (1988). *The sources of innovation.* New York: Oxford University Press.

Wade, J. (1996). A community-level analysis of sources and rates of technological variation in the microprocessor market. *Academy of Management Journal, 39,* 1218-1244.

Wholey, D. R., & Brittain, J. W. (1986). Organizational ecology: Findings and implications. *Academy of Management Review, 11,* 513-533.

Yoshitake, D. (1997). ISPs hold on to their market. http://www.news.com (13 February 1997).

[16]

Journal of International Entrepreneurship 1, 103–119, 2003
© 2003 Kluwer Academic Publishers. Manufactured in The Netherlands.

Acquiring Competence at a Distance: Application Service Providers as a Hybrid Organizational Form

ANNETTA FORTUNE
Drexel University, LeBow College of Business, Philadelphia, PA 19104, USA

HOWARD E. ALDRICH*
Department of Sociology, CB 3210, University of North Carolina, Chapel Hill, NC 27599-3210, USA

Abstract. Application service providers (ASPs) are an innovative way for firms to outsource business functions by renting software as a service via the Internet. ASPs bring state of the art technology within the reach of firms that have been denied access to such advances in the past. The novelty of the ASP model results from the use of the Internet in the provision of services and the virtual inter-organizational tie that it creates between ASP and customer. The novelty of the ASP model has generated legitimacy concerns among the potential pool of customers, which has slowed the diffusion of this innovation. The recent dot-com fall-out has also had negative effects on the diffusion of the model. Nonetheless, the ASP model has managed to survive by adapting to the trends of the market. Entrepreneurship researchers have two reasons to pay more attention to ASPs. First, the emergence of the ASP business model has opened up opportunities for entrepreneurial activity by those seeking to capitalize on this new business model. Second, the proliferation of ASPs has the potential to affect other new ventures by altering their technology options.

Keywords: Application service providers, legitimacy, innovation, Internet, outsourcing, hybrid organizational forms

Introduction

Application service providers (ASPs) are an innovative way for firms to outsource business functions by renting software as a service via the Internet. ASPs have the potential to transform competitive forces within an industry. They make state of the art software available to new and established firms that have been denied access to such advances in the past. We believe that giving small- and medium-sized firms fast and easy access to innovative business practices has profound implications for entrepreneurship. We have identified two ways in which the emergence of the ASP business model is of concern to entrepreneurship researchers. First, the emergence of the ASP business model has opened up new opportunities for entrepreneurial activity. Second, the proliferation of ASPs has the potential to affect other new ventures by altering their technology options. In particular, depending on the course and speed of the model's adoption across industries, a firm's size and age may no longer prevent it from enjoying access to up-to-date technology.

*Corresponding author

From a conceptual viewpoint, ASPs stand at the intersection of the transaction cost economics (TCE) and the innovation literatures because of the novelty of their business model and the relationship that it engenders between ASPs and their clients. By making business process software tools available through a web interface, ASPs provide firms with another alternative to the traditional make-or-buy decision framework. The new choice set now becomes one of make, buy, or rent.

An ASP provides its customers with access to software hosted at a remote location via the Internet. ASPs acquire the necessary infrastructure to provide network space and applications for customers through purchase, leasing, or alliances with hardware and software vendors, and then charge their customers a "rental fee" to access the applications via the Internet (Aldrich and Fortune, 2000). In essence, an ASP provides access to software and hardware on a rental basis, thus eliminating the need for entities to incur the large investment associated with the purchase of comparable technology. Consequently, firms with limited resources, such as many new ventures and small- to medium-sized enterprises (SMEs), have the ability to access contemporary technology. In addition to the benefits of a low initial cash investment, this arrangement provides customers with a degree of flexibility that is intrinsic to the semi-permanent nature of a rental agreement.

ASPs give firms access to a wide range of business process software applications that have been historically performed in-house, or through traditional outsourcing venues, including financial accounting, human resource management, data storage, enterprise resource planning (ERP), and customer relationship management (CRM). ASPs differ widely in the nature and breadth of the applications they offer. However, the common denominator across the population of firms that designate themselves as ASPs is the use of the Internet in providing services. Internet technology not only provides the infrastructure for the ASP model, but also enables ASPs themselves to outsource many of the services they need to make the model work. We believe that the use of Internet technology in the provision of services sets ASPs apart from traditional outsourcing firms, and therefore distinguishes this business model as innovative.

Use of the Internet to deliver services also facilitates firms' participation in the global economy. Internet technology enables users to transcend temporal and geographical boundaries as they communicate and access information via the Web. For example, students can do research for term papers when the library is closed, or business colleagues can exchange information across the Atlantic just as easily as they can exchange information inside their office building. Firms wanting to enter the ASP space, or those wanting to employ the services of an ASP, are not constrained by geographical boundaries, because the Internet alleviates the necessity for proximity between customer and service provider.

The emergence and evolution of ASPs

The launch of the ASP industry in 1998 (Benton, 2002; Davidson, 2002) was made possible in 1995 when online interactivity was provided by the development of mobile code (Marks, 2001). The development of the ASP Industry Consortium (ASPIC) signaled the growing maturity of the ASP industry, as varied stakeholders came together to form an industry advocacy group. When the commercial community of the Web first emerged (Hunt and Aldrich, 1998), various consortia and trade associations formed and acted as advocates, and the ASPIC followed a similar path. Its goal was to increase the legitimacy of the ASP industry by "sponsoring research, fostering standards, and articulating the measurable benefits of this evolving delivery model" (ASPIC 1999). As with all trade associations in the United States, which operate under strict antitrust scrutiny, membership was open to any organization with an interest in the consortium's goals. The ASPIC membership included a wide range of organizations, such as computer software and hardware firms, network service providers, Internet service providers (ISPs), ASPs, consulting firms, public accounting firms, and telecommunications firms.

The ASPIC was founded in May 1999 by 25 of the largest firms involved in the budding industry, including well-known names such as AT&T, Cisco Systems, Citrix Systems, Ernst & Young LLP, Interpath Communications, IBM, and Sharp Electronics (ASPIC, 1999). The ASPIC had a two-tiered membership structure, with executive members paying $15,000 and associate members paying $5,000. The growth and expansion of the ASPIC is detailed in Table 1. The truly international nature of the ASPIC was demonstrated by the variety of countries represented by ASPIC membership. By March 2000, the ASPIC membership included representation from the following countries: Australia, Canada, France, Germany, Hong Kong, Ireland, Israel, Italy, Japan, Korea, Malaysia, The Netherlands, Norway, Singapore, United Kingdom, and Venezuela (ASPIC, 2000a). By September 2000, the ASPIC had also added members from the following countries: Brazil, Denmark,

Table 1.   The growth of the ASP Industry Consortium.

Date	Milestone
May 11, 1999	ASP Industry Consortium founded with 25 members
June 22, 1999	Membership more than doubles as 31 new members join since the launch in May
July 26, 1999	ASPIC establishes four new operating committees: Education and Outreach, Research, Best Practices, and Membership
July 28, 1999	ASPIC membership reaches 90
August 11, 1999	ASPIC membership reaches 100
October 29, 1999	ASPIC announces a Japanese affiliate, based in Tokyo ASPIC Japan includes over 40 Japanese companies
November 8, 1999	ASPIC membership reaches 200
March 21, 2000	ASPIC membership reaches 400
June 22, 2000	ASPIC membership reaches 500
September 27, 2000	ASPIC membership reaches 650
December 21, 2000	ASPIC establishes four new territorial committees and the appointment of a new European Director as ASPIC now has over 100 members in Europe
November 28, 2001	ASPIC acquired by the CompTIA and becomes the ASP section of this IT trade association

Finland, Iceland, Portugal, Russia, Saudi Arabia, Sweden, and Switzerland (ASPIC, 2000b).

By late 1999, the emerging industry was marked by media hype and fueled by the optimism of industry analysts and their lofty forecasts. Initially, the ASP business model itself was seen as possessing unlimited potential. The ASP model was heralded as the "Next Big Thing" (Aurebach, 1999) and the next "killer app" (Dean and Gilchrist, 2000). However, by early 2001, the overly optimistic sentiments surrounding the emerging ASP industry had been tempered (Paul, 2001). What was hype in the beginning had morphed into anti-hype. Many firms had even resorted to disassociating themselves with the term ASP in an effort to avoid the negative connotations associated with the term ASP (Wainewright, 2001a, 2001b). The dot-com crash precipitated a shakeout among ASPs, forcing a reassessment of how media and industry analysts viewed the ASP phenomenon, in addition to forcing a transformation of the industry itself.

Four new themes emerged in discussions by industry analysts and the media concerning the future of ASPs. First, a shift from domination by pure-play start-ups to divisions or business units of established information technology (IT) firms suggested the demise of the ASP industry as a separate entity. Instead, the ASP model increasingly moved under the umbrella of mainstream IT services (Wainewright, 2001a). Second, ASP offerings were no longer viewed as substitutes for in-house IT. Instead, they were beginning to be viewed as a piece of the IT puzzle that should be complementary to existing IT within firms. The pure-play, low customization business model that dominated the initial proliferation of ASPs had fallen out of favor. It was replaced by service packages that offered multiple options and some degree of customization to mesh with a client's needs and existing IT infrastructure (Benton, 2002; Davidson, 2002). In essence, the ASP market had shifted from being largely supply driven to being demand driven (Bernard, 2002).

The third indication that the ASP business model had moved within the IT industry was the acquisition of the ASPIC by Computing Technology Industry Association (CompTIA) in late 2001. The membership of the ASPIC had fallen from over 700 to slightly under 400, and thus even the advocacy group founded to support the ASP industry had to yield to the prevailing evolutionary pressures precipitated by the dot-com fall-out (Muse, 2001). The ASPIC has become the ASP section of the CompTIA, which is a full-fledged trade association of IT professionals (Muse, 2001). The CompTIA, which represents the converging communications and computing market, has over 8,000 corporate members and over 9,000 individual professional members in 63 different countries (ASPIC, 2002).

Fourth, the rising interest of independent software vendors (ISVs) and their customers in ASP offerings suggests not only that the ASP model now resides within the IT industry, but also that the ASP model is not a passing fad. Interest in hosted applications arose among ISVs due to customer demand for their hosted applications (Bernard, 2002). Small businesses, in particular, have shown an increased interest in hosted applications for accessing advanced e-business technology or initiating a web presence (Wainwright, 2001b). Evidence of the increased interest among ISVs has been demonstrated at IBM, an initiator of an ASP enabling program, and at Agiliti, an ASP enabler firm. IBM graduated 400 ISVs from its xSP Prime enabling program since its launch in April 2000 as ASP Prime, and more ISVs signed up to take part in the program in the last half of 2001 than in all of 2000. Similarly, 80% of the new business of Agiliti came from ISVs over the last 6 months of 2001 (Bernard, 2002).

Overall, the evidence shows the continued viability of the ASP business model, despite its volatile and rocky beginning. Research by the Boston-based market analysis firm Aberdeen suggested that, regardless of negative publicity, the ASP model is still sound and offers many of the features touted during its emergence. Aberdeen's research on successful ASPs found that ASPs actually do offer benefits such as cost reduction, more efficient use of IT staff, and rapid deployment of software (ASP Island staff, 2002). Total revenues and total customers of ASPs have continued to rise as new ASPs appear daily and large enterprises join the ranks of those offering an ASP model (Wainwright, 2001c).

A local case study of an accounting ASP from the Triangle area of North Carolina demonstrates the viability of the ASP business model. During an interview in March 2000, a company executive was optimistic about the continued success of their ASP offering. They were doing enough business to justify expanding the infrastructure to accommodate a larger number of ASP customers simultaneously. Similar to many others at this time, the executives of this accounting ASP had a positive outlook regarding the potential of their ASP offering. Contact with this company during late 2001 revealed that it was still doing well with its ASP offering. Unlike many other high-technology firms that were feeling the repercussions of the dot-com crash, this accounting ASP was still acquiring new customers and getting referrals from CPAs, who saw the ASP offering as beneficial for small firms. However, ASP success stories, such as this one, took a back seat to the news of ASP failures that dominated the media in 2001.

ASPs and entrepreneurship

The ASP phenomenon is important to the field of entrepreneurship not only because the ASP business model represents an opportunity for entrepreneurial activity, but also because it expands the technology options available to other new ventures, such as application hosting firms and service integrator firms. The nascent stage of ASP emergence was marked by the creation of pure-play start-up firms hoping to take advantage of the opportunity afforded by contemporary Internet technology (Wainewright, 2001a). In addition, new kinds of firms are entering the ASP space, because divisions or business lines of established companies have set up ASP operations (Wainewright, 2001a). Consequently, the emergence of the ASP industry and its transformation represents a rich opportunity to apply principles from the field of entrepreneurship.

By providing a lower cost alternative to a large, up-front capital investment, ASPs provide new ventures and SMEs of any age with access to technology that would otherwise be available only to larger, more established firms. ASPs can reduce the initial outlay for the acquisition of contemporary technology, in addition to reducing the ongoing investment of internal resources required to maintain a comparable level of functionality in-house. Because entrepreneurs can obtain effective routines and competencies for a wide variety of business functions via the Web, they can concentrate on the specific value proposition their businesses bring to the market. The ability to focus on core value propositions, coupled with access to advanced technology, has the potential to positively affect the performance of new ventures that take advantage of ASP offerings. ASPs are relevant to the field of entrepreneurship in much the same way as venture capital activity, because both enrich the institutional infrastructure for new ventures.

ASPs: the issues and obstacles

The innovative features of ASPs

Outsourcing is an arrangement in which a firm pays an external party to perform an agreed upon business function, thus moving a particular business function to a location outside the firm boundary. The outsourced business function remains connected to the focal firm through a cooperative inter-organizational relationship between the entity and the provider of the service. Because the ASP model involves moving a business function from within the firm to a virtual location in cyberspace that spans the boundaries of the client firm and the ASP, it represents a form of outsourcing. By comparison, Ulset (1996) studied R&D outsourcing that involved contracting out part of a firm's R&D effort to an external party, such as a university or an R&D company. Ulset (1996) described such outsourcing as a hybrid mode of contracting, and we see ASPs as embodying a similar hybrid form.

Even though the outsourcing of business functions is not a new idea, ASPs possess certain characteristics that mark them as an innovation. Almost 30 years ago, Zaltman et al., (1973) defined an innovation as a change that includes a degree of newness. His definition persists today, as indicated by contemporary citations to Zaltman's work (e.g. Van de Ven et al., 1999) and the similarity of current definitions. For example, in the most recent edition of his book, Rogers (1995: 11) defined an innovation as "an idea, practice, or object that is perceived as new by an individual or other unit of adoption." Rogers' (1995) definition suggests that the essential aspect of an innovation is its novelty to the people involved. Accordingly, ASPs can be considered an innovation because they are perceived as a new phenomenon in the business environment.

Using Rogers' definition, the ASP business model is an innovation because of two characteristics: it is based on a new technology, the Internet, and it creates a novel organizational tie—a virtual inter-organizational relationship. The ASP model brings a new dimension to the well-established idea of outsourcing business functions because it uses Internet technology for the delivery of business services. Given that commercial access to the Internet was established in 1991, and mobile code, which provided online interactivity, was established even more recently in 1995 (ASPscope, 2001), use of the Internet to conduct business activity might be considered, by itself, an innovation. In addition, the resulting virtual connection and interaction between an ASP and its customers gives the business model an innovative twist, as shown in Figure 1. Unlike traditional forms of outsourcing, the ASP model builds a virtual inter-organizational relationship in which most interaction occurs via the Internet, with little face-to-face contact.

The ASP model can be construed as a hybrid form of contracting because the outsourced business function remains connected to the focal firm through a cooperative inter-organizational relationship between the entity and the service provider. Due to the necessity of an ongoing instrumental relationship between an ASP and its customers, the ASP business model can be described as a cooperative inter-organizational relationship that extends the traditional TCE make-or-buy question, to a question of make, buy, or rent. ASPs are similar to other hybrid contracting relationships in general, and outsourcing specifically, because they represent an alternative to the hierarchy and the market. Because an ASP moves the location of a business activity outside the boundaries of the firm, it constitutes an alternative to a hierarchical arrangement in which business activity remains within a firm's boundaries. An ASP also represents an alternative to a market purchase because the external relationship, or transaction, between the ASP and the customer is ongoing, rather than a one-time event.

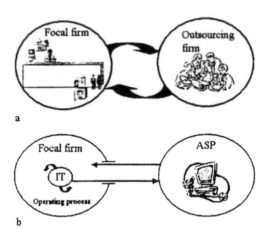

Figure 1.   Contrast between traditional outsourcing and ASP models. (a) Traditional limited boundary spanning outsourcing; (b) New boundary crossing relationship.

Like other hybrid forms, the ASP business model shares some elements of the market and hierarchy models, but also stands apart from them. It represents a unique and separate type of hybrid contracting because of two specific characteristics of the ongoing relationship between the ASP and its customers. First, the relationship between an ASP and its customer is both instrumental and cooperative. Like some other forms of outsourcing, the relationship between an ASP and a customer is instrumental because a customer is purchasing a service from the ASP. However, the relationship is also cooperative because the ASP and the customer must interact with each other on an ongoing basis, as the provision of the service requires continuous computer-mediated interaction between them.

Second, the relationship between an ASP and its customer is a virtual one, which also distinguishes the ASP business model from other forms of hybrid contracting modes. The ASP and its customers are connected and work with each other via the Internet, with very little face-to-face contact. Even the support service component of most ASPs, such as Intacct (Parrish, 2001), an accounting firm, is executed via the Internet and via the telephone. Furthermore, the initial contact between ASPs and users often takes place without face-to-face interaction. For example, through the NetLedger website, prospective customers or interested parties can access short-term free trials of the service (www.netledger.com). The ongoing virtual relationship that is the hallmark of the ASP business model makes this business model truly unique.

The innovative characteristics of the ASP business model have created challenges for ASP firms, as well as for their customers and potential customers. In spite of the optimism and media hype surrounding the ASP model, many industry analysts admit that the diffusion of the model has been much slower than expected (e.g. Maselli, 2000; Torode and Follett, 2000; Clancy, 2001; Gilmore, 2001; Paul, 2001). The pressing question now is why firms have been so slow to adopt the ASP business model.

The legitimacy concerns of ASPs

We address the challenges facing ASP firms within the framework proposed by Aldrich and Fiol (1994) in their model of the emergence of new industries. Legitimacy is the perception of an entity, or its activity, as just and suitable (Suchman, 1995), which is a substantial problem for new firms that are participating in novel activities. As an Internet-based venture, ASPs inherit the legitimacy issues surrounding the interface of the Web and business activities (Hunt and Aldrich, 1998). As suggested by the Aldrich and Fiol (1994) framework, the two types of legitimacy that are a concern for ASPs are cognitive and sociopolitical legitimacy. Cognitive legitimacy refers to the acceptance of a new activity such that the existence of activity becomes a taken for granted part of the environment, and sociopolitical legitimacy refers to the acceptance of a new activity as ethical and appropriate (Aldrich, 1999: 229–230). As a vehicle for the provision of client services, the Internet creates both cognitive and sociopolitical legitimacy issues for ASPs.

Using the Internet for the provision of outsourcing creates cognitive legitimacy issues because the novelty of this approach hinders this activity from becoming a taken for granted aspect of the business environment. Sociopolitical legitimacy issues arise because laws, norms, and standards have not yet been established to govern the activity or the parties involved.

The lack of legitimacy surrounding ASP firms has precipitated skepticism among potential customers who have questioned the potential benefits of the model. The lack of legitimacy, especially cognitive legitimacy, and the slow diffusion of the ASP model resulting from this lack of legitimacy can be linked to five attributes of an innovation that influence its diffusion or rate of adoption. These five attributes were set forth by Rogers (1995) as follows: (1) the relative advantage of adopting the innovation, (2) the innovation's perceived compatibility with existing practices, (3) its perceived complexity, (4) its trialability, and (5) the observability of the innovation including the outcomes of adoption. Table 2 provides descriptions of these five attributes, with examples taken from case studies of local ASP firms we have studied.

The Achilles heel of the ASP model lies in its lack of perceived relative advantage, based on negative perceptions of the benefits or returns to adopting the innovation. However, the issues of compatibility and observability suggest that even those willing to acknowledge the potential benefit of adopting the ASP model may still be discouraged from using it due to the uncertainty surrounding its effects on existing business practices. Lastly, the attributes of trialability and complexity emphasize the importance of potential adopters' perceptions of an innovation. For example, ASP executives interviewed from the Triangle area of North Carolina spoke confidently

Table 2.   Innovation attributes influencing diffusion.

Rogers' (1995) five dimensions	Description	Example from our case studies
Relative advantage	Degree to which the innovation is viewed as an improvement	Each of the ASP executives felt that their services provided efficiency benefits for customers
Compatibility	Degree to which the innovation is viewed as consistent with existing practices	*WebAccount*: The majority of customers using the web-based product were young, high tech firms
Complexity	Degree to which the innovation is viewed as hard to use and comprehend	*WebAccount and HrEval*: Customer training was offered to facilitate customer use and satisfaction of the service
Trialability	Degree to which the innovation can be used on a trial basis	All ASP services offered online trials of the service via the web site
Observability	Degree to which the innovation and the results of its use are visible	Each of the ASP executives spoke of an organized strategic marketing plan to raise awareness of the ASP model

about the online trials that their ASPs provided, the ease with which their offering could be employed within customer environments, and the availability of customer training. However, the customer resistance mentioned by these same executives indicated that potential customers are not looking at the ASP model from the same perspective as the ASP firms.

The slow diffusion of the ASP model confirms that the ASP model suffers from a lack of legitimacy, but continued interest surrounding the ASP model also indicates that legitimacy is slowly growing. In spite of the problems experienced by many of the ASP firms, interest in the ASP model continues to develop among ISVs (Wainewright, 2001c; Bernard, 2002). Customer demand has motivated many ISVs to adopt an ASP model (Bernard, 2002). Because customers are turning to their ISVs rather than signing up with existing ASP firms, it appears that potential customers may be more comfortable acquiring this service from a familiar party. Ironically, then, ISVs have greater legitimacy than ASPs, and they are thus having more success with the ASP model than the firms that introduced the model.

Case examples

The challenges faced by innovative ASP firms are daunting, as indicated by the demise of many ASP firms during the industry fallout. However, many ASP firms have found ways to address these challenges and survive. The two case analyses that follow demonstrate how some ASP firms are overcoming obstacles on the road to survival. NetLedger began as a web-native, pure-play accounting ASP start-up, but it has now been taken under the Oracle umbrella as the provider of an Oracle business service offering. Our other local case, of HRWeb, reveals the evolution of an ASP start-up to an HR business service provider. In this section, we also briefly look at the situation in the European ASP market, where we argue that on an international level, ASPs face the added challenge of an uncertain business environment.

NetLedger was founded in September 1998 and announced its five-dollar per month online accounting package in August 1999, which was targeted to small businesses with less than 50 employees (Wainewright, 1999). From the beginning, NetLedger had indirect connections to Oracle because its founder, Evan Goldberg, was a former Oracle vice president, and the company's initial investor was Oracle founder and CEO Larry Ellison (Wainewright, 1999). However, like numerous other ASP start-ups, NetLedger struggled to remain in the game, indicating that NetLedger was apparently not benefiting from its indirect ties to Oracle. Connections to Oracle may have given NetLedger a slight edge over other ASPs, but they did not provide it with enough legitimacy to survive as an independent entity.

NetLedger's development was marked by a deepening of its relationship with Oracle, until in October 2000, the two firms entered into a formal strategic partnership. The partnership was designed to bring a web-native online accounting solution to small businesses (Newcomb, 2000a). The formalized relationship further enhanced the legitimacy of NetLedger, given Oracle's reputation. NetLedger received another positive boost from Oracle when it was chosen to power Oracle's new Small Business Suite. The relationship resulted from a deal that stopped short of a merger or acquisition, but left that possibility open (Newcomb, 2001a).

In addition to the important strategic relationships that provided NetLedger with a degree of legitimacy, a transformation in the service offering of NetLedger also contributed to its continued survival. Following the demands of a market that called for more service options to meet more specific customer needs (Benton, 2002), NetLedger moved toward a broader, integrated service offering. In November 2000, it unveiled the new NetLedger 5.0, which added online commerce functionality to the package. This enhancement was the most significant to date and was intended to move the company closer to its goal of being an Internet-based, one-stop small business management service (Newcomb, 2000b). The transformation continued into 2001 when NetLedger announced the availability of an integrated business suite that included accounting, CRM, payroll, online bill paying, Web store, HR, and customer support within a single solution, the NetLedger 1 System. This package integrated the services that NetLedger had been offering separately on an a la carte basis, enabling it to offer an aggregated package of services at a lower price to the customers who desired this level of functionality (Newcomb, 2001b).

Our local case study of a firm from the Triangle area of North Carolina also revealed the evolution of ASP firms toward providing expanded, yet integrated, service solutions. This firm began as an ASP firm offering a Web-native, general human resource package that was targeted at small- to medium-sized firms that were at least in their "B" round of financing. This firm experienced early success, and they received only two outright rejections in their initial 30 sales presentations. Furthermore, executives of this firm did not even see the need for a sales force, given their success at exploiting existing distribution channels and the pools of potential customers provided through their strategic partners. However, early success did not exempt this ASP firm from keeping up with the evolution of the ASP sector. For this firm, adaptation included a new name, in addition to an expansion of the service offering to better suit the diverse needs of customers. In essence, the transformation of service offerings by successful ASPs demonstrates that the evolution of the ASP sector is truly one of adapt or die (Benton, 2002).

Our previous two examples were from the United States, where the industry has enjoyed its greatest level of success. In Europe, in addition to the problems we have noted, ASPs are faced with data protection laws that have not kept up with the reality of a mobile, online world. Research by a London-based law firm on behalf of the ASPIC revealed that in the 15 countries studied, each region had its own set of data protection laws, creating a highly uncertain environment (ASP Island, 2001). Therefore, European ASP firms and other firms hoping to take advantage of the potential of the European market have had to push for changes in local laws, while simultaneously adapting to global changes in the industry. This situation indicates that the evolution and proliferation of ASPs on an international level is further complicated by factors in the local business environment, especially a lack of sociopolitical legitimacy.

Continued interest in the ASP model and the existence of successful ASP firms indicates the viability of the ASP model. However, the transformation of ASPs suggests that industry analysts may be correct in predicting that the ASP model will be absorbed into the IT services industry to the point that the term "ASP" will fall out of use (Davidson, 2002). Regardless of whether the term "ASP" survives, the immediate survival of ASPs hinges on their continuing to build legitimacy and continuing to adapt to trends in the market. The combination of the movement of established companies, such as ISVs, into the ASP space and the involvement of other major players, such as those firms with Big 5 heritage (Wainewright, 2002a), has generated increased legitimacy for the ASP model. The evolution of the ASP model as a segment of the IT industry is demonstrated by the convergence between the service offerings of ASPs and other IT firms (e.g. ISVs, systems integrators, and management service providers). ASPs are adding the features of these other players to their service offering, while the other players are adding features of ASPs to their service offerings, generating a convergence toward providing real-time business and IT services within the IT industry (Wainewright, 2002b).

Implications

Technological innovation has been described as *either* competence-enhancing *or* competence-destroying (Tushman and Anderson, 1986). However, a third possibility exists. Technological breakthroughs might go beyond current organizational knowledge but still allow established populations to participate in a new community. Rather than a dichotomy between competence-destroying and competence-enhancing innovations, Hunt and Aldrich (1998) proposed a third category of innovations: *competence-extending*. Competence-extending innovations permit existing firms to pursue new opportunities that allow them to stretch existing competencies into complementary ventures.

Within the IT industry, the ASP model represents a competence-extending innovation because existing IT firms, such as ISVs, have been able to move into the ASP space. Unlike a competence-enhancing innovation, implementation of the ASP model is not a straightforward extension of existing competencies, requiring minimal effort, as indicated by the existence and popularity of ASP enabler programs provided by firms such as IBM and Intel. However, unlike a competence-destroying innovation, the ASP model is not a direct threat to the existing competencies of IT firms, because some of these firms have clearly been successful in launching ASP offerings. Consequently, the acceptance of the ASP model within the IT industry provides an opportunity for firms that accept the challenge.

Proposition 1. The near future will continue to see an increase in the number of IT firms that provide ASP offerings within their service packages.

An institutional perspective emphasizes the existence and power of external legitimating forces that pressure organizations to change their structures in an effort to conform to an institutionalized pattern (DiMaggio and Powell, 1983). One of the key outcomes of successful imitation of institutionalized patterns is enhanced organizational stability, and perhaps a higher level of efficiency (Tolbert, 1988). In other words, success may not only come from one's own technical achievements, but from following the whims of institutional trends. Specifically, institutional pressures appear to be more salient for late adopters, while economic pressures are more salient for early adopters (Burns and Wholey, 1993; Westphal et al., 1997; Walston et al., 1998). In other words, there is a temporal division between the effects of economic and institutional factors on the adoption of an innovation (e.g. Meyer and Rowan, 1977; DiMaggio and Powell, 1983; Tolbert and Zucker, 1983). Consequently, if the trends we have described continue, the proliferation of the ASP model may lead to institutional pressures on ISVs and other IT firms to incorporate this model into their service offering.

Proposition 2. Over time, institutional reasons may replace economic reasons for the inclusion of an ASP offering within IT firms.

An institutional perspective also suggests that the movement of the ASP model to a space within the mainstream of IT services industry may be beneficial for the continued existence of the ASP model, in general, and ASP firms, in particular. The institutional approach focuses on the objectified and taken-for-granted nature of organizations and organizational environments, as perceived by participants. It emphasizes the value-laden character of institutions and the way in which organizational actions are legitimated when cloaked in an institutionally acceptable rhetoric (Scott, 1995). Acceptance within the well-established IT industry provides the ASP model with the legitimacy that is needed for its survival. Consequently, existing ASPs and new ventures with an ASP focus stand to benefit from the inclusion of the ASP model within the IT industry, because their acceptance provides ASPs with the legitimacy that they lacked as members of an innovative, stand alone industry.

Proposition 3. Firms centered on the ASP model will increasingly prosper, as the ASP model becomes a feature of the IT industry.

For start-ups and SMEs, the proliferation of the ASP model provides a means of facilitating access to contemporary software and hardware technology in a cost-efficient manner. Resource- and knowledge-based theories of the firm emphasize the distinctive competencies held by firms that give them competitive advantages (Barney, 1986; Foss, 1999). Such theories emphasize the difficulty of developing and sustaining a unique set of competencies because of the resource constraints facing most firms. With only limited resources, managers face difficult tradeoffs between pursuing core competencies and staying current with developments in other aspects of business operations. ASPs can reduce the need of firms to invest internal resources in IT intensive business processes, which would free critical resources to focus on the core competencies, or the key value proposition of the business. The potential benefit of employing ASPs may be universal to all types of firms, but the use of ASPs may have the largest impact on new ventures and other SMEs that may be facing more severe resource constraints than larger, more established firms.

The IT needs of resource constrained new ventures and SMEs create a market niche for the ASP business model. Even though ASP offerings may lack some of the technological sophistication of the cutting edge offerings of larger, established firms, the ASP model possesses a new value proposition (i.e. software as a service via the Internet) that satisfies the needs of a subset of IT customers. Therefore, by definition, ASPs represent a disruptive technology because the ASP model under performs many existing product offerings, and yet manages to fulfill the needs of a set of customers residing on the periphery of the mainstream (Christensen, 1997). Similar to other disruptive technologies described by Christensen (1997), the ASP model offers a product that is less expensive, easier to implement, and more convenient relative to the product and service offerings of larger, established firms. Consequently, ASPs have the ability to serve the market created by resource constrained new ventures and SMEs, which larger, established firms are unable to reach within their product offerings. The new ventures and SMEs within this market that take advantage of the cost effective access to technology afforded by the use of ASPs will be able to gain ground on those forgoing this opportunity. With their IT needs satisfied, these firms will be able to redirect scarce resources toward developing their core competencies.

Proposition 4. New ventures, as well as other SMEs, using the services of ASPs, will gain a competitive advantage over those firms that do not use ASPs.

ASPs may level the playing field within any industry where the ASP model is widely adopted. First, ASPs may raise the level of competitive intensity in populations by reducing the competence gap between large firms, with their own IT staffs, and SMEs, which can now contract for applications that were formerly unattainable. Second, ASPs may also raise the level of competitive intensity in populations by reducing the boundary between competence-destroying, competence-enhancing (Tushman and Anderson, 1986), and competence-extending innovation (Hunt and Aldrich, 1998) within an industry. Currently, established firms, especially SMEs, are at a disadvantage when major innovations occur in their population, as their routines and competencies are often bundled in such a way as to make adaptation difficult (Hannan and Freeman, 1989). Adopting innovations requires reorganization, an often costly and difficult process (Aldrich, 1999: 163–195). However, when innovations occur in the business practices covered by ASPs, client firms gain immediate access to the latest developments.

Proposition 5. ASPs will raise the level of competitive intensity in industries where ASP use is widely adopted.

Conclusions

Our purpose in this paper was twofold. First, we wanted to draw entrepreneurship researchers' attention to the ASP phenomenon and the evolution of an innovative business model. Second, we developed five propositions to highlight promising research issues surrounding the evolution of the ASP business model. We believe that the proliferation of this model will have a substantial effect on the business landscape.

Based on our review, we believe the evolution of the ASP model offers an opportunity for entrepreneurship researchers to study some of the fundamental questions in resource- and knowledge-based views of the firm, institutional theory, and TCE. Researchers have the opportunity to study the evolution of ASPs as these changes are taking place, thus avoiding the bias of studying a phenomenon retrospectively. Historical analyses can uncover a wealth of information, but this approach often involves only a study of survivors. Such research suffers from a selection bias because many organizations do not survive long enough to be included in later investigations.

The contemporary nature of Internet growth affords entrepreneurship researchers an opportunity to avoid this bias by studying the organizations that are present during the nascent stages of the innovation. In particular, these circumstances give researchers access to the valuable knowledge that is present in the stories of the trailblazers that did not survive. The profusion of emerging and evolving ASPs constitutes a rich pool of subjects for future case studies.

References

Aldrich, Howard E. *Organizations Evolving*. London: Sage, 1999.

Aldrich, Howard E. and Marlene E. Fiol, "Fools Rush In? The Institutional Context of Industry Creation", *Academy of Management Review, 19*(4), 645–670, (1994).

Aldrich, Howard E. and Annetta Fortune, " 'Can't Buy Me Love' (But I Know Where You Can Rent It): The Emerging Organizational Community Around Web-based Application Service Providers", Paper Presented at the Annual Academy of Management Conference, Toronto, Ontario, Canada, 2000.

ASP Industry Consortium, Press Releases, Accessed December 6, 1999, http://www.aspindustry.org (1999).

ASP Industry Consortium, March, 30, 2000 Press Release, Accessed March 5, 2002, http://www.aspindustry.org (2000a).

ASP Industry Consortium, September 27, 2000 Press Release, Accessed March 5, 2002, http://www.aspindustry.org (2000b).

ASP Industry Consortium, "CompTIA and the ASP Industry Consortium Fact Sheet", Accessed January 21, 2002, http://www.aspindustry.org (2002).

ASP Island, "ASPs Warn: EU Data Protection Laws Fail to Keep Pace with Technology", Accessed January 23, 2002, http://www.aspisland.com (2001).

ASP Island, "Aberdeen Report Touts ASPs", Accessed January 21, 2002, http://www.aspisland.com (2002).

ASPscope, "Top 25", Accessed May 24, 2001, http://www.ASPscope.com (2001).

Auerbach, Jon G. "Technology (A Special Report): The Providers—Playing the New Order: Stocks to Watch as Software Meets the Internet", *The Wall Street Journal*, (November 15, 1999).

Barney, Jay B., "Types of Competition and the Theory of Strategy: Toward an Integrative Framework", *Academy of Management Review, 11*(4), 791–800, (1986).

Benton, Greg, "Adapt or Die: The Evolution of ASPs in Today's Economy", ASP Island Opinion, Accessed January 21, 2002, http://www.aspisland.com (2002).

Bernard, Allen, "ISVs Still Want to be ASPs", ASPnews.com, Accessed January 21, 2002, http://www.ASPnews.com (2002).

Burns, Lawton R. and Douglas R. Wholey, "Adoption and Abandonment of Matrix Management Programs: Effects of Organizational Characteristics and Interorganizational Networks", *Academy of Management Journal, 36,* 106–138, (1993).

Christensen, Clayton M., *The Innovator's Dilemma,* Boston, MA: Harvard Business School Press, 1997.

Clancy, Mark, "The Insidious Resistance to ASPs", Accessed May 20, 2001, http://www.aspnews.com (2001).

Davidson, Dean, "Who Will Survive the ASP Evolution", ASPnews.com, Accessed February 25, 2002, http://www.ASPnews.com (2002).

Dean, Gary H. and Wes Gilchrist, "ASPs: The Next Killer App", J.C. Bradford & Co., Accessed November 12, 2000, http://www.aspisland.com (2000).

DiMaggio, Paul J. and Walter W. Powell, "The Iron Cage Revisited: Institutional Isomorphism and Collective Rationality in Organizational Fields", *American Sociological Review, 48*(2), 147–160, (1983).

Foss, Nicolai J. "Research in the Strategic Theory of the Firm: 'Isolationism' and 'Integrationism'", *The Journal of Management Studies, 36,* 725–755, (1999).

Gilmore, Tom, "ITAA and ASPIC: Breaking Trail for Net Services", *IDC Newsletter—xSP Advisor,* No. 45. Accessed April 25, 2001, http://www.idc.com/newsletters/ (2001).

Hannan, Michael T. and John H. Freeman, *Organizational Ecology,* Cambridge, MA: Harvard University Press, 1989.

Hunt, Courtney S. and Howard E. Aldrich, "The Second Ecology: The Creation and Evolution of Organizational Communities as Exemplified by the Commercialization of the World Wide Web". In Barry Staw and Larry L. Cummings (eds), *Research in Organizational Behavior,* Vol. 20, pp. 267–302. Greenwich, CT: JAI Press, 1998.

Marks, Robert, "An Analysis of the ASP Delivery Model", Accessed May 10, 2001, http://www.aspscope.com (2001).

Maselli, Jennifer, "Growing Pains—ASPs and Their Customers Still Face Challenges with Pricing, Performance, and Training", *Techsearch Informationweek,* Issue 796, July 24, Accessed August 27, 2000, http://www.techweb.com (2000).

Meyer, John W. and Brian Rowan, "Institutionalized Organizations: Formal Structure as Myth and Ceremony", *American Journal of Sociology, 83*(2), 340–363, (1977).

Muse, Dan, "ASP Trade Group Joins CompTIA", ASPnews.com, Accessed December 3, 2001, http://www.ASPnews.com (2001).

Newcomb, Kevin, "NetLedger and Oracle Team Up", Internetnews—*ASP News Archives,* October 20. Accessed February 27, 2002, http://www.internetnews.com (2000a).

Newcomb, Kevin, "NetLedger: It's Not Just for Accounting Anymore", *Internetnews—ASP News Archives.* November 29. Accessed February 27, 2002, http://www.internetnews.com (2000b).

Newcomb, Kevin, "NetLedger to Power Oracle Small Business", Accessed February 27, 2002, http://www.internetnews.com (2001a).

Newcomb, Kevin, "NetLedger Moves Beyond Accounting", Accessed February 27, 2002, http://www.internetnews.com (2001b).

Parrish, Deidra-Ann, "The New School", *Small Business Computing,* (March 14, 2001).

Paul, Lisa, "The State of the ASP Market", ISP *Planet,* Accessed April 11, 2001, http://www.aspnews.com (2001).

Rogers, Everett M., *Diffusion of Innovations,* New York: The Free Press, 1995.

Scott, W. Richard, *Institutions and Organizations,* Newbury Park, CA: Sage, 1995.

Suchman, Mark C., "Managing Legitimacy: Strategic and Institutional Approaches", *Academy of Management Review, 20*(3), 571–610, (1995).

Tolbert, Pamela, "Institutional Sources of Organizational Culture in Large Law Firms". In Lynne G. Zucker (ed.), *Institutional Patterns and Organizations*, pp. 101–113. Cambridge, MA: Ballinger, 1988.

Tolbert, Pamela S. and Lynne G. Zucker, "Institutional Sources of Change in the Formal Structure of Organizations: The Diffusion of Civil Service Reform, 1880–1935", *Administrative Science Quarterly, 28*(1), 22–39, (1983).

Torode, Christina and Jennifer H. Follett (2000), "Empowering SMBs with Hosted Services—Selling ASP Services Presents New Opportunity for SMB Solution Providers", *Techsearch CRN*, Issue 908. Accessed August 27, 2000, http://www.techweb.com (2000).

Tushman, Michael L. and Philip Anderson (1986), "Technological Discontinuities and Organizational Environments", *Administrative Science Quarterly, 31*(3), 439–465, (1986).

Ulset, Svein (1996), "R&D Outsourcing and Contractual Governance: An Empirical Study of Commercial R&D Projects", *Journal of Economic Behavior & Organization, 30*, 63–82, (1996).

Van de Ven, Andrew H., Douglas E. Polley, Raghu Garud, and Sankaran Venkataraman, *The Innovation Journey*, New York: Oxford University Press, 1999.

Wainewright, Phil, "Debut by a $5-a-month Accounts App", ASPnews.com. Accessed May 24, 2001, http://www.ASPnews.com (1999).

Wainewright, Phil, "Weekly Review: Where Have all the ASPs Gone", ASPnews.com, Accessed December 3, 2001, http://www.ASPnews.com (2001a).

Wainewright, Phil, "The Year in Review", ASPnews.com, Accessed January 21, 2002, http://www.ASPnews.com (2001b).

Wainewright, Phil, "Don't Worry, Be Happy", ASPnews.com, Accessed July 30, 2001, http://www.ASPnews.com (2001c).

Wainewright, Phil, "What's the Big Deal with the Big 5", ASPnews.com, Accessed January 28, 2002, http://www.ASPnews.com (2002a).

Wainewright, Phil, "Weekly Review: Real Time is Right for ASPs", ASPnews.com, Accessed February 19, 2002, http://www.ASPnews.com (2002b).

Walston, Stephen L., Lawton R. Burns, and John R. Kimberly, "Institutional and Economic Influences on the Adoption and Extensiveness of Managerial Innovation: The Case of Reengineering in Hospitals", *Medical Care Research and Review, 58*, 194–228, (1998).

Westphal, James D., Ranjay Gulati, and Stephen M. Shortell, "Customization or Conformity? An Institutional and Network Perspective on the Content and Consequences of TQM Adoption", *Administrative Science Quarterly, 42*(2), 366–394, (1997).

Zaltman, Gerald, Robert Duncan and Jonny Holbek, *Innovations and Organizations*, New York: Wiley, 1973.

PART V

GENDER AND FAMILY

[17]

ENTREPRENEURSHIP & REGIONAL DEVELOPMENT, 9 (1997), 221–238

Invisible entrepreneurs: the neglect of women business owners by mass media and scholarly journals in the USA

TED BAKER, HOWARD E. ALDRICH and NINA LIOU

CB#3210, Department of Sociology, UNC-CH, Chapel Hill, NC 27599-3210, USA. email: bak@email.unc.edu; howard_aldrich@unc.edu; nliou@gibbs.oit.unc.edu; Home page: http://www.unc.edu/~healdric/

We examine a paradox: gains in women's business ownership in the USA have been extraordinary, whereas popular press coverage has actually declined, and academic articles on women owners are also exceedingly rare. We offer three simple explanations for this: (1) the media no longer consider women's business 'news'; (2) scholars are not interested in women's firms because they are mostly small and relatively unimportant; and (3) documented differences between men and women owners are few and thus reporters and scholars no longer look for them. Two dissenting voices, however, complicate the picture: small but significant gender differences have been found in studies of social behaviour and leadership; and, advocacy groups have strongly asserted that women owners possess unique advantages. Why haven't these voices been heard? We argue that androcentrism has clouded our perceptions of gender differences and blinded journalists and academics in two ways: (1) women's distinctive contributions have been muted as they have adapted to institutions of business that were already gendered, and (2) the search for distinctive contributions by women owners has been thwarted by assumptions that traditional ways of doing business are 'natural'.

Keywords: women; entrepreneur; androcentrism; gender; sex; business owner.

1. Introduction: the paradox

Some of the greatest gains achieved by US women in recent decades have been in business ownership, but media and academic attention to this progress and its consequences have been meager at best. Paralleling similar gains in the UK, Germany and other European nations (Cromie and Birley 1992, Marlow 1996, ENSR 1995), US women have achieved a six-fold increase in their percentage share of business ownership. However, as is shown in this paper, this phenomenal growth – this gender revolution in business ownership – has gone largely unnoticed by major US newspapers. Attention to women owners has actually decreased over the past decade. Similarly, despite burgeoning academic interest and writing about 'women's issues' and gender, little scholarly effort has been directed towards the study of women's business ownership. Academic articles on women business owners are still rare, and mainstream entrepreneurship journals pay little attention to gender issues. The discrepancy between achievements in business ownership and lack of attention to them poses a paradox for us: why has women's spectacular progress in business ownership been virtually *invisible*.

Our attempt to resolve the paradox is organized into four parts: (1) a description of the issue; (2) the development of a straightforward, gender-neutral explanation of what we observe; (3) a review of some dissident voices, rebutting our gender-neutral interpretation and arguing for more attention to gender differences; and (4) a call for more subtle research in the area of gendered differences in business ownership.

First, we demonstrate the extent of the paradox through detailed examination of patterns of popular newspaper and scholarly coverage of women's business ownership in the USA. We find that the paradox is powerful: a huge wave of women owners has flooded the US business landscape, but very few authors have taken notice. The patterns of neglect hold for two major national newspapers, for the general business press, and for scholarly business and entrepreneurship journals.

Second, we offer some simple, common-sense explanations that treat the paradox as largely unproblematic. If women are taking advantage of emerging ownership opportunities by creating firms that mimic men's, the story is simply old news. In the absence of a convincing demonstration that women's ownership of business really matters, reporters and scholars will ignore them. Additionally, élite academic journals tend to focus on patterns and issues important to large businesses, and a majority of women-owned firms are still small 'lifestyle' businesses – typically sole proprietorships. Documented differences between men and women owners are few and thus reporters and scholars no longer look for them.

Third, we review two sets of dissenting voices that have been raised, by scholars researching sex and gender issues, and by women's advocacy groups. Some scholars argue that there really are systematic empirical differences in the work-related behaviour of men and women. Likewise, some women's advocacy groups assert that women business owners are not only different but also possess unique advantages over men. If such gendered differences really exist, then women's rapid growth in ownership could result in distinctive differences between how women and men run their businesses. We argue that dissenting voices have been ignored because of 'androcentrism' (Bem 1993), in the form of the taken-for-granted notion that the traditional male-centred business model is the 'neutral' or 'normal' model. Androcentrism has lulled journalists and scholars into assuming that women and men business owners are interchangeable. This has in turn allowed the scant literature on differences to remain satisfied with documenting a few demographic differences between women's and men's businesses, and explaining the differences as a result of women owner's lesser qualifications in terms of human, social and financial capital.

Finally, we draw on the scholarly literature regarding gendered differences in social behaviour, and on writings on difference by women's business advocates, to highlight a variety of understudied areas where gendered empirical differences in ownership practices might be found. We conclude by speculating about what may be lost to a nation's economy when new approaches to business are disregarded.

2.   The quiet revolution: media and academic silence about the growth in women's ownership

The origins of this study were in casual conversation when it was realized that the common-sense question, 'how do women run businesses differently from men?' could not be answered. A cursory review suggested that very few papers published in entrepreneurship journals had approached this as an empirical question requiring a comparative design. It was difficult to find empirical studies of what women owners actually do, regardless of whether men were also studied. We were also struck by Joline Godfrey's (1992) letter to George Gendron, Editor-in-Chief of Inc. Magazine, noting that the annual competition for 'Entrepreneur of the Year' included remark-ably few women. Beginning with a working hypothesis that women owners were seriously under-represented in the academic literature, we decided to explore whether this was also true for the popular press.

Twenty-five years ago, an absence of articles on women's business ownership would have raised few eyebrows. As recently as 1970, women owned only about 5% of all the businesses in the USA. However, since 1970, growth has been rapid and steady. Women's proportional participation in entrepreneurship has been growing during a time in which entrepreneurship in general has flourished: by 1992, the Department of the Census estimated that women owned about 6.4 million businesses in the USA, representing over 33% of the US total of just under 19.3 million firms (US Department of Commerce 1996). Although the proportion of firms owned by women in EU nations is evidently not as high as in the USA, recent statistics none the less suggest that women are increasing their level of ownership in Europe as well. Kovalainen (1996), for example, noted that about 30% of the non-agricultural entre-preneurs in Finland are women. The 1995 ENSR report stated that the proportion of women starters was about 27% of the total across the EU (ENSR 1995: 91).

We conducted searches of indexes representing popular and scholarly outlets for coverage of US women's business ownership over time (detailed descriptions of the search methods are provided in the Appendix). Patterns of coverage for three groups were studied: general business periodicals, élite national newspapers and academic journals because of the varying time periods and periodicals covered by the indexes used, and also because we wanted to see whether overall patterns held for sub-groups of publications.

2.1 General business periodicals

Between 1982 and 1995, the number of articles on business ownership issues increased by more than five-fold, from 258 to 1326. The number of articles on women business owners also increased, but only by a factor of approximately 3, from 82 to 260 articles. Consequently, the proportion of ownership articles on women actually fell, from about 32% in 1982 to 20% in 1995. The long-term trend is shown in Figure 1. The number of articles on women in general, regardless of content, also increased substantially from 1982 to 1995, rising from 333 to 3,258. Thus, the decline shown in Figure 1 is not a result of the business media becoming more conservative or paying less attention to women's issues. Instead, the decline represents a shifting of article content, proportion-ately away from ownership and towards other issues, such as equal employment opportunity, family/work conflicts and sexual harassment.

2.2 Élite national newspapers

The underlying mix of articles in the Information Access Company index that we used (see Appendix for details) expanded and changed during the period being considered, and this may partially account for the results in Figure 1. Moreover, the data in Figure 1 begin in 1980 and show a decline thereafter, but tell us nothing about what happened during the 1970s, when women's business ownership first took off.

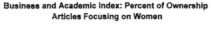

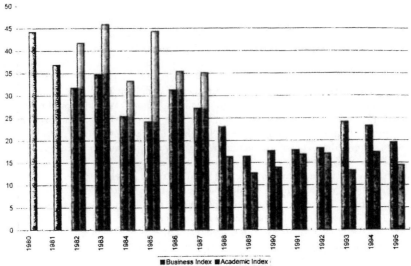

Figure 1.   **Business and academic index: percentage of ownership articles focusing on women.**

We therefore examined two élite national newspapers: *The New York Times* (*NYT*) and *The Wall Street Journal* (*WSJ*) for which a longer time series is available.

The *NYT* index is incomplete prior to 1981, but as shown in Table 1, the data for the 1970s fits very well with the long-term trend in the *NYT*'s coverage of women's business issues for the 1980s and 1990s. The percentage of all business ownership articles that specifically mentioned women increased slowly over this period, to a maximum of about 4% in the early 1990s. Thus, the *NYT* only slightly increased its coverage during the period of explosive growth in women's business ownership.

The low level of interest in women's business ownership was not driven by declining interest in either business issues or women's issues. The number of articles on business ownership remained almost constant over this period, at about 2,500 per year from 1981–1994. The number of articles covering 'women' in some way rose slightly in the *NYT*, from 12,017 in 1981 to 14,145 in 1994. Note that this is in contrast to the five-fold increase noted in the general business periodicals index.

The pattern of the *WSJ*'s coverage of women business owners was very similar to what we have described for the *NYT*. As shown in Table 1, the *WSJ* published few articles on women owners, proportionately, in the late 1970s and early 1980s, and then increased its coverage slightly.

Table 1.   Business ownership articles mentioning or focusing upon women.†

Year	Percentage business articles mentioning women				Percentage business articles with women as main focus					
	ETP	JBV	AMR	AMJ	WSJ	NYT	ETP	JBV	AMR	AMJ
1969	‡	‡	‡	6	‡	1	‡	‡	‡	0
1970	‡	‡	‡	3	‡	2	‡	‡	‡	0
1971	‡	‡	‡	11	‡	1	‡	‡	‡	0
1972	‡	‡	‡	0	‡	1	‡	‡	‡	0
1973	‡	‡	‡	10	0	1	‡	‡	‡	2
1974	‡	‡	‡	11	0	0	‡	‡	‡	3
1975	‡	‡	‡	19	0	1	‡	‡	‡	4
1976	10	‡	2	39	1	1	10	‡	0	14
1977	10	‡	6	34	0	2	10	‡	0	13
1978	11	‡	7	40	1	1	5	‡	2	13
1979	11	‡	4	30	1	2	5	‡	2	16
1980	0	‡	7	40	2	3	0	‡	2	10
1981	6	‡	7	53	2	3	6	‡	2	16
1982	8	‡	8	29	0	2	4	‡	3	13
1983	3	‡	10	50	1	3	3	‡	2	17
1984	7	‡	7	43	4	3	3	‡	2	15
1985	0	0	10	39	4	3	0	0	5	11
1986	11	8	10	39	5	3	0	0	6	8
1987	25	0	6	28	1	4	17	0	4	2
1988	36	11	3	35	4	3	18	5	3	8
1989	43	8	8	45	2	3	14	8	4	8
1990	33	20	7	26	1	3	0	12	4	5
1991	17	5	4	22	2	3	17	5	4	4
1992	11	26	24	40	3	4	11	4	16	9
1993	24	24	19	29	4	4	6	10	14	3
1994	25	20	9	48	5	4	20	8	9	14

†All numbers rounded to nearest integer.
‡Not available.

2.3   Academic journals

Across a broad spectrum of academic journals, between 1980 and 1995, the annual number of articles on business ownership issues – regardless of gender – increased by more than three-fold, from 129 to 447 articles. The number of articles on women business owners changed only slightly over that period, fluctuating at around an average of about 70 articles per year. Consequently, the proportion of ownership articles on women *fell* substantially, from about 44% in 1980 to 14% in 1995. The long-term trend is shown in Figure 1.

The number of articles on women in academic journals covered by the Information Access Company (IAC) index, regardless of content, increased substantially from 1980 to 1994, rising from 792 to almost 7,000. Thus, the decline shown in Figure 1 is not a result of academic researchers paying less attention to women's issues. Instead, the decline represents an actual shifting of article content, proportionately *away* from ownership and towards other issues regarding women.

2.4   *Management and entrepreneurship journals*

We chose four US academic journals for further investigation, based on their reputations as publication outlets for articles on entrepreneurship and business ownership: the *Academy of Management Journal* (*AMJ*), the *Academy of Management Review* (*AMR*), *Entrepreneurship: Theory and Practice* (*ETP*) and the *Journal of Business Venturing* (*JBV*). These journals have recently published more articles that at least mention gender/sex than they did in the 1980s. Our measure of 'mentioning' gender is quite generous, giving a journal credit for any article that collected data on the sex of subjects, even if sex was not included in the analysis. For three of the four journals, however, the proportions are still quite small. In the entrepreneurship journals *JBV* and *ETP* (Table 1), about one in six of the articles in the last decade has mentioned gender/ sex, and in *AMR*, about one in ten has mentioned gender/sex. Only in *AMJ* have articles mentioning gender/sex figured prominently, averaging about 30% in the late 1970s and about 35% over the last ten years.

Using a more restrictive coding than merely 'mentioning' gender/sex, the total number of articles with gender as the main focus of interest was recorded as shown in Table 1. The absolute number of articles falling into this category by journal is as follows: *JBV*: 13; *ETP*: 24; *AMR*: 30; *AMJ*: 120. Even in the *Academy of Management Journal*, only 26% of the 457 articles that mentioned gender/sex actually used it as an independent variable. Clearly, gender/sex has *not* been a major issue of interest in any of these four journals.

Of the 187 articles with gender as a main focus, the number which had studied women *as owners of businesses* was counted. For the four journals, the totals were: *ETP*: 10; *JBV*: 10; *AMR*: 1; *AMJ*: 1. Thus, for the two entrepreneurship journals, 20 of the 37 articles with gender/sex as a central focus dealt with ownership, but these 37 articles represented only 7% of all the articles published in that period. For *AMR* and *AMJ*, the two articles on women owners were lost in the 2,650 papers published over the period of our investigation.

European researchers apparently have no more interest in women-owned firms than do Americans. Although we did not conduct the same thorough search through major publication outlets as we did for US sources, we picked two that were recent and broad in scope. First, the authors examined the first four Annual Reports produced by the European Observatory for SMEs in 1993, 1994, 1995 and 1996 (see ENSR (1995) for reference). We found: in the 1993 report, one overt reference to gender; in the 1994 report, one page devoted to 'women and entrepreneurship'; and in the 1995 report, one page on 'entrepreneurial background', devoted mostly to 'female starters'. All three reports contained major reviews of trends and policies regarding labour markets, education, business training needs, and so forth, and none of the sections mentioned women. Thus, in approximately 1300 pages of text, tables, and figures, women occupied about 0.0002% of the space in the first three volumes. Only in the 1996 report was a separate section introduced on women owners, covering 21 pages, and that section will be dropped in the 1997 report.

Second, we examined a comprehensive review of entrepreneurship and small business research in 16 European nations, prepared by experts in each nation (Landström *et al.* 1996). In the sixteen chapters, three references to research on women were found: a study carried out in Ireland in 1987; 3 studies from Norway, focusing mainly on family issues; and 3 studies in the UK. This review of these two extensive sources on national developments in research on entrepreneurship and small business convinced us that European scholars view this field through a gender-lens very similar to that of American scholars. As Holmquist and Sundin (1989: 1) noted, 'entrepreneurial theories are created by men, for men, and are applied to men'.

2.5 Summary of findings

Our review of business periodicals shows that coverage of women as business owners and entrepreneurs declined between 1982 and 1995. Coverage in two national newspapers changed slightly, with the *NYT* increasing its percentage of business ownership articles mentioning women to around 4%, and the *WSJ* recently showing an increase to slightly higher levels. Our review of academic journals indicates that coverage of women in general increased substantially between 1982 and 1995, but coverage of women as entrepreneurs and owners declined substantially. Coverage of women in general in four entrepreneurship and management journals changed slightly, with only the *AMJ* publishing a substantial number of papers on women in the 1990s. Over 85% of the articles published in the two entrepreneurship journals over the period studied made no mention of women, whether as employees or owners. More importantly, women as owners and entrepreneurs were simply *invisible* in these four journals – only 22 of the 3206 articles published over the study period featured women owners or entrepreneurs.

3. Simple explanations for the silence

We present three simple explanations for women owners' relative invisibility: (1) the media only cover what editors and reporters consider to be 'news', and women's business is no longer 'news'; (2) scholars are interested in economically important entities, and women's firms are small and relatively unimportant; and (3) documented differences between men and women owners are few and thus reporters and scholars no longer look for them. After reviewing these three explanations, we will examine two lines of argument that claim gender differences are not only visible but also consequential for work-related behaviour. We believe that these two lines of inquiry have been inadequately pursued because of androcentric assumptions built into journalistic and scholarly work.

3.1 Media inattention

Perhaps there is good news in our findings: women's ownership of businesses does not get much coverage in popular business journals and newspapers because it is no longer novel or new. As opportunities for business ownership and entrepreneurship have opened up to them, women have responded by rapidly increasing their percentage ownership of US businesses, and are moving – on this measure – towards parity with men. Back in the late 1970s, or very early 1980s, when the two broadest series (Figure 1) begin and also show their highest levels of coverage, women business owners were still remarkable. However, as their numbers have grown and time has passed, women proprietors have simply slipped silently into the generic category of 'business owners' and disappeared.

News gathering routines are likely to ignore stories that don't lead to copy that stands out, as McCarthy *et al.* (1996) argued in their study of media coverage of demonstrations in Washington, DC. Newsworthy 'pegs' on which to hang a story must refer to notorious, consequential, extraordinary, or culturally resonant events. As Scollard (1995: 77) noted, 'routine fascination' with women who are successful entrepreneurs (and executives) 'has become as passé as frying two eggs easy over for breakfast every morning'. As women business owners have become taken-for-granted, gender has ceased to be a salient or newsworthy dimension of business ownership stories. The slight increase in newspaper coverage may simply be a result of the greater number and increasing variety of women's businesses. Articles are written when interesting things happen concerning some of these businesses, not because they are run by women.

3.2   Scholarly disinterest

Lack of coverage of women business owners by academic journals is also easy to understand. Mass media fascination with an issue seems to affect the choices that academic authors make about what topics to study (Barley *et al.* 1988), and declining media coverage may have reduced overall scholarly interest. Moreover, reward systems in business schools have systematically favoured research that focuses on large firms, preferably Fortune 500 firms and others whose stock is publicly traded. Such firms are overwhelmingly managed by men executives (Blau and Ferber 1986, Reskin and Padavic 1994). In 1995, women only held about 10% of the 6,274 positions available on the boards of Fortune 500 firms, although more than 80% of Fortune 500 firms had at least one woman on their board (*Women's Business Exclusive* 1995). Within business schools, research on small and family-owned businesses has sometimes been dismissed as trivial. Elite academic journals tend to focus on patterns and issues related or important to large businesses. Thus, we are not surprised to see that *AMJ* and *AMR* have all but ignored women entrepreneurs and business owners. As more women build large firms, they and their businesses will become more central to mainstream academic business research.

Just as business school curricula and management journals reflect the needs of large and growing firms, so too do the leading entrepreneurship journals. Since the early 1980s, a great deal of entrepreneurship research in the USA and Europe has been oriented to economic dynamism and job growth (Birch 1979, Davis *et al.* 1993, Davidsson *et al.* 1996). Leading entrepreneurship researchers have repeatedly attempted to distinguish between 'entrepreneurial' versus 'lifestyle' businesses, or between 'small business' versus 'entrepreneurship' (Reynolds 1993). The entrepreneurship literature has shown less concern with 'lifestyle' businesses and sole proprietorships than with fast-growing, job-generating enterprises. Only about 20% of women-owned businesses in the USA have any employees, a figure remarkably similar to the average of 22% of women-owned firms in the EU that have employees (ENSR 1995: 92). Some research has found that women are more likely to become self-employed for 'lifestyle' reasons such as attempts to balance work and family (Brush 1992, Elam 1997, Marlow and Strange 1994, Starr and Yudkin 1996). Consequently, we are not surprised to find that women have been invisible in entrepreneurship journals. As more women's businesses grow rapidly and generate large numbers of jobs, they will perhaps get more attention from entrepreneurship researchers.

3.3   *Limited findings of gendered differences in ownership style and practices*

If researchers were to document substantial differences between how women and men practice business ownership, sex/gender issues might become very hard to ignore. Gender would become particularly salient if, as some women's business advocates claim, women's leadership style was shown to provide women with a significant business advantage (Helgensen 1995) or if empirical findings showed 'styles of success' that strongly differentiated between successful women and men (Stover 1995). Instead, very few systematic empirical differences have been uncovered, either between women and men business owners or between the businesses that they run. The strongest differences uncovered have been demographic, with few 'style' differences documented.

The short list of differences between *businesses* shows that women's businesses, on average, are: (1) younger, (2) smaller, (3) more likely to be in retail or services, and (4) more likely to be sole proprietorships than are businesses owned by men (Brush 1992, Starr and Yudkin 1996; US Dept. of Commerce 1996). Comparing *owners* by gender, women tend to: (1) have less experience in their firm's industry, (2) have less experience as managers, (3) be more likely to have liberal rather than technical education, and (4) be more likely to start businesses to gain flexibility. Overall, 'along many psychological and demographic characteristics, women entrepreneurs are more similar to than different from men' (Starr and Yudkin 1996: 11; see also Birley 1989). Moreover, neither the differences in women's businesses, nor the differences in the characteristics that they bring to ownership, appear to convey clear 'advantages'. Rather, it appears that women approach business ownership similarly to men, but that they often bring less human, social, or financial capital to bear when they come to business ownership, due largely to structural differences in the overall position of women and men in US society.

An institutional market-oriented approach would predict that women business owners behave much like men. All entrepreneurs, men and women alike, operate their firms in a business environment structured by laws, standard practices, norms of behaviour, and a complex set of institutional contingencies to which owners adapt if their businesses are to persist. For example, Holmquist (1996) suggested that the effects of gender are primarily limited to women's choice of industries in which to operate. In a study of Swedish entrepreneurs, she found tangible gender differences overall, but when she focused on a specific industry, behavioural differences between men and women business owners all but disappeared. As Holmquist (1996: 107–108) explained, 'to be able to work in a specific industry, the entrepreneur has to adapt to the rules of the industry, regardless of gender'.

A market-based perspective thus sees differences among men and women, and individual differences between men and women, as fundamentally subordinated to economic and institutional requirements. Although 'odd' behaviour is occasionally associated with fabulous entrepreneurial success, indulgence of personal difference at the expense of responding to business needs is more likely to be a recipe for failure. As Campbell (1960) noted, most variations from established practices are deleterious. According to this view, business is business, for men and women alike.

4.   Complicating the simple explanations

Despite huge growth in the numbers of women business owners, few findings of interesting gender differences have emerged and national media and academic interest in women business owners has dwindled. We have presented a series of simple explanations that we think are reasonably powerful in resolving this paradox.

However, our claim for a simple resolution of the paradox is substantially at odds with two sets of voices that have grown increasingly bold over the past two decades: academics writing about sex and gender roles, and advocates offering arguments about women owners' distinctive advantages. We now turn to an examination of these voices.

4.1   Academic research on gendered differences in social behaviour

Sociologists and others have investigated a variety of structural or contextual explanations of gendered differences in behaviour. These explanations differ from the dispositional arguments of many psychologists by stressing differences in men's and women's current social circumstances that account for observed differences in patterns of behaviour. Fairly strong evidence supports arguments regarding consequential differences in women's role requirements and how they integrate them (Brush 1992, Kolvereid *et al.* 1993). By contrast, recent investigations into gender differences in use of social networks (Aldrich *et al.* 1996) and in access to financing (Schragg *et al.* 1992, Buttner and Rosen 1992, Van Auken *et al.* 1993, Loscocco and Robinson 1991, Neider 1987, Read 1994), have produced limited evidence of convincing gender differences.

Arguments that men's and women's social behaviours differ are also common across a variety of psychological and social psychological orientations, including bio-social (Buss 1995, Nielsen 1994, Udry *et al.* 1992, Wilson and Daly 1992), Freudian, feminist reformed Freudian, cognitive developmental (Chodorow 1978, Gilligan 1982, Miller 1976) and gender role (Eagly 1995, Eagly and Wood 1991, Eagly *et al.* 1992, 1995) approaches.

In a review of meta-analytic studies of sex differences in social behaviour, Eagly and Wood (1991: 315) 'challenged the consensus view-point in psychology that women and men behave either equivalently or so nearly identically that any differences are trivially small'. They found patterns of gendered behavioural differences whose magnitude is evidently typical of other research findings in psychology. Their largest and most robust finding – holding even in organizational contexts – was that women tend to have more democratic and participative leadership styles than men, who are more likely to display autocratic and directive styles. Small to moderate and reasonably consistent gendered differences were found, supporting the notion that women in groups tend to be more 'socially skilled, emotionally sensitive', 'expressive', and more 'concerned with personal relationships than men'. Women were also found to be 'more concerned than men about the social aspects of interaction and others' feelings' while men in groups tend to focus on task completion and more tangible outcomes (Eagly and Wood 1991: 307).

Sociological and psychological approaches both raise questions about the contexts that influence whether overall gendered differences will be expressed as gendered differences in particular types of behaviour. In a review of meta-analytic studies of sex differences in social behaviour, Eagly and Wood (1991) noted that little of the psychological research on sex differences had examined behaviour in *any* work organizations, where gender differences may be less predictive and formal role requirements more salient than in the laboratory studies frequently conducted by social psychologists. Indeed, in later meta-analyses, Eagly and her colleagues (Eagly *et al.* 1992, 1995, Eagly 1995) found consistent and non-trivial average differences between men and women in organizational leadership behaviour and how they were evaluated, but these differences were generally smaller than in those found in studies focusing on non-work contexts. Apparently, organizational contexts diminished – but did not extinguish – gendered behavioural differences.

What workplace contexts permit the most free expression of gender differences? Relatively small gendered differences in behaviour would be expected among employees in the same jobs in large, formalized organizations. The play of gender differences is probably more likely among employees in smaller organizations with less formalized job systems and role requirements than in larger organizations (Baker and Aldrich 1994). We would expect owners of small and medium-sized businesses to possess the greatest freedom from corporate hierarchy and formal role requirements. A strong expression of gendered behavioural differences would be possible between men and women business owners.

Therefore, whatever the differences between men and women, they should be increasingly embodied within the ranks of entrepreneurs and their firms. Our intent is not to engage in gender polarization or to essentialize the nature of behavioural differences between men and women (Bem 1993). Even where gendered behaviour differences have been found, there is a great deal of overlap between men and women, and variability within each sex generally dwarfs the behavioural differences between the sexes. None the less, differences do exist.

4.2   Advocates for women's business ownership

Women's business advocates tend to ignore the similarities between men and women, as well as the variation among women. These advocates constitute a committed force fighting against the invisibility of women business owners. Many of the contrasts claimed in the practitioner and policy-oriented research closely mirror the differences found in more narrowly-focused academic work. The main difference is that advocates characterize almost all differences as if they were large. In addition, context-specific behavioural differences are often represented as essential sexual distinctions.

We review a number of exemplars of policy-oriented writing to show the style of thinking that they represent. Helgensen (1995) argued that successful women owners, compared to men, (1) tend to communicate directly, rather than through hierarchical channels, (2) emphasize process, not just goals, (3) use health of relationships as an important criterion by which to judge business success, (4) do not compartmentalize their lives and identities into work and domestic spheres, and (5) are scornful of 'excessive' concern with rank, position and perks. The National Foundation for Women Business Owners issued a report on 'Styles of Success', a survey of 127 women and men conducted in 1994 (Stover 1995). The report suggested that men and women think differently and have correspondingly different styles of management.

Kearney and White (1994) claimed that men in business are oriented to tasks and women are oriented to relationships, and White argued that these different orientations, combined with 'an automatic, unthinking tendency to prefer to be surrounded by people like ourselves' (White 1995: 75) result in potential and actual problems when men manage women, or women manage men. In contrast, Scollard (1989, 1995) downplayed gendered differences in managing people, but claimed that with the exception of small numbers of very high level corporate executives and founders of large successful firms, women are hampered in business by fear of taking risks, and therefore usually found and build only small firms. Similarly, Stolze (1989, 1995) alleged that women's businesses are smaller and less successful than men's because women fear losing control if they accept money from outside investors.

In summary, the practitioner literature presents plausible descriptions of differences in how women and men think about their businesses and the people in them, how the businesses fit into their lives, and how they judge whether a business is successful. The first two columns of Table 2 summarize some of the differences between men and women suggested by the research we have reviewed. Column three describes the stereotypically similar – but often exaggerated – set of differences claimed by proponent researchers.

4.3   Androcentrism and why the dissenting voices have been ignored

We complicated our three simple explanations for the invisibility of women business owners by reviewing arguments from sex and gender scholars and women's business advocates, claiming that significant gender differences really do exist. Why, then, does invisibility persist?

We suggest that women are rendered invisible by a particular form of reification labelled androcentrism (Bem 1993). Reification of social constructions is a common and probably functionally necessary aspect of social life (Berger and Luckmann 1966), but it can have deleterious consequences. The concept of 'androcentrism', a specific

Table 2.   Descriptions of difference: academic and advocate literature.

Academic literature		Advocate/policy literature
Women	Men	Women entrepreneurs
Mothering	Non-mothering	Non-hierarchical communication
Nurturing	Ethics of justice	Emphasize process
Relational	Separation	Evaluate business by relationships
Connected	Tangible outcomes	Integrated work/family lives
Selfless	Task completion	Scornful of hierarchy and perks
Ethics of care	Dominant	Fear of risks
Feelings	Controlling	Fear of losing control
Interaction	Independent	Internally directed
Sensitive	Agentic	Instinct
Friendly	Leadership style:	Sensitivity
Integrate role requirements	autocratic and directive	Values
Expressive		Emphasize relationships
Leadership style:		
democratic/participative		

type of reification, describes the taken-for-granted notion that the traditional male-centred business model is the 'neutral' (or 'normal' or 'natural') model. We suspect that androcentrism affects both business owners and the scholars and journalists who study business owners.

Many authors have claimed that academic researchers wear androcentric blinkers. Gendered norms and values have been shown, in various contexts, to affect even disciplined observers' interpretations and explanations. For example, McGrayne (1993) argued that women scientists who teamed with men in research projects have been repeatedly overlooked by the Nobel Prize committee because of stereotypic assumptions about women's place. Calàs (1993) argued that management theorists' conceptions of 'charismatic leadership' have been based implicitly upon male leaders and ignore leadership characteristics associated with femininity. Calàs and Smircich (1992) asserted the presence of a more general gender bias in organization studies, and Hurley (1991) claimed that entrepreneurship research has historically been biased toward men, with writers ignoring gender-based realities.

Our own simple explanations are androcentric. We argued above that because men *and* women are subject to common institutional and economic structures, they adapt by behaving similarly and creating similar businesses. Playing by the same rules in the same game, women's ownership behaviour looks much like men's ownership behaviour. In short, they become isomorphic because they have adapted to, or been selected by, the environment they share in common (DiMaggio and Powell 1983).

However, our explanation of isomorphism ignores the historical fact that women owners enter a business world largely constructed and dominated by men. Thus, the simple structural explanation exemplifies androcentric reification. Men and women play by identical rules, but the rules were written, over long periods of time, by men.

Of course, androcentrism would not matter were there not reason to believe that an institutional business world constructed by women would differ in some way from that constructed by men, or that – given the chance – some women would approach business ownership differently from men. Is there a basis for such beliefs? Our review above of recent writings on gender differences leads us to suspect that under looser institutional constraints, women's ownership behaviour *would* differ more from men's. A careful look may find gender differences that have survived or even flourished and we now consider some hypotheses regarding gender differences that may well be consequential for the long-term viability of the business population.

5. Directions for future research on gendered differences in business ownership

In this section we suggest directions for future research on gendered differences in ownership that go beyond demographic comparisons by drawing on some of the evidence and claims about gendered behaviour that were reviewed in Table 2. Regardless of whether these differences provide *an advantage or a disadvantage*, they should be interesting to reporters, academics, and women's business proponents alike. If future research fails to uncover interesting differences, it will speak to the powerful ability of the marketplace to render dispositional differences moot.

5.1   Differences in leadership

One of the most robust findings of the gender differences literature is that women use leadership styles that are democratic and participative, compared to men's more autocratic and directive styles (Eagly and Wood 1991). Researchers could search for direct evidence of this difference through comparative study of organizational decision-making. Do women-owned firms have more people involved in decision processes, on average, than men-owned firms? Do they have distinctive decision-making processes that result in different decisions? In any industry undergoing significant changes, do men-owned firms respond differently than women-owned firms, on average, to the changes?

5.2   Nurture and social sensitivity

If women are more nurturing, relational, and socially sensitive than men, we would expect this to be reflected across a wide variety human resource practices. For example, do women-owned firms establish more 'family-friendly' policies, including flexible working arrangements and support for employees who balance work and family concerns? Are women-owned firms able to make productive use of employees who might be viewed as 'problems'? Do women-owned firms draw upon a broader population of potential employees than men-owned firms?

5.3   Role integration and balance

If women tend to be motivated to ownership by a desire to achieve integration and balance across role requirements, thus placing less value on rapid growth, then 'smallness' means something different for women-owned than for men-owned businesses (Cliff 1995). Are women's businesses on average more likely to be small through choice, rather than through lack of competence, compared to men's? Are small businesses owned by women more successful than small businesses run by men who have tried but failed to develop their businesses, controlling for industry?

5.4   New organizational forms

A burgeoning literature describes the increasing importance of hybrid and network form of organization (Powell 1990). These new forms are generally characterized as less hierarchical than traditional businesses, constructed using many ties between relationally connected firms and individuals. The skills that these new forms are said to demand sound a lot like the attributes that are claimed to differentiate women from men: 'there is little disagreement about what business must become: less hierarchical, more flexible and team oriented, faster and more fluid. In my opinion, one group of people has an enormous advantage in realizing this new vision: women' (Peters 1990: 216, quoted in Fletcher 1995: 2). Following this argument, are women-owned businesses particularly successful when they are organized in hybrid and network forms? Are women's hybrid organizations – or their parts of network firms – more successful than men's hybrid and network firms?[3]

6. Summary and conclusions

We have described a powerful paradox of women's business ownership in the USA today, demonstrating that despite spectacular gains, women business owners have remained virtually invisible in journalistic and academic discourse. We offered simple solutions to the paradox, and then suggested that the simple solutions could be improved by taking account of discordant voices.

We then argued that androcentrism muted these voices. Women have had to adapt to institutions of business ownership which are *already gendered*, in the sense of having been built and dominated by men. Additionally, efforts to find evidence of women's distinctive contributions to business ownership may have been retarded by an assumption that the traditional model of business ownership is gender neutral and 'natural'. Perhaps greater differences will be found in the future, with the huge increases in women's entrepreneurship, because an increasingly heterogeneous group of women is being drawn into ownership (Starr and Yudkin 1996).

New businesses add to the diversity of organizational solutions available to a society (Aldrich and Fiol 1994), enhancing economic vitality and expanding the variety of workplaces available. Conceivably, even in the absence of institutional pressures, women would build businesses just like men's. If – for whatever reason – women-owned businesses are really just like those owned by men, then diversity will not increase as women increase their ownership share. Something may have already been lost, if – in response to institutional and market pressures – women have merely mimicked men and created businesses in a traditional mould. However, we also wonder whether women are offering new ways of managing, new solutions to problems, and they just aren't being noticed. Very little scholarly empirical research has focused on this question. We suggest that entrepreneurship researchers consider the question still open, and design research that explores whether there are really are distinctive differences, or merely deceptive distinctions (Epstein 1988).

References

Aldrich, H. E. and Fiol, M. C. 1994 Fools rush in? The institutional context of industry creation. *Academy of Management Review*, 19, 645–670.

Aldrich, H. E., Elam, A. B. and Reece, P. R. 1996 Strong ties, weak ties, and strangers: do women business owners differ from men in their use of networking to obtain assistance?, in Birley, S. and MacMillan, I. (eds), *Entrepreneurship in a Global Context* (London: Routledge), 1–25.

Baker, T. and Aldrich, H. E. 1994 Friends and strangers: early hiring practices and idiosyncratic jobs, *Frontiers of Entrepreneurship Research* (Wellesley, MA: Babson College).

Barley, S., Meyer, G. and Gash, D. C. 1988 Cultures of culture: academics, practitioners and the pragmatics of normative control, *Administrative Science Quarterly* 33(1): 24–60.

Bem, S, 1993 *The Lenses of Gender: Transforming the Debate on Social Inequality* (New Haven, CT: Yale University Press).

Berger, P. L. and Luckmann, T. 1966 *The Social Construction of Reality* (New York Doubleday).

Birch, D. 1979 *The Job Generation Process: Final Report to Economic Development Administration* (Cambridge, MA: MIT Program on Neighborhood and Regional Change).

Birley, S. 1989 Female entrepreneurs: are they really any different? *Journal of Small Business Management*, 27(1): 32–37.

Blau, F. E. and Ferber, M. A. 1986 *The Economics of Women, Men, and Work* (Englewood Cliffs, NJ: Prentice-Hall.

Brush, C. G. 1992 Research on women business owners: past trends, a new perspective and future directions, *Entrepreneurship Theory and Practice*, 16(4): 5–30.

Buss, D.M. 1995 Psychological sex differences: origins through sexual selection, *American Psychologist*, 50(3): 164–168.

Buttner, E. H. and Rosen, B. 1992 Rejection in the loan application process: male and female entrepreneurs' perceptions and subsequent intentions, *Journal of Small Business Management*, 30(1): 58–65.

Calàs, M. 1993 Deconstructing 'Charismatic Leadership': re-reading Weber from the darker side, *Leadership Quarterly* 4(3/4): 305–328.

Calàs, M. and Smircich, L. 1992 Re-writing gender into organization theorizing: directions from feminist perspectives, in Reed, M. and Hughes, M. (eds), *Rethinking Organization* (London: Sage), 227–253.

Campbell, D. T. 1960 'Blind variation and selective retention in creative thought as in other knowledge processes', *Psychological Review*, 67: 380–400.

Chodorow, N. 1978 *The Reproduction of Mothering* (Berkeley, CA: University of California Press).

Cliff, J. 1995 Does one size fit all? Exploring the relationship between attitudes towards growth, gender, and business size. Unpublished paper, Faculty of Commerce and Business Administration, University of British Columbia.

Cromie, S. and Birley, S. 1992 Networking by female business owners in Northern Ireland, *Journal of Business Venturing*, 7: 237–251.

Davidsson, P., Lindmark, L. and Olofsson, C. 1996 The extent of overestimation of small firm job creation – an empirical examination of the 'regression bias'. Paper presented at the 41st ICSB World Conference, Stockholm, June.

Davis, S. J., Haltiwanger, J. and Schuh, S. 1993 Small business and job creation: dissecting the myth and reassessing the facts. Working Paper No. 4492. National Bureau of Economic Research, Cambridge, MA.

DiMaggio, P. J. and Powell, W. W. 1983. The iron cage revisited: institutional isomorphism and collective rationality in organizational fields, *American Sociological Review*, 48; 147–160.

Eagly, A. H. 1995 The science and politics of comparing women and men, *American Psychologist*, 50: 145–158.

Eagly, A. H. and Wood, W. 1991 Explaining sex differences in social behavior: a meta-analytic perspective, *Personality and Social Psychology Bulletin*, 17: 306–315.

Eagly, A. H., Karau, S. J. and Makhijani, M. G. 1995 Gender and the effectiveness of leaders: a meta-analysis, *Psychological Bulletin*, 117: 125–145.

Eagly, A. H., Makhijani, M. G. and Klonsky, B. G. 1992 Gender and the evaluation of leaders: a meta-analysis, *Psychological Bulletin*, 111(1): 3–22.

Elam, A. B. 1997 Small business ownership as a more flexible work option. Paper presented at University of North Carolina Department of Sociology Entrepreneurship Seminar, April.

ENSR (European Network for SME Research) 1995 *Third Journal Report: The European Observatory for SMEs* (Zoetermeer, The Netherlands: EIM Small Business Research and Consultancy).

Epstein, C. 1988 *Deceptive Distinctions* (New York: Russell Sage).

Fletcher, J. K. 1995 Radically transforming work for the 21st Century: a feminist reconstruction of 'Real' Work. Paper presented at the 1995 Academy of Management Meeting, Vancouver, BC, August.

Gilligan, C. 1982 *In a Different Voice: Psychological Theory and Women's Development* (Cambridge, Mass: Harvard University Press).

Godfrey, J. 1992 *Our Wildest Dreams: Women Entrepreneurs Making Money, Having Fun, Doing Good* (New York: HarperCollins).

Helgensen, S. 1995 One key strength of women: an emphasis on relationships, *Small Business Forum*, Vol. 13 Spring: 70–72.

Holmquist, C. 1996 The female entrepreneur: woman and/or entrepreneur, in *Aspects of Women's Entrepreneurship* (Stockholm: Swedish National Board for Industrial and Technical Development), 107–108.

Holmquist, C. and Sundin, E. 1991 The growth of women's entrepreneurship: push or pull factors? in Davies, L. and Gibb, A. (eds) *Recent Research in Entrepreneurship: The Third International EIASM Workshop: 1989* (Aldershot, UK: Avebury).

Hurley, A. E. 1991 Incorporating feminist theories into sociological theories of entrepreneurship. Unpublished paper presented at the Annual Meeting of the Academy of Management, Miami, Florida.

Kearney, K. G. and White, T. I. 1994 *Men and Women at Work* (NJ: Career Press).

Kolvereid, L., Shane, S. and Westhead, P. 1993 Is it equally difficult for female entrepreneurs to start businesses in all countries? *Journal of Small Business Management*, 31(4): 42–51.

Kovalainen, A. 1996 Female entrepreneurship in Finland and the Nordic countries, in *Aspects of Women's Entrepreneurship* (Stockholm: Swedish National Board for Industrial and Technical Development), 143–154.

Landström, H. Frank, H. and Veciana, J. (eds) 1996 *Entrepreneurship and Small Business Research in Europe – An ECSB Survey* (Aldershot, UK: Avebury).

Loscocco, K. and Robinson, J. 1991 Barriers in women's small-business success in the United States, *Gender and Society*, 5: 511–532.

Marlow, S. and Strange, A. 1994 Female entrepreneurs: success by whose standards?, in Tanton, M. (ed.), *Women in Management. A Developing Presence* (London: Routledge), 172–185.

Marlow, S. 1996 Women in self employment – do they mean business? Unpublished working paper, April 1996, Leicester Business School, UK.

McCarthy, J. D., McPhail, C. and Smith, J. 1996 Images of protest: dimensions of selection bias in media coverage of Washington demonstrations, 1982 and 1991, *American Sociological Review*, 61(3): 478–499.

McGrayne, S. B. 1993 *Nobel Prize Women: Their Lives, Struggles and Momentous Discoveries* (New York: Birch Lane Press).

Miller, J. B. 1976 *Toward a New Psychology of Women* (Boston: Beacon Press).

Neider, L. 1987 A preliminary investigation of female entrepreneurs in Florida, *Journal of Small Business Management*, 25(3): 22–29.

Nielsen, F. 1994 Sociobiology and sociology, in Hagan, J. and Cook, K. S. (eds), *Annual Review of Sociology 20* (CA: Annual Reviews Inc.), 267–303.

Peters, T. 1990 The best new managers will listen, motivate, support: isn't that just like a woman?, *Working Woman*, Vol. 15 September: 216–217.

Powell, W. W. 1990 Neither market nor hierarchy: network forms of organization, in *Research in Organizational Behavior*, vol. 12 (Greenwich, CT: JAI Press), 295–336.

Read, L. 1994 Raising finance from banks: a comparative study of the experiences of male and female business owners, *Frontiers of Entrepreneurship Research* (Wellesley, MA: Babson College), 361–372.

Reskin, B. and Padavic, I. 1994 *Women and Men at Work* (Thousand Oaks, CA: Pine Forge Press).

Reynolds, P. 1993 High performance entrepreneurship: what makes it different?, in *Frontiers of Entrepreneurship Research* (Wellesley, MA: Babson College), 88–103.

Schragg, P., Yacuk, L. and Glass, A. 1992 Study of barriers facing Alberta women in business, *Journal of Small Business and Entrepreneurship*, 9(4): 40–49.

Scollard, J. R. 1989 *Risk to Win: A Woman's Guide to Success* (New York: MacMillan).

Scollard, J. R. 1995 Management has become unisex – but managing risks hasn't, *Small Business Forum*, Vol. 13 Spring: 76–79.

Starr, J. and Yudkin, M. 1996 Women entrepreneurs: a review of current research, Monograph published by Center for Research on Women, Wellesley, MA CRW 15.

Stolze, W. J. 1989 *Startup: An Entrepreneur's Guide to Launching and Managing a New Venture* (New York: Rock Beach Press).

Stolze, W. J. 1995 A very important gender-related issue in control, *Small Business Forum*, Spring, 80–82.

Stover, C. 1995 Styles of success: research on gender differences in management styles, *Small Business Forum*, Vol. 13 Spring 52–69.

Udry, R. J., Kovenock, J. and Morris, N. 1992 A biosocial paradigm for women's gender roles. Paper presented at annual meeting of the Population Association of America, Denver, CO, April.

US Department of Commerce 1996 1992 Economic census: survey of women-owned businesses, US Government Printing office, Washington, DC.

Van Auken, H., Gaskill, J. and Kao, S.-S. 1993 Acquisition of capital by women entrepreneurs: patterns of initial and refinancing capitalization, *Journal of Small Business and Entrepreneurship*, 10(4): 44–55.

White, T. I. 1995 Men and women judge subordinates differently, *Small Business Forum*, Vol. 13 Spring: 74–76.

Wilson, M. and Daly, M. 1992 The man who mistook his wife for a chattel, in Markow, J. H., Cosmides, L. and Tooby, J. (eds), *The Adapted Mind: Evolutionary Psychology and the Generation of Culture* (Oxford: Oxford University Press), 289–322.

Women's Business Exclusive 1995 Most Fortune 500 companies have women on boards, 3(7): 4–5.

Appendix. Indexes used.

General business press: Information Access Company's (IAC) computerized Business and Company Index, both the full index (ASAP) and the Backfile. This index covers over 1,000 periodicals, back to 1982, with coverage more complete in later years.

Academic journals: IAC's Academic Index, which covers over 1600 journals and other periodicals, back to 1980, with coverage more complete in later years.

Elite newspapers: Lexis/Nexis electronic database, which covers the *NYT* fully back to 1980 and partially back to 1969, and covers the *WSJ* fully back to 1989 and partially back to 1973.

Search routines: The same routine was used in each index to develop measures of: (1) articles about business ownership, regardless of gender; (2) articles mentioning women, regardless of other content; and (3) articles about ownership that mentioned women. All articles that mentioned any of the following words were searched for by year:

   1 Business ownership: entrepreneur(s), entrepreneurial, entrepreneurship, owned business(s), businessman business man, businessmen, business men, business woman, business-woman, business women, businesswomen, business owner(s).

   2 Women: woman, women, womyn, female(s).

3 Women and business ownership: the same terms as in the business ownership search were searched for, but with the modifying adjectives: 'woman', 'women', or 'female' combined with the terms, except for those that already had woman as part of the term.

Elite management and entrepreneurship journals: For *AMR, AMJ, ETP,* and *JBV,* all issues were searched through for refereed papers, including research notes, classifying articles into one of the categories:

1 no mention of gender/sex;
2 demographic data on gender/sex collected, but not reported;
3 gender/sex composition of sample reported, but not used in analysis;
4 controlled for gender/sex of subjects in analysis and
5 used gender/sex as an independent variable in analysis.

For the last category, papers were further classified by whether gender/sex was the main issue of interest, and of those, whether ownership was the focus of the article.

[18]

Family Matters: Gender, Networks, and Entrepreneurial Outcomes*

LINDA A. RENZULLI, *University of North Carolina at Chapel Hill*
HOWARD ALDRICH, *University of North Carolina at Chapel Hill*
JAMES MOODY, *Ohio State University*

Abstract

In this article, we explore several factors that may have an effect on business start-ups, focusing on possible gender differences. We conceptualize social capital as inhering in people's relations with others and examine the association between men's and women's social capital and their likelihood of starting a business. Two aspects of respondents' social capital are highlighted: the extent to which their business discussion networks are heterogeneous and the extent to which they contain a high proportion of kin. We show that a high proportion of kin and homogeneity in the network, rather than a high proportion of females in the network or being female, are critical disadvantages facing potential small business owners.

Historically, men have enjoyed several advantages over women in their life chances. For example, men have had, on average, higher occupational status, a higher rate of self-employment, and higher incomes than women (Reskin 1993). Female-dominated occupations have been devalued, in part, because Americans consider work done by women less valuable, less important, and less difficult (England 1992). Men have also owned and controlled the great majority of businesses. In 1990 the self-employment rate[1] for men was 12%, whereas it was only 6% for women (Devine 1994). However, in the past several decades, women have made gains in occupational status, income, and business ownership. Many women are now employed in traditionally male occupations, and the pay gap between men and

A draft of this article was presented at the 1998 Conference on Entrepreneurship, Insead, Fontainebleau, France. We thank Rachel Rosenfeld, Jeremy Reynolds, and the two reviewers for their helpful comments on earlier drafts. Direct correspondence to Linda A. Renzulli, University of North Carolina at Chapel Hill, Department of Sociology, CB #3210 Hamilton Hall, Chapel Hill, NC 27599. Telephone: 919-962-5044. E-mail: linda_renzulli@unc.edu.

women has decreased (Reskin 1993). In addition, female business ownership has risen dramatically. Since the 1970s, women have experienced a sixfold increase in their share of U.S. businesses (Baker, Aldrich & Liou 1997; Devine 1994).

In this article, we explore the effects that social networks may have on women's inroads into business ownership, using unique social network data from a longitudinal sample of owners and potential owners in the Research Triangle Park area of North Carolina. We examine the actions of *nascent entrepreneurs* — persons who are seriously attempting to start a business, a category that includes persons who are not currently business owners as well as existing owners. We focus on social capital in business start-up, following Lin's (1999) conception of social capital as channels of access to resources that inhere in someone's social relations. Such ties provide differential incubation prospects for new business ideas, depending on the quality of the information and resources flowing through them. Indeed, few founders begin their businesses as solo endeavors (Reynolds & White 1997). Instead, they draw upon support and assistance from others to whom they are tied by personal and professional connections.

The viability of a new venture depends, in part, on how well nascent entrepreneurs gauge the environment in which they choose to start a business and on how well they can capture resources in order to survive after start-up. We argue that the diversity and composition of nascent entrepreneurs' social networks provide access to information and resources that change the likelihood of starting a business. We examine men's and women's networks and focus specifically on heterogeneity and kin composition, because much of the network literature points to gender differences in these dimensions of personal networks. Research has shown that men tend to have more diverse networks than do women, which, in turn, may provide subtle advantages to men.

Social Capital

Theorists have disagreed over the definition and interpretation of the term *social capital* (for the multiple definitions and usage, see Bourdieu 1986; Burt 1997; Coleman 1988; Lin 1999; Putnam 1993). Bourdieu (1986) and Putnam (1993) used the group as the level of analysis in their arguments that groups collectively enhance their members' life chances through social capital. By contrast, Lin (1999) used the individual as the unit of analysis to argue that social capital is instrumental for business and work in a way similar to that of human capital investments. Coleman (1988) seemed to use the term with both a collective and individual referent. He saw social capital as a resource for social action that could lead to the acquisition of other forms of capital, human and physical. Similarly, Burt defined social capital as a quality created between people, and Sik and Wellman (1999) referred to valuable social ties as "network capital." We use *social capital* to indicate the relationship characteristics of a person's ties to others who may provide access to important resources.

Arguments concerning the value of social capital suggest that part of the difference in business start-up rates between male-owned and female-owned businesses might be explained by differences in social capital accumulation created through ties. Interpersonal connections are a significant informal source of information about opportunities and available resources for occupational mobility and improved life chances (Campbell 1988; Campbell, Marsden & Hurlbert 1986; Marsden & Hurlbert 1988). By extension from these arguments, social capital can play a similar role in business start-ups. If there are consistent differences between the social networks in which men and women are embedded, and if such information affects business start-ups, then a partial explanation for differential start-up rates by gender could be found in people's differential possession of social capital.

We are specifically interested in the effects of network composition and heterogeneity on the likelihood of an individual's attempt to start a business. We focus on information and social support networks. These are very different from resource, exchange, or joint-venture organizational networks, which involve the flow of tangible capital resources. Our theoretical interest rests in the immediate circle of discussion partners surrounding a nascent entrepreneur, defined as a set of alters with whom a given entrepreneur discusses business matters. Such persons have the potential to influence nascent entrepreneurs' recognition of business opportunities, as well as the quality of their economic decision making. A key characteristic of such networks, affecting the types and quality of information obtained, is the relationship heterogeneity of the alters.

Our hypotheses thus focus on the informational and social support resources provided by business discussion networks, guided by three principles. First, people can maximize the value of the information they receive if they have low redundancy among the alters in their discussion network (Granovetter 1973). Therefore, the greatest returns to social capital occur for nascent entrepreneurs with many nonredundant ties. Second, kinship ties — by virtue of their common origin in the family — are likely to generate information drawn from a homogeneous pool. Kinship ties thus provide lower levels of new information (Marsden 1990). Third, access to information about opportunities and social support from peers are key bridges between one's intention to start a business and actually doing so (Denison, Swaminathan & Rothbard 1994).

Before explaining the rationale for our hypotheses, we review the central concepts of social network analysis relevant to gender differences. We illustrate our two major independent variables — heterogeneity and composition — and explain their theoretical significance.

526 / Social Forces 79:2, December 2000

GENDER AND NETWORKS

Researchers have found that men and women are embedded in different social networks and have suggested that network differences lead to divergent economic consequences (Popielarz 1999). Several studies have shown that women tend to nominate more kin as people with whom they "discuss important matters" (Marsden 1987; Moore 1990). In fact, women in the same social situation as men tend to have more homogeneous networks in terms of kin composition (Marsden 1987; Moore 1990), either because of induced homophily or choice homophily (McPherson & Smith-Lovin 1987).

In studies of business owners, researchers have replicated many of the findings from surveys of the general population. Evidence from a limited number of surveys suggests that men and women business owners resemble the general public in the composition of their personal networks. For example, using the Research Triangle Entrepreneurial Development Study (EDS), Renzulli (1998) found that women business owners included more kin in their business discussion networks than did men. By contrast, men owners included more coworkers in their networks than did women.

Researchers have interpreted gender differences in network composition as posing a disadvantage for women in the business world (Liao & Stevens 1994; Moore 1990). Women who include greater proportions of kin in their discussion networks may secure greater social support than men, but at the cost of sacrificing the necessary instrumental support needed for economic achievement (Fischer & Oliker 1983; Hurlbert 1991). Social support provides the emotional strength owners and managers need to cope with daily exigencies, but such ties may also limit the diversity and reach of women's networks.

However, despite men and women owners' differences in network characteristics, researchers have not found differences in the *consequences* of these characteristics for how owners use their networks (Katz & Williams 1997). Reese and Aldrich (1995) found that networking activity, defined as the time spent building and maintaining business contacts, was not essential to business survival. Furthermore, they found that survival rates and general economic performance were not significantly related to global measures of networking activity. Aldrich, Elam, and Reese (1997) reported that women owners were just as aggressive as men in searching for advice and assistance through their networks and just as successful in obtaining what they sought. These findings suggest that the type of information and support provided by business discussion networks may have little impact on the survival of businesses after they are founded. However, the likelihood of business start-up may still depend on network heterogeneity and composition.

HETEROGENEITY

Granovetter (1973, 1974) argued that people who have contacts in more places (a greater range) have greater access to resources and information. Heterogeneity is the most direct indicator of the diversity of an individual's interpersonal environment. High diversity implies integration into several spheres of society, which is often advantageous for instrumental action (Marsden 1987). Networks that are diverse help people reach other social realms and avoid redundant information. A redundant relation is one in which the same information or resource could be obtained from other relations (Burt 1992). A given piece of information obtained from a member of a heterogeneous network is likely to be unique because actors in the network draw information from different sources. However, most people's relations are within clusters containing people who are similar to themselves along multiple dimensions, such as race, sex, and age (Blau 1994).

The more heterogeneous someone's discussion networks, the greater the likelihood that they can obtain nonredundant or diverse information (Blau 1977). For example, Popielarz (1999) argued that an organization's demographic mix affects a member's opportunity to form network ties with dissimilar others. Heterogeneity may increase potential owners' social capital by deepening or extending their knowledge through indirect ties to others beyond their immediate circle. A heterogeneous network may also compensate for an individual's biased or incomplete perceptions and raise expectations for business start-up.

Hypothesis 1: The greater the heterogeneity in an individual's discussion network, the greater the likelihood he or she will start a new business.

KIN COMPOSITION

The concept of network composition refers to the precise mixture of alters in a social network (Marsden 1987, 1990). Whereas heterogeneity captures the mere diversity of network alters, the concept of composition captures the type and mix of alters as well. The category of kin includes spouse, parents, siblings, and in-laws; that of nonkin includes friends, neighbors, coworkers, consultants, and group or association members. Figure 1 illustrates the possible difference between the extent of heterogeneity and the percentage of kin in someone's discussion network. Networks A and B have the same heterogeneity scores: each actor reaches the same number of diverse alters. The two networks, however, differ in their composition. Network A has a higher proportion of coworkers and network B has a higher proportion of kin. Thus, both concepts, heterogeneity and composition, are crucial in understanding someone's personal discussion network.

528 / *Social Forces* **79:2, December 2000**

FIGURE 1: Heterogeneity and Composition

Network A

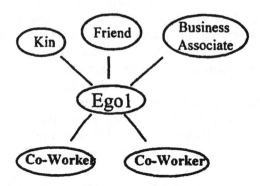

Composition = 2/5 coworker
1/5 kin

$$\left[\left(\frac{1\ \text{kin}}{5}\right)^2 + \left(\frac{1\ \text{business associate}}{5}\right)^2 + \left(\frac{2\ \text{coworkers}}{5}\right)^2 + \left(\frac{1\ \text{friend}}{5}\right)^2\right] = .72$$

Network B

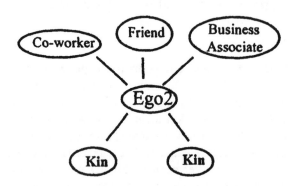

Composition = 1/5 coworker
2/5 kin

$$\left[\left(\frac{2\ \text{kin}}{5}\right)^2 + \left(\frac{1\ \text{business associate}}{5}\right)^2 + \left(\frac{1\ \text{coworker}}{5}\right)^2 + \left(\frac{1\ \text{friend}}{5}\right)^2\right] = .72$$

Note: For heterogeneity, see equation 1.

Previous research has suggested that kin ties are less likely than nonkin ties (especially coworker ties) to provide instrumental resources and unique information (Fischer & Oliker 1983; Moore 1990; Wellman 1990; Wellman, Carrington & Hall 1988; Wellman & Wortley 1990). For example, family members are much more likely to share information with each other than are nonkin members. Therefore, if individuals have a large proportion of kin members in their network, they may be at a disadvantage in the business community because their social ties are more inward-looking. A high proportion of kin in a network may indicate a high level of redundancy in information sources.

Hypothesis 2: The greater the proportion of kin in an individual's discussion network, the lower the likelihood he or she will start a new business.

OTHER FACTORS

Our two hypotheses focus exclusively on social capital for business start-up. We concentrate on heterogeneity and kin composition because the main thesis of our article is that quality of ties facilitates business start-up. Because men and women also differ in the number of women in their networks, our analysis takes into account the gender composition of nascent entrepreneurs' networks.[2]

Our analysis also includes factors such as life stage, employment status, and human capital to fully specify our model and ensure that our results are not spurious. We discuss previous research in which these factors have been the focus of analysis, and we comment on the effects of these other factors, but we do not present formal hypotheses about them.

Across entrepreneurial samples, researchers have found that the average age of business owners is generally greater than that of employees (Aldrich, Elam & Reese 1997; Aldrich, Renzulli & Langton 1998; Carter 1997). A nascent or established owner's age is important because throughout their life course, people pick up additional contacts and social support through their involvement in associations, work, and family activities. Marriage and parenthood are life-stage events that may also affect ownership. The presence of a spouse indicates that a respondent has a social tie to at least one other person and thus is not a social isolate. A tie to a spouse can, in turn, link respondents to others who can provide information and possible resources.

Marriage is not only a tie but also a potential constraint on economic activities due to gender-based expectations. For example, single women are similar to married men, and unlike married women, in their ability to allocate their time to business activities with little regard to domestic responsibilities (Starr & Yudkin 1996). Thus, it would seem likely that single female owners could begin and pursue business start-up activities more easily than their married counterparts. However, according to a Wisconsin study and data from the Current Population Survey,

530 / *Social Forces* 79:2, December 2000

female owners are at least as likely to be married as are male owners (Carter 1997; Devine 1994). Because these studies focus on respondents' current employment, rather than the process of moving into new employment, we do not know whether their results will hold for people in the process of starting a business. Children can also constrain someone's likelihood of entering self-employment. Married people with children are likely to face the competing demands of family life and business ownership and be more constrained in how much time they can devote to business than are nonparents (Shelton & Daphne 1996).

A person's employment status may also influence business start-up chances. Prior employment histories can affect a person's likelihood of following through on intentions to be self-employed by raising or lowering their stock of human capital and their career expectations. Thus, career histories and specific career trajectories push or pull someone into self-employment. Although some research points to unemployment as a push factor into self-employment (Evans & Leighton 1989; Storey 1991, 1994), other data reveal that the great majority of new owners have full-time employment directly prior to ownership (Aldrich, Renzulli & Langton 1998; Carter 1997; Manser & Picot 1999; Reynolds & White 1997).

Starting a business is a process that includes intentions or serious thought about business ownership. Thus, people who had an idea or inclination toward self-employment are more likely to actually move into the nascent stages of ownership if other influences are present (Carter 1997). However, intentions do not always come to fruition. Many people think about starting a business but never actually go through the stages to become an owner (Carter 1997; Reynolds & White 1997). Nevertheless, intentions are a first step toward ownership and thus should be included in analyses of start-ups.

Human capital is the investment in technical skills and knowledge that boosts someone's earning power (Becker 1964). People invest time and money in their education so that they will be able to negotiate for better jobs and more income based on their skills (Lin 1999). Thus, sociologists and economists alike have used years of education to measure human capital. In the case of business owners, some research has found that they have about the same level of educational attainment as the general public (Aldrich, Renzulli & Aldrich 1998; Gartner 1988), whereas others have found contrary results (Reynolds & White 1997).

Previous research has shown that women tend to have more ties to women than to men (McPherson & Smith-Lovin 1986; Popielarz 1999). Even though women have made substantial gains in occupational status and authority over the past few decades, they still on average occupy more disadvantaged positions than men do (Reskin 1993). Thus, if someone's ties are primarily to other women, this could also be a disadvantage in the business community for gathering information and other resources.

Research Design

The data consist of a panel of individuals in the early stages of business formation, owners of established organizations, and people providing services to new organizations. We tracked respondents over a two-year period, from 1990 to 1992.

DATA

We use data from the Research Triangle Entrepreneurial Development Study to explore the networks of nascent entrepreneurs and business owners. Participants were located in the Research Triangle area of North Carolina, an area previously studied by Aldrich et al. (1989), Campbell (1988), Kalleberg et al. (1990), and others. Campbell (1988) analyzed gender differences in job-related networks by contacting people through the firms that employed them in the region. Kalleberg et al. (1990) and Aldrich et al. (1989) used the same region to study differences in the coverage of various organizational sampling frames. Luger and Goldstein (1991) found that economic development efforts in the Research Triangle area were similar to programs in other regions that attempted to promote growth through science parks. Based on these studies and others, we believe the Research Triangle area of North Carolina is a valuable laboratory in which to study business start-up and growth.

The respondents in this sample were selected from people with entrepreneurial or business activity memberships and involvement, drawn from organizations in Durham and Wake Counties, North Carolina,[3] participants in technical-college small business classes in Wake County, and a random sample of new business owners in Wake County. The sample thus includes information on current small business owners (those with an active business) and two groups of people qualifying as nascent entrepreneurs: people actively trying to start a business and those who are thinking about becoming business owners. According to Reynolds and White (1997), our sample includes nascent entrepreneurs because we have included people who have taken action in the first steps toward business ownership, such as joining a business organization and taking an entrepreneurial class. Reese (1993) conducted analyses in which she included a dummy variable for her randomly drawn subsample, contrasting it with her purposively drawn subsamples, and showed that sample source was not a statistically significant predictor of network composition or networking activities.[4]

Two waves of information were collected, the first between 1990 and 1991 and the second in 1992 (see Reese 1993 and Reese & Aldrich 1995 for a full description of the data). Phase 1 of the first wave was a short mailed questionnaire, and phase 2 involved an in-depth telephone interview with those who returned the questionnaire. In the first phase, 659 questionnaires were mailed out and 444 returned. Telephone interviews were completed for 353 of the respondents who returned a mailed questionnaire. The survey thus had a completion rate of 67% of those who received a mailed questionnaire and a response rate of 54% of the original sample who completed a mailed and telephone questionnaire. We used only those wave 1 respondents who completed a phone interview, as they were asked the social network questions we used to construct our independent variables.

For the second wave (collected in 1992), a mailed questionnaire was sent to all the people who had completed a mailed questionnaire in wave 1. All respondents were also telephoned. Of the 353 who had completed the mailed and telephone questionnaire in wave 1, we received at least some follow-up information on 328 respondents, for a follow-up rate of 93%. These rates are comparable to those in other studies of entrepreneurs (Birley, Cromie & Myers 1990; Cooper & Dunkelberg 1987; Kalleberg 1987; Kalleberg 1986). See Table 1 for the demographic characteristics of our sample.

VARIABLES

We present information on the coding and definition of all variables in Table 2. For the dependent variable and the four central independent variables, we present additional information below.

Business Start-Up

We used the second wave of data to obtain information about business start-ups. Two groups of people were identified on the basis of their business status at wave 1 — business owners and nonowners. Interviewers asked the business owners a series of questions to tap additional business start-ups as well as new business start-ups.[5] Interviewers asked the nonowners if they had started or bought a business since wave 1. Fifty-two respondents started a new business between wave 1 and wave 2 of our interviews. Of the respondents already in business at wave 1, 16% had started a new business by wave 2. Of the respondents who were not owners at wave 1, 31% had started a new business by wave 2.

To measure business formation, we constructed a dichotomous variable for start-up in wave 2 that indicated whether respondents from wave 1 had started a business by wave 2. We have information on 276 cases for business start-up events between wave 1 and wave 2.[6]

Gender

Gender was measured with a dichotomous variable, taking the value 1 for male and 0 for female respondents.

Heterogeneity

Interviewers in the first wave of data asked respondents about the people with whom they talked about business. The respondents were asked the following: "Now I would like to talk about your business contacts. Please tell me the first five people with whom you feel especially willing or able to discuss your ideas for a new business or your ideas about representing or running your current business." The five people with whom respondents talked about business matters are "strong ties,"[7] and we will refer to these people as the "business discussion network."

Networks are composed of people with many different attributes. An investigator needs to decide which dimension of heterogeneity is relevant, as a person's network can be heterogeneous in some respects and homogeneous in others (Blau 1977; Marsden 1987). For example, someone can have a network made up of all kin members, and that network is homogeneous with respect to kin. Yet each of the kin members may have a different occupation, and thus the network is heterogeneous with respect to occupation. Because we were interested in whether potential owners gleaned information from multiple sources, we focused on the differing social dimensions within which relationships with alters arose: work, friendship, family, and membership groups.

Moore (1990) and other researchers have used separate OLS models for each relationship type to measure absolute network composition. By contrast, we prefer to use a general measure of heterogeneity, because it is a concise measure of network diversity. We asked respondents their relationship to each of the persons in their discussion network. Respondents could list up to three relationship categories for each alter (similar to the General Social Survey format). For the heterogeneity measure, we categorized an alter by using the first relationship the respondent named. The name generator provided six categories that make up the absolute composition of business discussion networks: kin, friends, coworkers, business associates, consultants, and fellow group or association members. We defined network heterogeneity as the probability of randomly choosing people with two different attributes from the possible six attributes. We calculated it as follows:[8]

$$1 - \left[\left(\frac{\# \text{ kin}_i}{\text{total}} \right)^2 + \left(\frac{\# \text{ business associates}_i}{\text{total}} \right)^2 + \left(\frac{\# \text{ coworkers}_i}{\text{total}} \right)^2 \right.$$
$$\left. + \left(\frac{\# \text{ consultants}_i}{\text{total}} \right)^2 + \left(\frac{\# \text{ friends}_i}{\text{total}} \right)^2 + \left(\frac{\# \text{ group members}_i}{\text{total}} \right)^2 \right]. \tag{1}$$

A heterogeneity score equal to 0 indicates a perfectly homogeneous network, whereas a heterogeneity score approaching 1 indicates a more heterogeneous network.

Proportion of Kin

We measured the percentage of kin members that ego nominated in the business discussion network as the ratio of kin to all persons named. As we note above, respondents had the opportunity to classify each alter into three relation categories.

534 / *Social Forces* 79:2, December 2000

TABLE 1: Demographic Characteristics of Respondents in Wave 1 Who Were Followed Up in Wave 2

Characteristic	Men	Women
Education		
High school or less	8.0 (20)	12.4 (12)
2 years of college	6.8 (17)	22.7 (22)
Bachelor's degree	48.2 (121)	37.1 (36)
Master's degree	26.3 (66)	22.7 (22)
Ph.D. degree	10.8 (27)	5.2 (5)
Race		
White	94.8 (237)	91.8 (89)
Black	3.6 (9)	8.2 (8)
Other	1.6 (4)	0
Family status		
Married	84.5 (212)	69.1 (67)
Single	15.5 (39)	30.9 (30)
Number of children		
0	50.4 (113)	64.8 (57)
1-4	43.4 (109)	32.0 (31)
5+	.8 (2)	0
Run own business		
Currently an owner	77.7 (195)	72.2 (70)
Currently not an owner	22.3 (56)	27.8 (27)
Intend to start a business	29.2 (73)	22.7 (22)
Source of respondent		
Random sample	8.8 (22)	16.5 (16)
Organizational rolls	91.2 (229)	83.5 (81)
Industry		
Manufacturing	7.2 (18)	7.2 (7)
Business services	17.5 (44)	18.6 (18)
Consulting services	16.3 (41)	7.2 (7)
Retail	11.6 (29)	20.6 (20)
Other (R&D, computers, real estate)	25.1 (63)	18.6 (18)
Work history		
Number of years employed full-time		
0	12.8 (30)	24.2 (22)
1-5	25.5 (60)	24.2 (22)
6-11	61.7 (145)	51.8 (47)
Number of years self-employed		
0	33.2 (78)	38.5 (35)
1-5	38.3 (90)	36.2 (33)
5-11	28.5 (67)	25.3 (23)
Start-up between waves 1 and 2	19 (40)	15 (11)

TABLE 1: Demographic Characteristics of Respondents in Wave 1 Who Were Followed Up in Wave 2 (Continued)

Characteristic	Men	Women
Mean age	42	40
N	251	97

Note: Figures preceding those in parentheses are percentages, and those in parentheses are total numbers.

We coded an alter as kin if the respondent classified him or her as kin as the first, second, or third relation type to ensure that we captured all kin alters.[9]

Total Number of People in the Network

The total number of people with whom respondents discuss business is a crude measure of the number of direct contacts but does not limit respondents to listing strong ties. Interviewers asked the respondents to indicate the total number of people with whom they discussed aspects of starting or running a business. The mean number of people was 8.8 and the mode was 5, but the data were highly skewed, with an interquartile range of 3 to 10.[10]

Results

We tested the hypotheses about network characteristics and business start-up in two steps. First we computed descriptive statistics for gender and network characteristics. Then we used multivariate logistic regression models to predict start-up by gender and network characteristics.

GENDER AND NETWORK CHARACTERISTICS AT WAVE 1

Our analyses only weakly confirm previous studies showing that gender is related to network characteristics.[11] Because the distributions of heterogeneity and proportion of kin are discontinuous in very small networks (less than 5), it is important to evaluate the size of each person's business network. Therefore, we explored whether the distribution of number of alters nominated by men and women was the same. The mean number of alters nominated by men and women was 4.7. About 82% of men and 84% of women nominated 5 business discussion ties (the difference between men and women is not statistically significant). Men and women have the same number of diverse alters and similar heterogeneity scores. The mean heterogeneity score for men is .45 and for women is .49, a

536 / *Social Forces* 79:2, December 2000

TABLE 2: Variables and Coding for Business Discussion Network

	Definition	Coding
Dependent Variable		
Business start-up	Respondents who started or bought a business between waves 1 and 2	0 = didn't start a business by wave 2 1 = started a business by wave 2
Independent Variables		
Social capital variables		
Heterogeneity score	Probability that each alter in the network will have a different relation to respondent from that of all other alters	Range of 0 to 1 (theoretical) where 0 = completely homogeneous network, 1 = absolutely heterogeneous network
Proportion of kin	Number of kin mentioned / total number of alters mentioned (as a function of the number of alters) at wave 1	0-.80 (observed) 0-1 (possible)
Total number in network	Total number of people with whom respondents discuss business at wave 1. Open-ended question not solicited through the name generator.	Range of 0 to 200 (mean = 8.8, mode = 5)
Proportion of female alters	Number of females mentioned / number of alters mentioned (as a function of the number of alters) at wave 1	0-1 (observed)
Life stage		
Marital status	Respondent married at wave 1	0 = not married, 1 = married
Age	Age of respondent at wave 1	22-78 (mean = 41.2)
Presence of children	Total number of children 18 years old or younger living with nascent or established owner	Range of 0 to 8 (mean = .86, s.d. = 1.1)
Human capital		
Education	Level of education attained	4 dummy variables: 1 = some college 1 = Bachelor's degree 1 = Master's degree 1 = Ph.D. degree 0 = Other education level, for each dummy

TABLE 2:   Variables and Coding for Business Discussion Network
(Continued)

	Definition	Coding
Human capital (cont'd)		
Work history	The respondent's work history over the past 10 years: number of years employed full time and number of years self-employed	Continuous variables: Employed: range of 0 to 11 years (mean = 5.2, s.d. = 3.9) Self-employed: range of 0 to 11 years (mean = 3.3, s.d. = 3.7)
Stage of business ownership	Running own business at wave 1	0 = no, 1 = yes
Continuity of business ownership	Running same business at wave 2	0 = no, 1 = yes
Intent to start a business	At wave 1, respondent planned to start a business in the future	0 = no plans, 1 = plans

statistically insignificant difference, as Table 3 shows. Women and men differ substantially in the proportion of female alters in their business networks (.48 versus .18, respectively).

Bivariate analysis, however, supports the typical finding that women nominate more kin in their networks than do men (Marsden 1987; Moore 1990; Renzulli 1998). Fifty-six percent of women nominate one or more kin as part of their business discussion network, compared with only 40% of men. The average proportion of kin for men is .14 and for women is .20, as shown in Table 3, and the difference is statistically significant. The proportion of kin for men and women in this sample was lower than in Wellman (1992a), who found that 55% of men and women named kin in their active networks. Moore (1990), using the General Social Survey, found that the proportion of kin in personal discussion networks was .51 for men and .58 for women. We believe that we found a smaller proportion of kin in our respondents' networks because they were specifically asked to name alters in their *business* networks. General discussion networks may draw more heavily on kin because they often provide emotional support, whereas business networks may draw less heavily on kin and more heavily on other kinds of ties that provide instrumental support.

START-UP BY GENDER AND NETWORK CHARACTERISTICS

In the final part of our analysis, we used logistic regression in two steps to test our hypotheses about the association between discussion network characteristics and business start-ups. We first ran a baseline model (model 1) without any network

TABLE 3:   Mean Network Characteristics for Men and Women in
           Business Discussion Network

	Men	Women
Number of business discussion alters nominated	4.68 (.84)	4.70 (.75)
Heterogeneity score	.45 (.21)	.49 (.19)
Proportion of kin	.14*** (.21)	.20 (.23)
Proportion of females	.18*** (.21)	.48 (.27)

Note: Standard deviations are in parentheses.

*** p < .001   (one-tailed tests)

variables in order to predict start-ups, and then we added the network variables in model 2. The nested models show that the addition of the network variables significantly increases explanatory power from model 1 to model 2. Table 4 shows the results of the multivariate models for start-ups.

As predicted by hypothesis 1, we found that network heterogeneity significantly increased the odds of starting a business, net of intentions, demographic characteristics, and other control variables.[12] The coefficient for heterogeneity's effect on start-up is positive, indicating that diverse ties in a network facilitate the start-up process. In fact, a perfectly heterogeneous network increased the odds of starting a business by a factor of five, net of all other variables (significant at the .05 level, one-tailed). This supports our contention that heterogeneous discussion networks serve as an important resource for nascent owners.

Hypothesis 2 was also confirmed. With respect to kin, we found that the greater the proportion of kin in respondents' networks, the less likely they were to start a new business between the two waves of our study. For a unit increase in the proportion of kin, the chances of starting a business at wave 2 decreased by a factor of .05, net of other network characteristics, individual variables, work history, and human capital variables. In other words, a business network that changes from zero kin to all kin will reduce the odds of a person starting a new business by 95%. We interpret this result as suggesting that the information that kin provide and the time it takes to maintain kin ties create disadvantages for people contemplating a business start-up. Net of the network variables, the gender of a respondent had no significant effect on the likelihood of starting a new business.

When we tested for the possible effect of the gender composition of a respondent's network, we found that adding the proportion of females did not

Gender, Networks, and Entrepreneurial Outcomes / 539

TABLE 4: Logistic Analysis for Business Start-Ups

Predictor Variables	Model 1 No Network Variables			Model 2 Full Model		
	Coefficient	S.E.	Odds Ratio	Coefficient	S.E.	Odds Ratio
Intercept	−3.51	1.23		−3.89	1.44	.00**
Social capital						
Heterogeneity	—	—	—	1.65	.96	5.23†
Proportion kin	—	—	—	−3.02	1.22	.05*
Proportion female	—	—	—	.67	.89	1.96
Total network size	—	—	—	.00	.01	1.00
Individual variables						
Married	−.01	.49	.99	.13	.51	1.14
Gender (male = 1)	.04	.46	1.04	.22	.55	1.25
Age	.03	.02	1.04	.03	.02	1.03
Number of children	.02	.16	1.02	.01	.17	1.01
Human capital						
Some college	−.59	.87	.56	−.53	.92	.59
Bachelor's degree	.19	.63	1.21	−.08	.67	.93
Master's degree	.04	.68	1.04	−.16	.72	.85
Ph.D. degree	.54	.81	1.72	.22	.86	1.25
Running own business at wave 1	.46	.62	1.58	.44	.65	1.56
Running same business at wave 2	−.65	.51	.52	−.73	.54	.48
Intent to start a business at wave 1	1.21	.41	3.37*	1.22	.41	3.37**
Work history						
Employed	.01	.07	1.01	.01	.08	1.01
Self-employed	.01	.08	1.01	−.02	.08	.98
−2 log-likelihood (N = 246)			219.39†			209.926*

† p < .10   * p < .05   ** p < .01   (two-tailed tests)

significantly change our findings. Proportion of females is not significant, nor does it change the significant negative effects of proportion of kin. Therefore, we are confident that it is the type of relation individuals have to the alters in their personal networks, rather than the gender of the alters, that has the greatest impact on the likelihood of becoming an entrepreneur. We suspect that the proportion of women in our respondents' networks does not significantly affect business start-ups because respondents named people with whom they had discussed business and thus may have named only people (male or female) who have some business knowledge.

We found that the gender of our respondents did not affect the likelihood of business start-up: men and women are equally likely to start a business (in Table 4, gender is not statistically significant). Our sample of owners and nascent owners probably eliminates most women who have been occupationally steered away from business ownership or blocked from considering ownership because of other gender-related factors. According to our data, network composition, rather than gender, is a key obstacle for starting a business. Thus, we find that what differentiates people at this level of interest in ownership is their networks and not their gender.

Among the other variables we included, only intentions had a significant impact on start-ups. Individual variables such as age, education, marital status, and number of children did not significantly affect the likelihood of start-up. Our sample was fairly homogeneous with respect to education and marital status, and this lack of variation undoubtedly played a role in reducing the explanatory power of such factors. Also, because we followed respondents over a fairly narrow time period, factors associated with life-course events were less likely to be significant in our models. A person's work history also did not significantly affect start-ups. But intentions do matter.

Having intentions to start a business at wave 1 significantly increased the likelihood of actually starting one, raising the odds by a factor of 3.4 in both the fully specified model and the restricted model, net of all other variables. People who said they were going to start a business were very likely to carry their plans through. In keeping with the unpredictable world of entrepreneurship, we note that a few people who were neither running a business nor even contemplating a start-up in our first wave nevertheless went on to actually start one.

Conclusion and Discussion

Over the last few decades, women-owned businesses have greatly increased as a proportion of all businesses. We suspect that the observed trend toward a greater number of female-headed businesses stems from an increase in women's social capital. That is, increasing occupational opportunities for women may well be generating increased heterogeneity in the composition of their social networks. The composition of women's discussion networks, especially women with entrepreneurial interests, might have changed in the past few decades. We believe that historical research on trends in women's social networks may lead to a better understanding of the relative increase in female-owned businesses.

In this article, we used a sample of Research Triangle area owners and potential owners, gathered in the early 1990s, to examine the association between the characteristics of owners' and nascent entrepreneurs' social capital and the likelihood that they would start a business. We followed Lin's (1999) and Portes's (1998) conceptions of social capital as inhering in people's relations with others and focused on the degree to which respondents' business discussion networks were heterogeneous and contained kin members. We treated discussion networks as conduits for information about economic opportunities as well as sources of social support for people who might be hesitant about attempting to start a business.

We found that networks spanning multiple domains of social life apparently provide nascent entrepreneurs with greater access to multiple sources of information than do more homogeneous networks and thus enable them to make the transition from idea to action. Our analyses show that actors with networks that draw information from multiple sources — those with high heterogeneity and a low percentage of kin — are much more likely to start a new business than are those with more homogeneous networks. Evidently, the increased social support provided by kinship ties does not offset the loss of information due to restrictions on network range. Our finding complements research showing that the most valuable social capital a person can mobilize is found via dissimilar ties (Popielarz 1999).

The received wisdom on the relationship between gender and social network composition is replicated in our data. We found that women tended to have more homogeneous networks than men with respect to kin. The network effects we observed held *net* of gender differences, and in analyses not shown here we found no significant interactions between network composition and owner gender. This implies that although men's and women's discussion networks differ in their composition, the mechanisms that link network range and entrepreneurial activity are similar across the sexes. A central conclusion of our study is that networks made up of a greater proportion of kin create disadvantages in entrepreneurial start-up *regardless* of gender. Therefore, based on our results, we conclude that a high percentage of kin in people's networks, rather than their gender or the gender composition of their networks, is a critical disadvantage facing potential owners.

We also found that intentions to start a business may be an impetus for people to mobilize and use their social capital. Although most people who initially reported that they intended to start a business in the near future did not actually do so, enough people did carry through on their intentions to suggest that intentions to start one might affect the extent to which people call upon their networks for assistance. Further research should examine the relationship between intentions and use of social networks.

Future research in network analyses of business ownership should look at the content of the information that passes between individuals and the alters to whom they are tied. Our analysis shows that network composition and heterogeneity are important influences on business start-up, implying that the information found in heterogeneous networks with nonkin ties is unique and useful to nascent entrepreneurs. However, we have not captured the content of ties with our network measurements; that is, we do not know what people are actually talking about when

542 / *Social Forces* **79:2, December 2000**

they meet with the alters in their networks. Instead, we have the characteristics of the network as a whole.

Research on the content of ties by Podolny and Baron (1997) shows the importance of looking at tie content for performance and mobility in firms. They showed that consistent role expectations within dense intrafirm networks affect an employee's likelihood of moving to higher levels. Outside the relatively closed boundaries of firms, however, role expectations may be less important than nascent entrepreneurs' ability to recognize potential resource providers and sustain ties with them. Nevertheless, the content of tie information and the level of role expectations may play a powerful role in the business community.

This article provides insights derived from a unique sample of owners and nascent entrepreneurs. Like all such samples, there are limitations based on sample size and geographic specificity. Although such limitations constrain the generalizability and statistical power of our work, we feel the general processes identified are grounded in a conceptual frame that is not context-specific. Heterogeneous social ties are an important resource that people can tap to improve their life chances. Thus, we suspect that research on business start-ups in other regions should find similar outcomes.

Notes

1. The self-employment rate is calculated as the percentage of people 16 and older who reported themselves as self-employed in a nonagricultural sector.

2. Thanks to an anonymous reviewer who pointed out that some readers may see gender composition as a competing hypothesis to kin composition as a disadvantage in business ownership.

3. The sample was drawn from membership lists for the following organizations: the Council for Entrepreneurial Development, a private nonprofit entrepreneurship promotion based in Durham, North Carolina; six private nonprofit business networking organizations; participants in Wake Technical Community College Small Business Center classes; and a local chapter of the National Association of Women Business Owners. To check on possible sample selection bias, a random sample of businesses registered in Wake County in 1990 was drawn.

4. In analyses not shown here, we replicated and extended Reese's (1993) test for possible selection bias in our sample. We found that sample source was not a significant predictor of our dependent variable, as the groups did not significantly differ from one another.

5. Thirteen respondents were lost because they refused to participate further at the end of wave 1.

6. To check for bias in nonresponse, we created a new test variable, coding the missing cases for the start-up variable as 1 and the others as 0. We then regressed the missing data variable on the independent network variables (proportion of kin, heterogeneity, and network size) and gender. The results (not shown here) were not significant,

indicating that respondents who did not answer the business start-up questions in wave 2 are not significantly different from those who did. Thus we are confident that our results are not influenced by selection bias.

7. The respondents were restricted to naming a maximum of five alters. This restriction limits the inferences we can draw about weak ties, as research has shown that using the name generator method elicits reasonably strong ties (Marsden 1987). Because we asked the respondents to tell us about their business networks, a focused subsample of their networks, we believe that having five named alters will provide an accurate account of the business discussion network. Asking for just five alters may introduce distortions in the data; however, the six relation types were evenly distributed over the five alters. We found no pattern across any of the five alters for any of the relationship types. Thus, there is no reason to suspect that the general pattern changes beyond five people, and thus we do not suspect our data were distorted by limiting the number of alters to five.

8. "Except for modifications due to sampling without replacement or an effort to take into account the true range of possible values for a given number of categories, [our measure of heterogeneity] is basically the same as the Index of Qualitative Variation described by Mueller and Schuessler" (Lieberson 1969:852).

9. Multiplex ties for kin members and partners in the business were not great in this sample and were not more common for women. Only 13% of men named a kin alter as a partner, which was very similar to the 9% of women who did so.

10. The variable had a range of 0 to 200 and was slightly skewed, with a small number of high values. We corrected for skewness by logging the size of the network. However, logging it did not significantly change the results; therefore, for ease of interpretation we used the raw size of the network. The mean of 8.8 is reasonable, considering other findings of general network size by Fischer (1982) and Wellman (1992b). Their studies found a mean range of 11 to 17. Because our question was only about business networks, a lower mean is plausible.

11. Multivariate analyses regressing heterogeneity and proportion of kin on gender are not shown here.

12. We ran models that would test the interaction effects of gender with the other variables, curvilinear effects of age, and influence of industry. However, the interactions, curvilinear age effects, and industry were not significant and therefore were not included in the final model.

References

Aldrich, Howard, Amanda Elam, and Pat Ray Reese. 1997. "Strong Ties, Weak Ties, and Strangers: Do Women Business Owners Differ from Men in Their Use of Networking to Obtain Assistance?" Pp. 1-25 in *Entrepreneurship in a Global Context*, edited by Sue Birley and Ian MacMillan. Routledge.

Aldrich, Howard E., Arne L. Kalleberg, Peter V. Marsden, and James Cassell. 1989. "In Pursuit of Evidence: Five Sampling Procedures for Locating New Businesses." *Journal of Business Venturing* 4:367-86.

Aldrich, Howard E., Linda Renzulli, and Nancy Langton. 1998. "Passing On Privilege." *Research in Social Stratification* 17:291-317.

544 / Social Forces 79:2, December 2000

Baker, Ted, Howard E. Aldrich, and Nina Liou. 1997. "Invisible Entrepreneurs: The Neglect of Women Business Owners by Mass Media and Scholarly Journals in the United States." *Entrepreneurship and Regional Development* 9:221-38.

Becker, Gary S. 1964. *Human Capital.* University of Chicago Press.

Birley, Sue, Stan Cromie, and Andrew Myers. 1990. *Entrepreneurial Networks: Their Creation and Development in Different Countries.* Cranfield School of Management.

Blau, Peter M. 1977. *Inequality and Heterogeneity: A Primitive Theory of Social Structure.* Free Press.

———. 1994. *Structural Contexts of Opportunity.* University of Chicago Press.

Bourdieu, Pierre. 1986. "The Forms of Capital." Pp. 241-58 in *Handbook of Theory and Research for the Sociology of Education,* edited by John G. Richardson. Greenwood Press.

Burt, Ronald S. 1992. *Structural Holes: The Social Structure of Competition.* Harvard University Press.

———. 1997. "The Contingent Value of Social Capital." *Administrative Science Quarterly* 42:339-65.

Campbell, Karen E. 1988. "Gender Differences in Job-Related Networks." *Work and Occupations* 15:179-200.

Campbell, Karen E., Peter V. Marsden, and Jeanne S. Hurlbert. 1986. "Social Resources and Socioeconomic Status." *Social Networks* 8:97-117.

Carter, Nancy. 1997. "Entrepreneurial Processes and Outcomes: The Influence of Gender." Pp. 163-77 in *The Entrepreneurial Process: Economic Growth, Men, Women, and Minorities,* Paul D. Reynolds and Sammis B. White. Quorum.

Coleman, James S. 1988. "Social Capital in the Creation of Human Capital." *American Journal of Sociology* 94:S95-S121.

Cooper, Arnold, and William Dunkelberg. 1987. "Old Questions, New Answers and Methodological Issues." *American Journal of Small Business* 11:11-23.

Denison, Daniel R., Anand Swaminathan, and Nancy Rothbard. 1994. "Networks, Founding Conditions, and Imprinting Processes: Examining the Process of Organizational Creation." Paper presented at the meeting of the Academy of Management, August 15, Dallas, Texas.

Devine, Theresa J. 1994. "Characteristics of Self-Employed Women in the United States." *Monthly Labor Review* 17(3):20-69.

England, Paula. 1992. *Comparable Worth.* Aldine de Gruyter.

Evans, David S., and Linda S. Leighton. 1989. "Some Empirical Aspects of Entrepreneurship." *American Economic Review* 79:519-35.

Fischer, Claude S. 1982. *To Dwell among Friends.* University of Chicago Press.

Fischer, Claude S., and Stacey J. Oliker. 1983. "A Research Note on Friendship, Gender, and the Life Cycle." *Social Forces* 62:124-33.

Gartner, William B. 1988. "Who Is an Entrepreneur? Is the Wrong Question." *American Journal of Small Business* 12:11-32.

Granovetter, Mark S. 1973. "Strength of Weak Ties." *American Sociological Review* 78:1360-80.

———. 1974. *Getting a Job: A Study of Contact and Careers.* Harvard University Press.

Hurlbert, Jeanne. 1991. "Social Circle and Job Satisfaction." *Work and Occupation* 18:415-30.

Gender, Networks, and Entrepreneurial Outcomes / 545

Kalleberg, Arne L. 1986. "Entrepreneurship in the 1980s: A Study of Small Business in Indiana." Pp. 157-89 in *Entrepreneurship and Innovation*, edited by Gary Libecap. JAI Press.

Kalleberg, Arne L., Peter V. Marsden, Howard E. Aldrich, and James Cassell. 1990. "Comparing Organizational Sampling Frames." *Administrative Science Quarterly* 35:658-88.

Katz, Jerome A., and Paula M. Williams. 1997. "Gender, Self-Employed and Weak-Tie Networking through Formal Organizations." *Entrepreneurship and Regional Development* 9:183-97.

Liao, Tim Futing, and Gillian Stevens. 1994. "Spouses, Homophily, and Social Networks." *Social Forces* 73:693-707.

Lieberson, Stanley. 1969. "Measuring Population Diversity." *American Sociological Review* 34:850-62.

Lin, Nan. 1999. "Building a Network Theory of Social Capital." *Connections* 22:28-51.

Luger, Michael I., and Harvey A. Goldstein. 1991. *Technology in the Garden: Research Parks and Regional Economic Development*. University of North Carolina Press.

Manser, Marilyn E., and Garnett Picot. 1999. "The Role of Self-Employment in U.S. and Canadian Job Growth." *Monthly Labor Review* 122:10-25.

Marsden, Peter V. 1987. "Core Discussion Networks of Americans." *American Sociological Review* 52:122-31.

———. 1990. "Network Data and Measurement." *Annual Review of Sociology* 16:435-63.

Marsden, Peter V., and Jeanne Hurlbert. 1988. "Social Resources and Mobility Outcomes: A Replication and Extension." *Social Forces* 66:1039-59.

McPherson, J. Miller, and Lynn Smith-Lovin. 1986. "Sex Segregation in Voluntary Associations." *American Sociological Review* 51:61-79.

———. 1987. "Homophily in Voluntary Organizations: Status Distance and the Composition of Face-to-Face Groups." *American Sociological Review* 52:370-79.

Moore, Gwen. 1990. "Structural Determinants of Men's and Women's Personal Networks." *American Sociological Review* 55:726-35.

Podolny, Joel M., and James N. Baron. 1997. "Resources and Relationships: Social Networks and Mobility in the Workplace." *American Sociological Review* 62:673-93.

Popielarz, Pamela A. 1999. "Organizational Constraints on Personal Network Formation." *Research in the Sociology of Organizations* 16:263-81.

Portes, Alejandro. 1998. "Social Capital: Its Origins and the Application in Modern Sociology." *Annual Review of Sociology* 24:1-24.

Putnam, Robert D. 1993. *Making Democracy Work: Civic Traditions in Modern Italy*. Princeton University Press.

Reese, Pat Ray. 1993. "Entrepreneurial Networks and Resource Acquisition: Does Gender Make a Difference?" Ph.D. dissertation, Department of Sociology, University of North Carolina.

Reese, Pat Ray, and Howard E. Aldrich. 1995. "Entrepreneurial Networks and Business Performance." Pp. 124-44 in *International Entrepreneurship*, edited by Sue Birley and Ian C. MacMillan. Routledge.

546 / Social Forces 79:2, December 2000

Renzulli, Linda. 1998. "Small Business Owners, Their Networks, and the Process of Resource Acquisition." Master's thesis, Department of Sociology. University of North Carolina at Chapel Hill.

Reskin, Barbara. 1993. "Sex Segregation in the Workplace." *Annual Review of Sociology* 19:241-70.

Reynolds, Paul D., and Sammis B. White. 1997. *The Entrepreneurial Process: Economic Growth, Men, Women, and Minorities.* Quorum.

Shelton, Beth Ann, and John Daphne. 1996. "The Division of Household Labor." *Annual Review of Sociology* 22:299-322.

Sik, Endre, and Barry Wellman. 1999. "Network Capital in Capitalist, Communist, and Post-Communist Countries." Pp. 225-54 in *Networks in the Global Village,* edited by Barry Wellman. Westview Press.

Starr, Jennifer A., and Marcia Yudkin. 1996. "Women Entrepreneurs: A Review of Current Research." Center for Research on Women, Wellesley College, Research Report.

Storey, David J. 1991. "The Birth of New Firms—Does Unemployment Matter?" *Small Business Economics* 3:167-78.

———. 1994. *Understanding the Small Business Sector.* Routledge.

Wellman, Barry. 1990. "The Place of Kinfolk in Personal Community Networks." *Marriage and Family Review* 15:195-228.

———. 1992a. "Men in Networks: Private Communities, Domestic Friendships." Pp. 74-114 in *Men's Friendships,* edited by Peter M. Nardi. Sage Publications.

———. 1992b. "Which Ties Provide What Kinds of Support." *Advances in Group Processes* 9:207-35.

Wellman, Barry, Peter J. Carrington, and Alan Hall. 1988. "Networks as Personal Communities." Pp. 80-85 in *Social Structures: A Network Approach,* edited by Barry Wellman and S.D. Berkowitz. Cambridge University Press.

Wellman, Barry, and Scot Wortley. 1990. "Different Strokes from Different Folks: Community Ties and Social Support." *American Journal of Sociology* 96:558-88.

ELSEVIER   Journal of Business Venturing 18 (2003) 573–596

JOURNAL
of BUSINESS
VENTURING

The pervasive effects of family on entrepreneurship: toward a family embeddedness perspective

Howard E. Aldrich [a,*], Jennifer E. Cliff [b,1]

[a]*Department of Sociology, University of North Carolina, CB#3210, Hamilton Hall, Chapel Hill, NC 27599-3210, USA*
[b]*Faculty of Business, University of Alberta, Edmonton, AB, Canada T6G 2R6*

Abstract

Families and businesses have often been treated as naturally separate institutions, whereas we argue that they are inextricably intertwined. Long-term changes in family composition and in the roles and relations of family members have produced families in North America that are growing smaller and losing many of their previous role relationships. Such transformations in the institution of the family have implications for the emergence of new business opportunities, opportunity recognition, business start-up decisions, and the resource mobilization process. We suggest that entrepreneurship scholars would benefit from a *family embeddedness perspective* on new venture creation.
© 2003 Elsevier Science Inc. All rights reserved.

Keywords: Family; New venture creation; Opportunity recognition; Start-up; Emergence

1. Executive summary

After decades of debate, scholars now agree that a crucial aspect of entrepreneurship involves the recognition of emerging business opportunities, which are often exploited through the creation of new business ventures. Although research on opportunity emergence and venture creation has grown considerably, very little attention has been paid to how family

---

* Corresponding author. Tel.: +1-919-962-5044.
E-mail addresses: howard_aldrich@unc.edu (H.E. Aldrich), jcliff@ualberta.ca (J.E. Cliff).
[1] Tel.: +1-780-492-0648.

0883-9026/03/$ – see front matter © 2003 Elsevier Science Inc. All rights reserved.
doi:10.1016/S0883-9026(03)00011-9

dynamics affect fundamental entrepreneurial processes. To some extent, this oversight is understandable. After all, business and families are commonly considered to be distinct social institutions and, as such, are typically investigated by scholars in separate faculties. Nonetheless, the vast majority of businesses are family businesses, and accumulated research findings show that family and business dynamics are highly interrelated.

In this paper, we encourage entrepreneurship researchers to incorporate family considerations in their conceptual models and empirical investigations of the emergence of new business opportunities and new business ventures. To establish the case for a *family embeddedness perspective*, we review the sweeping sociohistorical changes that have occurred in the North American family system over the past century. We document how several of these transformations have already spawned entrepreneurial opportunities, and we speculate on their implications for opportunity recognition, the venture creation decision, and the resource mobilization process.

In our review of trends in family composition, we describe how the traditional North American family, comprised of a married couple with children, is not only shrinking in size but also becoming less prevalent—the result of significant changes in marriages, divorce, and birth rates. In our review of the trends in family members' roles and relationships, we document dramatic changes in the roles of women and children, and present evidence illustrating the weakening social bonds between family members. Throughout our review, we provide numerous examples of the new product and service opportunities created by these changes in the North American family system, as well as examples suggesting that exposure to family transitions can provide individuals with idiosyncratic knowledge that heightens their ability to identify entrepreneurial opportunities. We further discuss how changes in family composition and family members' roles and relationships have equivocal implications for the venture creation decision and the resource mobilization process, simultaneously facilitating and impeding entrepreneurial activities.

In Section 5, we present a conceptual framework based on a family embeddedness perspective on new venture creation. The framework emphasizes how the characteristics of entrepreneurs' family systems (i.e., transitions, resources, and norms, attitudes, and values) can influence the processes involved in venture creation (i.e., opportunity recognition, the launch decision, resource mobilization, and the implementation of founding strategies, processes, and structures). The framework also stresses that outcomes of the new venture creation process (i.e., survival, objective performance, and subjective perceptions of success) can affect an entrepreneurial family's resources, potentially trigger certain family transitions, and ultimately even change family members' norms, attitudes, and values.

The family embeddedness perspective on entrepreneurship implies that researchers need to include family dimensions in their conceptualizing and modeling, their sampling and analyzing, and their interpretations and implications. Connecting the "unnaturally separated" social institutions of family and business will pave the way for more holistic—and more realistic—insights into the fascinating processes by which new business opportunities and new business ventures emerge. Scholars, educators, and policymakers will benefit from such a broadened perspective on entrepreneurship.

H.E. Aldrich, J.E. Cliff / Journal of Business Venturing 18 (2003) 573–596 575

2. Introduction

One hundred years ago, "business" meant "family business," and thus the adjective "family" was redundant. In the interim, the two social institutions have become more highly differentiated from each other. Today, scholars studying "family business" feel compelled to use the adjective "family," even though they note that 90–98% of all businesses owned by households are family businesses, using the broadest of definitions (Heck and Trent, 1999). Why is this the case? We believe the massive sociohistorical changes of the past century have led us to think of the two institutions as disconnected systems, needlessly fragmenting the study of each. This distinction has become enshrined in academia, as the scholarly study of "families" and "business" now takes place in different departments, even colleges. As Stafford et al. (1999, p. 198) noted: "The prevailing view claims that families and businesses are believed to be two 'naturally separate' institutions or systems."

Although understandable in terms of disciplinary identities and career needs, this unwarranted separation has blinded scholars to the significant causal processes connecting family systems and entrepreneurial phenomena. This separation persists despite observations that "entrepreneurs are usually family members manoeuvring in concert or disharmony with an array of other family members" (Heck and Trent, 1999, p. 209). Building on the pioneering work of others (Heck, 1998; Rosenblatt et al., 1985; Stafford et al., 1999), our primary objective is to encourage scholars to embrace a *family embeddedness perspective* on entrepreneurship, in which family factors figure more prominently in conceptual models and empirical investigations. To establish the case that families do, in fact, warrant greater research attention, we describe how the processes involved in two fundamental entrepreneurial phenomena—the emergence of new business opportunities and the emergence of new business entities (Davidsson et al., 2001; Shane and Venkataraman, 2000)—are inextricably linked to transformations in family composition and family members' roles and relationships.

3. Research on opportunity and venture emergence: the neglect of family embeddedness

After years of vigorous debate, a growing consensus holds that entrepreneurship can be defined as the process by which people discover and exploit new business opportunities, often through the creation of new business ventures (Davidsson and Wiklund, 2001; Shane and Venkataraman, 2000; Timmons, 1999). As noted by Davidsson et al. (2001), for example, the field has converged around the view that entrepreneurship is about *emergence*, albeit with some scholars emphasizing the emergence of entrepreneurial opportunities and others emphasizing the emergence of new organizations. Gartner (2001) argued that entrepreneurship researchers were studying such a diverse set of organizational forms that they were forced to use divergent theories. He suggested that entrepreneurship research should be organized into distinct communities of practice, with specific research questions guiding them, including the area of family businesses. Although research on the emergence of new business opportunities and the emergence of new business ventures has grown considerably over the past two decades, scholars within both streams have paid comparatively little attention to the role of the family (Stafford et al., 1999; Upton and Heck, 1997).

3.1. New business opportunities

3.1.1. Opportunity emergence

The lack of attention to families is particularly evident in the literature on the genesis of entrepreneurial opportunities. Whether interested primarily in the emergence of new products and markets (Shane and Venkataraman, 2000; Venkataraman, 1997) or in the emergence of new processes and ways of organizing (Abrahamson, 1996; Dijksterhuis et al., 1999; Lewin et al., 1999), scholars posit that entrepreneurial opportunities are spawned when environmental changes create information asymmetries, gaps, or "other vacuums in an industry" (Timmons, 1999, p. 81). Although some of these researchers include demographic and social changes as environmental triggers of entrepreneurial opportunities, most work has emphasized the effects of technological, regulatory, political, and economic changes. Scholars often assert that technological change drives entrepreneurship (Shane, 2000), in spite of Drucker's (1985, p. 35) assertion that demographic change is a more reliable and predictable source. Interestingly, even when demographic change is presented as a trigger of entrepreneurial opportunities, transformations within the family system are rarely mentioned.

3.1.2. Opportunity recognition

In addition to being absent from writing on the emergence of entrepreneurial opportunities, family considerations rarely appear in research on why, when, and how these opportunities are discovered by some individuals but not others. Shane and Venkataraman (2000) persuasively argued that an individual's idiosyncratic prior knowledge strongly influences the process of opportunity recognition. Rather than being perfectly distributed, information about "underutilized resources, new technology, unsated demand, and political and regulatory shifts" is dispersed "according to the idiosyncratic life circumstances of each person in the population" (Shane and Venkataraman, 2000, p. 222). Studies have tended to focus on the idiosyncratic knowledge obtained through prior work experience and education (see, for example, Shane, 2000). Although personal events are often acknowledged as another source of idiosyncratic knowledge (Venkataraman, 1997), researchers have not yet considered how family embeddedness can trigger events that stimulate the recognition of entrepreneurial opportunities.

3.2. New business ventures

3.2.1. Venture creation decision

Research on the emergence of new business ventures exhibits a similar lack of attention on families. The classic perspective on venture creation, for example, focused primarily on the traits and dispositions of founders (Aldrich and Wiedenmayer, 1993). In light of minimal empirical support for the trait approach (Gartner, 1988), researchers have looked in different directions for insights into the venture formation process. Some have adopted a cognitive

H.E. Aldrich, J.E. Cliff / Journal of Business Venturing 18 (2003) 573–596   577

perspective (Baron, 1998, 2000; Herron and Sapienza, 1992; Shaver and Scott, 1991; Simon et al., 1999), whereas others have adopted an ecological approach (Aldrich, 1999, pp. 75–112; Mezias and Kuperman, 2001). A third group favors a social embeddedness stance (Aldrich and Zimmer, 1986; Cramton, 1993; Larson and Starr, 1993). The embeddedness perspective argues that people are not atomized decision-makers, but rather, are implicated in networks of social relations. Thus, individuals do not decide to start a business in a vacuum; instead, they "consult and are subtly influenced by significant others in their environment" (Aldrich and Zimmer, 1986, p. 6). Although the social embeddedness approach on organizational emergence "appreciates the embeddedness of economic relationships within social settings (Larson and Starr, 1993, p. 11), it has paid little attention to the influence of one fundamental social institution—the family. As Cramton (1993, p. 233) noted, researchers have not yet focused their attention on how a new venture might spring from family relationships.

3.2.2. Resource mobilization

Much research on the resource mobilization process also reflects a social embeddedness approach, emphasizing the importance of founders' social ties in constructing a firm's base of financial, physical, human, and other resources (see Brush et al., 2001 for a review). Within this literature, some scholars have explicitly highlighted the role of family connections. Aldrich (1999) and Aldrich and Zimmer (1986), for example, argued in support of the resources provided by the "strong ties" of family members. Similarly, Starr and MacMillan (1990) suggested that kinship ties—in addition to previous work relationships, volunteer connections, and community ties—"lay the groundwork for new ventures" (p. 81). More recently, Chrisman et al. (2003) asserted that family represents a critical and often used resource for startups. Nevertheless, very few studies have expanded upon the role that families play in resource mobilization.

The neglect of family considerations in research on the new venture creation process is rather surprising, particularly in light of three sets of empirical findings. First, a sizeable proportion of new organizations are founded by two or more related individuals. Ruef et al. (2002), for example, found that married couples or cohabitating partners constituted about one-fourth of the nascent entrepreneurial teams in their nationally representative sample, and kin ties were involved in another 27% of the teams. Similarly, Reynolds and White (1997) found that people related by marriage or kinship initiated one-third of the start-ups in their sample. Second, Cramton's (1993) case study provided compelling evidence that organizational foundings may represent responses to changing family relationships rather than outcomes of the rational assessments of discovered economic opportunities. Third, several studies indicate that, during the start-up process, family plays an important role in the mobilization of financial resources (e.g., Aldrich and Waldinger, 1990; Steier and Greenwood, 2000), the provision of human resources (Aldrich and Langton, 1998), and physical resources in the form of space in the family household (U.S. Bureau of Labor Statistics, 2002).

In sum, mounting empirical evidence suggests that families play an important role in the venture creation process and thus deserve greater consideration in the entrepreneurship literature. In the following section, we identify the major transformations in the North American family system over the past half-century and discuss the relevance of these trends for the entrepreneurial phenomena of opportunity emergence, opportunity recognition, venture creation decisions, and resource mobilization processes.

4. Sociohistorical changes in the family system: implications for opportunity and venture emergence

In the mid-20th century, "family" usually meant a nuclear two-generational group with parents and children sharing the same household. Few women worked outside the home, children were in school, and, if they worked, contributed their wages to the family purse. Strong ties bound multiple generations together, and limited geographic mobility kept many extended kinship groups in the same or nearby communities. In North America at the beginning of the 21st century, almost everything has changed. Below, we describe two sets of the most significant transformations in the family system. The first set pertains to changes in the composition of households, both family and nonfamily, and the factors contributing to these compositional transformations. The second set pertains to changes in the roles and relationships of family members. Table 1 lists the trends we discuss. Table 2 summarizes examples of how these changes can influence, or have already influenced, the emergence of new business opportunities and new business ventures. In organizing our review, we were guided by research and writing from a life course perspective, which provides a model of how to study family and workplace interaction (Elder et al., in press; Moen, 1998).

Table 1
Trends in family composition and family members' roles and relationships (1900–2000)

Family composition	Family members' roles and relationships
Prevalence, nature, and size	*Roles*
• Families represent a decreasing proportion of all households	• Women's employment rate has increased
• The proportion of single-person households has increased	• Women are spending less time on housework but still assume primary responsibility for this task
• The proportion of cohabiting-couple households has increased	• A greater proportion of children work for their own discretionary income
• A greater proportion of children live in single-parent families and step-families	*Relationships*
• Average household size has decreased	• Parents are less directly involved in their children's activities
	• Parents are playing a reduced role in the socialization of their children
Contributing factors	• Intergenerational contact has declined
• Average age at first marriage has increased	
• Marriage rates have declined	
• Divorce rates have risen	
• Birth rates have dropped to population replacement levels	
• An increasing proportion of births occur to single women	

H.E. Aldrich, J.E. Cliff / Journal of Business Venturing 18 (2003) 573–596

Table 2
Implications of family transformations for opportunity and venture emergence

Entrepreneurial phenomenon	Examples of transformations' consequences	
	Family composition	Members' roles and relationships
Opportunity emergence	Shrinking family size is creating opportunities for accommodations and consumables offered in small sizes. Rising births to unwed mothers and increasing divorce rates are creating opportunities for such unusual product and service offerings as the "Baby Think it Over Doll" and "Divorce X".	The increasing number of working women in dual-earner families has stimulated growth in childcare services, away-from-home foods, and household cleaning industries. Decreasing parental supervision of children is creating opportunities for such products as security systems, remote controls, and other appliances that young children can operate on their own.
Opportunity recognition	Coping with (or witnessing others cope with) changes in family composition due to marriage, divorce, and childbirth can stimulate recognition of new products and services to fulfill unmet needs.	Undertaking new family roles may stimulate recognition of new methods of organizing: working women who become mothers, for example, may realize that others such as themselves represent an opportunity for firms to create novel work arrangements.
Venture creation decision	Shrinking family size may facilitate nascent entrepreneurship by lowering the perceived family risk of start-up and reducing the proportion of kin involved in start-up discussions. This trend may simultaneously impede nascent entrepreneurship by lowering perceptions of adequate start-up resources available from family.	The growing number of working women may facilitate the launch decision by increasing the proportion of women who perceive that they have sufficient human, social, and financial capital to launch a business. However, given working women's dual burdens of work and household responsibilities, few may perceive that they have adequate time to launch a business.
Resource mobilization	Shrinking family size may make the mobilization of financial resources more difficult during the start-up process; however, the increasing prevalence of stepfamilies may increase the pool of potential financial capital available from "quasi" family members.	The increasing number of working wives and teenagers may make the mobilization of human resources more difficult during the start-up process, as these family members no longer represent accessible sources of underpaid or unpaid labor.

The life course perspective focuses on movements into and out of roles and relationships, such as moving from school into employment and marriage. As an inherently dynamic approach to study social life, the life course perspective "reflects the interweave of work, family, and community role trajectories, the interdependencies of paths among family members, and the changing circumstances and options of both families and family businesses" (Moen, 1998, p. 16). In our review, we thus focus on the timing of events, within the life course of individuals and their families. We also focus on process, emphasizing transitions into and out of difficult life events. Finally, we focus on the changing context

580   *H.E. Aldrich, J.E. Cliff / Journal of Business Venturing 18 (2003) 573–596*

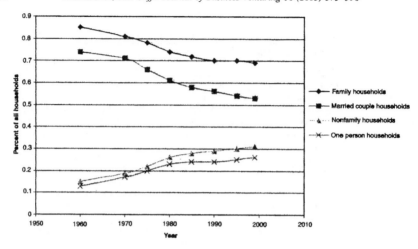

Fig. 1. Trends in household composition (1960–2000).

within which families and businesses are embedded, noting the importance of major historical changes over the past half century.

4.1. Trends in family composition

4.1.1. Characteristics of families: prevalence, nature, and size

Between 1960 and 1999, the number of households in the United States roughly doubled, from about 53 million to about 104 million households (U.S. Bureau of the Census, 2000b).[2] As the population grew, significant changes occurred in household composition (see Fig. 1). In 1960, families constituted about 85% of all households, as defined by the Census Bureau.[3] By 1999, families made up only 69% of households, and nonfamily households had grown from only 15% to about 31% of all households. Single-person households comprised the great majority of the nonfamily households, and cohabiting couples constituted most of the remaining households. One consequence of the increase in single-person households was a decline in average household size from 3.33 in 1960 to 2.61 in 1999 (U.S. Bureau of the Census, 2000a).[4]

---

[2] Throughout the text, we report many statistics on families. Unless otherwise noted, our figures come from U.S. Census reports.

[3] The U.S. Census defines a family as "two or more persons living together and related by blood, marriage, or adoption."

[4] Unlike much of Europe, in North America, unmarried adults usually do not reside with their parents.

H.E. Aldrich, J.E. Cliff / Journal of Business Venturing 18 (2003) 573–596 581

With respect to opportunity emergence, shrinking household size is clearly creating markets for new products and services. Proctor & Gamble, for example, recently launched "Folger's Singles," a single-serving coffee bag for people who live alone and thus do not need to make a full pot (Solomon et al., 2002, p. 410). Furthermore, the substantial increase in the number of single-person households "suggests that apartments, appliances, and food containers should be produced in sizes appropriate for single individuals" (Hawkins et al., 2001, p. 195). This trend is also expected to generate an increased demand for social and recreational club memberships as a means of alleviating the isolation associated with living alone (Sheth et al., 1999, p. 264).

As for venture creation, shrinking family size may both facilitate and impede the genesis of nascent entrepreneurs, i.e., individuals who are taking action to start their own business. On the one hand, people from smaller-sized families may perceive venture creation as less risky. Such individuals may find it easier to forego their salary and launch a business because they are not also financially responsible for a spouse, children, and/or aging parents. Moreover, these individuals will have fewer kin members in their discussion networks who might talk them out of becoming an entrepreneur. Research indicates that the greater the proportion of kin in a nascent entrepreneur's discussion network, the lower the odds of that person actually starting a business (Renzulli et al., 2000). On the other hand, individuals from smaller-sized families may perceive that they have inadequate potential resources available from kin members, and thus decide against starting their own firm.

Shrinking family size clearly has negative implications for the resource mobilization process, particularly for securing human resources. When it comes to attracting employees, many entrepreneurs rely on family members, whether paid or unpaid. Aldrich and Langton (1998), for example, found that 25% of the firms in their sample employed family members at the time of start-up. Although not restricted to start-ups, Heck and Trent's (1999) study of business-owning households provides further data on the importance of family members as a supply of human resources. About 73% of the business-owning households in their sample had at least two residential household members working in the business, approximately 24% had one or more employed relatives working for pay who did not live in the household, and 27% had nonhousehold relatives who were unpaid workers. Given the extent to which business owners rely on family members as a source of employees, shrinking family size complicates the human resource mobilization process for many organizational founders.

Smaller families may also make the mobilization of *financial* resources more difficult. Although Aldrich et al.'s (1998) empirical findings dispute the common assumption that family members represent a frequently used source of start-up funding, other studies indicate that, within some ethnic communities, kin provide a great deal of financial capital (Aldrich and Waldinger, 1990). Moreover, Steier and Greenwood's (2000) case analysis showed that although family members may not represent a *direct* source of funding, they are often an important source of *indirect* ties to other individuals capable and willing to inject financial capital. Their study indicates that family ties are sometimes part of the resource mobilization process, if nascent entrepreneurs are able draw on the network contacts of other family members (Brush et al., 2001, p. 69; Starr and MacMillan, 1990, p. 88). Our review suggests that shrinking family size might be hampering the ability of organizational founders to secure financial capital.

4.1.2. Contributing factors: marriage, divorce, and birth rates

Why has household composition changed so dramatically over the past four decades? Changing patterns of marriage and divorce provide a partial explanation. First, age at first marriage has gradually increased, from 22.8 in 1960 to 26.8 in 2000 for men and from 20.3 to 25.1 for women. Second, marriage rates have dropped slightly over time, as more people have chosen to remain single or cohabitate. Third, divorce rates have increased substantially, as indicated by age-specific studies of ever-married women. For example, the proportion of white women aged 40 to 44 who were divorced from their first marriage increased from 20% in 1975 to 35% in 1990; for black women, the proportion increased from 30% to 45% (Teachman et al., 2000).

Families are also choosing to have fewer children. At the beginning of the 19th century, women typically had about seven children, only some of whom survived to adulthood (Ahlburg and DeVita, 1992, p. 18). Birth rates dropped steadily throughout the 19th century, and in 1900, the average number of children per woman was only 3.6. Fertility rates continued to decline to the population replacement level of 2.1 children per woman, but then jumped dramatically after World War II. The "baby boom" peaked in the late 1950s, and the rate fell again, actually dropping below the replacement level for a few years in the 1970s. Today, the birth rate hovers near the replacement level for white women and is higher for black and Hispanic women (Bianchi and Casper, 2000).

Although the birth rate declined during the latter half of the past century, the proportion of births to unwed women increased dramatically during this period (see Fig. 2). In 1940, only 4% of all births were to unmarried women, and in 1960, the level was still only 5%. The rate rose dramatically in the 1970s and 1980s, but seems to have levelled off now. In 1999, the

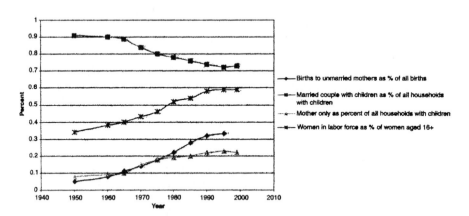

Fig. 2. Trends in family functioning (1950–2000).

proportion of births to unmarried women was 33%.[5] As Bianchi and Casper (2000, p. 17) noted, however, "a similar plateau in the early 1970s proved to be temporary, so demographers cannot predict whether the stability of non-marital birth rates in the late 1990's is a temporary lull or an end to one of the most pronounced trends in the latter half of the 20th century."

The increasing prevalence of divorce, as well as the rising proportion of births to single women, has transformed the household context in which many children are raised. The stereotypical "married couple with children" household dropped from approximately 44% of all households in 1960 to only 24% in 1999. Today, one out of every five children under the age of 18 lives with a mother only (see Fig. 2). Approximately 50% will spend at least some time in a single-parent family, and "about one-third of U.S. children will live in a remarried or cohabiting stepfamily household before they reach adulthood" (Coleman et al., 2000, p. 1290).

These trends in the life course transitions of marriage, divorce, and childbirth have implications for the emergence and recognition of entrepreneurial opportunities. Rising divorce rates, for example, have generated several new business opportunities. Many professional service firms have arisen to help individuals manage the new role relationships created by separation and divorce. Other entrepreneurs have discerned unusual opportunities in the aftermath of family dissolution events. A Canadian entrepreneur, for example, has recently introduced "Divorce X," a digital imaging service that removes ex-spouses from family pictures (Solomon et al., 2002). In response to the rise in nonmarital births to teenage girls, another entrepreneur has produced the "Baby Think it Over" doll: designed to convince teenagers that having a baby isn't all fun, this doll shrieks at random intervals and must be held for up to 30 min before stopping (Mowen and Minor, 1998, p. 535).

Life course transitions such as marriage, divorce, and childbirth often bring new business opportunities into focus. As individuals experience such family disruptions, their product/ service needs and buying habits change. Some may discover that existing vendors or means are not adequately fulfilling their needs, and may realize that these unmet needs present attractive prospects for new venture creation (Bhave, 1994). In other words, while striving to resolve a personal problem, individuals may become aware of a "customer problem"—one of the three major dimensions of knowledge considered important in the process of entrepreneurial discovery (Shane, 2000). Becoming a parent is one life course transition likely to trigger such awareness. As noted by Debelek (2001), parents often devise novel solutions to the problems associated with caring for children. A case in point is the "Baby B'Air Flight Vest," a safety vest for babies and toddlers to wear on planes. The idea for the product originated from a new mother's complaints about the difficulty of carrying car seats onto planes and her concerns about holding a child on her lap without a restraining device. Market research and subsequent sales of over US$1 million confirmed the business opportunity associated with the product (Debelek, 2001).

---

[5] The proportion of births to unmarried women varies greatly by ethnicity. For white mothers the rate is 22% whereas for black mothers the rate is 69%. In contrast, the rates are extremely low for Chinese-Americans and Japanese-Americans, at 6% and 10%, respectively (Bianchi and Casper, 2000). Some of these unmarried mothers are cohabiting with a partner, rather than living on their own.

Changes in marriage, divorce, and childbirth rates not only have implications for opportunity emergence and recognition, but may also have mixed effects on the new venture creation process. Consider the increasing number of couples choosing to cohabitate rather than get married. Many nascent entrepreneurs who are married pursue a start-up plan that involves one member of the couple working so that they are both covered by health insurance, and thus cover an important risk factor. Given that health insurance coverage to unmarried couples is not yet universal, how will cohabitation affect the venture creation decision? And what about the venture creation implications of the rising divorce rate? On the one hand, such family dissolutions might have negative consequences for resource mobilization. On the other hand, this type of family disruption may provide the impetus for organizational formation. Neider's (1987) research, for example, indicated that many women start their own firms after becoming divorced. Moreover, the increasing prevalence of stepfamilies arising out of divorce and remarriage suggests that a growing number of organizational founders have access to an expanded pool of current and former "family" members, which may facilitate the resource mobilization process. However, people often lose touch with nonresident family members after a divorce.

4.2. Trends in family members' roles and relationships

4.2.1. Women's roles

One of the most dramatic changes affecting the North American family system during the latter half of the 20th century was the huge increase in the proportion of women working outside the home (see Fig. 2). In 1960, 90% of adult men were in the labor force, compared to only 30% of adult women (Bianchi and Casper, 2000). By 1998, men's participation rate had declined to 78%, while women's participation rate had increased to 60%. As a result, dual-income households are becoming more prevalent: in 1998, both spouses were working in 60% of all married couples.

Historically, women with children withdrew from the labor force, especially if their children were less than 6 years old. Currently, young children are much less of a deterrent to women's employment: "in 1998, 71 percent of married mothers of children under age six did some work for pay during the year" (Bianchi and Casper, 2000, p. 29). Only about one-third of them, however, worked full-time. Bianchi and Casper (2000, p. 29) summarized these changes by noting that "although U.S. mothers of young children are much more likely to work in the 1990's than they were in the 1970's, which implies an increasing attachment of women to market work, married mothers tend to scale back their hours during their children's preschool years."

One might expect the growing number of employed women, and their increasing contribution to household income, to lead to more sharing of household tasks with husbands and children. Although Goldscheider and Waite's (1991) research suggested that this is indeed the case, women continue to carry the bulk of the responsibility, and the division of household labor remains traditional. Coltrane (2000, p. 1208), for example, noted that: "On average, women perform two or three times as much housework as men, and the vast majority of men, as well as most women, rate these arrangements as fair." The primary response of

H.E. Aldrich, J.E. Cliff / Journal of Business Venturing 18 (2003) 573–596   585

women who work full-time has been to do less housework. The number of hours per week that women spend doing household work declined from about 30 in 1965 to about 17.5 in 1995 (Bianchi and Casper, 2000, p. 29). Over this same period, men only increased their time on housework from 4.9 to 10 hours per week, clearly leaving some work simply undone (or done by nonfamily members).

Women in dual-income families with young children face an especially difficult burden. Presser (1998) noted, "For the modal family type in the United States, two-earner couples, one in four includes at least one spouse who works evening, night, or rotating schedules. The presence of children, and particularly young children, increases the likelihood of a split-shift arrangement among spouses. So, in one out of three two-earner couples with children under age 5 in the United States, one spouse works in the day and the other works evening, night, or rotating schedules."

These changes in women's roles have certainly spurred the growth of several industries, and have created opportunities for organizations within them to develop new products and services (Solomon et al., 2002). Consider, for example, the outsourcing of four common and time-consuming household chores: childcare, cooking and cleaning, and shopping. Private daycare employment has increased by more than 250% over the past two decades (Mowen and Minor, 1998, p. 519), reflecting the current reality that 48% of working families with children under the age of 13 have childcare expenses (Giannarelli and Barsimantov, 2000). The demand for food prepared outside the home has also increased: in 1970, only 26% of total food expenditures was spent on away-from-home foods; by 1996, this figure had risen to 39% (Lin et al., 1999). In 1999, expenditures on away-from-home food totalled over US$340 billion in the United States alone (Clauson, 2000). The housecleaning industry has also grown: in 1986, only 6% of households employed a house cleaner or housekeeper; by 1999, that figure had reached 11% (Sheth et al., 1999, p. 63). Several academic studies have directly linked the consumption of away-from-home foods and housecleaning services to women's increased labor force participation (Cohen, 1998; Hochschild, 1989; Oropesa, 1993). Shopping services for people too busy to shop for themselves have also sprung up.

The increasing number of working women has interesting implications for the recognition of entrepreneurial opportunities. For example, working women who become mothers may recognize that individuals on temporary child leaves, such as themselves, represent "underutilized resources" (Shane and Venkataraman, 2000, p. 222) who might be available to work on a limited-period, work-from-home basis. Acting upon such a realization could trigger the emergence of novel work arrangements and processes that ultimately transform the production processes within an industry—a form of entrepreneurship identified by Schumpeter (1934).

With respect to venture creation, the growing number of working women may both facilitate and inhibit the launch decision. By gaining work experience, an increasing proportion of women might perceive that they have secured sufficient human, social, and financial capital to launch a business. Moreover, the work-related inequities experienced by many women, such as hitting the "glass ceiling," may actually provide the motivation for venturing out on their own. As Brush (1992) noted in her literature review, female organizational founders are often motivated by job frustration. Members of a dual-income family might also perceive less risk in new venture creation than those who depend on only one income, as a dual-earner family would still have the employed spouse's salary as a source of income. All of these factors point to women's employment as facilitating venture creation decisions.

Nevertheless, working women may have difficulty finding the time to launch a business. Working women still bear primary responsibility for household chores, even when they also work full-time outside the home. Perhaps this inhibiting factor partially explains why proportionately fewer women than men attempt to start businesses, and fewer succeed in actually doing so (Carter, 1994). The dual burden of work and household responsibilities may also explain Ruef et al.'s (2002) finding that a large proportion of women involved in business start-ups do so as part of a spousal team rather than on their own. However, it is also possible that spousal pairs exert reciprocal positive influences on one another, increasing the likelihood that both will become involved in a new venture. For example, Budig's (2002) dynamic analysis of the 1978–1998 years of the National Longitudinal Survey of Youth found that having a spouse who was self-employed substantially increased the likelihood of someone being self-employed.

As with the venture creation decision, the increasing number of working women (and the corresponding rise in the number of dual income families) has mixed implications for the securing of start-up resources. One positive implication of this trend is an increase in the proportion of families with ample entrepreneurial capital that can be mobilized during the start-up process (Marshack, 1993). A less obvious negative implication of this trend is that fewer start-ups will be able to rely on the human capital provided by female spouses. Female spouses are a commonly tapped source of unpaid (or at least underpaid) labor during an organization's early years (Aldrich and Langton, 1998). It is unlikely, however, that already-employed female spouses would have either the time or the willingness to forego their salaries to help their husbands' firms in this traditional manner.

4.2.2. Children's roles

Children's and young adults' roles in families have changed as dramatically as wives' roles during the latter half of the previous century. "Until the mid-20th century, most young people lived in their parents' home until marriage. Since people married later before the baby boom, they remained at home for a decade or more after completing schooling to contribute to the family economy" (Goldscheider and Waite, 1991, p. 17). Only in the 20th century did men, as family heads, make enough money to allow their children not to work, and thus to attend school full-time. In the early days of the industrial revolution, children's incomes were a significant contributor to family income (Zelizer, 1994). Not having to work outside the home made children available, potentially, as household and small business help.

However, children have been contributing less and less in recent years to the family purse[6] (Goldscheider and Waite, 1991). Many of them have taken on paid work outside the household, thus enhancing their own economic welfare. A 1997–1998 Consumer Expend-

---

[6] Goldscheider and Waite (1991) found, however, that children in mother-only families assumed a greater responsibility for housework, with their contribution continuing even after the mother remarried. They also found that nontraditional family experiences, such as going through a divorce, increased the likelihood that a woman would share housework with children.

H.E. Aldrich, J.E. Cliff / Journal of Business Venturing 18 (2003) 573–596 587

iture Survey revealed that about one-third of all teenagers were employed sometime during that year (Johnson and Lino, 2000). Most did not work for family necessities. Rather, they were earning money for their own personal needs and to buy work-related items. Even in low-income families, a teenager's earnings accounted for only a modest proportion of the family's budget: about 9%.

The greater proportion of teenagers working away from home for their own disposable income may by creating a large pool of nascent entrepreneurs who perceive that they possess adequate human, social, and financial capital to one day launch their own business ventures. At the same time, teenage employment outside the home may be reducing the likelihood that organizational founders can rely upon their children as an inexpensive source of labor during the start-up period. Employed teenagers may be reluctant to trade the guaranteed hours and pay of an outside job with the variable hours and deferred pay of a job in their parent's business.

4.2.3. Relationships between family members

The final type of transformation in the North American family system that we identified pertains to the ties between family members. The media frequently contains statements announcing the "death of the family unit"—a claim based not only upon the declining prevalence of traditional family households but also upon data documenting the deterioration of social bonds within even intact nuclear families. Putnam (2000, p. 101), for example, pointed out that "between 1976 and 1997, according to Roper polls of families with children aged 8 to 17, vacationing together fell from 53 percent to 38 percent, watching TV together from 54 percent to 41 percent, attending religious services together from 38 percent to 31 percent, and 'just sitting and talking' together from 53 percent to 43 percent." These figures suggest that parents are spending less time interacting with, and thereby socializing, their children. As noted by Bianchi and Casper (2000), other institutions have taken over many of the traditional social functions of families, and some functions have simply disappeared, such as parental regulation of teenage sexual behavior.

Not surprisingly, social bonds between parents and children are even weaker within families disrupted by divorce. Divorce seems to particularly strain a father's relations with his biological children. Using figures from the 1981 National Survey of Children, Furstenberg (1988, pp. 202–203) argued that "many, if not most, non-custodial fathers are only weakly attached to their children." Almost half the children living in mother-headed households had not seen their biological father in the previous year.[7] The increasing prevalence of divorce, as well as the growing number of births to unwed women, has also weakened mother–child relationships. Bianchi's (2000) review revealed a growing gap between two groups of households: those with fathers present and those without. When fathers are not present, "mothers have neither adequate time nor money to invest in children" (Bianchi, 2000, p. 412).

---

[7] Furstenberg argued that contact appears to diminish rapidly one or two years after divorce (Furstenberg and Nord, 1985), and in a subsequent article, he presented other evidence of noncustodial fathers losing touch with their children (Furstenberg, 1990).

Intergenerational family relations have also been undergoing a fundamental change (Rossi, 1989). Even as longevity was increasing substantially, creating more families in which grandparents were still alive when children reached adulthood (Uhlenberg, 1996), residential co-location across generations has been declining. Over the past century, a very sharp drop occurred in the proportion of elderly persons residing with their adult children, especially among whites (Ruggles and Goeken, 1992).[8] In 1900, among whites aged 60 and over, about 53% were living in multigenerational families, defined as sharing a residence with children who are older than 21 or ever married. By 1980, only 14% were living in such arrangements.[9] Although most parents and children "live near one another and continue to interact on a regular basis throughout life" (Bumpass, 1990, p. 491), the frequency of contact appears to be diminishing. Bumpass (1990, p. 492), for example, noted that between 1962 and 1984, "the proportion of the elderly seeing a child at least once a week declined by 25 percent."

Although unfortunate, these changes in the social bonds between family members are creating entrepreneurial opportunities. For example, one company has capitalized on the diminishing frequency of joint parent–child activities by developing the "Weemote"—the first programmable TV remote control designed for kids (InventiveParent, 2002). Similarly, the increasing amount of time spent by children without adult supervision has created sizeable markets for such products as convenience foods, security systems, and appliances that young children can operate on their own (Hawkins et al., 2001, p. 196; Solomon et al., 2002, p. 407).

As an example of how the process of opportunity emergence and recognition can also be stimulated by changing intergenerational relations, consider the experience of an individual who recently found himself responsible for his aging father's care.[10] Consistent with the societal trend of not wanting his father to reside with him, but not knowing what options were available, he searched for information. Frustrated by the lack of easily accessible material to help him with this important family decision, yet aware of the prevalence of this major demographic change, he realized that the personal problem he was facing actually represented a potentially lucrative business opportunity. He subsequently published a book to help others with the process of arranging suitable eldercare.

Weakening bonds between family members surely carry implications for the venture creation process, but the nature of these implications is not clear-cut. On the one hand, for example, declining parental interaction with their offspring may reduce the preparation and motivation of children from business families to continue in their parent's entrepreneurial footsteps. On the other hand, an increasing proportion of children may be willing to make

---

[8] Three explanations have been offered for this trend. First, it has become more socially acceptable for unmarried women to live on their own. Second, norms regarding the obligation of children to care for parents in their old age have declined. Third, since World War II, the rising economic status of the elderly has allowed them to live alone, particularly as social security payments have improved (Ruggles and Goeken, 1992, p. 32). However, Johnson (2000) noted that estimates of residential proximity between parents and their grown children suggest that between 51% and 75% of parents have at least one child in their vicinity.

[9] As with many other characteristics of families in America, there are substantial ethnic differences in social relations within multigenerational families. For example, the decline has been much less pronounced for blacks, as 23% still lived in multigenerational families in 1980 and another 16% lived in other types of extended families.

[10] This example is taken from the personal experience of a friend of one of the authors.

H.E. Aldrich, J.E. Cliff / Journal of Business Venturing 18 (2003) 573–596 589

themselves available as a source of inexpensive human resources for their parent's business, as a means of potentially increasing the level of parent–child interaction.

5. Toward a family embeddedness perspective: implications for entrepreneurship and family business research

During the past two decades, the notion that entrepreneurs are embedded in social relationships has become almost axiomatic in the entrepreneurship literature (Aldrich and Zimmer, 1986; Burt, 1992; Larson and Starr, 1993). Rather ironically, however, the embeddedness approach has virtually neglected the one social institution in which *all* entrepreneurs are embedded—the family. This gap persists in spite of evidence that: family transitions can trigger organizational emergence (Cramton, 1993), founding teams are frequently composed of family members (Ruef et al., 2002), and families play an important role in resource mobilization process during start-up (Aldrich and Langton, 1998).

Guided by the literature on life course theory (Elder et al., in press; Moen, 1998), we have argued that family considerations should figure more prominently in entrepreneurship research. We illustrated how major sociohistorical transformations in family composition and family members' roles and relationships can influence, or have already influenced, the entrepreneurial phenomena of opportunity emergence and recognition, the venture creation decision, and the resource mobilization process. We turn now to some conceptual and methodological suggestions for researchers interested in connecting family systems with organizational emergence, and summarize the implications of a *family embeddedness perspective* for the literature on entrepreneurship, family businesses, and business families.

5.1. An emergent "family embeddedness perspective" on new venture creation

In Fig. 3, we present a conceptual framework to help guide research adopting a family embeddedness perspective on new venture creation. The left-hand side of the framework suggests that the characteristics of entrepreneurs' family systems (i.e., transitions, resources, and norms, attitudes, and values) influence the processes involved in venture creation (i.e., opportunity recognition, the launch decision, resource mobilization, and the implementation of founding strategies, processes, and structures). The right-hand side of the framework suggests that venture creation processes result in outcomes for the new organization (i.e., survival, objective performance, and subjective perceptions of success) that may alter the entrepreneurial family's resources, potentially trigger certain family transitions, and ultimately even change family members' norms, attitudes, and values.

Many of the relationships depicted in the left-hand side of the framework were implicit in our discussion of the dramatic transformations in the North American family system during the previous century and their implications for entrepreneurship. For example, we presented examples of how experiencing a family transition, such as childbirth, can provide family members with new information about unmet customer needs. This change in the family's informational resources may subsequently trigger the recognition of an entrepreneurial

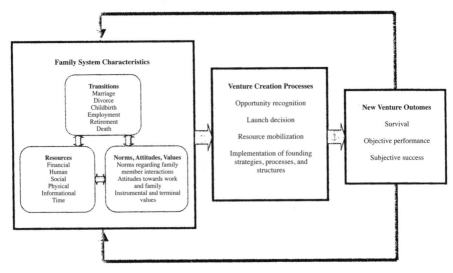

Fig. 3. A family embeddedness perspective on new venture creation.

opportunity, and possibly the other processes involved in venture creation. As another example, the increase in a family's financial resources associated with a woman's transition to employment might facilitate her spouse's decision to start his own firm.

Other relationships within the left-hand side of the framework were not derived directly from our sociohistorical essay but are plausible, based on existing research on either organizational emergence or family systems, and consistent with a family embeddedness perspective on new venture creation. Several entrepreneurship scholars, for example, have suggested that the venture creation process is not limited to opportunity recognition, the launch decision, and resource mobilization, but also includes the implementation of founding strategies, processes, and structures. The norms, attitudes, and values held by entrepreneurial family members likely influence these founding strategies, processes, and structures.

Similarly, the postulated relationships depicted in the right-hand side of the framework represent extensions of the arguments implicit in our sociohistorical review of family system changes. If families and businesses truly are as inextricably intertwined as we have claimed, then not only should family systems affect business systems, but the reverse should also hold. That is, business systems should also affect family systems. In the context of organizational emergence, this logic of interdependency implies that venture creation processes—particularly the outcomes associated with these processes—are likely to contribute to changes in the characteristics of founders' family systems.

The family embeddedness perspective on new venture creation summarized in Fig. 3 suggests a wide-ranging set of intriguing and important questions for future research. Those

H.E. Aldrich, J.E. Cliff / Journal of Business Venturing 18 (2003) 573–596 591

pertaining to the impact of family system characteristics on venture creation processes include:

- Is venture creation more prevalent among individuals who have recently experienced a major family transition?
- Is the incidence of venture creation higher among families with greater resources?
- Under what conditions do a family's norms, attitudes, and values affect the different elements of the venture creation process?
- To what extent do changes in family system characteristics affect the timing and pacing of venture creation processes?

Questions pertaining to the impact of new venture outcomes on family system characteristics include:

- Does new venture failure or success play a role in family system transitions such as divorce?
- Under what conditions does venture failure disrupt a family's resources so strongly that the family itself is affected?
- To what extent can new venture performance (whether objectively recorded or subjectively perceived) trigger changes in a family's norms, attitudes, and values?
- Does the relationship between venture performance and changes in a family's norms, attitudes, and values depend on the extent to which the family's resources are affected by the business failure?

We offer these questions not as an exhaustive list but rather to illustrate the provocative avenues for future research made possible by a family embeddedness perspective on entrepreneurship.

We note that the conceptual framework presented in Fig. 3 is consistent with other models connecting family and business systems—most notably, Stafford et al.'s (1999) "sustainable family business model." Like Stafford and her colleagues, we view family transitions (or disruptions, as they are called in the sustainable family business model) and family resources as important contributing factors to business processes and achievements. Similarly, we view business outcomes (particularly disruptive ones, as noted by the Stafford et al. model) as important contributing factors to family changes and outcomes. Our framework, however, focuses specifically on the *creation of new ventures*, regardless of whether they are deemed family businesses. In contrast, the sustainable family business model examines *existing* firms considered to be family businesses. Researchers might utilize either framework, depending on the purposes of their investigations.

We believe that both frameworks could benefit from further conceptual refinement. Both models posit sets of key events and transitions, and both could be further developed to spell out relations *within* sets of processes and events. Perhaps most important, from a modeling perspective, analysts could identify key feedback loops within the models and assess which are deviation amplifying and which are deviation reducing. For example, by reducing available financial resources, marital dissolution might further reduce the attractiveness of new ventures to women with young children, as well as increasing the likelihood of taking a wage or salary job. Some of the questions we have identified in our bulleted list explicitly posit feedback loops, suggesting where researchers could begin to fill in the models. For example, as a next step, investigators could model the valence of posited relations (positive or negative), and indicate the presumed strength of relations. As empirical generalizations accumulate, the dynamic implications of the models would become clearer.

5.2. Methodological implications and suggestions

5.2.1. Operationalizing "family"

The family embeddedness perspective encapsulated in Fig. 3 also raises a number of methodological implications. For example, what does the term "family" mean for organizational founders? Does this construct refer to founders' immediate nuclear families, which was the focus of Cramton's (1993) research, entrepreneurs' families of origin, which was the focus of Aldrich, Renzulli, and Langton's (1998) study, or entrepreneurs' extended and step family members? Researchers will need to explicitly define the notion of "family" in their conceptual models and empirical investigations.

The trends in family composition that we have discussed in our sociohistorical review highlight the importance of working with as inclusive a definition of "family" as possible. Researchers should not limit themselves to narrow definitions that are constrained by historical conceptions of what constitutes a family. We suggest focusing on households, regardless of size, and not simply on multiperson units in which two or more people are related. Many of the new business opportunities that will emerge in the 21st century will reflect a changing mix of household forms, which increasingly include single people and multiple unrelated people under the same roof. Similarly, patterns of family formation and dissolution have created extended kinship networks that cut across household boundaries, creating "business families" that may include multiple single-person households and family members living elsewhere.

5.2.2. Developing dynamic designs

Entrepreneurship research will need to be much more process oriented to capture the kinds of relationships suggested by Fig. 3. Investigators will need to build more longitudinal study designs so that they can make dynamic inferences about the effects of family system changes on the new venture creation process, as well as about the effects of new venture outcomes on family system changes. We suggest that more resources be invested in ethnographic approaches in particular, in which investigators spend considerable amounts of time within families, conducting systematic observations and collecting detailed field notes (Gartner and Birley, 2002). Disciplined field research gives us the possibility of making sense of what can only be indirectly inferred through other methods.

H.E. Aldrich, J.E. Cliff / Journal of Business Venturing 18 (2003) 573–596 593

5.2.3. Capturing the reciprocal causality of family and business system changes

Conceptual frameworks such as that presented in Fig. 3, which explicitly include characteristics of family systems, should enhance the comprehensiveness of our explanations for entrepreneurial phenomena and deepen our understanding of the complexities and compromises involved in entrepreneurial processes. Designing rigorous studies consistent with a family embeddedness perspective, however, will undoubtedly require research teams comprised of scholars with interests and skills in both "families" and "businesses." We hope that our paper will encourage at least some researchers to bridge these currently separate domains.

6. Conclusion

We need more research on how family systems affect opportunity emergence and recognition, the new venture creation decision, and the resource mobilization process. We need to learn more about the role that family characteristics and dynamics play in why, when, and how some people, but not others, identify entrepreneurial opportunities and decide to start business enterprises. In turn, we need to better understand the effects that venture creation can have on family systems. Such research projects would extend the scope of the existing social embeddedness approach to entrepreneurship, paving the way for a more holistic (and thus more realistic) approach to our understanding of entrepreneurial phenomena. The family embeddedness of most entrepreneurial activities—particularly new venture creation—necessitates broadening our perspective.

Acknowledgements

We thank Glen Elder, Guang Guo, Karen Benjamin Guzzo, Kathie Mullan Harris, Maria Haydey, Devereaux Jennings, Linda Renzulli, Ron Rindfuss, Lloyd Steier, and Peter Uhlenberg for their help. The Guest Co-Editors of this Special Issue were especially generous with their time in helping us improve earlier drafts. We are grateful for the financial support provided by the University of Alberta's Centre for Entrepreneurship and Family Enterprise as well as the Entrepreneurship and Small Business Research Centre in Stockholm, Sweden. Because both authors contributed equally to this paper, they are listed in alphabetical order.

References

Abrahamson, E., 1996. Management fashion. Acad. Manage. Rev. 21 (1), 254–285.
Ahlburg, D.A., DeVita, C.J., 1992. New realities of the American family. Popul. Bull. 47 (2), 1–35.
Aldrich, H., 1999. Organizations Evolving. Sage, London.
Aldrich, H.E., Langton, N., 1998. Human resource management and organizational life cycles. In: Reynolds, P.D., Bygrave, W., Carter, N.M., Davidsson, P., Gartner, W.B., Mason, C.M., McDougall, P.P. (Eds.), Frontiers of Entrepreneurship Research 1997. Babson College, Center for Entrepreneurial Studies, Babson Park, MA, pp. 349–357.

Aldrich, H.E., Waldinger, R., 1990. Ethnicity and entrepreneurship. Annual Review of Sociology, vol. 16. Annual Reviews, Palo Alto, CA, pp. 111–135.

Aldrich, H.E., Wiedenmayer, G., 1993. From traits to rates: an ecological perspective on organizational foundings. In: Katz, J., Brockhaus, R.H. (Eds.), Advances in Entrepreneurship, Firm Emergence, and Growth, vol. 1. JAI Press, Greenwich, CT, pp. 145–195.

Aldrich, H.E., Zimmer, C., 1986. Entrepreneurship through social networks. In: Sexton, D., Smilor, R. (Eds.), The Art and Science of Entrepreneurship. Ballinger, New York, pp. 3–23.

Aldrich, H.E., Renzulli, L., Langton, N., 1998. Passing on privilege: resources provided by self-employed parents to their self-employed children. In: Leicht, K. (Ed.), Research in Social Stratification and Mobility. JAI Press, Greenwich, CT, pp. 291–318.

Baron, R.A., 1998. Cognitive mechanisms in entrepreneurship: why and when entrepreneurs think differently than other people. J. Bus. Venturing 13 (4), 275–294.

Baron, R.A., 2000. Counterfactual thinking and venture formation: the potential effects of thinking about "what might have been". J. Bus. Venturing 15 (1), 79–91.

Bhave, M.P., 1994. A process model of entrepreneurial venture creation. J. Bus. Venturing 9 (3), 223–242.

Bianchi, S.M., 2000. Maternal employment and time with children: dramatic change or surprising continuity? Demography 37 (4), 401–414.

Bianchi, S.M., Casper, L.M., 2000. American families. Popul. Bull. 55 (4), 1–46.

Brush, C.G., 1992. Research on women business owners: past trends, a new perspective and future directions. Entrep. Theory Pract. 16 (4), 5–30.

Brush, C.G., Greene, P.G., Hart, M.M., 2001. From initial idea to unique advantage: the entrepreneurial challenge of constructing a resource base. Acad. Manage. Exec. 15 (1), 64–80.

Budig, M.J., 2002. Gender, Family, and Job Characteristics: Determinants of Self-Employment Participation for a Young Cohort, 1979–1998. Unpublished paper, Department of Sociology, University of Massachusetts. Amherst, MA.

Bumpass, L., 1990. What's happening to the family? Interactions between demographic and institutional change. Demography 27, 483–498.

Burt, R.S., 1992. Structural Holes: The Social Structure of Competition. Harvard Univ. Press, Cambridge, MA.

Carter, N., 1994. Reducing Barriers Between Genders: Differences in New Firm Startups. Academy of Management Meetings, Dallas, TX.

Chrisman, J.J., Chua, J.H., Steier, L.P., 2003. The influence of national culture and family involvement on entrepreneurial perceptions and performance at the state level. Entrep. Theory Pract.

Clauson, A., 2000. Spotlight on national food spending. Food Rev. 23 (3), 15–17.

Cohen, P.N., 1998. Replacing housework in the service economy: gender, class, and race–ethnicity in service spending. Gend. Soc. 12 (2), 219–231.

Coleman, M., Ganong, L., Fine, M., 2000. Reinvestigating remarriage: another decade of progress. J. Marriage Fam. 62 (4), 1288–1307.

Coltrane, S., 2000. Research on household labor: modeling and measuring the social embeddedness of routine family work. J. Marriage Fam. 62 (4), 1208–1233.

Cramton, C.D., 1993. Is rugged individualism the whole story? Public and private accounts of a firm's founding. Fam. Bus. Rev. 6 (3), 233–261.

Davidsson, P., Wiklund, J., 2001. Levels of analysis in entrepreneurship research: current research practice and suggestions for the future. Entrep. Theory Pract. 25 (4), 81–99.

Davidsson, P., Low, M.B., Wright, M., 2001. Editor's introduction: low and MacMillan ten years on: achievements and future directions for entrepreneurship research. Entrep. Theory Pract. 25 (4), 5–15.

Debelek, D., 2001. Infantile inventions. Entrep. Mag. 20 (October).

Dijksterhuis, M.S., Van den Bosch, F.A.J., Volberda, H.W., 1999. Where do new organizational forms come from? Management logics as a source of coevolution. Organ. Sci. 10 (5), 569–582.

Drucker, P.E., 1985. Innovation and Entrepreneurship: Practice and Principles. Harper & Row, New York.

Elder, G.H., Johnson, M.K., Crosnoe, R., in press. The emergence and development of life course theory.

H.E. Aldrich, J.E. Cliff / Journal of Business Venturing 18 (2003) 573–596 595

In: Mortimer, J., Shanahan, M. (Eds.), Handbook on the Life Course. Plenum, Amsterdam, The Netherlands.

Furstenberg Jr., F.F., 1988. Good dads–bad dads: two faces of fatherhood. In: Cherlin, A.J. (Ed.), The Changing American Family and Public Policy. The Urban Institute Press, Washington, DC, pp. 193–218.

Furstenberg Jr., F.F., 1990. Divorce and the America family. In: Scott, W.R., Blake, J. (Eds.), Annual Review of Sociology, vol. 16. Annual Reviews, Palo Alto, CA, pp. 379–401.

Furstenberg Jr., F.F., Nord, C.W., 1985. Parenting apart: patterns of childrearing after marital disruption. J. Marriage Fam. 47 (4), 893–905.

Gartner, W.B., 1988. "Who is an entrepreneur?" is the wrong question. Am. J. Small Bus. 12 (4), 11–32.

Gartner, W.B., 2001. Is there an elephant in entrepreneurship? Blind assumptions in theory development. Entrep. Theory Pract. 25 (4), 27–39.

Gartner, W.B., Birley, S., 2002. Introduction to the special issue on qualitative methods in entrepreneurship research. J. Bus. Venturing 17 (5), 387–395.

Giannarelli, L., Barsimantov, J., 2000. Child Care Expenses of America's Families. Urban Institute, Washington, DC.

Goldscheider, F.K., Waite, L.J., 1991. New Families, No Families? University of California Press, Berkeley, CA.

Hawkins, D.I., Best, R.J., Coney, K.A., 2001. Consumer Behavior: Building Marketing Strategy. Irwin McGraw-Hill, Boston, MA.

Heck, R. (Ed.), 1998. The Entrepreneurial Family. Family Business Resources Publishing, Needham, MA.

Heck, R.K.Z., Trent, E.S., 1999. The prevalence of family business from a household sample. Fam. Bus. Rev. 12 (3), 209–224.

Herron, L., Sapienza, H.J., 1992. The entrepreneur and the initiation of new venture launch activities. Entrep. Theory Pract. 17 (1), 49–55.

Hochschild, A., 1989. The Second Shift: Working Parents and the Revolution at Home. Viking, New York.

InventiveParent, 2002. Weemote: making TV safer for kids. Inventive Parent. Accessed on: September 2, 2002. Available at: http://www.inventiveparent.com/weemote.htm.

Johnson, C.L., 2000. Perspectives on American kinship in the later 1990s. J. Marriage Fam. 62 (4), 623–639.

Johnson, D., Lino, M., 2000. Teenagers: employment and contribution to family spending. Mon. Labor Rev. 123 (9), 15–25.

Larson, A., Starr, J.A., 1993. A network model of organization formation. Entrep. Theory Pract. 17 (2), 5–15.

Lewin, A.Y., Long, C.P., Carroll, T.N., 1999. The coevolution of new organizational forms. Organ. Sci. 10 (5), 535–550.

Lin, B., Guthrie, J., Frazao, E., 1999. Away-From-Home Foods Increasingly Important to Quality of American Diet. U.S. Department of Agriculture, Washington, DC, pp. 1–22.

Marshack, K.J., 1993. Coentrepreneurial couples: a literature review on boundaries and transitions among copreneurs. Fam. Bus. Rev. 6 (4), 355–369.

Mezias, S.J., Kuperman, J., 2001. The community dynamics of entrepreneurship: the birth of the American film industry, 1895–1929. J. Bus. Venturing 16 (3), 209–233.

Moen, P., 1998. A life course approach to the entrepreneurial family. In: Heck, R. (Ed.), The Entrepreneurial Family. Family Business Resources, Inc., Needham, MA, pp. 16–29.

Mowen, J.C., Minor, M.S., 1998. Consumer Behavior. Prentice-Hall, Saddle River, NJ.

Neider, L., 1987. A preliminary investigation of female entrepreneurs in Florida. J. Small Bus. Manage. 25, 22–29.

Oropesa, R.S., 1993. Using the service economy to relieve the double burden: female labor force participation and service purchases. J. Fam. Issues 14 (3), 438–473.

Presser, H.B., 1998. The future of work and health. The California Wellness Foundation. Accessed on: September 19, 2002. Available at: http://www.tcwf.org/conference/hpresser.htm.

Putnam, R., 2000. Bowling Alone: The Collapse and Revival of American Community. Simon and Schuster, New York.

Renzulli, L., Aldrich, H.E., Moody, J., 2000. Family matters: consequences of personal networks for business startup and survival. Soc. Forces 79 (2), 523–546.

Reynolds, P.D., White, S.B., 1997. The Entrepreneurial Process: Economic Growth, Men, Women, and Minorities. Quorum Books, Westport, CT.

Rosenblatt, P.C., deMik, L., Anderson, R.M., Johnson, P.A., 1985. The Family in Business: Understanding and Dealing with the Challenges Entrepreneurial Families Face. Jossey-Bass, San Francisco, CA.

Rossi, A.S., 1989. A life-course approach to gender, aging, and intergenerational relations. In: Schaie, K.W., Schooler, C. (Eds.), Social Structure and Aging: Psychological Processes. Earlbaum, Hillsdale, NY, pp. 207–236.

Ruef, M., Aldrich, H.E., Carter, N.M., 2002. Don't go to strangers: homophily, strong ties, and isolation in the formation of organizational founding teams. American Sociological Association Meeting, Chicago, IL.

Ruggles, S., Goeken, R., 1992. Race and multigenerational family structure, 1900–1980. In: South, S.J., Tolnay, S.E. (Eds.), The Changing American Family: Sociological and Demographic Perspectives. Westview Press, Boulder, CO, pp. 15–42.

Schumpeter, J., 1934. The Theory of Economic Development. Harvard Univ. Press, Cambridge, MA.

Shane, S., 2000. Prior knowledge and the discovery of entrepreneurial opportunities. Organ. Sci. 11 (4), 448–469.

Shane, S., Venkataraman, S., 2000. The promise of entrepreneurship as a field of research. Acad. Manage. Rev. 25 (1), 217–226.

Shaver, K.G., Scott, L.R., 1991. Person, process, choice: the psychology of new venture creation. Entrep. Theory Pract. 16 (2), 23–45.

Sheth, J.N., Mittal, B., Newman, B.I., 1999. Customer Behavior: Consumer Behavior and Beyond. Dryden Press, Fort Worth, TX.

Simon, M., Houghton, S.M., Aquino, K., 1999. Cognitive biases, risk perception, and venture formation: how individuals decide to start companies. J. Bus. Venturing 15 (2), 113–134.

Solomon, M.R., Zaichowsky, J.L., Polegaro, R., 2002. Consumer Behavior. Prentice-Hall, Toronto.

Stafford, K., Duncan, K.A., Danes, S., Winter, M., 1999. A research model of sustainable family businesses. Fam. Bus. Rev. 7 (3), 197–208.

Starr, J.A., MacMillan, I.C., 1990. Resource cooptation via social contracting: resource acquisition strategies for new ventures. Strateg. Manage. J. 11 (1), 79–92.

Steier, L., Greenwood, R., 2000. Entrepreneurship and the evolution of angel financial networks. Organ. Stud. 21 (1), 163–192.

Teachman, J.D., Tedrow, L.M., Crowder, K.D., 2000. The changing demography of America's families. J. Marriage Fam. 62 (4), 1234–1246.

Timmons, J.A., 1999. New Venture Creation. Irwin McGraw-Hill, Boston, MA.

U.S. Bureau of the Census, 2000a. America's Families and Living Arrangements: March 2000. U.S. Bureau of the Census, Washington, DC. Current Population Reports, Series P20-537.

U.S. Bureau of the Census, 2000b. Statistical Abstract of the United States: 2000. U.S. Government Printing Office, Washington, DC.

U.S. Bureau of Labor Statistics, 2002. Work at Home in 2001. U.S. Bureau of Labor Statistics. Accessed on: September 19, 2002. Available at: http://www.bls.gov/news.release/homey.t01.htm.

Uhlenberg, P., 1996. Mortality decline in the twentieth century and supply of kin over the life course. The Gerontologist 36 (5), 681–685.

Upton, N., Heck, R., 1997. The family business dimension of entrepreneurship. In: Sexton, D.L., Smilor, R.W. (Eds.), Entrepreneurship 2000. Upstart, Chicago, IL, pp. 243–266.

Venkataraman, S., 1997. The distinctive domain of entrepreneurship research. In: Katz, J.A. (Ed.), Advances in Entrepreneurship, Firm Emergence, and Growth, vol. 3. JAI Press, Greenwich, CT, pp. 119–138.

Zelizer, V.A., 1994. Pricing the Priceless Child: The Changing Social Value of Children. Princeton University, Princeton, NJ.

PART VI

STRATIFICATION
AND INEQUALITY

[20]

PASSING ON PRIVILEGE:
RESOURCES PROVIDED BY SELF-EMPLOYED
PARENTS TO THEIR SELF-EMPLOYED CHILDREN

Howard E. Aldrich, Linda A. Renzulli, and
Nancy Langton

ABSTRACT

We examined the argument that a "property barrier" explains the high degree of
self-employed inheritance between propertied families and their children. Our
study used data on 229 self-employed business owners in the Greater Vancouver
area of British Columbia, Canada, obtained in 1995 via face to face interviews.
We found little evidence for the property barrier hypothesis, as physical and financial capital had very little impact on business start-ups, through either inheritance
of the business or transfer of wealth. We then tested the hypothesis that entrepreneurial capital—including childhood exposure, work in a family business, and
jobs with managerial responsibility—is a resource differentiating children of
self-employed parents from others. Our results were again negative, because we
found no direct evidence that business owners with self-employed parents gained

Research in Social Stratification and Mobility, Volume 16, pages 291-317.
Copyright © 1998 by JAI Press Inc.
All rights of reproduction in any form reserved.
ISBN: 0-7623-0279-8

any more entrepreneurial capital than other owners. Notwithstanding our negative findings, we speculated that entrepreneurial capital is a resource needed for starting a business, and proposed further research to examine how entrepreneurial capital is obtained.

Theories about social classes, whether from a Marxist or Weberian perspective, treat the reproduction of social class advantage over generations as a central issue. Relative persistence in positions, from parents to children, has been taken as a sign of the success of privileged groups in closing off access to better locations, as well as the failure of disadvantaged groups to mount effective challenges to dominant groups. Persistence has also been attributed to a lack of permeability produced by the success of relatively privileged parents in passing on resources that are highly valuable to their children in various markets, such as managerial expertise. Analysts who view social classes from a Marxist perspective are more likely to see a unity of interests among the privileged and thus treat class relations in political terms, with classes standing in antagonistic relation to one another (Western and Wright 1994, p. 610). By contrast, Weberian analysts tend to see individuals' life chances as influenced by their own unique constellation of resources—financial, social, cultural—and thus the concept of class relations itself is relegated to secondary importance.[1]

Regardless of theoretical orientation, analysts agree that the extent to which class positions are inherited should be a central concern of social mobility research, and thus researchers have focused on the association between social origins and destinations. In more open and permeable social structures, intergenerational transmission of inequality is low and children's positions may diverge widely from those of their parents. In more closed and impermeable social structures, barriers to mobility keep children from drifting very far from their social origins.

Origins and destinations are quite narrowly defined in many Weberian-inspired schemes, and the locations examined are typically occupations or socioeconomic status. In more Marxist-oriented schemes, ownership and control of property and labor are added to the occupational classification system favored by Weberians and neo-Weberians (Wong 1992). The two traditions converge, however, in the special attention they pay to self-employed persons. The category of "self-employed people" is rather heterogeneous, as it includes mostly people who work on their own account and do not have employees, but it also includes a sizable number of people who have employees and work out of fixed premises—people who are traditionally thought of as owners of small and medium-sized businesses. Because many of the self-employed possess capital and have control over others in an employment relation, Marxist and Weberian theorists have seen them as well-positioned to pass on their privileged positions to their children.

Although Lipset and Bendix (1959) argued that the process of modernization in industrial societies had led to a relative decline in inheritable positions, occupational inheritance persists at a high level among the self-employed. Beginning with Blau and Duncan's (1967, pp. 41-43) historic study, social scientists have noted an extremely high degree of occupational inheritance and self-recruitment among the self-employed. More recent studies have confirmed their finding and generalized it across other industrialized nations. Wong (1992, p. 407) found that occupational inheritance among the self-employed varied significantly across the six nations he studied, with inheritance strongest in two socialist nations and weaker in the United States than in either England or Japan. Western and Wright (1994) found that the "property boundary" to intergenerational mobility was significantly less permeable in the United States than the other class boundaries they identified. Dunn and Holtz-Eakin's (1996, p. 15) event history analysis of the National Longitudinal Survey of Labor Market Experience found that parents' self-employment experience had "very large and significant effects, just about doubling the probability of the son's entering self-employment." Similar effects have been found in other well-designed studies (Fairlie 1994; Lentz and Laband 1990, 1993)

What accounts for the relatively high degree of occupational inheritance between propertied families and their children? Curiously enough, despite the existence of a strong empirical generalization that has been replicated over time, across different sampling frames, and in many different nations, we know very little more now than we did three decades ago. For example, here is what Western and Wright (1994, p. 611) had to say, just a few years ago: "Mobility across the property boundary is *likely* [emphasis added] to be limited because (1) financial and physical capital is transferable to the offspring of property owners..., and (2) capitalist parents can finance their children's businesses out of profits or borrowings...The rigidity of the property boundary may be compounded by the preferences of children of property owners for self-employment rather than wage labor." Wong (1992, p. 400) speculated that "self-employment often reflects *strong* and *positive* influences from parents who are also self-employed and prior experiences of working for the family business....The socialization and internalization of the self-employed generate inheritance and perpetuate inequality, a basic condition for class formation." Similar speculation marks another discussion concerning occupational inheritance among the self-employed, suggesting that the time has come for a closer look at the processes underlying the well-accepted empirical generalization.

In this paper we use data on self-employed business owners, in the Greater Vancouver area, in Canada, to describe in rich detail the process of intergenerational transmission of this class location. Within the limits of our sample—selected because they were already in business—we test hypotheses about the various modes by which self-employed parents could have affected their children's life chances.

THE CONTINUING IMPORTANCE OF
THE SMALL BUSINESS SECTOR

Small businesses play important economic, social, and political roles in modern industrial societies. Despite repeated claims that it is disappearing or irrelevant, the small and medium-sized business sector of most industrialized societies is alive and well (SBA 1994; Wong 1992, pp. 399-400). The proportion of the workforce that is self-employed has actually risen in the United States in recent years, and small businesses employ a sizable minority of the labor force. In 1990 about 40 percent of the labor force worked in firms with less than 100 employees (SBA 1994), and in European Union nations in 1988 about 55 percent of workers were employed in firms with under 100 employees (ENSR 1993). The contentious debate over how much of a contribution small firms make to job generation has obscured the fact that they represent a significant sector of our economy that is growing in absolute and relative terms; for example, in 1994 about 807,000 new firms were created. Preliminary results from the Entrepreneurship Research Consortium's study conducted in 1996 show that about 37 percent of U.S. households include someone who, over their life course, has had a primary role in a new or a small business (Selz 1996).

Small businesses and self-employment hold out the dream of social promotion and thus play a major role in the social and political ideology of industrial nations (Lipset and Bendix 1959). The dream of social promotion involves a belief in one's prospects for upward mobility and an opportunity to rise above the class position of one's parents. Culturally, small businesses are a visible symbol of a perceived path for mobility and a sign of the system's openness. Wong (1992, p. 400) noted that, "Self-employment is important in social mobility—not only does it provide an alternative to paid employment, but it also offers an avenue of upward mobility to those who lack the educational or technical qualifications to move up in large organizations." People can use the prevalence and visibility of those who move in and out of this stratum as evidence of fluidity.

The dream—Nicos Poulantzas called it the "myth" of social promotion—is not unique to the United States. Beckhhofer and Elliot (1985) examined the symbolic significance of the petite bourgeoisie in Scotland, and Carroll and Mosakowski (1987) pointed out that Germany—unlike the United States—has an official categorization scheme for types of self-employment. Wong (1992, p. 400) argued that "because the historical context of the self-employed class varies across countries, the degree of mobility among the self-employed may be an important source of cross-national variation in overall social mobility."

Small business owners tend to position themselves politically with large business and property owners who are conservative in their political ideology and in their voting behavior. Small business owners are usually not activists and typically shun organized political activity, and their conservative beliefs place them squarely within the values of the middle class.

Politically, socially, and economically, then, owners of small and medium-sized businesses continue to play an important role in industrial societies. They are a conservative voice on the political scene, a symbol of the dream of social promotion, and a significant source of employment opportunities, especially for younger and less educated workers.

MODES BY WHICH SELF-EMPLOYED PARENTS CAN INFLUENCE THEIR CHILDREN'S LIFE CHANCES

A life-course framework is useful for examining the ways in which self-employed parents' resources and actions may affect the life chances of their children (Elder and O'Rand 1995). Among others, Goldthorpe (1980, p. 258) has noted that the high degree of occupational inheritance within what he called the "petty bourgeoisie" suggests long-term continuity in family dynamics:

> some collection of individuals and families does exist in modern British society which is identifiable over time not so much by the continuity with which its members occupy the self-employed positions of [the petty bourgeoisie] but rather by what could be regarded as their "tradition" of self-employment:…by the propensity of its members to move into self-employment when opportunity arises and to do so, perhaps, in spite of previous disappointments or failures in self-employed ventures. It is in this sense…that the petty bourgeoisie may best be thought of as presently existing as a social formation within the British class structure.

Bechhofer and Elliott (1985, p. 200) echoed a similar theme, as they argued that many small businesses "are not simply run by families, they are run for families." Such arguments imply that growing up in a family in which parents are self-employed shapes the life course of children in ways that increase the likelihood that they will also become self-employed. What is it about self-employed families that sustains this tradition over generations?

Following Stier and Grusky (1990, p. 740), we have identified two kinds of resources that self-employed parents may provide to their children: (1) physical and financial capital, either via passing on an operating business or making loans and gifts that make possible a business startup, and (2) entrepreneurial capital, encompassing the traditional notion of "human capital" but focusing specifically on attitudes, values, skills, and emotions that are relevant to business ownership. After reviewing the various types of resources potentially available to the children of self-employed parents, we describe our study design and present evidence from our own study.

Physical and Financial Capital

First, there are two ways that parents' accumulation of capital and property can affect their children's life chances: through a succession process, whereby a child takes over the parents' business, or through a transfer of other wealth that enables a child to purchase some or all of a business. Passing on an actual operating business entity to a child, either through a gift or a sale, is actually a fairly rare event among business owners. Dunn and Holtz-Eakin (1996) estimated that, at most, about 10 percent of the sons they studied could have entered the same business as their parents. Lentz and Laband (1990), using a sample of NFIB members in the United States collected in 1980, found that 14.2 percent of proprietors had inherited their business. Other research in the United States and England has produced estimates of slightly less than one in 10 businesses being acquired via inheritance (Aldrich, Cater, Jones, and McEvoy 1983; Aldrich, Kalleberg, Marsden, and Cassell 1989; Zimmer and Aldrich 1987).

Transfer of wealth, in the form of gifts or loans, is a more indirect route through which self-employed parents may influence their children's chances of entering self-employment. Western and Wright (1994, p. 611) argued that "parental ownership of property is…'insurance' against downward mobility into wage labor for the offspring of capitalists, and the requirement of capital ownership is a barrier to entry for the children of most employees." Actually, most business owners begin at a very small scale and with very little capital. In 1987 almost one-quarter of all nonminority male business owners in the United States reported they began with *no* initial capital, and another 42 percent began with less than $10,000 (U.S. Department of Commerce 1987). About two-thirds reported they did not borrow any capital, either because they did not need it or were able to rely on their own funds. Only 7 percent raised capital from family members.

Relative to the wealth that the children themselves have accumulated, parental wealth is not very consequential. Dunn and Holtz-Eakin (1996, p. 14) found that parental assets exerted a positive but quantitatively small influence on sons' odds of becoming self-employed, finding that a "$10,000 increase in parents' total assets raises the probability of a son's transition into self-employment by 0.0009, which is small relative to both the sample transition probability of 0.031 and the son's own-asset impact." They did not examine, however, whether parents became co-owners in the sons' businesses.

Contrary to what many sociologists apparently believe, personal wealth is *not* a major determinant of becoming self-employed or founding a business. Even if parents help children accumulate their own capital, the capital thus amassed would make a relatively small contribution to occupational inheritance via wealth transmission. (Dunn and Holtz-Eakin [1996] make this same point.) We have noted that most owners in the United States begin with very small amounts of capital, raised from their own resources.

Our first hypothesis, then, with regard to occupational inheritance among business owners, is:

Hypothesis 1. Financial and physical capital will play a minor role in business ownership among children of self-employed parents.

We will examine four indicators of a privileged position: inheriting a business, buying a business from one's parents, obtaining capital from parents, and having parents as business co-founders.

Entrepreneurial Capital

The second major kind of resource that self-employed parents may provide their offspring is entrepreneurial capital. In coining this new term—entrepreneurial capital—we have expanded the traditional notion of "human capital" so as to include the experiences and skills that are relevant to business ownership. Experiences and skills, in turn, promote attitudes and values that facilitate business ownership. Relevant attitudes created by experience include a willingness to work long hours, foregoing leisure activities and holidays, and perhaps sacrificing family life to the needs of the business. Relevant skills include managing a workforce and keeping track of a firm's cash flow. Self-employed parents may foster the development of entrepreneurial capital in their children through socialization, work experience, and the development of social capital. They may also replenish and reinforce the results of earlier experiences by contributing emotional and other nonfinancial forms of support to their adult children.

Socialization during adolescence may lead to children taking on the attitudes and values necessary for entering self-employment. By serving as role models, self-employed parents may give children an understanding of self-employment as a career and help them to see self-employment as "a realistic alternative to conventional employment" (Carroll and Mosakowski 1987, p. 576). Referring to Hout's (1989) study of social mobility in Ireland, Western and Wright (1994, p. 611) observed that, "In small businesses, the experience of unpaid family labor may lead the offspring of the self-employed to place a high value on self-employment." Valuing self-employment more highly than other forms of employment may lead children to pursue work experiences that eventually culminate in business ownership, even without direct financial support from their parents. For example, we might expect them to seek jobs with managerial responsibility, rather than jobs in which they are supervised.

Children of parents in jobs permitting a high degree of self-direction are disciplined in ways encouraging self-control. The children take on the values of their parents, favoring autonomy and control in their own lives (Kohn 1981; Kohn and Schooler 1978). As Goldthorpe (1980, p. 41) noted, the high degree of economic insecurity and severe market constraints faced by the "petty bourgeoisie" are partly offset because "they have the advantage...of a high degree of autonomy, in the sense of freedom from direct supervision, in the performance of their work tasks." We would expect the children of self-employed parents to value hard work and self-sacrifice and to be willing to put in long hours to achieve their goals. However, the incessant demands of managing a small business may well require *all* owners to labor long hours, regardless of their social origins.

A second way self-employed parents may influence their children's life chances is through on-the-job experiences (Becker and Tomes 1986). Children may gain valuable skills and competencies via working for their parents (Carroll and Mosakowski 1987), such as time and financial-management skills. However, such skills can also be learned elsewhere, so this process is probably not as critical as the acquisition of attitudes and values. As Stier and Grusky (1990, p. 737) argued, "the reproduction of classes is now mediated by a socioeconomic metric, with most parents passing on generalized resources to their children (e.g., financial support) rather than job-specific ones (e.g., on-the-job training)."

Testing for the influence of parental socialization practices on children's acquisition of skills is difficult because children might find the opportunity to acquire the same skills in a variety of ways, including formal education and in jobs as young adults. Following Kohn and others, we would expect the children of self-employed parents to seek out jobs that allow for occupational self-direction and control. Thus, they would have many opportunities to acquire the skills needed for managing a business, although not necessarily the skills needed to start one.

A third way in which self-employed parents may influence their children's life chances in nonfinancial ways is via social capital and personal networks. Parents may act as brokers and put their children in touch with people able to provide valuable resources for running a business (Granovetter 1993). Studies of personal networking by small and medium-sized business owners, however, show that friendship and work-related connections are much more numerous and significant than family ties in mobilizing business resources (Aldrich, Elam, and Reese 1996). We will not examine social capital in our study.

More problematic is the argument that self-employed parents provide their offspring with social and cultural capital that affects their self-employment prospects (Joppke 1986; Bourdieu 1987). Theorists holding to a "cultural capital" view have treated educational attainment not only as a symbol of generalized cultural competence but also as a relatively impermeable boundary to intergenerational mobility. Apart from businesses requiring a high degree of technical competence, such as in the high-technology sector, there is no a priori logic to justify a prediction that level of educational attainment affects entry into self-employment. Well-designed dynamic analyses of work careers, such as Carroll and Mosakowski (1987) and Dunn and Holtz-Eakin (1996), have failed to find any evidence that advanced educational credentials have a significant net effect on entering self-employment. We cannot examine this issue, given our study design.

Finally, a fourth way that self-employed parents may influence their self-employed offspring's' life chances, *after* they have entered business, is by providing nonfinancial as well as financial support. Parents may provide funds to help self-employed children over a temporary cash crisis, and they may also provide household help for time-strapped children. Emotional support for self-employed children may also boost their spirits when their businesses are generating personal stress. We will examine this issue in subsequent papers.

Our second hypothesis, then, with regard to occupational inheritance among business owners, is:

Hypothesis 2.   Entrepreneurial capital will play a more significant role than financial capital in business ownership among children of self-employed parents, giving them an advantage over owners whose parents were not self-employed.

We will examine four indicators of exposure to an entrepreneurial lifestyle: duration of exposure to a self-employed lifestyle, work experience in parents' businesses, holding jobs with managerial responsibility, and the development of an entrepreneurial work ethic, as reflected in a willingness to work long hours in one's current business.

STUDY DESIGN

A full test of propositions about the influence of self-employed parents on their children would require a research design that is difficult and costly to implement. First, an investigator would need to follow cohorts of parents and then their children over those portions of their life course when the parents are likely to be self-employed—typically in their 30s and 40s. Second, the investigator would have to follow those children who had been exposed to an entrepreneurial lifestyle until they had also reached the time when they had acquired enough experience and capital to become self-employed—again, typically in their 30s and 40s. Information would be collected on parents' relations with their children during adolescence—child rearing and discipline practices, education and training in business matters—as well as during the transition to self-employment, during adulthood. Unable to meet the daunting demands of such a design, researchers have had to make compromises.

Cross-sectional studies, such as those used by Wong, and Western and Wright, provide detailed information about occupations and some accumulated experiences, but do not provide the rich details needed either on what happened during adolescence or on the transition into self-employment. Dynamic studies, such as the NLS used by Dunn and Holtz-Eakin or the West German Life History Study used by Carroll and Mosakowski, provide more details on the circumstances surrounding the transition to self-employment and parents' possible contributions to the transition. However, the NLS and the West German studies give only limited information about financial and social-psychological background factors. For an informative discussion of inflow or recruitment data versus outflow or inheritance data, see Myles and Sorensen (1975).

In designing our own study of business owners, we were highly cognizant of the compromises necessary to field an affordable study of a special group that constitutes a small proportion of the population, and thus we made two decisions. First, we created a comprehensive survey for an initial cross-sectional data collection effort, but built in a panel component so that we could follow the owners over the next several years, with repeated interviews. In this paper we only report data on the first wave. Second, in our initial interviews we asked retrospective questions designed to tap the respondents' experiences over their life course, guided by an extensive pilot-testing project during which we evaluated respondents' abilities to recall the information we sought.

Our study was conducted in the Greater Vancouver area of British Columbia, Canada in the summer and fall of 1995. We sampled firms from records obtained from the Greater Vancouver Contacts Target Marketing database for 1994 and 1995. Because we were interested in gender differences in business practices for some aspects of our overall research plan, we sampled industries from three categories: male-dominated, female-dominated, and mixed. Because we were interested in human resource issues, we chose firms that had six employees or more, to ensure that our questions about hiring, promotion, and other human resource practices would be relevant to the firms. Choosing firms with more than five employees also had two advantages for our study of occupational inheritance. First, it decreased the likelihood of including transitory or "lifestyle" businesses in the sample. Second, it increased the likelihood of including firms that have a significant "property" barrier to entry, a key concern of previous research. Firms were excluded from our sampling frame if they were franchises, branches, or subsidiaries.[2]

To obtain enough women owners, we included all female-owned firms and a random sample of male-owned firms as targets for possible interview. In our initial contacts with firms, they were excluded if: (1) we discovered that a franchise, branch, or subsidiary had been included by mistake; (2) they were no longer in business; (3) the owner was untraceable or not involved in the management of the company; or (4) the owner had participated in our pilot study. This resulted in a total of 594 eligible firms. Of these, 229 owners agreed to participate, resulting in a response rate of 39 percent.[3] Of the 229, 141 were men and 88 were women; 204 were Caucasian, 15 were Chinese, and the rest were of other ethnicities. We were able to compare those who agreed to participate in our study with those who did not agree (for any reason) on gender of owner, age of firm, industry, and size of firm. Only size of firm showed a significant difference, with larger firms less likely to participate in our study. In some cases this reflected the owner's report that he or she was not responsible for employee issues and a suggestion that we interview the person in charge of human resources (a nonowner) instead. We did not pursue these businesses. Our sample is representative of the population of firms available for study, particularly those firms for which the owner is still acting in a "hands on" capacity.

Table 1. Variable Description, Means, and Standard Deviations

Variable Name	Description	Mean	Standard Deviation
Hours worked per week	Number of hours per week (10-100)	52.74	14.47
Evening work	Coded 0 if no, 1 if yes	.79	.41
Weekend work	Coded 0 if no, 1 if yes	.80	.40
Parents own Business	Coded 0 if no, 1 if yes	.55	.5
If parents owned a business:			
a) Number of years parents owned business	Continuous variable (1-71)	27.58	16.27
b) Worked in parents' business	Coded 0 if no, 1 if yes	.71	.49
c) Number of years worked for parents	Continuous variable (.20-37)	9.86	7.56
Education	Continuous variable (7-20)	14.36	2.74
Sex	Coded 0 if female, 1 if male	.62	.49
Age	Continuous variable (26-73)	47.2	9.47
Hours spent on housework and child-care	Continuous variable (0-131)	12.47	15.66
Married	Coded 0 if no, 1 if yes	.85	.36
Own other business	Coded 0 if no, 1 if yes	.36	.48

Information was obtained in personal interviews and typically took between 50 and 80 minutes to complete. The main part of the survey instrument included questions on: the nature, structure, size, and profitability of the company; human resource practices, policies, and hiring intentions; the background of the owner; and the interplay between work and personal domains. In the final interviewed sample, the industry distribution was as follows: manufacturing firms, 10.9 percent; transportation services, 4.8 percent; wholesale trade, 18.3 percent; retail trade, 13.5 percent; printing, 8 percent; personal services, 7.9 percent; and business services, 35.8 percent.

Full descriptions of our variables and their operational definitions are given in Table 1.

RESULTS

One goal of our paper is to correct some misconceptions concerning what resources self-employed parents provide for their children, and thus part of our analysis is descriptive. Thus, we will present some rich empirical details not available in other reports on this sector. Another of our goals, however, is to test whether the self-employed children of self-employed parents differ in predictable ways from other business owners.

Table 2.   Financial and Physical Capital

	Percent	Number
1. Percent whose parents were self-employed:	55.5	(229)
Father:	35.8	
Mother:	3.1	
Both:	16.6	
2. Percent who inherited their business:		
a. as percent of all owners	5.2	(229)
b. owners whose parents were self-employed	7.9	(127)
3. Percent who bought their business from their parents:		
a. as percent of all owners	3.1	(229)
b. owners whose parents were self-employed	5.5	(127)
4. Percent who used capital from an inheritance to fund their business:	0.0	(229)
5. Percent who obtained capital from:		
a. self-employed parents	8.7	(127)
b. non-self-employed parents	7.8	(102)
		N.S.[a]
6. If parents contributed funds, average percent of capital obtained from:		
a. self-employed parents	77.3	(11)
b. non-self-employed parents	32.0	(8)
		p=.01
7. Percent whose original co-owners included a parent:		
a. self-employed parents	7.9	(127)
b. non-self-employed parents	0.0	(102)
		p=.01
8. Accumulative percent who inherited and/or bought from parents and/or obtained capital from parents and/or had parents as co-owners:		
a. self-employed parents	24.0	(127)
b. non-self-employed parents	8.0	(102)
		p=.01

Note: [a]N.S. = difference between self-employed and non self-employed parents not significant.

As we expected, a majority of all respondents (55%) reported that one or both of their parents were self-employed at some point in their lives, as shown in the first row of Table 2. Our estimate is almost the same as that of Lentz and Laband (1990), who found that 53 percent of all the owners in their U.S. sample had a self-employed parent. Of the 127 people in our sample whose parents were ever self-employed, 82 reported it was their father, 38 said it was their father and mother, and 7 said it was only their mother. Similar findings have been reported in other studies of small business owners, in the United States and internationally (Aldrich, Cater, Jones, and McEvoy 1983; Aldrich and Sakano 1995).

Physical and Financial Capital

We examined two ways in which parents' accumulation of capital and property could have affected their children's life chances: a child inheriting a business, or a child receiving a loan or gift of capital. Direct inheritance of a business was highly unlikely in our sample, accounting for only 5.2 percent of all business ownership, as shown in row 2 of Table 2. By definition, business inheritance could only occur among the children of the self-employed, and when we restrict our analysis to that group, we still find only 7.9 percent inherited their business. Inheritance of the business tended to occur fairly late in the work careers of the 10 inheritors in our sample, as the median age of inheritance was 41 and only two were younger than 35. This is consistent with Hout's (1989) finding that in the agricultural sector, direct inheritance led to comparatively late entry to farm ownership.

Some parents sold their businesses to their children, rather than making a gift of the firm, and such sales accounted for 3.1 percent of all ownership. Again, restricting ourselves to only that subset of respondents whose parents could have made such a sale, we found that 5.5 percent of the children of self-employed parents bought their firm from the parents. Just as most respondents who inherited firms were well into their careers, so too are the respondents who bought their parents' businesses—three of the five were over 50 and only one was under 35. Thus, for the small fraction of children inheriting or buying a parent's business, the event occurred well after the sons and daughters had launched their own work careers and had accumulated substantial resources on their own.

Turning from ownership succession to more indirect avenues through which propertied parents could confer advantages to their children, we asked owners how they had raised the capital to buy their businesses. *None* of them mentioned using capital from an inheritance, such as from the estate of a deceased parent. About 8 percent, however, received capital from their parents, with 8.7 percent of the children of self-employed parents raising funds this way, compared to 7.8 percent of the other respondents (the difference is not statistically significant). In general, the amount of outside capital raised by our respondents was low, amounting to approximately five percent of the total start-up capital used. However, for the 8 percent of our sample who received funds from family, these funds were a much larger portion of the start-up capital. The average percent of total capital required that was raised from parents was larger for respondents of self-employed parents than others, and although there was a significant difference between the two groups, the numbers of respondents to whom this situation applies are quite small. It is perhaps not surprising that the offspring of self-employed do not receive substantial capital from their parents. Though both Marxist and Weberian theorists see the self-employed as well positioned to pass on help and resources to their

Table 3.   Entrepreneurial Capital

1. Duration of parents' business ownership:

Years	Percent
1-9	16.5
10-19	14.1
20-29	27.3
30-39	18.1
40-49	12.4
50+	11.6
	100.0 (121)

2. Duration of respondent's exposure to parents' business ownership, prior to age 22:

Years	Percent
0	16.5 (20)
1-9	20.7
10-19	32.2
20-21	30.6
	100.0 (121)

3. Children of business owners only: percent worked in parents' business: 61

4. Age at which respondent began working in parents' business:

Years	Percent
1-9	24.4
10-14	26.9
15-19	33.3
20+	15.4
All	100.0 (78)

5. Total years worked in parents' business:

Years	Percent
1-4	29.5
5-9	21.8
10-14	23.1
15-19	14.1
20+	11.5
	100.0 (78)

Table 4.   Previous Jobs: Ownership and Responsibility

A. *Most recent job, before current ownership, if employed before owning this business*

	Not a manager	Manager	Business Owner	All jobs
Parents self-employed	26.2	53.3	20.5	100.0 (122)
Parents not self-employed	26.7	52.0	20.8	100.0 (101)
All	26.5	52.9	20.6	100.0 (223)
				N.S.

B. *Next-to-last job (if employed)*

	Not a manager	Managed/ Owned	All jobs
Parents self-employed	43.3	56.7	100.0 (97)
Parents not self-employed	49.4	50.6	100.0 (87)
All	46.2	53.8	100.0 (184)
		N.S.	

children, the average small business owner is not financially better off than the average wage earner, as Kalleberg and Leicht (1991) note.

One final route to business ownership in which parents could participate is via becoming a co-owner with their children. As shown in row 7 of Table 2, 7.9 percent of the children of self-employed parents brought their parents in as co-owners, whereas *none* of the other owners were able to do so. Three of the 10 owners who said they inherited their business also had their parents as co-owners, and four of the 12 whose parents were initially co-owners also borrowed capital from them (these four said they did not inherit their businesses). Thus, for these two small subsets of the children of self-employed parents, the advantages of parental property were cumulative.

Summary of Financial/Physical Capital

We examined the total cumulative advantages for children of self-employed parents by aggregating the four types of resources parents could supply to children, as we have described above, and the results are shown in line 8 of Table 2. Most of the business owners we studied had very little financial help from their parents, self-employed or otherwise. For those owners whose parents were self-employed, 24 percent obtained one or more of the resources with which to acquire a business, compared to 8 percent of the children of other parents (the difference is statistically significant). The approximately 16 percent gap between these two groups

Table 5a. Influence of Self-Employed Parents on Respondent's Work Ethic: Unstandardized Regression Coefficients

| | Hours worked per week | |
Independent variable	Equation (1)	Equation (2)
Parents self-employed	1.17	−1.41
	(2.45)	(3.00)
Years parents s-e	—	0.11
		(.08)
Worked in parents' business	1.932	0.83
	(2.56)	(3.26)
Years worked in parents' business	—	0.00
		(.21)
Sex	1.04	.71
	(2.08)	(2.11)
Education	.49	.51
	(.34)	(.34)
Age	−0.29**	−0.31**
	(.10)	(.11)
Married	−0.76	−0.83
	(2.79)	(2.78)
Own other business	1.37	1.36
	(1.99)	(2.00)
Hours spent on housework/childcare	−0.24***	−0.24***
	(.06)	(.06)
Intercept	60.85	61.62
Adjusted R^2	0.09***	0.09***
N	229	229

Notes: ***$p = .001$, **$p = .01$, *$p = .05$, #$p = .10$.

thus represents a fairly slight initial advantage for the children of the self-employed. The great majority of business owners mobilized the resources they needed from nonfamily sources, and thus *not* having been born to self-employed parents did not constitute a property barrier for them.

Our sample of firms includes mostly larger than average firms that have been in operation for many years. If there truly is a property barrier to becoming a small business owner, then our sample composition should heighten the likelihood that we will find such a barrier, as these are individuals who have managed to survive the initial incidence of failure common to small business owners. Nonetheless, our hypotheses should be tested on other samples of firms, including smaller and younger ones.

Table 5b. Influence of Self-Employed Parents on Respondent's Work Ethic: Logistic Regression Coefficient.

| | Work evenings? | | | | Work weekends? | | | |
| | Equation 3 | | Equation 4 | | Equation 5 | | Equation 6 | |
Independent variable	coef.	effect on odds	coef.	effect on odds	coef.	effect on odds	coef.	effect on odds
Parents self-employed	0.29	1.34	0.60	1.82	-0.11	0.90	-0.30	0.74
Yrs. parents self-employed	—	—	-0.01	0.99	—	—	0.01	1.01
Worked in parents' business	-0.57	0.56	-0.89	0.41	1.08*	2.94	0.61	1.83
Yrs. worked in parents' business	—	—	0.04	1.04	—	—	0.05	1.05
Sex	0.60	1.82	0.68#	1.98	0.28	1.33	0.27	1.31
Education	0.07	1.07	0.07	1.08	0.00	1.00	0.00	1.00
Age	-0.05**	0.95	-0.05*	0.95	-0.02	0.97	-0.03	0.97
Married	-0.99	0.37	-0.95	0.39	-0.82	0.44	-0.81	0.44
Own other business	0.70*	2.01	0.72#	2.05	-0.49	0.61	-0.49	0.61
Hours spent on housework/childcare	-0.02	0.98	-0.02	0.98	-0.02*	0.97	-0.02*	0.98
Intercept	3.46	—	3.26	—	3.44	—	3.46	—
R^2	0.10**	—	0.11**	—	0.08**	—	0.08*	—
N	229		229		229		228	

Notes: ** $p = .01$; * $p = .05$; # $p = .10$.

307

Because our sample consists of relatively successful businesses (i.e., the majority had been alive for at least one year) we are not able to say anything about businesses that fail early on in their life cycle. It is possible that those failed businesses were more heavily funded by parents, but if this is the case it would be hard to argue that wealth transfer results in successful business operations. In general, then, we would conclude that businesses that survive beyond the first critical year do not appear to receive substantial capital from parents.

Entrepreneurial Capital

We hypothesized that a more important resource than financial capital is the entrepreneurial capital that self-employed parents may provide their offspring. We use the term entrepreneurial capital to include the attitudes, values, and skills that are relevant to business ownership. Our study provides information on the development of several types of entrepreneurial capital: childhood exposure to a self-employed lifestyle, work experience alongside one's parents, taking jobs with managerial responsibility, and the development of an entrepreneurial work ethic.

On average, the self-employed parents of our respondents owned their businesses for almost 28 years (standard deviation of 16 years), with only 16.5 percent in business less than 10 years, as shown in Table 3. Such stability is rather unusual, given high failure rates among new and small businesses, and the long periods of ownership give us an opportunity to assess whether exposure to self-employment affects children's behavior.[4] Business ownership of long duration seems to fit well with Goldthorpe's (1980) speculations about families that are well-placed to sustain a tradition of self-employment. About 84 percent of our respondents were 21 or under for at least some of the years during which their parents owned a business, as shown in Table 3. Almost 63 percent lived for 10 years or more with parents who were running a business. Thus, a high proportion of the children of business owners lived under conditions where it would have been possible for them to see first-hand the rewards, and the demands, of an entrepreneurial lifestyle.

Exposure to an entrepreneurial lifestyle while children are living at home, however, may not teach them the attitudes and values necessary to carry on the entrepreneurial tradition within a family. Accordingly, we examined whether our respondents had worked in their parents' businesses, when they had started, and how long they had worked. As shown in Table 3, 61 percent of the respondents whose parents owned businesses had worked in the business. Moreover, most began working at a very young age: almost a quarter started before they were 10, and over half had started working for their parents by the time they were 15. Only 15.4 percent began working for their parents after they turned 20.

Even though most of the employed children started at a young age, very few stayed in the business as either a career or, eventually, as the owner. About 29.5 percent stayed less than five years, and 51.3 percent left after their ninth year. Only 11.5 percent reported they worked 20 years or more for their parents, even though many more had the opportunity to do so. Of the 62 respondents whose parents owned a business for 20 years or more, only nine worked in the business for 20 years or more. Thus, although a majority of the children whose parents owned a business began working in it at a fairly young age, the work was short term and most left for other jobs before they turned 21.

Living with parents who own a business, or working for them, is significant for an analysis of social mobility only insofar as children in such circumstances are socialized differently. We did not interview the parents of our respondents, and we did not ask our respondents to describe their childhood for us. Thus, our evidence of the consequences of a presumably privileged childhood is necessarily indirect. We examined two sets of indicators of parental influence on entrepreneurial capital: the route our respondents had followed into business ownership, and their current work habits.

Was the route to business ownership different for those children whose parents owned businesses, compared to those whose parents did not? We asked respondents about the last two jobs they held, before assuming ownership of their current business For the two jobs, we asked whether they had managerial or ownership responsibility.

In their most recent jobs, prior to becoming an owner, the children of self-employed parents were absolutely indistinguishable from wage- and salary-earning parents, as shown in Table 4. For both sets of respondents, slightly more than one-fourth had held nonmanagerial jobs, about one-fifth had been business owners (of a business they had subsequently left), and the rest had held jobs with managerial responsibility. The average number of people supervised on their last managerial job was also almost the same for the two groups—13 for the children of self-employed parents and 15 for others. For their next-to-last job, respondents whose parents were self-employed were only slightly more likely to have held jobs with managerial responsibility (which includes ownership—we did not distinguish between managerial and owner responsibility for that job), and the difference is not statistically significant.

In future papers we will conduct a multivariate analysis of career paths, but introducing controls could not materially change the results in Table 4. Within our sample of small and medium-sized enterprises, the recent employment history of business owners reveals that children of self-employed parents followed fundamentally similar paths to other future owners. Some owned a previous business, some held nonmanagerial jobs, and most were gaining managerial experience in a business owned by someone other than their parents. Based on the numbers of people they were supervising, the level of responsibility delegated to the future owners did not differ by their parents' status.

Our final analysis of the potential entrepreneurial capital gained by the children of self-employed parents involves examining the work habits of our respondents. Following Kohn (1981; Kohn and Schooler 1978), we hypothesized that children of parents in jobs permitting a high degree of self-direction might be disciplined in ways encouraging self-control, self-sacrifice, and valuing hard work for long-term goals. We therefore looked to see if, in fact, the children of self-employed parents were putting in longer hours than other owners.

We asked our respondents how many hours, on average, they worked per week; whether they worked evenings; and whether they worked on weekends. Building explanatory models for variations in working style poses a substantial difficulty for a sample of business owners, as this group is already putting in more hours than other workers: on average they were working almost 53 hours per week; 79 percent reported they sometimes worked in the evening; and 80 percent reported they occasionally worked on weekends. In a random sample of workers, business owners would stand out because their self-employed status would be a major predictor of time spent at work. Within our more homogeneous sample, we cannot expect to explain as much of the variation in their working style as we could in a more heterogeneous sample.

Using ordinary least squares regression, we examined whether parents' self-employment and working in a parent's business made a significant contribution to weekly hours worked, net of some factors that might also affect working hours: sex, education, age, marital status, owning another business, and hours spent per week on housework and childcare. As shown in the first column of Table 5, which reports unstandardized regression coefficients for equation (1), neither having self-employed parents nor having worked in a parent's business has a significant impact on hours worked. Age has a substantial negative affect, while hours spent on housework and childcare clearly were subtracted from hours spent on the business.

In equation (2) we added two indicators of the *intensity* of possible parental socialization and training of children: the number of years parents had owned businesses, and the number of years the respondent had worked in the businesses. Neither of these variables significantly affected the number of hours worked. Parental self-employment itself is still not significant, nor is working in the parents' business.

Equations (3) and (4) give the results of a logistic regression in which a dummy variable for evening work—coded 0 for *not* working evenings and 1 for working evenings—is regressed on the same predictors as in equations (1) and (2). Parental self-employment and work experience in parents' businesses are not significant in either the baseline equation or the expanded equation, with the duration of possible socialization experiences taken into account. Owning another business roughly doubles the odds of working evenings. By contrast, aging lowers the odds of working evenings.

Equations (5) and (6) present results of a logistic regression for weekend work, coded as a dummy variable, using the same variables as in equations (3) and (4). Again, having self-employed parents has no impact on whether owners worked weekends. However, having worked in a parent's business roughly triples the odds of working weekends, suggesting a possible long-term effect from such experience. Adding the two indicators for the duration of each potential socialization experience only has the effect of reducing the zero-order effect of working in a parent's business to statistical insignificance. The only significant control variable in equations (5) and (6) is hours spent on housework and childcare, which reduces the odds of working on weekends.

Our analysis of the possible influence of self-employed parents on their children's work habits fails to confirm our hypothesis. Out of six possible coefficients for the effects of either having self-employed parents or working in their firm, none is statistically significant. Of the six possible coefficients for the effects of the duration of socialization experiences, again only one is statistically significant. Within our sample of small and medium-sized firms, conditions associated with owners' life-course circumstances are more consequential than their social origins: age and having household and childcare responsibilities are critically important.

Summary of Entrepreneurial Capital

We have found only weak and inconclusive support for our hypothesis that entrepreneurial capital is more important for the children of self-employed parents than financial or physical capital. Without question, given the length of time their parents were business owners, the respondents in our study had ample opportunity to observe the role requirements of an entrepreneurial life, as well as to sample its advantages and disadvantages. The great majority experienced an entrepreneurial lifestyle during their childhood and adolescence, and more than half worked for at least a few years in their parents' business.

Nonetheless, very few worked in their parents' firms when they reached adulthood, and by their mid-twenties, most had struck out on their own. Most of the owners not only finished high school but attended college (under the Canadian system), and the majority have at least some university education. Formal education and work experience in businesses other than their parents' added to these future owners' entrepreneurial capital, and with our research design, we face great difficulties in attributing current capital specifically to self-employed parents. Tracing back through the past two jobs held by our respondents, we found that the offspring of self-employed parents were evidently on the same track as others. Our indicator of a strong entrepreneurial work ethic—putting in long hours, during the week and on evenings and weekends—failed to separate the children of self-employed parents from others. Instead, our results imply what previous studies have also argued—the constraints of the small and medium-sized business niche within capitalist economies keep all business owners on their toes, cutting into family time and gradually wearing down those owners who continue to manage their firms as they near retirement age.

CONCLUSIONS

We have taken up the challenge posed by Wong (1990, P. 571), in his analysis of cross-national variation in occupational mobility, who noted that, "The family plays a dynamic role in the intergeneralizational transmission of status, possibly via other institutions such as the educational system....Of course, families are not always successful in transferring status either directly or indirectly. Future research should investigate how and why certain societies are more successful in one form of transmission than another." Within the limits of our sample—selected because they were already in business—we tested hypotheses about the various modes by which self-employed parents could have affected their children's life chances.

Summary

Many studies have found a high degree of occupational inheritance between propertied families and their children, posing a puzzle for theories of modernization that predict a decline in inheritable positions in industrial societies. Most investigators have been content to merely speculate about causes of the high rate of persistence of self-employment and business ownership across generations. We chose instead to probe more deeply into the possible resources that self-employed parents may provide to their children.

We identified two kinds of resources: (1) physical and financial capital, either via passing on an operating business or making loans and gifts that make possible a business startup, and (2) entrepreneurial capital, encompassing the traditional notion of "human capital" but focusing specifically on attitudes, values, skills, and emotions that are relevant to business ownership. Our analysis of these two kinds of resources was guided by two hypotheses, based on our literature review: (H1) that financial and physical capital will play a minor role in business ownership among children of self-employed parents, and (H2) that entrepreneurial capital will play a more significant role than financial capital in business ownership among children of self-employed parents. We found substantial support for the first hypothesis, but little support for the second hypothesis.

With respect to Hypothesis 1, few owners acquired their businesses via inheritance or purchase from their parents, with more owners bringing in parents as co-owners than borrowing capital from them. Most raised the capital they needed from other sources, rather than drawing upon family resources. We found only a 16 percent gap between the children of self-employed parents and other owners in the total array of resources derived from parents. Moreover, very few owners had any financial help from their parents, self-employed or otherwise.

For Hypothesis 2, we found that the great majority of owners of self-employed parents had first-hand experience with an entrepreneurial lifestyle during their childhood and adolescence. Not only did they live in a business-owner's family, but they also worked alongside their parents, at least for a few years. Thus, the conditions were suitable for the acquisition of entrepreneurial capital from their parents. However, the children of self-employed parents were no more likely to have held immediately prior managerial jobs than other owners in the sample. Children of self-employed parents also were indistinguishable from others in their willingness to work long hours, nights and weekends, in the service of their firm. Gaining managerial experience and being willing to work long hours are clearly ways of accumulating entrepreneurial capital, but these avenues are not the exclusive province of children whose parents were business owners.

Because our data are inflow, or recruitment, rather than outflow, or inheritance data, we cannot examine the effects on parental characteristics on the propensity of their children to enter self-employment. Obviously, outflow data would allow us to address whether self-employed parents pass on the desire to be self-employed, whether or not they help their children achieve these goals. We can, however, speculate on this with the data we have. Specifically, we asked our respondents whether they had siblings, and over 90 percent reported that they did, with no significant difference between those with self-employed parents and the others. For those who had siblings, 50 percent reported that they had siblings who currently owned a business. There was a slight difference ($p = .10$) between those with self-employed parents (55%) and those without (42%). This result mostly supports the idea that preference for self-employment is learned from one's parents. However it also suggests that there is considerable permeability in the entrepreneurial ranks.

Implications

Our findings have several implications for future research on the extent to which one relatively privileged class position in industrial societies—owners of small and medium-sized businesses—is successful in passing on resources that enable their children to maintain their privileged position. We believe that property barriers are *not* an explanation for the high rate of occupational inheritance among the self-employed. First, we argued that life course constraints make inheritance of parents' businesses quite difficult, and our results confirm that few children take over their parents' firms. The low rate of direct inheritance of a family business is understandable from a life course perspective, given the low probability of several necessary events occurring within a fairly narrow window of opportunity. Neither owning a business nor having children is sufficient to ensure intergenerational transmission of ownership. Parents must not only found or purchase a business, but also maintain it as a viable entity until their children are of an age when they can manage the business. Moreover, if income from the business is not sufficient to support both the parents and the children, then the children must either wait until the parents retire or take over the business prior to their parents' retirement and try to increase its profits so that multiple generations can be supported. Even if income from the business is sufficient to support parents and children, many studies of family firms have shown that parents are often extremely reluctant to give up ownership until they are of retirement age. By that point, their children have, in all likelihood, made substantial investments in other careers and are therefore hesitant to take over their parents' business. Accordingly, we would be very surprised if direct inheritance of business ownership figured very heavily in the reproduction of the propertied classes. While class analysts imply that direct status inheritance must go on among the self-employed, our results suggest that one must look elsewhere for an explanation of occupational inheritance among the self-employed.

Second, given the low capital requirements for the great majority of business startups, transfer of wealth from parents to children is unnecessary to ensure ownership among the children. Our findings show that self-employed parents were no more likely to loan money to the businesses of their children in our sample than were other parents. With the widespread availability of alternative forms of credit in advanced capitalist economies, parental wealth is relatively insignificant except, perhaps, for the truly elite group at the very top of the financial pyramid (Aldrich forthcoming). But sociological analyses of mobility are not really about such people. For the ordinary propertied classes, the capital required to own a business is obtained from jobs and other personal resources.

Third, entrepreneurial capital—which is nonfinancial—can be obtained through many sources, only one of which is self-employed parents. Our results show that self-employed parents had ample opportunity to socialize their children into an entrepreneurial way of life, but few were able to keep the adult children in the family business. Most children went on to colleges and universities, and then to jobs with managerial responsibility, acquiring along the way many of the skills, and probably the attitudes, needed to create and manage (if not to succeed in) businesses. Entrepreneurial capital, as we have defined it, cannot be easily monopolized, and we found that owners whose parents were not self-employed also have acquired it.

Fourth, we are left with a daunting challenge. If inherited financial and physical capital do not account for business ownership among the children of self-employed parents, and entrepreneurial capital is widely available from other sources, why should parental self-employment raise at all the likelihood of their children's entering self-employment? Robinson (1984; Robinson and Garnier 1985) suggested that fathers hand over the businesses and/or provide capital to their sons. We find little evidence of this. Instead, we suspect that the answer to increased likelihood of becoming self-employed lies in a more subtle and sophisticated conception of entrepreneurial capital, and a better understanding of the life course of people who become business owners. Most children of self-employed parents are exposed to an entrepreneurial life during their childhood and adolescence. During those impressionable years, exposure to a self-employed lifestyle and working alongside their parents could have had a fundamental influence on their personalities. Over the course of their adult lifetime, they will be repeatedly exposed to entrepreneurial opportunities, as is the rest of the population. If their propensity to respond is only slightly but significantly higher than other adults, we predict that by the end of their working careers, it is likely that they will have had more spells of self-employment than other adults. Testing this proposition would require information not only on the work histories of adults, but also on events during their formative years.

ACKNOWLEDGMENTS

An earlier version of this paper was presented at the 1997 American Sociological Association meetings. The research reported in this paper was funded by the Social Sciences and Humanities Research Council of Canada (SSHRC Grant No. 412-93-0005). We would like to acknowledge Jennifer Cliff and Jane Olsen for their numerous contributions to the project, Allen Lehman, Jodi McFarlane, John Oesch, and Indira Prahst for their assistance in data collection, and Amy Ewert for her help with data entry. We would also like to thank Ted Baker, Amanda Brickman Elam, Lisa Keister, Kevin Leicht, Jeremy Reynolds, Rachel Rosenfeld, Mark Western, and Raymond Wong for helpful comments on an earlier draft of this paper.

NOTES

1.   Goldthorpe, Lockwood, Bechhofer, and Platt (1969), for example, in their widely cited study of workers in Luton, focused on issues of *embourgeoisement* and alienation, rather than the availability of workers for collective class-based action.

2.   While Bills (1997) shows that franchises are an intermediate step between salaried employment and self-employment, our data do not indicate this. When respondents were asked whether they owned previous businesses, very few mentioned franchises.

3.   This response rate was calculated by dividing the number of completed interviews by the number of people who were interviewed, who refused to participate, and who did not respond to our faxes after repeated attempts.

4.   We did not collect data on number of businesses owned by parents, or whether there were cycles of start-up and failure. Obviously this information could provide further insight into the lessons these entrepreneurs learned from their parents.

REFERENCES

Aldrich, H.E. forthcoming. *Organizations Evolving*. London: Sage.
Aldrich, H.E., A.B. Elam, and P.R. Reese. 1996. "Strong Ties, Weak Ties, and Strangers: Do Women Business Owners Differ from Men in Their Use of Networking to Obtain Assistance?" Pp. 1-25 in *Entrepreneurship in a Global Context*, edited by S. Birley and I. MacMillan. London: Routledge Ltd.

Aldrich, H.E., and T. Sakano. 1995. "Unbroken Ties: How the Personal Networks of Japanese Business Owners Compare to Those in Other Nations." In *Networks and Markets: Pacific Rim Investigations*, edited by M. Fruin. New York: Oxford Press.

Aldrich, H.E., J. Cater, T. Jones, and D. McEvoy. 1983. "From Periphery to Peripheral: The South Asian Petite Bourgeoisie in England." Pp. 1-32 in *Research in the Sociology of Work*, Vol. 2, edited by I.H. Simpson and R. Simpson. Greenwich, CT: JAI Press.

Aldrich, H.E., A.L. Kalleberg, P.V. Marsden, and J. Cassell. 1989. " In Pursuit of Evidence: Strategies for Locating New Businesses." *Journal of Business Venturing*, 4 (November): 367-386.

Aldrich, H.E., C. Zimmer, and T. Jones. 1986. "Small Business Still Speaks with the Same Voice: A Replication of 'The Voice of Small Business and the Politics of Survival.'" *Sociological Review* 34(May): 335-356.

Bechhofer, F., and B. Elliott. 1985. "The Petite Bourgeoisie in Late Capitalism." *Annual Review of Sociology* 11: 181-207.

Becker, G.S., and N. Tomes. 1986. "Human Capital and the Rise and Fall of Families." *Journal of Labor Economics* 4(3) (Part 2, July): S1-S39.

Bills, D.B. 1997. " A Community of Interests: Evolving Relationships Between Franchisors and Franchisees." Paper presented at the 1997 Midwest Sociological Society Meetings, Des Moines Iowa.

Blau, P.M., and O.D. Duncan. 1967. *The American Occupational Structure*. New York: The Free Press.

Bourdieu, P. 1987. "What Makes a Social Class? On the Theoretical and Practical Existence of Groups." *Berkeley Journal of Sociology* 32: 1-17.

Carroll, G.R., and E. Mosakowski. 1987. "The Career Dynamics of Self-Employment." *Administrative Science Quarterly* 32(4) (December): 570-589.

Dunn, T., and D. Holtz-Eakin. 1996. "Financial Capital, Human Capital, and the Transition to Self-Employment: Evidence from Intergenerational Links." Working Paper 5622. Cambridge, MA, National Bureau of Economic Research.

Elder, G., and A.M. O'Rand. 1995. " Adult Lives in a Changing Society." Pp. 452-475 in *Sociological Perspectives on Social Psychology*, edited by K.S. Cook, G.A. Fine, and J.S. House. Boston: Allyn and Bacon.

ENSR. 1993. "The European Observatory for SMEs: First Annual Report." Zoetermeer, The Netherlands: European Observatory for SME Research and EIM Small Business Research and Consultancy.

Fairlie, R.W. 1994. "The Absence of the African-American Owned Business: An Analysis of the Dynamics of Self-Employment." Center for Urban Affairs and Policy Research Working Paper No. 94-9, Northwestern University.

Goldthorpe, J.H. 1980. *Social Mobility & Class Structure in Modern Britain*. Oxford: Clarendon Press.

Goldthorpe, J.H., D. Lockwood, F. Bechhofer, and J. Platt. 1969. *The Affluent Worker in the Class Structure*. London: Cambridge University Press.

Granovetter, M. 1993. "The Nature of Economic Relationships." Pp. 3-41 in *Explorations in Economic Sociology*, edited by R. Swedberg. New York: Russell Sage Foundation.

Hout, M. 1989. *Following in Father's Footsteps: Social Mobility in Ireland*. Cambridge, MA: Harvard University Press.

Joppke, C. 1986. "The Cultural Dimensions of Class Formation and Class Struggle: On the Social Theory of Pierre Bourdieu." *Berkeley Journal of Sociology* 31: 53-78.

Kalleberg, A., and K. Leicht. 1991. "Gender and Organizational Performance: Determinants of Small Business Survival and Success." *Academy of Management Journal* 34(1) (March): 136-161.

Kohn, M.L. 1981. "Personality, Occupation, and Social Stratification: A Frame of Reference." *Research in Social Stratification and Mobility* 1: 267-297.

Kohn, M.L., and C. Schooler. 1978. "The Reciprocal Effects of the Substantive Complexity of Work and Intellectual Flexibility: A Longitudinal Assessment." *American Sociological Review* 38: 97-118.

Lentz, B.S., and D.N. Laband. 1990. "Entrepreneurial Success and Occupational Inheritance among Proprietors." *Canadian Journal of Economics* 23 (August): 563-579.

———. 1993. "Like Father, Like Son: Toward an Economic Theory of Occupational Following." *Southern Economic Journal* 50(2): 474-493.

Lipset, S.M., and R. Bendix. 1959. *Social Mobility in Industrial Society.* Berkeley: University of California Press.

Myles, J.F., and A.B. Sorensen. 1975. "Elite and Status Attainment Models of Inequality of Opportunity." *The Canadian Journal of Sociology* 1(1): 75-88.

Robinson, R.V. 1984. "Reproducing Class Relations in Industrial Capitalism." *American Sociological Review* 49(2) (April): 182-196.

Robinson, R.V., and M.A. Garnier. 1985. "Class Reproduction among Men and Women in France: Reproduction Theory on Its Home Ground." *American Journal of Sociology* 91(2) (September): 250-280.

Selz, M. 1996. "Entrepreneurship in U.S. is Taking Off." *Wall Street Journal*, December 13, p. B15A.

Small Business Administration. 1994. *Handbook of Small Business Data.* Office of Advocacy, Small Business Administration. Washington, DC: U.S. Government Printing Office.

Small Business Administration. 1983. *The State of Small Business: A Report of the President.* Washington, DC: U.S. Government Printing Office.

Stier, H., and D.B. Grusky. 1990. "An Overlapping Persistence Model of Career Mobility." *American Sociological Review* 55(5) (October): 736-756.

U.S. Department of Commerce. 1987. Bureau of the Census. *Characteristics of Business Owners.* Washington, DC: U.S. Government Printing Office.

Western, M., and E.O. Wright. 1994. "The Permeability of Class Boundaries to Intergenerational Mobility Among Men in the United States, Canada, Norway and Sweden." *American Sociological Review* 59: 606-629.

Wong, R.S-K. 1990. "Understanding Cross-National Variation in Occupational Mobility." *American Sociological Review* 55(4) (August): 560-573.

———. 1992. "Vertical and Nonvertical Effects in Class Mobility: Cross-National Variations." *American Sociological Review* 57(3) (June): 396-410).

Zimmer, C., and H.E. Aldrich. 1987. " Resource Mobilization Through Ethnic Networks: Kinship and Friendship Ties of Shopkeepers in England." *Sociological Perspectives* 30: 422-455.

A LIFE COURSE PERSPECTIVE ON OCCUPATIONAL INHERITANCE: SELF-EMPLOYED PARENTS AND THEIR CHILDREN

Howard E. Aldrich and Phillip H. Kim

ABSTRACT

Using a life course perspective, we develop a theoretical model of how parents can influence their children's propensity to enter self-employment. We draw on the sociological, economic, psychological, and behavioral genetics literatures to develop a model in which parental influence occurs in different ways, depending on someone's stage in their life course. We review and summarize existing findings for parental influences on entrepreneurial entry using a three-part life course framework: childhood, adolescence, and adulthood. We also analyze new data from the Panel Study of Entrepreneurial Dynamics on the extent to which children were involved in their parents' businesses. From our review, we propose strong effects from genetic inheritances and parenting practice (during childhood); moderate effects from reinforcement of work values and vocational interests (during adolescence); and little influence from financial support but stronger effects from other tangible means of support (during adulthood).

The Sociology of Entrepreneurship
Research in the Sociology of Organizations, Volume 25, 33–82
Copyright © 2007 by Elsevier Ltd.
All rights of reproduction in any form reserved
ISSN: 0733-558X/doi:10.1016/S0733-558X(06)25002-X

33

HOWARD E. ALDRICH AND PHILLIP H. KIM

INTRODUCTION

Since the pioneering studies of social mobility in the 1950s, sociologists have shown that children tend to choose occupations that are very similar to those of their parents. Self-employed professionals and farmers are especially likely to have children following in their footsteps, but that tendency has been muted by the disappearance of solo professional practices and family farms. The term "occupational inheritance" was coined as a general label for this tendency, although strictly speaking, most studies of the intergenerational transmission have been of occupational status, rather than of specific occupational choices. Some sociologists have focused on the intergenerational transmission of occupational status because of their interest in patterns of inequality and stratification in modern societies, whereas others have been more interested in what occupational inheritance tells us about the importance of human capital and wealth for occupational choices.[1]

In this paper, we focus on one occupational status, self-employment, rather than the more general issue of occupational inheritance. We are especially interested in exploring why the sons and daughters of self-employed parents have a heightened tendency to attempt entrepreneurship (and thus become self-employed) at some point during their working careers.[2] Cross-national studies of self-employment and entrepreneurship over the past few decades have repeatedly confirmed this pattern, and theorists have offered a broad variety of explanations for it. Although we focus narrowly on self-employment, we draw on the larger literature on social mobility and occupational attainment to provide concepts and principles for our review.

We offer a life course perspective on work careers as a framework for integrating previous work and generating new propositions, building on previous researchers who used diverse data sets, different analytic approaches, and focused mainly on adults. By taking a long-term view of parent–child relationships, we turn a critical eye on the literature, revealing gaps and suggesting new research directions. A unique feature of our review is the addition of the concept of nascent entrepreneur to a model of occupational inheritance among the self-employed. A great deal of research on self-employment conflates selection into entrepreneurship with survival in that status, whereas we propose keeping the two states analytically distinct.

Our paper is organized as follows. First, we suggest a number of reasons for why sociologists ought to care about such links. Second, we propose a life course model of occupational attainment and apply it to work careers and self-employment. We break the life course into semi-discrete segments for ease of exposition: childhood and adolescence, adolescence into adulthood, and adult status. Because no single data set covers all the points we wish to make, we draw on many. We rely heavily on two data sets in which we were principal investigators: a study of business owners in British Columbia and a national study of nascent entrepreneurs in the United States.

WHY CARE ABOUT PARENT TO CHILD OCCUPATIONAL TRANSMISSION?

Analysts have offered at least three reasons for focusing our attention on the issue of occupational inheritance among the self-employed. First, *inequalities* of income, wealth, and power characterize nearly all societies, but the extent to which such inequalities persist over generations varies widely across societies and over time. Sociologists refer to the persistence of intergenerational inequality as *stratification*: the degree to which families and their offspring remain in roughly the same level in the hierarchy of inequality over time. In a highly stratified society, origins and destinations are highly correlated. Thus, studying occupational inheritance can provide a clue to the open or closed nature of a society's reward structure (Rytina, 1992).

Second, studies of occupational inheritance can identify the sources of values and attitudes that prove useful to entrepreneurs. Miller and Swanson's (1958) oft-cited Detroit Area Study of parenting practices claimed that youth could be imprinted with "bureaucratic" or "entrepreneurial" values by their parents. Kohn and Schooler's (1983) research on parenting practices associated with different parental work environments also suggested that parents could induce predispositions in youth toward particular kinds of occupations, such as a desire for autonomous work. The child's preference for such work might then be fulfilled by self-employment. We thus have theoretical as well as policy-oriented reasons for studying occupational inheritance among the self-employed.

Third, a society's degree of occupational inheritance sheds light on the importance of educational experiences during childhood, adolescence, and even adulthood. Questions arise such as, "does more training in entrepreneurial practices among youth result in more adults becoming self-employed?" To the extent that education and work experience moderate the link between parental origins and children's occupational destinations, it is human capital, rather than parental self-employment, that enables people to enter self-employment.[3] Thus, governments wishing to sever the link between social origins and destinations would be advised to invest heavily in the education and training of young people.

A LIFE COURSE PERSPECTIVE ON WORK AND CAREERS

In this section we present a brief overview of the life course perspective. We draw on the work of Elder (1999) to explain the principles underlying the perspective. Full application of the life course perspective to an empirical question makes huge demands on research designs and analyses. Accordingly, in our subsequent review we note the strengths and weaknesses of the data sets that we draw upon.

The Life Course Perspective

The life course perspective has developed across a variety of social and behavioral sciences during the past three decades and refers to the social patterning of events and roles over a person's life span, a process shaped by the interaction of individuals' behaviors and changing historical contexts. Temporal organization is embedded in people's work histories and careers, making the life course perspective especially suited for examining the cumulative effects of career choices. In all capitalist societies, work constitutes an important context for the expression and further development of people's identities and knowledge. Elder (1999) noted four primary principles of the life course perspective.

First, individuals' life trajectories are embedded in and shaped by their experiences of historical times and places over their entire lifetimes. Individuals develop their skills and expectations within specific socio-historical contexts. Second, the developmental impacts of life transitions and events are contingent on when they occur in people's lives. For example, the impact of an event such as parents starting their own businesses may depend on whether it occurs in someone's childhood, adolescence, or adulthood. Third, social and historical influences on individual development are mediated through networks of shared relationships and linked lives. As they move through their lives, individuals take on some roles and give up others, and these roles link them to important others in their environments. Fourth, the life course perspective assumes that people play a constructionist role in shaping their own life course. Within the constraints and opportunities of changing historical circumstances, individuals make choices and take actions that shape their own life courses. The perspective is not deterministic.

The life course perspective on work careers focuses on issues of timing, and the interaction between individuals' actions and environmental contingencies. It assumes no single fixed cycle or set of stages. For example, workers' likelihood of entering self-employment depends in part on the strength of their attachment to current employers. Individuals enter the labor force in their late teens or early twenties and remain until reaching retirement age or becoming disabled. Depending on their occupations, they may thus be in the labor force for three to five decades, although many interrupt their work careers with spells of other activities, such as unemployment, child rearing, or further education and training (Rosenfeld, 1992). Younger individuals change jobs frequently: in January 2004, median employee tenure was only 2.9 years for workers 25–34, whereas it was approximately four years for the entire workforce. Older workers averaged much longer tenure: 9.6 years for workers ages 55–64 (US Department of Labor, 2004). Age and job tenure are thus quite strongly associated, partially accounting for the curvilinear relationship between aging and becoming an entrepreneur.

Importance of History

In his various reviews of the perspective, Elder has painted an expansive and complex view of life course explanations for individual development. Understanding how and why adults select entrepreneurship as a career option thus requires that we take account of workers' social origins, family environment, early work experiences, proximate opportunities, and many other factors. Historical influences lie at the heart of the perspective and may be classified into three types of effects: cohort, period, and maturation or aging.

Aging or maturation effects, as defined by demographers, describe the secular process of aging. For example, Evans and Leighton (1989) found that transition probabilities into self-employment did not increase as people aged, but people did remain in self-employment for longer spells. Consequently, the likelihood of being self-employed rose with age. Uusitalo (2001) found a similar pattern for Finland, with the entry rate constant at 1.5 percent up until age 40 and then declining slightly to a constant 1 percent until retirement. A *cohort effect* occurs when historical events have a differential impact on younger versus older persons. For example, younger children, especially boys, were most adversely affected by the economic strains of the Great

38   HOWARD E. ALDRICH AND PHILLIP H. KIM

Depression in the 1930s and this might have colored their view of the importance of security in choosing an occupation such as shopkeeper (Elder,
1999). Similarly, desperation led many middle-aged men to attempt
self-employment during the Great Depression. A *period effect* occurs when
historical events have similar consequences on different age cohorts. For
example, the Internet explosion of the 1990s and the resulting dot com bubble were so intense that they affected all age groups' propensities to enter
entrepreneurship, raising the entrepreneurial entry rate to an historic high.

Fig. 1 shows a simple schematic diagram of the time span encompassed by
a comprehensive application of the life course perspective to entrepreneurial
entry. For ease of exposition, we have broken the life course into three
segments: childhood, adolescence, and adulthood. In subsequent sections,
we will discuss each segment separately. In keeping with the life course view,
the picture we have drawn is contextual, contingent, and social, and posits
that individuals play an active role in constructing their work careers. For
example, for children, their family determines their genetic makeup and
their nurturing environment. As adolescents, children begin playing an

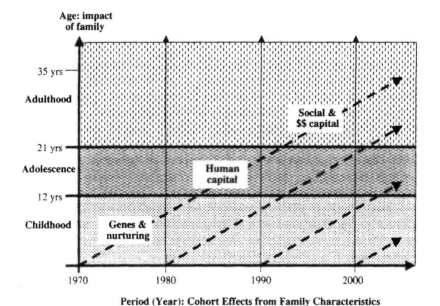

Fig. 1.   Lifecourse Perspective of Parental Influences on Entrepreneurial Entry.

active role in choosing compatible peer groups and those peers often become influential enough to displace the primary role of the family.

Relevant Research: Data Sets

A life course perspective on work careers poses severe demands on analysts. To fully capture the historically contingent nature of person–environment interactions, a research design should follow people over a lengthy period and include a substantial number of individual, family, and contextual measures. We uncovered no data sets that met the most stringent tests for a life course analysis of entry into entrepreneurship. Instead, we found data sets that did reasonably well on a few key criteria: (1) clear sampling design, (2) truly longitudinal or very good retrospective information, and (3) adequate controls for important covariates. Table 1 presents a few details on the studies we will mention often in our review. Although Arum and Mueller's (2004) edited book is a compendium of multiple studies, we also include it in Table 1 because we make several references to it in our review.

In the second column we show the years in which data collection occurred, and in parentheses the years covered by the retrospective questions asked in the surveys. We only searched for English language publications and thus most of the studies cover North America and Great Britain, with a few others from Northern European nations. In the fourth column, we note whether the study used a retrospective or a prospective panel design. Seven of the 15 studies are based on surveys in which people were asked retrospective questions about their lives, and seven are panel studies in which information was collected prospectively about people, either through interviews or archival information. People were then followed over time for at least one more wave of data collection.

From a life course perspective, five of the seven longitudinal studies have the undesirable property of being based on one or more fixed cohorts of individuals. Accordingly, researchers have difficultly separating out "aging" from "cohort/period" effects in most of the longitudinal studies. However, they do permit investigators to calculate transition probabilities. In retrospective designs, investigators are usually limited to analyze inflow/outflow statistics, although if complete work histories are collected, the information can be broken into spells (Carroll & Mosakowski, 1987). The studies also differ widely in how they defined "self-employment." For example, Sørensen (2006) only counted employers with employees, whereas Uusitalo (2001) included anyone reporting self-employment earnings or membership in a self-employment pension scheme and Burke et al. (2000) included all

Table 1. Studies of Occupational Inheritance.

Authors	Dates of Data Collection and (Years Covered, if Retrospective)	Nation(s)	Data Description
Retrospective			
Aldrich et al. (1998)	1994 (1921–1994)	Canada	229 small business owners in Vancouver area
Carroll and Mosakowski (1987)	1979 (1929–1979)	West Germany	West German life history study: Three birth cohorts
Fairlie (1999)	1996	USA	Characteristics of business owners
Gartner et al. (2004)	1999 (?–1999)	USA	PSED
Hout and Rosen (2000)	1973–1996 (1909–1996)	USA	Pooled GSS surveys
Lentz and Laband (1990)	1979 (?–1979)	USA	Study of 514 NFIB members
Taylor (1996)	1991 (?–1991)	Great Britain	British Household Panel Study
Panel			
Arum and Mueller (2004)	1980–2002	12 industrialized countries	Time period studied varies with country
Burke, FitzRoy, and Nolan (2000)	1958–1991 (1958–1991)	Great Britain	National Child Development Study: single cohort born in 1958
De Wit and Van Winden (1989)	1952–1983 (1939–1983)	The Netherlands	Single Cohort of 6th grade students
Dunn and Holtz-Eakin	1966–1982 (1942–1982)	USA (men only)	National longitudinal surveys of labor market experience: 10-year cohort (born in 1942–1952)
Evans and Leighton (1989)	1966–1981 (1942–1981)	USA (men only)	Series of 2-wave panels from national longitudinal survey of men
Sorensen (this volume)	1980–1997	Denmark	Three cohorts of Danish-born children (born 1966–1968)
Van Praag and Cramer (2001)	1952–1993 (1939–1993)	The Netherlands	Single cohort of 6th graders

those reporting self-employment as their main economic activity plus those who reported self-employment income and met three other conditions.

Most of these studies include very few measures from a respondent's pre-adult years, and thus we found only limited data from their childhood and adolescence. All of them, however, do report at least the occupation of the father when the child was growing up. Some also report the occupation of the mother. The panels begun when children were born or in primary school contain some personality and educational achievement information, but none provide information on parenting styles. Accordingly, in our review we draw upon other studies of children and adolescents that contain occupationally relevant information.

Most of these studies also include very few respondents from ethnic minority groups. Blacks, Hispanics, and other racial and ethnic groups were overlooked until the 1970s, when their growing political presence led to special government surveys of their business ownership. In their analysis of data from the 1973 through 1996 General Social Surveys, Hout and Rosen (2000) noted that Latino and black men were at a triple disadvantage with regard to self-employment. First, their fathers were less likely than others to be self-employed. Second, even if their fathers were self-employed, they were significantly less likely to become self-employed themselves, compared to other groups. Third, if their fathers were not self-employed, they were less likely than others with similar backgrounds to become self-employed. Using the Panel Study of Income Dynamics (PSID), Fairlie (1999) estimated that African-American men are one-third as likely to be self-employed as white men. He found that much of the gap arose from lower asset levels among blacks and their lower likelihood of having self-employed fathers. Thus, future research projects collecting data on occupational inheritance should over-sample African-Americans and Hispanics so that these issues can be pursued in more depth.

Parent to Child Transmission: Previous Findings

The data sets we have reviewed, plus several others, permit us to offer three empirical generalizations about the connection between parental self-employment and the self-employment of their sons and daughters. We break the research into three groups: inflow, outflow, and transition probability studies.

Inflow Studies
Inflow studies start with destination statuses – people who are currently self-employed – and examine the social origins of their parents. Most studies ask about parents' occupations when the respondent was 15 or 16 years of age or when they were growing up, but some simply ask if parents were ever self-employed. Studies consistently find that a high proportion of self-employed

people report that their parents were also self-employed. For example, Lentz and Laband (1990) found that 52 percent of the proprietors they surveyed had parents who were proprietors. Studies in Canada, the United States, and many European nations have found that about one-quarter to one-third of self-employed men report that their fathers were self-employed when they were growing up. When we expand the time frame to parental self-employment over their entire life course, we find that about half of the self-employed people report self-employed parents (Fairlie & Robb, 2005; Kim, Aldrich, & Keister, 2006).

Outflow Studies

In contrast to inflow studies, outflow studies start with origin statuses – people who are self-employed – and examine the destination occupations of their children. Beginning with occupational mobility studies in the 1950s, sociologists have found that children of self-employed parents are much more likely to be self-employed themselves than would be expected if destinations and origins were independent. For example, Blau and Duncan (1967) showed that the sons of self-employed professionals in the United States were about 12 times more likely to be self-employed professionals than expected by chance. The ratios of observed-to-expected frequencies were much lower for self-employed proprietors and farmers (2.3 and 3.2). Even when not choosing their father's exact occupation, they chose occupations that were similar in autonomy and prestige. For example, sons of proprietors were more likely to become managers and about as likely to become salaried professionals as they were to follow in their fathers' footsteps.

Transition Probability Studies

Inflow and outflow studies usually work with cross-sectional data, whereas transition probability studies examine the likelihood of someone transitioning to self-employment from another status and are based on repeated observations of the same individuals over time. Some examine only a worker's first transition into self-employment, whereas others examine all transitions and include measures of whether the worker previously had a spell of self-employment. The shortest time intervals typically involve panel studies over two years, whereas studies such as the PSID follow respondents over several decades.

Labor force and life course studies, using dynamic data, have consistently found that having self-employed parents (fathers more than mothers) raises the likelihood of transitioning into self-employment by two or three times the baseline rate, e.g. Dunn and Holtz-Eakin (2000). For example, in a collection of papers from 11 nations assembled by Arum and Mueller (2004), having a self-employed father typically raised the odds of a son transitioning to self-employment by a factor of between 1.3 and 2.2. Thus, at the extreme, the odds of entering self-employment were slightly more than doubled if a respondent's father had been self-employed. However, a more conservative estimate would be that father's self-employment raises the odds by about one-third. The effects differ substantially by whether the father was a professional, skilled, or unskilled self-employed person.

The Meaning of "Occupation" in Occupational Inheritance Research

We note several issues that cloud our ability to generalize from these data sets. First, occupational inheritance is not unique to the self-employed. Many other occupations show a disproportionate number of children taking up the same or a very similar occupation as their parents. Even though occupational inheritance can thus occur across the entire occupational spectrum, most researchers have been interested in intergenerational continuity among the more prestigious and highly rewarded occupations, such as lawyers, doctors, and business owners.

Second, most of the transition probability studies – the most technically sophisticated approach – measure only whether the parents were self-employed and do not include other aspects of the parents' occupations or social and psychological environments. For example, Hout and Rosen (2000) included a seven-category occupational coding scheme in their analysis, but nothing else. Thus, any features that "self-employment" shares as a social status with other occupations will be encompassed by this simple coding scheme. "Parent self-employed" could be tapping characteristics of the parents' socialization practices, social networks, financial assets, genomes, and so forth.[4]

Third, almost all sociological studies of intergenerational social mobility use measures of occupational status or prestige, not actual occupational destinations, as independent and dependent variables.[5] Fourth, the virtue of using occupational prestige as a marker of destination, rather than "self-employment," is that "prestige" captures the possibility that children will transition to similar but not identical occupations as their parents'. Even though the children of self-employed parents may never serve a spell as self-employed themselves, they may choose an occupation that is similar in many respects on dimensions such as autonomy, prestige, income potential, and so forth. If we are interested in the advantages self-employed parents provide for their children, then studies focusing only on a limited set of

occupations may cause us to miss many of the benefits derived from particular parental origins.

LIFE COURSE MODEL OF PARENTAL INFLUENCES ON CHILDREN'S SELF-EMPLOYMENT

From a life course perspective, processes of socialization and control extend
from childhood until old age, with succeeding generations linked by age-
graded role sequences and social roles. A person's experience within a particular sequence is historically and contextually dependent, with cumulative
advantages and disadvantages seamlessly altering transitions and turning
points. However, for presentation purposes, we have broken the life course
into three discrete segments: childhood, adolescence, and adulthood. For
each segment, we review the theoretical principles relevant to understanding
which causal forces affect someone's eventual transition into attempting self-
employment and succeeding in it. Because genetic endowments interact with
environmental factors to influence outcomes across all segments, we begin
with a discussion of genetic influences on childhood development. We note
that previous studies have tended to err on the side of attributing most of the
similarity in parents' and children's occupations to socio-economic factors.
We believe that research taking account of genetic influences establishes a
more balanced context within which to assess all forms of parental influence.

Genetic Influences: General Considerations

Over the past few decades, research on various developmental outcomes has
confirmed the importance of taking account of the genetic inheritance as
well as the social origins of people attaining certain occupations (Bouchard
& McGue, 2003; Shanahan & Hofer, 2005). When born, children possess a
plethora of innate genetic potentials as a result of genes inherited from their
parents.[6] Whether these potentials will be fully expressed depends upon the
environment in which children are raised. For example, in supportive environments, a child's potential with regard to intelligence has a high probability of being expressed, whereas in impoverished environments, the
potential may be suppressed. Thus, the realization of a child's genetic potential is highly conditioned by environmental factors. Note that this implies
an interaction between genes and environment, and not a simple additive
process, substantially complicating research on the topic.[7] Maccoby (2000),

in her critical review of behavioral genetics research on parents and children, made this point forcefully, arguing that we should not assume a zero-sum game between genes and environment.

To the extent that children and adolescents actively seek out conditions allowing them to develop their potential, the impact of favorable environments is amplified.[8] Poorer environments suppress the potential range of genetic variation of children raised in them. Thus, somewhat paradoxically, genes have a greater impact in highly resource-rich environments than in poor ones. For example, Guo and Stearns (2002) found that heredity not only had a major effect on children's intellectual development but that parental unemployment and ethnicity had a significant effect on the extent to which a child's genetic potential was realized.

Genetic variation has significant effects on a surprising range of behaviors. In their early summary of results from the Minnesota Study of Twins Raised Apart, Bouchard, Lykken, McGue, Segal, and Tellegen (1990) reported that "for almost every behavioral trait so far investigated, from reaction time to religiosity, an important fraction of the variation among people turns out to be associated with genetic variation."[9] For example, current research suggests that from 50 to 70 percent of the observed variation in general intelligence may be due to genetic variation. Bouchard et al. (1990) argued for many characteristics, being reared by the same parents in the same physical environment does not, on average, make siblings any more alike as adults than they would have been if reared separately in adoptive homes.[10] They noted that people might select environments, e.g. peer groups, under pressure from their genomes, thus finding situations that allow a greater expression of their genetic potential.[11]

In a more recent review of the heritability of five major personality characteristics, Bouchard and McGue (2003) found broad consensus on the significant effects of heritability across a range of twin studies and research reviews. One trait with high heritability is "conscientiousness," which Bouchard and Loehlin (2001) suggested encompassed sub-traits such as self-discipline, control, and locus of control. Rotter's measure of locus of control is the only such trait we found measured in any of the occupational inheritance studies we reviewed. In the NLS panel used by Evans and Leighton (1989), Rotter's scale was administered in 1976, when the men were between the ages of 24 and 34. When included in a cross-sectional analysis of the 1981 panel data, individuals who had a more internal locus of control were more likely to be self-employed than wageworkers, as psychological theory would predict. Controlling for locus of control reduced the coefficient for education to statistical insignificance.

Uusitalo (2001) examined three personality characteristics in his panel study of Finnish army recruits from 1982 until 1993: leadership, dynamism, and cautiousness. Psychological theory assumes that these are stable personality traits with roots in genetic differences and childhood rearing environments. All were measured with paper and pencil tests given by the army in 1982, when the men were aged 20. In a cross-sectional logit analysis of the likelihood of being self-employed in 1993, all three variables were statistically significant, with "leadership" and "dynamism" positive and "cautiousness" negative in their effects. Without the original questions, we had difficulty in interpreting precisely what these three really mean, but Uusitalo (2001, p. 1636) argued that "the cautiousness score appears to be very close to what the economists mean by risk aversion." The significance of the three personality characteristics was maintained when parents' income and self-employment were included in the equation.

Burke et al. (2000) included four personality traits in their probit analysis of the probability of self-employment in their sample in 1991. The National Child Development Study began in 1958, and respondents were tested in 1965 at age seven to assess their "creativity," "unforthcomingness," "anxiety acceptance," and "hostility toward others." No details were given on the origins of these tests or their interpretation, and we have no way to assess the magnitude of their effects. Two of the four had statistically significant positive effects on self-employment probability: creativity and anxiety acceptance. We report Uusitalo's and Burke et al.'s results because they represent one of the very few longitudinal studies of entry into self-employment that assessed psychological characteristics years before measuring entrepreneurial entry. Their results suggest that childhood experience within particular environmental contexts may well affect personality development in ways that lead some people to prefer self-employment later in life.

Genetic Influences on Occupational Attainment and Work Values

Sociologists have historically been skeptical of arguments positing a major role for genes in explaining between-family variance in social behavior, but accumulating evidence from studies of twins reared together and apart suggests an important role for genetic endowments. Discerning readers may recall that Aldrich and Wiedenmayer (1993) argued strongly against a simple "traits" explanation for entrepreneurial behavior. However, we also note that Aldrich and Ruef (2006, p. 61) argued against a sociological alternative of moving to a very macro-level of analysis. Instead, they suggested a multi-level

approach, connecting individuals, organizations, and social contexts. We believe the emerging cooperation between social scientists and genetics researchers will help us avoid the simplistic "traits" approaches of the past.[12]

Lichtenstein, Herschberger, and Pedersen (1995) pointed out that sociologists have observed similarities in occupational position and status between fathers and sons and have taken them as evidence for the influence of
socio-economic factors, e.g. childhood socialization. However, they noted
that "fathers and sons share 50 percent of their genes" (Lichtenstein et al.,
1995) and the observed similarities could thus be due to genetic as well as
environmental influences. They used the Swedish Adoption/Twin Study of
Aging (SATSA), a sample of twins (monozygotic and dizygotic) similar to
the Minnesota study mentioned earlier, to study father/son similarities in
occupational status. Lichtenstein and his colleagues used a simple six-part
occupational category scheme to classify the 308 men and 288 women in
their sample, and showed that two dimensions adequately described the
multi-dimensional occupational space: "status" and "farm." The same solution worked for twins reared together and apart. Then, they performed a
second analysis, using the occupational status dimension, to asses the relative importance of genetic and environmental influences on the similarities
in twins' occupational statuses. For men, genetic effects accounted for
slightly more than 50 percent of the between-family variation in occupational status, whereas the effects were not significant for women.[13]

In a follow-up study of a smaller sample, they investigated the extent to
which the genetic variation in occupational status could be attributed to
genetic variation in cognitive abilities (Lichtenstein & Pedersen, 1997). They
found significant genetic variance in educational attainment and occupational status that was not due to genetic variance in cognitive abilities,
suggesting other genetic-based factors were at work. For example, standard
cognitive tests might not capture genetic variance in personality, interests, or
talents. In reviewing this research, Pedersen, Spotts, and Kato (2005, p. 81)
noted that the "rearing environmental effects of educational achievement
and occupational status were completely overlapping, which implied that
the same factors in the rearing home made family members similar to each
other for both education and occupation." Thus, the social context in which
the twins were raised also contributed to their similarity as adults.

Cognitive abilities can be assessed through IQ tests, which can then be
linked to occupational attainment. The heritability of IQ is generally estimated at between 50 and 70 percent and thus if IQ were strongly related to
self-employment, it could be offered as partial explanation for occupational
inheritance among the self-employed. However, only two of the studies

listed in Table 1 included the IQ of respondents, as measured when they were children aged 12. Both studies used the same data set from the Netherlands, which suffers from severe missing data problems. De Wit and Van Winden (1989) found that IQ had a positive effect on children being self-employed in 1983. Using an updated data set, Van Praag and Cramer (2001) used as their dependent variable whether a person had ever been self-employed from the time they entered the labor force until 1993, and also found that IQ had a positive effect. Although provocative, without replications in other nations and across different periods these two Dutch studies remain mostly an interesting curiosity.

In summarizing research over the past several decades on genetic influences on vocational values and interests, Bouchard and McGue (2003) noted "while the number of studies of interests and work measures is much more limited than in the domains of abilities and personality, there are enough studies using different kinships to make a convincing case that reliable measures in this domain are significantly influenced by genetic factors." In particular, we speculate that genetic influences may account for between 25 and 50 percent of the association between fathers' and sons' self-employment status, in part because of the strong genetic component in the sons' work values.

Childhood: Parental Practices and Work Values

Whiston and Keller (2004) identified 77 high-quality studies published between 1980 and 2002 in 29 different journals related to the impact of family of origin on career development and occupational choice. Although directed primarily at child psychologists, their comprehensive review provided a valuable summary of the available evidence. They were surprised to find few studies that examined family influences on the career development of young children, given other research on family and parental influence. Bouchard et al. (1990, p. 223) noted that the "evidence for the strong heritability of most psychological traits, sensibly construed, does not detract from the value or importance of parenting, education, and other propaedeutic interventions."

Parenting
Parents have many routes through which they can influence the occupational attainment of their children: serving as role models, choosing particular child-rearing practices, acting as vocational advisors, and so on. They may also try to shape the educational experiences and peer-group

choices of their children by sending them to private schools and otherwise controlling their rearing environments. Later, in adolescence, they may invest in vocational or college educations for their children, and eventually, provide capital for business ventures.

Early sociological and economic research on occupational inheritance implicitly posited within-family homogeneity in the experiences of children and adolescents. Family characteristics such as parental self-employment and educational attainment were often treated as having the same meaning for all children, but subsequent research has shown substantial within-family variability in outcomes such as educational attainment and occupational status (Conley, 2004). For example, Conley and Glauber (2005) noted that in the PSID, the sibling correlation between occupational prestige scores in 2001 was only 0.225 for sisters, 0.302 for brothers, and 0.233 for all siblings. When controls were introduced for educational attainment, the correlations dropped substantially. Thus, any model of occupational inheritance must allow for substantial within-family diversity in occupational outcomes. In short, we should not expect that all children of self-employed parents themselves become self-employed.

We focus on two types of parental influence in this section. First, we examine research on the sources of *work values* among children. Second, we examine research on children's choices of *specific vocational interests and occupations*. Note that parental influences may lead children to value entrepreneurship, but children may nevertheless fail to develop the other values and skills needed to succeed. They may also simply encounter an unfavorable environment or a run of bad luck.

Parenting: Work Values

With regard to *work values*, Kohn and his colleagues (1983, 1986) produced perhaps the best-known model linking parents' occupations to their values, and their values, in turn, to the orientation toward work they foster in their children. In this respect, they followed the lead of Miller and Swanson (1958) in arguing that parents' work environments influence how they socialize their children. However, whereas Miller and Swanson used the Detroit area study survey to argue that the entrepreneurial or bureaucratic nature of a father's work setting affected maternal child rearing values and practices, Kohn emphasized the distinction between intrinsic versus extrinsic work values.[14] Kohn argued that work high in substantive complexity, intellectual flexibility, and autonomy led workers to value self-direction and internal standards, whereas work lacking these features led workers to value conformity to externally imposed rules.

In their studies in the United States and Poland, Kohn, Slomczynski, and Schoenbach (1986) confirmed these predictions and found that work values influenced parents' child-rearing practices. Workers with high occupational self-direction tended to value self-direction in their children, whereas workers low in occupational self-direction favored conformity. Most important, interviews with their children confirmed that parental values did, in fact, affect children's values. A follow-up study collected a third wave of interviews for the American sample in 1994–1995 and showed that the effects of occupational self-direction on intellectual functioning and valuing self-directedness persisted over many decades (Schooler, Mulatu, & Oates, 2004).

Parenting: Gender Differences
In a portion of the study conducted only in the United States, Kohn et al. (1986) found that the effect of mothers' values on what their children valued was mediated by whether the children accurately perceived their mothers' values. However, for fathers, they found that the effect of values was largely direct and mostly independent of whether the children accurately perceived what their father valued. Thus, fathers had apparently used child-rearing practices that conveyed what they expected, without necessarily articulating those values in a form that children consciously understood.

Kohn's research on gender differences suggests that an inquiry into childhood socialization, parenting, and institutional constraints might prove fruitful in understanding the gender gap in business start-up rates. Until the early 1970s, self-employment rates were very low among women, and women-owned businesses constituted only about 5 percent of all businesses in 1970. As women's proportional representation among business owners began to grow, researchers paid more attention to the phenomenon and a subfield of "women's entrepreneurship" was created. Our review suggests several promising lines of inquiry into forces that created, sustained, and are now closing the gap.

First, women entered the labor market in growing numbers in the 1950s and then began starting their own businesses in greater numbers in the 1970s. Accordingly, daughters of the self-employed raised in the 1970s and later might have experienced a different rearing environment than those raised earlier. Second, parenting styles for boys versus girls may have differed more widely in the 1950s than later (Buldroft, Carmody, & Buldroft, 1996), as mothers' participation in the labor force grew and self-employment rates increased. Period and cohort differences in the transmission of occupational values may thus account for the growing number of women-owned businesses.

Parenting: Ethnographic Studies

Most studies of parenting practices rely on self-reports from parents and children, or reports from third parties, such as teachers. Ethnographic studies that observe parents and children as they go about their daily activities are clearly needed, such as the research carried out by Lareau (2002). She argued that childrearing practices differ between middle class and working class parents because of resource differences, as well as differences in occupational experiences. In her ethnographic study of black and white 10-year-old children, she contrasted the "concerted cultivation" of middle class children with the "accomplishment of natural growth" of working class children. Among middle class children, the complex organization of their every day activities, parental encouragement of sophisticated language use, and extensive social connectedness beyond kin led to an emerging sense of entitlement. In contrast, working class children gained an emerging sense of constraint in their lives because of their less structured daily lives, little monitoring or coaching of their verbal fluency, and heavy reliance on kin-based socializing.

Lareau's analysis has ambiguous implications for class-based explanations of entrepreneurial entry, as her findings do not map neatly onto an extrinsic/intrinsic divide in work values. Middle class children's greater sense of entitlement could give them the confidence they need to mobilize needed resources, whereas working class children's greater experience with more autonomy in their personal lives could stimulate a similar desire for occupational autonomy. Lareau's findings suggest that we must look to occupation-specific family experiences to understand the genesis of work values. Unfortunately, her study did not include any self-employed people or employers. Nonetheless, her detailed account of parenting illustrates the potential value of ethnographic studies of self-employed parents and their children.

Returning to our theme of the neglected role of genetic influences, we note that Keller, Bouchard, Arvey, Segal, and Dawis (1992) examined the heritability of work values. Specifically, they examined the aspects of work that people came to value as they grew up with their genetic potential within a particular environment, using a subset of cases from the Minnesota study of twins. After adjusting for age and sex effects, they found that about 40 percent of the variance in measured work values (achievement, comfort, status, safety, and autonomy) was associated with genetic differences within the sample. Keller et al. (1992) pointed out that people are not "born" with work values, but rather learn or acquire them as they mature. Nonetheless, this small study reinforces findings from others that showed genetic factors influence vocational interests, e.g. Waller, Lykken, and Tellegen (1995), and reminds us that parental influence operates along several dimensions.

Parenting: Vocational Interests and Occupational Choices
With regard to *specific vocational interests and occupational choices*, a number of studies have suggested that parents play at least a moderately significant role, although the design of most has not matched parents' to children's reports of influence (Whiston & Keller, 2004). Such influences are already apparent in pre-school children (Barak, Feldman, & Noy, 1991). We have already noted that Kohn and his colleagues found strong evidence that parents' occupations shape their children's orientations to general conditions of work via the parents' value systems. In addition, children's attitudes and aspirations toward specific occupations might be sensitive to parental influence.

However, Trice's research raises questions about children's awareness of parents' jobs. In a study of 11 to 14-year-olds, Trice and Knapp (1992) found that only 68 percent accurately reported their father's occupations, and children's occupational aspirations had no statistically significant relationship to their fathers' occupations (occupations were classified into a six-category scheme). Fewer than 10 percent of the children they interviewed reported that "parental suggestions" in response to the question, "has anyone ever told you that when you grow up you should be something or that you would be good at something?" Even when parental suggestions were reported, the children had *not* described these suggestions as either their own first or second choices. In their study of 949 elementary school children from 11 different schools, Trice, Hughes, Odum, Woods, and McClellan (1995) again found no significant relationship between boys' or girl's expressed job preferences and their fathers' jobs, whereas mothers' jobs were associated with children's preferences (jobs were coded in a six-category scheme).

Longitudinal studies of children's occupational aspirations and expectations are rare, and one of the few to observe how parental influence wanes over time was Helwig's (2004) decade-long study of 208 second graders from the Denver area interviewed six times.[15] He also obtained information about their parents. Students were asked what job they would like to have as an adult, what job they think they will actually have, and what job do they think their mothers and fathers would like them to have.[16] Although sample attrition makes interpretation of the results ambiguous, there was a clear tendency for older children to report that parents became less directive and more willing to let them choose "anything I want."

In addition to their role as socializing agents, parents also affect their children's interests via their genetic endowments. A number of studies using the Minnesota twins study has concluded that variation in occupational interests is strongly correlated with genetic factors. For example, Lykken, Bouchard, McGue, and Tellegen (1993) found that genetic influences accounted for as much as half of the variance across a battery of specific vocational and recreational interests. They noted that individuals learn such interests and precursor traits of aptitude and personality shape people's interests in specific aspects of occupations. Whiston and Keller's (2004) review of child development research over the previous two decades suggests that parental contributions to their children's aptitude and personality constitute probably a bigger influence on their occupational interests and expectations than either directive suggestions or specific occupational role modeling.

Adolescence into Adulthood

Children move into their teenage years with very general vocational interests and expectations, having shed their "fantasy occupations" of childhood, e.g. an astronaut or doctor, but without fixing on any specific future jobs. Their families have influenced their development through the structuring of home environments, such as through discipline practices that encourage self-direction. Adolescence is a time of vocational exploration and identity development, as aptitude and personality traits interact with environmental contingencies to open some avenues and close others. During this period of transition, studies have documented that children perceive their families, including siblings as well as parents, as influencing their career choices (Whiston & Keller, 2004). Not surprisingly, children who perceive their families as supportive and having high expectations tend to have higher occupational aspirations than others.

Given the obvious importance of the transition from school and adolescence to begin a career, we might expect adolescents to be quite active in exploring possible jobs and occupations. However, as Mortimer, Zimmer-Gembeck, Holmes, and Shanahan (2002, p. 221) noted in summarizing the work of Schneider and Stevenson (1999) "only a minority of high school students seriously considers potential career paths by seeking information or by engaging in appropriate activities, even though almost all report

occupational aspirations when asked. In addition, many lack basic information about how much education they need for the occupations they are
considering." Thus, we should not think of youth as preparing for future
self-employment in any systematic way, but instead consider ways in which
family contexts shape work values, preferences, and possibly skills.

Difficulties in Linking Adolescent Experience to Entrepreneurship
We face several difficulties in establishing a connection between family contexts during children's adolescent years and their becoming entrepreneurs
sometime in the future. First, very few people choose self-employment as their
first job. For example, Dunn and Holtz-Eakin (2000), using the PSID, found
that the average age of first self-employment for sons ranged from 26 to 27.5
years, depending on whether their father or mother was self-employed.
Standard deviations for these estimates were about 5 years, indicating that
many sons were in their early 30s before becoming self-employed for the first
time. Also using the PSID, Williams (2004) noted that less than 1 percent of
youth aged 16 and 17 were self-employed, with the percent increasing to
about 3.5 percent by age 24.[17] Lentz and Laband (1990), using National
Federation of Independent Businesses (NFIB) survey data, reported that the
age of first-time owners following in their parents' footsteps, but not inheriting their business, was about 36, compared to 37 for non-followers and 32
for people who inherited their business. In their national survey of 692 youth
aged 14–19, Kourilsky and Walstad (2000) asked their respondents how many
years they would wait before they acted on their desire to start a business, and
53 percent said at least seven years or more.

Most entrepreneurs therefore gain work experience at other jobs before
tackling self-employment. Thus, from a life course perspective, the time lag
between children leaving home and actually becoming self-employed as
adults provides many opportunities for intervening events to dampen or
amplify earlier experiences. Over such long durations, disruptive or catalytic
events might disrupt the linked lives of parents and children. Additionally,
conditions promoting entrepreneurial aspirations might not be the same as
those promoting entrepreneurial success. Young adults may come to value
an entrepreneurial career but not have the skills and resources to succeed in
their attempts. Accordingly, we must be cautious in searching for direct
links between adolescent experiences and adult occupational attainment.

Second, most studies of occupational inheritance, whether retrospective
or panel, obtain very little information about processes of socialization and
control that are household specific. Most questions about parents' occupations ask about fathers' and mothers' jobs when the respondent was 16 years

old. However, they typically obtain no information about business size, years of self-employment, whether the respondent worked in the business, and so forth. For example, we found no studies asking the kinds of questions necessary to examine the family dynamics studied by Kohn and his colleagues.

Adolescent Occupational Aspirations

In this section, we review studies that link occupational inheritance to parental activities that occurred in late adolescence, such as Mortimer's study of students at the University of Michigan. We examine findings from previous studies that included age-specific information on self-employment durations in families, such as Aldrich, Renzulli, and Langton's (1998) Vancouver study and Sørensen's (2006) Danish study. In the next section, we offer some new findings from the Panel Study of Entrepreneurial Dynamics (PSED).

Beginning in the 1950s, researchers found that many adults expressed an interest in being self-employed or owning their businesses (Chinoy, 1955; Lipset & Bendix, 1959). For example, Steinmetz and Wright (1989, p. 973) noted that in 1980, "57% of all people in the American working class and two-thirds of all male workers say that they would like to be self-employed someday." Adult interest in self-employment has apparently been matched by that of high school students. For example, a Gallup Organization poll of 967 youths aged 14–19 in 1995 (Kourilsky & Walstad, 1998) found that 72 percent of the young men and 62 percent of the young women answered yes to a question, "Would you like to start a business of your own?" The study was repeated in 1999 with a national sample of 1,148 youth and 1,104 young adults, aged 21–30 (Kourilsky & Walstad, 2000). At that time, 61 percent of the youth and 58 percent of the young adults said "yes."[18] Very similar results were obtained 10 years later in a Junior Achievement online poll of 1,155 students in 2005, which found that 69 percent of students expressed an interest in starting their own business (Bell, 2005).

Over the past few decades, many non-profit organizations have been founded around the world to promote "entrepreneurship education" among young people, e.g. the Consortium for Entrepreneurship Education in the USA, the National Collegiate Entrepreneurship Organization in the USA, the Junior Achievement Worldwide Association, the Enterprise and Industry Initiative of the European Union, the Enterprise Insight program sponsored by the British government, and many state-level initiatives in the United States, such as those sponsored by the Appalachian Regional Commission. In the United States, the Ewing Marion Kauffman Foundation of

Kansas City has funded many initiatives aimed at age groups ranging from elementary school children to high school youth. Thus, today's youth live and work in an environment saturated with information and images about entrepreneurship and business ownership. Indeed, the period beginning with the 1980s revival of interest in entrepreneurship changed American culture to such an extent that research results on occupational inheritance from earlier decades may no longer be valid. As we noted in Table 1, most of the occupational inheritance data sets cover a period in which the respondents were growing up in the 1940s through the 1960s, and their findings may thus be historically specific.[19]

Even though their environments are rich in information about entrepreneurship, research on occupational aspirations and expectations suggests that interest in specific occupations develops from more immediate experiences. Extrapolating from the research we have reviewed on career development and counseling among youth, we assume that most adolescents lack knowledge of the occupationally specific skills needed for self-employment. Moreover, because typically a decade or more passes before high school graduates attempt to become self-employed, we doubt that learning entrepreneurially specific skills during adolescence makes much of a difference. By contrast, youth can develop a preference for occupational autonomy, flexibility, and substantive complexity while observing parents engaged in their chosen occupations. If their parents are self-employed, of course, youth may acquire some specific skills in business management.

Jumping too quickly into self-employment during adolescence actually seems to harm the future career prospects of youth. In his analysis of youth over the period 1979–1989, using the PSID, Williams (2004, p. 334) found that "time spent in self-employment as a youth is negatively correlated with current earnings, and ... the returns to self-employment experience are significantly lower than the returns to wage employment experience in the wage and salary sector." Most of the youth were self-employed for very short periods, but apparently they lost out on the development of new skills and also lost opportunities to gain experience about the functioning of the labor market.

Acquiring and Reinforcing Occupational Values
Does growing up in an entrepreneurial household make a difference in young adults' career choices? We found no large-scale research projects focusing on family dynamics involving adolescents within self-employed households. However, we found a well-designed study that explored the effect of fathers' occupational attributes on their 18–22-year-old sons' career

choices. Mortimer (1974, 1976) used survey data collected from two entering classes of University of Michigan students in 1962 and 1963, who were also interviewed in 1967 and 1968. Within this group of middle and upper middle class sons, most had fathers in high prestige occupations: 12 percent had fathers who were doctors, dentists, or lawyers, and 27 percent had fathers who were self-employed businessmen. Sons were asked which occupation they were planning on entering after graduation.

Mortimer used the Dictionary of Occupational Titles to code occupations on the basis of "interests," and applied them to all 129 occupational groups. The groups were collapsed into a 13-category code, using "interests," for a smallest space analysis of fathers' and sons' occupational choices. Results showed that the students had a strong tendency to choose their father's occupations. If they did not choose exactly the same occupation, they chose ones with similar levels of autonomy, reward structure, and work activities (as inferred from the smallest space analysis). Parental values – as revealed in the occupations they held – regarding work thus seemed to strongly influence their sons' expectations for careers. The closeness of father and son relationships had a mediating effect on whether sons adopted their fathers' occupations.

Several studies have tried to assess the extent to which adults were exposed to an entrepreneurial lifestyle when they were children. Aldrich et al. (1998) studied 229 business owners in the Greater Vancouver area of British Columbia, Canada, in 1995, collecting a great deal of information about parents who were self-employed. About 55 percent reported that one or both of their parents were self-employed at some point in their lives, with the average duration of business ownership almost 28 years (standard deviation of 16 years). Under these conditions, children could gain experience with an entrepreneurial lifestyle in two ways: by simply living in the same household and by actually working in the business. About 83 percent of the children of owners had some experience with an entrepreneurial household prior to age 22, with 63 percent having 10 or more years of exposure.

Exposure to an entrepreneurial lifestyle while living at home, however, may not be sufficient to gain the tacit knowledge and values involved in being self-employed. Children may gain an appreciation of an entrepreneurial life but not learn enough to succeed at it. Working in the business involves a commitment that can drive home the lesson of the demands of self-employment. With regard to working, only 61 percent had actually worked for their parents. About 25 percent began working before the age of 10, 27 percent between 10 and 14, 33 percent between 15 and 19, and 15 percent at 20 years of age or older.

Even though most of the employed children started at a young age, very few stayed in the business as a career. About 30 percent worked less than five years, and 51 percent left after their ninth year. Only 12 percent reported working 20 or more years for their parents, even though many more had the opportunity to do so.[20] Thus, although a majority of the children whose parents owned a business began working in it at a fairly young age, the work was short term and most left for other jobs before they turned 21. These results show that a minority of the children of self-employed parents is not only actively exposed to the lifestyle but also have first hand working knowledge of the activities involved. Unfortunately, none of the transition probability studies we reviewed contained any information about the duration of exposure of children to self-employment or the extent of their involvement.

Occupational Inheritance in Denmark

Sørensen (2006) tried to separate the consequences of being exposed to an entrepreneurial lifestyle during adolescence from exposure during adulthood in his study of the transition to being a self-employed person with employees in Denmark. He found that parental self-employment had a significantly positive effect on the transition to self-employment, regardless of whether it occurred during adolescence or adulthood. For exposure during adolescence only, the odds increased by 1.52, for adulthood only by 1.68, and for exposure during both periods by 1.84. (The last coefficient is statistically significantly different from the first but not the second.) Sørensen explained the adolescent exposure effect by invoking role modeling, noting that even if parents were no longer self-employed by the time their children entered the labor force, the consequences of early exposure persisted.

He explained the effects of adult-only exposure by positing that self-employed parents provide social capital to their children, who aspire to become entrepreneurs, such as by passing on knowledge of opportunities to them and making introductions for them. This interpretation is strengthened by his finding that prior work experience in a parent's industry and having a self-employed parent increases the likelihood that a child will enter the same industry. Returning to our theme of including a consideration of genetic endowments in a life course model, we note that if children inherit aptitudes and abilities that require a favorable environment for their development, parental self-employment during adolescence could enhance their effects. However, if the aptitudes and abilities can be developed in *any* familial context that fosters occupational self-direction and autonomy, then parental self-employment during a child's adulthood is not a sign of the transfer of social capital. Instead, it could be taken as a marker of a genetic endowment combined with a child-rearing environment that allowed the development of entrepreneurial-relevant skills and values during childhood.

Assessing the extent to which Sørensen's results reflect children acquiring their parents' occupational values and skills versus social capital would require additional information: for how many years was the child exposed to parental self-employment and did the child actually work in the business, and what occupational route did siblings follow. (If a disproportionate share of siblings also enters self-employment, then we have added grounds for investigating between-family variance.) Sørensen's analysis ended when the children were aged 29–31, and thus he captured only the entrepreneurial early movers, as well as those with enough capital and organizing ability to hire employees for their first venture. We will return to Sørensen's analysis when we consider what resources self-employed parents can offer their adult children.

Evidence from the PSED: Parental Influences on becoming a Nascent Entrepreneur

Many of the studies we have drawn upon include information about parental occupations but not about the businesses they owned. In contrast, the PSED includes extensive information on business characteristics. In this section, we use the PSED to look more closely at possible sources of parental influence.

PSED Study Design

The PSED's module on parents built on some of the findings from the Greater Vancouver project, as more information was obtained about the businesses owned by respondents' parents. Unlike the other studies we have reviewed, the PSED focused on *nascent entrepreneurs* rather than people already in business. Respondents were included in the nascent entrepreneur sample if they reported that had taken action, alone or with others, within the past year to start a new business. It thus identified people very early in the start-up process, before the outcome of their efforts was known, and is arguably an indicator of people's interest in self-employment without regard to their abilities to actually succeed.

The PSED also included a comparison sample of people who identified themselves as not trying to start a business. Thus, by combing the two samples, properly weighted, we can assess the extent to which parental characteristics differentiate people who say they were trying to start a business from those who were not during the period 1999–2000. Because the respondents were not followed over their working careers, we cannot use the PSED to calculate transition probabilities. Instead, we have a snapshot of who was attempting a start-up at a moment in time when entrepreneurial interest was rising rapidly in the United States. The combination of a different period and a different outcome means that we expect differences in our results, compared to other projects that examined people reporting their occupations as "self-employed."

We can use the PSED to gain an understanding of how much experience respondents have had with parental self-employment. The survey asked people if their parents were ever self-employed, how many businesses they owned, for how many years their parents ran their businesses, the size of the largest business they owned, and whether the respondent had ever worked for any of the parents' businesses. Using this information, we can assess the 1999–2000 PSED sample's experience of parental self-employment, but we must note two limitations that prevent us from generalizing about the past. First, differential parental fertility means that our sample of sons and daughters may not accurately capture the historical distribution of self-employment by parents. Second, differential cohort survival and other factors affecting sample selectivity mean that we must be careful in inferring cohort differences, using the age of our respondents.

All respondents were asked, "Did your parents ever work for themselves or run their own businesses, alone or together?" and 50 percent answered "yes." Although this percent may seem high, note that it refers to any spell of self-employment, however brief, over the parents' entire life span.[21] For comparison purposes, we note that Dunn and Holtz-Eakin (2000) reported that 30 percent of the fathers and 16 percent of the mothers of sons in the PSID experienced at least one year of self-employment over the 15 years of their study (1966–1981). Fairlie and Robb (2005) reported that about 52 percent of all business owners in the 1992 CBO had at least one self-employed family member prior to starting their firm. Reynolds and White (1997) showed that between 40 and 42 percent of the respondents aged 40–69 in the 1968–1988 waves of the PSID reported at least one spell of self-employment. In the national longitudinal survey of youth (NLSY) 1979–1998 waves, at least 25 percent of the original respondents experienced at least one self-employment spell (Budig, 2006). This percentage is biased downward as it is unadjusted for sample attrition and only covers the early working years (aged 18–41). Thus, at the outset, we know that a large proportion of the American work force has parents who have experienced at least one spell of self-employment over their working careers.

Many occupational inheritance studies either include only whether a respondent's father was self-employed, or include both parents into a single indicator of parental self-employment. As we will show, however, family employment dynamics are different for children, depending upon the business's ownership structure. Among the PSED respondents reporting parental self-employment, 43 percent reported that only their father had owned a business, 11 percent said only their mother, 31 percent reported joint ownership by both parents, and in 8 percent of the cases, each parent owned a separate business. (Some other combination of activity was reported by 3 percent of the respondents.) In the following tables, we will report statistics separately for three types of ownership: father's business, mother's business, and joint ownership.

Because the startup propensity for women has historically been lower than that for men, we also report statistics separately for men and women respondents so that we can observe any possible contributions of parental self-employment to the sex differential. To anticipate our results, the only significant sex difference we found concerned whether respondents had worked in their parents' businesses, with men much more likely to work for their fathers' or a jointly owned business than were women.

Results from the PSED Analysis

In most cases, respondents reported that their parents owned only one business, as shown in Table 2. Some of the parents were serial entrepreneurs, owning more than one business, with 11 percent of the fathers owning three or more and 15 percent of the joint owners having three or more. Only 9 percent reported that their mothers had owned more than one business. As might be expected from variation in numbers of businesses owned, parents varied greatly in the total number of years they had owned businesses, as shown in the second panel of Table 2. Women and men were equally likely to report their parents were serial entrepreneurs and the duration of ownership was also the same.

Comparison data are rare, but we note that Reynolds and White (1997), summarizing PSID data, reported that about half of the self-employed heads of households aged 40–59 had self-employment spells lasting six or more years. Dunn and Holtz-Eakin (2000) reported that over the 15 years covered by their study, father who were self-employed at any time during the study years spent nearly three-quarters of their working time in that state. Interestingly, in their equations predicting the transition to self-employment, they

Table 2. Parental Ownership Characteristics: PSED.

	Father (N = 252)			Mother (N = 111)			Joint (N = 159)		
	Female (%)	Male (%)	Total (%)	Female (%)	Male(%)	Total (%)	Female (%)	Male (%)	Total (%)
Number of businesses owned									
1	70	59	64	89	95	92	68	66	67
2	22	28	25	2	1	2	12	23	18
3 or more	8	14	11	9	3	7	19	11	15
Total percent	100	100	100	100	100	100	100	100	100
P			0.55			0.44			0.49
Number of years as owner									
1–9	26	24	25	47	58	51	8	20	14
10–19	25	20	22	37	39	38	39	20	30
20–39	37	39	38	16	3	11	33	40	36
40 or more	12	18	15	0	0	0	20	20	20
Total percent	100	100	100	100	100	100	100	100	100
P			0.86			0.35			0.42
Largest business owned									
No employees	23	12	17	50	30	43	14	2	9
1–4 employees	50	34	41	24	45	32	35	35	35
5–9 employees	17	24	21	9	1	6	23	32	27
10 or more employees	10	30	21	17	24	19	28	31	30
Total percent	100	100	100	100	100	100	100	100	100
P			0.11			0.35			0.36
Worked for parent									
Full-time	1	24	14	8	1	6	8	53	30
Part-time	36	32	34	18	26	21	50	26	38
Did not work at all	63	44	52	73	73	73	42	20	32
Total percent	100	100	100	100	100	100	100	100	100
P			0.01			0.39			0.00

found that taking account of the duration of parents' self-employment, as well as its timing, produced coefficients of the same magnitude as their preferred "any parental exposure over the sample period" indicator of parental involvement in self-employment. Thus, the duration of exposure to parental self-employment was no more significant than the exposure itself.

Most of the businesses owned by parents were quite small, as shown in panel 3 of Table 2. About 58 percent of businesses owned by fathers and 75 percent of businesses owned by mothers had fewer than five employees. In contrast, jointly owned businesses were larger: only 44 percent had fewer than five employees, and 30 percent had more than 10. Again, we found no significant sex differences. Unfortunately, none of the studies listed in Table 1 reported information on the number of businesses owned or their size, and so we cannot offer comparative statements. However, the size distribution of the parents' businesses compares quite closely with that of all US businesses (Aldrich & Ruef, 2006).

Children's Employment in Parents' Businesses

Very few of the PSED respondents worked full time for their parents' businesses, as shown in the last panel of Table 2. Indeed, for those without jointly owned business in their families, most did *not work at all* in the business owned by one parent.[22] Full time work was also rare. Just 14 percent of the children whose fathers owned businesses and only 6 percent of those whose mothers owned businesses worked full time. By contrast, children whose parents jointly owned businesses were much more involved in the running of the business: 30 percent worked full time and 38 percent worked part time. These jointly owned businesses fit the classic notion of a family-owned and managed business: father and mother as joint owners and at least one child working in the business. Thus, about one in twenty respondents in our sample spent at least part of their working lives in a traditional family-owned business.[23]

Sons and daughters differed significantly in their involvement in parents' businesses. For businesses owned by respondents' fathers, about 24 percent of the men reported working full time and 32 percent part time, compared to only 1 percent of the women who worked full time and 36 percent who worked part time. Thus, almost two out of three women reported not working at all in their father's business. Even more dramatically, 53 percent of the men reported working full time in a jointly owned family business, compared to only 8 percent of women. Only 20 percent of the men reported not working at all in a jointly owned business, compared to 42 percent of the women. In contrast, neither men nor women were very involved in their mothers' businesses, as 73 percent of each sex reported not working at all in the business. From this information, we were tempted to infer that part of the gender gap in business start-up and persistence rates stems from the differential involvement of sons and daughters in their parents' businesses. However, as we shown in Table 3, controlling for involvement in parental businesses does not significantly reduce the gender gap in the entrepreneurial entry rate.[24]

To determine whether parental business ownership might have influenced the likelihood of their children attempting entrepreneurial entry, we conducted a logistic regression analysis. We coded our dependent variable (nascent entrepreneur = 1, otherwise = 0) if the respondent qualified based on whether he/she answered yes to the following question: "Are you, alone or with others, now trying to start a new business?" In addition, we only included individuals as nascent if they expected to be owners or part owners in the firm, reported being active in trying to start the new business in the past 12 months, and were still in the start-up phase. The fully specified model included measures of education, work experience, current employment status, age, marital status, sex, race and ethnicity, and region, as developed in Kim et al. (2006). In this analysis, we report only the coefficients relevant to parental business ownership, as shown in Table 3.

In Model 1 of Table 3 we show the simple additive effects of three forms of parental business ownership on a respondent being a nascent entrepreneur in 1999–2000, and none of the three is statistically significant. Prior to entering these three variables into the equation, the coefficient for sex (male = 1, female = 0) in an equation with all the control variables was 0.515 ($p < .01$), and adding the three ownership variables does not change the coefficient significantly. Men were about 1.67 times as likely as women to be nascent entrepreneurs, a result similar to that observed in the studies in Table 1 where the dependent variable was actual self-employment rather than attempting to start a business.

We checked to see whether the effects of parental self-employment might differ by sex, as shown in Model 2 of Table 3, by including an interaction term for ownership by sex. None of the interaction terms is statistically significant and the coefficient for sex increases slightly. Thus, the gender gap in becoming a nascent probably does not result from a differential effect of parental ownership on men and women.

As a final check on the impact of parental ownership, we included two of the four parental ownership characteristics in another logistic regression, as shown in Model 3. We included number of businesses owned by fathers, mothers, and joint parental ownership because we felt it was the best

Table 3. Logistic Regression Results of Entrepreneurial Entry on Parental Ownership Characteristics: PSED.

Independent Variables	Model		
	1	2	3
Male	0.535**	0.640**	0.592**
	[0.176]	[0.219]	[0.180]
Father owns business	−0.331	0.058	
	[0.225]	[0.328]	
Father owns business × male		−0.592	
		[0.430]	
Mother owns business	0.075	−0.332	
	[0.291]	[0.417]	
Mother owns business × male		0.771	
		[0.589]	
Joint parental ownership	−0.056	0.085	
	[0.245]	[0.360]	
Joint parental ownership × male		−0.251	
		[0.475]	
Number owned: father's bus			−0.114*
			[0.069]
Work for father's bus			−0.116
			[0.312]
Number owned: mother's bus			−0.131
			[0.287]
Work for mother's bus			0.928
			[0.586]
Number owned joint bus			0.224*
			[0.118]
Work for joint bus			−0.422
			[0.350]
Constant	1.354	1.294	1.537
	[1.512]	[1.535]	[1.561]
Observations	1021	1021	1021
−2LL	−212.25	−211.6	−210.93
DF	26	29	29
χ^2	119.12	122.36	120.6

Robust standard errors in brackets, two-tailed test. The fully specified model included measures of education, work experience, current employment status, age, marital status, sex, race and ethnicity, and region, as developed in Kim et al. (2006).
*Significant at 10%.
**Significant at 5%.

indicator of whether parents had pursued an entrepreneurial lifestyle. We did not use number of years owned or the size of the largest business because without measures of business profitability, we were uncertain of how to interpret them. We included whether respondents had worked for their parents' businesses not only because it indicated that children might have acquired some entrepreneurial skills, but also because it might have affected their occupational aspirations and values. None of the parental ownership variables in Model 2 were significant and so we left them out of Model 3.

Our results paint an equivocal picture of parental influence on children's desires for self-employment. Of the two indicators for fathers' businesses, having worked for their father had no effect, and the number of father-owned businesses actually *decreased* the likelihood of becoming a nascent entrepreneur. The effect is fairly small: each additional business owned, compared to never owning a business, reduced the odds of nascency by about 10 percent. If some fathers owned a succession of marginal or failed businesses, the negative effect we uncovered might reflect children's reactions to observing unsuccessful serial entrepreneurship. Alternatively, parental serial entrepreneurship might actually have been successful, thus allowing sons and daughters to pursue the managerial or professional careers that most small business owners desire for their children. Without more information about the performance of parents' firms, we cannot adjudicate between these interpretations.

Neither of the indicators for mothers' businesses had a statistically significant effect, although we note that again, the coefficient for number of businesses owned is negative. Finally, for jointly owned businesses, the number of businesses owned has a positive effect, whereas working in the business has no significant effect. Having a jointly owned parental business in the family increased the odds of being a nascent entrepreneur by a factor of 1.25, an effect apparently not due to the son or daughter having worked in the business. Indeed, the non-significant coefficient for having worked in a jointly owned parental business is negative.

Our findings in Tables 2 and 3 show that parental ownership has little discernable effect on children's propensities toward becoming nascent entrepreneurs. About half of all adults in our 1999–2000 survey reported at least some parental business ownership in their families, with most reporting the business was either their father's or was jointly owned by their mothers and fathers. Of those reporting some ownership, most said their parents experienced only one spell of ownership, especially for their mothers. However, the spells were of fairly long duration. Most businesses were very small, in keeping with the overall organizational landscape of the American economy. Very few worked full time for their parents' businesses, with only those reporting jointly owned parental businesses seemingly very much involved in the business.

Strikingly, people's involvement in nascent entrepreneurship in 1999–2000 was not associated with whether their parents were owners, or how much they were involved in the businesses. Indeed, experience with father-owned businesses appears to have decreased people's interest in starting a business themselves. The only hint of a possible lingering effect of family-run businesses is the positive effect of a family being heavily involved in ownership through multiple firms. Finally, the gender gap in becoming a nascent entrepreneur was not narrowed, regardless of which indicators of parental ownership we included in our models.

Adulthood: Do Parents Assist Adult Children with Business Ventures?

To this point, we have examined two of the three life course segments portrayed in Fig. 1: childhood and adolescence. We turn now to the issue of the extent to which parents help their adult children enter self-employment. By the time they enter adulthood, institutional environments have imposed constraints on children and have interacted with family, school, and genetic endowments to establish most of the human capital people bring to their working careers. In the previous sections, we noted that occupational values and expectations have been established by late adolescence. Nonetheless, self-employed parents could potentially serve as role models and provide some on-the-job training that affects the likelihood of adult children taking up self-employment.

In the life course perspective, the principle of linked lives reminds us that parental assistance depends upon the conjuncture of parents' and children's stages in the life course. Are parents in a position to help? Do children time their pursuit of business opportunities to coincide with parental abilities to make resources available? Or, do children pursue their occupational goals, regardless of current parental resources, meaning that parents may not be in a position to help at a critical juncture. In this section, we focus on two types of resources that have been discussed in the literature on occupational inheritance of self-employment: financial support and social capital.

Financial Support

Three types of financial support have been studied: the inheritance of a business, the inheritance of capital such as through an estate settlement, and the availability of parental assets through loans or grants. Most studies indicate that very few self-employed people *inherited* their businesses from their parents or other family members. The 1994 Vancouver study found that 5.2 percent of all owners inherited their business directly from parents (Aldrich et al., 1998), and another 3.1 percent bought their businesses from their parents. Using the 1993 CBO data, Fairlie and Robb (2005) estimated that only 1.6 percent of all the small businesses were inherited.

Fairlie and Robb (2005) noted that two federal reserve surveys have provided information on businesses obtained through "inheritances and gifts," thus commingling possible parents' passing on businesses to children with other people's "gifts" to new owners. The Survey of Small Business Finances estimated that 4 percent of firms were inherited or acquired as gifts, and the Survey of Consumer Finances estimated that 3.5 percent of businesses were similarly obtained. The 1992 CBO survey reported that 6.6 percent of owners acquired their businesses through a transfer of ownership or a gift. However, after removing owners who did not have self-employed family members prior to starting their businesses, Fairlie and Robb (2005) estimated that only about 4 percent obtained their firms through transfers of ownership or gifts.[25]

Inherited wealth can facilitate the founding of a business, and a number of studies have found that sudden increase in wealth appear to increase the likelihood that someone will enter self-employment (Blanchflower & Oswald, 1998). Other studies have investigated the association between parental wealth and becoming self-employed (Dunn & Holtz-Eakin, 2000), and we will consider them shortly. Fewer studies, however, have looked specifically at wealth inherited from parents and applied to entrepreneurial entry. In their Vancouver study, Aldrich et al. (1998) explicitly asked owners if they had used capital from an inheritance to fund their business, and all *denied* receiving such a bequest.

In Finland, Uusitalo (2001) was able to obtain information about who had received an inheritance or other unusual income during the previous five years, but this information was available only in the first wave of the panel study. About 18 percent had received an inheritance, but when a dummy variable for inheritance was included in an equation for the transition into self-employment, the coefficient was not significant. In contrast, Burke and Oswald (2000), using an updated version of the data set employed by Blanchflower et al. (1998) found a sizeable effect for inheritances. However, as with Uusitalo's study, the actual source of the inheritance was not given.

Loans and grants comprise a more likely way for parents to make resources available to the children, who are contemplating becoming self-employed. However, most studies have found that parents seldom provide startup capital to their children. In Vancouver, Aldrich et al. (1998) found that only 8.7 percent of the owners obtained any capital from self-employed parents, comparable to the 7.8 percent who obtained capital from their non-self-employed parents. In the 1992 CBO study, only 6.4 percent of the owners borrowed capital from their family (Fairlie & Robb, 2005).

Several studies have investigated the possible effects of parental assets on children's transitions to self-employment, although they cannot provide evidence that the children actually *received* any assets from the parents. Dunn and Holtz-Eakin (2000, p. 298) found that parents' total assets had a statistically significant but quite small effect on sons' self-employment: "a $10,000 increase in parents' total assets raises the probability of a son's transition into self-employment by 0.0009, which is small relative to both the sample transition probability of 0.031 and the impact of the son's own assets." By contrast, they noted that the parents' self-employment experience – measured simply as whether father, mother, or both were ever self-employed during the survey years – had a powerful effect, almost doubling the probability of a son's entering self-employment. Similarly, in his study of transitions to self-employment in Denmark, Sørensen (2006) concluded that parental wealth did not have a substantively significant effect on entrepreneurial entry. Based on our review, we believe that direct financial transfers are not a major cause of the association between the self-employment of parents and their children.

Social Capital

If parents do not provide much in the way of financial resources to their children who are considering entrepreneurial entry, what else might they provide? Aldrich and Zimmer (1986) proposed that resources obtained via social networks could supplement or even supplant the financial and physical resources that a nascent entrepreneur controlled. Subsequently, other theorists have offered the more general concept of "social capital" to refer to advantages that people obtain through direct and indirect ties with resource providers.

For example, Sørensen (2006) argued that parents with work experience in a particular industry can pass on their valuable knowledge to their children, thus saving them some of the costs of trial and error learning. Dunn and Holtz-Eakin (2000) drew a similar inference from their finding that transition probabilities to self-employment were increased to the extent that parents were self-employed longer, had higher business assets, or higher business income than others. They also noted that because the majority of sons entered different industries and occupations than their fathers, the expertise being passed within families was not entirely specific to a particular job or industry. Because of their research designs, neither study could directly assess the extent to which children obtained skills and knowledge from their parents as opposed to other sources during their adolescence and adulthood, such as via work experience or networks of advisors. For example, Fairlie and Robb (2005) reported that slightly more than half of all the small business owners reported that, before starting their own business, they worked in a similar business for someone else. Sørensen noted that children whose parents were self-employed were much more likely to choose their parents' industry than children whose parents were not self-employed, but having parents in the same industry made no difference in their degree of business success, as measured by exit rates or self-employment income. Thus, whereas parents might have influenced their children's choice of industry, they did not seem to actually pass on any valuable industry-specific skills to them.

Unfortunately, the studies of occupational inheritance in Table 1 contain no information about actual interactions between parents and adult children, nor have many studies – survey or ethnographic – examined parental contributions to children's businesses. The literature on family business mostly focuses on families already in business, rather than the conditions that may lead to children launching their own ventures (Aldrich & Cliff, 2003). Thus, in this section, we draw on a few selected studies to convey a sense of what might be included in future research projects.

In a series of reports on business owners in the Research Triangle Park Area of North Carolina, Aldrich and his colleagues investigated the extent to which social ties within families affected business start-ups and business practices. They found that networks spanning multiple domains of social life, beyond kinship networks, provided nascent entrepreneurs with greater access to multiple sources of information than homogeneous networks (Renzulli, Aldrich, & Moody, 2000). The higher the proportion kin in nascent entrepreneurs' networks, the *less* likely they were to subsequently start a business. They argued that the increased social support provided by family ties did not offset information lost because people relied so heavily on insiders. After nascents started their businesses, however, having a high proportion of kin in their core networks did not affect owners' abilities to mobilize resources from the core (Renzulli & Aldrich, 2005). Nonetheless, most did *not* turn to family members for help.

When owners were asked who they relied on for legal, financial, business loan, and industry expert advice, they rarely mentioned family members.

Instead, they turned to people with the necessary qualifications, rather than their parents or other kin (Aldrich, Elam, & Reese, 1996). For legal and financial assistance, and help with business loans, almost no one turned to family members (less than 5 percent of men and women for any of these three resources). Most relied on accountants for financial assistance and lawyers for legal advice, rather than kin. Finally, for expert advice, owners turned to business associates and friends, rather than family.

We have noted that rates of entrepreneurial entry remain fairly constant over most of the life courses (Evans & Leighton, 1989). For most people, years and even decades elapse between leaving home and attempting self-employment. During that time, they accumulate work experiences that both build on and supersede what they learned from their parents, such as by taking a job with managerial responsibility. Using the PSED, Kim et al. (2006) found that years of managerial experience was a strong predictor of being a nascent entrepreneur in 1999–2000. In the Vancouver study, about 53 percent of all owners' held jobs as managers before their current ownership, and parental self-employment made no difference in who held such jobs. The next-to-last job for about 54 percent of the owners also involved managerial responsibility, and again, parental self-employment made no difference. We suspect that over the life course, workers' career trajectories gradually attenuate the advantages they might have gained as children and adolescents with self-employed parents.

From a life course perspective, what happens to the children of self-employed parents during adulthood, before they attempt entrepreneurial entry, is the key to sorting out the influences we portrayed in Fig. 1. To the extent that people gain experiences during childhood and adolescence that change their career aspirations and identities, they may subsequently seek self-affirming environments that accentuate parental influences. However, adults' environments may not permit them to select contexts that ensure continuity. Instead, disruptive events may attenuate parental influences, making adult entrepreneurial entry much more contingent on proximate environmental factors. The research designs we have reviewed are not complex enough to allow us to decide between alternative interpretations.

CONCLUSIONS AND IMPLICATIONS

Previous research has tried to explain why the sons and daughters of self-employed parents have a heightened tendency to attempt entrepreneurship (and thus become self-employed) at some point during their working careers. As such, investigators might have framed the problem too narrowly, looking for patterns of association between two discrete states: parents' and children's self-employment. We have noted that the issue actually requires a more general consideration of the forces producing occupational inherit-ance. We suggested following the lead of social mobility researchers and conceptualizing the problem as one of the intergenerational continuity in classes of occupational attainment, rather than simply thinking of specific occupations. Framing the problem more generally helps us see that instead of looking only for occupation-specific skills, resources, and training, we should look for more general factors, such as occupational self-directedness, which predisposes children not only to self-employment but also to other occupations with high autonomy.

The Life Course Perspective

We offered a life course perspective on work careers as a framework for integrating previous work and generating new propositions, taking a long-term view of parent–child relationships. The life course view brings two benefits to the study of occupational inheritance. First, it makes salient the role of timing, duration, and historical change in the patterning of events and roles over a person's life span. Understanding how temporal organi-zation affects people's careers requires that we build theories about the cumulative effects of career decisions as shaped by changing historical con-texts. We noted that historical influences can be classified into three types of effects (age, period, and cohort) and that untangling their separate and joint effects requires dynamic research designs.

Second, the life course perspective makes salient the special methodological requirements of studying transitions and turning points in people's lives. Inflow and outflow studies provide snapshots of linked lives across generations, but they fail to capture duration-dependent processes that are sensitive to changing historical circumstances. In Table 1, we noted that investigators have used panel studies to estimate the effects of various con-tingencies on the likelihood of switching into self-employment from other states. However, few of these studies contained more than a handful of time-varying covariates and most used fixed cohorts, rather than adding new cohorts as the sample aged. Given the limited historical period covered by these studies, it would be advantageous to begin new transition probability studies to ascertain whether factors leading to self-employment have changed in the new millennium.

Explaining Occupational Inheritance among the Self-Employed

In our review, we have summarized dozens of empirical projects and offered empirical generalizations about parents' affects on their children's occupational attainment in three discrete life course segments: childhood, adolescence, and adulthood. For each segment, we noted the conceptual principles relevant to developments during that segment and reviewed selected studies. For our summary, we revisit those segments in reverse order, starting with adults. Table 4 contains a list of the key propositions emerging from our review.

Adulthood
We think it is unlikely that more than a small portion of the association between parents' and children's self-employment can be accounted for by activities undertaken by adults for their adult children. We noted that few children inherit their parents' businesses or receive any startup capital from

Table 4. Propositions of a Life Course Model of Parental Influences on Children's Self-Employment.

Impact throughout life course
P1: Parents influence their children's propensity to share similar occupational status, generally, and to enter self-employment, specifically, through the interaction of genetic inheritances and environmental conditions (within and between families)

Childhood
P2: Parents strongly influence their children's propensity to enter self-employment through parenting practices that affect their children's work values
P3: Parents moderately influence their children's propensity to enter self-employment through parenting practices that affect their children's awareness of vocational interests and occupational choices

Adolescence
P4: Parents moderately influence their children's propensity to enter self-employment by reinforcing work values during adolescence developed through childhood
P5: Exposure to their parents' occupational environment during adolescence has little effect on the likelihood that individuals with self-employed parents will enter self-employment themselves, except in traditionally structured family businesses

Adulthood
P6: Parents rarely influence their children's propensity to enter self-employment by providing financial support during adulthood
P7: Parents slightly influence their children's propensity to succeed in self-employment by providing advice and other tangible means of support

them. Extraordinary examples of second and third generation family firms have probably misled family business theorists into thinking that parent-to-adult child capital assistance is routine. We found no evidence to support such a belief. With regard to *social capital*, we found mostly speculation rather than empirical confirmation regarding the extent to which parents offer their adult children valuable entrepreneurial assistance. Indeed, parents and family seem to play a minor role in business operations by other family members.

Adolescence

With regard to adolescence, we began with an assumption that much of what parents can provide to their children that might eventually affect their decisions to enter entrepreneurship lies outside the realm of parental "investment" strategies. In the section on childhood, we laid out the foundations of this argument: genetic endowments cannot be altered, child-raising practices are driven by dynamics much more short-term oriented than concern for future occupations, adolescent children are mostly consumers of financial resources rather than investment vehicles, and investments in educational attainment after high school probably represent the most forward-looking human capital planning carried out by parents. Thus, we looked for parental activities that could happen in the natural course of events, when parents interact with their adolescent and college-age children.

We noted that most adolescents' and young adults' first jobs are as employees, and most will spend years in this state before attempting self-employment. Studies show adolescents lack basic information about the occupations they report considering, and few engage in robust search activities to learn more. Thus, they are susceptible not only to parental influence but also to peer and media influence. For example, we reported that very high proportions of youth and young adults in recent years have expressed an interest in starting their own business, although they are quite cautious about actually following through on their interests. Perhaps self-employed parents who employ their children during their teenage years reinforce values such as occupational self-directedness that eventually lead to entrepreneurship.[26] However, our analysis of the PSED found little indication that parental business ownership directly influenced their children's decisions regarding nascent entrepreneurship, at least in 1999–2000. Nonetheless, Mortimer's (1976) research showed that college students' career choices are apparently influenced, to some extent, by how they perceive their parents' occupations. Perhaps collecting such information from survey respondents, in addition to occupational data, will shed light on this conundrum.

Our review of the few studies with information on the involvement of the children of self-employed parents in their families' businesses found that as many as half of all the adults had parents who had experienced at least one spell of self-employment in their careers. Thus, potential exposure to an entrepreneurial lifestyle has been widespread in the United States over the past half century. However, most did not work in their parents' businesses, and if they did, they worked only part time. The one exception was businesses jointly owned by both parents, which seemed to involve their children much more actively than other businesses. However, we found that involvement in parents' businesses made no difference in who became a nascent entrepreneur in 1999–2000 (Kim et al., 2006).

Childhood

With regard to childhood, few studies of occupational inheritance among the self-employed have considered either studies of parental genetic contributions to their children's aptitude and personality or studies of parental socializing influence on children's occupational values and interests. A great deal of research on parenting has attributed most outcomes to the effects of parenting per se, without regard to the possibility that the outcomes result from a much more complex mix of genetic, environmental, and genetic/environmental interaction (Maccoby, 2000). Studies show that genetic variation has significant effects on a wide range of behaviors and personality traits, including occupational interests and values. We noted that the new thrust in genetic research views genetic endowments as developing within environmental contexts that can allow their full expression or hinder their development, and moreover may interact with them magnify or dampen their effects. Moreover, children and adolescents can be active in seeking out environments that allow the development of their potential. Although few genetics researchers have tackled the issue of occupational inheritance, one tantalizing study argued that about half of the between-family variance in occupational status could be attributed to genetic effects. We envision future research on occupational inheritance among the self-employed as paying much more attention to genetic endowments, to parental values as reflected in occupational working conditions, and to the interaction between genetic endowments and child-rearing environments.

NOTES

1. One reader of our paper, Philip Cohen, noted that we make heavy use of the term "choice" in this paper, even though self-employment might better be thought of

as an "achievement" rather than a preference. We note that the literature on occupational attainment, work values, career mobility, and work more generally also
uses the term "choice," even when an analysis clearly implies that few options might
have been open to people. We have tried to restrain ourselves, but trying to avoid the
agentic implications of "choice" by substituting more cumbersome circumlocutions
can bog a paper down. Thus, readers should be aware that we often use "choice"
while being fully aware that the available options in the process we are analyzing
might have been heavily constrained.

2. The occupational inheritance literature uses the term "self-employment" to
characterize people who fall into the broad category of earning a living that does not
depend on being employed by someone else. Within the category of the self-
employed, researchers have made distinctions between self-employed professionals,
skilled workers, and unskilled workers as well as between farmers and other self-
employed persons (Arum & Mueller, 2004). Blau and Duncan (1967) distinguished
between self-employed professionals, proprietors, and self-employed farmers. By
contrast, the entrepreneurship literature typically distinguishes between entrepreneurs with employees and those without, between low- and high-growth businesses,
and between innovative and non-innovative businesses (Aldrich & Ruef, 2006; Kim
et al., 2006). For our purposes, we will use the generic terms "self-employed" and
"entrepreneur" to cover all persons who attempt to start a business, regardless of its
size or growth orientation, by themselves or with others, and who are not engaging in
such activity for a third party.

3. To the extent that self-employed parents have more resources to invest in their
children's education, their children will benefit from greater acquired human capital.

4. Despite the potential for serious specification error, most empirical projects
include only a few characteristics of a self-employed person's social origins, such as
parents' occupations and education.

5. Rytina (2000) argued that prestige scores are constructed strictly on empirical
grounds from two components, education and income, and it is therefore improper
to equate prestige scale scores with "occupation."

6. Although the term "potential" seems to convey an inherent positive conno-
tation, we use it in a neutral way to mean an ability, skill, or trait that can be put to
any ultimate use, positive or negative.

7. As our colleague Glen Elder reminded us, genetic effects involve not only main
effects but also gene environment interaction effects. Shanahan and Hofer (2005,
p. 65) noted the complex relationship between genotypes and phenotypes introduced
by gene–environment interactions, "which occur when genes alter the organism's
sensitivity to specific environmental features or environmental features exert differential control over genetic influences."

8. Behavioral geneticists do not argue that individuals necessarily consciously seek
out environments favorable to their genetic endowments. Rather, the pressures are
mostly pre-conscious.

9. For a review of the strengths and weaknesses of twin studies, see Bouchard and
McGue (2003). We note that twin studies give an upper bound estimate of possible
genetic effects, rather than an unequivocal point estimate.

10. Researchers are able to estimate the heritable fraction of behaviors and traits
using studies of monozygotic ("identical") and dizygotic ("fraternal") twins raised

together and apart. By making comparisons of the extent of similarity in monozygotic twins raised apart versus together, versus dizygotic twins raised apart versus together, researchers can estimate the relative impact of environmental and genetic influences.

11. Similarly, within a family, children in competition with siblings might move to a niche that best suits their temperament and skills. Some psychologists have referred to this as the principle of "niche picking."

12. For a critique of studies of gene–context interactions, see Shanahan and Hofer (2005).

13. One explanation Lichtenstein offered for the sex difference in heritability is that the women were raised in much more constraining environments in which the tendencies latent in their genomes were suppressed. By contrast, men were raised in less constrained environments in which they were more free to pursue their natural tendencies.

14. Halaby (2003) used the 1993 follow-up study of Wisconsin high school seniors, who were first interviewed in 1957 to argue that a basic entrepreneurial versus bureaucratic dimension of work values is the key to understanding workers' achievement motivation and mobility. However, Johnson, Mortimer, and Lee (2006) challenged his argument. In re-analysis of the Wisconsin data, plus four other data sets, Johnson et al. found that the extrinsic–intrinsic schema was a better fit to the data in samples that included men and women, as well as among women in the samples where such comparisons were possible. They expressed appreciation for Halaby's inclusion of one specific aspect of extrinsic rewards – security – into studies of work values and suggested that researchers include "risk tolerance" in future studies of occupational choice.

15. Attrition reduced the sample size to half by the time of the final interviews. Tests for possible sample bias indicated no significant difference by sex or parental education or age for those interviewed at all six points and those who missed one or more interviews.

16. Unfortunately, parents were not asked what occupations they would like their children to have, and so Helwig could only report children's perceptions of parents' goals for them.

17. Youth self-employed in their teenage years were about three times as likely as others to be self-employed at age 27.

18. Six percent of the young adults said that they had already started a business.

19. In a personal communication, Jeylan Mortimer suggested that in an earlier era, self-employment conveyed more tolerance of risk than it does today, as well as a more distinctive organizational environment. With the media painting a picture of increasing turbulence among large firms – outsourcing, downsizing, mergers, temporary employment, and so forth – many workers may perceive self-employment as no more risky than being employed by a large firm.

20. Of the 62 children whose parents owned a business for 20 years or more, only nine worked in the business for 20 years or more.

21. As we might expect, the percent reporting parental self-employment is moderately related to a respondent's age. By age cohort, the percent reporting parental self-employment is 20–29, 50 percent; 30–39, 54 percent; 40–49, 64 percent; 50–59, 58 percent, and 60–69, 56 percent.

22. We do not have information on how many years they worked in their parents' businesses.

23. In this small subset of businesses, we might expect some grown children to return to their parents' businesses to take them over, after their parents have retired. Elder and Conger (2000) noted this pattern in the case of farm families.

24. For comparison purposes, recall that in the Vancouver study, 61 percent of the respondents whose parents owned businesses worked in them, with most beginning to work in their teenage years. Very few began work in their parents' businesses in their 20s. In Fairlie and Robb's (2005) analysis of the 1992 CBO data, about 44 percent of the owners worked in a family member's business, but they did not report data on whether the work was full or part time. None of the studies listed in Table 1 provided any information on children's involvement with a parent-owned business, making it difficult for us to assess the extent to which the occupational inheritance they observed was due, in part, to on-the-job training.

25. Lentz and Laband (1990) reported that 14.2 percent of their NFIB sample had inherited their businesses, but the sample was not representative of the business population of the United States, as it contained many large firms.

26. Kourilsky and Walstad (1998) noted that a "desire to be my own boss" was the most often-mentioned reason youth and young adults wanted to start their own businesses.

ACKNOWLEDGMENTS

We thank Philip Cohen, Amy Davis, Glen Elder, Lisa Keister, Steve Lippmann, Michael Lounsbury, Jeylan Mortimer, Linda Renzulli, Martin Ruef, Michael Shanahan, and the editors for their helpful comments on earlier drafts of this paper.

REFERENCES

Aldrich, H., Renzulli, L. A., & Langton, N. (1998). Passing on privilege: Resources provided by self-employed parents to their self-employed children. In: K. Leicht (Ed.), *Research in stratification and mobility*, (Vol. 16, pp. 291–317). Greenwich, CT: JAI Press.

Aldrich, H. E., & Cliff, J. E. (2003). The pervasive effects of family on entrepreneurship: Toward a family embeddedness perspective. *Journal of Business Venturing*, 18(5), 573–596.

Aldrich, H. E., Elam, A., & Reese, P. R. (1996). Strong ties, weak ties, and strangers: Do women business owners differ from men in their use of networking to obtain assistance? In: S. Birley & I. C. MacMillan (Eds), *Entrepreneurship in a global context* (pp. 1–25). London: Routledge.

Aldrich, H. E., & Ruef, M. (2006). *Organizations evolving*. London: Sage.

Aldrich, H. E., & Wiedenmayer, G. (1993). From traits to rates: An ecological perspective on organizational foundings. In: J. Katz & R. H. Brockhaus (Eds), *Advances in entrepreneurship, firm emergence, and growth*. (Vol. 1, pp. 145–195). Greenwich, CT: JAI Press.

Aldrich, H. E.. & Zimmer, C. (1986). Entrepreneurship through social networks. In: D. Sexton & R. Smilor (Eds), *The art and science of entrepreneurship* (pp. 3–23). New York: Ballinger.

Arum, R.. & Mueller, W. (2004). *The reemergence of self-employment: A comparative study of self-employment dynamics and social inequality.* Princeton. NJ: Princeton University Press.

Barak, A.. Feldman. S.. & Noy, A. (1991). Traditionality of children's interests as related to their parents' gender stereotypes and traditionality of occupations. *Sex Roles, 24.* 511–524.

Bell, S. (2005). *JA enterprise poll on teens and entrepreneurship.* Colorado Springs, CO: Junior Achievement Worldwide.

Blanchflower, D. G.. & Oswald, A. J. (1998). What makes an entrepreneur? *Journal of Labor Economics, 16*(1). 26–60.

Blau, P. M.. & Duncan, O. D. (1967). *The American occupational structure.* New York: Wiley.

Bouchard, T. J.. Jr.. & McGue, M. (2003). Genetic and environmental influences on human psychological differences. *Journal of Neurobiology, 54*(1). 4–45.

Bouchard, T. J.. Jr.. & Loehlin. J. C. (2001). Genes, personality, and evolution. *Behavioral Genetics, 31.* 243–273.

Bouchard, T. J.. Jr.. Lykken. D. T.. McGue, M.. Segal, N. L.. & Tellegen, A. (1990). Sources of human psychological differences: The Minnesota study of twins reared apart. *Science, 250*(4978). 223–228.

Budig, M. (2006). Intersections on the road to self-employment: Gender, family, and occupational class. *Social Forces, 84,* 2223–2239.

Buldroft, R. A.. Carmody, D. C.. & Buldroft, K. A. (1996). Patterns of parental independence giving to adolescents: Variations by race, age, and gender of child. *Journal of Marriage and Family, 58*(4). 866–883.

Burke, A. E.. FitzRoy, F. R.. & Nolan, M. A. (2000). When less is more: Distinguishing between entrepreneurial choice and performance. *Oxford Bulletin of Economics & Statistics, 62*(5). 565–587.

Carroll, G. R., & Mosakowski, E. (1987). The career dynamics of self-employment. *Administrative Science Quarterly, 32*(4). 570–589.

Chinoy, E. (1955). *Automobile workers and the American dream.* Garden City, NY: Doubleday.

Conley, D. (2004). *The pecking order: Which siblings succeed and why?* New York: Pantheon Books.

Conley, D.. & Glauber, R. (2005). *Sibling similarity and difference in socioeconomic status: Life course and family resource effects.* New York: Center for Advanced Social Science Research.

de Wit, G., & Van Winden, F. A. A. M. (1989). An empirical analysis of self-employment in the Netherlands, *Small Business Economics, 1,* 263–72.

Dunn, T. & Holtz-Eakin, D. (2000). Financial capital, human capital, and the transition to self-employment: Evidence from intergenerational links, *Journal of Labor Economics, 18*(2), 282–305.

Elder, G. H. (1999). *Children of the great depression: Social change in life experience,* Boulder, CO: Westview Press.

Elder, G. H., & Conger, R. D. (2000). *Children of the land: Adversity and success in rural America,* Chicago: University of Chicago Press.

Evans, D. S., & Leighton, L. S. (1989). Some empirical aspects of entrepreneurship, *American Economic Review, 79*(3), 519–535.

Fairlie, R. W. (1999). The absence of the African-American owned business: An analysis of the dynamics of self-employment. *Journal of Labor Economics, 17*(1), 80–108.

Fairlie, R. W., & Robb, A. (2005). *Families, human capital, and small business: Evidence from the characteristics of business owners survey.* Santa Cruz, CA: University of California.

Gartner, W. B., Kelly, G. S., Nancy, M. C., & Paul, D. R. (Eds) (2004). *Handbook of entrepreneurial dynamics: The process of business creation in Contemporary America.* Thousand Oaks, CA: Sage.

Guo, G., & Stearns, E. (2002). The social influences on the realization of genetic potential for intellectual development. *Social Forces, 80*(3), 881–910.

Halaby, C. N. (2003). Where job values come from: Family and schooling background, cognitive ability, and gender. *American Sociological Review, 63*(2), 251–278.

Helwig, A. A. (2004). A ten-year longitudinal study of the career development of students: Summary findings. *Journal of Counseling & Development, 82*(1), 49–57.

Hout, M., & Rosen, H. S. (2000). Self-employment, family background, and race. *Journal of Human Resources, 35*(4), 671–694.

Johnson, M. K., Mortimer, J. T., & Lee, J. C. (2006). *Dimensions of work values revisited.* Pullman, WA: Washington State University.

Keller, L. M., Bouchard, T. J., Arvey, R. D., Segal, N. L., & Dawis, R. V. (1992). Work values: Genetic and environmental influences. *Journal of Applied Psychology, 77*(1), 79–88.

Kim, P. H., Aldrich, H. E., & Lisa, A. K. (2006). Access (not) denied: The impact of financial, human, and cultural capital on entrepreneurial entry in the United States. *Small Business Economics, 27,* 5–22.

Kohn, M. L., & Schooler, C. (1983). *Work and personality: An inquiry into the impact of social stratification.* Norwood, NJ: Ablex Publishing Corporation.

Kohn, M. L., Slomczynski, K. M., & Schoenbach, C. (1986). Social stratification and the transmission of values in the family: A cross-national assessment. *Sociological Forum, 1*(1), 73–102.

Kourilsky, M. L., & Walstad, W. B. (1998). Entrepreneurship and female youth: Knowledge, attitudes, gender differences, and educational practices. *Journal of Business Venturing, 13*(1), 77–88.

Kourilsky, M. L., & Walstad, W. B. (2000). *The e generation: Prepared for the entrepreneurial economy?* Dubuque, IA: Kendall/Hunt Publishing.

Lareau, A. (2002). Invisible inequality: Social class and childrearing in black families and white families. *American Sociological Review, 67*(5), 747–776.

Lentz, B. F., & Laband, D. N. (1990). Entrepreneurial success and occupational inheritance among proprietors. *Canadian Journal of Economics, 23*(3), 563–579.

Lichtenstein, P., Herschberger, S. L., & Pedersen, N. L. (1995). Dimensions of occupations: Genetic and environmental influences. *Journal of Biosocial Science, 27,* 193–206.

Lichtenstein, P., & Pedersen, N. L. (1997). Does genetic variance for cognitive abilities account for genetic variance in educational achievement and occupational status? A study of twins reared apart and twins reared together. *Social Biology, 44,* 77–90.

Lipset, S. M., & Bendix, R. (1959). *Social mobility in industrial society.* Berkeley: University of California Press.

Lykken, D. T., Bouchard, T. J., McGue, M., & Tellegen, A. (1993). Heritability of interests: A twin study. *Journal of Applied Psychology August, 78*(4), 649–661.

Maccoby, E. E. (2000). Parenting and its effects on children: On reading and misreading behavior genetics. *Annual Review of Psychology, 51*(1), 1–27.

Miller, D. R.. & Swanson. G. E. (1958). *The changing American parent: A study in the Detroit area.* New York: Wiley.

Mortimer, J. T. (1974). Patterns of intergenerational occupational movements: A smallest-space analysis. *American Journal of Sociology, 79*(5), 1278–1299.

Mortimer, J. T. (1976). Social class, work and the family: Some implications of the father's occupation for familial relationships and sons' career decisions. *Journal of Marriage and the Family, 38*(2), 241–256.

Mortimer, J. T., Zimmer-Gembeck, M. J., Holmes, M., & Shanahan, M. J. (2002). The process of occupational decision making: Patterns during the transition to adulthood. *Journal of Vocational Behavior, 61*(3), 439–465.

Pedersen, N. L., Spotts, E., & Kato, K. (2005). Genetic influences on midlife functioning. In: S. L. Willis & M. Martin (Eds), *Middle adulthood: A lifespan perspective.* Newbury Park, CA: Sage.

Renzulli, L. A., & Aldrich, H. E. (2005). Who can you turn to? Tie activation within core business discussion networks, *Social Forces, 84*(1), 323–342.

Renzulli, L., Aldrich, H. E., & Moody, J. (2000). Family matters: Consequences of personal networks for business startup and survival. *Social Forces, 79*(2), 523–546.

Reynolds, P. D., & White, S. B. (1997). *The entrepreneurial process: Economic growth, men, women, and minorities.* Westport, CN: Quorum Books.

Rosenfeld, R. A. (1992). Job mobility and career processes. In: J. Blake & J. Hagan (Eds), *Annual review of sociology,* (Vol. 18, pp. 39–61). Palo Alto, CA: Annual Reviews, Inc.

Rytina, S. (1992). Scaling the intergenerational continuity of occupation: Is occupational inheritance ascriptive after all? *American Journal of Sociology, 97*(6), 1658–1688.

Rytina, S. (2000). Is occupational mobility declining in the U.S.? *Social Forces, 78*(4), 1227–1276.

Schneider, B. L., & Stevenson, D. (1999). *The ambitious generation: America's teenagers: motivated but directionless*, New Haven, CT: Yale University Press.

Schooler, C., Mulatu, M. S., & Oates, G. (2004). Occupational self-direction, intellectual functioning, and self-directed orientation in older workers: Findings and implications for individuals and societies. *The American Journal of Sociology, 110*(1), 161–197.

Shanahan, M. J., & Hofer, S. M. (2005). Social context in gene-environment interactions: Retrospect and prospect. *Journal of Gerontology, 60B*(Special Issue I). 65–76.

Sorensen, J. (2006). Closure vs. exposure: Mechanisms in the intergenerational transmission of self-employment. In: M. Ruef & M. Lounsbury (Eds). *Research in the sociology of organizations*, Elsevier: JAI.

Steinmetz, G., & Wright, E. O. (1989). The fall and rise of the petty bourgeoisie: Changing patterns of self-employment in the Postwar United States. *American Journal of Sociology, 94*(5), 973–1018.

Trice, A. D., Hughes, M. A., Odum, C., Woods, K., & McClellan, N. C. (1995). The origins of children's career aspirations: IV. Testing hypotheses from four theories. *The Career Development Quarterly, 43*(4), 307–322.

Trice, A. D., & Knapp, L. (1992). Relationship of children's career aspirations to parents' occupations, *Journal of Genetic Psychology, 153*(3), 355–357.

Uusitalo, R. (2001), Homo entreprenaurus? *Applied Economics, 33*(13), 1631–1638.

Van Praag, C. M., & Cramer, J. S. (2001). The roots of entrepreneurship and labour demand: Individual ability and low risk aversion, *Economica, 68*(269), 45–62.

82   HOWARD E. ALDRICH AND PHILLIP H. KIM

Waller, N. G., Lykken, D. T., & Tellegen, A. (1995). Occupational interests, leisure time interests, and personality: Three domains or one? Findings from the Minnesota twins registry. In: R. Dawis & D. Lubinski (Eds), *Assessing individual differences in human behavior* (pp. 233–259). Palo Alto, CA: Davies-Black.

Whiston, S. C., & Keller, B. K. (2004). The influences of the family of origin on career development: A review and analysis. *The Counseling Psychologist, 32*(4), 493–568.

Williams, D. (2004). Youth self employment: Its nature and consequences. *Small Business Economics, 23*(4), 323–336.

US Department of Labor. (2004). *Employee tenure summary*. Washington, DC: United States Department of Labor.

[22]

Small Business Economics (2006)
DOI 10.1007/s11187-006-0007-x

Access (Not) Denied: The Impact
of Financial, Human, and Cultural
Capital on Entrepreneurial Entry
in the United States*

Phillip H. Kim
Howard E. Aldrich
Lisa A. Keister

ABSTRACT. Entrepreneurship contributes to business dynamics in all economies, and the individual benefits of starting a business are clear. Nonetheless, access to business start-ups may not be available to all people because of resource constraints. Using a unique new data set for the United States, we examine the relative importance of three forms of resources in pursuing start-up ventures: financial, human, and cultural capital. Our analysis of the Panel Study of Entrepreneurial Dynamics shows that neither financial nor cultural capital resources are necessary conditions for entrepreneurial entry. By contrast, potential entrepreneurs gain significant advantages if they possess high levels of human capital. Specifically, advanced education and managerial experience are significantly positively associated with entrepreneurial entry. Our findings suggest that attempts at entering entrepreneurship, at least in the short-term, may be increasing, as opportunities to acquire human capital are becoming more widespread.

KEY WORDS: Entrepreneurial entry, nascent entrepreneur, financial resources, human capital, cultural capital

JEL CLASSIFICATION: C21, J23, J24, M13

1. Introduction

In spite of numerous risks, the appeal of being self-employed lures many workers in the United States into attempts at starting new businesses. Buoyed by prospects of greater job autonomy and a chance to be their own boss, their pursuit of business ownership fits into the American ideal of grasping opportunities for

Final version accepted on February 4, 2006

Phillip H. Kim, Howard E. Aldrich, Lisa A. Keister
Department of Sociology
University of North Carolina at Chapel Hill
C. B. #3210, Hamilton Hall, Chapel Hill,
NC. 27599-3210, USA
E-mail: pkim@unc.edu

advancement and upward social mobility without regard to one's current status (Chinoy, 1955). For example, Steinmetz and Wright (1989) noted that in 1980, "57% of all people in the American working class and two-thirds of all male workers say that they would like to be self-employed someday" (974). Aspirations for an entrepreneurial career cut across the occupational spectrum, reflecting the tradition of "ideological equalitarianism" in the United States – a belief in equal access to widely available opportunities (Lipset and Bendix, 1959). About 10 percent of the U.S. labor force is self-employed full time at a given time, and over their lifetimes, about 40 percent of U.S. adults will experience a spell of self-employment. Despite this evidence concerning widespread access, some scholars have nonetheless asked whether opportunities to become an entrepreneur are distributed evenly across workers or whether such chances fall disproportionately to those who are already advantaged. For example, nearly four decades of social mobility research, driven principally by Blau and Duncan's (1967) status attainment model, have shown that rates of recruitment into self-employment depend heavily upon the occupations of one's parents.[1]

In this article, we explore whether wealthy and high-income individuals are more likely to attempt transitions into entrepreneurship than less advantaged individuals. We know that factors other than wealth and income are important in business formation, and thus to avoid specification bias, we build a model of nascent entrepreneurship that includes human and cultural capital factors.

First, with regard to financial capital, if prior wealth or high current income is necessary for starting a business, people who are already financially advantaged will be most likely to attempt entrepreneurship. Second, having sufficient human capital to begin the organizing process may embolden potential entrepreneurs. We focus on several dimensions of human capital, such as educational background and work experience that may give potential entrepreneurs necessary skills and qualifications. Third, individuals contemplating entrepreneurship might benefit from high levels of cultural capital. Obtaining key business skills, especially tacit knowledge, occurs most easily through direct exposure to an entrepreneurial environment, and thus individuals with family business backgrounds might have an advantage over others.

To fully see the impact of the three forms of capital on people's pursuit of entrepreneurship, we need to study people at the earliest stage of the process, when they are still trying to pull their ideas and resources together. We refer to this initial transition as *entrepreneurial entry*. Researchers have typically studied entrepreneurs fairly far along in the business formation process, despite the fact that questions about access to entrepreneurship really address behaviors and processes that occur very early in the process. Designs that fail to capture individuals in the early stages of planning their ventures have thus hampered investigators. Some researchers have used cross-sectional studies to compare self-employed persons with wage and salary workers, whereas others have used longitudinal designs and observed wage and salary workers making successful transitions into self-employment. Studying those who have succeeded, however, does not reveal the characteristics of those who were initially attracted to the role but subsequently failed. Thus, in this article, we refer to *entrepreneurial entry* as a decision to attempt a start-up, rather than the successful establishment of a new business.

Ideally, research should focus on *nascent entrepreneurs*, people still in the process of organizing and assembling the resources they need for a new business (Reynolds and White, 1997). By focusing on nascent entrepreneurs, we also avoid a common misperception that entrepreneurship is

concerned only with large, successful firms. Instead, the study of entrepreneurship encompasses a much larger population of small and often unsuccessful start-ups. Studying nascent entrepreneurs requires overcoming a major data collection hurdle: only about 4–6 percent of the adult population enter the nascent entrepreneur pool each year (Reynolds and White, 1997). Identifying enough nascent entrepreneurs to ensure statistical power and finding them early in the planning process further compounds the difficulty of data collection. We use a unique dataset, the Panel Study of Entrepreneurial Dynamics (PSED) to overcome difficulties encountered in previous empirical efforts.

We begin by reviewing research on the relationship between financial, human, and cultural capital and entrepreneurship and develop a series of seven hypotheses. Then, we explain the design of the PSED, our operationalization of independent and dependent variables, and the logic of our statistical analysis. After presenting our results, we discuss how they compare with previous findings and conclude with some research and policy implications derived from our analysis.

2. Financial resources and entrepreneurial entry

Financial resources can be viewed along two dimensions: household wealth and household income. Given the moderate correlation between the two, typically around 0.5 or less, we contend both forms of resources affect attempts at transitions into entrepreneurship (Keister and Moller, 2000). We conceptualize financial resources at the household level. For example, a decision to pursue a start-up venture by a married couple may involve jointly owned resources (such as a home) to raise additional capital. Other household members can provide income while a nascent entrepreneur plans the new venture.

2.1. Household wealth

The possible benefits nascent entrepreneurs enjoy from wealth can be linked to a theory of *liquidity constraints* (Evans and Jovanovic, 1989). According to this theory, business start-ups often require substantial start-up capital. If personal financial resources are inadequate, entrepreneurs must turn to credit markets to capitalize their new businesses. However, for several reasons, obtaining financing through bank loans or investors can be difficult. First, because these businesses are small and high risk clients, lenders are often unwilling to provide capital and some compensate by increasing borrowing costs (Jurik, 1998). Second, new businesses incur the cost of identifying potential financiers and undergoing bonding activities to ensure firm legitimacy. To overcome these barriers, nascent entrepreneurs often use personal capital from family wealth holdings as collateral. As another option, entrepreneurs can bypass the credit markets altogether by investing their own funds in the business venture to cover ongoing expenses until sufficient revenues are generated. In support of the liquidity constraint model, Holtz-Eakin et al. (1994) found a positive influence of family assets on transitions to self-employment. We note, however, that their research focused on successfully completed transitions, not attempts.

Liquidity constraint arguments suggest a direct positive association between wealth and starting a business, but at very high wealth levels, people have other career options. Proponents believe that very high wealth individuals may be more inclined to fund other nascent entrepreneurs rather than be directly involved in pursuing their own entrepreneurial pursuit. The potential pecuniary gains from a successful venture for high wealth individuals may not be worth making the personal sacrifice required to plan a start-up. Based on previous theorizing and research findings from the liquidity constraints perspective, we propose that *household wealth has a positive curvilinear association with the likelihood of entrepreneurial entry (H1a)*.

Skeptics might note two potential difficulties with the liquidity constraints view as applied to the situation of nascent entrepreneurs. First, its empirical support comes entirely from studies carried out on people already in business, rather than people still working toward that goal. Whereas it might be the case that persons who succeed in establishing a viable business long enough to be interviewed indeed have more wealth than others, they represent the fortunate few. Only about half of nascent entrepreneurs succeed

in founding a new firm, and fewer than one in ten new ventures grow (Reynolds and White, 1997).

Second, most businesses do not require large amounts of financial capital in their start-up phase. Data from the 1992 United States Census – Characteristics of Business Owners survey showed that the majority of business owners in the United States started their firms with less than $5,000 (Census, 1992). Home-based businesses, for instance, which accounted for half of all new businesses in 1992, often require little capital up front. Although certain industries such as technology and manufacturing have high capital requirements, start-up capital requirements are generally low across all industries. In addition to minimal start-up costs, most businesses do not have many employees. In the United States, 89 percent of the approximately 5 million firms have less than 20 employees (SBA, 1994). Even industries often thought of as having high capital requirements are dominated by small firms. For example, 73 percent of manufacturing firms in 2001 employed fewer than 20 employees (SBA 2004).

In contrast to the attractive dilemma facing high wealth individuals of whether to invest in their own startup or those of other people, low wealth individuals confront an altogether different situation. Although low wealth individuals cannot invest in other peoples' ventures, the low initial capital requirements for most types of business put a startup attempt within easy reach of most households. Many aspiring business owners use financial bootstrapping methods to decrease external capital needs in their start-up phase. Harrison et al. (2004) described three types of bootstrapping: reliance on internal funding sources; low cost acquisition of financial resources; and low cost acquisition of other start-up resources. For example, in the first category of bootstrapping, a second mortgage on a house – which is the single largest asset for most households – may generate enough funds to start an internet consulting business or a landscaping service. In the second category, informal credit sources such as credit cards and rotating credit associations provide short-term liquidity options. Family members serve as another source of funding, especially if capital needs are modest (Parker, 2004). In the third category, new businesses often do not require a separate office location, as nascent entrepreneurs conduct initial operations in their homes. Given the low initial barriers to entry, we are thus somewhat skeptical of the liquidity constraint hypothesis with regard to *attempted initial entry*. We therefore propose an alternative hypothesis: *household wealth has no association with the likelihood of entrepreneurial entry (H1b)*.

2.2. Household income

Individuals may weigh their participation in a start-up venture in terms of the opportunity costs of reducing their present income from employment (Blanchflower and Oswald, 1998). A nascent entrepreneur makes two evaluations: prospects for additional income from a start-up relative to present income, and prospects for future income from current employment. At lower income levels, individuals may find the opportunity cost so low that they lose little or nothing by pursuing the uncertainties of income from a new venture. For example, if a venture fails, an individual may be able to find wage employment elsewhere at a similar income level. Or, the projected minimal income stream from a new venture may be similar, in the short-term, to an individual's current income stream. In such cases, an individual would pursue a new venture, given a higher projected long-term income stream. For example, Devine (1994) argued that many women choose self-employment as a response to a higher potential income from business ownership versus lower potential income from wage and salary work.

People in high paying occupations can undoubtedly invest more in the entrepreurial process, but we propose that those individuals find entrepreneurship less appealing. Sørensen (2000) reasoned that some higher income labor force participants benefit from rents generated from firm-specific skills. He highlighted a key decision faced by individuals in well-paying occupations. By remaining in their existing employment relationship, these individuals build wealth by accumulating rents from specialized and firm-specific skills. Decisions to obtain advanced professional degrees or certifications are made with the intention of recouping the initial investment and securing higher, long-term income. Therefore, in higher income brackets, individuals may find that the loss of present and future income from their current place of employment outweighs prospective gains from an entrepreneurial venture.

Consequently, individuals at higher income levels may perceive future income streams from their present occupation more favorably than an uncertain outcome from an entrepreneurial venture. Supporting this perception, findings by Hamilton (2000) (using the 1984 panel of the Survey of Income and Program Participation) and Moskowitz and Vissing-Jorgensen (2002) (using the 1989–1998 Survey of Consumer Finances) showed that earnings generated from self-employment lagged behind wage and salary employment.[2]

For these reasons, we propose that *household income has a positive curvilinear association with the likelihood of entrepreneurial entry (H2)*.

3. Human capital and entrepreneurial entry

In addition to financial resources, theoretical models of entrepreneurial attempts should include the role and impact of human capital characteristics (Åstebro and Bernhardt, 2005). Education and work experience are the most common dimensions of human capital used in labor force participation analyses, and they have been associated with successful transitions into entrepreneurship. We believe these characteristics also apply to nascent entrepreneurs. We further differentiate these dimensions in order to clarify which types of human capital affect the prospects of nascent entrepreneurs.

3.1. Education

Formal education can affect the likelihood of entrepreneurial entry through (1) the acquisition of skills, (2) credentialing, and (3) sorting people by ambition and assertiveness. However, the association between education and entrepreneurship is not necessarily straightforward (Bates, 1997). General business and technical skills can guide nascent entrepreneurs in setting up basic business functions and avoiding common mistakes; individuals are more likely to learn these in specialized courses and training, rather than in typical high school and college courses. Certain courses, such as vocational programs, enable students to learn specific trade and business skills. In other courses, students develop critical thinking, communication, teamwork, and other general skills that will be necessary as an entrepreneur. Formal education, as a credential, can also provide access to certain social networks (e.g., alumni network) or serve as a positive signal for nascent entrepreneurs when evaluated by resource providers (e.g., venture capitalists). The acquisition of skills and credentials may create valuable opportunities for individuals to work for others, rather than pursuing a new business venture.

As the U.S. labor market has become increasingly service- and information-based, education has played an increasingly important role in facilitating new business formation in some but not necessarily all industries.[3] For example, in knowledge-based industries, such as technology, finance, real estate, and insurance, education is clearly relevant to business acumen. Even if the knowledge and skills gained in formal education are not directly relevant to entrepreneurship, educational achievements may be an indicator of someone's ambition, achievement motivation, and endurance, as well as their social class background. Formal education thus allows individuals to gain knowledge and skills, earn credentials valued by others in the business community, as well as sorting people by ambition and assertiveness. However, people who start small businesses in trades such as construction or carpentry have little need for advanced formal education. Instead, they draw on their acquired technical skills and on-the-job experience.

Thus, given the ambiguity about education's possible value to entrepreneurial entry, we offer no hypothesis concerning educational attainment.

3.2. Work experience

Previous research has shown that work experience may be a very important component of human capital for nascent entrepreneurs (Brüderl et al., 1992). Without sufficient work experience, individuals may encounter difficulties in taking the first steps toward becoming an entrepreneur. We believe that individuals may be influenced to pursue entrepreneurship through multiple forms of work experience (Parker, 2004). In particular, we focus on four types of work experience: general full-time work experience, managerial experience, previous start-up experience, and current self-employment.

In addition to generating wide-ranging business-related skills, general full-time work experience provides two important learning opportunities. If such work experience occurs within the new venture's industry, individuals can rely on the knowledge of their industry to identify potential opportunities and other industry-related conditions (Shane, 2003). Furthermore, individuals gain access to various social networks for market information, access to capital, hiring employees, establishing reputations, and developing supplier and customer relationships. Previous managerial experience can give people skills needed to coordinate and administer diverse activities in the early phases of a start-up (Boden and Nucci, 2000). In previous research using age as a proxy for accumulated human capital, age exhibited a curvilinear effect, peaking at a certain level, beyond which its effects decreased (Bates, 1997). *Accordingly, we expect positive curvilinear relationships for entrepreneurial entry due to general (H3) and managerial work experience (H4).*

Prior start-up experience and current self-employment are two additional ways in which nascent entrepreneurs develop relevant planning and managerial experience for a new start-up (Kalleberg and Leicht, 1991). Individuals with prior experience starting a new business may develop confidence in their ability to identify promising opportunities (Shane, 2003). The success of their earlier ventures may further enhance their confidence. Therefore, we expect that *individuals with prior start-up experience will have a higher likelihood of entrepreneurial entry than people without such experience (H5).*

Research suggests that those who are currently self-employed are more likely to be involved in other new business ventures than those who are working for others (Renzulli et al., 2000). Studies also show that many business owners own more than one business. For example, Aldrich et al. (1983) found rates of multiple ownership among Asian and white shopkeepers ranging from 10 to 34 percent in four English cities, with the average around 19 percent. In Vancouver, Canada, Aldrich et al. (1998) found that 36 percent of business owners owned multiple businesses. People already in business have many opportunities to develop valuable contacts, as well as accumulate the additional wealth that can be used to begin a new venture. They are also well placed to spot new opportunities in their own or contiguous industries. Thus, we believe that *persons already in business will be more likely than others to attempt to start another one (H6)*.

4. Cultural capital and entrepreneurial entry

The children of entrepreneurial parents are more likely to become entrepreneurs in their adult careers (Blau and Duncan, 1967; Western, 1994). Steinmetz and Wright (1989) reported that among adults in 1980 in the U.S. labor force, "nearly 32% come from families in which the head of the household was self-employed most of the time while they were growing up, and 46% come from families in which the head of household was self-employed at least part of the time" (974). Butler and Herring (1991) and Hout and Rosen (2000) both found a positive association between father's self-employment and son's self-employment. Parents can pass down their businesses to their children upon retirement or provide capital for new businesses. These second-generation entrepreneurs benefit from exposure, perhaps at early ages, to an entrepreneurial environment, ranging from practical matters of running business operations to developing social networks to coping with the risks associated with entrepreneurship. Informal training and pre-market experiences are cultural capital resources that might increase interest in a start-up project (Lentz and Laband, 1990).

Parental role modeling of entrepreneurial values, such as autonomy and perseverance, provides a valuable cultural resource for future entrepreneurs (Hout, 1984; Miller and Swanson, 1958). These values may be transmitted to the children through direct encouragement and indirect cues by their parents. Children in a family business benefit from apprenticing with family mentors and as well joining business-related social networks. Some entrepreneurs devote considerable time and effort to sustaining this resource due to the high level of occupational commitment required establish a successful business (Blau and Duncan, 1967). For these reasons, we expect that *individuals with a parent as an entrepreneur will be more likely to attempt entrepreneurship than others (H7)*.

5. Data and methods

5.1. *The PSED data*

We analyzed data from the Panel Study of Entrepreneurial Dynamics (PSED). The PSED contains a nationally representative sample of nascent and non-entrepreneurs with detailed information about financial resources, work histories, and other individual and background traits. The PSED enhances our understanding of nascent entrepreneurs in three important ways. First, individuals qualified as a nascent entrepreneur based on a four-part definition, providing a more focused definition of self-employment than those used in other studies (e.g., Hamilton, 2000). Because of inconsistent definitions of self-employment used to categorize cases, previous findings are difficult to compare. Second, finding individuals early in their planning process minimizes the selection bias encountered by studies relying on small business databases that do not include entrepreneurs who have abandoned efforts prior to data collection (e.g., Bates, 1997). Third, key demographic variables, such as age, race, gender, and region are available, which were not included in earlier studies (e.g., Evans and Leighton, 1989). Over-sampling of minorities and women in the PSED enhanced the quality of the data in these respective groups. As a result of these enhancements, we are able to improve model specification in examining nascent entrepreneurs. A complete description of the study's background and sampling methodology can be found in Gartner et al. (2004b) and Reynolds et al. (2004).

Screening of the United States adult population (18 years of age and older, within the contiguous 48 states) took place between July, 1998 and January, 2000, using random digit dialing (RDD) methodology. In the screening interview of 59,575 individuals, respondents were identified as nascent entrepreneurs using four qualifying questions to form a potential pool of respondents. Individuals qualified if they expected to be owners of a new business they have been actively trying to start within the last 12 months. Owners reporting firms with positive cash flow for at least three months or majority institutional ownership did not qualify. From this pool of 1,492 eligible individuals, nascent entrepreneurs were randomly drawn and invited for participation in the study. 830 nascent firms comprise the final Nascent Entrepreneur sample. Additionally, women and minorities were over-sampled. Collection for the Comparison Group sample also occurred in two phases. In this screening interview of 5,047 individuals, 639 qualified to participate in a survey of work and career patterns in the United States. After randomly drawing individuals from this pool, 431 respondents completed final interview to form the Comparison Group sample. These respondents answered the same set of basic background questions as the Nascent Entrepreneur sample. Only minorities were over-sampled for Comparison Group.

Ideally, the PSED would have interviewed respondents who did not qualify as nascent entrepreneurs when initially selected in the Nascent Entrepreneur sample, hence eliminating the need for a Comparison Group sample. However, financial considerations made that design infeasible. Therefore, we combined the Comparison Group sample with the Nascent Entrepreneur sample into one final data set for analysis.

We used individual case weights for both Nascent Entrepreneur and Comparison Group samples in our analyses to ensure representativeness. We relied on weights calculated by the Institute for Survey Research at the University of Michigan for the PSED. These weights accounted for differences in selection probabilities based on age, education, race, and sex (based on the Current Population Surveys conducted by the U.S. Census) and correct for differences due to differential non-response rates (Curtin and Reynolds, 2004). Weights were originally calculated using the respective samples, and we recalculated them so that each case accurately represents their actual proportion of the United States' population when both samples are combined into one.

5.2. Dependent variable

We coded our dependent variable (nascent entrepreneur = 1) if the respondent qualified based on the following criteria. A respondent must have answered yes to the following question: "Are you, alone or with others, now trying to start a new business?" In addition, we only included individuals as nascents if they expected to be owners or part owners in the firm, reported being active in trying to start the new business in the past twelve months, and were still in the start-up phase.[4]

5.3. Independent variables

We used two measures of financial resources. The correlation between household net worth and income was low (0.29), consistent with previous research and suggesting that these two variables, in combination, provide a composite picture of an individual's financial well-being. *Household net worth* includes the value of total assets (e.g., physical property and investments, including primary residence) net of outstanding debt (e.g., mortgage, home equity and car loans). These questions are also used in the Survey of Consumer Finances conducted by the Federal Reserve Board. We transformed the raw wealth variable into a quadratic term, anticipating a non-linear relationship. We retained all cases, including cases where wealth is less than or equal to zero, for a more accurate assessment of how wealth is associated with becoming an entrepreneur.[5] *Household income* includes income from work, government transfers, pensions, and all other sources before taxes in the previous year. We transformed the raw income value into a quadratic term as well.

Respondents who did not provide a value for total household wealth or income responded to a series of questions in which they estimated their appropriate income and wealth range and provide information on specific wealth components. We recoded these responses based on a set of decision rules (Kim et al., 2004) and achieved complete information for 96 percent of the cases for the net worth and income variables. The median values for household net worth and household income are comparable to other survey data.[6]

We included five measures of human capital. *Education* is a categorical variable indicating the highest level of education completed. As Parker (2004) noted, "it is often informative to distinguish between different types of labour market experience" (70). He noted that results have been "scant but interesting." We included four indicators of work experience. We used *net full time work experience* with managerial experience subtracted (in years). *Managerial experience* is the number of years of managerial, supervisory, or administrative experience. We transformed both variables into their quadratic forms. We included a dichotomous indicator for *previous start-up experience*. We created three dummy variables for *current business ownership* based on a respondent's employment status: (1) people who said they were business owners or self-employed with no other jobs; (2) owners or self-employed persons who also worked for an employer for less than 35 hours per week; and (3) owners or self-employed persons who also worked for an employer for more than 35 hours per week. We reasoned that working for others, especially on a full-time basis, would interfere with current owners' ability to allocate time to starting a new venture. We believe these work experience measures improve the operationalization of the human capital concept for which previous studies relied on proxy measures, such as educational background and age (Bates, 1997; Dunn and Holtz-Eakin, 2000). We also followed other researchers who have measured work experience with multiple indicators (Bosma et al., 2004). To test for the effects of cultural capital resources, we included a dichotomous indicator of whether a *respondent's parents were business owners*.

We included four control variables in our models. We controlled for respondent's *age, gender, race, marital status, and region of residence*. We transformed raw age by taking its natural logarithm because previous research has shown that the likelihood of entrepreneurial entry increases up to a certain age and then plateaus (Evans and Leighton, 1989). We also controlled for whether the respondent was *foreign born* or the respondent's *parents were foreign born*. Descriptive statistics for the variables in our model appear in Table I.

6. Results

In Table II, we present the logit coefficients for our regression models.[7] We performed regression diagnostics to identify any potential outliers and influential cases.[8]

6.1. Financial resources

In Model A, neither financial resource variable had a statistically significant association with being a nascent entrepreneur, after controlling for other variables.[9] Our analysis thus supports the second of our two alternative household wealth hypotheses (H1b rather than H1a) and does not support H2, which predicted a positive association with household income. The insignificant finding for household income is consistent with Parker (2003).

These results contradict H1a, based on the expectation from liquidity constraint theory that financial resources limit transition attempts at entrepreneurship. Our findings are consistent with Hurst and Lusardi (2004) in their analysis of the Panel Study of Income Dynamics (PSID) and with Aldrich et al.'s study (1998) of business owners in British Columbia. Uusitalo (2001) also reported no relationship between net worth and transition attempts at entrepreneurship in Finland. Financial resources are not a barrier to attempting entrepreneurship for most individuals, allowing aspiring entrepreneurs to make voluntary attempts at a transition between formal wage employment and entrepreneurial activity (Parker 2004).

We offer five explanations for these findings. First, most nascent entrepreneurs started their ventures with very little financial capital. Approximately 75 percent of nascent entrepreneurs

TABLE I

Descriptive statistics for Panel Study of Entrepreneurial Dynamics, 1998–2000

Variable	Mean	SD	Min	Max
N = 1,050				
Dependent variable				
Nascent entrepreneurs	6%	0.23	0	1
Independent variables				
Financial resources variables				
Household net worth	$199,389	$477,856	–$378,000	$13,300,000
Median	$82,000			
Non-positive	7%			
$0–$100,000	49%			
Household income (annual)	$53,303	$43,506	$0	$1,800,000
Median	$45,000			
Human capital variables				
Education				
Up to high school degree	24%	0.43	0	1
Technical/vocational	5%	0.22	0	1
Some college	38%	0.49	0	1
College degree	18%	0.39	0	1
Post college	14%	0.35	0	1
Work experience (net of managerial experience – years)	10.70	9.00	0	60
Managerial experience (years)	8.02	8.60	0	50
Helped start other business	48%	0.50	0	1
Current business owner and not working for others	11%	0.31	0	1
Current business owner and working for others less than 35 hours/week	5%	0.22	0	1
Current business owner and working for others 35 hours/week or more	8%	0.28	0	1
Either parent business owner	50%	0.50	0	1
Control variables				
Age	42.69	13.72	18	93
Male	47%	0.50	0	1
Race				
White	73%	0.44	0	1
Black	11%	0.32	0	1
Hispanic	7%	0.26	0	1
Other	8%	0.27	0	1
Foreign born	6%	0.25	0	1
Either parent Foreign born	16%	0.37	0	1
Married	54%	0.50	0	1
Region				
Northeast	20%	0.40	0	1
South	33%	0.47	0	1
Midwest	25%	0.44	0	1
West	22%	0.41	0	1

contributed $10,000 or less into their ventures, while 50 percent began with about $2,500 or less. Removing professional and service industries, the initial investment was only slightly higher: less than $3,000 for about 50 percent of nascent entrepreneurs and less than $12,000 for about 75 percent of nascent

entrepreneurs. Second, 66 percent of nascent entrepreneurs reported developing their current venture at their residence or personal property, further reducing the need for start-up capital.

Third, we found few nascent entrepreneurs seeking funding from others for their ventures. As

TABLE II

Results from logistic regression analysis of being a nascent entrepreneur on financial resources, human, and cultural capital variables: Panel Study of Entrepreneurial Dynamics, 1998–2000

	Model A		Model B (24 month)†	
Financial resources				
Household net worth/$10,000	−0.007	[0.006]	−0.003	[0.006]
Household net worth^2	1.13E 05	[.0000117]	7.63E 06	[.0000134]
Household income/$10,000	−0.007	[0.044]	0.019	[0.049]
Household income^2	0.001	[0.001]	0.0002	[0.001]
Human capital				
Education				
Technical/vocation	0.333	[0.375]	0.491	[0.432]
Some college	0.364	[0.224]	0.34	[0.266]
College graduate	0.722**	[0.273]	0.807**	[0.318]
Post college	0.459	[0.319]	0.134	[0.389]
Work experience (net of managerial experience)	0.024	[0.032]	−0.013	[0.036]
Work experience^2 (net of managerial experience)	−0.001	[0.001]	−0.0003	[0.001]
Managerial experience	0.075*	[0.032]	0.083*	[0.041]
Managerial experience^2	−0.002*	[0.001]	−0.002*	[0.001]
Helped start other businesses	−0.704**	[0.190]	−0.655**	[0.226]
Current business owner and not working for others	1.724**	[0.283]	1.696**	[0.330]
Current business owner and working for others less than 35 hours/week	1.389**	[0.324]	1.049**	[0.384]
Current business owner and working for others 35 hours/week or more	0.954**	[0.305]	0.617*	[0.361]
Cultural capital				
Parents business owner	−0.085	[0.188]	−0.17	[0.221]
Control variables				
Age (LN)	−1.481**	[0.434]	−1.533**	[0.480]
Male	0.580**	[0.178]	0.325	[0.208]
Race				
Black	0.674**	[0.203]	0.608**	[0.233]
Hispanic	0.225	[0.302]	0.253	[0.378]
Other	−0.51	[0.374]	−0.920*	[0.509]
Foreign born	0.176	[0.380]	0.528	[0.473]
Either parent foreign born	−0.186	[0.380]	−0.401	[0.402]
Married	0.29	[0.184]	0.199	[0.218]
Region				
South	−0.112	[0.244]	−0.086	[0.284]
Midwest	−0.113	[0.269]	−0.133	[0.315]
West	0.249	[0.270]	0.09	[0.324]
Constant	1.193	[1.424]	1.836	[1.600]
−2LL	−205.25		−133.42	
DF	28		28	
χ^2	117.9		93.91	
	$N = 1050$		$N = 684$	

*Significant at 5%; **significant at 1% (one-tailed test for primary independent variables; two-tailed test for control variables).
†Sample restricted to nascent entrepreneurs who thought about starting a business within the last 24 months.
Reference categories: education (up to high school degree); race (white); region (northeast). Standard errors in [ ].

shown in the last row of Table III, only about 56 percent of nascent entrepreneurs pursued external funding sources. Among the financing options, 33 percent of nascent entrepreneurs used credit cards most often and 16 percent turned to friends and other family members. Nascent entrepreneurs borrowed from banks as secondary options, and may have followed a financial

TABLE III

Funding sources of nascent entrepreneurs by industry: Panel Study of Entrepreneurial Dynamics, 1998–2000

	Distribution of nascent entrepreneurs (%)	Requested funding (%)	Credit cards (%)	Friends & family (%)	Bank loan (%)	SBA loan (%)	Second mortgage (%)	Venture capital (%)	Personal finance company (%)	Current employer (%)
Agriculture, forestry, fishery	2.88	63.26	36.71	9.37	33.45	0.00	8.05	6.18	0.00	4.13
Construction	4.27	43.85	29.65	9.69	8.43	7.05	0.00	1.73	0.00	2.79
Manufacturing	4.38	60.78	15.81	21.94	13.57	8.03	11.65	4.15	3.35	0.00
Transportation, communication, utilities	1.98	72.67	36.45	9.00	57.82	9.19	0.00	7.42	6.02	0.00
Wholesale	2.52	66.43	49.47	13.04	22.22	7.51	9.18	8.39	0.00	13.04
Retail	20.78	59.90	32.95	19.45	11.13	4.95	3.61	4.06	5.83	2.57
Business services	30.76	52.30	33.93	10.03	11.27	3.67	3.84	3.10	1.61	2.46
Consumer services	14.09	59.48	37.79	20.64	10.04	4.88	2.39	0.68	2.61	0.00
Health, education, medical, government services	18.35	42.54	24.23	18.31	7.74	4.16	0.00	3.24	0.00	3.81
Total	100.00	56.19	33.08	15.59	13.03	4.79	3.70	3.30	2.77	2.37

The Impact of Financial Capital on Entrepreneurial Entry

resources priority order by applying for bank loans only after other primary options had been pursued (Myers, 1984). Capital-intensive industries such as transportation, communications, utilities, and wholesale exhibited higher external funding requests, where a higher proportion of nascent entrepreneurs sought third-party financing, presumably due to larger funding needs. However, for the majority of nascent entrepreneurs who were in retail or service-related industries, funding requirements remained low.

Fourth, as shown in Table IV, we found no substantively significant association between respondents' household net worth and whether they had pursued a bank loan or been approved for one. Although nascent entrepreneurs with zero or negative net worth applied for a bank loan slightly more often than higher net worth individuals, they were only slightly less likely to be approved, compared to positive wealth nascent entrepreneurs.[10] Although not a study of entrepreneurial loan approval rates, our descriptive findings point toward a credit market willing to fund individuals who do not have significant wealth. Our findings indicate that many aspiring business owners used financial bootstrapping methods to decrease external capital needs in their start-up phase (Harrison and Mason, 1997).

We ran one additional test to explore whether the relationship between financial resources and being a nascent entrepreneur was conditioned by the length of the organizing period. In their analysis of entrepreneurial motivation using the PSED, Gartner et al. (2004a) found differences when restricting the sample to nascent entrepreneurs who started organizing within the last 24 months. To see if our results still held under this restricted condition, we reduced our sample to those respondents who reported they had begun thinking about starting a new venture within the twenty-four months prior to the interview. We thus focused on "determined" nascent entrepreneurs who began their start-up project more recently, rather than nascent entrepreneurs who may have been "tinkering" with an idea over a longer period. When we tested our model on the reduced sample of the "determined" nascent entrepreneurs (Table II, Model B), our results were unchanged. Financial resources did not have a significant association

TABLE IV
Pursuing bank funding by wealth of nascent entrepreneurs: Panel Study of Entrepreneurial Dynamics, 1998–2000

Household net worth (in percents)	Will pursue bank loan	Approved bank loan
Zero or less	18.81	40.64
$1–$50,000	12.62	47.62
$50,001–$100,000	13.87	45.49
$100,001–$250,000	11.97	58.85
Over $250,000	11.12	48.13
Total	12.99	48.59
p value	0.71 (ns)	0.18 (ns)

with being a nascent entrepreneur, even for the "determined" group.

The statistically insignificant relationship for household income (H2) supports an inference suggested by Parker's (2003) results from his study of the 1994 British Household Panel Survey and Family Expenditure Survey. Parker examined whether individuals are more likely to pursue self-employment because of opportunities to increase their income through schemes for tax avoidance. Based on his results, Parker argued that individuals do not pursue entrepreneurship solely for potential tax incentives and other income maximization reasons, a position also argued by Hamilton (2000).

Endogeneity of our financial resources and human capital variables may create a possible threat to the validity of these findings. Ideally, with longitudinal panel data on these variables, we could verify whether our results remain robust after accounting for possible reciprocal relationships with appropriate instrumental variables (e.g., Hurst and Lusardi, 2004). However, we believe that potential biases due to endogeneity are limited for two reasons. First, when we ran our models with the net worth and income variables separately, neither variable was statistically significant when included by itself. Thus, we concluded that even if income often generates additional wealth and even if wealth produces additional income, their reciprocal association was not causing us to underestimate their individual impact on entrepreneurial entry. Only if either financial resource variable, by itself, had a direct and statistically significant association with being a nascent entrepreneur would we be concerned.

Second, we argue that if biases were present, our results actually may overstate the impact of

wealth. A critique of our analysis based on a concern for endogeneity implies that a possible causal association between human capital (experience and education) and financial resources produces a situation in which including human and financial capital in the same equation leads to problems. Ideally, we should know much of the impact of "income" and "wealth" is really due to significant experience or advanced educational credentials. Absent that knowledge, some of the impact of "income" and "wealth" is really due to the (unmeasured) effects of human capital. With our cross-sectional data, we cannot decompose the effects of financial capital into the "true" effects of income and wealth nor the specific effect of human capital's impact on these financial resource variables. As we interpret this situation, our statistical analysis thus should, if anything, overstate the impact of the financial resource variables.

6.2. *Human capital*

In contrast to our results for financial resources, several human capital variables were significantly associated with being a nascent entrepreneur. Advanced formal education had a positive association with being a nascent entrepreneur. College graduates were twice as likely (i.e., $100 * e^{0.722}$) to be nascent entrepreneurs as people with high school degrees or less, but post-college education made no additional contribution to being a nascent entrepreneur. Our results thus suggest a curvilinear impact of education: both too little and too much education discourages attempted entrepreneurship.[11]

Two of the four work experience variables were significantly positively associated with being a nascent entrepreneur. Full-time work experience was not positively associated with being a nascent entrepreneur (H3), whereas managerial experience was positively associated (H4). The positive effect of managerial experience rose at a decreasing rate, peaking at approximately 19 years. We believe that our measures of work experience improve upon previous proxy indicators, such as education and age, which have conflicting effects on nascent entrepreneurship. Age is negatively associated with being a nascent entrepreneur, whereas both education and managerial work experience are positively associated.[12] Clearly, aging workers face an intersection of conflicting forces if they are in managerial positions.

Individuals with previous start-up experience (H5) were actually about 50 percent less likely to attempt another startup, compared to individuals without start-up experience. Individuals who were currently business owners or self-employed were about 2.6–5.6 times more likely to be nascent entrepreneurs, depending on the hours they spent working for others (H6). The three current-owner coefficients form the logical hierarchy that one would expect if working for others dampened the potential gains from owing one's own business or being self-employed. People who reported they were self-employed or a business owner but who also worked 35 hours or more a week clearly faced greater time and resource constraints than those reporting business ownership as their sole occupation. Our results support Ronstadt's "corridor principle" wherein current business owners perceive more opportunities than non-owners through what they have learned from their initial successful attempts to start a business (Ronstadt, 1988).

One possible explanation for the failure of H5 centers on what people learn from previous business startup experience. In retrospect, our H5 presumed a cycle of positive feedback that clearly cannot be sustained over the life course of most entrepreneurs. If it were, a far greater proportion of the working population would be small business owners. Given the difficulties entrepreneurs generally face, people who have been involved in previous startups, especially abandoned ones, may become discouraged and thus less likely to take part in another startup.

Indeed, due to the high mortality rate of new ventures, abandoned attempts must comprise the majority of previous attempts reported by our respondents (Reynolds and White, 1997). By learning from experience, these discouraged or disillusioned former entrepreneurs become more likely to opt for a wage and salary career. Therefore, our negative coefficient probably reflects the discouraging effects of previous experience and an assessment that another try would not reward the effort required.[13]

6.3. Cultural capital

Somewhat surprisingly, levels of entrepreneurial involvement among family had no association with being a nascent entrepreneur (H7). Although the proportion of entrepreneurial parents in our sample – 50 percent – was similar to earlier findings (e.g., 46 percent – Steinmetz and Wright, 1989), the presumed advantages of having at least one entrepreneurial parent were not apparent in our results – these people were no more likely than the children of wage and salary workers to be nascent entrepreneurs. We found no evidence to match previous findings of intergenerational immobility. We offer four possible explanations. First, perhaps this confirms that a goal of entrepreneurial parents was finally achieved in the last decade of the 20th century: to have their children pursue careers that do not involve the difficulties of starting and running a business (Aldrich et al., 1998). The prospects for working long hours and enduring economic uncertainties may dissuade children of entrepreneurial parents from following in their footsteps. Second, the limitations of impoverished cultural capital may only become obvious after a business begins operations, rather than at the planning and organizing stage. Third, our parental business ownership measure does not distinguish between parents who ran a successful business venture versus those for whom the enterprise was a miserable failure. We would need more information about parents' businesses to determine whether the transmission of cultural capital depends upon the achievements of one's mentors. Fourth, having parents in business may not sufficiently motivate children to enter entrepreneurship, but it is still possible that they provided help to their children via wealth transfers, which we did not capture in our data (e.g., Dunn and Holtz-Eakin, 2000).

6.4. *Control variables*

Among the control variables, we highlight the significant results for African-Americans. Fairlie (1999) argued that African-American men were one-third as likely to be self-employed as white men, citing lower asset levels and rate of self-employed fathers. Similarly, Butler and Herring (1991) and Hout and Rosen (2000) reported that African-Americans and Latino men were less likely to pursue self-employment after controlling for father's self-employment status. In contrast to previous results, we found that blacks were twice as likely as whites to be nascent entrepreneurs, net of other variables. This may be a leading indicator that foreshadows a shift in the rate of entrepreneurship in these minority groups, relative to whites. Fairlie (2004b) reported a growth rate of 87 percent in the number of self-employed blacks between 1979 and 1998, compared to a growth rate of 36 percent for whites, based on the Current Population Survey. However, it could also reflect special circumstances during a period when mass media outlets, politicians, and others trumpeted "entrepreneurship."

Women were less likely than men to be a nascent entrepreneur, as men were 1.8 times as likely as women to pursue a new venture in the full sample. These findings are consistent with previous research; after controlling for other factors, men are more likely than women to be entrepreneurs. In a Wisconsin study with a similar design to the PSED, Reynolds and White (1997) found that women were 60 percent less likely than men to be nascent entrepreneurs. Thus, although the rate of women attempting to start businesses increased between 1975 and 1990 (Devine, 1994), it still lags behind that for men.

7. Discussion

We examined whether lack of financial, human, and cultural capital resources poses a barrier to entrepreneurial entry. Previous findings on attempts at transitions into entrepreneurship have

been inconclusive because of poor data quality and the limited availability of information on people attempting to become entrepreneurs. We found that net worth did not have a statistically significant association with being a nascent entrepreneur, contrary to what liquidity constraint theory predicts. Rather than the wealthy having greater opportunities for creating additional wealth through business startups and the less-privileged having fewer opportunities, we found a human capital effect. Educational background and work experience (managerial experience and current business ownership) were positively associated with being a nascent entrepreneur, whereas previous start-up experience had a negative effect. Although lack of advanced education and lengthy managerial experience potentially pose obstacles to entrepreneurial entry, opportunities to invest in these forms of human capital are widely available. Additionally, experience with entrepreneurial family members, as a form of cultural capital, did not promote a transition to entrepreneurship. These findings suggest that intergenerational immobility among entrepreneurs, at least in the short-term, could be declining, as budding nascent entrepreneurs encounter semi-permeable rather than impermeable barriers. With appropriate human capital, transitions into entrepreneurship are possible, without significant financial resource constraints or having come from an entrepreneurial family background.

7.1. *Comparison with previous findings*

Our results take into account some of the shortcomings of previous research and thus contrast with previous findings in several ways. First, we employed a fairly stringent set of criteria to qualify an individual as a nascent entrepreneur. In previous studies, the concept of "entrepreneurship" depended on more general indicators for the dependent variable, such as "self-employment" or "small business owner." Definitions established by researchers varied from survey to survey, lacking a clear baseline for reference. Previous researchers have mostly examined people who are *already* running an operating business. In contrast, the PSED focused on nascent entrepreneurs who were in the initial phase of pursuing a start-up venture. Specifically, we examined individuals actively involved over the last twelve months in a start-up, securing ownership rights and operating with a degree of autonomy. These individuals cannot be directly compared to successful entrepreneurs and small business owners because a significant proportion of nascent entrepreneurs do not survive the start-up phase (Reynolds and White, 1997). In this respect, our findings speak to the factors involved in drawing people into entrepreneurship, rather than those enabling them to succeed at it.

Second, the PSED was specifically designed to study the nascent entrepreneurial population. We thus were able to include more precise measures of financial resources, work histories, and various socio-demographic characteristics of potential entrepreneurs than previous studies. Such measures reduced the model misspecification problems encountered in other data sets. For example, we believe that having separate measures of self-employment, past and current, as well as differentiating among owners with varying degrees of employee obligations to other firms, advances the measurement of this concept. Previous studies simply treated start-up experience and business ownership/self-employment as single variables.

Third, we disaggregated the process of a founding a new business by differentiating between the attempt at transitioning into entrepreneurship and running a viable new venture. Although we found that lack of income or wealth did not inhibit people from taking action to start new businesses, financial resources may play a major role in the subsequent success of the established entities. However, research suggests that the relationship between startup capitalization and subsequent success is not straightforward (Ruef, 2002). High capitalization does not guarantee business success. New firms face high levels of mortality because they must learn effective practices, adapt to competitors, and gain legitimacy. Therefore, we would expect a significant proportion of nascent entrepreneurs to disband their new ventures during the early phases of the start-up process. Future research will address that question.

7.2. Implications

Based on our findings, we propose two implications for research and theorizing on the factors affecting who becomes involved in trying to start a new business. First, the prospects for entrepreneurial entry do not appear to be concentrated among those financially advantaged. The lack of liquidity constraints and importance of education and work experience for nascent entrepreneurs might help explain the persistence of entrepreneurship during the late 20th century. Findings by Steinmetz and Wright (1989) and Wong (1992) indicated that the proportion of entrepreneurs in the labor force and the rate of entrepreneurship ceased their long-term decline during the late 20th century. In our sample, over one-half of the nascent entrepreneurs were attempting their first new venture – a strong sign of a resurgent entrepreneurial segment in the labor force. Indeed, opportunities for wealth accumulation among successful entrepreneurs are increasing. In 2000, small businesses accounted for over 40 percent of the total wealth within the U.S. business sector (SBA, 2002). Moreover, extensive government funding of educational institutions has created widespread opportunities to invest in and obtain human capital. Such democratization of the process of acquiring human capital may have lessened the importance of financial resources.

Second, structural changes within the environment, especially the diffusion of technical innovations, have created new opportunities for individuals which may not require significant start-up resources. Notably, a new generation of entrepreneurs has emerged using internet-based infrastructure to create home-based businesses with virtual storefronts (Pratt, 1999). For example, eBay transformed from just a website for people to sell miscellaneous items through online auctions into a platform for merchandising online. Rapid technological changes in digital media and communications have promoted a convergence of telecommunications, entertainment, and other forms of commerce that has opened up many new niches to innovative entrepreneurs with fresh ideas.

Policymakers should recognize the importance of distinguishing between policies that encourage more startup attempts and policies that assist emergent firms further along the start-up process. Policymakers may decide to encourage more people to pursue entrepreneurship in anticipation of several benefits. First, additional start-up attempts lead to more opportunities for innovative organizational forms to emerge. Second, an increasing start-up rate enhances the public's perception of an economy open to ambitious people who want to strike out on their own. By contrast, policymakers who wish to invest more resources in developing emergent firms would devote their attention to assisting them to survive and succeed as viable, operating firms, rather than spurring additionally attempts. Benefits from this approach include the generation of additional employment opportunities in successful start-up firms.

Our results suggest that entrepreneurial entry does not depend upon wealth or income, but instead, education and managerial experience promote entrepreneurial attempts. Higher education is a generalized public good and thus need not be targeted by policy makers. Policies promoting entrepreneurship should focus on developing managerial experience. Providing meaningful and responsible positions for workers inside organizations promotes the kind of experience that apparently gives employees entrepreneurially-relevant skills and confidence. For example, ten years of managerial experience approximately doubles the likelihood of someone trying to start their own business. Encouraging employers to create internal labor markets in which job ladders provide cumulate managerial experience for workers can lead to some of them leaving to start their own businesses. As the global economy spawns more knowledge-based occupations, experienced managers with specialized skill sets may find opportunities to exploit these skills if they start their own firms. Thus, policies designed to enhance the quality of working life carry the added benefit of potentially increasing the supply of nascent entrepreneurs in the American economy.

As a caveat, we must acknowledge that the data collection for the PSED took place during a period of strong economic growth within the United States. Our results should be interpreted within the context of low unemployment,

significant returns from equity markets, and greater access to both credit markets and venture capital funding. During this period of "irrational exuberance," nascent entrepreneurs may have been drawn into the prospects of a starting a successful new venture. Given these macroeconomic conditions, especially in terms of increasing household wealth, any possible relationship between financial resources and entrepreneurial intentions may have been attenuated. However, in 2003, the rate of entrepreneurship in the United States remained steady at about 12 percent (Reynolds et al., 2004), undermining simple macroeconomic cyclical explanations of our results. Even when the Internet boom ended, the promise of an entrepreneurial career still attracted people, just as Lipset and Bendix described for workers in the 1950s. Therefore, even though our data were gathered during extraordinary economic times, we believe our findings would also hold during less economically robust times.

Notes

* We appreciate the suggestions and comments from Simon Parker and our anonymous reviewers. We thank Michelle Budig, Randy Collins, Mary Fischer, Tom Lee, Colin Mason, Stephanie Moller, Ted Mouw, Kaye Schoonhoven, Olav Sorenson, Jesper Sørensen, Mark Western, and participants at the 2005 Nascent Entrepreneurship Conference at the University of Durham for their helpful advice. Paul Reynolds and Nancy Carter provided guidance in using the PSED. Beth Crosa provided research assistance early in the project. We gratefully acknowledge support from the National Science Foundation to Howard Aldrich under grant SBR-9809841 and the Kauffman Foundation for making the PSED available to the academic community.

[1] Blau and Duncan (1967) reported high self-recruitment (i.e., a high concentration of inflows along the diagonals of mobility tables) as well as low outflow among entrepreneurs. Within the European context, Erikson and Goldthorpe (1992) also described highest immobility among entrepreneurs.

[2] However, Fairlie (2004a) discovered that earnings from self-employment were higher than wage and salary employment for African-American and Hispanic men. They may thus have an incentive to start a new venture, even at high income levels.

[3] To the extent that educational attainment is related to business performance, we would expect a stronger relationship between education and business survival than between education and trying to start a business (Gimeno et al., 1997).

[4] A start-up firm was considered an infant firm if the start-up had a positive monthly cash flow that covered

expenses and the owner-manager salaries for more than three months. Such firms were excluded from further analyses. We focused on independent start-ups and excluded any respondents who reported starting their new businesses with their current employers.

[5] In contrast, Evans and Jovanovic (1989) deleted negative net worth cases in their analysis.

[6] 2001 Survey of Consumer Finances vs. PSED (in parentheses) – Median net worth: $86,000 ($82,000); household income: $39,900 ($45,000).

[7] We also analyzed our data using a complementary log-log model, which is suitable for analyzing rare events. Based on the Akaike's Information Criteria (AIC) values, the complementary log-log model (AIC = 467.92, df = 29) fit slightly better than the logistic regression model (AIC = 468.51, df = 29). However, because coefficient estimates were very similar between the two models, we relied on the logistic regression approach since it is more widely used.

[8] Based on the distribution of the Cook statistic, we reviewed one case more closely that appeared influential. Upon further inspection, we discovered a coding error leading to a miscalculation of the wealth variable. We reran our analysis with the corrected wealth variable.

[9] The financial resource variables were also not significant when included in a model with only the control variables.

[10] The correlation between net worth and pursuing a bank loan was 0.04 (*p* value = ns) and the correlation between net worth and approval was 0.21 (*p* value = 0.07).

[11] We thank one of our reviewers for pointing this out to us.

[12] We also explored whether age exhibited a quadratic effect, but did not find a statistically significant effect.

[13] We believe the negative effect of previous startup attempts may have been missed in other studies because of a failure to control for factors associated with trying to start a business, and also because studies examined only outcomes that produced operating businesses, rather than attempts.

References

Aldrich, H. E., J. Cater, T. Jones, and D. McEvoy, 1983, 'From Periphery to Peripheral: The South Asian Petite Bourgeoisie in England', in I. H. Simpson and R. Simpson (eds.), *Research in the Sociology of Work*, vol. 2, Greenwich, CT: JAI Press, pp. 1–32.

Aldrich, H., L. A. Renzulli and N. Langton, 1998, 'Passing on Privilege: Resources Provided by Self-Employed Parents to their Self-Employed Children', in K. Leicht (ed.), *Research in Stratification and Mobility*, vol. 16, Greenwich, CT: JAI Press, pp. 291–317.

Åstebro, T. and I. Bernhardt, 2005, 'The Winner's Curse of Human Capital', *Small Business Economics* 24, 63–78.

Bates, T. M., 1997, *Race, Self-employment, and Upward mobility: An Illusive American Dream*, Baltimore: Johns Hopkins University Press.

Blanchflower, D. G. and A. J. Oswald, 1998, 'What Makes an Entrepreneur?', *Journal of Labor Economics* 16, 26 60.

Blau, P. M. and O. Dudley Duncan, 1967, *The American Occupational Structure*, New York: Wiley.

Boden, R. J. and A. R. Nucci, 2000, 'On the Survival Prospects of Men's and Women's New Business Ventures', *Journal of Business Venturing* 15, 347–362.

Bosma, N., M. Praag, R. Thurik and G. Wit, 2004, 'The Value of Human and Social Capital Investments for the Business Performance of Startups', *Small Business Economics* 23, 227 236.

Brüderl, J., P. Preisendörfer and R. Ziegler, 1992, 'Survival Chances of Newly Founded Business Organizations', *American Sociological Review* 57, 227 242.

Butler, J. S. and C. Herring, 1991, 'Ethnicity and Entrepreneurship in America: Toward an Explanation of Racial and Ethnic Group Variations in Self-Employment', *Sociological Perspectives* 34, 79 94.

Census, U.S. Bureau of the, 1992, *Characteristics of Business Owners*, Washington, DC: U.S. Government Printing Office.

Chinoy, E., 1955, *Automobile Workers and the American Dream*, Garden City, NY: Doubleday.

Curtin, R. and P. D. Reynolds, 2004, Appendix B – Background for Analysis: Data Documentation, Data Preparation and Weights, in W. B. Gartner, S. K. G., N. M. Carter and P. D. Reynolds (eds.), *Handbook of Entrepreneurial Dynamics: The Process of Business Creation in Contemporary America*, Thousand Oaks, CA: Sage, .

Devine, T. J., 1994, 'Changes in Wage-and-Salary Returns to Skill and the Recent Rise in Female Self-Employment', *American Economic Review* 84, 108–113.

Dunn, T. and D. Holtz-Eakin, 2000, "Financial Capital, Human Capital, and the Transition to Self-Employment: Evidence from Intergenerational Links', *Journal of Labor Economics* 18, 282-305.

Erikson, R. and J. H. Goldthorpe, 1992, *The Constant Flux: A Study of Class Mobility in Industrial Societies*, Oxford: Clarendon Press.

Evans, D. S. and B. Jovanovic, 1989, 'An Estimated Model of Entrepreneurial Choice under Liquidity Constraints', *The Journal of Political Economy* 97, 808–827.

Evans, D. S. and L. S. Leighton, 1989, 'Some Empirical Aspects of Entrepreneurship', *American Economic Review* 79, 519–535.

Fairlie, R. W., 1999, 'The Absence of the African-American Owned Business: An Analysis of the Dynamics of Self-Employment', *Journal of Labor Economics* 17, 80-108.

Fairlie, R. W., 2004a, Does Business Ownership Provide a Source of Upward Mobility for Blacks and Hispanics, in D. Holtz-Eakin and H. S. Rosen (eds.), *Public Policy and the Economics of Entrepreneurship*, Cambridge, MA: MIT Press, 153-180.

Fairlie, R. W., 2004b, 'Recent Trends in Ethnic and Racial Self-Employment', *Small Business Economics* 23, 203-218.

Gartner, W. B., N. M. Carter and P. D. Reynolds, 2004a, Business Start-up Activities, in W. B. Gartner, K. G. Shaver, N. M. Carter and P. D. Reynolds (eds.), *Handbook of Entrepreneurial Dynamics: The Process of Business Creation in Contemporary America*, Thousand Oaks, CA: Sage, 285-298.

Gartner, W. B., K. G. Shaver, N. M. Carter and P. D. Reynolds, 2004b, *Handbook of Entrepreneurial Dynamics: The Process of Business Creation in Contemporary America*, Thousand Oaks, CA: Sage.

Gimeno, J., T. B. Folta, A. C. Cooper and C. Y. Woo, 1997, 'Survival of the Fittest? Entrepreneurial Human Capital and the Persistence of Underperforming Firms', *Administrative Science Quarterly* 42, 750–783.

Hamilton, B. H., 2000, 'Does Entrepreneurship Pay? An Empirical Analysis of the Returns of Self-Employment', *Journal of Political Economy* 108, 604–631.

Harrison, R. T., C. M. Mason and P. Girling, 2004, 'Financial bootstrapping and venture development in the software industry', *Entrepreneurship & Regional Development* 16, 307–333.

Harrison, R. T. and C. M. Mason, 1997, 'Entrepreneurial Growth Strategies and Venture Performance in the Software Industry', *Frontiers of Entrepreneurship Research* 18, 448–449.

Holtz-Eakin, D., D. Joulfaian and H. S. Rosen, 1994, 'Sticking it Out: Entrepreneurial Survival and Liquidity Constraints', *Journal of Political Economy* 102, 53–75.

Hout, M., 1984, 'Status, Autonomy, and Training in Occupational Mobility', *American Journal of Sociology* 89, 1379–1409.

Hout, M. and H. S. Rosen, 2000, 'Self-Employment, Family Background, and Race', *Journal of Human Resources* 35, 671–694.

Hurst, E. and A. Lusardi, 2004, 'Liquidity Constraints, Household Wealth and Entrepreneurship', *Journal of Political Economy* 112, 319–347.

Jurik, N. C., 1998, 'Getting Away and Getting By: The Experiences of Self-Employed Homeworkers', *Work and Occupations* 25, 7–35.

Kalleberg, A. L. and K. T. Leicht, 1991, 'Gender and Organizational Performance: Determinants of Small Business Survival and Success', *Academy of Management Journal* 34, 136–161.

Keister, L. A. and S. Moller, 2000, 'Wealth Inequality in the United States', *Annual Review of Sociology* 26, 63–81.

Kim, P. H., H. E. Aldrich and L. A. Keister, 2004, Household Income and Net Worth, in W. B. Gartner, K. G. Shaver, N. M. Carter and P. D. Reynolds (eds.), *Handbook of Entrepreneurial Dynamics: The Process of Business Creation in Contemporary America*, Thousand Oaks, CA: Sage, 49–61.

Lentz, B. F. and D. N. Laband, 1990, 'Entrepreneurial Success and Occupational Inheritance among Proprietors', *Canadian Journal of Economics* 23, 563–579.

Lipset, S. M. and R. Bendix, 1959, *Social Mobility in Industrial Society*, Berkeley: University of California Press.

Miller, D. R. and G. E. Swanson, 1958, *The Changing American Parent; A Study in the Detroit Area*, New York: Wiley.

Moskowitz, T. J. and A. Vissing-Jorgensen, 2002, 'The Returns to Entrepreneurial Investment: A Private Equity Premium Puzzle?', *American Economic Review* 92, 745–779.

Myers, S. C., 1984, 'The Capital Structure Puzzle', *Journal of Finance* 39, 575–592.

Parker, S. C., 2003, 'Does Tax Evasion Affect Occupational Choice?', *Oxford Bulletin of Economics and Statistics* 65, 379–394.

Parker, S. C., 2004, *The Economics of Self-employment and Entrepreneurship*, New York: Cambridge.

Pratt, J. H., 1999, *Homebased Business: The Hidden Economy*, Washington, DC: Small Business Administration.

Renzulli, L. A., H. Aldrich and J. Moody, 2000, 'Family Matters: Gender, Networks, and Entrepreneurial Outcomes', *Social Forces* 79, 523–546.

Reynolds, P. D., N. M. Carter, W. B. Gartner and P. G. Greene, 2004, 'The Prevalence of Nascent Entrepreneurs in the United States: Evidence from the Panel Study of Entrepreneurial Dynamics', *Small Business Economics* 23, 263.

Reynolds, P. D., W. D. Bygrave and E. Autio, 2004, *Global Entrepreneurship Monitor: 2003 Executive Report*, Kansas City, MO: Kauffman Center for Entrepreneurial Leadership.

Reynolds, P. D. and S. B. White, 1997, *The Entrepreneurial Process: Economic Growth, Men, Women, and Minorities*, Westport, CT: Quorum Books.

Ronstadt, R., 1988, 'The Corridor Principle', *Journal of Business Venturing* 3, 31–40.

Ruef, M., 2002, 'Unpacking the Liability of Aging: Toward a Socially-Embedded Account of Organizational Disbanding', in M. Lounsbury and M. J. Ventresca (eds.), *Research in the Sociology of Organizations*, vol. 19, Greenwich, CT: JAI Press, pp. 195–229.

SBA, 1994, *Handbook of Small Business Data*, Washington, DC: Small Business Administration.

SBA, 2002, *Estimation of Small Business Wealth*, Washington, DC: Small Business Administration.

SBA, 2004, *Firm Size Data: Statistics of U.S. Businesses and Nonemployer Statistics*, vol. 2004, Washington, DC: Small Business Administration.

Shane, S., 2003, *A General Theory of Entrepreneurship: the Individual-Opportunity Nexus*, Cheltenham, UK: Edward Elgar.

Sørensen, A. B., 2000, 'Toward a Sounder Basis for Class Analysis', *American Journal of Sociology* 105, 1523–1558.

Steinmetz, G. and E. O. Wright, 1989, 'The Fall and Rise of the Petty Bourgeoisie: Changing Patterns of Self-Employment in the Postwar United States', *American Journal of Sociology* 94, 973–1018.

Uusitalo, R., 2001, 'Homo entreprenaurus?', *Applied Economics* 33, 1631–1638.

Western, M., 1994, 'Class Structure and Intergenerational Class Mobility: A Comparative Analysis of Nation and Gender', *Social Forces* 73, 101–134.

Wong, R. S.-K., 1992, 'Vertical and Nonvertical Effects in Class Mobility: Cross-National Variations', *American Sociological Review* 57, 396–410.

[23]

ENTREPRENEURSHIP AND INEQUALITY

Stephen Lippmann, Amy Davis and Howard
E. Aldrich

ABSTRACT

Nations with high levels of economic inequality tend to have high rates of entrepreneurial activity. In this paper, we develop propositions about this relationship, based upon current research. Although we provide some descriptive analyses to support our propositions, our paper is not an empirical test but rather a theoretical exploration of new ideas related to this topic. We first define entrepreneurship at the individual and societal level and distinguish between entrepreneurship undertaken out of necessity and entrepreneurship that takes advantage of market opportunities. We then explore the roles that various causes of economic inequality play in increasing entrepreneurial activity, including economic development, state policies, foreign investment, sector shifts, labor market and employment characteristics, and class structures. The relationship between inequality and entrepreneurship poses a potentially disturbing message for countries with strong egalitarian norms and political and social policies that also wish to increase entrepreneurial activity. We conclude by noting the conditions under which entrepreneurship can be a source of upward social and economic mobility for individuals.

Entrepreneurship
Research in the Sociology of Work, Volume 15, 3–31
Copyright © 2005 by Elsevier Ltd.
All rights of reproduction in any form reserved
ISSN: 0277-2833/doi:10.1016/S0277-2833(05)15002-X

3

4   STEPHEN LIPPMANN ET AL.

INTRODUCTION

Nations vary widely in their levels of entrepreneurial activity, ranging from
countries in which large employers and the state dominate labor markets to
countries in which small firms and self-employed craft workers play much
the same role they did a century ago. Nations also vary widely in their levels
of economic inequality, ranging from countries in which wealthy families
dominate the economic scene to countries in which wealth is widely shared
and ostentatious displays of wealth are frowned upon. We have reason to
believe that these two phenomena are linked. The same social and economic
dynamics that increase societal levels of economic inequality – the uneven
distribution of a society's financial resources within its population – may
also lead to increases in rates of entrepreneurial activity. In addition, institutional factors, such as wealth transfer and labor market policies, may
strengthen the link between inequality and entrepreneurship.

In this paper, we offer two contributions. First, we review the existing
literature on the relationships between societal level inequalities and entrepreneurship, and second, we develop theoretically based propositions to
suggest future empirical projects. Although we provide some descriptive
analyses to support our propositions, our paper is not an empirical test but
rather a theoretical exploration of new ideas related to this topic. We draw
on various research streams in what we believe is one of the first attempts to
integrate the literature on societal level inequalities and entrepreneurship.

Our plan is as follows. We briefly note the historical importance of
inequality and explore two sides of an argument concerning inequality's
possible consequences for individual opportunities. We then offer a definition of entrepreneurship at the individual and societal levels, explaining
the difference between necessity- and opportunity-based entrepreneurship. We incorporate that distinction into our propositions concerning
cross-national differences in entrepreneurial activities. Next, we review
sociological theories of how and why various social and economic struc-
tures, including economic development and inequality, affect the distribution of resources needed by entrepreneurs across societies. We draw on
these literatures to develop propositions intended to provide theoretical
linkages between the causes of inequality and the great variation in entrepreneurial activity among nations. If certain types of entrepreneurial activity
require financial resources, then the unequal distribution of these resources
and differential access to them could restrict entrepreneurship to certain
groups and suppress entrepreneurial activity generally. Alternatively, if
inequality limits individuals' opportunities to participate in the formal

labor market, they may pursue self-employment as a last resort. We conclude by discussing the implications of our arguments for further research.

INEQUALITY

Concern with inequalities in access to power and valued resources has been central to sociological research since the discipline's inception (e.g. Marx 1852). On one side, some social theorists have emphasized the systematic reproduction of wealth and privilege inequalities that favor the well off at the expense of the less fortunate. On the other side, some theorists have emphasized the expanded opportunities available to people from humble origins as economies grow. Thus, both sides in this debate have argued that the extent to which resources are unequally distributed within and between societies has a profound impact on whether social and economic inequality increases or declines.

Conceptualizing Wealth Inequality

Although the distribution of wealth is understudied by sociologists, it is a crucial aspect of inequality in the United States and throughout the rest of the world. Most studies of economic inequality focus on income, but wealth and income are not highly correlated. In addition, for a variety of reasons, wealth inequality is much more severe than income inequality (Keister and Moller 2000). For our purposes, wealth is more relevant than income to the relationship between economic inequality and entrepreneurship. To the degree that financial resources are necessary for becoming an entrepreneur, wealth, in the form of real and financial assets, is more likely than income to be the resource that nascent entrepreneurs rely on.

Unfortunately, severe data limitations with regard to measuring actual household wealth have hampered attempts to clear up the relationship between wealth and entrepreneurship. Accordingly, previous research gives us little guidance concerning the impact of financial capital on new business formation (Dunn and Holtz–Eakin 2000; Reynolds and White 1997; Kim, Aldrich and Keister 2003). For example, research in the United States on the relationship between household wealth and new business formation has yielded mixed results (Reynolds and White 1997; Kim et al. 2003).[1] We are not aware of any research that has used the same definitions of inequality

6   STEPHEN LIPPMANN ET AL.

and entrepreneurship across nations, except for the Global Entrepreneurship Monitor project, described later in our paper. We offer propositions the
testing of which would require such data and thus justify a new research
thrust in the field of entrepreneurship.

Economic Inequality and Opportunity

Arguments concerning the *negative* consequences of inequality note that the
social structures of modern societies severely inhibit mobility chances for
some people (Blau and Duncan 1967; Fijiwara-Greve and Greve 2000).
Through direct inheritance of wealth, privilege and status structures can be
reproduced from one generation to the next (Keister and Moller 2000).
People occupying advantageous levels in the occupational structure often
manage to pass along educational opportunities to their offspring, as shown
by the high rate at which children of self-employed professionals become
professionals themselves (Blau and Duncan 1967; Sobel, Becker and Minick
1998).

The unequal distribution of resources often magnifies other disadvantages
associated with the ascriptive characteristics of individuals, including race
and gender (Blau 1977; Tilly 1998). People born into poor families and
residing in impoverished areas face bleak prospects for upward mobility
(Wilson 1996). If underrepresented and underprivileged groups are consistently excluded from sources of access to resources, then their life chances are
damaged (Tomaskovic-Devey 1993).

When two social dimensions are highly correlated with other social distinctions, such as wealth with race or gender, theorists call them "consolidated" (Blau 1977). To the degree that inequality is consolidated and a lack
of resources inhibits entrepreneurship, the founding of new businesses contributes to the reproduction of social and economic inequalities. In addition,
by limiting entrepreneurial opportunities, persistent inequalities may narrow
the range of startup types in a society, thus limiting organizational and
industrial diversity.[2]

Arguments concerning the *positive* role of inequalities in wealth and income turn on the proposition that self-employment can be a source of social
and economic mobility for individuals (Keister 2000). Since the industrial
revolution spread from England to other western capitalist societies in the
19th century, one widespread socio-political ideology has encouraged a
"belief in success among the unsuccessful" (Bendix 1956). To be sure, when
economies were growing rapidly, expanding opportunities allowed many

immigrants and children of the working class to become prosperous business owners. The spurt of economic growth in the 1990s seems to have reawakened that dream. Indeed, some research suggests that entrepreneurship may be impervious to some of the posited constraints on business startups and therefore still represents an important source of mobility for entrepreneurs and their families.

ENTREPRENEURSHIP

Entrepreneurial activities are central to the evolution of capitalist societies because new businesses drive economic and employment growth. In capitalist societies, continued economic growth depends on the extent to which potential entrepreneurs can obtain and effectively utilize the social and economic resources they need. Moreover, new firms' foundings and disbandings generate a great deal of employment volatility through job creation and destruction. For example, between 1992 and 1996, newly founded organizations created about 28 million jobs in the United States (Birch 1997). In the first years of the 21st century, fewer new businesses were founded and the rate of job creation slowed.

Entrepreneurship at the Level of Individuals and Teams

"Entrepreneur" and "entrepreneurship" constitute somewhat contested terms, especially outside of the community of scholars who regularly publish in entrepreneurship journals (Gartner 1985). Debates over the meaning of the terms became a regular feature of conference presentations and journal articles in the 1970s, as the field struggled for academic legitimacy. Some of the debates reflected the field's attempt to distinguish the field of "entrepreneurship" from the field of "small business studies," which had been the traditional home of people studying business startups. The debate also reflected disciplinary disputes over units and levels of analysis, period, methods, and theoretical perspectives (Aldrich 2004).

Over the past decade, several teams of researchers have used a scheme developed by Katz and Gartner (1985) to study the emergence of new organizations, with the largest project being the Panel Study of Entrepreneurial Dynamics, or PSED. Their investigations have shown that researchers must accept some degree of imprecision and ambiguity in deciding when entrepreneurs have truly "created" an organization. Working

8   STEPHEN LIPPMANN ET AL.

within this perspective, researchers do not sharply delimit the concepts of "self-employment" from "creating an organization," or make someone's status as an entrepreneur dependent on whether he or she employs others. Sociologically, an "organization" exists to the extent that a socially recognized bounded entity exists that is engaged in exchanges with its environment. In the remainder of this chapter, we focus on the study of entrepreneurship as the creation of new organizations and we will label the people who create organizations and manage them during their early years as "entrepreneurs," in keeping with the way sociological research on entrepreneurship is characteristically framed.

Entrepreneurship at the Level of the Nation-state

Theorizing cross nationally requires a generic conceptualization of entrepreneurship. Most entrepreneurship research has been conducted within single countries and thus has not been concerned with societal level rates. Investigators doing cross-national research have mainly studied differences in individual entrepreneurs across countries, rather than differences in societal level rates. In response to this lack of truly comparative national level data, the Global Entrepreneurship Monitor (GEM) project set out to provide internationally comparable data from multiple countries concerning entrepreneurial activity (Reynolds et al. 2002). GEM, which began in 1999, conducts surveys of at least 2,000 adults in each nation studied, as well as a smaller number with national experts.

GEM reports the level of total entrepreneurial activity (TEA) for a nation based on two indicators. The first indicator is the percentage of the labor force actively involved in starting a new venture that has not yet become an operating business. The second indicator is the percentage of individuals in the labor force who either own or manage a business that is less than 42 months old. Taken together, the TEA indicators provide a reasonable estimate of the level of entrepreneurial activity in a nations labor force. In 2001, its values ranged from 1.8 in Japan to 18.9 in Thailand.

Types of Entrepreneurship

Ambitions to start a business are widespread in the populations of many capitalist societies, but resources are not. Researchers have debated the role that *financial resources* play in influencing an individual's likelihood of becoming a nascent entrepreneur. Financial resources refers to property, stocks and bonds, tangible goods, and other assets that can be pledged in exchange for credit or actually turned into a liquid form, such as money used in leasing or purchasing resources.

Some researchers have asserted that financial resources are critical for entrepreneurship and that liquidity constraints inhibit start-ups (Evans and Jovanovic 1989; Bates 1997; Blanchflower and Oswald 1998; Fischer and Massey 2000). They reason that business start-ups often require a substantial sum of money and that entrepreneurs' access to credit markets will be constrained due to the risks associated with a new venture. This viewpoint emphasizes that equity, particularly from family wealth holdings, allows entrepreneurs to obtain credit, and those with little personal wealth simply will not secure necessary start-up loans and capital (Bates 1997). Thus, we would expect those with high net-worth to be more likely than others to become self-employed (Evans and Leighton 1989; Fischer and Massey 2000).

Researchers who disagree with the emphasis on financial resources argue that economists and others have placed too much importance on the availability of monetary assets (Aldrich 1999). Many small businesses do not require large amounts of financial capital in their start-up phase and most founders begin their businesses with little or no capital. In the U.S., well over half of all owners in the mid-1990s required less than $5,000 dollars to start their businesses (U.S. Census 1997). Home-based businesses, for instance, which accounted for half of all new businesses in 1992, often require little capital up front.

Even though most small businesses start very small and with low levels of capital investment, financial resources have nonetheless been linked to the subsequent success of new business ventures (Fichman and Levinthal 1991). Newly founded organizations face severe obstacles to their survival (Aldrich and Auster 1986). Starting a new business requires human and physical resources, and financial reserves can help struggling new businesses acquire relevant competencies and market share (Aldrich and Auster 1986; Aldrich and Fiol 1994). Entrepreneurs starting with more assets survive the liabilities associated with newness more readily than entrepreneurs with fewer assets (Stinchcombe 1965).

Whereas financial resources may play a critical factor in the *success* of a newly formed business, its role in determining whether a person *becomes* a nascent entrepreneur is unclear. We feel that some clarity can be brought to this debate by distinguishing between two broad types of entrepreneurial activities: *opportunity* entrepreneurship and *necessity* entrepreneurship

10   STEPHEN LIPPMANN ET AL.

Table 1.   Necessity and Opportunity Entrepreneurship and Their
Relationships to Social, Human, and Financial Capital.

Necessity Entrepreneurship: Undertaken when there are few or no other opportunities for
gainful labor market participation
- Typically relies on little or no financial capital
- Once decision is made, success partially dependent upon social and human capital

Opportunity Entrepreneurship: Undertaken to take advantage of perceived market opportunities
- Recognition of such opportunities is positively related to social and human capital
- Once decision is made, financial capital becomes relevant to success

---

(Reynolds et al. 2002), as defined in Table 1. This distinction is an important
one, we argue, because it helps to explain the conditions under which financial resources affect entrepreneurial decisions. We summarize the relationships between types of entrepreneurship and resources in Table 1.

Necessity Entrepreneurship
People undertake necessity entrepreneurship when there are few, if any,
other options for finding suitable work. We believe that entrepreneurs often
undertake this type of entrepreneurial activity with little or no financial
capital because it constitutes a final effort to secure an income when other
employment options fail. In short, it represents a failure of labor markets to
provide opportunities that are more attractive than self-employment. One
can easily imagine that this type of entrepreneurship will be more prevalent
in certain economic and social contexts than others, as we discuss below. In
addition, one might reasonably expect that this type of activity will provide,
on average, substantially fewer opportunities for individual upward mobility and organizational and economic growth than the second type of entrepreneurial activity.

Opportunity Entrepreneurship
People undertake opportunity entrepreneurship when they perceive an opportunity in the market, which can include underserved, poorly served, or
newly emerging niches. Knowledge of these niches can be considered a form
of human capital, typically gained from industry experience (Burton et al.
2002). In addition, people embedded in wide-ranging and diverse social
networks have greater access to such knowledge. Opportunity entrepreneurship probably depends more than necessity entrepreneurship on the
possession of human capital. If so, then opportunity-based endeavors

provide the greatest potential for individual mobility, organizational growth, and job creation. Therefore, opportunity entrepreneurship will be, on average, more beneficial to economies and societies than that arising out of necessity.

SOCIETAL LEVEL ECONOMIC INEQUALITY AND ENTREPRENEURSHIP

Countries with higher levels of wealth inequality tend to have higher rates of entrepreneurship. The GEM project found that the greater the level of wealth inequality in a society, the higher its level of total entrepreneurial activity, necessity entrepreneurship, and opportunity entrepreneurship. The GEM measured wealth inequality using the Gini index, which assesses the extent to which the population of a country shares unequally in a nation's total wealth. It is calculated as the extent to which the distribution departs from perfect equality, and is scaled from a minimum value of 0 to a maximum value of 1, with 0 representing no inequality and 1 representing complete inequality. For example, if every household had exactly the same wealth holdings, then there would be no inequality and the Gini index would be 0. At the other extreme, if a small fraction of all households held all the wealth in a nation, the Gini index would be almost one. Although it has some limitations, the Gini index is the most widely used measure for making cross-national comparisons of inequality.

In Fig. 1, we plot the relationship between economic inequality, as measured by the Gini index, and total entrepreneurial activity. This relationship is linear, with a correlation of 0.451, demonstrating that inequality and total entrepreneurial activity rise in tandem. However, when total entrepreneurial activity is broken down into its two component parts, the relationships between economic inequality and both necessity and opportunity entrepreneurship become nonlinear. For each of these bivariate relationships, a quadratic form provides the best fit, as represented by the following equation:

$$Y = X + X^2$$

where Y is the rate of entrepreneurial activity, and X is the Gini index of economic inequality. These quadratic relationships are presented in Figs. 2 and 3.[3] In Fig. 2, we see that increases in wealth inequality raise a nation's level of necessity entrepreneurship at an increasing rate, whereas Fig. 3

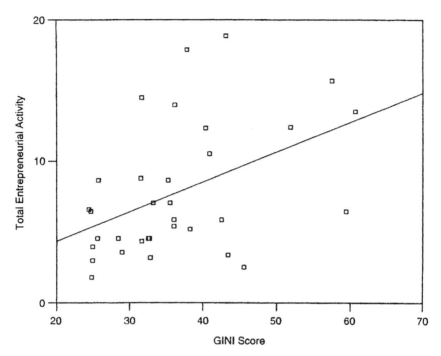

Fig. 1.   Total Entrepreneurial Activity and Economic Inequality. *Source:* Reynolds
et al. (2002). $R^2 = 0.415$.

shows that opportunity entrepreneurship has a curvilinear relationship with
inequality. Opportunity entrepreneurship is highest at an intermediate level
of wealth inequality.

What might account for these relationships? Based on other information
in the GEM report, at least two complementary explanations appear plausible. First, countries with higher levels of wealth inequality have larger poor
and low-income/wealth populations. For such groups, which also typically
have low levels of education and few connections to sources of power and
influence, necessity entrepreneurship might be the most readily available
option for earning a living. Therefore, high levels of wealth inequality
should be positively related to high levels of necessity entrepreneurship.

A second explanation, which focuses on wealth held by the most privileged groups in society, posits that higher levels of wealth inequality may be
an indication that some segments of the population have surplus capital to
invest in new ventures, and therefore increase opportunity entrepreneurial

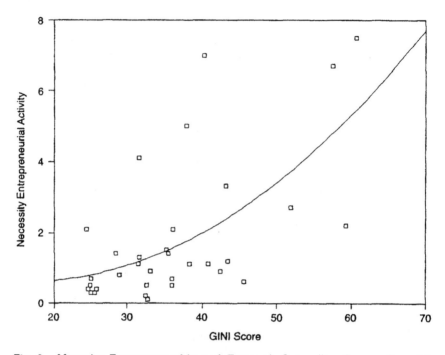

Fig. 2. Necessity Entrepreneurship and Economic Inequality. *Source:* Reynolds
et al. (2002). $R^2 = 0.385$.

activity. They could either invest it in their own startups or act as angel
investors for the startup activities of others. At moderate levels of inequality, "elite mobilization can activate the community field and encourage
other groups to become involved – if cultural or financial capital of the elites
and other residents is not so unequally distributed that inter-group trust is
lacking" (Flora 1998: 500). Therefore, rising inequality indicates that elites
have begun to accumulate a disproportionate share of resources that they
can use to initiate economic development. By investing surplus capital in the
pursuit of perceived market opportunities, elites increase the level of opportunity entrepreneurship. In addition, the improved life chances and lux-
urious life style associated with greater wealth serve as an incentive for
potential entrepreneurs.

The four countries with the highest levels of inequality – Mexico, Chile,
South Africa, and Brazil – have low-to-moderate levels of opportunity entrepreneurship. Rapid industrialization in Mexico may largely account for

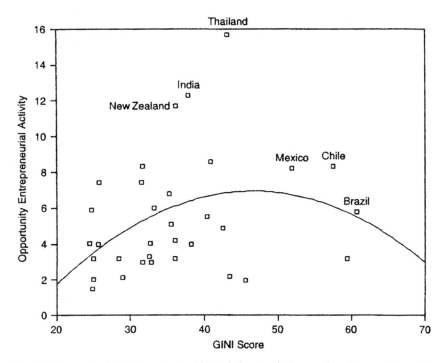

Fig. 3. Opportunity Entrepreneurship and Economic Inequality. *Source:* Reynolds et al. (2002). $R^2 = 0.127$.

its high level of inequality. Firms from advanced industrial nations, particularly the U.S., have found it attractive for its low labor costs and its proximity to domestic markets and infrastructure. This trajectory increased inequality as low-wage manufacturing work became an increasingly dominant part of Mexico's labor market. In addition, foreign firms have controlled much of the economic growth in Mexico in the past several decades, thus limiting opportunities for high-quality entrepreneurship among Mexico's citizenry.

The Chilean economy, while growing, remains primarily dependent on capital intensive extractive industries including mining, fishing, and forestry, which may explain its relatively limited opportunity in entrepreneurial activity. These industries provide relatively few opportunities for new business formation. In addition, the Chilean economy continues to feel the enduring effects of the coup of 1973, as the country struggles to find its footing after the repressive Pinochet regime. South Africa suffers from extremely high levels of unemployment and poverty, which account for its high Gini score. In addition, persistent crime and corruption, and the enduring legacy of apartheid, help to suppress opportunities for successful entrepreneurship among a large portion of the population. Chaotic fiscal policies, high inflation, and steadily rising foreign debt in Brazil have left it an unattractive place for foreign investment, thus limiting its opportunity in entrepreneurial activity. In addition, Brazil's stagnant economy has led to very high levels of inequality.

Thus, it appears that moderate levels of inequality do help *opportunity entrepreneurship* to flourish. Countries with high levels of inequality do not experience as much opportunity entrepreneurship because people lack the resources and information required to take advantage of opportunities essential for such activity.

Furthermore, as revealed in Fig. 3, the three countries with the highest levels of opportunity entrepreneurship, New Zealand, India, and Thailand, fall very close to the mean Gini score for the entire sample.[4] Thailand and India are known for having large populations of highly educated workers and high numbers of businesses engaged in outsourcing and subcontracting arrangements with foreign firms. The increasing prevalence of these arrangements continues to create many high-quality opportunities for entrepreneurs in a variety of industries. When we remove these nations from the analysis, the inverted-U shaped curve remains virtually unchanged. This result further supports our contention that *moderate* levels of economic inequality are favorable for opportunity entrepreneurship.

These proposed explanations for the positive association between economic inequality and entrepreneurship posit a direct effect of inequality on entrepreneurship. Recent theories of the causes of inequality suggest other forces that may indirectly strengthen the link between inequality and entrepreneurship because of their direct effects on one or both.

INEQUALITY AND ENTREPRENEURSHIP IN THEORETICAL PERSPECTIVE

Studies from a variety of theoretical backgrounds have found that the factors that affect countries' levels of income inequality also affect their labor market structures, dynamics, and outcomes. These studies have focused mainly on how a country's level of economic development (Kuznets 1953; Nielsen and Alderson 1995) or position in the world system (Wood 1994) affects the size and growth of various economic sectors, and how these sectoral dynamics affect income and wealth inequality and opportunities for social mobility. Typically, however, these studies ignore self-employment and entrepreneurial activity, even though they are an increasingly important part of labor markets across the globe (Aldrich 1999; but see Aronson 1991). In this section, we review the literature on economic and industrial development in order to develop a set of propositions about factors that may create a link between inequality and entrepreneurship.

We examine seven structures and processes linked with varying levels of entrepreneurship and inequality: economic development, government policies, foreign direct investment, growth in the service sector, increasing labor market flexibility, wealth transfer programs, and variation in the strength of the working class. We review each and explain how we feel it should be included in a comprehensive explanation of the linkage we identified. All seven are listed in Table 2.

Development and Economic Inequality

We begin with the pioneering work of Kuznets (1953, 1955), who argued that inequality follows an inverted U-shaped path coincident with economic and industrial development. According to his logic, as countries begin to develop an industrial infrastructure, newly created wealth becomes concentrated in the hands of those who control that infrastructure. In Marx's terms, others are forced to sell their labor power or engage in agriculture or small-scale production and thus do not share equally in the newly created wealth. However, as development continues, opportunities for increased income spread to more segments of the population; the agricultural sector shrinks and participation in the industrial economy becomes more widespread. Kuznets' theory has been supported for income inequality in a variety of settings (Lindert and Williamson 1985), and a similar trend has been documented for wealth inequality (Lampman 1962).

Since a country's level of economic development constitutes a major predictor of its level of inequality, we offer the following proposition:

Proposition 1. Developing nations experience higher rates of entrepreneurship.

Proposition 1 gains some support from the GEM data, as shown in Fig. 4. At low levels of development, as measured by energy consumption per capita, total entrepreneurial activity was high in 2001. According to the

Table 2.   Explanations for the Positive Relationship Between
Entrepreneurship and Inequality.

Structure/Process	Effect on Inequality	Effect on Entrepreneurial Activity
Economic development	(+) U-shaped pattern (Kuznets 1953)	(+) Provides new markets for goods and services
Government policies favoring development	(+)Creates new class of industrial elite, new industrial working class	(+) Provides finances and market opportunities for nascent entrepreneurs
Foreign Direct investment	(+) Creates an elite managerial and financier class, increases the number of low wage, low skill manufacturing jobs	(+) Provides finances and market opportunities for nascent entrepreneurs
Rapid service sector growth	(+) Bifurcation of labor market into highly skilled, high-wage service jobs and low skill, low-wage service jobs	(+) Creates new market demands
Increasing employment flexibility	(+) Returns to skill through occupational labor markets, increasing employment insecurity	(+) Individuals less tied to particular firms, responses to employment insecurity through individual opportunity
Wealth transfer programs	(−) Redistributes wealth equitably across the population	(−) Reduces the need to rely on necessity entrepreneurship as a last resort
Strong working class	(−) Helps to encourage the redistribution of wealth, the formation of occupational labor markets, and protect their economic interests	(−) Reduces the need to rely on necessity entrepreneurship because jobs are more secure due to occupational labor markets

GEM, developing Latin American countries and developing countries in Asia had entrepreneurship rates over 10%, figures well above the average rate of 7% for all of the GEM countries.[5] As countries develop, more opportunities for entrepreneurship may emerge as underserved markets expand and more people move into self-employment because traditional sectors of the economy shrink. However, it appears, in the quadratic relationship shown in Fig. 4, that after development reaches a certain

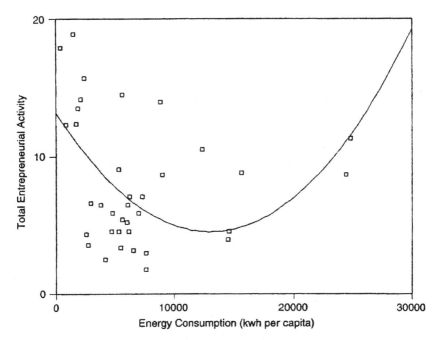

Fig. 4. Total Entrepreneurial Activity and Economic Development. *Source:* Reynolds et al. (2002) and World Bank Group (2004). $R^2 = 0.260$.

stage, entrepreneurial activity declines and then picks up again at higher levels of development.

Government Support for New Businesses

Several key factors associated with national economies in both developing and developed nations may account for variation in economic inequality and entrepreneurial activity. Clearly, development may be the result of an active strategy pursued by governments wishing to compete in the global economy. State agencies and programs in developing nations play a large role in industrial development through fiscal policies that favor business and entrepreneurial activity, including taxation, investments, loans, and other policies (Evans et al. 1985; Wade 1990). To compete in an increasingly global economy, developing nations may encourage the growth of certain targeted industries, which can create an industrial elite and increase economic inequality. These same policies may also provide the seeds for new businesses.

Similar processes can occur in developed nations, as well. In Ireland, for example, the Industrial Development Authority worked throughout the 1990s to recruit existing high-tech companies. Ireland also formed an organization called Enterprise Ireland to encourage and support entrepreneurship in similar industries (Florida 2002). As a result, Ireland has the second highest rate of opportunity entrepreneurial activity (7.8) among Western nations, behind only the United States. We therefore expect that countries actively pursuing such strategies generate favorable contexts for opportunity entrepreneurship.

Proposition 2. Governments whose policies and regulations favor the emergence of a market economy and industrial development will experience more opportunity entrepreneurship.

Rona-Tas (1994) provided support for this idea in his research on Hungary's transition from socialism to capitalism, which distinguished between countries experiencing an *erosion* of socialism versus countries experiencing a *transition* from socialism. The erosion of socialism was a passive process in which socialist institutions dissolved. The transition from socialism, on the other hand, has become an active strategy followed by governments to create a market economy. According to Rona-Tas, countries undergoing a transition provided many more opportunities for entrepreneurs and experienced greater levels of entrepreneurial activity.

Foreign Direct Investment

Industrial development may also be the result of foreign direct investment (FDI) in industrial infrastructure, with firms taking advantage of welcoming environments in many developing nations, including cheaper labor costs and more lax regulatory standards. FDI has been criticized by world-systems theory because of its role in developing countries (Bornschier and Chase-Dunn 1985). Critics argue that FDI creates long-term dependence of developing nations upon transnational corporations and contributes to inequality by creating a group of highly paid managers and professionals, in addition to low-wage manufacturing and other marginal jobs. However, recent research has shown that FDI might actually be of some benefit to the economies of developing nations (Alderson and Nielsen 1999; Soysa and Oneal 1999). As foreign firms invest money directly in their own operations

20   STEPHEN LIPPMANN ET AL.

or through subcontracting and other outsourcing arrangements, they also create opportunities for entrepreneurial activity by stimulating new markets and pumping new financial resources into the economy.

Proposition 3. Foreign investment in developing nations increases their opportunity entrepreneurship rates.

Sectoral Shifts

Developing nations often undergo a dramatic sectoral shift away from agriculture and into manufacturing and services. As agriculture shrinks, those individuals or families formerly engaged in agricultural activity must compete in a new economic order. Early on, this process disrupts traditional means of securing a living and leads to increased economic inequality. Although many make the adjustment by becoming employees of larger firms, many also turn to entrepreneurial activities (Rona-Tas 1994). For some, the decline of agriculture reduces traditional opportunities for securing a living. As the sectoral balance shifts away from agriculture, these individuals may have few opportunities in the new industrial sectors that emerge. Entrepreneurship may be their best or only option. At the same time, the growth of the service sector may create new economic opportunities that entrepreneurs can exploit.

Proposition 4. As developing countries' economies shift away from agriculture, both necessity and opportunity entrepreneurship increase.

Whereas developing nations industrialize and experience declines in agriculture and increases in their manufacturing activity, advanced industrialized nations suffer a concurrent decline in their manufacturing sector. This dual dynamic represents the essence of globalization, as firms in advanced countries move production abroad to take advantage of cheaper labor, production chains span political boundaries, and economies become global (Alderson 1997). A major outcome of the globalization of production has been a relative decline in the size of the manufacturing sector in advanced industrial economies, and an overall shift in labor market demands in these nations, as highlighted by the U.S. case. Labor market restructuring has created an increasingly bifurcated labor force of high-skill, high-wage and low-skill, low-wage service work (Harrison and Bluestone 1988). For this reason, the dynamics of globalization have allegedly increased inequality among advanced industrial and post-industrial nations, leading to "the great U-turn" in the Kuznets curve (Alderson and Nielsen 2002; Harrison

Table 3.   Entrepreneurial Activity in the United States and Other
Developed Nations in 2002.

	Total Entrepreneurial Activity[a]	Opportunity Entrepreneurship[b]
All nations	8.08	5.63
Developed nations	6.52	5.20
United States	10.5	8.6

Source: Reynolds et al. (2002).
[a]Percent of labor force either actively involved in starting a new venture or the owner/manager of a business that is less than 42 months old.
[b]Percent of labor force electing to start a business as one of several possible career options.

and Bluestone 1988). In addition, the labor market options facing workers in the "new" economy have changed dramatically.

According to the GEM reports, the U.S. rates of total entrepreneurship and opportunity entrepreneurship are well above the average for all countries included in the dataset, and remarkably above countries at similar levels of industrial development, as reported in Table 3. Models that focus on general characteristics of developing nations that might foster entrepreneurship fall well short of explaining the United States' unique level of entrepreneurial activity. Deindustrialization has had unique and significant effects on employment and labor market dynamics in the United States, which may account for its comparatively higher levels of entrepreneurial activity.

Why might deindustrialization in the U.S. lead to increases in entrepreneurial activity as well as inequality? Some have argued that deindustrialization constitutes a natural outcome of economic growth, and that as societies become affluent and productivity rises, the demand for services increases (Alderson 1999). A hallmark of economic maturity is a decline in the manufacturing sector and an increase in the service sector. Therefore, the rapid growth of the service sector may create more opportunities for engaging in entrepreneurial activity to serve new and underserved niches.

Proposition 5. The rapid growth of the service sector during deindustrialization leads to an increase in opportunity entrepreneurship.

Changing Employment Institutions

Others argue that deindustrialization, instead of being a natural outcome of the advanced stages of industrial development, constitutes one component of an active strategy by firms to move manufacturing overseas. According to Bluestone and Harrison (1982), deindustrialization is not simply the outcome of a natural evolutionary process, but rather part of a managerial strategy undertaken in the U.S. in response to increasing global competition. In addition to massive reductions in capital investment and development, a large part of this strategy involved reducing labor costs. Millions of workers lost their jobs in unprecedented numbers as employers dismantled the social contract that had governed employer–employee relations after World War II. Workers were no longer guaranteed employment security in return for their commitment and loyalty. Union-busting campaigns undercut the structural sources of labor's power and employment in the U.S. became increasingly unstable.

Early on, such instability generated a good deal of concern from labor market analysts (Bluestone and Harrison 1982; Harrison and Bluestone 1988; Osterman 1988) and policy makers (Reich 1983). However, as downsizing and employment instability became a regular occurrence in the U.S. labor market, these processes also became a more "institutionally regular" part of employment relations and career development (Osterman 1999). Employees have slowly developed adaptive responses to this instability by making new investments in education and taking a more pro-active role in identifying opportunities for career advancement and mobility.

Not only are firms becoming less committed to long-term relationships with their employees, but employees also feel less committed to specific firms over the course of their careers (Osterman 1999). Perhaps in response to the decline of firm internal labor markets and stable employment, many workers have taken on a more individualistic approach to career development (DiTomaso 2001). Often, this means taking on more self-directed work within firms. As employment instability and an emphasis on self-direction evolve in tandem, however, many workers opt out of binding relationships with firms and behave like independent contractors. In particular, workers with high levels of education and valuable skills are seeking new opportunities for themselves. People in the emerging "creative class" often seek these opportunities through business start-ups (Florida 2002).

Proposition 6. Increasing employment flexibility leads to an increase in opportunity entrepreneurship.

We are not making a deterministic argument. Dynamic relationships between development, inequality, and entrepreneurial activity create specific political and social structures at particular historical conjunctures. The political and social structures that affect economic inequality do so in large part by changing labor market structures and processes (Kalleberg and Berg 1987). Political policies influence the degree to which individuals must rely on the labor market to gain a living, and taxation policies determine how much wealth is transferred from those with large wealth holdings to those without. Class structures in societies depend upon the size of occupational and industrial groups and their degree of mobilization. When groups are highly mobilized and influential, they can protect their interests more effectively. These structures alter the choices individuals must make about their labor force participation. Therefore, as we explain below, they should have an effect on entrepreneurial activity.

Welfare State Structure

The policies and provisions provided by modern welfare states vary greatly from nation to nation. In his path-breaking work, Esping-Andersen (1990) categorized these structures into three regime types. The regime types differed in the level and type of provisions they guaranteed citizens and the effects they had on labor market dynamics. Esping-Andersen argued that the three regime-types – liberal, corporatist, and social democratic – differed in the degree of decommodification they allowed. The most generous social democratic welfare states go the furthest in allowing citizens to maintain a livelihood without reliance on the market, whereas liberal regimes tie benefit provision directly to market participation and stigmatize recipients, furthering dependence on the market for all except the most desperate citizens.

What effect does regime-type have on levels of income and wealth inequality? Nations with social democratic welfare state regimes often have a strong egalitarian ethic. Such nations bring down levels of wealth inequality by decommodifying labor and redistributing large amounts of wealth. On the opposite end of the spectrum, liberal regimes have high levels of wealth inequality and mechanisms to encourage participation in the labor market as a source of income and mobility. We propose that welfare state policies also affect entrepreneurial activity, reinforcing the relationship between inequality and entrepreneurial activity. If necessity entrepreneurship is, by definition, a final effort to secure a living when other labor market options fail, then strong welfare state policies in the form of unemployment insurance and job training programs should reduce the need to rely on necessity entrepreneurship.

Proposition 7. Nations with more generous welfare state policies have lower rates of necessity entrepreneurship.

Figs. 5 and 6 show the total and necessity entrepreneurial rates of countries categorized by Esping-Andersen's (1990) regime typology. As Fig. 5 makes clear, corporatist and social-democratic regimes, both of which decommodify labor and transfer more wealth than liberal states, have lower rates of total entrepreneurial activity. The relationship between regime type and necessity entrepreneurship is even more striking. Social democratic regimes have two-thirds the amount of necessity entrepreneurship of

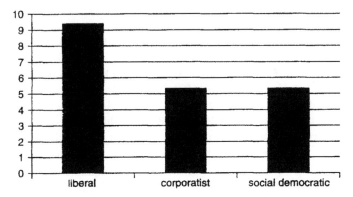

Fig. 5. Total Entrepreneurial Activity by Welfare State Regime Type. (Percentage of Labor Force involved in Nascent Entrepreneurship.) *Source:* Reynolds et al. (2002).

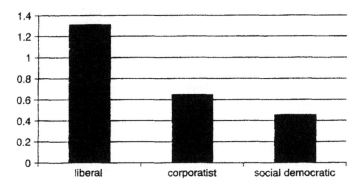

Fig. 6. Necessity Entrepreneurship by Welfare State Regime Type. (Percentage of Labor Force involved in Nascent Entrepreneurship.) *Source:* Reynolds et al. (2002).

corporatist regimes, and only one-third of that of liberal regimes. According to the GEM data, citizens of regimes that decommodify labor rely less on necessity entrepreneurship to secure a living than citizens of other regime types.

Strength of the Working Class

Some theorists have argued that the negative relationship between economic equality and entrepreneurial activity stems from the strength of a nation's working class. Nations with highly organized and influential working classes experience less inequality because unions and other working class organizations are able to exert their influence to gain a larger share of the economic and social fruits of their labor. In many industrially advanced European nations, labor parties after World War II were able to pursue policies of full employment, unemployment benefits, and related social benefits (Korpi 1989; Korpi and Palme 2000). In addition, many egalitarian countries have a strong working class (Esping-Andersen 1990, 1994). The presence of a strong working class curtails many of the negative effects of globalization and employment instability that we previously argued may cause an increase in entrepreneurial activity.

Proposition 8. The presence of a highly mobilized and influential working class will reduce necessity entrepreneurship rates.

McManus (2000) confirmed this association in her research on the quality of self-employment in Germany and the U.S. In Germany, the presence of influential union–employer associations and strong occupational labor market has contributed to more labor market stability and a higher earnings floor for many of the same occupations that are in decline in the U.S. These factors, in turn, have led to a lower rate of poor quality self-employment in Germany than in the U.S. Strong occupational labor markets and more labor market stability resulted in more stable, higher quality self-employment in Germany.

DISCUSSION AND CONCLUSION

We have focused on the way in which societal-level inequalities in resource distributions affect entrepreneurial activity. Interestingly, those countries with higher levels of wealth inequality have higher levels of entrepreneurial activity. High levels of wealth inequality might indicate that those in the upper end of the income distribution have surplus capital to invest in new business ventures. Conversely, in societies in which large segments of the population have few financial resources, self-employment may be the only viable form of employment for many people.

We outlined a perspective that focuses on cross-national comparisons of the factors that influence a country's level of economic inequality. We asked what effect economic inequality may have on labor markets and rates of entrepreneurship. Identifying the structural causes of this relationship will generate valuable information for all nations interested in business start-ups, job growth, and social and economic opportunity. Table 2 summarizes the seven factors we identified in our literature review. Note that all seven have similar effects on inequality and entrepreneurship and that many are inter-related. We suggest that states interested in policies favoring entrepreneurship could begin with any of the seven.

Policy Implications

Unequal possession of resources can hamper a social group's abilities to engage in entrepreneurial activity, but entrepreneurship can also disrupt patterns of inequality and may be a source of upward mobility for individuals (Stinchcombe 1965). In the U.S., entrepreneurship has been a significant source of upward mobility for minority and immigrant groups who are more likely to be excluded from opportunities for mobility in conventional labor markets. In formerly socialist nations, however, the human and social capital advantages that accrued to cadres seemed to persist during the transition to capitalism. In these societies, it appears that entrepreneurship is less likely to be a source of mobility. Nonetheless, the situation may change because capitalist institutions have yet to become fully developed and firmly entrenched in many countries still in transition.

Wealth and gender inequality are widespread and persistent in advanced capitalist societies. Even as women's labor force participation approaches that of men, they continue to be segregated into lower-paying, lower-status occupations. The inheritability of wealth ensures its unequal distribution from generation to generation. In fact, after years of stability, wealth inequality in the United States has been increasing (Keister and Moller 2000). We have not addressed the role that the entrepreneurship might play in overcoming these structured and durable forms of inequality. However, we do know that starting a business appears to require very little financial capital and represents a possible source of mobility for individuals. There-fore, although entrepreneurship might not seriously erode the level of struc-tured wealth inequality, it may provide individuals with the opportunities to move out of their current class locations. Gender, on the other hand, is highly consolidated with inequalities in access to human and social capital (Aldrich, Elam, and Reese 1996). Given the importance that these resources have in the founding process, prevailing patterns in gender inequality might do more to restrict entrepreneurial opportunities than entrepreneurship will do to upset gender inequality.

Schumpeter, a dominant voice in the entrepreneurship literature of the last century, emphasized the role that entrepreneurs play in introduc-ing variation into organizational populations and societies (Becker and Knudsen 2002). Variation across social groups represents a potential source of diversity in organizational populations. When some groups are less likely to start new organizations than others, diversity suffers. Moreover, problems of social justice arise when social groups have unequal access to economic and social resources that are important in the process of entrepreneurship. When members of disadvantaged groups no longer believe in the possibilities of "success among the unsuccessful," they may turn to other, socially dis-ruptive channels in the pursuit of economic advancement.

The positive relationship between economic inequality and entrepreneur-ial activity poses a disturbing message for those nations with strongly egal-itarian norms that seek to increase business start up rates. We have argued that state policies encouraging social and economic equality may suppress entrepreneurial activity, while those favoring entrepreneurship may unin-tentionally lead to higher levels of economic inequality. Pursued unthink-ingly, programs promoting entrepreneurship may thus cause unwanted consequences. However, once forewarned, policy makers can watch for un-intended consequences and plan for them.

NOTES

1. Many entrepreneurs use various "boot strapping" methods to secure the fi-nances required during the initial stages of new business formation. Borrowing money from family members, withholding their own wages, or using personal credit cards to purchase supplies and equipment are the primary ways that entrepreneurs can get around capital constraints (Winborg and Landstrom 2000).

2. Diversity is an important source of variation in organizational populations (Aldrich 1999), and variation across organizations increases the likelihood of inno-vations and the level of competitive intensity in industries (Kaufman 1991). It is

28   STEPHEN LIPPMANN ET AL.

important, therefore, to understand the factors that encourage or inhibit such diversity.

3. For readability, we have suppressed case labels in all figures except in Fig. 3, where particular cases merit identification and further discussion.

4. The mean score on the Gini index for the entire sample is 36.32 (S.D. 10.00). The respective Gini scores for New Zealand, India, and Thailand are 36.17, 37.83, and 43.15.

5. Mexico – 12%, Brazil – 13%, Argentina – 14%, Chile – 16%, China – 12%, Korea – 14%, India – 18%, Thailand – 19%.

ACKNOWLEDGMENTS

We would like to thank Arthur Alderson, Clinton Key, Kammi Schmeer, and Steve Vaisey for their comments on earlier versions of this paper.

REFERENCES

Alderson, Arthur S. 1997. "Globalization and Deindustrialization: Direct Investment and the Decline in Manufacturing Employment in 17 OECD Nations." *Journal of World Systems Research* 3:1–34.

------. 1999. "Explaining Deindustrialization: Globalization, Failure, or Success?." *American Sociological Review* 64:701–721.

Alderson, Arthur S. and Francois Nielsen. 1999. "Income Inequality, Development, and Dependence: A Reconsideration." *American Sociological Review* 64:606–631.

Aldrich, Howard. 1999. *Organizations Evolving*. London: Sage.

------. 2004. "Entrepreneurship." Pp. 451–477 in *Handbook of Economic Sociology*, edited by R. Swedberg and N. Smelser. Princeton, NJ: Princeton University Press.

Aldrich, Howard E. and Ellen R. Auster. 1986. "Even Dwarfs Started Small." Pp. 165–198 in *Research in Organizational Behavior* Vol. 8, edited by B.M. Staw and L.L. Cummings. Greenwich, CT: JAI Press.

Aldrich, Howard E., Amanda B. Elam, and Pat R. Reese. 1996. "Strong Ties, Weak Ties, and Strangers: Do Women Business Owners Differ from Men in Their Use of Networking to Obtain Assistance?." Pp. 1–25 in *Entrepreneurship in a Global Context*, edited by S. Birley and I. MacMillan. London: Routledge Ltd.

Aldrich, Howard E. and Marlene C. Fiol. 1994. "Fools Rush In? The Institutional Context of Industry Creation." *Academy of Management Review* 19:645–670.

Aronson, Robert L. 1991. *Self-Employment: A Labor Market Perspective*. Ithaca, NY: ILR Press.

Bates, Timothy. 1997. *Race, Self-Employment, and Upward Mobility: An Illusive American Dream*. Washington, DC: Woodrow Wilson Center Press.

Becker, Markus C. and Knudsen Thorbjørn. 2003. "The Entrepreneur at a Crucial Juncture in Schumpeter's Work: Schumpeter's 1928 Handbook Entry Entrepreneur." *Advances in Australian Economics* 6:199–234.

Bendix, Reinhard. 1956. *Work and Authority in Industry: Ideologies of Management in the Course of Industrialization.* New York: Wiley.

Blanchflower, David G. and Andrew J. Oswald. 1998. "What Makes an Entrepreneur." *Journal of Labor Economics* 16:26–60.

Blau, Peter M. 1977. *Inequality and Heterogeneity: A Primitive Theory of Social Structure.* New York: Free Press.

Bluestone, Barry and Bennett Harrison. 1982. *The Deindustrialization of America: Plant Closings, Community Abandonment, and the Dismantling of Basic Industry.* New York: Basic Books.

Burton, M. Diane, Jesper Sorenson, and Christine Beckman. 2002. "Coming From Good Stock: Career Histories and New Venture Formation." in *Social Structure and Organizations Revisited,* edited by M. Lounsbury and M. Vantresca. Amsterdam: JAI/Elsevier.

DiTomaso, Nancy. 2001. "The Loose Coupling of Jobs: The Subcontracting of Everyone?." in *Sourcebook of Labor Markets: Evolving Structures and Processes,* edited by Ivar Berg and Arne L. Kalleberg. New York: Klewer Publishers.

Dunn, Thomas A. and Douglas Holtz-Eakin. 2000. "Financial Capital, Human Capital, and the Transition to Self-Employment: Evidence from Intergenerational Links." *Journal of Labor Economics* 18:282–304.

Esping-Andersen, Gosta. 1990. *The Three Worlds of Welfare Capitalism.* Princeton, NJ: Princeton University Press.

Evans, David S. and B. Jovanovic. 1989. "An Estimated Model of Entrepreneurial Choice Under Liquidity Constraints." *Journal of Political Economy* 7:808–827.

Evans, David S. and Linda S. Leighton. 1989. "Some Empirical Aspects of Entrepreneurship." *American Economic Review* 9:519–535.

Evans, Peter B., Rueschemeyer Dietrich, and Theda Skocpol, eds. 1985. *Bringing the State Back In.* Cambridge: Cambridge University Press.

Fichman, Mark and Daniel, A. Levinthal. 1991. "Honeymoons and the Liability of Adolescence: A New Perspective on Duration Dependence in Social and Organizational Relationships." *Academy of Management Review* 16:442–468.

Fischer, Mary and Douglas Massey. 2000. "Residential Segregation and Ethnic Enterprise in U.S. Metropolitan Areas." *Social Problems* 47:410–424.

Flora, Jan L. 1998. "Social Capital and Communities of Place." *Rural Sociology* 63:481–506.

Florida, Richard. 2002. *The Rise of the Creative Class: And How It's Transforming Work, Leisure, Community, and Everyday Life.* New York: Basic Books.

Fujiwara-Greve, Takako and Henrich R. Greve. 2000. "Organizational Ecology and Job Mobility." *Social Forces* 79:547–585.

Harrison, Bennett and Barry Bluestone. 1988. *The Great U-Turn: Corporate Restructuring and the Polarizing of America.* New York: Basic Books.

Kalleberg, Arne L. and Ivar Berg. 1987. *Work and Industry: Structures, Markets, and Processes.* New York: Plenum Press.

Keister, Lisa A. 2000. *Wealth in America.* New York: Cambridge University Press.

Keister, Lisa A. and Stephanie Moller. 2000. "Wealth Inequality in the Unites States." *Annual Review of Sociology* 26:63–81.

Kim, Phil H., Howard E. Aldrich, and Keister, Lisa A. 2003. "If I Were Rich? The Impact of Financial and Human Capital on Becoming a Nascent Entrepreneur" Paper presented at the annual meetings of the Academy of Management, Seattle, WA.

Korpi, Walter. 1989. "Power, Politics, and State Autonomy in the Development of Social Citizenship: Social Rights during Sickness in Eighteen OECD Countries since 1930." *American Sociological Review* 54:309–328.

Korpi, Walter and Joakim Palme. 1998. "The Paradox of Redistribution and the Strategy of Equality: Welfare State Institutions, Inequality and Poverty in the Western Countries." *American Sociological Review* 63:661–687.

Kuznets, Simon. 1953. *Shares of Upper Income Groups in Income and Savings.* New York: National Bureau of Economic Research.

------. 1955. "Economic Growth and Income Inequality." *The American Economic Review* 45:1–28.

Lampman, Robert J. 1962. *The Share of Top Wealth Holders in National Wealth, 1922–1956.* Princeton, NJ: Princeton University Press.

Lindert, Peter H. and Jeffrey, G. Williamson. 1985. "Growth, Equality, and History." *Explorations in Economic History* 22:341–377.

Marx, Karl. 1852. "The Eighteenth Brumaire of Louis Bonaparte."

McManus, Patricia A. 2000. "Market, State, and the Quality of New Self-Employment Jobs Among Men in the U.S. and Western Germany." *Social Forces* 78:865–905.

Nielsen, Francois and Arthur S. Alderson. 1995. "Income Inequality, Development, and Dualism: Results from an Unbalanced Cross-National Panel." *American Sociological Review* 60:674–701.

Osterman, Paul. 1988. *Employment Futures: Reorganization, Dislocation, and Public Policy.* New York: Oxford University Press.

------. 1999. *Securing Prosperity: The American Labor Market, How it has Changed, and What to Do About it.* Princeton, NJ: Princeton University Press.

Reich, Robert B. 1983. *The Next American Frontier.* New York: Times Books.

Reynolds, Paul D., Michael Hay, William D. Bygrave, Michael Camp and Autio, Erkko, 2002. "Global Entrepreneurship Monitor: Global Executive Report." *Kauffman Center for Entrepreneurial Leadership* Accessed on: November 20, 2003. http://www.gemconsortium.org/download/1080500608703/WebGlobalGEMReport11.12_1.pdf

Reynolds, Paul D. and Sammis B. White. 1997. *The Entrepreneurial Process: Economic Growth, Men, Women, and Minorities.* Westport, CT: Quorum Books.

Róna-Tas, A. 1994. "The First Shall Be Last? Entrepreneurship and Communist Cadres in the Transition from Socialism." *American Journal of Sociology* 100:40–69.

Sobel, Michael E., P. Mark Becker, and Susan M. Minick. 1998. "Origins Destinations and Association in Occupational Mobility." *American Journal of Sociology* 104:687–721.

Soysa, Indra and John R. Oneal. 1999. "Boon or Bane? Reassessing the Productivity of Foreign Direct Investment." *American Sociological Review* 64:766–782.

Stinchcombe, Arthur L. 1965. "Social Structure and Organizations." in *Handbook of Organizations,* edited by J.G. March. Chicago, IL: Rand McNally.

Tilly, Charles. 1998. *Durable Inequality.* Berkeley, CA: University of California Press.

Tomaskovic-Devey, Donald. 1993. *Gender and Racial Inequality at Work: The Sources and Consequences of Job Segregation.* Ithaca, NY: ILR Press.

U.S. Census Bureau. 1997. Characteristics of Business Owners, 1992 *Economic Census.* Washington, DC: U.S. Department of Commerce.

Wade, Robert. 1990. *Governing the Market: Economic Theory and the Role of Government in East Asian Industrialization.* Princeton, NJ: Princeton University Press.

Wilson, William J. 1996. *When Work Disappears: The World of the New Urban Poor.* New York: Alfred A. Knopf, Inc.

Winborg, Joakim and Hans Landstrom. 2000. "Financial Bootstrapping in Small Business: Examining Managers' Resource Acquisition Behaviors." *Journal of Business Venturing* 16:235–254.

Wood, Adrian. 1994. *North-South Trade, Employment, and Inequality.* New York: Oxford University Press.

World Bank Group. 2004. *Development Data Online.* Accessed March 9, 2004 http://devdata.worldbank.org/dataonline/

PART VII

CONCLUSION

[24]

Conclusion and Further Reflections

The essays reprinted in this volume reflect three goals that have guided my writing. First, with my co-authors, I have tried to convey a sense of the full scope of contemporary entrepreneurship, and not just analyses of the large publicly traded firms that appear in many entrepreneurship papers. Second, I have written about the emergence of organizations, populations, and communities, as well as their strategies and structures. As revealed in this collection, I am more interested in the genesis of social entities than in their subsequent activities. Third, I have used an evolutionary approach to understand the process through which new social units emerge because it provides a generic framework for studying entrepreneurship. It explains patterned change in social systems, of whatever type, by focusing on the processes of variation, selection, retention, and struggle. In this concluding Chapter, I want to raise some promising issues for future work.

Conceptualizing and studying variation

The essays in this book have investigated emergence at all levels of analysis and I want to mention two issues in particular that deserve further attention. First, we need greater understanding of the role of nascent entrepreneurs and their role in assembling and preserving organizational knowledge. The availability of large-scale public databases on nascent entrepreneurs, such as PSED II and the Kauffman Firm Study, should certainly help that effort. Second, collective action, in various guises, appears in nearly every paper. We need to study the process by which organized action by groups of entrepreneurs and managers contributes to the development of new organizations, populations, and communities.

Nascent entrepreneurs are the key agents of organizational creation. In the past, organization theorists might have overlooked them because the entrepreneurship literature offered implausible tales of entrepreneurs as super action heroes. Researchers endowed them, after the fact, with competencies beyond belief, as I noted in Chapter 5. In Chapter 3, Amy Kenworthy and I offered a more modest portrayal of their achievements, focusing on organizational founding as a disorderly process in which people improvise as best they can, given their situation. Lacking clairvoyance, nascent entrepreneurs mostly reproduce common forms characteristic of the populations they enter, rather than creating new ones.

What might we study next? First, is there an optimal mix of reproducers and innovators that can sustain a population's pool of routines and competencies? Perhaps the periodic appearance of innovative forms sets in motion forces that awaken drifting reproducers from their slumber. Perhaps population reproduction depends on a core set of entrepreneurs and organizations that faithfully reproduce its routines and competencies, regardless of a multitude of poorly adapted innovators. Second, given the level of improvisation required, every founding has the potential of introducing variations into a population. However, most evidently do not. Is innovation so infrequent because entrepreneurs habitually rely on powerful copying rules that outweigh idiosyncratic entrepreneurial learning? Alternatively, do selection pressures simply eliminate most innovators very early in the process, as implied in the study of Swedish firms reported in Chapter 13?

To what extent do successful routines and competencies come in bundles as opposed to discrete practices? Human and social capital theories of new venture foundings often imply that valuable knowledge is transportable, such as between self-employed parents and their children. However, to the extent that entrepreneurial knowledge is embedded in organization- and population-specific contexts, most attempts to transfer knowledge across contexts will fail. What kinds of entrepreneurial knowledge are portable, and under what conditions is transfer most likely? Perhaps the only managerial skills that are relevant to entrepreneurial foundings are those people learn in exactly the same industries in which the foundings will occur.

Throughout these essays, I have emphasized purposive collective action as a potent evolutionary force. Most of the examples in this edited book involve purposive collective action by individuals and organizations organizing around shared interests for a limited period. I emphasized the advantages accruing to organizations that created vehicles for collective action and then used them to acquire more resources in competitive situations. In my writings, I have paid less attention to collective action involving parallel activities by organizations that might unintentionally create joint benefits. Both kinds of collective action need greater attention from entrepreneurship theorists.

Over the course of the 20th century, formal organizations have squeezed out individuals and informal organizations as significant actors. Are collectivities of organizations now beginning to squeeze out single organizations? Organizations are assuredly the central actors in all facets of social, economic, and political life. Throughout my work, I have presented examples of their roles in many sectors of society, from shaping individual identities to influencing the course of political decisions. At the beginning of the 21st century, over 90 percent of the population works for an organization rather than themselves, and organizations employing 100 or more people now contain over half of the workforce. As Jennifer Cliff Jennings and I pointed out in Chapter 19, relatively few goods and services are produced at home any more, as formerly family-based activities such as recreation, sustenance, and leisure activities are now produced by organizations and obtained on the open market.

Selection

Evolutionary accounts rest on identifying the selecting forces that interact with particular variations to produce organizational and population change. Two issues surrounding selection deserve more attention. First, can we identify the conditions under which different units of selection are most likely to be favored by selection forces? A related issue concerns the extent to which supra-organizational levels of analysis can be used not only as contexts for action in our models but also as units of selection in their own right. Second, are levels of analysis merely an analytic device, or do they represent selection filters? In models with multiple levels of analysis, investigators need to find ways of analyzing selection at multiple levels that may occur at different rates of change.

Consider first the question of choosing units of selection. Theorists disagree over the relative significance of different units of selection: routines and competencies, bundles of routines and competencies, organizations, and various supra-organizational entities. Because of its behavior-centered approach, the organizational learning perspective has unwittingly reinforced the routines and competencies view. TCE theorists, by focusing on implicit decisions involving specific transactions, have also encouraged this view. Organizational sociology has been more ambivalent in this regard. Resource dependence and institutional theorists have often treated organizations as units of analysis. However, because they have typically favored interpretations based on adaptation rather than selection, their explanations have been by default very similar to organizational learning accounts: organizations change, rather than being selected out of a population. By contrast, organizational ecology has been forthright in its treatment of organizations as units of selection, while still encompassing studies of entrepreneurial adaptation.

Adopting an explicitly evolutionary perspective will raise such issues to the top of our research agenda. Are organizations inseparable bundles of routines and competencies on which selection forces operate, selecting entire entities? Such a view would largely negate the notion of population-level knowledge, because surviving organizations would be unable to choose selectively from the successful practices developed by failing organizations. However, if organizations are merely carriers of population-level routines and competencies and thus temporary repositories of the real stuff of organizational evolution, then the fate of individual organizations is decoupled from the fate of their routines and competencies. From this perspective, changes within existing organizations, as well as foundings and disbandings, play a major role in evolution. Selection forces would affect the mix of routines and competencies in organizations as well as their distribution in populations.

In Chapter 16, Annetta Fortune and I argued that new firms could selectively acquire what they need from other organizations, rather than having to do everything internally themselves. As they acquired competence from a distance, they could integrate those best practices with what they had developed internally, based on previous experience. In Chapter 13, my co-authors and I argued that this is how subsidiaries acquired their routines and competencies, in contrast to autonomous organizations, which learned from their experiences. Because we did not have access to how each type of firm had changed internally over time, we relied on plausible inference, rather than a precise test of this argument. Pursuing such a test would shed light on the issue of whether organizations can disaggregate their routines and competencies such that learning from outsiders is possible.

Another selection issue concerns units of selection larger than single organizations. In Chapter 14, Marlena Fiol and I discussed the genesis and reproduction of organizational populations, and in Chapter 15 Courtney Hunt and I examined organizational communities. I have discussed other supra-organizational levels of analysis, such as networks (in Chapter 11) and population-level learning (in Chapter

16). Organizational ecologists have offered a convincing case that not only an organization but also a population constitutes a unit of selection, although few analyses have actually explored the genesis of new populations. Nonetheless, theorists and researchers from a variety of perspectives now routinely write about populations as if they exist as coherent units of selection.

Retention: preserving patterned pehaviors and knowledge

Retention occurs when selected variations are preserved, duplicated, or otherwise reproduced so that the selected activities are repeated on future occasions and the selected structures appear again in future generations. Without the constraints on variation provided by retention mechanisms within organizations, the selected variations represented by routines and competencies would rapidly dissipate. Daily errors in reproduction would gradually destroy the legacy of historical accumulation (Darr, Argote et al., 1995). At the population level, retention mechanisms preserve the administrative, technological, and social competencies that all members of the population use to exploit their niche. A tenuous balance exists between the stability gained from preserving organizational knowledge and the stagnation created by not departing from that same knowledge.

Two issues involving retention seem particularly interesting. First, to what extent do organizations reproduce or mitigate the structure of economic inequality in a society? The chapters in the Part V on 'gender and family' and Part VI on 'stratification and inequality' tackle this question. Second, is the pace of organizational evolution destroying the relevance of the past at a faster pace than a generation ago? The chapters in Part II on 'theory' and Part IV on 'strategy' address this question.

Organizations have contradictory effects on reproducing the structure of economic inequality in a society. Their potential leveling influence arises from the nearly unfettered access nascent entrepreneurs from diverse social origins have to the founding process, as Phil Kim, Lisa Keister, and I argued in Chapter 22. Universalistic and merit-based selection criteria in modern organizations have also somewhat diminished the association between people's social backgrounds and their life chances, although it is still relevant for many immigrant groups as Roger Waldinger and I argued in Chapter 2. Organizations' potential stratifying influence arises from their role as the key generators of wealth in capitalist societies. As Stinchcombe (1965) and other sociologists have pointed out, access to ownership and control of organizational assets now separates the privileged from the rest of society. Competitive struggles not only sort organizations into positions of dominance and subordination but also allocate life chances to individuals affiliated with them (Aldrich and Weiss 1981).

The potential leveling influence of organizations is reflected in the small effect family background has on access to ownership. As I noted in the chapters in Part VI, on stratification and inequality, parental wealth has a substantively insignificant effect on the odds of becoming self-employed. Few owners inherit their businesses or obtain any capital from their parents or family. The low threshold of resources required for founding a business allows people from very diverse social origins to enter the field. Organizations thus substantially reduce the association between the socio-economic status of families and their children.

Nonetheless, the social capital provided by organizations affects the life chances of people because some affiliations are more valuable than others. Research in social stratification has found that the largest effect of family background on children's mobility is through educational attainment. For example, family background affects the kinds of schools children are able to attend. Attending certain private schools or elite colleges generates networks of contacts that enable graduates to enter the managerial ranks of major corporations or take high ranking public sector appointments (Useem, 1984). Once employed by centrally placed organizations, individuals can build valuable networks that enable them to recognize and exploit opportunities for further advancement (Fernandez, Castilla et al., 2000). In this respect, organizations may amplify, rather than dampen, the effects of parental privilege.

An evolutionary model of the production of economic inequality would start with the process by which entrepreneurs found organizations and the wealth-creating potential of such activities. It would also take into account the genesis of new populations that create opportunities for rapid increases in the wealth of pioneering entrepreneurs. For example, the commercialization of the World Wide Web, described in Chapter 15, involved thousands of startups and employment opportunities for people linked to the new technologies. Social scientists interested in the generation of wealth and the production of inequality are paying more attention to organizational affiliation. For many years, a reliance on sample surveys of individuals blinded sociologists to the primary role played by organizations in structuring the life chances of individuals. The concepts of socioeconomic status and occupational mobility dominated models of stratification and theorists failed to acknowledge the dominant role played by organizations as selecting and sorting agents. In contrast, today researchers interested in stratification and mobility pay much more attention to the centrality of organizations.

As I argued in Chapter 4, concerning historical and comparative approaches, historical analysis is relevant to evolutionary models in two senses. First, theorists are concerned with the manner in which the past appears in the present. For example, in some systems theories, the best prediction of the next state of the system uses only the current structure of the system and the values of the variables characterizing the system. An 'understanding' of what has happened in the past is contained in the current state. In several chapters in this book, I have argued that organizational evolution does not work in the same way. Historical trajectories and current contexts matter a great deal. Second, theorists today build synthetic models of organizational change from the results of studies conducted over the past several decades and some statistical models may include information from many decades. How reasonable are such aggregations from an evolutionary perspective?

Aldrich and Ruef (2006) urged adoption of an age, period, and cohort model for interpreting the effects of social change on organizational evolution. Such models retain the past in three ways. First, individual organizations display the cumulative effects of a unique life course in their current organizational knowledge. Routines and competencies imprinted during the founding process occur in combination with subsequent knowledge earned through experience. Second, the effects of previous periods show up in the mix of current populations and communities, the diversity or similarity of forms within populations, and in adaptations made by organizations surviving those periods. Third, the shared experiences of cohorts of organizations living through the same periods are also evident in the current composition of organizational routines and competencies.

We need to be on the alert for current research methods that disguise such lingering variability. Because selection forces rarely produce homogeneity within or across populations, the retained routines and competencies lurking within these organizations will be quite diverse. Some unused but harmless routines and competencies may persist for years in subunits that are shielded from selection pressures. Others that would be maladaptive if directly exposed to external selection may have been retained because of perverse internal selection criteria. At the population level, resource partitioning might have preserved extremely specialized organizations whose ancient routines and competencies are poorly understood (Carroll and Swaminathan, 2000). Universities, foundations, research institutes, and other non-market-based organizations can also serve as holding tanks for unconventional or apparently irrelevant knowledge.

The diverse pool of routines and competencies represented by the totality of these retention mechanisms can become relevant to organizational evolution whenever entrepreneurs draw on them again. Under the most unlikely of circumstances, entrepreneurs may discover long dormant routines that solve a current problem, thus activating a link to some distant selection event. During the founding process, when entrepreneurs improvise under severe time constraints, they may hire employees from completely unrelated populations. Suddenly, competencies abandoned as outmoded in another population become useful again.

More generally, as long as retention mechanisms somewhere preserve routines and competencies, they are potentially available as the raw material for evolutionary processes. For example, social movements can make salient once again an organizational model that was dormant or under-appreciated (Clemens, 1993). What implications does this have for entrepreneurship studies? Researchers devote a great deal of attention now to discovering what works. Perhaps more attention should be devoted to finding apparently useless or irrelevant organizational knowledge. Many large organizations allocate some of their efforts to re-engineering their processes, which means finding and discarding routines thought no longer useful. What mechanisms in organizations and populations retain routines and competencies that lie dormant, rather than being used?

The second question I posed above concerns the long-term stability of retention mechanisms, within organizations, populations, and communities. Entrepreneurship theory needs to make some assumptions about environmental stability so that it can claim generality for its findings. For example, what features of environments have remained unchanged for the past few decades? What features have changed? Unless we can confirm such stability, research would be of purely historical interest, in the best sense of that term. However, researchers allocate little effort to this task. If our research practices reflected an evolutionary sensibility, meta-analyses testing the stability of results obtained in different periods would fill entrepreneurship journals. The issue is not simply one of reliability, because the term 'reliability' presumes that results should be the same. By default, however, researchers seem to have adopted an assumption that empirical generalizations hold over all eras and epochs. As I noted in Chapter 4, this assumption seems unwarranted.

As we begin the 21st century, we can raise a more general question about retention mechanisms. Have improvements in the speed and scope of information technology increased the pace of information diffusion to such an extent that societies are abandoning their histories more quickly than before? In Chapter 15, Hunt and I noted that the commercialization of electronic commerce occurred on an unprecedented scale and at such speed that they caught many established organizations and populations off guard. Although they scrambled to catch up, many have found themselves in a repetitive cycle of costly adaptations to continuous technological improvements.

Finally, a great irony characterizes the current literature on entrepreneurship. Investigators have chosen to focus much of their efforts on extremely prominent organizational events, such as mergers and acquisitions, the restructuring of large publicly-held corporations, and venture capital deals. In contrast, ubiquitous but essential events, such as foundings, have received relatively little attention. For example, in several chapters I noted that the vast majority of organizations do not grow significantly after their early days. We might expect, therefore, to find questions framed along the lines of 'why is growth such a rare phenomenon?' instead of 'are larger organizations more inert than smaller ones?'.

Organizations constitute the fundamental foundation of modern societies. Entrepreneurs, individually and collectively, construct these foundations. As we enter the 21st century, organizations are remaking our world through collective action. Studies of why and how entrepreneurs succeed and fail are crucial for analyzing social change. We need encompassing schemes for understanding what is happening to us, and for putting local actions into their historical and global context. I think evolutionary theories of entrepreneurship can do that.

References

Aldrich, H.E. and J. A. Weiss (1981), 'Differentiation Within the U.S. Capitalist Class: Workforce Size and Income Differences', *American Sociological Review*, **46**(3), 279–89.

Carroll, G.R. and A. Swaminathan (2000), 'Why the Microbrewery Movement? Organizational Dynamics of Resource Partitioning in the U.S. Brewing Industry', *American Journal of Sociology*, **106**(3), 715–62.

Clemens, E.S. (1993), 'Organizational Repertoires and Institutional Change: Women's Groups and the Transformation of U.S. Politics, 1890–1920', *American Journal of Sociology*, **98**(4), 755–98.

Darr, E.L., L. Argote, et al. (1995), 'The Acquisition, Transfer, and Depreciation of Knowledge in Service Organizations: Productivity in Franchises', *Management Science*, **41**(11), 1750–62.

Fernandez, R.M., E.J. Castilla, et al. (2000), 'Social Capital at Work: Networks and Employment at a Phone Center', *American Journal of Sociology*, **105**(5), 1288–1356.

Stinchcombe, A.L. (1965), 'Social Structure and Organizations', in J.G. March, *Handbook of Organizations*, Chicago, IL: Rand McNally, 142–93.

Useem, M. (1984), *The Inner Circle: Large Corporations and the Rise of Business Political Activity in the U.S. and U.K.*, New York: Oxford University Press.